The Gospel of Mark

D1596748

FAITH MEETS FAITH

An Orbis Series in Interreligious Dialogue
Paul F. Knitter, General Editor

Editorial Advisors
John Berthrong
Julia Ching
Diana Eck
Karl-Josef Kuschel
Lamin Sanneh
George E. Tinker
Felix Wilfred

In the contemporary world, the many religions and spiritualities stand in need of greater communication and cooperation. More than ever before, they must speak to, learn from, and work with each other in order both to maintain their vital identities and to contribute to fashioning a better world.

FAITH MEETS FAITH seeks to promote interreligious dialogue by providing an open forum for exchanges among followers of different religious paths. While the Series wants to encourage creative and bold responses to questions arising from contemporary appreciations of religious plurality, it also recognizes the multiplicity of basic perspectives concerning the methods and content of interreligious dialogue.

Although rooted in a Christian theological perspective, the Series does not endorse any single school of thought or approach. By making available to both the scholarly community and the general public works that represent a variety of religious and methodological viewpoints, FAITH MEETS FAITH seeks to foster an encounter among followers of the religions of the world on matters of common concern.

FAITH MEETS FAITH SERIES

The Gospel of Mark

A Mahāyāna Reading

John P. Keenan

ORBIS BOOKS

Maryknoll, New York 10545

The Catholic Foreign Mission Society of America (Maryknoll) recruits and trains people for overseas missionary service. Through Orbis Books, Maryknoll aims to foster the international dialogue that is essential to mission. The books published, however, reflect the opinions of their authors and are not meant to represent the official position of the society.

The Gospel of Mark in *The New Jerusalem Bible: Reader's Edition* (Garden City, N.Y.: Doubleday, 1985) served as an underlying text in this work; it has been thoroughly revised, and retranslations from the Greek have altered most texts in this volume.

Library of Congress Cataloging-in-Publication Data

Keenan, John P.
    The Gospel of Mark : a Mahāyāna reading / John P. Keenan.
      p. cm.—(Faith meets faith)
    Includes bibliographical references and index.
    ISBN 1-57075-041-6 (alk. paper)
    1. Bible. N.T. Mark—Commentaries.   2. Bible. N.T. Mark—
Buddhist interpretations.   3. Mahayana Buddhism—Doctrines.
4. Christianity and other religions—Mahayana Buddhism.   5. Mahayana
Buddhism—Relations—Christianity.   I. Title.   II. Series.
BSBS2580.3.K44   1995
226.3'077'0882943—dc20   95-20341
                                       CIP

For Forest and Gwen

What happened in . . . the history of Christianity's earlier relation with another religious tradition, the philosophico-religious Platonism of the early centuries of the Christian era . . . was the emergence of Platonic forms of Christian theology, in which the insights of a religious Platonism played a coordinating role in ordering the insights of Christian history and Christian symbolism. We might look forward in a similar way to the emergence of Islamic or Buddhistic forms of Christian theology. These would take insights emerging from the dialogue with the other religions and use them in a similar way to provide a new ordering of Christian resources. They would stand as particular forms of Christian theology alongside others, but would also have implications for those other theologies, sometimes calling for the bringing to the fore of relatively submerged elements within them and at other times calling for the correction of old beliefs now seen to be no longer worthy of assent.

Maurice Wiles
Christian Theology and Inter-religious Dialogue

Contents

Acknowledgments

I would like to thank a handful of critical readers who have taken the time carefully to examine this book and point out errors and overstatements: Dr. Bonnie Thurston of Wheeling Jesuit College, Dr. James Fredericks of Loyola Marymount, and the Rev. Karen Sheldon, Rector of St. John the Baptist Episcopal Church in Hardwick, Vermont.

Also to be thanked for their comments and suggestions are members of the Diocesan Study Program of the Diocese of Vermont, Class of 1994: Jean Austin, Sally Curtis, Nanci Gordon, Karen Janus, Betty Lamb, Bob Lamb, Dotty McCarty, Dinny Monroe, Colleen Shover, and Cynthia Watters.

My thanks go also to Paul Knitter, general editor of the Faith Meets Faith Series at Orbis Books. He is a careful and sometimes excruciatingly demanding editor. And to William Burrows of Orbis Books for his insightful reading and suggestions.

I appreciate their criticisms and suggestions very much indeed.

PART I

Introduction

A Mahāyāna Reading of Mark

Hermeneutical Moves

Samuel Sandmel once told a friend of his intention to write a commentary on the gospel of Mark. The friend replied: "What the devil do you have to say that hasn't been said a hundred times already?" Sandmel, recounting this incident over twenty years ago, before the recent volcanic explosion of books on Mark, observed that "there is, of course, a large sense in which he is right, for much that appears in a commentary simply repeats, out of requirements of completeness, what is the common property of commentaries."[1] Still, he remained undeterred in his intention: ". . . the context and the form of Mark intrigue as a puzzle might, and as an essay might not. I think that I have seen, or at least glimpsed, in Mark things which others seem to me not to have seen. Perhaps I have seen correctly, perhaps I have not. But if there is something which I have seen and others have not, this is due not to better eyesight on my part, but to the accident of the angle of vision."[2] I too find the Gospel of Mark to be intriguing and think that a reading of Mark from the perspective of Mahāyāna Buddhist philosophy may perhaps shed some light on this gospel from a new angle and provide another avenue for reading the text.

In an earlier work, *The Meaning of Christ: A Mahāyāna Theology*, I proposed a new theological model for christology, based on the philosophies of the Mahāyāna themes of emptiness and dependent co-arising, the two truths of ultimate meaning and worldly convention, and the three patterns of conscious understanding. Insights gained from such an approach may perhaps coax new meanings from the Markan text. The present Mahāyāna reading

---

1. Sandmel, *Two Living Traditions,* 148. In Markan studies, the explosion of commentarial literature has made it impossible for all but the most dedicated specialist to consult all the relevant material. Indeed, single volumes of commentary are of such size that they are, as one interpreter remarks, predestined to "be consulted on a piecemeal basis only" (Anderson and Moore, *Mark and Method,* 11).

2. Sandmel, *Two Living Traditions,* 149. To my knowledge Sandmel never did write his projected commentary, yet in the "Prolegomena to a Commentary on Mark," 153, from which the citations have been taken, he is, it would appear, the first unambiguously to "allege that Mark regards [the disciples] as villains," a theme much developed in more recent Markan scholarship, especially by Theodore Weeden.

of Mark is an application of the same philosophic methodology to the tasks of scriptural hermeneutics.

This Mahāyāna reading of Mark is an attempt to realize that possibility of "passing over" into the faith and way of life of another culture, "in order to return to one's own time and culture with one's outlook, faith and understanding both deepened and broadened."[3] Readings of Mark to date have been so conditioned by the history of Christian exegesis that it is difficult to move beyond the filters of the existing commentarial literature. Robert Fowler wishes it were otherwise: "If I were a storyteller, I would like to write a Gospel that places Mark's successors in such a light that the shadows they have cast upon Mark for centuries would be dispelled and the highlights they have shown upon Mark would be muted. I would like to construct a grid for reading [Mark] that blocks out Matthew and allows only Mark's Gospel to be seen as it was before Matthew came along. Nevertheless, such a reading experience is a pipe dream—no such magical reading grid will ever be produced—so I shall continue to trust the powers of criticism to serve reading."[4] I propose that Mahāyāna thought can afford such a grid, for the Markan rhetoric of indirection and irony is the narrative analogue to the Mādhyamika dialectical rhetoric employed in Nāgārjuna's *Stanzas on the Middle* (*Mūlamadhyamakakārikā*), more so in fact than any Buddhist narrative I have come across. Furthermore, Mahāyāna eschews precisely those clarifying elements that Matthew and Luke have added to domesticate Mark's story and discourse, preferring the opacity of ultimate meaning to the full explication of stated truths, opting for the emptying of all themes and ideas in order to reclaim them with an awakened mind.

Yet the commentarial tradition is indeed daunting in urging its accustomed patterns of interpretation. Readings of the gospel of Mark have enjoyed a long and diverse history, and until relatively recent times have regarded Mark as an abridgement of the Gospel of Matthew.[5] Mark was so much in the shadow of Matthew and Luke that the first commentary devoted exclusively to Mark was not written until the fifth century. During the middle ages various commentaries were written on this gospel, each from the theological vantage point of its times. In recent decades, with the emergent consensus for the priority of Mark among the Synoptics,[6] more attention has been focused upon it as the (newly discovered) charter document of the Christian Gospel.

---

3. Dunne, *The Way of All the Earth,* quoted in Kealy, *Mark's Gospel,* 235.
4. Fowler, *Let the Reader Understand,* 266.
5. The view of Augustine, *De consensu evangelistarum,* 1.2.4.
6. Taylor, *The Gospel According to St. Mark,* 11, claims that "in modern commentary it is no longer necessary to prove the priority of Mark." Yet others, such as Farmer, *The Synoptic Problem,* and Mann, *Mark,* 47–66, argue for the Griesbach thesis that Mark is dependent on both Matthew and Luke. So also Johnson, *The Griesbach Hypothesis and Redaction Criticism.* Yet the majority of New Testament scholars hold for Markan priority. Most enlightening is Fowler, *Let the Reader Understand,* 228–260, which argues for Markan priority by turning the question around to ask which gospel turns another into its precursor and attempts to supplant it by creative misreading.

Numerous techniques have been employed in the task of interpretation, moving away, more recently, from attempts to identify the text's original community and its function therein, and toward an examination of its literary, rhetorical structure. Indeed, the identification of the intent and community of Mark, as well as its relationships with the other Synoptic gospels, has been carried out mostly in the subjunctive mood. Even attempts at dating, relying as they do on the dating of other related texts, present no definitive demonstrations.[7] The present attempt, performed outside the scholarly guild of biblical interpreters, will not be so bold as to adjudicate between scholarly opinions about the original significance of Mark, for that is beyond the ken of one who is by profession a student of Buddhist texts and doctrinal development and not a New Testament scholar.[8]

The present adoption of Mahāyāna philosophy as a reading grid for Mark can perhaps recommend itself in that it stresses both the emptying of all preconceived notions of just how to proceed, as well as the reclamation of such notions in terms of their dependently co-arisen and conventional validity, for insight into emptiness entails insight into the dependent co-arising of all things. That is to say, it entails an alternate hermeneutical procedure, generated from the Mahāyāna understanding of the function of text and doctrine, driven by Mahāyāna philosophy. It may perhaps be reckoned as one version of "a criticism twinned to philosophical theology and content to labor (as philosophical theology sometimes does) without epistemological or ontological guarantees."[9] Such a reading is deconstructive in the extreme, tearing down any fixed textual stability, maintaining that truth is empty of any fixed essence and in the final analysis beyond the grasp of discriminative thinking. It precludes one from following redactional or compositional strategies aimed to uncover the latent ideational content of a text and then to formulate its theological viewpoint in propositional language.[10] Any viewpoint whatsoever is emptied of essential content, for all are based, the Mahāyāna thinker claims, on futile attempts to identify a permanent something that might be seen as

---

7. Kealy, *Mark's Gospel,* 150, reports the observation of Farrer: "The datings of all these books are like a line of tipsy revelers walking home arm-in-arm; each is kept in position by the others and none is firmly grounded. The whole series can lurch five years this way or that, and still not collide with a solid obstacle."

8. In this I follow the example of Kermode, *The Genesis of Secrecy,* 137–38: "Some kinds of speculation I shall forbid myself. I shall not peer into the past for a glimpse of a man writing, out of a need I cannot know, a book of which the content derived from perhaps a few pieces of paper, and a quantity of oral material organized on principles that must be guessed at, and ordering his materials on some principle (catchwords, topics, the requirements of a lectionary) which seem not to have been in any easy sense biographical, yet involved something recognizable, in part at any rate, as a narrative."

9. Felperin, *Beyond Deconstruction,* 40 n. 9, quoted in Moore, *Literary Criticism and the Gospels: The Theoretical Challenge,* 129.

10. Moore, *Literary Criticism,* 59: "For redactional critics (as for composition critics), a gospel's content is *ideational*—specifically, an overarching theological viewpoint, extrapolated from the narrative form, and reexpressed in propositional language."

basic, stable meaning. This approach seems particularly congenial to a text such as the Gospel of Mark, for if Mark did have any clear and consistent ideological point of view, he chose a most awkward method of imparting it.[11] The Mahāyāna notion of emptiness, however, is the dispeller of all views, leaving the reader of Mark in the vertiginous prospect of, in Moore's phrase, "leaping into the epistemological abyss" of a constant whirlwind of negative results, wherein no abiding foothold in abiding essences can be found.[12] Yet, a leap of this nature could be a boon for biblical commentary, where essential-ist views, pretending to have ascertained the inner substance of the narrative rhetoric, often have permeated and distorted interpretative endeavors.[13]

True, there is some danger in steadfastly insisting on emptying all notions and ideas, for in the end the very text may vanish from one's desk in swirls of deconstructive double-backs. Indeed, Stephen Moore titles a section of his *Literary Criticism* "The Vanishing Text." Scholars critique the work of Stanley Fish and Richard Rorty, warning that the text is in danger of becoming unhinged from its semantic moorings to float free in a constant interplay of interpretations, grounded only by the normative rules of interpretative communities. Mark becomes then not the charter document of the Church, but nothing more than one expression of the hermeneutical needs of a specific community in a particular situation. To a large extent it is deprived of its authoritative status, for, if the text itself has no internal structure that might tie it down and guarantee its privileged position, one can envision any number of divergent interpretations. Indeed, what if the Church has no charter docu-ment at all?

Post-modernist readings of texts do indeed hurl a disturbing challenge at the practice of biblical hermeneutics, arguing that there is no overarching "signified" to be discovered through any hermeneutics. Jacques Derrida launches attacks on the "logocentrism and the metaphysics of presence as

---

11. Which is perhaps why some scholars have regarded Mark, in the words of *The Anti-Marcionite Prologueas* as "colobodactylus," that is, stumpy fingers, in an apparent reference to the inelegant style of his writing, leading to the rather general consensus that Mark was a somewhat poor writer. Yet, perhaps Mark's stylistic deficiencies have been exaggerated. Sandmel, *Two Living Traditions,* 155, writes: "The simplicity of Mark's style . . . is misleading; interpreters who have stressed the unornate character of his writing have failed to grasp that involved sentences and orotundity result not from skill so much as from pretentiousness, and that in Greek, as in English, it is more difficult to write simply than to write complicatedly." Also see Enslin, "The Artistry of Mark," written in 1947.

12. I am then much in agreement with Crossan's attempt to recover a negative theology, as expressed in his *Raid on the Articulate* and *Cliffs of Fall,* for that too was my design in *The Meaning of Christ: A Mahāyāna Theology,* although when writing that book I was unaware of Crossan's work.

13. Moore, *Literary Criticism,* 121: "With little exaggeration it can be said that the modus operandi of the biblical guild has generally consisted of an *adequatio intellectus et rei,* the aim of interpretation being one of correspondence to the essential semantic properties of the biblical texts, properties contained within the texts, awaiting discovery." Again 125: "Essentialist views of the biblical text are rife in biblical scholarship."

the exigent, powerful, systematic, and irrepressible desire for such a [transcendental] signified."[14] Human beings want very much to reach the far shore of firm meaning, some meaningful signified beyond the flux of all signs and symbols. It is disconcerting not to know the central core of settled meaning. Indeed, Derrida, like others before him, sees that quest for surety as the motor power behind metaphysics in all its permutations.[15] His deconstructive strategies pull one back from a disinterested focus on a given text to the far from disinterested, yet unconscious, structures and infrastructures of the inquirer.[16] One begins to question not the text, but the self one sees reflected in interpreting that text. And this in Mahāyāna terms is indeed a necessary propaedeutic, for without awareness of the emptiness of all things, including the questioning self, one cannot move forward to the tasks of compassionate and reengaged enunciation of doctrine. Yet, while the Mahāyāna philosophy urges an emptying of all viewpoints, it also warns that emptiness itself can be ineptly apprehended and turned into a most pernicious viewpoint—by one's very insistence on emptying each and every idea and affirmation. Disengagement from unconsciously projected assumptions in interpretative procedures becomes simply disengagement from those procedures. The postmodernist strategies of suspicion are blinding in their incisiveness, deferring all semantic content from vision. It is not surprising then that such a strategy is rather meager in its actual performance. One could, I suppose, write a deconstructive account of Mark by copying his doubling back moves in a post-modern critical encirclement to set free all previous interpretations in an unending play of illuminative, but personal, one-upmanship. In such a scenario, one might accuse capital-D Deconstruction with sneaking in a transcendental signified in the guise of a normative free play of doubling back. The Mahāyāna thinkers equate such a deconstructive procedure with the figure of the *pratyekabuddha*—"a solitary enlightened person" who indeed realizes the emptiness of all things, but then departs from this world to roam blissfully free but alone like the rhinoceros in the depths of whatever forests are available. But that is emptiness ineptly apprehended as itself an essentialist viewpoint that there are no viewpoints.

Nāgārjuna, the founder of the earliest, Mādhyamika school of Mahāyāna philosophy and thus the father of Mahāyāna thought, identifies emptiness with dependent co-arising. Emptiness means not that things simply do not exist, but rather that nothing has any firm and fixed essence. Their essenceless

---

14. Derrida, *Of Grammatology,* 49.

15. Moore, *Literary Criticism,* 133, on Derrida: "His project is directed against that Western nostalgia for full presence that bespeaks a dread of insecurity—that *ontotheological* yearning, which has petrified philosophical thought from the overt metaphysics of Plato to the covert metaphysics of Heidegger." One should not, however, restrict such a yearning to Westerners, for Buddhist thought evinces parallel attempts to rest in a "transcendental signified," such as a logocentric notion of Buddha nature. See Hakamaya, *Hihan bukkyō.*

16. Gasché, *The Tain of the Mirror,* 185–224 on infrastructure.

existence is described in terms of their mutual conditioning, their co-arising in mutual dependency. Insight into emptiness does entail a loss of epistemological certitude and entails the recognition that all notions and all images arise in virtue of clusters of particular causes and conditions. Asaṅga and Vasubandhu, the principal proponents of Yogācāra philosophy, the second school of Indian Mahāyāna, shifted this focus on dependent co-arising inward, to explicate the language-formed infrastructures of consciousness (*trisvabhāva*). They were proponents of a hermeneutics of suspicion, describing the genesis of deluded thinking as the pattern of imputing essences to images. They pointed out that that pattern, however, once broken by insight into emptiness, recovers its "originally present" validity—precisely in its contextual and conventional truth.

It is, I think, such a recovery of the dependently co-arisen validity of the scriptural texts that recent structuralist and narrative criticisms have been accomplishing in biblical studies. Taking a clue from the notion of Ferdinand de Saussure's *Course in General Linguistics* that language signs are not referential to external realities, but conventional indicators of an internal structure of binary relationships in search of mediation, Structuralist thinkers see verbal signifiers as referring to the intelligible content signified within the text. Structuralist New Testament scholars have accordingly attempted to read biblical texts in terms of their internal dynamism. A good example is Elizabeth Struthers Malbon's *Narrative Space and Mythic Meaning in Mark,* which employs a creative reading of Claude Lévi-Strauss to coax meanings from the text heretofore unnoticed.

The Deconstructive critique of such procedures is that, while language indeed refers to no external reality, even the distinction between signifiers and signifieds is itself conventional, representing nothing more than a mistaken quest for a firm ground of self-enclosed meaning beyond the play of language. In a Mahāyāna understanding, such a Deconstructive criticism does not itself escape from the deconstructive thrust of emptiness, for a menu of rigorously followed deconstructive procedures can be as fixed as any static essence. The sword of emptiness cuts both ways: to undermine all attempts to erect an absolute viewpoint of signified reality, and to disallow the deconstruction of conventionally constructed viewpoints. Mahāyāna attitudes are pragmatic, moving as needed now to construct and now to identify that construct as nothing more than a conventional model (*saṃvṛtimātra*). Stephen Moore incisively points out that a number of scholars, such as John Dominic Crossan and Werner Kelber, oscillate awkwardly between deconstructive strategies that would abandon extra-linguistic realms of reference, and less rigorous moves that might take one beyond such free play back to more conventional discourse.[17] They are examples, Moore explains, of soft deconstruction, for they do not maintain a consistent rigor in emptying imputed

---

17. Moore, *Literary Criticism,* 136–51 on Crossan, and 151–59 on Kelber.

assumptions of extra-linguistic references in their actual interpretative practices. Such a soft deconstruction is precisely what the Mahāyāna theme of
the two truths (*satyadvaya*) recommends: that one skillfully and with care
(*upāya*) oscillate between the ineffability of the truth of ultimate meaning that
is beyond any signification and the language-formed constructs of worldly,
conventional truth. Ultimate meaning is not a matter of language at all, but
of that which can only be "traced" by language; in the Zen notion, words
trace the ultimate as the flight of birds trace their course through the sky. Moore
himself recognizes the tension: "We can oscillate between two conflicting
perspectives and settle on one of them. But the repressed perspective generally
returns to unsettle our attempted repose. . . . Certain pragmatic constraints
do lend a temporary stability to our constructions. And since they make our
lives livable—or cast long dark shadows over them, as the case may be—our
constructions can not be taken lightly."[18] In Mahāyāna terms, however, it is not
a question between "two conflicting perspectives," but between an ultimate
meaning that is described as no perspective at all, and the constructed perspectives of worldly convention. Truth does not come in levels, nor in layered
strategies of interpretative operations. Rather, the issue for Nāgārjuna, as for
all Mahāyāna thinkers, is how linguistic worldly convention "manifests" an
ultimate, from which it is forever completely other. All strategies, even the
deconstructive logic of emptiness, remain conventional, without ever invading
a realm of signified ultimate meaning. Yet, in their very failure to grasp
something ultimately meaningful, they mark the reality of its absence, i.e.,
as a deferred presence. The bodhisattva, the Mahāyāna epitome of a skillful
practitioner of wisdom, abides in a tensive awareness which differentiates the
two truths of ultimate meaning (*paramārtha-satya*) and worldly convention
(*saṃvṛti-satya*), aware that no conventional construct ever leads to ultimate
meaning, yet totally engaged in just such constructs. The Mahāyāna philosophic discourse on bodhisattva practice is not simply a rigorous and consistent emptying, but a shifting, seemingly shifty, moving point that, beginning
from an initial journey toward ultimate meaning, both constructs and deconstructs (along) the way, at length arriving at a final point that has been emptied
of any fixed finality. The outcome is not the attainment of an abiding haven
of repose, but an attainment of awakening described as non-abiding
(*apratiṣṭhita-nirvāṇa*). One finds rest (*nirvāṇa*) only in the journeying
(*saṃsāra*). Thus the Mahāyāna assertion that this world of constant journeying
is itself final repose (*nirvāṇa* is *saṃsāra*).[19]

---

18. Moore, *Literary Criticism,* 136.
19. Nagao, *The Foundational Standpoint of Mādhyamika Philosophy,* 78: "The path
promises awakening at its end, but that is a tentative promise and not a preestablished
guarantee. If it were the latter, no matter how far off in the future the awakening might
be, the very idea of pilgrimage would be rendered meaningless. . . . Only a path that is
dark and empty in both its beginning and its end, in its starting point and its destination,
only a path that bespeaks a journeying, can fulfill the requirements of a process that casts
a bridge from the initial conventional awareness to ultimate meaning." Such a bridge leaps

The Yogācāra thinkers interpreted this to mean that all constructs are precisely that: just conscious constructs (*vijñaptimātra*). Such constructs are not by this recognition rendered inane, but themselves become the practice of enunciated wisdom, so long as they do not pretend to capture any final viewpoint of "the way things really are." In light of the persistent metaphysical grasping for logocentric essences, post-modern deconstructive strategies are indeed much to be welcomed. They do tend toward the emptying of any theory proposed as absolutely true. Christopher Norris describes Derrida's intent (is that not a philosophic blasphemy?) in terms that echo Mahāyāna concerns: "What he calls into question is the right of philosophy to erect a wholesale theory of mind and language on the basis of commonsense notions that work well enough for all practical purposes but take on a different, more doctrinaire aspect when applied as a matter of philosophic principle."[20] Jerry Camery-Hoggatt echoes a similar idea: "The attempt to boil down metaphorical language to its bare bones informational content may preserve some small measure of its nutritional value, but it does so at the expense of its palatability and texture."[21]

Crossan's and Kelber's "oscillation" is their recognition of the need both for undermining essentialist presumptions and for constructing conventional structures. Yet, I think Moore's criticism is valid in pointing out that they are unable either to validate the need for such oscillation or even to explicate it clearly. A Mahāyāna reading can perhaps be of some service here. Responding to a now-ancient "post-modern" context in which the essentialist notions of previous Buddhist schools had been emptied, Mahāyāna thinkers turned to issues of how to reclaim conventional thinking as the valid construction of discourse within a context of emptiness.

Attempts then to structure approaches to scriptural exegesis are to be heartily welcomed as conventionally valid approaches, none of which can succeed in stating the final meaning of the text. Rhetorical criticism, the present leading contender among hermeneutical challengers, has proven by its fruits to be a productive method of reading the text. Narrative analysis issues not simply in an understanding of the meaning of a text in a suppositional context, but focuses attention on the impact of the narrative on the reader.[22] The insistence of such scholars as Robert Fowler is that the reading of the text is a temporal experience occasioned by the rhetorical structure of what is read, not a grasp of fixed propositions distilled from the texts by an

---

to ultimate meaning in discontinuity from all conventional journeying. Thus awakening is present at every stage of the journey, even the final state of buddhahood, as that which is completely other. Again 80: "Hence, one can attain awakening at any stage. Even the first stage can become the stage of awakening and even at the buddha stage awakening must still remain attainable."

20. Norris, *Derrida*, 179, quoted in Moore, *Literary Criticism*, 159.

21. Camery-Hoggatt, *Irony in Mark's Gospel*, 25.

22. Moore, *Literary Criticism*, 80: "More often than not, reader-response criticism in the New Testament context amounts to a reader-oriented narrative criticism."

intellectual wrestling.[23] One cannot then separate the context of the text from its inner message.

Moore again points out regarding narrative criticism, that in their desire to exorcize the demons of invasive propositional theology from the story text, such critics often wind up in a most unpleasing paradox. Following the interpretative schema of Seymour Chatman's *Story and Discourse: Narrative Structure in Fiction and Film,* New Testament scholars distinguish discourse (termed rhetoric by Rhoads and Michie in *Mark as Story*) and story, and then separate the formal discourse from the story content.[24] By paraphrasing the content of the story plot, one may well wind up with a literary pretender to the vacated throne of metaphysical essences. One may be led by the exigencies of re-presenting a gospel narrative to "hold strongly (if implicitly) to the view that the gospel text has a primary, recoverable meaning: what its author intended,"[25] offering one's reconstruction of that intent as the point of the story itself. The assumption, as described by Moore and evidenced by Rhoads and Michie, that the text is a holistic, formal unity, to be paraphrased in a Targum-like commentary, does seem curiously like a new quest for an unmetaphysical essence, and herein lies the unpleasing paradox.[26]

All of which indicates that the yearning for some firm shore of certitude pops up everywhere. Yet, shorn of such essentialist viewpoints, narrative criticism does seem to supply an apt tool for dealing with the text on the desk. One may agree with Moore who foresees a reinvigorated narrative criticism that is aware of the pervasiveness of discourse form throughout the story content of a text.[27] If one employs narrative, reader-response strategies skillfully, much as Fowler does in his *Let the Reader Understand,* one need not adopt the essentialist baggage of a reified unitary text or a reified identified authorial intent. One is, after all, employing nothing more than a conventionally valid strategy in order to reengage in the task of interpretation.[28]

---

23. See Fowler, *Let the Reader Understand,* 47–58.

24. I thus agree with Moore, *Literary Criticism,* 44, 60, in his critique of Rhoads and Michie's *Mark as Story* that they fail to apply their narrative strategy with consistency, for the rhetorical discourse of the story is not merely the framework within which it is told, but the ubiquitous structuring of the story itself.

25. Moore, *Literary Criticism,* 12. Again 23: "The evangelist's narrative is paraphrased, not by means of discrete statements of propositional content as in the verse-by-verse commentary, but by means of a second plotted narrative, the commentator's own, that explicates the primary narrative for the reader by augmenting it. Commentary thus retains a targumic form."

26. Moore, *Literary Criticism,* 35–38.

27. Moore, *Literary Criticism,* 61: "Reconceived with a rigor that narrative criticism demands but has yet to realize, the notion of form encompasses everything in the presentation of the contentual set of events to which the given gospel refers."

28. I do not agree with Moore's critique, *Literary Criticism,* 73–78 of Tannehill's "The Disciples in Mark," for it appears to me that Tannehill's explication of the author's intent is no more than an interpretative strategy and need not imply that he thinks he has actually unearthed the true intent of the flesh and blood author. Similarly, the Yogācāra scholars, in awareness that everything is empty of essence (*svabhāva*), often employ the term essence (*svabhāva*) as the conventionally valid content of an equally conventionally valid

The theme of the two truths offers a philosophic ground for a reclamation of the dependently co-arisen validity of conventional strategies. It acknowledges that, since all words and ideas are empty of fixed inner content, language can never attain any transcendental content. All discourse is therefore identified as worldly and conventional (*saṃvṛti*), a covering (from *saṃ-vṛt,* to cover over) of the empty nakedness of human understanding by words.[29] Anything then identified through words as an ultimately meaningful content falls from its linguistic perch to ground itself among human and conventional discourse. Any naming of ultimate meaning (*paramārtha*) is itself conventional. Emptiness undermines the duality between an essential apprehender (*grāhaka*) and an essence apprehended (*grāhya*), together with all derivatory dualities. Yet, the identity of emptiness with dependent co-arising resurrects a dualistic pattern of a subject understanding an object, now recognized as worldly convention-only. Not just in the sense that that is sadly all we have at our limited disposal, but also in the sense that the linguistic coverings do indicate something so covered which escapes all verbal signification. The quest for logocentric presence is affirmed as valid, so long as one expects to attain no such presence.[30] Ultimate meaning is described by the Mahāyāna texts as ineffable (*anabhilapya*), and cannot itself be signified in any way.

The Mahāyāna literature speaks of ultimate meaning as the very contentless content of awakening. It is described as an ineffable (*anabhilapya*), non-discriminative wisdom (*nirvikalpa-jñāna*), to be distinguished from the subsequently attained wisdom of verbal mediation (*tat-pṛṣṭalabdha-jñāna*). This itself, of course, is a verbal distinction, and thus appears to drag ultimate meaning into its verbal net as some kind of a transcendental signified: that which is verbally described by saying it is never indicated by language. Do the Mahāyāna thinkers uncritically sneak in the back door what they exclude from the front?

There are, I think, many examples in Mahāyāna doctrinal history of a doctrine of "pure mind" that do subtly affirm such a "transcendental signified," apart from the flux of language and grounded in extra-linguistic experiences. The East Asian focus on Buddha Nature as the originally and always present ground for awakening often does seem to escape the realm of language altogether and float free, as for example in the Zen teaching of Bankei with its insistence on the "unborn mind," or in the American Zen preaching of D.T. Suzuki with its basic theme of intuitionism.[31] In such lineages, for the

---

idea. They are not thereby negating the philosophy of emptiness, but reengaging in language-formed discourse.

29. On the etymology of the Chinese and Sanskrit terms for worldly convention, see Nagao, *The Foundational Standpoint,* 39–45.

30. See Eckel, *To See the Buddha,* 49–128, for an insightful discussion of "the dimensions of the Buddha's absence."

31. Keenan, "The Doctrine of Buddha Nature in Chinese Buddhism," and "Introduction," *The Realm of Awakening.* For a modern philosophical discussion of Zen rhetoric and practice, see Bernard Faure, *The Rhetoric of Immediacy: A Cultural Critique of Chan/Zen Buddhism.* Professors Hakamaya and Matsumoto, Soto Zen scholars, have elicited a

most part pastoral in their orientation, the pure mind functions as the calm
ocean depth which underlies all the language that whirls in bootless falsifica-
tion upon that ocean calmness. But, the Indian Mahāyāna philosophers took
a more critical approach, outlining their understanding in terms of differentiating the two truths.

Mahāyāna philosophy is constituted by its two principal Indian schools:
the Mādhyamika (the philosophy of the middle way) and Yogācāra (the
practice of yogic meditation), also known as Vijñaptimātratā (the philosophy
of conscious construction only). The basic themes were set by the Mādhyamika thinkers, especially Nāgārjuna. The Yogācāra thinkers came slightly
later and attempted to explicate the significance of Mādhyamika insights in
terms of their critical theory of consciousness.

Mādhyamika functions in terms of two basic themes. The first is that of
the identity between emptiness (*śūnyatā*) and dependent co-arising (*pratītya-
samutpāda*). Emptiness entails dependent co-arising, for it describes the
essenceless being of that which arises in mutual dependency. Dependent co-
arising entails emptiness, for it describes the mutual dependency of that which
arises without essence. The second theme is the differentiation of the two
truths of ultimate meaning (*paramārtha-satya*) and worldly convention
(*saṃvṛti-satya*). While the first theme is horizontal in its inspection of existence, the second is vertical, sketching an awareness of the "revelatory"
power of doctrine. Since that which is "revealed" is the content of awakening,
it is beyond all language, and thus is completely other than any conventional
expression. The two truths are then to be differentiated, not identified, for
there is no literal, propositional grasp of the silence of ultimate meaning.
One is to hold the silence of ultimate meaning in dynamic tension with the
conventional awareness of the language-constructed world of convention.
Neither truth is to be granted any final priority over the other, for to the mind
of a buddha, an awakened person, both are empty of any fixed essence that
might ground such a priority. Yet, as the very terms imply, ultimate meaning
is granted a precedence over worldly convention, for to the yet-unawakened
practitioner the goal is the attainment of awakening from the delusions of
the world, a world itself generated through one's absorption in language. One
engages in practice for the sake of that attainment.[32] Indeed, without the hope
of such an attainment, no one would ever expend the effort. The practice of
the middle path (*madhyamā*), however, demands that the practitioner not
collapse the two truths into a single, all-inclusive unity. "The reason for
describing worldly convention and ultimate meaning as unrelated and absolutely other is to avoid overemphasizing either. . . . When one is unclear about
their differentiation, talk about the 'identity' of emptiness and dependent co-
arising cannot but slip into a purely rational ontology biased in the direction

---

most lively debate in Japan on the issue of just what constitutes authentic Buddhism.
They present a most insistent Mādhyamika critique of any substantialist themes.

32. Nagao, *The Foundational Standpoint of Mādhyamika Philosophy,* 25.

of conventional thinking, or into an unmediated mysticism biased in the direction of ultimate meaning."[33] Mahāyāna presents a negation of essentialist views which reaffirms dependently co-arisen views. If one fails to hold in differential tension the two truths, then dichotomies result, and one is forced to choose between a world seen as always captured in subtle linguistic affirmations of logocentric being, or a world forever emptied of any final significance. Yet, that very dichotomy results from a focus on the conventional attainments of verbal awareness. A rigorously consistent emphasis on deconstructive procedures can easily stress the always-deferred presence of what is signified to such an extent that one hardly ever is moved to practice the path. And that is emptiness ineptly apprehended, true indeed in its intellectual thrust, but skill-less in its negation of dependently co-arisen meaning.

Meaning is always dependently co-arisen. There is no non-linguistic meaning, apart from human thinking and secure in its ineffable realm.[34] The emptying of all views, including those thought to be ultimately meaningful, means that the expressed differentiation between the two truths is itself nothing more than another conventional designation. No absolute negation of all essentialist views can be carried out in language, for as soon as one begins to speak, one is immersed in the fabrication of words and ideas. Such a deconstructive negation consists in a silence beyond all language, for silence is the only opposite of linguistic fabrication (*prapañca*). "Everything that comes to be in language, including all worldly conventional negations, is not in fact negation at all. The true working of negation is found in silence. This is the import of the identification of dependent co-arising (verbal worldly convention) with emptiness (ultimate meaning)."[35]

If then, the description of truth as ultimately meaningful, as spoken, remains worldly and conventional, the question urges itself: why bother? If no final signified, no pure mind, no absolute viewpoint can be identified beyond linguistic construction, what is there to attain? If one doubles back only to find a depressing opacity, why not simply conclude that that is about as far as we can go? And go fishing?

In Mahāyāna the doubling back to empty all viewpoints results not in a despair over the limits of linguistic signification but in awareness of those limits, and thus the boundaries, of language. Once emptied of essential referents, the very quest for ontological security is reclaimed in terms of quest-only, not of any expected attainment. "Ultimate meaning can only occur

---

33. Nagao, *The Foundational Standpoint,* 102.

34. Nagao, *The Foundational Standpoint,* 56. See Fowler, *Mark and Method,* 52: "Reader-response criticism is only one among many forms of criticism today that advocate a change in our understanding of meaning. A shift is taking place, away from a static, objective meaning bound to the text to a more subjective meaning experienced by the reader in the temporal flow of the reading experience." Also Malbon, *Mark and Method,* 24: "The move from historical to literary questions represents a paradigm shift in biblical studies."

35. Nagao, *The Foundational Standpoint,* 67.

as something beyond the pale of language and worldly convention, whose borderline in any case can never be delineated. The limits of language and worldly convention are forever receding further and further."[36] The otherness of ultimate meaning is not grounded in some intuition into a logocentric essence beyond the flux of signification but in the exigency to push against the borders of language in a quest for a silence beyond language. In silencing the quest, one does not stifle it. One negates that it is capable of grasping any final reality, not that it is indeed present. Rather, in a silent awareness, the goal of awakening to some absolute truth realized by some pure mind is itself deconstructed. "The pure mind does not exist in the form of an ultimately meaningful essence; it is identical with the conversion . . . [of the mind from delusion to awakening] and hence is conditioned and subject to change."[37] Any pure mind attained in awakening is not a transcendental signified, but the originally present conventional ground of all dependently co-arising insight, and it is such conventional insight that enables one to interpret both text and experience. One knocks at an unopened door in awareness that—for the moment—the boundary is approached, yet the door remains closed and the boundary recedes before it can be transgressed.[38] What is signified by the description of ultimate meaning is an awareness of human seeking, now conscious of such ever-expanding boundaries. Ultimate meaning is present only in an awareness of its absence, but it is the absence of a presence, for its "trace image within worldly convention . . . tends to grow faint and the contours of its reflection of ultimate meaning fade from view."[39] Phantom-like images are all that remain, seen as through a glass darkly.[40] Yet, the construction of such glasses remains a valid interpretative strategy.

The design of the present Mahāyāna commentary on Mark parallels such constructive Mahāyāna strategies. But I do not paraphrase the content of Mark, for fear of filtering out the text on the desk in favor of the paraphrase. Although the traditional commentarial form may be somewhat in decline, the commentary which follows is traditional in its format, presenting the text of Mark for those unfamiliar with it and offering whatever insights a Mahāyāna reading grid can coax to mind. When it coaxes nothing much to mind, I will, I hope, like Martin Luther, be wise enough to leave the text alone.[41]

A Mahāyāna reading is not identical with structuralist or post-structuralist strategies. It is a more theologically driven endeavor, looking through the

36. Nagao, *The Foundational Standpoint,* 76.

37. Nagao, *The Foundational Standpoint,* 106.

38. Nagao, *The Foundational Standpoint,* 78: "The destiny of one following the path consists in knocking repeatedly at a door that remains eternally unopened, in waiting expectantly, even in despair, before that unopened door, in the pilgrimage of knocking again and again."

39. Nagao, *The Foundational Standpoint,* 75. Eckel, *To See the Buddha,* 73–113, on the Buddha's absence.

40. Nagao, *The Foundational Standpoint,* 116–19.

41. Kealy, *Mark's Gospel,* 44.

glasses of basic Mahāyāna philosophical themes, while gratefully accepting assistance from any quarter, not only from traditional Christian scholars who have produced the major commentaries and from those, such as Theodore Weeden, Werner Kelber and Howard Kee who attempt to identify Mark's theological purpose and community, but also from the structuralist readings of Elizabeth Struthers Malbon, the literary criticism of Mary Ann Tolbert, the literary-theological analyses of Dan Via, the political reading of Ched Myers, the study of Mark's irony by Jerry Camery-Hoggatt, the reader-response critique of Robert Fowler, the examination of the Markan miracle stories by Edwin Broadhead, the tradition-history approach of Adela Yarbro Collins, and the emphasis on parable and story of John Dominic Crossan.

This attempt is akin to structuralist interpretations, for it moves within the binary tension of the two truths. Yet that Mahāyāna structure of thought is not only constructed and employed, but also deconstructed and emptied at every turn, for binary oppositions remain conventional strategies in Mahāyāna. It resembles Robert Fowler's reader-response criticism in that any Mahāyāna doctrine is seen as valid only in terms of the practice it elicits and encourages in its hearers. This Mahāyāna reading is also a literary criticism, for it attends to the constant interplay of symbols and allusions in the text. It does not, however, try to construct and filter the gospel through its original literary context, as does Mary Ann Tolbert, for it may well be that Mark was using the conventions of his day only to undermine them. It also has political implications, as does Ched Myers, for Mark does indeed undermine the ideologies of his time. But I do not think he counterpoises a rival ideological structure of liberation. Rather, he leaves that task to the concrete actions of his readers in their dependently co-arisen lives and situations. As John Meier remarks, ". . . the historical Jesus subverts not just some ideologies but all ideologies."[42] The approach used here has perhaps the closest affinity with parable theory, for all teaching in Mahāyāna points beyond itself to that which is not said and indeed cannot be said apart from realization in concrete practice. And that concrete practice is not an uncovering of ancient intentions, but an always decidedly modern engagement in living the middle path. "An artistic work like Mark's gospel, once written, takes on a life of its own which even the original author cannot control as it is handed down from generation to generation in a variety of contexts."[43] The

---

42. Meier, *A Marginal Jew: Rethinking the Historical Jesus,* 199.

43. Kealy, *Mark's Gospel,* 8. Similarly Kee, *Community of the New Age,* ix: "The New Testament theologian can approach his task with considerable freedom. He is at liberty to choose his perspective from which he will launch his inquiry from a number of New Testament possibilities. . . . Once a norm is established, one has a framework within which interpretation can take place." Mahāyāna was not of course a possibility for traditional New Testament scholarship, yet it seems to me that such a reading can coax meanings from the text that both are faithful to and explicative of the text. Kee, 162, remarks that: "Unlike the Pharisees' acquiescence . . . and unlike the Essenes' withdrawal, the Markan community is discernible from the pages of Mark as at once esoteric and evangelistic, as both inclusive and voluntaristic, as affirming both divine determination and hard decisions

Sitz im Leben for Mark is not a fixed context to be discovered by careful reconstruction, but an ongoing history in the life of the Christian communities which have, at least in part, read themselves through this gospel. The present attempt may perhaps be described as a Mahāyāna pesher on Mark, for it freely reads Mark within a philosophic context which is foreign to the text, attempting to explicate its meaning within the experience of one taken with the beauty of such a context.[44] Such a Mahāyāna philosophy serves as the grid and screen for viewing Mark's narrative and will operate in terms of a number of basic themes, outlined below.

The Gospel of Mark is an obvious choice for such an endeavor, for at every turn its rhetoric and strategy reflect in a narrative mode the Mahāyāna themes of emptiness and dependent co-arising, ultimate meaning and worldly convention. Mahāyāna teaches a doctrine that all things, all ideas are empty of essence, referring to no fixed, external reality in the outer world. Mark's rhetoric of indirection likewise empties the clarities one has been led to anticipate, leaving one in the lurch of many mind-numbing puzzles and conundrums. By his use of metaphor and irony, paradox and ambiguity, all surrounded by an abiding opacity which veils both the beginning and the end, Mark accomplishes in narrative what Nāgārjuna was effecting through dialectics: the emptying of expectancies and a tensing of consciousness which may work to trigger awakening.[45] The text twists and turns, employing one trope after another,[46] with the result that the reader begins to sweat in its tropical climate, searching through the literary jungle for a secret meaning.[47] And so I will search, knowing that whatever secrets are found must then be emptied. Emptiness means that "once this experience [of a dynamic, temporal reading] is the focus of criticism, the meaning of meaning also needs to be

---

to be made by members." It is Mark's tensiveness that reflects perhaps not simply the movement of its community, but also a more general awareness of truth and its manifestation, central to any Mahāyāna philosophy.

44. Donahue, *Are You the Christ? The Trial Narrative in the Gospel of Mark,* 76.3: "The three elements which make up the pesher mode, (a) freedom with the text, (b) the actualization of the text in terms of the interpreter's own experience, and (c) the tendency to make a narrative text, are seen now by commentators as explaining the formation of many New Testament narratives."

45. On Mark's rhetoric of indirection, see Fowler, *Let the Reader Understand,* 155–227. Also *Irony in Mark's Gospel* by Camery-Hoggatt.

46. Fowler, *Let the Reader Understand,* 163: " 'Trope,' that which gives language a turn and thereby turns the uses of language along with it, nicely reminds us of the dynamism of indirect language. To the theoretically minded critic, talking about dual semantic structures is a futile attempt to distill a static essence from what is a dynamic temporal experience of following the turn of a word, a phrase, or a longer utterance."

47. Fowler, *Let the Reader Understand,* 166: "The tropical language in Mark's Gospel turns with and within itself when different indirect moves occur simultaneously, it turns over against and on itself when one indirect move gives way to or prepares the way for another, and it also turns from one move into another when a single move takes on new shape and complexion in retrospect as the reading experience progresses. Indirection is protean; just when we think we have it figured out, it transfigures itself."

reinterpreted. No longer can meaning be understood to be a stable, determinate content that lies buried in the text, awaiting excavation. Rather, meaning becomes a dynamic event in which we ourselves participate. . . . No longer can the language of the Gospel be regarded as primarily referential or informative; it has become rhetorical, affective, and powerful."[48] The meaning of Mark, once emptied, becomes then a dependently co-arisen meaning, marking the ambiguity and temporality of all human living.[49]

Mark's text does exhibit a double structure. "On the surface the characters in the drama play out their roles as they understand them; beneath is the level at which only the reader understands the real meaning of events."[50] This distinction does not parallel the Mahāyāna notion of the two truths of ultimate meaning and worldly convention, however, for ultimate meaning signifies not a deeper or higher viewpoint, but the abeyance of all viewpoints, of all signification.[51] Both the story Mark portrays and the discourse through which he weaves that story remain conventional rhetorical strategies.[52] Yet

---

48. Fowler, *Let the Reader Understand,* 3. Also Camery-Hoggatt, *Irony in Mark's Gospel,* 47: "The fundamental presupposition of narrative analysis is this: narratives articulate a field of signification to which readers may assign meaning."

49. Fowler, *Let the Reader Understand,* 4: "I also strive to persuade my reader to focus on the discourse as opposed to the story of the Gospel narrative, on the temporal experience of reading rather than the static structure of the text, and on the omnipresent reception history of the Gospel rather than its lost production history."

50. Juel, *Messiah and Temple,* 178–79, quoted in Fowler, *Let the Reader Understand,* 22. Also Camery-Hoggatt, *Irony in Mark's Gospel,* 179: "So the core of the ironies lies in the tension between exclusionary strategies and veiled revelations. The exclusions prevent the story's characters from hearing or understanding the full implications of the story in which they are a part. The revelations make certain that the reader is continually and subtly confronted with just that deeper level of significance. In the play between these two, the reader is not only allowed to view the silhouette of Jesus' full messianic identity, but he is also asked to take a position, to declare himself." It seems to me, however, that what is involved is more than taking a position or declaring one's assent, for even the assent-declaring Peter is portrayed as totally missing the point. Readers are presented not with a clear definition of Jesus' messianic status, but only with a shadowy silhouette.

51. Fowler, *Let the Reader Understand,* 23, critiques: "*Story* and *discourse* are preferable to Juel's *upper level* and *lower level* because the former pair is less prejudicial. If, as Juel says, Mark is preoccupied with what I would call the discourse level, then the story level is not at all aptly described as the 'first level' or the 'upper level.' The discourse, not the story, is the main concern of the author, so it should be graced with the language of preeminence. Juel is here reflecting the bias of modernity toward the referential function of language, whereby the content of an utterance is regarded as its raison d'être. Such a view of language stands over against the understanding of language common in the ancient world, namely, that the chief function of language is pragmatic or rhetorical and intended to persuade or somehow affect the reader." On the persistent focus on referential meaning in Markan scholarship, see Fowler, 55–56.

52. Bryan, *A Preface to Mark,* 46: "Mark's techniques for presenting his subject are, like his understanding of it, conventional. He expresses directly his own authorial opinion of his hero by his opening words, 'Christ, [Son of God],' and by at once applying to him the words of God's promise (1:1–3). John the Baptist speaks of Jesus, Mark tells us, 'as

both story and discourse close back upon themselves to demarcate the opacity of the boundary of all conventional strategies. "The paratactic-episodic style in which the story is told presents gaps and moments of indeterminacy at every turn. More like lace than a carpet, actually, many patterns in the narrative consist of outlined but empty space."[53] That empty space marks the presence of what cannot be mind-digested by conventional methods. Not only are there gaps, but Mark's conventional narrative abounds in an opacity that reflects the Mahāyāna teaching of the indicated hiddenness of ultimate meaning.[54] That hiddenness is never abated in the text, which ends without a proper story ending and forces the reader to wrestle with its abruptness. "The empty and open tomb is a narrative gap par excellence. The emptiness of the tomb is a story-level figure for the emptiness the narratee encounters in the discourse of this episode: it becomes meaning-full only when the reader fills it with meaning. The empty tomb awaits the fulfillment only the reader can supply."[55]

There is a host of books which attempt to conflate Buddhist and Christian thought. Some suggest now-lost historical connections or attempt to show that, in essence, both traditions are teaching the "same thing."[56] These are, in the main, misguided endeavors, and yet they do signal perceived convergences in doctrinal and philosophical notions between these traditions. The present commentary, by contrast, is not based on parallel doctrinal notions. Rather it employs Mahāyāna philosophical themes as a grid for reading Mark, precisely because Mahāyāna focuses on themes which are neglected in Christian tradition and thus differs from the mainstream of that tradition.[57] This is a weighted philosophical reading of Mark.

---

it is written, . . . the voice of one crying, Prepare the way of the Lord.' Thereafter, who Jesus is and what he is emerges through his words and actions . . . It is all perfectly conventional."

53. Fowler, *Let the Reader Understand,* 153.

54. Fowler, *Let the Reader Understand,* 162, notes Mark's "frequent use of opacity (and ambiguity) to put not only characters but also the audience in the dark." Nagao, *The Foundational Standpoint of Mādhyamika Philosophy,* 51–55, notes that the truth of worldly convention is a covering over (saṃvṛti) of ultimate meaning, which is then indicated as that which is so covered or hidden (saṃvṛta)

55. Fowler, *Let the Reader Understand,* 154.

56. For example, Roy Amore in his *Two Masters, One Message: The Lives and Teachings of Gautama and Jesus,* following the line of thinking in R. Seydel, *Das Evangelium von Jesu in seinan Verhältnissen zu Buddha. Saga und Buddha—Lehre mit fortlaufender Rücksicht auf andere Religionkreise untersucht* of 1882, not only points out the similarity of message, but further argues that the famed Q source was, at least in part, derived from Buddhist circles. There are, I grant, doctrinal parallels to cite, and perhaps even cases of indirect borrowing, but Amore's argument fails, it seems, for lack of clear textual evidence in the sources. See the largely negative conclusions of Lamotte on the closeness of Buddhist accounts to extra-canonical Christian literature in his *History of Indian Buddhism,* 675–688 (740–47 in the original French), and a similar evaluation by Thomas, *The Life of Buddha as Legend and History,* 237–48.

57. Schulz, "Mark's Significance," 159, describes Luke as "the father of the West and

Mark is a subtle writer, sprinkling allusions not only to the Hebrew scriptures but back and forth to earlier and later portions of his own text. Martin Kähler held that the gospels were passion narratives with extended introductions, and thus that Mark actually composed his text backwards, beginning at the end and moving forward to the earlier life of Jesus.[58] That notion rested on a now little-accepted opinion that Mark's passion narrative constitutes a relatively unedited core tradition of historical events, while the first thirteen chapters obviously show the traces of Mark's editorial efforts. Yet the gospel shows no regular process of narrative unfolding that leads to a defined conclusion.[59] It has no single, identifiable thematic glue. "In different ways many have sought the figure in Mark's carpet, [the hidden thematic meaning that lies under the surface of the text], and no one has ever failed to find it. That no two versions of the figure are ever identical simply makes critics try harder. . . . The number of figures in the carpet equals the number of readers and reading experiences. This multiplicity is a sign of the narrative's wealth, not a sign of our criticism's poverty."[60] The text constantly turns on itself, moving both forward to sketch a life of Jesus and backward from the deferred darkness of the crucifixion and resurrection.[61] It begins in the midstream of Jesus' life and ends with the absence of the risen Christ. The cross itself not only casts its shadow backwards on the life of Jesus, but seems to be the emptying of that life. In such a constantly doubling-back and stretching-forth structure, "we are jostled from one puzzle to the next— immediately, again *euthus, palin*—as if the purpose of the story were less to establish a comfortable sequence than to pile one crux upon another, each instituting an intense thematic opposition."[62]

---

promoter of emergent early catholicism." Thus, the Lukan story, much more than Mark, forms the dominant reading of most Christian traditions.

58. Kähler, *The So-Called Historical Jesus and the Historic, Biblical Christ,* 80.11.

59. Kermode, *The Genesis of Secrecy,* 53–54, speaking of the enigmatic man in the mackintosh from Joyce's *Ulysses:* "It is a prior expectation of consonance, the assumption that as readers we have to complete something capable of completion, that causes us to deal as we do with the man in the mackintosh." That is, to try earnestly and insistently to find a definite meaning for what may be but a literary cipher.

60. Fowler, *Let the Reader Understand: Reader-Response Criticism and the Gospel of Mark,* 150–52. Fowler criticizes his scholarly guild: "We are a guild of Jamesian critics, proposing one version of the [thematic] figure [in Mark's narrative carpet] after another with no end to this critical game in sight. . . . What the guild needs to recognize is that the reader deals with the seemingly fragmented, pearls-on-a-string narrative by processes of gap filling, of prospection and retrospection, and of continuous encounters with many kinds of repetition or duality. In episodic narrative the discrete episodes are connected, held together in fluid and ever-changing association, and thus receive their coherence only in the act of reading. The narrative invites us to tie together its disparate pieces ourselves." In Mansfield's words, "Mark did not write with one single theological theme in mind. Instead he utilized multiple motifs in both traditional and redactional passages to portray the richness of 'Gospel' (Good News) to his hearers and readers in his community (Church)" (*"Spirit and Gospel" in Mark,* 2).

61. See Marxsen, *Introduction to the New Testament,* 193.

62. Kermode, *The Genesis of Secrecy,* 141. Again 142: "Behind them all we sense an

The present approach will not attempt to set Mark in his historical context and identify extra-textual references that may lead to fuller understandings of the text itself. There are numerous attempts to coax from the text the concrete situation of the community that produced it and for which it was written.[63] There have been persuasive analyses of that community and thus of the gospel's *Sitz im Leben,*[64] and each seems conclusively convincing while one is engaged in reading that particular analysis—despite the conflicting interpretations offered. In the end, it seems to me that, like the people of Kansas City, we have gone about as far as we can go in reconstructing suppositional contexts for Mark, and must be content with a lack of definitive result. "The history of recent research on the Gospel of Mark can be seen as the record of an attempt to discern the aim of the evangelist and so to discover the perspective which gives coherence to all the features of the Second Gospel."[65] Yet, "whatever we may find to say about the community for which it was originally written (and the evidence will come largely from the gospel itself, in defeating circularity), it is far beyond us to reproduce the tacit understandings that existed between this dead writer and his dead audience. Those accords are lost. We cannot know the original generic set of Mark; and to read it against our own is to read it differently."[66]

To paraphrase Pogo, we have found the *Sitz im Leben* for Mark, and it is us.

Thematic Design

With the hermeneutical prerequisites momentarily out of the way, the thematic design of a Mahāyāna reading of Mark, developed more fully in the running commentary to follow, can be briefly sketched.

On the Way

The Gospel of Mark depicts Jesus' entire life as a journey along the way.[67] Recapitulating the ongoing journey of Israel—out of Egypt, out of Sinai, out

---

algebra, some formal principle of opposition and contradiction." I argue that that algebra can be fittingly expressed by the Mahāyāna theme of the two truths, as explained below.

63. Tolbert, *Sowing the Gospel: Mark's World in Literary-Historical Perspective,* 71, however, does not think that it has a specific community at all, but is directed to the broad range of Hellenistic readers familiar with popular literature.

64. I find most convincing Kee, *The Community of the New Age: Studies in Mark's Gospel,* and Kelber's *The Kingdom in Mark: A New Place and a New Time,* both of which stress the eschatological trajectory of Mark. But see Broadhead, *Teaching With Authority,* 189, for a critique of the circular reasoning of proposed identifications of Mark's *Sitz im Leben.*

65. Kee, *The Community of the New Age,* 353.

66. Kermode, *The Genesis of Secrecy,* 138.

67. Kelber, *The Kingdom in Mark,* 67–68. Also his *Mark's Story of Jesus,* 17: "The very first time Mark alludes to an aspect of Jesus' life, he does so in terms of a 'way' (1:2–3). The reader knows that Jesus will be traveling a way. We shall observe that the

of Babylon,[68] and into the promised land—Mark structures his gospel around Jesus' journeys along his way.[69] The very opening of the text announces that Jesus is God's eschatological messenger who will build the way, who will prepare the way of the Lord and make his paths level.[70] The message, however, is not some privileged piece of information offered to the reader,[71] but a call to set out on a journey toward what such good news might mean. And this is more a journey of seeking and questioning than of geographical transition.[72]

Jesus returns from the wilderness by journeying into Galilee, preaching conversion and faith in the gospel newness. He immediately calls disciples to follow him, to practice the way he both embodies and announces. Throughout his career, Jesus travels from place to place, first in and around Galilee, and then through the climactic events to Jerusalem, to return, once risen, back to Galilee. The journey does not end in Jerusalem. After the resurrection, the young man informs the frightened women that Jesus is going before them into Galilee: so the journeying does not even halt with Jesus' resurrection.[73] "Jesus' whole career is conceived in Mark as a journey."[74]

Markan Jesus is in constant movement from place to place, from region to region, frequently back and forth, and all the way from life to death. Jesus' whole career is conceived by Mark as a journey. . . . There is a logic to Jesus' journey, to grasp that logic is to grasp the meaning of his mission and identity."

68. Via, *The Ethics of Mark's Gospel—in the Middle of Time,* 160.

69. Fowler, *Let the Reader Understand,* 224: "Knowledge . . . is exactly what many have gone looking for in Mark's Gospel; nevertheless, capability or a way is what readers experience. I have already embraced indirection as my own term for the incongruous and uncertain turns of Mark's narrative discourse. Now, too, I embrace capability and way as apt images for what Markan indirection accomplishes. . . . 'The way' appears in the story so many times that it seems to become a metaphor for the temporality of experience within the story itself, and it definitely becomes a metaphor of temporality at the discourse level."

70. Following Tolbert's interpretation, *Sowing the Gospel,* 239–248.

71. For example, Rhoads and Michie, *Mark as Story: An Introduction to the Narrative of a Gospel,* 57: "The reader . . . is in a better position to understand these riddles than the characters are, since from the outset the reader knows Jesus' identity and his relation to the rule of God. . . . This understanding in turn increases the reader's alignment with the world views of Jesus and the narrator." I rather see Mark's opening confession as the setting forth on a journey, both for the characters in the story and for the reader, toward an understanding of just what that initial confession might mean.

72. Malbon, *Narrative Space and Mythic Meaning in Mark,* 69: "That 'on the way' is an enacted spatial metaphor of discipleship is made even clearer by the questions and discussions raised as characters are in movement on the road."

73. Fowler, *Let the Reader Understand,* 224: "The resumed way at the end of the narrative implies that the reader who wishes to continue to follow Jesus on past Mark 16: 8—to see where the way might now lead—must continue to read on past where the narrator ceases to narrate. The reader must read right off the bottom of the last page of the Gospel and on into the dark and the silence. Mark's way trails off into realms of enduring opacity, and the reader must decide at the end of the discourse whether to continue the story."

74. Kelber, *Mark's Story of Jesus,* 17. Malbon, *Narrative Space,* 68: "The initial and final references of the topological sequence of the Gospel of Mark are, more or less explicitly, to 'the way,' forming a spatial frame for the narrative. The first narrative fact or relation presents a prophecy from the past (1: 2–3), the final one a promise for the future (16: 7), and both past and future impinge upon the narrative present. Between these

Jesus' geographical travels are interwoven with the path that he models and preaches. The road leads from Galilee through Jerusalem back again to Galilee, but also from ignorance and incomprehension through awakening to ultimate meaning and then back to a "Galilean" engagement in the practice of the kingdom. It is both a horizontal path, allowing movement from beginning to end, and a vertical path ascending up to and descending back from a Jerusalem death and resurrection. Both aspects are entailed in the practice of the path of Jesus and are held in dynamic tension throughout the narrative.[75] His horizontal awareness is expressed by his movement through and within the settings of the story, along the surface of the earth.[76] His vertical awareness is seen in the constant interplay and tension between his eschatological wilderness experiences (which culminate in his abandonment on the cross) and his engagement in social relationships (reaffirmed in the return to Galilee).[77]

But that way is not the narrative unfolding of a cosmic plan whereby Jesus is divinely fated to travel through Galilee to meet his death in Jerusalem. It is not a numinous design, moving toward the goal God has set for him: death

---

poles, further references to the way occur throughout the sequence, and a significant cluster is presented between 8: 27 and 11: 9. Thus the way provides a unifying framework for the topological suborder." Again, 70: "While many commentators have noted the more-than-spatial significance of one or another Markan reference to 'on the way,' few, if any, have considered the pattern of *all* such references as a unifying framework." And 71: "*Hodos* and *proagein* signal not so much one place among others as a way between places, a dynamic process of movement." Similarly Bratcher and Nida, *A Translator's Handbook on the Gospel of Mark*, 293: "*On the way* must be rendered in some languages by an expression containing a verb, 'as you walked along the path' (or 'along the road'), since *on the way* implies a process of journeying, not simply a position." In similar terms, Mahāyāna teaches that the practice of the middle path leads to no final point of absolute reference, but engages one in the concrete world of dependent co-arising in awareness of the complete otherness of ultimate meaning.

75. Kermode, *The Genesis of Secrecy*, 141: ". . . strong thematic oppositions are forming. John is associated with public baptism, the public fulfillment of his type, Elijah; Jesus with private epiphany and the private fulfillment of his type, Messiah. Moreover, Jesus accepts a baptism of repentance (suggesting prior uncleanness) and at the same time is called the son of God. The paradoxes continue: unmistakable public recognitions alternate with demands for and withdrawals into silence. Demons infallibly recognize him, disciples do not. The Law is now kept and now broken. The canons of purity are challenged; a purity which is itself accused of uncleanness opposes and purges the unclean. If the general sense that this is a movement of special force in the eighth chapter is well-founded, it must be so because so many of these paradoxes come together there in a great knot. But there are many knots; they occur in the riddling parables, in the frequent collocation of perceptive demons and imperceptible saints, in the delight and gratitude of the outsider who is cured, and the astonishment, fear, and dismay of the insiders." Such rhetorical tenseness results, I think, from the constant narrative interplay between what in Mahāyāna is expressed through the themes of emptiness and dependent co-arising and the differentiation of the two truths of ultimate meaning and worldly convention.

76. See Rhoads and Michie, *Mark as Story*, 64–65.

77. Via, *The Ethics of Mark's Gospel—In the Middle of Time*, 160: "A 'road' (hodos) is a spatial phenomenon, but it is one that enables the expression of movement, process, and change and allows the differentiating of points that belong to time: before/beginning—now/ middle—afterwards/end."

in the service of proclaiming God's rule.[78] The way Jesus travels is not a road map leading from start to finish.[79] Indeed, the beginning Mark describes is not Jesus' beginning, but that of the good news about Jesus (1: 1) and the ending is hardly his ending (16: 8), for the risen Jesus is reported still to be journeying back to Galilee.[80] The present tense at 16: 7, "he is going before you" (προάγει) emphasizes the process of going before on the way as opposed to the resultant arrival.[81] The disciples expect Jesus to reach the goal of a final messianic triumph, yet he does not do so.

Although interpreters often take their clues from Mark's treatment of these beleaguered disciples, they often present a mirror image of the disciples, describing the achieved goal as Jesus' enthronement on the cross according to the divine plan. The path ends for them either with the Jerusalem death and resurrection of Jesus, or with a projected parousia in Galilee.[82] By contrast, in a Mahāyāna reading, Jesus is still going before us to Galilee. The understanding of path that guides this commentary is not that of a road map between two points, whether cosmically designed or spiritually fulfilled. Rather, it is drawn from Mahāyāna sources to emphasize the practice of conversion and

---

78. Among many other interpreters who assert such a cosmic plan, see Rhoads and Michie, *Mark as Story,* 64. Donahue, *Are You the Christ?* 230, is perhaps closer to the mark: "In contrast to Paul who says that Jesus was put to death by the 'powers of the age' (1 Cor 2: 8), what immediately strikes one about the Markan passion narrative is its 'secular' character. In Mark the dramatic action is explained in terms of human causality and human decisions. It is true that the fulfillment of scripture is a motif in the passion narrative, but the Markan *dei* functions much like the tragic necessity or *moira* of Greek tragedy."

79. Thus I disagree with Beardslee, *Literary Criticism of the New Testament,* 17: "By creating its own ordered world, wherein, through struggle or action an end is achieved, the story expresses faith in the ultimate reality of order and life." Rather, Mark's world seems placed in the tension between order and wilderness, moving all the while to an ending is hardly a proper ending at all. Kermode, *The Genesis of Secrecy,* 143, perceptively writes about Mark's rhetoric: "We are most unwilling to accept mystery, what cannot be reduced to other and more intelligible forms. Yet that is what we find here: something irreducible, therefore perpetually to be interpreted, not secrets to be found out one by one, but secrecy."

80. Malbon, *Narrative Space,* 49: "At the close of the Gospel of Mark, Jesus' spatial location is neither Jerusalem nor its environs, neither Judea nor Galilee, but somewhere in between; Jesus is in movement (16: 7). For the followers of Jesus—after the strange and surprising event of the resurrection outside Jerusalem—nothing, not even the familiarity of home in Galilee, is likely ever to be the same."

81. Malbon, *Narrative Space,* 54.

82. Malbon, *Narrative Space,* 181.71: "Although the Markan tension is clear, the equation of it—to a greater (Marxsen and Kelber) or lesser (Lightfoot) degree—with the expectation of a literal, imminent parousia in late first-century Galilee is not." See also Malbon, "Galilee and Jerusalem: History and Literature in Marcan Interpretation," *Catholic Biblical Quarterly,* 44 (1982) 242–55. The tension of the middle path (*madhyamā-pratipād*) is collapsed by any literal reading of Mark's plot, for that would interpret the text only in the light of a supposed original context, ignoring the long history of the text in Christian rereadings. Note that the term παρουσία occurs nowhere in Mark's text; it is strange therefore to make it the overriding theme of the text.

faith, the central message of Mark (1: 15). Path means journeying, a practicing of faith. Not as a means to an end, but as an ongoing realization of an awakened practice. That practice is described by the Mahāyāna masters in terms of a number of interlocking themes.[83] They speak of a middle path in terms of the identity between emptiness and dependent co-arising, the differentiation of the two truths of ultimate meaning and worldly convention, and the three patterns of consciousness. This Mahāyāna doctrine of the middle path will form the hermeneutical template guiding the following interpretation at every turn.

Emptiness

The Japanese translation of the first verse of *Qoheleth* employs the same term used to translate emptiness (*śūnyatā*) into Chinese characters. It says: "Emptiness of emptiness, all is empty." As a further reading of *Qoheleth* will confirm, that emptiness issues in a most desolate and pessimistic view of life itself. Perhaps the translators of the Bible into Japanese had the Buddhist notion in the back of their minds when they chose emptiness (*kū*) to translate the Hebrew *hebhel* (an ephemeral mist), but, if so, they misunderstood the Mahāyāna notion of emptiness. In the Mahāyāna literature, emptiness does not lead to bemoaning one's sad fate nor does it sink one into pessimistic tedium. Rather, emptiness functions as a liberator from illusions. It is meant to counter the security of self-centered knowledge by undermining the belief that human ideas and images represent the very essences of things.[84] Although the specific doctrinal context in which the Mahāyāna notion of emptiness was first propounded in India has long since passed, emptiness remains the banner cry of Mahāyāna.[85] Emptiness refutes all assurances that one has grasped the core of reality, that one's understanding has a fixed and secure point of reference in the real, external world, that it is grounded in the underlying being (substance) of beings. There is a pervasive naive realism which pretends to have reached unassailable knowledge of the way things really are. Yet in Mahāyāna doctrine such a pretense to certitude occludes the very possibility of awakening, for it clings to ideas and images in place of the unexpected and unanticipated experience of insight and awakening. All ideas are described as nothing more than (and nothing less than) "descriptive

---

83. For a brief summary of the historical unfolding of Mahāyāna doctrine, see Keenan, *The Meaning of Christ: A Mahāyāna Theology,* 123–186.

84. See Crossan, *The Dark Interval: Toward a Theology of Story,* 34–46.

85. The Perfection of Wisdom Scriptures and the Mādhyamika philosophy of Nāgārjuna were aimed at refuting specific schools of Abhidharma scholasticism and their claim to have reached the essences (*svabhāva*) of things through proper and exhaustive analysis. Thus, the *Heart Scripture* announces that all is empty, even the most central Buddhist doctrinal notion of emptiness. (See Lopez, *The Heart Sutra Explained,* 33). Nāgārjuna, *Stanzas on the Middle,* 13.8, teaches that "The Victors have declared emptiness as the expeller of all views."

designations," supported indeed upon sensed images, concepts and judgments, but never corresponding directly to the very being of things.[86] Naive realism is regarded as self-centered clinging to fixed ideas projected onto external realities, supporting a false belief in an independent inner self (*ātman*) in firm control of outer reality (*dharma-svabhāva*). Emptiness is a Mahāyāna commentary on the basic doctrine of no-self (*anātman*), i.e., no self apart from and independent of the contextual conditioning of all being. There is, Mahāyāna teaches, an all but innate tendency to view the personal, inner self apart from all relationships as the core at the center of all one's relationships, but in Mahāyāna a person is more an onion than an apple—no inner core at all. Emptiness is then the peeling away of the onion layers of fixed and firm ideas that support a false belief in self to reveal the emptiness within.[87]

If we read Mark through such a Mahāyāna lens, the disciples typify just such an obdurate clinging to their own ideas about precisely who they are and who Jesus is.[88] From their self-perspective, they repeatedly reject Jesus' predictions about how the messiah is to suffer and die, and they never seem to get the point that only by losing one's life is one saved. Indeed, Mark's portrait of the disciples is so negative that it has engendered a number of attempts to explain this surprising portrayal.[89] After all, Jesus' first disciples were the first Christians, and one would expect them to have both understood Jesus and to have followed the path he taught.[90] The recent emphasis on the

86. Nāgārjuna, *Stanzas on the Middle,* 24.18, depicts the Buddha as saying: "It is dependent co-arising that I term emptiness. Taking on this designation, [emptiness] is established." See Nagao, *The Foundational Standpoint of Mādhyamika Philosophy,* 11–12. Ideas describe things not because they are supported upon or have recourse to the essences of things, but because they are grounded in the dependent co-arising of things, because they are part and parcel of a mutually interdependent world. The Yogācāra thinkers take the theme a step further and explicate the very nature of understanding in terms of the mutual dependence of the processes of thinking and understanding.

87. That does not, however, imply the negation of an existential self, only of an essential self. See Nagao, "Buddhist Subjectivity."

88. Tannehill, "The Disciples in Mark," 140, explains that Mark first draws the reader to identify with the disciples by presenting them in a positive light and then forces that reader "to distance from them and their behavior. . . . This tension between identification and repulsion can lead the sensitive reader beyond a naively positive view of himself to self criticism and repentance." Thus Mark "intended to awaken his readers to their failure as disciples and call them to repentance."

89. See Weeden, *Mark—Traditions In Conflict,* which sees Mark's strategy as countering the false claims of a divine man christology; Kelber, *The Kingdom in Mark,* which interprets the context in terms of Mark's critique of the then already destroyed Jerusalem Church, represented in the story by the disciples. By contrast, Tannehill, "The Disciples in Mark," 141, sees that portrayal not as a "polemic against any particular group," but against the faulted discipleship of Christians generally. Fowler, *Let the Reader Understand,* 256, credits Weeden with breaking the grip of the Matthean and Lukan rehabilitation of the disciples on the reading of Mark. He lists Weeden's precursors in note 53, to which Sandmel should be added, for in *Two Living Traditions,* 153, the latter states: "I allege that Mark regards them [i.e., the disciples] as villains."

90. The Prajñāpāramitā texts of the Mahāyāna tradition present a similar literary strategy when they present the disciple Śāriputra as the consummate master of analytical knowledge who consistently fails to get the point of the Buddha's teaching. Note, however, that no

narrative character of Mark as a literary composition does lead one to seek a literary reason for the structure of the text, particularly one which will explain why the story ends so abruptly and elliptically without any definitive conclusion. Yet that very abrupt ending demonstrates the deliberately unfinished nature of this gospel. The final γαρ clause at 16: 8 serves as a sign of an unfinished narrative. The plot implicitly carries over into the lives of the "Galilean" readers. Mark's plot is not merely information to be apprehended about its characters and then implemented in terms of knowledge gained. The extra-textual ending is an intrinsic part of the narrative. All the plot expectations a reader may entertain are emptied of any final validation, even as regards the role of the disciples.[91] Remarkably, even Jesus' resurrection goes unreported and unwitnessed. There is simply nothing left to hold onto. It is not surprising that quite early the Christian communities felt compelled to fill in the apparent lack, adding post-resurrection appearances and rehabilitating the sorry disciples. Indeed, as the text reads, the last chapter has not been written. It remains to be filled in by subsequent readers. A commentary is then a filling in of the empty spaces left by the text. But that exercise

---

one has yet claimed that Śāriputra represents anything more than a well-meaning but rather dense disciple.

91. Fowler, *Let the Reader Understand,* 173: "Note that the dramatic irony that is cultivated by elaborate repetition almost always involves the disciples at story level. Significantly, the disciples are usually the unknowing victims of the dramatic irony that is created by means of repetition. Could the victimization of the disciples be merely fortuitous? They are the companions of Jesus through the long haul of the story, and perhaps they are victimized the most merely because they are present the most. That does not explain why they should be victimized at all, however, nor does it explain why their obtuseness grows rather than diminishes." Perhaps they are so victimized merely because of their august position in the Christian communities of Mark's time, in full awareness of the reverence Christians exhibited toward their apostolic predecessors, yet not because of any specific theological struggle or debate, but simply because, being august and revered, they tended to become regarded as a sacral class representing a sacral time. Eliade, *Myths, Dreams, and Mysteries,* 34, writes about the quest to escape from the present in order to recapture by recapitulation a primordial time: "The Polynesians, when setting out upon a grandiose maritime adventure, are careful to deny its 'novelty,' its unprecedentedness, its spontaneity; for them, it is only a case of repeating the voyage that was made by some mythical hero *in illo tempore,* to 'show the way,' to set an example." See also *The Sacred and the Profane,* 68–113. It is perhaps significant that the phrase *in illo tempore,* which occurs frequently in the other Synoptics, is absent in Mark. To establish a privileged sacral time or a privileged sacral class suggests a practice that is but a pale imitation of that time and directed by that class. Mark then, while deconstructing the sacredness of the official classes of the Jews, does the same for his own Christian community. There is no need to imagine that the flesh-and-blood Mark actually thought all the apostolic representatives were in fact as obtuse as the disciples, nor that he thought the Pharisees as uniformly unenlightened as he presents them. Their role in his story is literary and not referential. Similarly, Ivan Illich's treatise "The Vanishing Clergyman," which harshly criticizes clerical professionalism, does not mean that Illich himself saw all clerics as professional, deluded usurpers of religious faith practice. He, perhaps like Mark, merely wanted to disestablish their sacred hegemony. When he wrote his article, Illich was himself a cleric. Similarly, Mark himself was apparently a disciple of Jesus.

should not so conclude the text that its plot is brought to closure, for then Mark would lose its creative design.

Dependent Co-Arising

The emptying of all expectations and all ideas is not a nihilistic endeavor. Rather, emptiness entails dependent co-arising. In Mahāyāna, dependent co-arising refers to the existence we in fact experience, apart from the reifying delusion of naive realism. Emptiness refutes essential being, while dependent co-arising affirms being as it arises from the convergence of clusters of causes and conditions. Nothing exists independently, but the world with all its variety does exist in a mutual conditioning and support.[92] Even the most cherished notions of self are subjected to the logic of emptiness and declared to be non-existent. But that very non-existence affirms their dependently co-arisen being, and makes possible the enunciation of true doctrine and the authentic practice of the middle path.[93] The course of the events reported by Mark is not the cosmic unfolding of a divine design, but the dependently co-arising convergence and conflict between the authentic practice of the path and the deluded opposition to that practice, a drama that continues beyond the text into the lives of all Christian practitioners. "In the end the Gospel beckons us to leave the relative security of its nest behind and to try out our new wings, by plunging ahead into the void beyond Mark 16: 8."[94] It is a human drama that unfolds, not a divine plan. Furthermore, it is simply inappropriate to take the life of Christ as the exact model for each and every Christian, as if all Jesus' followers would repeat his experiences of arrest, suffering, and execution. When Jesus talks in his prediction of suffering (8: 31) about the necessity (δεῖ) that he suffer and die at the hands of the authorities, or about the inevitability of wars and rumors of wars (13: 7), he is foreseeing the dependently co-arisen outcome of the forces placed in conflict. His practice of the kingdom directly counters the religious fixations of his opponents and leads inevitably to his rejection and suffering. But the Father is not his executioner. Rather, Jesus' emptying of accustomed traditions and reified practices engenders fear all around and elicits from the unconverted the compulsion to remove him from the scene.

---

92. For a restatement of these themes in dialogue with modern existentialist thinking, see Nishitani, *Religion and Nothingness,* especially the first article, "What is Religion?"

93. Nāgārjuna, *Overcoming Vain Discussions,* 71: "I pay homage to the unequalled Buddha who taught that emptiness, dependent co-arising, and the middle path are one in meaning."

94. Fowler, *Let the Reader Understand,* 262. Fowler, 137–140, sees Mark's plot as a blending of a predestined, divine inevitability with one of contingency and freedom. I disagree. In Mahāyāna terms, freedom opens up only within the field of karmic conditioning, without any appeal to a cosmic or divine inevitability. It is sufficient in Mark's story that the necessity of Jesus' future derives from the complex of actions (*karma*) performed by the characters.

Yet that very emptying opens the way to the true practice of the eschatological kingdom, in which Jew and Gentile, male and female, share in a common practice of the path.[95] Mark is not a world-denying gospel, but a preparing of the way of the Lord. Even the eschatology of chapter 13 does not entail the rejection of the world. Rather, one is left with a new journeying back to Galilee, as announced in 14: 26.[96] Interpreters argue over whether Jesus is present to or absent from the Markan community. Are they—as we—left with his absence until he comes in glory on the clouds of heaven? In a Mahāyāna reading, his essential absence as the central presence of the Christian community entails his dependently co-arisen presence in all the journeys of practice. The middle path is not the following of a sacral ideal set up in the understanding mind, but entails the emptying of all ideals to reclaim the concreteness of living in the interdependence of the new community. There are no privileged representatives of that community, for the inner circle of Jesus' family, friends, and disciples are all disqualified from such an honor. The only characters who respond to Jesus with faith and understanding are

---

95. Nāgārjuna, *Stanzas on the Middle*, 24.18: "It is dependent co-arising that I term emptiness. Taking on this designation, [emptiness] is established. It alone is the middle path." Without the initial emptying, views are taken to represent the reality of the path in a rigid fashion, thus precluding the actual engagement in practice. Camery-Hoggatt, *Irony in Mark's Gospel,* 22 writes: "If our experiences of reality were . . . fixed, growth would be unnecessary, and conversion impossible. The varying textures of experience could be flattened out and assimilated to a single, coherent, rationally defensible system." In like fashion, Nāgārjuna in *Mūlamadhyamakakārikā* is criticized by an opponent who claims that if everything is empty, then no practice could result in change or conversion, since everything is emptied of reality. Nāgārjuna answers in 24.20 that: "If everything is not empty, there would be no arising and no passing away. According to your [opinion that all things are fixed essences], you would have to say that the four truths are nonexistent." The four truths are the bedrock teaching of the Buddha Śākyamuni, leading to the realization of cessation (*nirvāṇa*) of suffering (*duḥkha*) through the practice of the path (*mārga*) that reverses the causal origin (*samudāya*) of that suffering. Thus, Nāgārjuna's point is that a universe fixed in some metaphysical program precludes the realization of cessation, i.e., awakening.

96. Fowler, *Let the Reader Understand,* 262: "Apparently the Jesus who was present in the past will again be present in the future, but he is not present in the present. Yet does that make sense? This puzzle may be less irksome if we consider that perhaps again we have confused story content with narrative discourse because the Jesus of Mark's past, present and future is always *Mark's* Jesus. . . . In one sense the Galilee alluded to in 14: 28 and 16: 7 is the experience beyond 16: 8 of following Jesus on the way into an unknown future. In another sense, what is Galilee but the way in which we have already followed Jesus through the experience of reading the sixteen chapters of Mark's Gospel? Could not the very last word of the Gospel (the awkwardly placed conjunction *gar*) be analogous to the musical notation of a coda, which signals the musician to return to a marked passage and to keep on playing?" Similarly Donahue, *Are You the Christ?* 222: "In his penetrating analysis of the Markan understanding of *euaggelion* Marxsen has shown that gospel is less a matter of content than a way of re-presenting Jesus to the time of the reader. The gospel 'makes contemporary the one who has come and the one who will come' [*Mark,* 148]." Again, 231: "One function of narrative in Mark is to create a time scheme where the past of Jesus becomes the present of the reader."

outsiders—the scribe who understands the great commandment, the Syro-Phoenician woman, the synagogue president Jairus, the centurion at the cross. Even when outsiders want to join the following of Jesus, they are not allowed to do so, as with the healed and restored Gerasene demoniac. The sighted Bartimaeus, the last person healed by Jesus, follows Jesus along the way, but he soon disappears and is not identified as a representative of the kingdom. As soon as people respond to Jesus in faith, Mark whisks them from the story, disallowing these "little people" from remaining long enough to constitute a sacral elite.[97] The absence of representatives who might structure and thereby close off the new community denotes the emptiness of that community, and thus its radical openness and interdependence. Emptiness is identical with dependent co-arising.

The Truth of Ultimate Meaning

The practice of the middle path involves more than insight into emptiness and living in the dependently co-arisen world. Jesus' way is not merely a journeying away from and back to Galilee. Rather, Jesus comes into his Galilean ministry as an eschatological voice crying in the wilderness. He is empowered by the wilderness splitting-open of the heavens and the divine voice of his Father. At strategic points throughout the narrative, he again withdraws into the wilderness to pray.[98] Wilderness, however, is not a geographical term, but serves a theological purpose.[99] It denotes the abeyance of all societal intercourse. The theme is set in the prologue, where the cosmic forces are represented by the voice from heaven, the presence of Satan to test Jesus, the wild beasts and angels.[100] These cosmic forces signal the truth of ultimate meaning as completely other. Even when demonic, they are symbols for that which is apart from the conventional meanings engendered among human beings. Thus Jesus is drawn out from the towns to the mountains—to pray, to be transfigured, to the anguished prayer on the Mount of Gethsemane, and finally he is lifted up on the cross where he utters his last lonely prayer. Each time he leaves the crowd, his disciples pursue him to bring him back to town. They share only in his mountain transfiguration, but even there they do not understand what is happening. They fall asleep during his anguish in the garden. And they all abandon him on the cross.

---

97. Rhoads and Michie, *Mark as Story,* on "The Little People," 129: "In contrast to both the opponents and the disciples, minor characters in the gospel consistently exemplify the values of the rule of God. The minor characters make brief cameo appearances and then disappear, yet the role of each is often quite memorable."

98. Kermode, *The Genesis of Secrecy,* 141: "His authority is widely recognized, his miraculous cures are seen by great crowds. But once again he withdraws (a repeated movement, which Starobinski calls *esseulement*)."

99. The central theme of Mauser, *Christ in the Wilderness.*

100. See Tolbert, *Sowing the Gospel,* 111. Malbon, *Narrative Space,* 63: "Like the wilderness, the mountain is generally an isolation in the Markan context."

The truth of ultimate meaning is other than all conventional representations of truth, and thus throughout the gospel Jesus consistently undermines expected notions of religious truth. He does not simply set himself over against the falsity of the scribes and Pharisees, as if he proposes one viewpoint and they another. Rather, all viewpoints are subjected to eschatological critique and judgment, even those of his inner circle of friends, family, and disciples.[101] None of those cameo characters who manifest faith presents any doctrinal viewpoint. The content of his teaching "is generally not given at all, or only summarized very briefly or illustrated by a single example."[102] Mark is not an omniscient narrator who informs the reader of the truth of the events he describes. Rather he himself, whoever he was, is engaged in the enigma of following Jesus. His point is not that one assents to the content of some verbal teaching, but that one is converted and attains faith. When Jesus teaches in the synagogue at Capernaum (1: 22), Mark stresses not the content of that teaching, but that it is given with authority. Jesus teaches the shore-bound crowd from the boat many things (4: 2), and, Mark explains, in the course of that teaching he presents the parable of the sower, focusing not on what is taught but on the receptivity of his hearers. Later in Jerusalem Mark says that Jesus was teaching in the temple (12: 35–37), but offers no hint at what the substance of that teaching might be. Rather, he presents Jesus as deconstructing the necessity of the teaching, as aiming to empty false practice (12: 38–40), rather than to impart true viewpoints. Even Peter's confession at Caesarea Philippi (8: 30–33), although it faithfully echoes Mark's initial confession that Jesus is the Christ, is found to be mistaken, for no verbal orthodoxy assures the presence of conversion. Jesus counters Peter by speaking plainly about the sufferings he is to undergo. Yet "even this uncoded speech is totally misunderstood, even by Peter who has just made his confession of Christ. Again we see the infinite difference between God and man. There is no bridging here."[103] Peter moves only within the

---

101. Tolbert, *Sowing the Gospel,* 233, writes: "In the Gospel of Mark that cause [of deforming the disciples' expectations] has to do with the clash of worldviews held by participants in the kingdom of God and by members of this sinful and faithless generation." Yet, those kingdom participants, those who have faith and are healed by Jesus—the good earth—appear only briefly in the narrative to fall almost immediately out of the picture. They present no worldviews. Only Mark and Mark's Jesus offer any extended teachings, and then usually in parables that preclude unconverted understanding.

102. Schweizer, "Mark's Theological Achievement," 45. So Bultmann, *Jesus and the Word,* 79: "This really means that Jesus teaches no ethics at all in the sense of an intelligible theory valid for all men concerning what should be done and left undone. . . . A man cannot control beforehand the possibilities upon which he must act; he cannot in the moment of decision fall back upon principles, upon a general ethical theory which can relieve him of responsibility for the decision; rather every moment of decision is essentially new. For man does not meet the crisis of decision armed with a definite standard; he stands on no firm base, but rather alone in empty space."

103. Schweizer, "Mark's Theological Achievement," 52.

realm of worldly convention, the things of humans (τὰ τῶν ἀνθρώπων) and not within the realm of ultimate meaning, the things of God (τὰ τοῦ θεοῦ).

The gospel is so empty of positive content that it has led scholars to supply that absence, usually by focusing on the person of Jesus. What then becomes important is a recognition of the identity of Jesus himself. Jesus, rather than the conversion and faith he preaches (1: 13), becomes the content of the gospel. Yet efforts to pin down Jesus' identity seem to flounder at every turn, for Mark describes Jesus in rather loose terms by titles that are susceptible of a variety of interpretations.[104] In the text the people who do identify him are mistaken. The home town folks at Nazareth are sure that he is the woodworker they all know (6: 3). The authorities identify him as a demoniac (3: 22), bent upon destroying the temple (14: 58). His disciples, confessing him to be the christ, seem to think he is a divine personage.[105] For centuries Christian exegetes and theologians read the christological creeds back into the gospels and naturally assumed that they knew who Jesus is, the second person of the Trinity.[106] With the arrival of more textually sensitive exegesis that approach, no matter how it may be evaluated as Church doctrine, is seen as theologically and scripturally naive. The ultimate meaning escapes all worldly convention and all theological narrative. "World and book, it may be, are hopelessly plural, endlessly disappointing; we stand before them, knowing that they may be narratives only because of our own impudent intervention, and susceptible of interpretation only by our hermetic tricks. Hot for secrets, our only conversation may be with guardians who know less and see less than we can, and our sole hope and pleasure is in the perception of a momentary radiance, before the door of disappointment is finally shut on us."[107] Yet, that rhetoric of disappointment is aimed not at the negation of meaning, but at countering the intrusive attempts of worldly and conventional

---

104. Fowler, *Let the Reader Understand,* 180: "Another important category of metaphorical expressions in Mark is the nicknames and titles given to various characters at story level. The chief example is Jesus, who receives numerous honorific titles or epithets: 'Christ,' 'Son of God,' 'Son of man,' 'Son of David,' 'King of the Jews,' and others. For generations scholars have labored to clarify the meaning of these titles in Mark in the light of their popular usage in first-century Palestine and the broader Mediterranean world, but I shall insist on staying within Mark's Gospel and focusing on the metaphorical, riddlelike nature of the epithets used for Jesus and for other characters. In Mark's narrative the titles for Jesus are not clearly defined or interpreted, either in the story or in the discourse. The title that gets the most exposure is Son of man, but it remains a metaphorical puzzle to the end."

105. Weeden, *Mark—Traditions in Conflict,* sees the turning point in the gospel at Peter's confession, all preceding it presenting the disciples' view of Jesus within a "divine man" christology, and all following it as Mark's critique from a perspective of a *theologia crucis*. Without following Weeden's identification of the disciples as representatives of an extra-story heretical christology, it seems that he has indeed pinpointed their intrastory misidentification of Jesus as beyond suffering and failure, i.e., as a "divine man."

106. See Keenan, *The Meaning of Christ: A Mahāyāna Theology,* for an interpretation of the Incarnation and Trinity through Mahāyāna themes.

107. Kermode, *The Genesis of Secrecy,* 145.

thinking to locate a final point of reference. No final point of reference shall be given. "Mark 8: 11 is a request for certainty, resolution, and clear referential ('sign') meaning. The Pharisees ask Jesus for an escape from uncertainty, and he turns them down."[108] The blind Bartimaeus, sighted by the word of Jesus, does not mope around but follows Jesus joyfully in his path. None of the faithful who pop in and out of Mark's narrative seeks for signs of certitude, but are content to experience the saving force of Jesus' word to them. To be caught in sad disappointment is to be caught in a mind-set that insists, despite its impossibility, on capturing the truth of things in clear ideas and images. Mark's narrative, however, "implies that a person should be able to live with uncertainty and gaps in understanding. It gives us practice in living without full illumination."[109] In a Mahāyāna reading, that very lack of illumination is itself illumination, aware of the hidden presence of that which recedes behind the veils of all words and images. Any final illumination is an unachievable goal, for awakening itself is empty of abiding essence. Once emptied, the quest for a resting point is replaced by engagement in the dependently co-arisen world, suffused with an awareness of the omnipresence of that which is hidden.

The eschatological imagery throughout the text coalesces in the "little apocalypse" of chapter 13. Jesus comes to announce the arrival of the end time, the kingdom of God is at hand (1: 15). He predicts his suffering and death to undermine the expected messianic role his disciples imagine for him. He further answers his disciples who wonder at the marvelous buildings of the Temple by describing in mythic terms the eschatological judgment on all structures and all constructs that would circumscribe—in whatever temple—the immediately available presence of Yahweh as other. The eschatology of Mark is then not a revelation of the shape of the future course of any divine plan, but a stricture against constructing any fixed and delimited plan whatsoever. Thus even Jesus, the eschatological son of man, ends his discourse on the future by stating that he does not know the hour or the day of the end time and his advice is to engage in watchfulness and practice in the middle time (13: 34–37). Markan eschatology is the mythic expression in Mark's narrative for the reversal of all expectancies and all constructs. It is not, I think, to be demythologized or reduced to more manageable terms, such as ethics or millenarian projections. Rather, the cosmic and dramatic descriptions are to be seen as mythic narrative elements signifying the complete otherness of ultimate meaning from all conventions and all plans.

The Truth of Worldly Convention

Yet Jesus does teach and preach the Gospel. He relies both on a wilderness emptiness and on conventional discourse.[110] He counters the mistaken views

---

108. Fowler, *Let the Reader Understand*, 195–96.
109. Fowler, *Let the Reader Understand*, 220.
110. Nāgārjuna, *Stanzas on the Middle*, 24.8–10: "The Buddha's doctrine relies on the

of both opponents and disciples with parables and plainly spoken teachings. He comes out from the wilderness of his testing into Galilee, preaching the arrival of the kingdom and calling for conversion and faith.[111] At the transfiguration on the mountain the voice of the Father tells both the disciples and the reader to listen to what he teaches. Jesus is not an "empty cipher, merely signifying freedom from superstitious observance of the law and incomprehensible cultic practices."[112] Rather, he preaches the way, the middle path that brings the otherness of Abba into speech, without collapsing its otherness into the categories of worldly convention. The practice of the middle path entails living in a tensive awareness of the otherness of ultimate meaning and its translation into conventional teachings. Indeed, the Markan narrative strategy is to heighten the tensive awareness of the hiddenness of ultimate meaning within the enunciation of Jesus' teaching so as to trigger a renewal or reorientation of consciousness. "Mark's rhetoric of indirection is maieutic: it performs the role of a midwife, lending encouragement and assistance to the reader's . . . self-transformation in the experience of reading."[113] Yet even Jesus' teachings do not capture ultimate meaning, which remains forever other and disjunctive from all teaching. Rather, they are skillful rhetorical strategies directed toward insights that go beyond words and images, that finally fall silent in the wilderness of no-speaking. There is no linear connection between the silence of the wilderness and the proclamation of the gospel. Ultimate meaning triggers conventional discourse but is not captured therein. The Markan narrative strategy of emptying and indirection cock the pistol, but they do not pull the trigger. No rhetorical discourse brings about faith.

Like Jesus, however, the reader is not to remain silent, for, in awareness of the constant otherness of Yahweh, the call to discipleship means engagement in the task of skillful teaching and compassionate living. Emptiness and dependent co-arising are identical, two sides of the same philosophic coin. Conventional meaning, in contrast, never attains to any ultimate. We move toward that ultimate, seek it out, express it variously, and teach the path toward its realization, but never actually reach a verbal understanding of its nature. Faith is not a viewpoint. Yet that very understanding of the limitation of all viewpoints is itself a constant awareness of ultimate meaning as other, as that which draws forth the attempts at translation.

The term worldly convention is taken from the Chinese rendering of the original Mahāyāna term *saṃvṛti*, which literally means a "covering over" of

---

two truths: the worldly, conventional truth and the ultimate truth. Those who do not know the differentiation between these two truths do not understand the point of the Buddha's teaching. Without reliance on conventions, the ultimate is not taught. And without arriving at ultimate truth, cessation is not reached."

111. Malbon, *Narrative Space,* 73: "The Markan prologue draws significantly upon the rich (Hebrew) wilderness tradition, combining the themes of repentance and renewal."

112. Schweizer, "Mark's Theological Achievement," 43.

113. Fowler, *Let the Reader Understand,* 223.

truth by language. Conventional teachings both reveal and hide the truth thus revealed.[114] The veil in the temple not only hides from view the holy of holies, but also manifests its presence as veiled. Conventional teachings similarly manifest the ultimate truth by marking its concealment.[115] That does not imply that all teachings are equally valid or that logical presentation finds no place in biblical hermeneutics. Rather, reasoning and interpretation regain their dependently co-arisen validity as human constructs precisely by being freed from any pretension of capturing ultimate truth.[116] One is not to glory in overturning conventional language, even though it never captures the golden fleece of a final and identified meaning.[117]

There are interpreters who see the gospel as recommending a mystic union of life and death, celebrated in the folly of the cross. In this account Jesus has broken into history and teaches a mystical truth that abrogates all conventional, human experience. Both Jesus and Christians are inevitably to suffer, because that is the will of the Father. The cross then becomes the intersection point of the divine in human history, for it is God's intervention in the human sphere. Read back into Mark, this becomes a scriptural source for Tertulian's famous dictum: I believe because it's absurd. Going beyond all conventional thinking, God has come and revealed his truth in the identification of life with death, of crucifixion with resurrection. We then are to glory in the cross and abandon all thinking and operating. Yet, Mark does not present such a picture. Nor is his gospel so structured as to depict the irruption of the divine into human living. The manifestations of the divine are always veiled, never

---

114. See Nagao, *The Foundational Standpoint of Mādhyamika Philosophy,* 51: "In his *Lucid Exposition,* Candrakīrti uses the term *saṃvṛta* to contrast 'that which is worldly and conventional' with *saṃvṛti* or worldly convention. Now what is expressed as 'that which is worldly and conventional' is itself ultimate meaning and is synonymous with 'that which is clouded over'."

115. Similarly Via, *Ethics,* 175: "The concealment of revelation paradox (i.e., the first messianic secret paradox of a concealed revelation), the concealing of Jesus' identity, is more than a practical device for dealing with specific problems [as in Wrede's claim for a progressive revelation of that identity]. Along with the second messianic secret paradox (i.e., plain revelation misunderstood), it is the governing theme of the whole narrative, and . . . it interlocks with and closely parallels hardness of heart, also a characteristic Markan theme." For Via concealment is a structural part of revelation and is the reason why the disciples fail to understand. *Ethics,* 181: "The reason the disciples fail to appropriate existentially what they know intellectually is that the revelation itself is veiled or concealed. . . . Concealed revelation is the thematic counterpart to this plot as a whole and is in Mark's narrative world the necessary explanation for the disciples' failure of faith and understanding."

116. Nagao, *The Foundational Standpoint,* 121–41.

117. Crossan, *The Dark Interval,* 42–43 talks of the rumor that destroyed the classical vision of a centrist God overseeing all, quoting Emily Dickinson's version about poor Jason who not only doesn't find the fleece, but loses his crew, learns the fleece doesn't exist, and finally finds his very own questing self to be but a sham. In a Mahāyāna reading, the fleece here would stand for conventional attainment of ultimate meaning, and its loss represents the awareness of that ultimate as disjunctive and beyond the limits of all conventions.

taking center stage in full vision. The gospel itself is a product of Mark's theological skill, weaving parabolic revelations with the dependently co-arisen course of events. Life is not simply identified with death in the abeyance of all common sense. Rather, death is overcome in the raising of Jesus, and in his return to the everyday life of Galilean practice.

Yet, this mystic theology of the "cross and resurrection" does, I think, capture a central theme of the gospel: that Jesus is indeed, in his very humanness, the Son of God. This theme is encapsulated in the Mahāyāna summary that all is only worldly convention. The word "only" (*mātra*) here is not, however, merely privative, signifying that there is no transcendent dimension at all. Rather, "only" excludes facile identification of ultimate meaning with any viewpoint, any conventional expression of the final truth. In Luke, if one knocks on the door, it will be opened. In Mark, one knocks at a closed door that, remaining closed, rivets attention to the mystery it hides. To say that all is worldly convention-only means that the everyday practices of faith themselves signify the presence of God as a hidden presence. Any opening of that door, being conventional, issues only in further versions of conventional realities. Divine truth that can be verbally revealed falls from its august pinnacle and becomes yet another human construct. Revelation then is not a verbal manifestation of some divine truth, but an invitation to conversion and a dawning consciousness of God present as the ground of all human language and practice.

Likewise, the identity of Jesus turns out to be transparent, emptied of all defined content. Mark's narrative strategy, in all its turns and twists, labors to identify God with Jesus, not Jesus with God. The latter option would result in a "divine man" portrait, with Jesus assumed into a status beyond suffering and beyond human contingency. Yet, that is what is consistently denied in the text: Jesus, in virtue of being christ, is subjected to the same historical and social forces that mould all our lives. It is only after that is abundantly manifested in his death that the centurion, himself conditioned by birth and circumstance to be present at the cross, echoes the initial identification of Jesus as son of God (1:1; 15: 39). In Mahāyāna terms, since all is empty, in the awakened awareness of a buddha the realm of cessation (*nirvāṇa*) is identified with the realm of suffering (*saṃsāra*). The famed messianic secret of Mark's text seems to be the narrative analogue of such an identification: right here is the world of awakening, right here is the full embodiment of Abba in the very historically contingent humanity of Jesus, now identified as the christ, the messiah.

The Mahāyāna scriptures attribute such an insight into the identity of ultimate cessation and conventional living to the mind of an awakened buddha. Yet, for ordinary unawakened practitioners there remains the tension between the two truths. The ultimate all but crashes into the conventional, yet remains hidden therein as other, while the conventional constantly seeks to ascend to the ultimate, without ever succeeding. In Mark, the spirit not only descends upon Jesus, but into him.[118] That tensiveness is present throughout Mark's narrative, which reveals only to hide once more, and which makes things hidden only to bring everything to light. Many of Mark's rhetorical devices urge such a tensive reading. "To show how the tension between hiddenness and revelation determines the whole of Jesus' activity, Mark makes use of three different but connected motifs: the commands to silence which he imposes on the demons and those healed, the secret instructions he gives to the disciples, i.e., to 'those inside' in contrast to 'those outside' (4: 11) in the parables discourse, and the repeated failure of the disciples to understand Jesus' word and work (6: 52; 8: 17–21)."[119] One cannot abide in ultimate meaning, but, emptying even that, reengage in the conventional world.[120] Mark sets his story, i.e., the characters and events within the story, in tension with his discourse, i.e., the rhetorical ways in which Mark directs the reader to understand that story, in order to heighten the tensiveness of all conventional language and lead the reader to a conversion enabling her to abide therein in the practice of the middle path.[121] Living within the differential awareness of the two truths is not living in an intellectual riddle, but engaging in the dependently co-arisen world in the context of emptiness. "Mark himself would probably not agree that whatever he is trying to accomplish by means of his narrative could be adequately summarized in the form of a single paradoxical expression. Rather, the kind of paradoxical truth that Mark offers is the truth of paradox lived, not merely described verbally."[122]

---

118. Fowler, *Let the Reader Understand,* 16: "In discussions of Mark's baptism episode, for example, the spirit is usually said to descend 'upon' Jesus. A more literal rendering of the Greek preposition *eis,* however, would have the spirit descend 'into' Jesus. Each of the other evangelists uses *epi,* 'upon,' describing a more genteel resting of the spirit upon Jesus, and this understanding has usually been read into Mark, but inappropriately, because Mark is portraying for us a person being invaded and possessed by a spirit. In Mark, Jesus becomes spirit-possessed. See, for example, Mark 1: 12, where the spirit within Jesus throws him out (*ekballō*) into the desert. Jesus has not so much acquired a spirit; rather, a spirit has acquired Jesus."

119. Kertledge, "The Epiphanies of Jesus," 88. Kertledge, 89, continues: "We may therefore speak of Mark's indirect revelations, or in M. Dibelius' phrase, of Jesus' 'secret epiphanies' [*From Tradition to Gospel,* 297]."

120. Malbon, *Narrative Space,* 63: "But the crowd sometimes seeks out Jesus even on the mountain (5: 5, 11) or in the wilderness (1: 45; 6: 31, 32, 35; 8: 4); thus, not even topographically isolated areas can totally isolate the Markan Jesus. Furthermore, events on a mountain, a traditional setting of solemn divine acts, intensify Jesus' involvement with others—especially the disciples (3: 13; 9: 2, 9; 13: 3; 14: 26)."

121. Fowler, *Let the Reader Understand,* 259–60: "Because Mark is willing to put story and discourse into tension with each other, he is able to offer a narrative that instructs the narratee in the challenges of discipleship without a full and explicit portrayal of successful discipleship in the story." Again Fowler, 184–85, stresses such an abiding in tensive awareness: "The experience of paradox is the experience of being bracketed between seemingly incompatible but nevertheless coexisting polar opposites. Of all Mark's indirect moves, incongruity is at its sharpest in paradox."

122. Fowler, *Let the Reader Understand,* 191.

Yet, it is not, I think, that the reader, given privileged information by the rhetoric of the text, has by that very fact attained insight in advance of the disciples. Rather, by first identifying the reader with these first of Jesus' disciples and then inducing her to mentally withdraw from them as they increasingly become hard of heart, the reader ends the gospel in a most awkward position. Led, tricked by the narrative grammar, she is caught in entertaining a sense of privileged selfhood that is diametrically at odds with Jesus' injunction to abandon self. Indeed, what reader is free from such assertions? No theological position of the necessity of a suffering messiah or the glory of the cross alleviates that dilemma, for no verbal position can empty self. Mark is indeed a crafty writer. In the end, willy-nilly, the reader is drawn once more into identifying with the fleeing disciples, not by the force of the intra-story logic or the rhetorical discourse, but by the force of being both human and a disciple. We too must journey to Galilee to recapture the original, everyday practice of the kingdom of God.

The Three Patterns

The Mahāyāna themes employed above were developed by the Mādhyamika philosophers Nāgārjuna, Āryadeva, Candrakīrti, and Bhavya. The three patterns of consciousness represent a further elaboration of these notions within the Yogācāra framework of critical theory worked out by Asaṅga, Vasubandhu, Sthiramati, Asvabhāva, Dharmapāla, and Paramārtha. Over a millennium ahead of Western philosophers, the Yogācāra thinkers took a turn toward critical interiority, trying to develop an understanding of consciousness that could ground emptiness and dependent co-arising within the mind. They developed a philosophy of mind which attempted to delineate its patterns of understanding and misunderstanding, faith and hardness of heart. The outcome of their endeavors is contained in their explanation of the three patterns of consciousness: the other-dependent, the imagined, and the perfected.

The underlying structure of consciousness is itself other-dependent, i.e., dependently co-arisen, for consciousness operations entail a synergy of different, mutually-interdependent, levels and operations. The fundamental level is that of consciousness as the storehouse of past impressions, lying dormant and unrecognized in seminal efficacy. Each action, whether individual or communal, imprints its "seed" energy upon that preconscious ground, leading to similar actions that again imprint their energy on the deep mind.[123] Sensation and perception are not then neutral exercises, but are subtly directed in accord

---

123. Asaṅga, *The Summary of the Great Vehicle*, 1.15: "Here we treat the structural characteristics of this storehouse consciousness, which in sum are three: its defining characteristic, its characteristic as cause, and its characteristic as result. Its defining characteristic is that, relying on the impressions of all the defiled states, it is the basic repository of seeds whereby the arising of those states is maintained. Its characteristic as cause means that consciousness with all these seeds is the cause for the constant generation of those defiled states. Its characteristic as result means that this consciousness arises as the result of the beginningless impressions of these variously defiled states."

with the inner gestalts imprinted by the storehouse consciousness.[124] Thinking itself is defiled in virtue of such imprinting and habitually clings to perceived images as if they represent the reality of things. Ideas are similarly taken to capture the reality behind images, and the mind functions in primal ignorance (*avidyā*). Insight is frozen in pictorial world views, and awakening does not occur. In Mark, the religious authorities present examples of such frozen world views. The scribes and Pharisees have clear and definite views about ritual purity (2: 15–17, 23–28; 7: 1–5). The Sadducees defend their thesis of no resurrection (12: 18–23). So entrenched are they in these views that they cannot but see Jesus' attitude as demonic (3: 22), desire to arrest him (12: 12), and resolve to put him to death (14: 1). They never evince any sense of questioning or self-doubt, but remain "wicked tenants of the vineyard."[125] The disciples in the narrative are caught in their own imagined expectancies, countering Jesus' first prediction of suffering (9: 32), responding to his second prediction with a lack of understanding and preoccupation with self aggrandizement (9: 32–34), and reacting to his third prediction with requests for positions of self power (10: 35–37).[126] By strategies of occlusion, the Markan Jesus prevents access to any correct viewpoint and thus intensifies the tension that may trigger conversion.

Ordinarily human beings are caught in the net of their own verbal fabrication. Unawakened consciousness takes its images and ideas to represent the very being of beings. From whatever beginning one can identify, our minds are imbued with the effects of past actions and colored in all their perceptions. Language itself, mistaking its structuring of experience for reality, becomes a vehicle for furthering delusion.[127] And people function within an imagined

---

124. See Waldron, "A Comparison of the Ālayavijñāna with Freud's and Jung's Theories of the Unconscious," *Annual Memoirs of the Ōtani University Shin Buddhist Comprehensive Research Institute*, 6 (1988), 109–150.

125. Tolbert, *Sowing the Gospel*, 231–39.

126. Fowler, *Let the Reader Understand*, 212: "The third major way in which opacity is figured in the narrative is the imagery of sense perception and intellectual and spiritual discernment. . . . Sense perception opacity thus makes its presence felt suddenly and unexpectedly." When the reader thinks she finally sees, the veil descends to cut off all hopes of understanding. Mark consistently undermines both the perceptions and the views of the disciples.

127. In treating the nature of the storehouse consciousness Asaṅga, *The Summary of the Great Vehicle*, 1.18, explains that "there are three different kinds of impressions: those of language, those of belief in selfhood, and those of [the chain of] being." In the unawakened person, language itself arises from the impressions of latent seeds and accounts for the generation of imagined realities, such as the false belief in self and one's attachment to the transmigratory cycle of rebirth. The interpenetration of language and experience is one of the favorite themes of modern interpreters and philosophers. Following Sapir, Camery-Hoggatt, *Irony in Mark's Gospel*, 20, writes: "If language qualifies and shapes man's experience of the external world, it also creates and sustains the structures of his inner experience," and further on 22: ". . . the formation of identity is at once made possible and radically circumscribed by the structures of language as a primary vehicle of socialization." The Markan abundance of tropical twists and turns is aimed, so it seems to me, at dislodging such identities, formed in a bootless quest for the security of selfhood. Thus irony in Mark is not presented merely to play "upon the reader's own repertoire of

pattern of consciousness, adhering to images as a support for their self-centered expectancies.[128]

Yet, that imagined pattern is a superimposition over the basically other-dependent pattern of consciousness, i.e., over its dependently co-arisen structure and functioning. By meditative insight into emptiness, one becomes aware that images are just images, and ideas are just ideas (*vijñapti-mātra*). Gradually through intensified practice, the underlying "seed" energies are eliminated, and the basic structure of the mind is turned around, con-verted. Such a reorientation or con-version (μετάνοια; *āśraya-parivṛtti*) is itself awakening, becoming buddha. In Mark it constitutes the content of Jesus' proclamation, for he calls for conversion and faith at the very inception of his preaching (1: 15). The drama of the story turns around the response of Jesus' disciples, whether they will reorientate their minds and practice the way of Jesus. And it ends elliptically, insistently taking the troubling question beyond the confines of the story into the lives of the readers. The possibility of conversion is constantly present, for the other-dependent structure of the mind allows one to pivot from the pattern of imagined delusion to the perfected pattern of understanding, able to see that the dependently co-arisen mind is itself empty of any final validity, able to see that emptiness entails and enables one to attain the relative validity of enlightened practice, differentiating the unattainable truth of ultimate meaning from the worldly and conventional truths of teaching, skillfully designed (*upāya*) in accord with concrete circumstances.[129] Mark is a story about practicing the way, about the conversion of consciousness that enables that practice to occur.

Not only does Mark's story plot carry this significance. Even Mark's discourse style of constant cross-referencing and doubling, both back and

---

knowledge and convictions to produce a distinctive subtext" (Camery-Hoggatt, *Irony in Mark's Gospel,* 2), nor is it the case that "Mark's ironies express a crisis of loyalties between Christianity and traditional Judaism" (*Irony in Mark's Gospel,* 180). Rather, the rhetorical effect inscribed in Mark's discourse deconstructs the self-protective loyalties to all views and places the reader in the position of going beyond all verbal convictions and knowledge. The point is conversion and the practice of the kingdom, not doctrinal choices between verbal identities. In pursuit of such a goal, Mark craftily maneuvers the reader to identify with Jesus against his disciples in affirming as paradigm a messiah who is radically contingent, despite the dissonance of such an assumed identity with the reader's own sense of secure selfhood. The reader (at least this reader) winds up just like the disciples, committed to Jesus yet denying him at every turn!

128. Weeden's thesis, *Mark—Traditions in Conflict,* is that the disciples represent a specific *theios anēr* viewpoint, countered by Mark with his suffering messiah theme. There are indeed passages where the disciples do express their desires for power and greatness and clearly their hopes and Jesus' understanding are in conflict. Yet a suffering messiah is hardly a viewpoint at all, unless it be seen as part of a cosmic design, apart from the lived world of Mark's Jesus.

129. Asaṅga, *The Summary of the Great Vehicle,* 2.29: "In the Abhidharma Scripture the Bhagavat taught three aspects [to the other-dependent pattern]: the defiled aspect, the pure aspect, and the defiled and pure aspect. What was his intention in teaching these three aspects? While the defiled aspect is the imagined pattern within the other-dependent

forward, suggest an attempt to call into question imagined patterns of understanding on the part of the reader.[130] Some literary critics try to reconstruct the common consensual background in which Mark's audience would have heard the gospel, in light of which the text should be interpreted.[131] Such an analysis does offer many clarifications, yet it also confines the text within those mistaken, conventional assumptions. Moreover, it "assumes that the Gospel writer intended to communicate something to an audience who had the necessary competencies to understand it."[132] Yet both the content and the style of the narrative suggest that Mark's project was more subtle than that, for both Jesus and Mark are concerned with eliciting a conversion of consciousness from those not yet able to understand, and not with imparting information to a deluded pattern of consciousness.

The most important doubling-back concerns the understanding of the opening confession in 1: 1 that Jesus is christ and son of God.[133] Peter doubles back faithfully to repeat the confession in 8: 29, but without understanding its import. Then the centurion, seeing Jesus die on the cross, doubles back on Peter ambiguously to confess that indeed this man was God's son (15: 39). Things are not what they appear to be, for the initial confession is not understood until one has gone through an emptying of Peter's repetition of that confession, and on to the centurion's event-generated reaffirmation, seen by the reader as ironically true. By translating the initial confession into Peter's flawed version, and then drawing that forward to the centurion's observation, Mark reaches back into the reader's apparently assured understanding and catapults that forward to identify it with Jesus' executioner! New understandings are called for at every step of the process. And new understandings entail the abandonment of previously fixed ideas about who Jesus is, no matter how orthodox they may be.[134]

---

pattern, and the pure aspect is the fully perfected pattern within the other-dependent pattern, the defiled and pure aspect is the other-dependent pattern itself."

130. Neirynck, *Duality in Mark,* 49, has described, to the satisfaction of most scholars, a doubling, two step progression as "one of Mark's most characteristic features of style."

131. Tolbert, *Sowing the Gospel,* 13: A writer "cannot write without making certain assumptions about the readers' beliefs, knowledge, and familiarity with conventions." Again, 53, quoting Kellogg in note 16, "we must bring our view into line with the prevailing view of reality in the time of the work's composition." Bryan, *A Preface to Mark,* 155, writes: "If we are correct in our description of the gospel's origins [as a Hellenistic life of Jesus], then Mark's written text would have been understood from the beginning as a recollection of what had been said: it was *hupomnēmata* (memoranda), . . . *apomnēmoneumata* (recollections)."

132. Tolbert, *Sowing the Gospel,* 88.

133. Bryan, *A Preface to Mark,* 40.1, notes Mark may well have been the first to employ flashback in a *prose* narrative.

134. Here Tolbert is near the mark; *Sowing the Gospel,* 222–23: "Mark's use of disciples to illustrate the rocky ground thwarts conventional expectations. This defamiliarizing of normal patterns presses the reader to see something new happening in the text. Wolfgang Iser terms the strategy 'coherent deformation,' and its special grace is to force the reader into intense activity, seeking the cause of deformation. Texts that confirm customary norms allow readers to remain basically passive, whereas texts that cut away common

The theme of the way presents another doubling back strategy. Jesus comes to prepare the way (1: 2–3), and immediately comes from the wilderness into the Galilean phase of his career, preaching the gospel of conversion and faith. He travels back and forth across the Lake of Galilee, including both Jew and Gentile, men and women, within the kingdom he announces. He then sets his face toward Jerusalem, moving inexorably to his encounter with the authorities and his death. His death and resurrection occur there in Jerusalem, and yet during his last meal before his death Jesus tells the protesting disciples that his journey will not end in Jerusalem, for after he is risen, he will go before them into Galilee (14: 28), which is exactly what the women are told by the young man in the empty tomb (16: 7). They ran away without informing Peter or the disciples, but in the text itself, those disciples have already been informed by Jesus about his return to Galilee. The way leads up from Galilee to the climactic experiences in Jerusalem, and then doubles back to Galilee, the site of Jesus' everyday activity, the site where the disciples first were called (1: 16–20) and appointed (3: 13–19), where they first were sent out to exorcize demons and preach (6: 7–13). The elliptical ending of Mark's gospel leads back to the very beginning (ἀρχὴ), coaxing the reader away from Jerusalem hopes and expectancies to return to the wilderness/Galilee engagement of the original Jesus of the prologue.

The wilderness theme is itself another doubling back strategy. Jesus is announced as a voice crying out in the wilderness (1: 3), and immediately after his baptism is driven by the spirit into that wilderness (1: 10). He is hunted down in the wilderness by Simon (1: 36), and forced to remain outside in wilderness places by the increasing expectations of the crowds (1: 45). Wilderness signifies the eschatological emptying of all conventional norms and notions. Frequently he withdraws into that silence to pray, but he does not remain there alone. He draws the twelve up onto the mountain to appoint them disciples (2: 13), and leads Peter, James, and John to a high mountain off by themselves (9: 2). The wilderness becomes not only the origin and source of Jesus' mission, but a disclosure of transcendent truth.[135] Mark doubles back on the theme in his eschatological discourse, for the enigmatic "detestation that makes desolate" (τὸ βδέλυγμα τῆς ἐρημώσεως) in 13:

---

ground propel readers into active engagement." Yet interpreters are wont to envision themselves as living in the truth, in the light of insightful readings that explain, and thus once again control, the rhetoric of the gospel. They seem to repeat in hermeneutical swirls of insight the very trajectory followed by the disciples in the story.

135. Asaṅga, *The Summary of the Great Vehicle,* 1.45, raises the question of how the storehouse consciousness, which is the cause of delusion, can also cause the transcendent mind, since it is impressed with the seed energies of impure states. He answers that "the world transcendent mind arises because its seed is the impressions from hearing [the scripture] which flow from the purest realm of reality." The converted mind of faith is not engendered by self-realization, for attachment to self is an obstacle to transcendent insight. This Indian Mahāyāna theme is taken up in the Pure Land doctrine of salvation through other-power (*tariki*) and in the Zen teaching of the suddenness of awakening. It parallels the Markan theme of wilderness disclosure.

14, alludes back to the desolate wilderness (ἔρημος) from which Jesus comes in the prologue and forward to Jesus' desolate cry on the cross (15: 34), and then, beyond the scope of the narrative, to his resurrected, yet empty, return to Galilee (16: 7). One has to constantly reassess just what the empty wilderness signifies: the immediate presence of God, the goal of discipleship and practice, the eschatological climax of the cross that is detestable to God, Jesus' abandonment at death, and ambiguously his return to the everyday life of Galilean practice. The stress throughout is upon the mind of the reader and the invitation is to reorient and transform one's understanding from self-delusion to the practice of the kingdom.

Time and again in the story Jesus presents a teaching that his disciples do not understand. They just don't get it. And so he tells them that he teaches in parables so that "those who are outside" will never understand (4: 11–12). Those who externalize meaning cannot get the point, for the meaning of the practice of the kingdom must be internalized through practice in order to be understood. Parables are not simply examples, but tensive invitations to a conversion of consciousness, crafted in accordance with the capabilities of his hearers (4: 33).[136] The parables aim at undermining imagined patterns of understanding, awakening one to the constantly hidden presence of God in the conventional coverings of human words.

Jesus' journeying on the way is not only geographical, from here to there and back again. That horizontal way is enclosed within a vertical way, out from the wilderness into the towns and cities and back again. Mark interweaves descriptions of the differential tension between Jesus' wilderness experiences of the vertical, transcendent, and ultimate reality of the Father together with his engagement in worldly and conventional affairs that describe his horizontal awareness of the dependently co-arisen emptiness of all the events of his life. The result of that interweaving is a doubled doubling back, for all aspects of the way, both horizontal and vertical, interpenetrate. Together they constitute the middle path, the way followed by Jesus and offered to his disciples. And that middle way is the path to awakening to who Jesus is and what he is all about, for he has no discernible identity apart from his embodiment of the middle way.

---

136. Crossan, *The Dark Interval,* 63–128.

PART II

Commentary on the Gospel of Mark

1

Wilderness and Engagement

Jesus' Wilderness Voice
1: 1–3

¹The beginning of the Good News about Jesus Christ, son of God, as it has been recorded by the prophet Isaiah:
  ²Behold I am sending out my messenger before your face
  who will build your way,
  ³The voice of one calling out in the wilderness,
  Prepare the way of the Lord,
  Make his paths level.[1]

This "beginning (ἀρχὴ)" recalls the beginning of *Genesis*, "In the beginning God created heaven and earth" (Gen 1: 1). Mark envisages a new creation.[2] Such a beginning, however, is more than an inception point within

---

1. I follow Tolbert, *Sowing the Gospel*, 239–248, in connecting verses 2 and 3 to verse 1 as referring not to John, who is first named in verse 4, but to Jesus. She writes: "Mark 1: 2–3 . . . is intended to describe primarily Jesus, its most natural grammatical and rhetorical referent, and secondarily, John, since they both share the same mission" (240). The translations herein are primarily from *The New Jerusalem Bible* (see note on copyright page).

2. See Via, *The Ethics of Mark's Gospel*, 45: "It can hardly be doubted that the *archē* of Mark 1: 1 has a paradigmatic or metaphorical relationship to the *archē* (LXX) of Genesis 1: 1. . . . The very beginning of the story, even before Jesus actually appears in his public ministry, is the advent of the newness of creation which is also the establishing of the eschatological time. There is another first time despite the fatigue of world history." Mauser, *Christ in the Wilderness: The Wilderness Theme in the Second Gospel and its Basis in the Biblical Tradition*, 89, stresses Jesus' return to the wilderness as an acknowledgment of the history of Israel's unfaithfulness and a beginning over again "at zero. This reduction to nothing is . . . the starting point for a new history of grace." Such a new history of grace is not, however, a linear history, but an eschatological emptying of the sureties of history itself, new in that it is available at any present moment.

the linear flow of time. Rather, as an eschatological beginning it collapses the ongoing flow of human history, containing inchoately the fullness which subsequently unfolds. It points toward a final fullness that is likewise not just the end point of linear time, but a time beyond time. The opening lines of Mark's gospel set the "eschatological orientation of everything that follows."[3] But that eschatological end time is enfolded in the very beginning. The fullness of such an origin will be restored at the end time. The movement of the Markan Jesus is from Galilee to Jerusalem and back to Galilee after the resurrection. And yet origin and end time are not simply the first and last points of the time line, for the eschatological kingdom is present in every moment of linear time. Jesus' appearance recapitulates the beginning, and his death will signal the presence of the end time, although there is time before the beginning that is Jesus, and time goes on even after his death. The eschatological end time is the restoration of the archetypal origin in the present moment. Both undermine linear conceptions of time.

In a Mahāyāna reading, no point of time has any stable duration. All is marked by a radical transience and impermanence (*anitya*). Assertions of the permanence of selfhood against such a radical impermanence result in the primal ignorance that sinks people into the endless bondage of suffering (*saṃsāra*). Cessation (*nirvāṇa*) is the ending of that endless bondage, attained in an awakening modeled after that of the historical Buddha, Śākyamuni Gautama. In such an awakened mind, cessation itself has no stable permanence, and this very world of suffering (*saṃsāra*) is equated with cessation (*nirvāṇa*), for awakening issues not in some blissful withdrawal, but in enlightened historical activity, i.e., in human activity informed by compassion and wisdom. In like fashion, the beginning of Mark's good news invites the reader toward a conversion in which time itself becomes the acting out and unfolding of the kingdom of God, where the rule of justice and peace is embodied in the lives of Jesus' disciples.

After alluding to the beginning time, Mark sets his Gospel in the concrete, linear time of Jesus' preaching, specifically within the context of the wilderness and the preaching of John the Baptist. This contrasts, for example, with the Gospel of John, which envisages a beginning (ἀρχή) in the preexistence of the word with the Father. Some have seen this as a minor omission in Mark, who otherwise depicts Jesus as a "divine man," in harmony with the Pauline presentation.[4] But this opinion seems to underestimate the specific Markan setting, whose hallmark is that it moves not in the comforting spiritual presence of the Christ of Luke-Acts, or in the mystic ontology of John, but in terms of its theologically designed memories of John the Baptist and Jesus. Mark does not move in the realm of spiritual metaphysics and he does not present a prior philosophic viewpoint in which the story of Jesus must be

---

3. Camery-Hoggatt, *Irony in Mark's Gospel,* 93.
4. Bultmann, *History of the Synoptic Tradition,* 348.

read. The beginning of this gospel aims to actualize the good news in the lives of Mark's readers,[5] not to impart information about Jesus.

Mark does, however, immediately confess his faith that Jesus is son of God. This is the primal confession of Mark: that Jesus is messiah (christ) and son of God.[6] Yet, Mark does not explain just what these titles mean. Scholars have long argued the exact import of such titles. The grammar of the phrase, "son of God" does not explain its meaning, for in Hebrew it can mean nothing more than "a godly son," i.e., a good son. The later interpretations of the Fathers of the Church see in it a much more theological meaning of divine sonship, but Mark himself is unconcerned with pinning down its exact import at this stage. Rather, he leaves it ambiguous, to be worked out in the ensuing narrative. Throughout the gospel Jesus' identity is polysemous and its interpretation, both within the text and within the reader of the text, serves more to heighten the ambiguity of expected notions than to eliminate them. Some interpreters indeed do see this opening phrase as Mark's sharing information with the reader which the characters in the story do not have. Readers know who Jesus is, whereas the disciples remain in the dark and blunder towards what in the final outcome remains a misunderstanding.[7] Yet it appears that the point of the verse is not to give information about Jesus Christ, son of God, but to talk about the proclamation he embodies and practices. The titles "christ" and "son of God" were not clear-cut and definite identity markers, and do not suggest the assured possession of privileged information. Many meanings attached to the notion of messiah. It is not at

---

5. Kelber, *Mark's Story of Jesus,* 16.

6. Perrin, "The Christology of Mark," 101, notes that the term son of God "occurs at each of the places in the Gospel where cosmic phenomena (heaven opening and the like) indicate a revelatory moment." Yet, the initial appearance of the term in 1: 1 hardly qualifies as a revelatory moment. Fowler, *Let the Reader Understand,* 19, explains the function of 1: 1 as the structuring of tension between the discourse Mark directs to the informed reader and the story of the uninformed and obdurate disciples. In such a case, the title son of God serves not to impart objective content but to highlight that dissonance between the reader who knows that somehow Jesus is son of God and the story characters who have no clue who Jesus is.

7. Tolbert, *Sowing the Gospel,* 94: "In the first place, since the narrator tells the reader the identity of Jesus in the opening line, and in the first thirteen verses reinforces that identification by the authority of scriptural quotation, scriptural allusion, prophetic announcement, and a voice from heaven, the reader from the beginning has no doubt about who Jesus is or the basis of his authority." Camery-Hoggatt, *Irony in Mark's Gospel,* 92: ". . . at the very beginning of the narrative it discloses to the reader the critical information that Jesus—the protagonist of the story that follows—is both 'Christ'/'Messiah' and 'Son of God'." Again, 93: ". . . the superscription from the very beginning places in the reader's hands interpretative keys which are denied the story's characters until very much later in the narrative." Once again, 98: "Whatever else we read in Mark, we must bear this constantly in mind. The reader and Jesus have been told something which is carefully shielded from the story's characters. The ironic tensions in the points of view which are later all developed in one way or another play off this central distinction. The reader and Jesus know that he is 'Son of God' and 'Messiah,' the other characters do not."

all obvious what calling somebody the son of God signifies. Such terms encode the mystery of this new beginning and proleptically envisage the end time by calling the reader's attention to just what it means to refer to Jesus by these titles. Mark is concerned about conversion and faith, not merely intellectual assent.[8] What is apparently revealed turns out to be a matter of profound enigma and a challenge to all notions of identifiable selfhood and identity. Mark here is not, as is often assumed, a totally reliable narrator imparting straightforward information, nor is he an unreliable narrator, seeking to deceive. Rather, he is a skillful author who begins his narrative by engendering tension in the reader to see if that which follows indeed fleshes out the initial characterization of Jesus. As one moves through the text, one has constantly to reevaluate and reformulate the sense of all titles attributed to Jesus, and, in the end, to abandon the mind set that seeks revelation as information. Such a "tension in the text is necessary to its purpose. This tension enables the text to resist being digested by the prevailing patterns of interpretation and instead to challenge these patterns."[9]

The context of this beginning is set. Jesus comes not as a Hellenistic "divine man,"[10] but as a voice in the wilderness (ἐν τῇ ἐρήμῳ), immediately (1: 4) identified with the eschatological figure of John and with the prophetic tradition of Israel in that he fulfills the prophecy of Isaiah. Jesus is seen as a prophet, embodying the teachings (*tanach*) of Israel.

Verse 3 is cited from *Isaiah* 40: 3, but verse 2 is not a direct citation from *Isaiah,* or anywhere else in the Hebrew scriptures or in the Septuagint. Rather, it reworks *Malachi* 3: 1, which reads: "Look, I shall send my messenger to clear a way before me." In Malachi, the verse refers to the coming of the

---

8. I think that the initial titles are rhetorical devices to heighten the tension concerning Jesus' identity. They are ironic not only for the story-level characters, but also for the reader, who is drawn into the gospel not simply to assent to theological definitions, but to undergo a conversion of consciousness. The titles "christ," and "Son of God" are thus ironic to all participants, both within and outside the story. If I may quote Camery-Hoggatt against himself, *Irony in Mark's Gospel,* 10: "Irony implies that more is going on than mere information can grasp, and that discipleship must be an activity of personal response as well as an activity of intellectual assent." Again, 24: ". . . the reduction of language to informational content may represent a failure of vision."

9. Tannehill, *The Sword of His Mouth,* 55. In Markan studies there does seem to be a tendency to side with Jesus against the obtuse disciples. But that may enact on the discourse level of interpretation that same story recounted in the story level of the gospel.

10. A number of interpreters represent this opinion. Telford, "Introduction: The Gospel of Mark," 17, describes this interpretation: "In presenting Jesus as a powerful and charismatic figure awakening numinous awe in his followers, able to calm storms or walk on water, to heal at a touch or raise the dead, a mysterious being subject to metamorphosis or transfiguration, these traditions are said to reflect the influence of the 'divine man' or *theios anēr* concept, a type encountered in or deemed to underlie stories associated with hellenistic heroes such as Socrates, Apollonius of Tyana or Pythagoras." By contrast, Weeden, *Mark—Traditions in Conflict,* sees this divine man christology as the heresy that Mark counters by identifying it with the dense and unawakened disciples.

Lord himself, who will confound those who weary Yahweh by questioning his justice and concern. It is preceded by the sentence:

> You have wearied Yahweh with your talk. You ask, "How have we wearied him?" When you say, "Any evil-doer is good as far as Yahweh is concerned; indeed he is delighted with them;" or when you say, "Where is the God of fair judgment now?"

These are the sentiments which evoked the plaintive cries of Job in the face of the prosperity of the wicked and the suffering of the innocent.[11] It is in this context of the felt absence of Yahweh that Yahweh will send his messenger and then he himself will "suddenly enter his temple" (*Malachi* 3: 1). Mark's Jesus indeed enters the Jerusalem temple in Chapter 12.

A parallel is also found in *Exodus* 23: 20: "Look, I am sending an angel to precede you, to guard you as you go and to bring you to the place that I have prepared." The Hebrew term for angel is the same as for messenger: *male'ak.* In *Exodus,* the angel will lead the chosen people through the wilderness and into the promised land. He will lead the people against their enemies and strike the fear of the Lord into them. Mark is drawing upon these traditions of deliverance. He is saying that the work of Jesus and John will concretize the presence of Yahweh and be an answer to those who fail to see any discernible action of Yahweh in the world. He is saying that the work of deliverance will take place in the career of Jesus, from his first preaching to his death and resurrection. But he is not yet saying just how that takes place.

Verse 3 is taken directly from *Isaiah,* quoted from the Septuagint. There it recounts the "consolation of Israel," and suggests that the people of Jesus' time, like their forefathers languishing in Babylon, will be led out of the wilderness of their captivity into the land of promise. The allusion to the wilderness of the Babylonian captivity in *Isaiah* recalls the Sinai wilderness, through which the angel led Moses and the children of Israel. In these verses Mark identifies the context for his gospel as the deliverance of the people from alienation and bondage. He recalls the wilderness of Sinai and of the Babylonian captivity to contextualize the wilderness origin of Jesus' voice. The voice calling out in the wilderness is a voice flowing from direct contact with Yahweh, for Mark's wilderness serves as a spatial metaphor of transcendent wisdom, apart from societal communication and abiding in silence.

The wilderness is more than just a place to escape from. It is also "the site of the eagerly awaited future, of the eschatological 'new start' and total transformation."[12] Mark's spirituality, at least in one aspect, is eschatological and ascetic, as shown in Jesus' wilderness origin and in the description of

---

11. On skepticism among the Israelites, see Crenshaw, *Old Testament Wisdom,* 202, and "Popular Questioning of the Justice of God in Ancient Israel," *Studies in Ancient Israelite Wisdom,* 289–304.

12. Schillebeeckx, *Jesus,* 127. Mauser, *Christ in the Wilderness,* 88–89.

the Baptist that follows. The solitude of the wilderness forms a constant pole in the rhetorical structure of Mark, for there one meets with Yahweh directly, apart from any human encumbrances. A voice calling out in the wilderness means that one reengages in making straight the paths of the Lord in the world of men and women, the paths of true practice. These paths of true practice have been covered over by human traditions. The realization of ultimate meaning (*paramārtha*) toward which the path leads has been usurped by conventional truths (*saṃvṛti*) that cover over its manifestation. The world of religious traditions is crooked, occluding easy access to Yahweh. It is askew, and needs to be straightened out, in order to facilitate the passage of Yahweh's deliverance out from the desert wilderness into the cities of humans.

Yet, it is only from a wilderness consciousness that one can recognize the crookedness of human traditions. Jesus' way is presaged: he will open up the way toward awareness of Yahweh apart from all tradition, by abiding in the emptiness of the wilderness, by embracing the inner meaning of tradition and bringing its good news to proclamation. In fact a messenger such as that in verse 2 does appear in the Septuagint text of *Isaiah* 40: 8–9 as the bringer of good news (εὐαγγελιζόμενος) who proclaims that the word of God (τὸ δὲ δῆμα τοῦ θεοῦ) abides forever. Thus the beginning of the gospel (ἀρχὴ τοῦ εὐαγγελίου) about Jesus is located in the wilderness, for Jesus comes from the desert solitude to initiate that proclamation. Jesus announces the kingdom by returning to its origins in the wilderness experience of Yahweh.

The Mark narrative begins not with a clear piece of information about who Jesus is, but with the assertion that his voice issues from a wilderness awareness of ultimate meaning.

The Wilderness Spirituality of John
1: 4–8

[4]*John the Baptist was in the wilderness, proclaiming a baptism of conversion for the forgiveness of sins.*[13] [5]*All Judaea and all the people of Jerusalem made their way to him, and as they were baptized by him in the river Jordan they confessed their sins.* [6]*John wore a garment of camel-skin, and he lived on locusts and wild-honey.* [7]*In the course of his preaching he said, "After me is coming someone who is more powerful than I, and I am not fit to kneel down and undo the strap of his sandals.* [8]*I have baptized you with water, but he will baptize you with the Holy Spirit."*

John the Baptist is described in terms that evoke the figure of Elijah, for he is seen by Mark as Elijah returned to earth. *The Second Book of Kings* 1: 8 describes Elijah as "a man wearing a hair cloak . . . and a leather

---

13. Taking μετανοίας in verse 4 as the basic conversion that leads to repentance for one's entire sinful orientation, not just particular sins. See Bauer, *Lexicon*, 512.

loincloth." In the next chapter of *Second Kings* Elijah is taken up into heaven in the fiery chariot. Elisha, who witnessed the event, "took up the cloak of Elijah" (*2 Kings* 2: 13). By Mark's description, John too takes up the cloak of Elijah and fulfills the expectation that before the Lord comes, Elijah would return, as explicitly stated in Mark 9: 12. *Malachi* 3: 23–24 had prophesied:

> Look, I shall send you the prophet Elijah before the great awesome day of Yahweh comes. He will reconcile the hearts of parents to their children and the hearts of children towards their parents, to forestall putting the country under the curse of destruction.

Jesus too comes to soften the hardness of heart of his disciples, and warns about the sacrilege that will bring the eschatological desolation (Mark 13: 14) if that hardness continues. Mark alludes to *Isaiah* and *Malachi,* as he did explicitly in verses 2 and 3, both to assert that the long-promised deliverance of Yahweh is now at hand, and to suggest that hardness of heart may nullify that deliverance.

John's garb is indicative of his wilderness lifestyle.[14] He did not dwell among men and women, but remained in the wilderness (ἐν τῇ ἐρήμῳ). His is a wilderness spirituality, focused not on the everyday life of townspeople, but on the ultimate reality of Yahweh. He does not even move on the periphery of society where he might receive a meal or two in recognition of his worth, but remains totally apart. This is why all Judaea and Jerusalem have to come out to him. He represents a single-minded focus on the ultimate meaning of direct awareness of Yahweh. He has abandoned the city life of men and women to dwell in empty places and to live without attachments. This contrasts with the spirituality of Jesus, which is subsequently presented as encompassing both desert aloneness and engagement in the affairs of humans, a spirituality able to maintain a dynamic and creative tension between ultimate meaning and worldly convention, without negating one in favor of the other. Mark associates John only with the wilderness. The Markan Jesus, by contrast, follows a middle path which holds wilderness spirituality and societal engagement in dynamic tension.[15]

Mark simply describes John's activity as baptizing, but Matthew, in his account of Jesus' dispute with the chief priests, adds that John's baptism is "from heaven" (*Matthew* 21: 25). Such a heavenly baptism signaled a conversion away from sin and toward the transcendent reality of God. This baptism was "for repentance" or "for conversion" (μετανοίας) away from sin. The

---

14. Kraeling, *John the Baptist,* 10. Camery-Hoggatt, *Irony in Mark's Gospel,* 95: "The reference to his mantle of camel's hair (1.6) recalls the association of the garments of hair with which the lying prophets disguise themselves in Zechariah 13.4 (LXX), and the narrative itself recalls the Martyrdom of Isaiah, in which Isaiah withdraws from Jerusalem as an act of symbolic judgment, settling in the wilderness, on a mountain (2.8), clothing himself with garments of hair (v.9) and eating wild herbs (v.11)."

15. Tolbert, *Sowing the Gospel,* 244.

sin here spoken of is not just any random act of injustice or unfaithfulness, but specifically the penitents' confidence in the efficacy of the temple cult and sacrifice.[16] They come out to the Jordan from Jerusalem, the very site of the temple and its liturgies. In fact, during this time many questions had been raised among the Jews about the purity and efficacy of the temple cult.[17] The people came out from all Judaea and Jerusalem to John, so that, as Malachi prophesied about Yahweh's messenger, the Lord "will purify the sons of Levi and refine them like gold and silver, so that they can make the offering to Yahweh with uprightness. The offering of Judah and Jerusalem will then be acceptable to Yahweh as in former days, as in the years of old" (*Malachi* 3: 3–4). Malachi predicts the reformation and purification of religious practice.[18] Mark keeps up his allusion to Malachi. The hyperbole of saying that "all Judaea and all the people of Jerusalem made their way to him" is meant not to record John's popularity, but to allude to the passage from *Malachi* and to oppose John's wilderness spirituality to the Jerusalem temple cult. "John offered an alternative to the Temple but from another fixed location, from desert and Jordan rather than from Zion and Jerusalem. Jesus was . . . atopic, moving from place to place, he coming to the people rather than they to him."[19] Mark stresses the ultimacy of Jesus' wilderness voice: both he and John call to conversion those who mistakenly cling to the conventional forms of worship and substitute them for ultimate awareness of Yahweh in the wilderness. The baptism by John in the Jordan presents his hearers with an either/or between worldly, conventional religion and ultimate, transcendent conversion, between the conventional order of the Jerusalem cult and the wilderness immediacy of Yahweh.[20]

Yet in Mark John does not represent full deliverance, for there comes one after him. Traditionally, Christian exegetes and theologians have read this to mean that John is simply the forerunner of Jesus, that John leads to Jesus, who is the son of God and savior. How then is John a forerunner of Jesus? In verses 4–8, deliverance is seen as entailing a conversion and repentance (μετάνοια) away from the basic sin of taking conventional religious practice as itself ultimate. In this understanding, Jesus brings John's message to fulfillment through his engagement not only in the wilderness emptiness of direct awareness of God, but also by his reengagement in the conventional society of men and women. John lives in the wilderness apart from the

---

16. Schillebeeckx, *Jesus,* 134.

17. Cohen, *From the Maccabees to the Mishnah,* 131–32.

18. Yates, "The Form of Mark 1.8b," notes that the spirit in Mark's text is consistently understood as an agent of purification, and not as the result of having been baptized.

19. Crossan, *The Historical Jesus,* 355.

20. Crossan, *The Historical Jesus,* xii: "But the Jordan was not just water, and to be baptized in it was to recapitulate the ancient and archetypal passage from imperial bondage to national freedom." Again, 235: "For baptism you only need water, not necessarily Jordan water, but any such baptism anywhere would have cast aspersions, be they explicit or implicit, on the Temple cult. But a Transjordan desert location and a baptism in the Jordan, precisely the Jordan, had overtones, explicit or implicit, of political subversion."

conventional world. Jesus lives in the tension of practicing a middle path, differentiating the silent, transcendent truth of Yahweh from the language-covered truth of the conventional world, but never collapsing one into the other. People do not have to go out to hear his message. He intrudes himself upon their everyday activities where they are. That is why he is more powerful than John: baptism with water signals ultimate conversion, baptism with the holy spirit signals a reimmersion in the conventional affairs of the world.

Jesus' Experience of the Ultimacy of God
1: 9–11

⁹It was at this time that Jesus came from Nazareth in Galilee and was baptized in the Jordan by John. ¹⁰And at once, as he was coming up out of the water, he saw the heavens split open and the Spirit, like a dove, descending into him.²¹ ¹¹And a voice came from heaven, "You are my son, the beloved, my favor rests on you."

Jesus comes from Nazareth, a satellite village near the administrative city of Sepphoris in the heart of Galilee.²² Without fanfare, he arrives on the scene simply as one of those who come to be baptized in the Jordan by John.²³ Although identified by Mark as christ and son of God, there appears to be

---

21. Following Fowler, *Let the Reader Understand,* 16: "A more literal reading of the Greek preposition *eis,* however, would have the spirit descend 'into' Jesus. Each of the other evangelists uses *epi,* 'upon,' describing a more genteel resting of the spirit upon Jesus, and this understanding has usually been read into Mark, but inappropriately, because Mark is portraying for us a person being invaded and possessed by a spirit. In Mark, Jesus becomes spirit-possessed. See, for example, Mark 1: 12, where the spirit within Jesus throws him out (*ekballō*) into the desert. Jesus has not so much acquired a spirit; rather, a spirit has acquired Jesus. In the baptism scene Mark is laying the basis for a debate that will arise later in the Gospel. Whether Jesus is spirit-possessed is not a question in Mark but rather whether the spirit in him is good or evil, from God or Satan (3: 20–35)."

22. See Crossan, *The Historical Jesus,* 18–19 on the geographical location of Nazareth along one of the busiest trade routes of ancient Palestine at the very administrative center of the Roman provincial government.

23. Camery-Hoggatt, *Irony in Mark's Gospel,* 96, stresses the unfulfilled expectancy that Jesus would arrive on the scene with more vigor and a mightier presence. He is anticipated to be "one mightier" than John, who will immerse the crowd in the Holy Spirit. He is the Lord whose way John prepared. "Were this a drama, we might say that Jesus is an actor standing in the wings. But standing there, a silent figure, his shadow looms already across the stage. The implied presence of the Messiah is critical. Everything that has appeared thus far has pointed to it. The reader expects a messianic figure of gigantic proportions, what Thomas Howard has called 'a towering and furious figure who will not be managed.' It is only a shadow, to be sure, but that looming shadow, and the Baptist's self-effacement, such critical factors in vv. 8f, set up the reader and the story's characters for a terrific disappointment. We are hardly prepared for the understated way Jesus finally makes his appearance in verse 9: he simply appears, without fanfare, like everybody else who has come to be baptized by John in the Jordan."

nothing special about his appearance at the riverside. There is no account of any wondrous birth in Bethlehem, as in Matthew or Luke. While Bethlehem as the city of David serves an apologetic function in the infancy accounts of those gospels, Jesus' home town in Mark is simply Nazareth in Galilee. This is important, for not only does Jesus begin his public activity by coming from there, but after his resurrection he returns to Galilee (16: 7). In the context of ultimate meaning, Jesus is a voice from the empty wilderness, but in the context of the truth of worldly convention, he comes from Galilee.[24] He comes up out of (ἀναβαίνων) the water to encounter the spirit descending (καταβαῖνον) from heaven. At the end, from the ultimate silence of his risen absence, he goes before his disciples back to the conventional world of his everyday home town. He comes from obscurity into the dramatic light of his career, and risen returns back to that everyday obscurity.

In coming to John and being baptized by him, Jesus joins the Judaean crowds and accepts John's prophetic insistence on transcendent conversion with its disassociation from the ordinary forms of worship. The phrase "at once" translates an original Greek term (εὐθὺς) which means "immediately." It is often deemed to be no more than a stylistic characteristic of Mark's rhetorical style, simply indicating a transition. Here, however, it seems to bear a different sense, for it indicates not a temporal sequence, but a spontaneous linkage, for "immediately" upon "coming up" from the water, the heavens are split open (σχιζομένους) and the spirit descends into Jesus.[25]

The image presented is more than a simple "opening" of the heavens, the sky, but of a powerful tearing of the fabric of normal expectancies, for this

---

24. Malbon, *Narrative Space and Mythic Meaning in Mark,* 24–25, sees a symbolic linkage between this initial journey of Jesus from Galilee to Judaea and the final journey of Jesus from Galilee to Jerusalem: "In the beginning Jesus journeys to Judea to be baptized by John into a ministry that leads, in the end, to a journey to Jerusalem to be crucified. The Markan Jesus would appear to interpret the first journey as a metaphor for the second in asking James and John, 'Are you able . . . to be baptized with the baptism with which I am baptized?' (10: 38) But Jesus' initial return from Judea to Galilee also foreshadows Jesus' final return to Galilee from the tomb in Judea (16: 7). The crucial importance of 1: 14 as the inauguration of Jesus' ministry is generally recognized, but it must be noted that his ministry opens with a *return* to Galilee from Judea. In the opening of Mark, Jesus' return to Galilee is reported; in the closing of Mark, Jesus' return to Galilee is anticipated." In a Mahāyāna reading of Mark Galilee serves as an indicator of worldly convention, the everyday life in all its depth and ordinariness. Jesus' journey from ultimate awareness, either in the initial wilderness of the desert or from the wilderness of the tomb, to Galilee signify his awareness that all is worldly convention-only, as does his post-resurrection return. On "worldly convention only," see Nagao, *The Foundational Standpoint of Mādhyamika Philosophy,* 109–221.

25. Fowler, *Mark and Method,* 58–59, notes that in current literary discussions of Mark the term *euthys* (1: 18; 1: 20; 1: 21; 1: 23) sets "a mood of urgency for the actions of the characters in the story being told. . . . We might hazard the generalization that the cumulative effect of all the *euthyses* is to drill into the reader that this narrative has relentless forward thrust." That, I think, is to read *euthys* as if it actually were a time marker. I prefer to understand it as indicating the spontaneous linkage of actions and events not obviously related to each other within linear time, not a hurried-up flow of linear time.

baptism brings about direct realization of ultimate meaning: the passage is an enlightenment account. Jesus realized conversion and witnessed its confirmation in the tearing open of the heavens and the coming down of the spirit, i.e., in direct contact with the transcendent God. It anticipates the splitting of the temple curtain into two parts from top to bottom in Mark 15: 38, where the same verb is used (ἐσχίσθη εἰς δύο ἀπ' ἀνωθεν ἕως κάτω). That scene also has a revelatory significance, suggesting that the eschatological moment has arrived at the crucifixion of Jesus. Here, the spirit descends into him, and the voice ratifies the validity of that enlightened conversion. The phrase "my favor rests upon you" translates ἐν σοὶ εὐδόκησα. The verb indicates approval or favor, and signifies not merely that the voice of the transcendent God from heaven approves Jesus' baptism, but that God graces Jesus with insight into ultimate reality, for it repeats the initial identification of Jesus as God's son made in 1: 1. In Mahāyāna terms, such insight is described as the wisdom of "undefiled suchness," the realization of reality apart from any signs or symbols that might represent it. It contrasts with the "defiled suchness," which is embedded in signs and symbols. In Mark's context a similar association is to be drawn, for "the designation of the perfectly righteous one as a 'son of God' had been made in the *Wisdom of Solomon* 2: 18. To someone familiar with that work, it is God who gives wisdom (*Wisdom* 7: 7; 8: 21; 9: 6, 10), and the wisdom of God is a 'holy' 'Spirit' (*Wisdom* 7: 22). Thus the scene in Mark 1: 9–11 is a dramatic realization of the principle expressed in *Wisdom* 7: 27; 'in every generation she [Wisdom] passes into holy souls and makes them friends of God and prophets.' Mark not only links his account of Jesus to Israel's prophetic hope but he also situates it squarely in Israel's wisdom tradition and its hope for God's blessing of immortality upon the righteous."[26] At this point in the narrative, to be "son of God" indicates an awakened wisdom that splits the heavens and gains direct awareness of Yahweh, the sharing of which becomes the mission of Jesus' subsequent endeavors.[27] Such an immediate awareness of God bypasses all traditions and all cultic liturgy, emptying in eschatological judgment all forms that would intervene and hinder direct access. In contrast to John, who is localized in the wilderness, Jesus, "lest he be interpreted as simply the new broker of a new God, . . . moved on constantly, settling down neither at Nazareth nor Capernaum. He was neither broker nor mediator but, somewhat paradoxically, the announcer that neither should exist between humanity and divinity or between humanity and itself. Miracle and parable, healing and eating were calculated to force individuals into immediate physical and spiritual contact with God and unmediated physical and spiritual

26. Humphrey, *He Is Risen*, 21.
27. Humphrey, *He is Risen*, 25: "If the Spirit which descended upon Jesus at the baptism is understood as Wisdom who is a Holy Spirit (Wisdom 7: 22), who enters into the souls of the righteous, making them friends of God, then Wisdom has been shown to have presenced herself in Jesus, and Jesus, in turn, has taken up Wisdom's mission. . . ."

contact with one another. He announced, in other words, the brokerless kingdom of God."[28]

The heavenly voice does not impart any further information. There is in Mark no back and forth dialogue between God and the story characters, even Jesus. When Jesus speaks, even on the cross, God is silent. When God speaks, Jesus is silent. "Jesus does not enter into dialogue with God, as do Moses, Samuel, Isaiah, and Jeremiah. Therefore the specific features of Jesus' task and the accompanying characteristics of his speech and action, are undefined."[29] Jesus does not remain in the wonder of silent awakening following his baptism, but is driven into the wilderness to empty even the emptiness of ultimate truth.

Temptation in the Wilderness
1: 12–13

[12]*And at once the Spirit drove him out into the wilderness* [13]*and he remained there for forty days, and was put to the test by Satan. He was with the wild beasts, and the angels looked after him.*

The "immediate" (εὐθὺς, i.e., at once) and natural result of Jesus' enlightenment was that he was "thrown" into the desert. The presence of the Spirit of awakened wisdom disorients one and drives one apart from the conventional "realities" of town living. The whole passage depicts a violent experience. The sky is "split open" and Jesus is "thrown out" (ἐκβάλλει) into the wilderness, in the company of wild beasts and angels. This verb, "to drive out" is used of the driving out of demons, but here Jesus is driven out by the Spirit into his confrontation with Satan. He is taken from ordinary life and forced into direct contact with Satan, into a chaotic disorientation of any rigid attachment to human identities and social constructs. The temptations are the first trial of Jesus, here taking place outside the constructs of any social reality. They test the authenticity of his awareness of the ultimacy of God, about which he must contest with Satan. His mission, indeed his very

---

28. Crossan, *The Historical Jesus,* 422. Crossan goes on to remark, 424, that when Christianity "attempted to define as clearly as it could the meaning of Jesus, [it] insisted that he was 'wholly God' and 'wholly man,' that he was, in other words, himself the unmediated presence of the divine to the human." My *The Meaning of Christ: A Mahāyāna Theology* is meant to express that unmediated Christ wisdom in terms of Mahāyāna philosophy.

29. Robbins, *Jesus the Teacher: A Socio-Rhetorical Interpretation of Mark,* 81. Also: "As a result of the absence [of the conventional commands, directions, and explanations from God that exist in prophetic biblical literature] in Mark, the activities of Jesus' character, action, and speech unfold as he himself initiates the action in the next section of the narrative. The reader cannot be sure what Jesus will do next, but whatever he does will be appropriate since Jesus, the beloved Son of God, will do nothing displeasing to God (1: 11)."

person, are at issue. The scene is a foreboding of the later confrontations when Jesus is accused of himself being possessed by Satan and the final trial before the religious and secular authorities, where he is charged with blasphemy. Jesus' trial is ruled throughout by the demonic assumption of the unquestioned validity of the absolute reality of an establishment view of religious truth. The conflict is an increasingly agonistic drama between cosmic or ultimate forces, and the issue becomes who in fact is possessed by demons and who will drive out whom. Will Jesus' wilderness awakening to Abba overcome the demonic delusion of his accusers and their attachment to realpolitik? Or will they finally succeed in eliminating him once and for all?

Here in his wilderness testing Jesus is placed between beasts and angels, apart from all human contact in the empty awareness of direct experience, bereft of human constructs, as he will be upon the cross. This is not the philosopher's portico, where ideas are interchanged and ideologies argued. The Gospel is not a set of doctrinal ideas, but a record of and invitation to experience. The Gospel writers indeed do theologize. Yet, the primacy always remains with accounts of the paradigmatic experiences themselves. The trials or temptations from Satan test Jesus' insight into the ultimacy of God. Mark does not report the precise nature of these tests. Both Matthew and Luke, however, do: Jesus is offered conventional rewards to abandon his mission. Satan dangles fame and power before him; he is taunted to prove through the concrete act of throwing himself down from a high place that God really does favor him. He is tempted to manifest his august status in conventional form, thus circumscribing insight into ultimate meaning within conventionally identifiable terms.

But Mark does not give such detail; the testing is simply a wilderness experience and a solitary one. Just as only Jesus "sees" ($\epsilon\hat{\iota}\delta\epsilon\nu$) the heavens torn apart, so he alone is driven to the wilderness for forty days and nights. What happens is not a public fact, and he is not described as being tested by the allure of conventional power or reward. Rather, he has a personal and direct experience of the demands of the spirit. In Mark the test is not to renounce the wilderness in favor of conventional glories, but to stay there, prolonging the forty days. These forty days and nights allude to Moses and Elijah, who wandered for forty days in the wilderness of Sinai/Horeb (*Exodus* 24: 18 and *1 Kings* 19: 8). Moses and Elijah also appear in risen presence with the transfigured Jesus (9: 4–8), and Peter wants to construct three booths to perpetuate their wondrous presence. The temptation in the wilderness trial is to grasp onto emptiness and abide therein as if in a secure abode, remaining apart from reengagement. Yet the emptiness of the wilderness is not any kind of secure abode, not any kind of final truth or viewpoint. In the trial before the religious and secular authorities, the issue turns around the attachment to religious and social securities and viewpoints: who is king? does Jesus blaspheme against the Temple? will he destroy that Temple? If one holds onto a view of emptiness as the final truth, then that view becomes not the dispeller of false views, but a most pernicious view, a poison that eats away at one's innards and makes it impossible to see that all views are empty. Even emptiness must be emptied in order for one to reengage in the dependently co-arisen world wherein wisdom becomes concretized in compassionate actions. Jesus does not remain in that desert, but, unlike John, returns to the social life of his world to preach the gospel, healing the sick and curing the possessed.

In Mark the cosmic forces, the epiphanies and the demons, are narrative symbols for the realm of ultimate meaning, apart from the conventional realm of town living. They evoke fear and wonder, as does Jesus' performance of exorcisms (5: 1–20) and his power over the forces of nature (6: 45–52). The realm of ultimate meaning is ineffable and beyond any linkage with conventional language and striving. Thus set apart, the natural response to it is one of amazement and wonder, as will be exemplified again and again by both the disciples and the crowds. Yet that amazement is not the response of faith, for it regards the ultimate as a strange and alien sphere, unrelated to everyday living and irrupting into life only on special occasions. Amazement at miracles bypasses the practice of the middle path, making impossible the practice of differentiating the two truths of ultimate meaning and worldly convention because one remains attached to a dichotomy between a sacred realm projected above and a secular realm experienced below. The conventional and the ultimate come to be regarded as two separate spheres tied together only when some linkage is achieved through a prophet or a miracle worker. One's response may be momentary awe, but one's life is left securely in place.

The structure of this prologue to Mark (1: 1–13) is chiastic, doubling back upon itself and emphasizing "the two levels of the plot, the human and the divine or cosmic."[30] Verses 1: 1–3 present Jesus at the beginning, coming from the wilderness of direct contact with God to prepare the way of the Lord. Verses 1: 4–8 describe the activity of John's baptism of conversion, and the success of that enterprise. Verses 1: 9–10 depict Jesus' submission to John's baptism and identify him with John's call for conversion. Verse 1: 11 recapitulates the divine presence at the beginning with the splitting of the heavens and the voice of the Father. The gospel will move henceforth in interplay between these two levels, at first adumbrating the presence of the divine in the healings and miracles, but finally differentiating them not as two separate levels, but as differing aspects of wisdom. It is not enough to believe in a separate realm of divine activity: the disciples, witnessing all the healings and miracles, continue to see the ultimacy of the divine as a realm apart from the everyday, whereas Jesus practices a wisdom path by following the conventional course of his life in awareness of the otherness of the ultimate, manifested by the absence of the Father at the cross and by the risen Christ's return to the everyday life of Galilee. For the disciples the ultimate remains separate, and thus is rendered irrelevant to their practice. For Jesus, although always veiled and hidden from conventional attempts

---

30. Tolbert, *Sowing the Gospel,* 112.

at identification, the ultimacy of God is the ever-present reality veiled by conventional living. God is present not as a higher level reality, but as that which is other to all conventional endeavors. Jesus comes from the wilderness of divine presence to follow the way of John's baptism and preach conversion. Driven out into the wilderness to be tested, he emerges victorious precisely in his reengagement in the preaching of the gospel. He is not only the son of God, as proclaimed by the voice from heaven; he is also messiah, engaged in the liberating deeds of prophetic wisdom. Thus the prologue sets up the next section, wherein Jesus comes back into Galilee and into the affairs of men and women.[31]

Jesus' Reengagement
1: 14–15

[14]After John had been arrested, Jesus went into Galilee. There he proclaimed the Good News from God. [15]"The time has come," he said, "and the kingdom of God has arrived. Convert, and believe the Good News."[32]

This section introduces the public preaching of Jesus in Galilee in the first half of the gospel, for it is the first time when Jesus speaks in his own voice, announcing the need for conversion and faith in light of the arrival of the kingdom.[33] Just when John is arrested by Herod, as a potential threat to the political status quo, Jesus returns from his Judaean baptism and wilderness experience to Galilee. Note that Jesus does not directly challenge Herod and

---

31. Kelber, *Mark's Story of Jesus*, 19: "There is a tight logic which controls the Markan story of 1: 1–12 and sets the stage for the pivotal verses 1: 14–15. Jesus enters upon the way by traveling to the Baptist. Equipped with the Spirit, he is driven out into the wilderness to an initial encounter with Satan. Emerging victorious from that confrontation, he is now fully equipped to make his gospel announcement. To this end Jesus the Galilean returns to Galilee after John's imprisonment." In the present reading, especially following Tolbert's rendering of verses 1: 1–3, Jesus is already the voice crying out in the wilderness. His baptism-signaled conversion derives from his wilderness contact with the ultimacy of God apart from the conventions of traditional religion. Verse 1: 13 doubles back to reaffirm that wilderness spirituality by the splitting of the heavens and the voice of divine approval. The central theme of the way is structured throughout this reading of the gospel in terms of these two truths and their tensive relationship.

32. Again taking μετανοεῖτε in verse 15 in its basic meaning of conversion, a turning around of one's conscious orientation. I take ἤγγικεν in its grammatical perfect sense, in line with the preceding πεπλήρωται, also in the perfect tense. For scholars who support this interpretation, see Bratcher and Nida, *A Translator's Handbook on the Gospel of Mark*, 37, and Kelber, *Mark's Story of Jesus*, 19: "The RSV rendering of 'is at hand' does not convey the Markan meaning." Likewise Tolbert, *Sowing the Gospel*, 117: ". . . in Greek both main verbs are in the perfect tense: the time has been fulfilled (πεπλήρωται), the kingdom has come near (ἤγγικεν). The force of the perfect tense is to represent an action begun in the past and continuing into the present."

33. Tolbert, *Sowing the Gospel*, 114.

does not stay where John had been baptizing, around Jerusalem. Instead he returns to his home area. Jesus does not follow John's wilderness path, but begins his career, again without fanfare, by reengaging in the world of ordinary humans. The content of his message differs from that of John. Jesus preaches not only an eschatological conversion apart from worldly affairs,[34] but also the good news of the arrival of the kingdom.[35] According to an alternate but well attested reading of the present passage, Jesus preaches "the good news of the kingdom of God" (τὸ εὐαγγέλιον τοῦ βαοιλείας τοῦ θεοῦ), i.e., the good news is that the kingdom has arrived. The verb "has arrived" (ἤγγικεν) in verse 15 is perfect tense, denoting not that the kingdom is going to arrive, but that it has already come and thus is at hand, available here and now. This reading approaches Dodd's idea about "realized eschatology," that the kingdom is both here and not yet here.[36] But I will argue, particularly in the commentary on chapter 13, that it represents not so much a realized eschatology as an emptied eschatology, wherein the linear expectations of the end time are reversed to be reaffirmed in terms of dependent co-arising.

---

34. I follow Crossan, *The Historical Jesus,* 238, in understanding eschatology broadly as world-negation, one subspecies of which is apocalyptic, which includes some version of a belief that the world is actually soon to end. In this reading, John is the apocalyptic prophet, while Jesus is an eschatological prophet, in that he empties all worldly expectancies and social structures in favor of reengagement in dependent co-arising. Eschatology, I think, is a Jewish narrative form for the Mahāyāna doctrine of emptiness, deconstructing only to reconstruct.

35. Crossan, *The Historical Jesus,* 237–38, analyzes the relevant materials and concludes that "Jesus changed his view of John's mission and message. John's vision of awaiting the apocalyptic God, the Coming One, as a repentant sinner, which Jesus had originally accepted and even defended in the crisis of John's death, was no longer deemed adequate. It was now a question of being in the Kingdom. 'Jesus started his public life,' as Paul Hollenbach put it, 'with a serious commitment to John, his message and his movement, and . . . Jesus developed very soon his own distinctive message and movement which was very different from John'." I would prefer to say that, rather than changing his view, the Markan Jesus empties the other-worldly and eschatological focus of John's desert experience to reengage in the world in terms of the coming kingdom. It is not an issue about viewpoints, but about the structure of the wisdom experience Jesus is portrayed as having at his baptism and its testing in the wilderness.

36. Dodd, *The Parables of the Kingdom,* 28–40. Kelber, *The Kingdom in Mark,* 10–11 also argues for the accomplished realization of the kingdom, and identifies its location as Galilee: "The kingdom has accomplished its realization and it has done so in Galilee. Thus there is the gospel program of the Markan Jesus: There is full time in Galilee, for it is here that the kingdom of God has attained its earthly destination." Again, "Eschatology is of ultimate concern to Mark, and the realized eschatology of the Galilean Kingdom serves as a premise for and holds the hermeneutical key to Markan theology." I do not think that such an eschatological fulfillment can be localized, or that the Markan use of Galilee serves such a purpose. It rather seems to me to be a cipher for one's everyday life. See Marxsen, *Mark the Evangelist,* 93–94: "Mark does not intend to say: Jesus worked in Galilee, but rather: Where Jesus worked, there is Galilee." Also see Kee, *Community of the New Age,* 107, where he argues for the eschatological kingdom, as both drawing near and future.

It is disputed whether the verb "draw near" means actually to be present, or to still be slightly in the future, over the next hill as it were, yet not quite here now. This argument parallels a similar issue in Mahāyāna circles about Buddha Nature, for it is argued by some that humans have such a nature as a potential for future realization and by others that they have Buddha Nature as an already present, although unrecognized, fact of their existence.[37] Both issues, the kingdom of God and the presence of Buddha Nature, raise what is perhaps a deeper question about the time frame assumed by the posing of the question, in the case of the gospel, of the events depicted in Mark.[38] If, as Edward Schillebeeckx maintains, the kingdom of God means God's rule of justice on earth, then it is clearly not a present empirical reality. Nevertheless, Mark's Jesus says that "the time has come" and that it has arrived. What then does time (καιρὸς) mean? It is not evidently a point in the conventional continuum of measured time, before which the kingdom has not arrived and after which it has. Rather, the eschatological Jesus comes from the timeless wilderness, where his enlightenment into the transcendent reality of God is beyond measurement, into the measured, conventional time flow of yesterday, today, and tomorrow. The time is at hand when that ultimate meaning of God, realized in the emptiness of the desert wilderness, reengages one into the conventional meanings of human affairs, determined by the contextual web of dependently co-arising circumstances. But, the kingdom is not the irruption of God in all his might into time, for it has come simply with Jesus' preaching. It is the reengaged presence of the compassionate Jesus from the wilderness into the towns of human beings. That itself is the eschatological realization of the rule of God, present but yet not fulfilling linear expectancies. The Greek verb "to come near, to arrive" (ἐγγίζω) occurs only three times in Mark, here in Jesus' opening proclamation, at Mark 11: 1, where Jesus and his disciples are arriving at Jerusalem (historical present) and in Mark 14: 42, when the hour has arrived (perfect tense) for Judas to betray Jesus. "In the last instance, the use of the perfect tense is unsurprising, because Jesus' preaching and healing have led to that moment of arrest. However, to begin the ministry with such an assertion casts an atmosphere of urgency over everything: the . . . narrative opens with the acknowledgment that the time is already, almost past. The Markan narrative has no time; all is rushing to imminent conclusion."[39] That suggests that time in Mark is not measured clock time, but itself a rhetorical construct. The fulfillment is then to happen in the very experience of the reader. When Jesus comes announcing the arrival of the kingdom and the call to conversion, no one in the story seems to hear what he is saying. His message is unheard and unheeded within the confines of the story, yet it can have impact through the discourse directed

37. See Grosnick, "Buddha Nature as Myth," 65–74, and Keenan, "The Doctrine of Buddha Nature in Chinese Buddhism: Hui-K'ai on Paramārtha," 125–138.
38. The theme of Via, *The Ethics of Mark's Gospel—In the Middle of Time,* 40–60.
39. Tolbert, *Sowing the Gospel,* 117.

to the reader. "In other words, 1: 14–15 is an admission by the narrator of what he wants to happen to the reader in the course of the reading experience. . . . For the reader, the time is filled full and the kingdom of God draws nigh in the experience of reading Mark's Gospel."[40]

And so Jesus not only announces that the kingdom is at hand, but also demands that people repent, i.e., that they become converted to the reality of God and believe in the good news of the kingdom. Without such a conversion, that kingdom, present in their midst, remains nothing but an idea, experienced perhaps by others, but not by oneself. The point of Jesus' preaching is then to share his experience of God as alone ultimate, as empty of any conventional definition, and as propelling one to reengage in the world to further the actualization of justice and peace. The command to convert is accompanied by an injunction to believe in the Gospel. Here faith is clearly not the acceptance of doctrine.[41] Rather, it is the conscious awareness of a mind that has been so converted.[42] Jesus adds faith to John's call for conversion and that remains a distinctive mark of Jesus' ministry.[43]

The chiastic, doubling back structure of the prologue does not simply move on two levels, human and divine, but enfolds human activity within the ultimacy of the wilderness that allows faith to be engendered, for Mark is interested not just in a wilderness conversion, but in the concrete practice of the middle path of faith in the enfolding, yet hidden presence of God in the everyday affairs of Galilee. The kingdom (βασιλεία) Jesus announces is a spatial metaphor for the realm of reengaged practice, reflecting the verbal sense of God's active ruling, which is present in the Aramaic parallel (*malkuth*), for it calls for an ongoing engaged practice of the justice and peace that embodies the kingdom.[44]

The Social Nature of the Kingdom
1: 16–20

[16]*As he was walking along by the Sea*[45] *of Galilee he saw Simon and Simon's brother Andrew casting a net in the sea—for they were fishermen.* [17]*And*

---

40. Fowler, *Let the Reader Understand,* 90–91.

41. Robinson, *The Problem of History in Mark,* 75: "Mark has no single person or act as the object of faith, and no specific credal statement as the content of faith." Kelber, *The Kingdom in Mark,* 13: "Generally, the Markan *pistis* is not concerned with belief in somebody, i.e., this Christ of the cross, but *pistis* constitutes an attitude on the part of man. . . ." See Robbins, *Jesus the Teacher,* 111: "Jesus does not instruct his disciples in the details of his system of understanding. In fact only three verses contain statements by Jesus to the disciples (1: 17, 38; 2: 14)." I would doubt that Jesus exhibits anything like a system of understanding.

42. Schweizer, "Mark's Theological Achievement," 44: "The content of this proclamation is characterized by two terms that have come to Mark from the tradition. It is a call to metanoia ('repentance') and so is euaggelion ('gospel'), or message of salvation."

43. Tolbert, *Sowing the Gospel,* 117.

44. See Tolbert, *Sowing the Gospel,* 172, and Perrin, *The Language of the Kingdom,* 1–88.

45. I prefer "sea" for Mark's τὴν θάλασσαν τῆς Γαλιλαίας, to maintain the sense

Jesus said to them, "Come after me and I will make you fishers of men."
[18]And at once they left their nets and followed him.

*[19]Going on a little further, he saw James son of Zebedee and his brother
John; they too were in their boat, mending the nets. [20]He called them at once
and, leaving their father Zebedee in the boat with the men he employed, they
went after him.*

This account of the calling of the disciples is stark in the extreme. No
information is given about the disciples, except that they were fishermen and
that two of them left their father to follow Jesus and inaugurate the kingdom.
That kingdom then "consists of people and it bids for people (1: 17c), but
in the curious sense of dislodging these first participants from their native
environment. The nucleus of this kingdom is called into being . . . by a forced
departure of four men away from their professional and personal lives."[46]
Their immediate response is perhaps reminiscent of "the manner in which
the prophet Elijah suddenly and authoritatively called Elisha from his work
to be his follower (*1 Kings* 19: 19–21)."[47] If the Elisha story lies behind
Mark's account, then Jesus' new followers understood from the beginning
that they were to share in Jesus' prophetic task of announcing the kingdom.

Yet, the promise that they would be fishers of men is somewhat ambiguous.
There is a passage from *Jeremiah* 16: 16, "Watch, I shall send for many
fishermen, Yahweh declares, and these will fish them up. . . ." The point of
this passage from *Jeremiah* is that invading forces, acting as Yahweh's agents,
will fish up and hunt down the unfaithful. Perhaps Jesus is alluding to this
passage, suggesting that the disciples will be such agents of Yahweh. This
implies, however, that they will enjoy positions of power from which to
punish the unfaithful. After all, a caught fish is a dead fish! The more common
explanation of Jesus' metaphor here is that his disciples will gather human
beings together into the kingdom as fishermen gather fish into the net.[48] Yet
who wants to be netted by anyone?

There is always a tendency to read the Gospels as a record of the wondrous
being who was Jesus. The first disciples, without ever having met Jesus
before, immediately leave everything behind and follow him, merely at his
invitation. James and John leave their father not only in the boat, but perhaps
in the lurch as well. One can perhaps argue that they did know about Jesus
before this, for he is reported as preaching in the area—the reader can fill
in the gaps to assume that they are already disposed to follow Jesus. But
that is not what the passage says and thus is not, I think, what it is about.
Rather, following as it does directly after the report of Jesus' preaching about

---

of chaos that sea connotes. See Malbon, *Narrative Space,* 100 and 76; Mark first named
that sizeable but limited lake the Sea of Galilee. Maybe the Galilean Ocean would suggest
Mark's sense.

46. Kelber, *The Kingdom in Mark,* 15.

47. Heil, *The Gospel of Mark as a Model for Action,* 43.

48. Wuellner, *The Meaning of "Fishers of Men,"* explains the metaphor as an allusion
to an Old Testament metaphor for salvation and judgment.

the kingdom, the passage on the calling of the disciples is about the kingdom: that it is not a private wilderness reality, but a calling together of humans. The starkness of the story serves its point well, for it says only that Jesus discipled others in the bringing about of the kingdom, already at hand. The point is that, having been called to come after him, the disciples evinced no concern about their lost circumstances. And they did not come to him, he called them. Jesus is not a renowned master sought after by would-be disciples. He abruptly calls them and they come at once (εὐθύς), as the spontaneous and natural response to the reality of the kingdom. Here Mark's rhetorical structure moves not in a narrative linear perspective, but in the rhetorical time of the inner events of Jesus' eschatological preaching and its inevitable conclusion, often signaled in the text by a quickening of pace through the use of the adverb "at once" (εὐθύς).[49] The theological outflow of Jesus' wilderness experience of ultimate meaning is that he preaches the good news of the kingdom, resulting spontaneously in the calling of disciples and in their willing response.

Yet, their very spontaneity suggests a further meaning in the business about being fishers of men. Mark's implied reader knows that, as both Israelites and fishermen, the first disciples are aware of Jeremiah's passage about the invading fishermen acting as God's agents and punishing the unfaithful. Thus, when they heard Jesus' invitation, they easily understand it as promising positions of power over men and women. They see Jesus as a divine personage, powerful and "mightier than John."[50] They even now look forward, as later in the account they request, to sitting on judgment thrones over the twelve tribes of Israel, catching men from their positions of power. Because the metaphor is ambiguous, the reader is unsure if the spontaneous following of Jesus flows from faith or is driven by images of a bright and powerful future glory. This interpretation has in its favor Mark's subsequent treatment of the disciples, for in his portrayal they remain focused on their selfish concerns and never do quite get the point of what Jesus' message of the kingdom of God among humans is all about. Furthermore, the phrase "leaving their father" (ἀφέντες τὸν πατέρα, 1: 20) forebodes their leaving Jesus (ἀφέντες αὐτὸν) and fleeing at his arrest (14: 50), presaging ironically their future abandonment of disappointed hopes.[51] "From the standpoint of an ironic reading, what makes that response particularly noteworthy is that these four men drop everything to follow Jesus *without knowing who he is*."[52] In the subsequent

---

49. Tolbert, *Sowing the Gospel*, 117: "Everything happens 'immediately' in the Gospel, for εὐθύς is one of Mark's favorite words, appearing forty-nine times." Εὐθύς then is not a temporal indicator, but a rhetorical marker to move the story line along its theological path. It here stands for the spontaneity of their response.

50. In a word, they would have seen Jesus from the beginning as the 'divine man' to whom one might hitch one's chariot to glory, as presented by Weeden, *Mark—Traditions in Conflict*.

51. Tolbert, *Sowing the Gospel*, 154.

52. Camery-Hoggatt, *Irony in Mark's Gospel*, 101.

narrative, their understanding of who Jesus is constitutes a basic issue and they continue to cling to notions of a messiah who is beyond suffering and soon to enter into his glory. Their part in Jesus' eschatological mission remains an enigma for the reader.

Jesus Teaches at Capernaum and Cures a Demoniac
1: 21–28

[21]They went as far as Capernaum, and at once on the Sabbath he went into the synagogue and began to teach. [22]And his teaching made a deep impression on them because, unlike the scribes, he taught them with authority.

[23]And at once in their synagogue there was a man with an unclean spirit, and he shouted, [24]"What do you want with us, Jesus of Nazareth? Have you come to destroy us? I know who you are: the Holy One of God." [25]But Jesus rebuked it saying, "Be quiet! Come out of him!" [26]And the unclean spirit threw the man into convulsions and with a loud cry went out of him. [27]The people were so astonished that they started asking each other what it all meant, saying, "Here is a teaching that is new, and with authority behind it: he gives orders even to unclean spirits and they obey him." [28]And his reputation at once spread everywhere, through all the surrounding Galilean countryside.

This account is the first of four initial healing stories, portraying the effective power of Jesus' teachings.[53] The healing of the man with the unclean spirit is quickly followed by the healing of Simon's mother-in-law (1: 29–34), the healing of a leper (1: 40–45), and the healing of a paralytic (2: 1–12), which leads at once into a controversy over Jesus' authority to forgive sins. That controversy is quickly followed by three other controversy stories, over eating with sinners (2: 15–17), over fasting (2: 18–22), and over observance of the Sabbath (2: 23–26).[54] Mark presents the exorcising and healing power of Jesus' teaching as the means used by Jesus to translate the kingdom into action.[55] It is not merely an issue of Jesus' power to drive out demons or to heal, but, as indicated here, of the primal experience from which the powerful and healing teaching of Jesus derives and from which it takes its force to transform human beings.[56]

---

53. Broadhead, *Teaching With Authority,* 61: "Even before his presentation as a miracle worker, the story characterizes Jesus as teacher with authority."

54. See Tolbert, *Sowing the Gospel,* 131–42.

55. Kelber, *The Kingdom in Mark,* 17.

56. Crossan, *The Historical Jesus,* 310, notes that "There is something very strange about the miracles of Jesus," in that they have comparatively meager attestation in the earliest strata of texts. "One might almost conclude that miracles come into the tradition rather later than earlier, as creative confirmation rather than as original data. I think, however, that such a conclusion would be completely wrong. The better explanation is just the opposite. Miracles were, at a very early stage, being washed out of the tradition and, when retained, were being very carefully interpreted."

Capernaum, on the Sea of Galilee, is the scene of Jesus' first miracle, involving the power of his teaching over distortions of ultimate meaning. Demons symbolize such distortions, either insisting on ultimate meaning to the neglect of worldly convention, or trying to force ultimate meaning into the confining net of worldly convention. The unclean spirit in the man shouts out that Jesus should maintain his distance, for the holiness he embodies is seen as apart and aloof from the actual world of distorted and possessed people.[57] The deluded, demonic view of a separate, sacred realm dichotomizes ultimate truth from the everyday world of human suffering. And so the demon urges Jesus to keep away.

The action described in this passage continues Jesus' prior reengagement in the world of men and women. With rhetorical spontaneity (εὐθὺς),[58] Mark has Jesus go to town, and as would be expected, he enters the synagogue, for, unlike John, he is now reinvolving himself in the ordinary structures of religious life. His teaching is well received, for it flows from his wilderness contact with God and not from books, like the scribes. Jesus is not presenting ideas about the kingdom, but announcing an experience that others may share. He is not commenting on the scriptures, as do the scribes. That is an honorable task, and the passage does not denigrate it. But a scribal reading borrows the authority of the text and has none of its own. In Mark, Jesus speaks from his wilderness awareness and from his commitment to reengage in the world of humans. He practices the middle path of differentiating, but not dichotomizing, ultimate meaning and worldly convention.

Embodying the ultimate in human terms, Jesus encounters a person possessed of an unclean spirit. But this fellow is not possessed by a wilderness demon, for he is present in the synagogue, apparently taking part in its observances. He is, it would seem, familiar with and expecting to hear the verbal teachings of the scribes. This is not a question of a crazed person, living apart in the wilderness or even on the outskirts of the town. This man's spirit is unclean because, not having experienced the wilderness awakening to the ultimacy of God, he rests secure in the accustomed liturgies. The picture sketched by Mark is of a person who clings tenaciously to verbal doctrine, mistaking human fabrications for the very experience of God: this too signals an unclean spirit. For him the teachings are not verbally mediated and constructed upon the foundational experience of the wilderness, but themselves take over and usurp the very role of experience. This is why he shouts at Jesus, for he perceives Jesus to be the enemy of conventional

---

57. Heil, *The Gospel of Mark as a Model for Action,* 47: "The implication is that Jesus has no concern with or power over the demonic realm of evil."

58. Tolbert, *Sowing the Gospel,* 135: "Everything happens 'immediately,' and the narrative pace of the entire subsection [1: 16–3: 6] hardly allows an auditor time to assimilate the separate actions. . . . this fast progress reinforce[s] the claim . . . that the time has been fulfilled (1: 13)." Mark's rhetorical narrative breaks with linear time, and builds gradually toward the eschatological discourse in chapter 13.

religion.[59] He senses the otherness of Jesus' experience and message. He calls Jesus the "Holy One of God" and asks if Jesus wants to destroy, not just him, but "us," i.e., the entire synagogue structure and congregation. The man with the unclean spirit embodies the reaction of those who regard conventional truth and doctrine as the only ultimate they are willing to deal with. He recognizes that there are holy ones, *hasidah*. His objection is that there is no need for such persons to come into the synagogue. Let them stay in the desert wilderness, like John!

Up to this point in Mark, the theme is Jesus' wilderness experience and his reengagement in society. Here Mark makes a transition, setting the stage for the events that constitute the subsequent course of Jesus' life and death. The focus shifts to the question of the authenticity of Jesus' primal wilderness awareness and his reengagement in the world. From here on, Jesus will have to respond to charges that he should not intrude his awakening upon the conventional world of others. There is always in Mark a tension between ultimate meaning and worldly convention. Some, like the unclean man here, want to draw a protective cloak around their conventional awareness to exclude the silent emptiness of ultimate meaning. Others, perhaps like the Baptist, remain apart in total focus on ultimate meaning and find space only for a condemnation of the world. This tension will occur again and again in the events that follow in Mark's account.

Jesus' initial response is to rebuke the man and enjoin silence. This first use of the verb "to rebuke" (ἐπετίμησεν) signifies power over the cosmic forces that move beyond the realm of human control, as in Jesus' rebuking of the wind (4: 39), and foreshadows not only the rebuking of other unclean spirits (9: 25), but also the mutual rebuking of Peter (8: 32) and Jesus (8: 33). The use of the term is a signal that we are dealing with the realm of ultimate meaning, distorted in one way or another by Jesus' adversaries.[60] The command to remain silent is sometimes seen as Jesus' desire not to reveal himself as the Messiah yet. But the deeper significance is that Jesus'

---

59. Kelber, *Mark's Story of Jesus*, 21: "[The man with the unclean spirit] realizes that Jesus' mission is intended to oppose not merely a single exponent of evil but the demonic power structure itself." That religious structure is demonic because the demoniac usurps ultimate meaning within the traditions. It is not, as Best claims in *The Temptation and the Passion: The Markan Soteriology*, 61, that Jesus' achievement is the defeat of Satan, conclusively in the desert and subsequently in mopping up operations. Rather, the demonic is always in Mark a distortion of the differential relationships between the two truths, either trivializing ultimate meaning by binding it within conventions, or negating traditions by imposing a divine logic upon them. The man with the unclean spirit here wants to marginalize the emptiness of the wilderness in favor of the synagogue liturgies.

60. Kee, "The Terminology of Mark's Exorcism Stories," shows that the use of the verb ἐπετίμησεν is more than a corrective rebuke, but signals an aggressive attack on the demonic powers themselves. In a Mahāyāna reading, the context is basic, treating the understanding of emptiness and its distortions. It is not, as Kelber, *The Kingdom in Mark*, 16, argues, a struggle between two kingdoms, but of the very basis of God's kingdom in emptiness and dependent co-arising. Broadhead, *Teaching With Authority*, 60, notes that: "The command to silence (φιμώθητι) has reference to muzzling an animal."

revelation of God occurs in silence, not in verbal identifications, as will become apparent in Peter's confession (8: 29). What is thus silenced is the imagined pattern of mistaking words for meaning. Even Peter, who correctly identifies Jesus as the christ, using the terms of Mark's own initial identification (1: 1), fails to understand what that identification means. Crystal clear definitions of Jesus are beside the point, for what he reveals remains veiled from deluded perception.

But the man did not claim that Jesus was the christ, the messiah, only that he was a holy one of God, a description that could also apply to a number of prophets and saints.[61] Furthermore, the crowd takes no cognizance of the demon's identification of Jesus as the holy one of God.[62] They generally pay little attention to the titles attributed to Jesus in Mark and never respond to them. Mark's point seems to be theological, directed to the reader, for the Christian community to whom he wrote can be assumed to be interested in Jesus' titular identity. Yet the text does not expatiate upon titles at any length—with the exception of the title of messiah, about which Jesus' disciples will later be deeply confused. Here, he is simply identified as holy. In Mahāyāna parlance, emptiness is described as the silence of the saints. Jesus commands the man to empty his mind of attachments to convention and to gain insight into the silent emptiness of all verbal doctrine. He orders the unclean spirit to come out of the man, to free him from clinging to human constructs. And, the account relates, that unclean spirit did go out, throwing the fellow into convulsions. The term for convulsions (σπαράξαν) means "to pull to and fro," and thus to convulse. Mark depicts an inner struggle between clinging madly to one's own images or ideas about religion and being freed to experience God in emptiness. A similar anguish characterizes Jesus in the garden of Gethsemane, where he violently "throws himself upon the ground" (14: 35). The test there was also to abandon the wilderness awareness of the ultimacy of God and to let the cup of suffering pass by. Yet Jesus arises, healed through his prayer to the Father and prepared for the events to come. This man, too, is healed at Jesus' word and able perhaps to glimpse the reality behind all words. Whether they be exorcisms or physical cures, Jesus' healings restore people to their everyday lives.

The people in the synagogue are astounded and begin to question one another about this new teaching (διδαχὴ καινὴ). Christians often mistakenly equate this "new" teaching with that of the New Testament and see the passage as demonstrating the superiority of Jesus, who teaches a new teaching with authority, over the Tanach, with its old outmoded teachings. But this notion is unsupported by the text. Mark's Jesus does not in fact present any new teaching, either in this passage or in the preceding ones. His teaching is not new because of some new content, but because of its power to enliven

---

61. It recalls both Elisha in *2 Kings* 4: 9 and Elijah in *1 Kings* 17: 18. See Kee, *The Community of the New Age,* 34.

62. Via, *Ethics,* 176. See Dewey, *Markan Public Debate,* 177.

and liberate. After all, the liberation of the man from his unclean spirit is what elicits the wonder of the people. That is what they say: that it has effective power. Jesus' words have such power not because of magical potency, but because they can liberate one from clinging to conventional constructs as if those constructs were themselves realities. The unclean spirits obey his words because those words flow from the wilderness experience of the ultimacy of God, and heal demonic distortions about the truth of ultimate meaning and how it relates to conventional language and tradition.

Yet Jesus' reputation becomes a social reality. He becomes a known entity, socially defined as a miracle worker and healer. Rather than recognizing him as the empty and transparent mirroring of the Father, the people focus on him as the center of attention. The constant danger of deluded consciousness is to construct images of things and then to mistake those imaginings for reality itself. In such an imagined pattern of consciousness, the wilderness awakening of Jesus is trivialized in favor of his newly found fame as a powerful healer through these "new" teachings. This initial Galilean fame expands until Jesus is seen as embodying not the awareness of God in silence and reengagement, but as a threat against the nation and the social order.

Mark also manages to foist upon his implied reader a view about Jesus' reputation (ἡ ἀκοὴ), for the story begins to focus on just who Jesus is. Mark's rhetoric supplies the implied reader with added perspectives on Jesus. "Two traits of the story (21–29) deserve preliminary notice. First, the story initiates a concerted focus on the characterization of Jesus. Particular attention is directed to the character traits of Jesus through two narrative devices: crowd response (1. 22a) and an intrusion by the narrator (1. 22b). Secondly, the miracle act undergoes a narrative subordination to the more idiosyncratic characterization of Jesus as 'teacher with authority.' This strategy reflects the central plot action into an intense portrait of Jesus."[63] This indeed appears to be Mark's surface intent.

Yet there are other indications of who Jesus is, indications at variance with the portrait of Jesus as a teacher with authority. The unclean spirit identifies him as the holy one of God. This is the first of a series of demonic disclosures to the reader of who Jesus is (see 3: 7–12; 5: 7). One can readily conclude that "they constitute disclosures of Jesus' identity which the reader can overhear."[64] The demons and the reader are then endowed with privileged information which is denied to the characters in the story, who never seem to overhear anything. But there is, I think, a deeper irony, beyond that of a privileged reader watching the bumbling attempts of the disciples to understand Jesus. Mark's Jesus himself states later on the story level that the house of Satan is not divided against itself (3: 20–27) and he warns that false

63. Broadhead, *Teaching With Authority*, 62.
64. Camery-Hoggatt, *Irony in Mark's Gospel*, 103. Again, 105: "It (i.e., the demon's identification of Jesus) indicates to the reader that he is possessor of privileged information, information which has come from a supernatural source, and while it is a source that is antagonistic to Jesus, it is one which nevertheless recognizes his true identity."

prophets will come to identify the christ (13: 21–22). Such advice should reinforce one's instinctive mistrust of the witness of demons: they are unreliable, and unlikely to have been employed by Mark as purveyors of an overheard truth about Jesus. They, like the unclean spirit in the present passage, identify Jesus as separate from everyday life, as a special personage apart from worldly affairs. No matter how "correct" their information, they mislead the implied reader into settling for mere information. The rhetorical result is not, as some maintain, "that Jesus, the demons, and the reader stand together in a kind of occlusion, such that their common knowledge separates them from the remaining characters in the story."[65] Rather, the result is that, unlike the disciples who at least are confused on the issue, the reader, like the demons, begins to cling to a firm definition of who Jesus is. Both demons and reader are blocked from understanding Jesus' identity. The misguided disciples throughout the narrative remain the image of the implied reader, whatever privileged information that reader may access. Like Jesus who came not to call the righteous, but sinners (2: 17), Mark writes not for the informed and enlightened, but for the misguided and misinformed.

Jesus as Healer of Mothers-in-Law
1: 29–34

[29]*And at once on leaving the synagogue, he went with James and John straight to the house of Simon and Andrew.* [30]*Now Simon's mother-in-law was in bed and feverish, and at once they told him about her.* [31]*He went in to her, took her by the hand and helped her up. And the fever left her and she began to serve them.*

[32]*That evening, after sunset, they brought to him all who were sick and those who were possessed by devils.* [33]*The whole town came crowding around the door,* [34]*and he cured many who were suffering from diseases of one kind or another; he also drove out many devils, but he would not allow them to speak, because they knew who he was.*

The immediate consequence (καὶ εὐθὺς) of the healing in the synagogue is that Jesus is taken to the house of Simon, where the disciples straightaway (εὐθὺς) tell him about Simon's mother-in-law. Jesus now has a reputation as a healer, and the disciples immediately put him to use. The emergent pattern of Jesus' relationship with the disciples is here adumbrated, for they constantly attempt to use his power for their own benefit. Most interpreters have seen this passage as merely reporting the cure of Simon's mother-in-law, as a sign of Jesus' healing power. But that does not seem to be the impact of this account, for his power is not in question. The synagogue scene already amply shows that Jesus speaks with authority and that even the spirits obey him.

---

65. Camery-Hoggatt, *Irony in Mark's Gospel,* 105.

Mark's point here is that the disciples, and then the whole town, begin to define who he is—a miracle worker. They objectify his reengagement and, as becomes apparent in the subsequent account, take that definition as his meaning. His wilderness spirituality is increasingly lost to those who cling to hopes of being the beneficiaries of his powerful actions. The silent experience of ultimate meaning is always a fearful and disturbing event, provoking reactions to tame it down and reestablish accustomed securities. Jesus is certainly not the first miracle worker or healer in Israel.[66] Indeed, all ancient cultures have such figures. When the Gospel was first preached in India, the Christian claim for uniqueness because of Jesus' ability to perform miracles was met with incomprehension, for in India all yogis develop such powers (*ṛddhi*). Jesus' reputation as a healer tends to obfuscate his meaning. It is not merely that he effects healings. Rather, since the ancient world assumed sickness to be caused by the presence of evil spirits, his healings are "frontal attacks on the power structure of evil."[67] To relieve people of sickness is to liberate them from the powers that distort the presence of God. It is a practice of the middle path, abiding firmly in the conventional world of sick people through and in an awareness of the otherness of God. Throughout the gospel, those healed are never permitted to follow Jesus, but almost immediately disappear into the dependently co-arisen world of their everyday lives. They are restored not to the ultimate glory realm of a false kingdom imagined by the disciples and the readers, but to the conventional realm of human living in which alone the kingdom may be established.

Jesus casts out many devils but does not allow them to speak, because they know him (ὅτι ᾔδεισαν αὐτόν). Again, this passage is often taken to mean that Jesus wants to hide the fact that he is the messiah, an idea clearly reflected in the above translation from the Jerusalem Bible: "because they knew who he was." The text, however, merely says, "because they knew him." The unclean spirits and devils do have an inner affinity with Jesus, for both have gone outside the conventional norms of society, albeit in different directions.[68] Jesus forbids them to speak because, when unaccompanied by commitment to reengage in the world, wilderness experiences, either of the ultimacy of God or of the madness of possession, disrupt and harm the ordered world of humans. One cannot build the kingdom of God in society from a power position that is aloof from society. And so, Jesus silences

---

66. See Crossan, *The Historical Jesus,* 336–37 for the cultural background of Jesus' healing activity.

67. Kelber, *Mark's Story of Jesus,* 21.

68. Fowler, *Let the Reader Understand,* 131: "Confirming the statements by the heavenly voice are the utterances by other denizens of transcendent realms, the demons. Repeatedly the demons cry out that Jesus is the son of God (1: 24, 34; 3: 11–12; 5: 7), which confirms what the heavenly voice tells us, as well as what the narrator himself tells us about Jesus in the first verse of the Gospel." But again, that confirmation is merely information, leading the reader to entertain the delusion that she has a viewpoint higher than the disciples in the story. That would only be true if the gospel were trying to present a viewpoint.

the devils and their knowledge that he has indeed gone beyond, for their inept apprehension of emptiness is not the practice of the middle path. His life course evolves on two levels. On one level, he struggles in the wilderness both with devils and finally on the cross with the Father. Yet he returns from the wilderness to the world and by casting out devils and pointing to the silent presence of the Father frees the minds of those who fail in their practice. These devils of course recognize him, for they too have gone beyond, but, being unable to reengage, fall into madness. On the other level, Jesus struggles to carry out the conventional tasks of building the kingdom of God on earth, preaching the ultimacy of the love of God and insisting on justice in the concrete living of life. These two realms of meaning are always in tension, but they never collapse into one another. Ultimate meaning always remains other from any conventional embodiment; worldly convention develops only through worldly and conventional means. Even the miracles and healings, in their Israelite context, albeit strange and wondrous, remain worldly and conventional. But the distinctiveness of the two realms of truth does not mean that they are unrelated. Rather, in the mind of wisdom they are constantly held in dynamic tension, for Jesus' reengagement in the world of humans is informed and driven by his awareness of the otherness of God. And his awareness of the otherness of God remains constant, even in the midst of his weariness from dealing with the deluded world of men and women.

Jesus' Wilderness Prayer
1: 35–39

[35]In the morning, long before dawn, he got up and left the house, and went off to a lonely place and prayed there. [36]Simon and his companions hunted him down, [37]and when they found him they said, "Everybody is looking for you."[69] *[38]He answered, "Let us go elsewhere, to the neighboring country towns, so that I can proclaim the message there too, because that is why I came out."*[70] *[39]And he went all through Galilee, preaching in their synagogues and driving out devils.*

The two verbs "he left" (ἐξῆλθεν) and "he went off" (ἀπῆλθεν) express two separate movements. Jesus first leaves the house of Simon where the crowd had gathered and where one would expect it to reassemble. He leaves conventional expectations and definitions in the dark of the night. Then he goes off into a wilderness, i.e., "a lonely place" (εἰς ἔρημον τόπον), a place of direct contact with God in the nighttime darkening of all conventional

---

69. I translate "hunted him down," rather than "searched him out," following Tolbert, *Sowing the Gospel*, 138: "The Greek word καταδιώκω carries a very strong, often hostile sense: Simon and the others harassed him or hunted him down."

70. Following RSV translation of ἐξῆλθον, i.e., came out from the house.

expectations. The Japanese philosopher Nishitani Keiji talks about "the field of emptiness," the localization of the non-discriminative wisdom of awakening.[71] This is the fundamental wisdom that constitutes one a buddha, an awakened one. Jesus withdraws into this silent, wilderness place time after time, there to pray. "These times are characterized by isolation: he always goes alone and he goes to a lonely place."[72] The Greek term for prayer (προσηύχετο) means both "to pray" and "to wish." Jesus' prayer is also a firm wish, i.e., a commitment to maintain awareness of the silent ultimacy of God, even while reengaged in preaching the kingdom in the world, even in the coming trial and passion. It is a commitment to so reengage, similar to the vow of a bodhisattva selflessly to dedicate himself or herself to the salvation of all sentient beings, rather than to enter individually into the peace of salvific cessation.

But Simon and the disciples interrupt Jesus' silent prayer. They do not let him alone, fearing perhaps that, like John, he might go back to the wilderness and disappoint their hopes. They hunt him down and harass him, reminding him of just how much he is in demand as a healer and miracle-worker.[73] Jesus is not in the Markan story now tempted to abandon the conventional world. He moves now to renew his engagement, but not in the terms of the crowd's expectancies, or of the disciples' hopes.[74] The drama of the Gospel turns upon Jesus' differential awareness, of the ultimate meaning of Abba on the one hand, and on the other of the conventional meaning of social engagement. Thus Jesus disassociates himself from Peter's house and Peter's hopes: "that is why I came out" (εἰς τοῦτο γὰρ ἐξῆλθον). He has come out of Peter's house in order to preach to all the villages, not simply to bolster the status of his chosen disciples. It is significant that the content of that preaching is again not expressed,[75] despite the subordination of the miracle story to the portrait of Jesus as teacher.[76] He comes in order to preach (ἵνα καὶ ἐκεῖ κηρύξω) in words a conversion which cannot be verbally appropriated.

71. Nishitani, *Religion and Nothingness,* 119–67. That empty field is also one of dependently co-arisen reengagement, as explained by Nagao, *The Foundational Standpoint of Mādhyamika Philosophy,* 114.

72. Tolbert, *Sowing the Gospel,* 189.

73. Malbon, *Narrative Space,* 75 reads κατεδίωξεν as to "track down," a hostile action on the part of the disciples. In Mahāyāna their action is an incursion into the silence of ultimate meaning by the boisterous boasting of conventional religiosity.

74. Crossan, *The Historical Jesus,* 346: "Any Mediterranean person would recognize what should happen or is already happening. Peter's house is becoming a brokerage place for Jesus' healings, and Peter will broker between Jesus and those seeking help."

75. The New Jerusalem Bible adds "the message," which the Greek does not express.

76. Broadhead, *Teaching With Authority,* 70: ". . . the miracle focus has been subverted and refocused. Miracle stories carry no inherent orientation toward preaching (teaching); only through narrative manipulation do they focus on proclamation. Mark 1.21–39 reveals a narrative strategy which refocuses miracle stories toward a distinct portrait of Jesus and his proclamation." Yet that distinct portrait is itself an enigma, realized only through the reader's conversion (μετάνοια) from imagined realities to the dependently co-arisen identity of Jesus and his message.

In Mark, Jesus comes from such a direct awareness of God. There is no mention of him coming from the heavens, as in the Gospel of John. The drama of Mark turns on Jesus' attempts to show just how conversion reengages one in conventional truth while aware of the emptiness of all things. Thus, he does not identify with the awaiting crowd. Rather, Mark says that he preaches in "their" synagogues (εἰς τὰς συναγωγὰς αὐτῶν). There is a distancing of Jesus from the conventional religious practices and expectancies of the people, for they have not realized the emptiness of all conventional realities. Even though Jesus is in his home district, Mark describes him as if he were visiting. In virtue of his direct awakening, here reaffirmed through his silent prayer vow, all the conventional manifestations of religion are "theirs." He holds himself apart from absolutizing any forms of religion, for all religion is empty of essence, and in that emptiness it finds its true form.[77]

Hiding the Story
1: 40–45

[40]*A man suffering from a virulent skin disease came to him and pleaded on his knees saying, "If you are willing, you can cleanse me."* [41]*Feeling sorry for him, Jesus stretched out his hand, touched him and said to him, "I am willing. Be cleansed."* [42]*At once the skin disease left him and he was cleansed.* [43]*And at once Jesus sternly charged him,[78] and sent him away at once and said to him,* [44]*"Mind you tell no one anything, but go and show yourself to the priest, and make the offering for your cleansing prescribed by Moses as evidence to them."* [45]*The man went away, but then started freely proclaiming and divulging the story everywhere,[79] so that Jesus could no longer go openly into any town, but had to stay outside in deserted places. Even so, people from all around kept coming to him.*

Jesus, moved by visceral (σπλαγχνισθεὶς) compassion, heals the man, but then sternly dismisses him with the naive advice that, even after having shown himself to the priest and making the proper offering, public acts to be sure, he should say nothing to anybody about his healing. The passage is unintelligible on the story-level, if Jesus is really trying to keep his act secret.

In *Leviticus* 14: 2–8, it is explained that a declaration of purification from leprosy (any serious skin disorder) by the priest entails the priest's going

---

77. *The Heart Scripture,* in *Buddhist Wisdom Books, 81,* declares: "Here, O Śāriputra, form is emptiness and the very emptiness is form; emptiness does not differ from form, form does not differ from emptiness; whatever is form, that is emptiness, whatever is emptiness, that is form."

78. Following RSV translation of ἐμβριμησάμενος.

79. Taking διαφημίζειν τὸν λόγον more as the divulging of the meaning of the story, than as a simple telling of the story, for, as Mark presents the passage, that is not much of a secret.

outside the encampment of the people to perform the purification and declaration. Only then is the cleansed one allowed to return to the encampment of the people. This makes good sense, for the encamped people do not want to take chances on catching the disease. Mark introduces Jesus both as the healer of the disease and as an outsider to the declaration. He is not part of the "insider encampment," but a marginal figure to the priestly establishment and their legal procedures. The man is cleansed on the outside, i.e., his skin, but, by divulging the affair, remains diseased on the inside. Outwardly cleansed, he reenters the conventional world of the people, while Jesus himself must remain outside the towns in deserted places, i.e., wilderness places (45: ἔξω ἐπ' ἐρήμοις τόποις). Mark constructs the passage not to signify that Jesus has a secret that he does not want to reveal, but to begin to construct a theme of inner-outer. Those who externalize their understanding of the gospel message, by clinging to false conventional expectancies, become progressively alienated from the outsider Jesus, in fact proclaiming a different gospel. The cleansed man goes out and begins to proclaim such a gospel with intensity (ὁ δὲ ἐξελθὼν ἤρξατο κηρύσσειν πολλὰ). He mimics Jesus, who in verse 38, has himself come (ἐξῆλθον) to proclaim (κηρύξω) the word. But he goes one step further and divulges its meaning (καὶ διαφημίζειν τὸν λόγον), leading the observers to externalize the significance of Jesus' compassionate action, projecting images of a wonder worker, while Jesus, who does not move within their imagined pattern of understanding, becomes an outsider. Because of the expectations of those who see him as wondrously different, he can no longer abide in the conventional world of false expectations, but is again driven into the wilderness.

This is perhaps why Jesus is portrayed as angry. "The language and response of Jesus are more typical of exorcism than of healing. The use of ἐμβριμησά-μενος [sternly charged] points to a harsh expression of anger and is paralleled by the response of Jesus' opponents in Mark 14. 5."[80] The phrase is difficult. Crossan renders it: "And being angry at him, he tossed him out right away," noting that nobody has a very good explanation of its purpose.[81] Why is Jesus angry at the healed fellow? Why immediately (εὐθὺς) send him away? On the story level, the only explanation I can think of is that Jesus is embarrassed at the miracle, not wanting to be identified as a miracle worker. His anger is directed at being pigeon-holed and rendered even more marginal to the society around him. On the discourse level perhaps Mark is speaking to his readers with another intent: to forbid them the pleasure of identifying with the healed man. As the gospel unfolds it becomes more and more apparent that Jesus' chosen disciples, the obvious models for the implied readers, are miserable failures and not to be imitated. The reader wants to find replacement models, and often modern readers do, seeing in the cameo appearances of

---

80. Broadhead, *Teaching With Authority*, 73.
81. Crossan, *The Historical Jesus*, 323.

persons healed and favored by Jesus' brief images of discipleship.[82] That is an attractive interpretation, for the man does not merely talk about Jesus, but "went out and began to preach many things and spread the word" (δὲ ἐξελθὼν ἤρξατο κηρύσσειν πολλὰ καὶ διαφημίζειν τὸν λόγον), words that indeed suggest a discipleship role. Yet, such a reading only deepens the dilemma: why would Jesus be angry at having gained a new and enthusiastic disciple? A better interpretation, perhaps, is that the Markan Jesus is speaking to the implied readers, warning them not to identify with such cameo disciples, rhetorically forcing them to maintain their identification with the sorry disciples. Jesus literally kicks the healed leper out of the narrative scene precisely because he proclaims too many words about Jesus, words that he is something wonderful and marvelous, separated from the everyday and the object of crowd adulation.

The tension is between any reader who attempts to draw ultimate meaning within conventional terms and regards Jesus' significance as a wondrous secret able to be divulged verbally to the imagined pattern of false understanding, and the Markan Jesus, who calls for a reordering of understanding and faith in the gospel. The secret involved is not a view of who Jesus is, as if the issue is one of christological identity. The real secret about Jesus lies within the minds of the gospel characters, and the gospel readers. It cannot be revealed to false unconverted consciousness which tries to apprehend the gospel as religious information. It is the reversal of such consciousness that Jesus comes to preach (1: 14–15).

As a result of his growing reputation, Jesus cannot remain alone even in the wilderness. The prior separation between town and wilderness is here obliterated, for people now come to his wilderness place from all sides. Simon and the other disciples had hunted him down, wanting to bring him back to Simon's Capernaum house to continue his healing practices. Now, mimicking their actions, the crowds search him out in the wilderness. Although he will openly proclaim himself to be the eschatological messiah before the Sanhedrin questioning (14: 62), he has already undermined the expectancies the town people project upon that figure. In the ordering of the cleansed man to keep his mouth shut, Mark counterposes the gospel message over against the primal ignorance of those who try to grasp ultimate meaning in expected images. The messianic secret is not a special piece of new information, but the contentless truth that the messiah is Jesus himself, in his dependently co-arisen simplicity. The false understanding of Jesus' healing deed, which suggests that he exercises some supernatural power and might be the conventional deliverer of Israel, repeats the driving of Jesus into the wilderness (1: 12). The spirit drove Jesus into the wilderness to be tested by

---

82. Broadhead, *Teaching With Authority*, 73: " 'The victim responds' (1.45a) shows total oblivion of the command of Jesus. The victim goes out to preach and proclaim 'the word'. Like the victim of 1.31, the cleansed leper embodies the ideal of discipleship for the implied reader. The narrative result of this proclamation, however, is a limitation on the movement of Jesus."

satanic allurements toward unmitigated emptiness. The crowd drives Jesus again into the wilderness, but follows even there to draw him into the framework of their conventional expectations. There is a constant temptation either to immerse oneself in the dependently co-arisen world of human living, regarding it alone as the real world, or to seek transcendent surcease in the solitude of God-awareness, apart from any engagement in society or human affairs. Jesus is an outsider to both alternatives. He does not remain in the desert of John's withdrawal, nor does he confine himself within the conventional patterns of the town people. He is indeed a marginal person in Mark's account, practicing a middle path that embraces both without collapsing either.

2

Conflicts over Traditions

Return to Capernaum
2: 1–2

¹When he returned to Capernaum, some time later word went around that he was in the house; ²and so many people collected that there was no room left, even in front of the door.

Chapter 2 through 3: 6 constitutes a collection of conflict stories, arranged as a single literary unit and exhibiting a chiastic, ring structure. The cure of the paralytic (2: 1–12) is linked with the healing of the man with the withered hand (3: 1–6). The conflict over eating with sinners (2: 13–17) parallels the conflict over the observance of Sabbath (2: 23–28). The central section on fasting (2: 18–22) "is set apart from the other four controversy stories. It stands alone at the middle of the five."[1] These accounts of conflict have often been understood as an explanation of why Jesus was killed.[2] They increase in intensity until in 3: 6 his enemies begin to plot his destruction. In the first story, the scribes silently think that Jesus, by pronouncing the forgiveness of sins, has committed blasphemy, the actual charge leveled against him in 14: 64. In the second story, they question Jesus' disciples about Jesus' practice of sharing table with sinners. In the third they question Jesus himself on the issue of fasting. In the fourth they intensify their questioning by accusing him of violating the Sabbath, itself a legal accusation, and in the fifth they begin to plot his demise.[3] The entire unit of conflict stories, then, is understood

---

1. Dewey, *Markan Public Debate,* 115, and "The Literary Structure of the Controversy Stories in Mark 2: 1–3: 6," 109.

2. See Dewey, *Markan Public Debate,* 186, note 18, for references.

3. Dewey, *Markan Public Debate,* 116.

to show the inevitability of Jesus' suffering and death.[4] In the outer healing stories of the ring, Jesus is accused of blasphemy and plots are hatched to destroy him, suggesting "the possibility (or inevitability) of Jesus' death at the hands of the opponents."[5] The point is important, because later Jesus predicts his suffering and death by alluding to its inevitability. At times interpreters have seen a divine inevitability, associated with a christology of the suffering savior. Yet, the text itself does not depict such a divine inevitability, but sketches the growing opposition Jesus experienced and its inevitable outcome. In a Mahāyāna reading, the death of Jesus flows from practicing a middle path that refuses to absolutize ultimate meaning within human traditions. That practice is indeed the will of the Father, for it flows directly from Jesus' wilderness awareness of the otherness of Yahweh. When Jesus becomes engaged in social conventions, he cannot but engender opposition from those attached in delusion to those conventions. But there is no hint of any divine will that Jesus must, because of some divine design, suffer and die. The course of his life, as of all life, is dependently co-arisen, not fixed beforehand by a magical plan from on high.

In 1: 21 Jesus is reported to have gone to preach in Capernaum, where he cured a demoniac, and healed a number of people including Peter's mother-in-law. In 1: 29 he goes to the house of Peter and in 1: 35 he leaves that house to get away from the role in which Peter and the disciples want to cast him. He seeks a silent place to pray, after which he goes through Galilee as an itinerant preacher. At the very end of chapter 1, we are told that his fame has spread so that he cannot go openly into any town. Yet, here at the beginning of these conflict stories, the first thing Jesus does is to openly enter town and, apparently, even to set up house in town (ἐν οἴκῳ ἐστίν). Matthew 4: 13 clearly says that "he settled in Capernaum," i.e. he set up house there (κατῴκησεν εἰς καφαρναοὺμ), and Mark 2: 15 will speak of Jesus as having dinner "in his house."[6] Jesus moves into town, sets up a house different from that of Peter and thus apart from the wonder-worker role Peter desired for him. He leaves the wilderness behind. He visits wilderness places many times, but his abode is now firmly in the conventional world of towns. He apparently remains in Carpernaum for some time, since

---

4. Dewey, *Markan Public Debate,* 43 (explaining Martin Albertz, *Die synoptischen Streitsgespräche,* 6): "The purpose of the collection [2: 1–3: 6] was to demonstrate the necessity of Jesus' death by showing an overview of the historical conflict between Jesus and his enemies." Again, 119: "Jesus and the opponents are on a collision course toward Jesus' death."

5. Dewey, *Markan Public Debate,* 120.

6. Malbon, *Narrative Space,* 192.28: "The Gospel of Mark is not known as a model of clear pronoun reference, and the *autou* at 2: 15 is a case in point. While some commentators simply point out the ambiguity, most take 'his house' to refer to Levi's house. I find, however, that arguments from the immediate Markan context and from Matthean and especially Lukan alteration, as well as from the overall position of the 'house' as an architectural space in Mark's Gospel, suggest the opposite conclusion: *tē oikia autou* at Mark 2: 15 refers to Jesus' house."

the first clear indication that he actually begins the journeying announced in 1: 39 (and then only in Galilee) is found in 4: 35 when he announces his intent to cross the Sea of Galilee. Thereafter Jesus and his disciples are constantly traveling from place to place, until the final journey to Jerusalem. Even then it does not end, for the risen Jesus returns to Galilee. The ring of conflict stories from 2: 1 through 3: 6, and beyond to 4: 35, recount Jesus' initial attempt to settle down in the practice of the middle path, embodying his wilderness experience of the immediate availability of Abba in everyday life, an attempt for the moment rendered fruitless by the hardness of heart of his followers.

In Mahāyāna thought the bodhisattva first gains insight into the wisdom of emptiness: that all things are empty of any abiding essence. But that is not enough, for that would render one aloof from the concerns of people and incapable of compassion. Thus, the wisdom of emptiness must be completed by a wisdom of dependent co-arising, manifested by the immersion of the bodhisattva in the affairs of the world. Such an immersion is expressed through the vows of the bodhisattva, whereby he or she abandons the comfort of solitary contemplation in order to fulfill the tasks of compassion for all sentient beings. Likewise, Jesus' desert prayers issue in his commitment to act compassionately in the town and he sets up home in Capernaum. Note that he does not now preach in the synagogue, as he did in 1: 22. Rather, he addresses the crowd from right in front of the door to his house.

The tension grows between the silent emptiness of the wilderness and the tumultuous crowds of that town.

Jesus Forgives the Sins of a Paralytic
2: 3–5

He was preaching the word to them ³*when some people came bringing him a paralytic carried by four men,* ⁴*but as they could not get the man to him through the crowd, they stripped the roof over the place where Jesus was; and when they had made an opening, they lowered the stretcher on which the paralytic lay.* ⁵*Seeing their faith, Jesus said to the paralytic, "My child, your sins are forgiven."*

It was not mentioned where the earlier healing of the leper occurred. Here Jesus is at home and the crowd comes anyway. He cannot really settle in, despite his coming home. Neither the solitude of the wilderness nor the comforts of home are available to him. The people even proceed to dismantle the roof of his Capernaum house (apparently without reassembling it later). The insistence of the crowd is a common theme in Mark—how they insist on pursuing Jesus and how they regard him as a wonder-worker. Note that Jesus sees that their faith, i.e., the faith of the paralytic's porters, is faith in his ability to effect a cure. And so he pronounces a forgiveness of the man's sins! Consistently Mark sets up an expectation, here on the part of the crowd, the porters,[7] and the paralytic, and then describes Jesus as somehow pulling the rug out from under that expectation. Jesus does not pander to their faith. Note that he does not directly forgive the man's sins, as he will be accused of doing. Rather, he pronounces that they "are forgiven" (ἀφίενται).[8]

The Baptist in 1: 4 proclaims a conversion for the forgiveness of sin, and in 1: 14–15, Jesus takes up that role. Conversion itself (μετάνοια) is a turning away from sin and delusion, and so the paralytic is restored to health, both spiritual and physical. Jesus' announcement that the man's sins are forgiven focuses on the immediate availability of such conversion, not on the expected cure sought.

Jesus Cures the Paralytic
2: 6–12

[6]*Now some scribes were sitting there, and they debated in their hearts,*[9] [7]*"How can this man talk like that? He is being blasphemous. Who but God can forgive sins?"* [8]*And at once, Jesus, inwardly aware that this is what they were thinking, said to them, "Why do you have these thoughts in your hearts?* [9]*Which of these is easier: to say to the paralytic, 'Your sins are forgiven' or to say, 'Get up, pick up your stretcher, and walk'?* [10]*But that you might know that*[10] *the son of man has authority on earth to forgive sins,"—*[11]*he said to the paralytic—"I order you: get up, pick up your stretcher, and go off home."* [12]*And the man got up, and at once picked up his stretcher and walked out in front of everyone, so that they were all astonished and praised God saying, "We have never seen anything like this."*

The scribes accuse Jesus of trying himself to forgive the man's sins in his own name, as if he were usurping the place of God. They are questioning

---

7. Against Broadhead, *Teaching With Authority,* 76: "The persistence of the four helpers is described by the narrator as faith. Once again the role of the victim confronts the implied reader with the ideals of discipleship."

8. Broadhead, *Teaching With Authority,* 76.1: "The use of ἀφίενται is crucial. This form is best seen as a divine passive; thus, 'Your sins are forgiven (by God)'. For use of the divine passive, see Pesch, *Markusevangelium* I, pp. 155–56; BDF, p. 72."

9. *The New Jerusalem Bible* has: "and they thought to themselves." That seems too weak for καὶ διαλογιζόμενοι ἐν ταῖς καρδίαις αὐτῶν. Διαλογίζομαι is more than just thinking something; it signifies reasoning, debating, deliberating. Furthermore, since Mark here first uses the term καρδία, heart, which will take on increasing significance as Jesus' opponents, as well as his disciples, begin to harden their hearts, it is significant how he describes the process whereby one comes to reject Jesus' message.

10. *The New Jerusalem Bible* has: "To prove to you." Yet, the point is not rational demonstration, nor, I think, overcoming their inner reasoning by miraculous proof, but rather the actual restoration attained through conversion and forgiveness. Jesus is not engaging the scribes in a rational give and take.

not his powers, but what they see as his pretentions about being in direct, immediate contact with God, his wilderness awareness. It is in virtue of that awareness that he can say that God is immediately available to everyone without exception. Their charge is patently false in Mark, for Jesus declares that indeed it is God who has forgiven the man's sins. But that in itself is subversive, for the scribes represent the religious establishment which circumscribes God within the conventional structures of the accepted cult practices. "There is, first and above all, a terrible irony in that conjunction of sickness and sin, especially in first-century Palestine. Excessive taxation could leave poor people physically malnourished or hysterically disabled. But since the religiopolitical ascendancy could not blame excessive taxation, it blamed sick people themselves by claiming that their sins had led to their illness. And the cure for sinful sickness was, ultimately, in the Temple. And that meant more fees, in a perfect circle of victimization. When, therefore, John the Baptist with a magical rite or Jesus with a magical touch cures people of their sickness, they implicitly declared their sins forgiven or nonexistent. They challenged not the medical monopoly of doctors but the religious monopoly of the priests. And this was religiopolitically subversive."[11]

The scribes, as part of the crowd, expected simply a wonder worker, but that did not entail any direct awareness of the mind of God, or the power to declare forgiveness of sin.[12] Behind the scribal criticism lies not only the religious monopoly on issues of sin, but also the scriptural assertion in *Isaiah* 43: 25, that only Yahweh can forgive sins: "I it is, I it is, who must blot out everything and not remember your sins." The scribes are among the bystanders, looking on and hoping to see some sign or wonder. They judge things conventionally, reasoning (διαλογιζόμενοι) upon the scriptures and holding to their legalistic conclusions.[13] Jesus, by contrast is free from the imagined patterns of such discrimination through a wilderness awareness of God, beyond any thinking and apart from any institutional brokering. The imagined pattern of consciousness is explained by the Mahāyāna philosophers as itself discriminative (*vikalpa*). Mistaking inner images for outer realities (external essences), one begins to reason, judge, and evaluate things within frozen perspectives, occluding the very possibility of any awakening to what lies beyond those delusions. Mark describes the scribes' thinking in similar terms: they reason within their hearts (διαλογιζόμενοι ἐν ταῖς καρδίαις αὐτῶν), i.e., they construct problems in their minds, hardening their thoughts against

11. Crossan, *The Historical Jesus,* 324.

12. Crossan, *The Historical Jesus,* 324: "[Jesus' action and response] makes the whole challenge quite explicit. The authorities are trapped in their own theology. If sickness is a divine punishment, then the one who cures sickness has forgiven sin and manifested divine power." That connection is made, however, only by Mark. Not every healer was equated with forgiving sins.

13. Camery-Hoggatt, *Irony in Mark's Gospel,* 113: "If the fact that they are sitting suggests something like a tribunal, that suggestion is deepened by the recurring διαλο-γίζεσθαι which in these verses might be translated 'debating'."

any availability of God's forgiveness apart from accustomed patterns. This is the first use by Mark of the term "heart" and it describes the misunderstanding of Jesus' critics and opponents.[14] Such "reasoning" within fixed parameters of a tradition considered absolute is the root cause of the "hardening of hearts," later attributed both to the opponents and to the disciples. They get caught in the net of their own reasoned fabrications (*prapañca*). Yet, reasoned thinking itself is not to be rejected, only the imagined pattern of set realities in which it occurs. One is to restore thinking to its original, dependently co-arisen context, understanding traditions as traditions, and thus affirming traditions.

In this set of Galilean conflict stories, Jesus negates the validity of any tradition imagined as fixed and set: he eats with sinners, ignores counsels to fast, and breaks Sabbath rules. Later, in a second series of Jerusalem conflict stories spread through chapters 11 and 12 (11: 27–33 on the source of Jesus' authority, 12: 13–17 on paying the Roman tax, 12: 18–27 on the resurrection, 12: 28–34 on the fundamental demand of God for love, and 12: 35–37 on Christ as the son of David),[15] a series much closer to the Passion narrative, Jesus affirms his agreement with the tradition.[16] The gospel of Mark is not offering a new ideology, a new set of religious truths, as much as calling for a conversion in the way traditions and truths are understood. In Mahāyāna thinking, the mind of false discrimination is the source for the sufferings that accompany life in the world, both the personal sufferings one experiences and the social sufferings that are inflicted on others. The hardening of the heart that derives from such inner debating is the source of the inevitability of suffering, no less for Jesus than for anyone else.[17]

Jesus sees immediately what they are debating and reasoning about, for he knows the inward thoughts of other people. The Buddha also is said to have the power to know the thoughts of others. But one need not think this is some kind of special, supernatural ability. Having been freed from clinging to images as if they represented reality, one easily recognizes the patterns of common delusion. Besides, it looks as if Jesus was deliberately eliciting their response, setting them up, as it were. And so, to answer their doubt, he performs the wondrous healing they were expecting, in order to subvert the notion of wonder-worker they entertained.

14. Dewey, *Markan Public Debate,* 111: In the first story at 2: 1–12 "Jesus knows that they debate in their 'hearts,' in the last [at 3: 1–6] Jesus is grieved at their hardness of 'heart.' These are the first uses of 'heart' in the gospel and the word is not used again until 6: 52 in which the disciples' hearts are hardened."

15. Dewey, *Markan Public Debate,* 55–63 and 164–67.

16. Dewey, *Markan Public Debate,* 164 argues that "the fact that the debates exhibit *agreement* with basic Jewish beliefs explains their rhetorical function in the narrative of the Jerusalem public ministry."

17. Kelber, *Mark's Story of Jesus,* 24: "It is of course Jesus' message and lifestyle which generates the mounting antagonism among the authorities. As his journey continues it becomes ever more obvious that the Kingdom he announces and puts into practice is diametrically opposed to the conventional piety and morality guarded by the authorities."

And yet, the proof Jesus offers demonstrates little. Even if he is able to effect a cure, how does that prove he is capable of making pronouncements about the forgiveness of sins? Wonder workers and healers abounded in Jesus' day, but nobody would have concluded from that that they had authority to pronounce the forgiveness of sins. Jesus is, I suspect, doing more than subverting a deluded notion of wonder-worker. He is also overturning the notion of sin as a direct offense against God that results in sickness. Sin is not simply a private affair between a human person and God, subject to consequent divine punishment. Rather, it is a closing of one's consciousness to God by clinging to set realities and ideas. It is the action (*karma*) of opting for self and exercising that option through habitual attachments to false realities in protecting that false self.

Jesus' characterization of the paralytic man is significant in this regard, for he addresses him bluntly as "my child" (τέκνον), surely a strange way to address a man. "It is an insult for an adult to be compared to children."[18] Mark's Jesus is, it would appear, proleptically alluding to the child-like mind of 10: 13–16 and thus his address characterizes the paralytic as having attained such a mind, free from discriminating conceits and open to the immediate presence of God's forgiveness. Child-like consciousness is characterized by the absence of sophisticated reasoning, by a readiness to experience the world as it is given. To be both adult and child-like in Mark is to see through the language-formed conventions that parade as absolute truths. The paralytic has recovered his originally dependently co-arisen mind. There is perhaps an allusion to the same passage from *Isaiah* 43: 25 which lay behind the scribes' criticism, "Cast your mind back, let us judge this together." That is just what the paralytic has done, turning his mind back to recover its pristine child-like condition, and thus being forgiven.

It is significant, I think, that after the healing Jesus sends the man home, for the point of recovering the child-like mind of non-discrimination (*nirvikalpa-jñāna*) is to return to the everyday world of practice. The pattern will repeat itself throughout the gospel: Jesus heals and sends the healed back to their former lives. What he is not able himself to attain in his Capernaum sojourn, he sends those he saved to do—immerse themselves in the conventional world in an abiding awareness of the immediate presence of God as that which goes beyond everything everyday. Such persons are models of discipleship only inasmuch as they disappear from the scene, for there is in Mark no universally applicable model of discipleship. All depends on just what the conditions of one's everyday life are. No prescriptions, no guarantees. Only the invitation to enter into contact with a forgiving God and reengage in one's daily living.

The text refers to the authority of the son of man on earth (ἐξουσίαν ἔχει ὁ υἱὸς τοῦ ἀνθρώπου . . . ἐπὶ τῆς γῆς) to forgive sins. The interpretation of the title "son of man" is an oft-debated issue. It has a generic usage,

---

18. Cotter, "Children Sitting in the Agora," 70.

meaning simply one, anyone.[19] In this reading, Jesus as son of man is a very human person, as denoted by the general Hebrew sense of the term. A son of man is simply a human being.[20] Yet, 'son of man' is also a well-known eschatological term; in the Hebrew scriptures the son of man is he who will usher in the end times that bring closure to the world. It draws on the images in *Daniel* 7: 13–14 of the visionary appearance of "one like a son of man" coming on the clouds of heaven to assume an everlasting rule and suggests the harbinger of the eschatological kingdom, announced by Jesus himself in 1: 15. Mark's readers could scarcely have missed such a messianic implication.

But, nowhere is any earthly authority or power ascribed to this eschatological, messianic son of man; he has power over the earth, but not upon the earth, for his coming marks the severance of all earthly authority and power. Yet, here Mark has Jesus say that the son of man has authority on earth, and in 28 that the son of man has authority over the Sabbath. Yet Mark in no way explains this innovation.[21] "In each saying [in verses 10 and 28], the claim of authority (ἐξουσία κύριος) is placed first. . . . From our knowledge of Daniel and Enoch, one would not expect the figure to have authority *on earth* or *over the sabbath*."[22] Once again, it would appear, Mark is undermining common expectancies, for he uses a phrase with clear eschatological connotations most uneschatologically, bereft of any heavenly description and immersed in the affairs of this world. It is not the final judge that Mark

---

19. See Crossan, *The Historical Jesus,* 241–43, for a discussion of the dispute over the generic usage and the circumlocutional usage for "I, myself" between Fitzmyer and Vermes. Crossan opts for the former, 243: "In summary, therefore, if Jesus spoke about a son of man, his audience would not have taken the expression in either a titular or a circumlocutionary sense, but, following normal and expected usage, in either a generic (everyone) or an indefinite (anyone) sense. He is talking, they would presume, about human beings, making claims or statements about humanity."

20. Tolbert, *Sowing the Gospel,* 134.15: "Whether 'Son of man' in Mark 2: 28 refers to Jesus as a title, apocalyptic or not, or is only being used here as a synonym for 'human, being,' which is its general function in Hebrew and Aramaic, is a difficult issue to decide. Clearly, the phrase 'sons of men' in Mark 3: 28 is being used in the general sense, while the earlier singular usage of 'Son of man' in 2: 10 appears to refer definitely to Jesus with no apocalyptic overtones. Given the repeated gnomic type of conclusions to these controversies and the general point they are all making, I am inclined to view 'son of man' in 2: 28 as a general reference to humanity and 'Lord' (κύριος) as meaning master or director; so human beings are directors even of the Sabbath."

21. Perrin, "The Christology of Mark," 103: "Mark . . . first takes the step of using *exousia* of that earthly ministry and linking it with the Son of Man." Dewey, *Markan Public Debate,* 77–78: "Perhaps the most debated issue in scholarship on Mark 2: 1–12 is the question of how to understand the use of the Son of Man in v. 10. It is the first use of the term in Mark; it is not prepared for in the text; it is not explained. The Son of Man as pardoner of sins does not occur elsewhere in the synoptic or Jewish tradition. Further, Mark 2: 10 and 28 (and par) are the only instances in the synoptic tradition which refer to the earthly authority of the Son of Man. Unlike many later uses of the title, the use here is public, before hostile witnesses. And the term does not occur again after 2: 28 until 8: 31 in the first passion prediction."

22. Dewey, *Markan Public Debate,* 99.

identifies with Jesus. It is not that the Markan Jesus is claiming an exalted status and authority as an eschatological figure, but that that eschatological figure has been emptied of any other-worldly status whatsoever by being identified with Jesus. Jesus does not come with any divine pedigree or guarantee. Rather, by introducing Jesus as an earthly son of man, Mark empties the term of imagined content. When Jesus again uses the phrase "son of man" as the subject who necessarily must suffer and die, that necessity is to be similarly understood in terms of the "son of man" in these conflict stories in 2: 1–3:6, i.e., in terms of the sufferings that result from deluded reasoning and hardened hearts, not from any divine necessity for Jesus to experience suffering or die by execution.[23]

Jesus acts not on his own special authority, but as the son of man with authority "on the earth" (ἐπὶ τῆς γῆς), for all authority is worldly and conventional (*saṃvṛti*), in virtue not of any supernatural status, but of Jesus' function as the announcer of the kingdom, as the son of man. In fact, he does not deny the scribes' point—only God can forgive sin. Yet, anyone, recovering the mind of original openness, can pronounce forgiveness of sins, for sins are themselves worldly and conventional. Jesus' authority is then derived from God simply by being human, as son of man. The miracle is then not meant to refute the scribes, but to show the genuineness of Jesus' conventional action of forgiving, deriving not from any power model of messiah, but simply and deeply from his awareness of the kingdom.

Note that here there is no attempt to escape notoriety—quite the opposite. The action takes place in front of everyone (ἔμπροσθεν πάντων).

The Call of Levi
2: 13–14

[13]He went out again to the shore of the sea; and all the people came to him, and he taught them. [14]As he was walking along he saw Levi the son of Alphaeus, sitting at the tax office, and he said to him, "Follow me." And he got up and followed him.

---

23. I disagree with Perrin, who in "The High Priest's Question and Jesus' Answer," 90–91, argues that the function of the son of man title in Mark moves from 2: 10 and 2: 28, which "equate the authority of Jesus with that of the Son of Man," on to 8: 27–10: 45, where "we find the *apocalyptic* authority of Jesus as Son of Man (8: 38), [and] the necessity for the passion of Jesus as the passion of the Son of Man (8: 31; 9: 31; 10: 33)," further into the apocalyptic discourse of Chapter 13, which restates "the theme of the *apocalyptic* Son of Man (13: 26)," and to the passion narrative where the Son of Man is delivered up and becomes a "very passive figure in the narrative." Perrin sees a crescendo of authority and power from the earthly son of man to the heavenly, which is then superseded by the passivity of Jesus in the passion account, which is "Mark's way of dramatizing the element of divine necessity in the passion."

In 1: 16 Jesus began his Galilean ministry by walking along the shore of the sea and calling the first set of disciples. Mark opens this account of Levi's call by placing Jesus again (πάλιν) by the sea. He calls his disciples from the edge of chaos to follow him and learn the practice of the middle path that embodies insight into emptiness with engagement in the dependently co-arisen world. Jesus has been teaching the crowds, but there is no mention of just what that teaching is. Its content is not specified by Mark in any detail, only that he preached the kingdom and the need for repentance (1: 15). Evidently it was a moving sermon, for it attracted not only the bystanding crowd. Levi's commitment to follow Jesus, however, is not elicited from hearing Jesus' teaching, for he was not in the crowd, but in his office. Nevertheless, without hearing any doctrinal teaching, he rises up to follow (ἀναστὰς ἠκολούθησεν) Jesus upon hearing his invitation, just as the paralytic had risen up (ἠγέρθη).[24] Yet, Levi is even more of a cipher than the paralytic. He is not listed among the twelve in 3: 16–19 and immediately after rising up to follow Jesus, disappears from the story altogether. He is described as sitting at the tax office. He is a tax collector, and thus guilty of the sins of extortion.[25] He seems to parallel the paralytic in that he is crippled socially and morally, but Mark does not report either that his sins are forgiven or that he returns home. Rather, he accepts Jesus' call to follow him as a disciple. Those who are healed and forgiven are sent home, while those who are not follow Jesus. Levi is not able to return home and embody the practice of Jesus' middle path in everyday living; he needs to learn just what it means to follow Jesus.

There is, I think, a two-tiered irony in Mark's narrative. On the first level, Mark draws his implied reader to identify neither with the obtuse disciples who follow Jesus nor with the religious authorities who challenge him, but with the cameo characters who briefly appear to be healed and immediately withdraw back into their everyday lives. The reader begins to feel that she has attained an insight above the story-level disciples and a status far above

---

24. The imagery of the healing of the paralytic suggests resurrected life. See Farrer, *A Study in St. Mark,* 47: "The man is carried by four bearers, like the dead going to burial. Unable to come at Christ otherwise they dig out (Mark's word) a hole and lower him into his grave. Thus descending, he falls in the presence of the Son of God, and 'stands up on his feet.' . . . The miracle of the paralytic carries the symbolism of resurrection almost as far as it will go."

25. Myers, *Binding the Strong Man,* 157: "Levi, a customs official, will have represented a socially outcast—though economically secure—class. Distinct from the so-called tax farmers, who oversaw the collection of the major land taxes and tributes, toll collectors were usually under the employ of the Roman or Herodian administrators. They handled the myriad of local transportation taxes and tariffs, and such a customs station would be expected in a commercial center such as Capernaum, which was 'the first town within Herod Antipas' territory after one crossed the border . . . from Herod Philip's territory, necessitating provision for import taxes and security' (Harrison 1985: 75f). The toll collectors' widespread reputation for dishonesty, and the fact that they were bureaucratic representatives of the oppressive politico-economic order, meant that they were a shunned caste in Judaism, even to the point of often being denied basic civil rights."

the authorities.[26] Herein lies the second tier of irony, for the reader begins to entertain a sense of religious status that on the story-level characterizes the scribes who cling to their righteousness and the disciples who cling to their own viewpoints. Mark doubles back on his reader not only in that his discourse positions her to adopt a point of view that distances her from the story's main characters, but also in that that rhetorically-generated point of view and sense of righteousness associates the reader with the story-level followers of Jesus, who are not healed and do not understand.

Jesus at Home with Sinners
2: 15–17

[15]When Jesus was at dinner in his house, a number of tax collectors and sinners were also sitting at table with Jesus and his disciples; for there were many of them among his followers. [16]When the scribes of the Pharisee party saw him eating with sinners and tax collectors, they said to his disciples, "Why does he eat with tax collectors and sinners?" [17]When Jesus heard this, he said to them, "It is not the healthy who need the doctor, but the sick. I came to call not the upright, but sinners."

The scene unfolds at Jesus' house (ἐν τῇ οἰκίᾳ αὐτοῦ). As noted above, Jesus had set up a home in Capernaum.[27] Capernaum seems to have been the home base for the initial Galilean phase of the Markan Jesus' activity, and to some degree he tried, despite his notoriety among the people, to live a normal life as a householder. This has some bearing on the story, for it is into his own home that Jesus admitted sinners and tax collectors. Sinners (ἁμαρτωλοί) are not simply those who disregard the Mosaic teachings. Rather, they are the people of the land (*amme ha-aretz*), i.e., commoners without any social standing whatsoever.[28] The call of John the Baptist, and Jesus after him, had been to such people. Jesus is at home with them.

---

26. Camery-Hoggatt, *Irony in Mark's Gospel,* 116: "The narrative passes implicit judgment against the scribes [who question Jesus' authority to forgive sins], and it is a judgment which the reader is called upon to share. As he does so, as he accepts as his own the point of view from which that judgment proceeds, he is led to make his own declaration of 'unrighteousness,' and in that way to come under the aegis and urgency of Jesus' call."

27. The text is not clear about just whose house is meant, for it is possible that it was Levi's house. Yet, I favor the opinion that it was Jesus' own house, since after Jesus returned to Capernaum in 2: 1, he is said to be "at home" (ἐν οἴκῳ). It is unlikely that he would have returned to Peter's house (1: 29), for the text says that he had "come out" (1: 38) of that house and thus from Peter's role expectations. Matthew in describing the call of Matthew (9: 10), has Jesus "at table in the house" (ἐν τῇ οἰκίᾳ), while Luke (15: 1) omits any reference to any house. As all the Markan action until 4: 35 takes place in Galilee around Capernaum, it seems likely to me that Jesus had indeed for a period set up "house" in Capernaum.

28. Camery-Hoggatt, *Irony in Mark's Gospel,* 114: ". . . the term 'sinners' does not stand in apposition to 'tax collectors.' Rather, it refers to the *amme ha-aretz* with whom

Even the bureaucratic tax collectors (τελῶναι) are not rejected and Jesus does not demand that they renounce their unpopular livelihood. Returning home he calls (καλέσαι) everybody to share his table, yet his healing does not entail any social transformation of sinners into virtuous people as understood by the scribes of the Pharisee party. In the Pure Land tradition of Mahāyāna Buddhism, one is saved only by recognizing that no self-power (*jiriki*) avails for anything. Only through the grace of Amida Buddha's other-power (*tariki*) is one saved. Thus, Shinran, the Japanese Pure Land master, is reported to have said that "even a good person can attain birth in the Pure Land, so it goes without saying that an evil person will."[29] The recognition that one is a sinner, a common mortal caught in webs of karmic evil, entails insight into no-self (*anātman*), without which one is unable to experience the grace of salvation.

The story of Mark's gospel presents the reader with a similar recommendation: without joining Jesus' table fellowship of common sinners one is unable to be associated with him. Note that the text mingles these tax collectors and sinners with the disciples—they form one group with Jesus. He simply calls them all to share dinner—no other teaching and no other healing is mentioned in the passage. The reader must also identify with this motley crowd. It will not do to stand apart in the bright light of an interpretative overview that distances the reader from her own identity as a sinner. In the story of the cure of the paralytic, Jesus is thought to commit the sin of blasphemy when he forgives sins. Here, he is portrayed by Mark as a doctor who cures sinners, not the upright.[30] Jesus' words are directed over the heads of the fictive scribes to the reader.

Jesus then sets himself against the ossified conventional norms of just what constitutes virtue and righteousness and throughout the gospel he manifests a clear preference for the marginal and officially excluded "sinners" who, precisely because they are unable to function within the constructed ideology, are open to the immediacy of truth.[31] "The distinct needs of human beings in every special moment in time always take precedence over the established rules, rituals, and customs dictated by tradition."[32]

Jesus was accustomed to dine; in that sense, it simply means 'commoners'." Ahn, "Jesus and the Minjung in the Gospel of Mark," 139, 149–50, argues that Mark understood the more generic term "the crowd" (ὁ ὄχλος) to refer to *amme ha-aretz*. The implication is that Jesus himself belongs to the common poor of the land. See Myers, *Binding the Strong Man*, 156–57.

29. *Tannishō: A Primer*, tr. Dennis Hirota, 23 (3: 1–2).

30. Dewey, *Markan Public Debate*, 85.

31. Klosinski, *The Meals in Mark*, 17: "The dominant paradigm of the Pharisees, that holiness required a separated community, was challenged by this commensality. Thus, given the social environment of Israel, Jesus' inclusive table fellowship was a political protest against contemporary structures and assumptions about holiness, as well as the introduction of an alternate understanding of Torah and holiness."

32. Tolbert, *Sowing the Gospel*, 133.

The scene depicts a party affair, leading into the criticism in verses 18–22 that Jesus and his friends neglect fasting.

Feasting and Fasting
2: 18–20

[18] John's disciples and the Pharisees were fasting, when some people came to him and said to him, "Why is it that John's disciples and the disciples of the Pharisees fast, but your disciples do not?" [19] Jesus replied, "Surely the bridegroom's attendants cannot fast while the bridegroom is still with them? As long as they have the bridegroom with them, they cannot fast. [20] But the time will come when the bridegroom is taken away from them, and then, on that day, they will fast."

The accepted religious ideal is set by the Pharisees' practice of strict observance and fasting, embodied also by the followers of the ascetic John. This issue is not as weighty as blasphemy or violation of the sabbath. Rather it is one of recommended practice.[33] In regard to fasting, the Pharisees' disciples are aligned with those of John, himself described as an ascetic and a wilderness personality.[34] Once again there is an ironic contrast set up between the single-focused, wilderness spirituality of the fasters and the town—even the party—mentality of Jesus. Jesus has fused the wilderness and the town. He needs no lonely fasting, no locusts or wild honey, but a bit of cheerful wine.[35]

The preceding literary context was one of sharing a dinner. Here the imagery is that of a wedding feast. It is precisely because Jesus and his followers are celebrating that the questioners come to question—and to make abundantly clear the difference between the ideal of fasting and the carousing of a wedding celebration. When the bridegroom is taken away from them, they will experience a time of human sorrow, of absence, death, and separation.

Who is this bridegroom? "Though it is inevitable that the bridegroom should have been supposed to be a reference to Jesus himself, it is much

---

33. See Cohen, *From the Maccabees to the Mishnah,* 143–50, on the Pharisees' adherence to "the tradition of the elders," above and beyond the Mosaic law.

34. See Brown, *The Gospel According to John I–XII,* Introduction, LXII–LXX, on the Sectarians of John the Baptist, and 42–92. Note also Cohen, *From the Maccabees to the Mishnah,* 149: "When Paul boasts of his zeal for the ancestral traditions (Gal. 1: 14), he is probably boasting of his former Pharisaic piety. That piety included not only observance of the laws. Within a space of four chapters the Paul of Acts proclaims three times that he was or is still a Pharisee."

35. Crossan, *The Historical Jesus,* 259: "I have argued that John the Baptist was an apocalyptic prophet preparing his followers for the imminent advent of God as the Coming One but that Jesus, after having originally accepted that vision, eventually changed his response some time after the execution of John. He then emphatically contrasted a follower of John and a member of the Kingdom. He never spoke of himself as the apocalyptic Son of Man. . . ."

more likely that Jesus himself is alluding to the well-known Old Testament idea of God as the husband of Israel. The response of the common people is that God is gaining his bride."³⁶ Jesus has just gathered around himself the common people, i.e., sinners and disciples. In so doing, it is implied, God is present also, as marriage partner of the common people. This is why partying is appropriate. The other meal scenes in Mark urge the same point: everyone can be included. The twin feedings of the crowds in 6: 30–44 and 8: 1–10 take place respectively in Jewish and gentile territory, thereby including both within the circle of Jesus' table companions. The meal at Bethany in the house of Simon the leper when Jesus is anointed by an unnamed woman (14: 3–9) suggests that even the most insignificant are included. The last table scene recorded, the Passover meal of Jesus with his disciples in 14: 12–25, refers one to an eschatological meal which will be shared with all "in the kingdom of God."³⁷ But there are times when such an all-inclusive community fails to function, and then God is absent and there is a time for fasting.

Yet, even granted that the bridegroom refers to God, it seems to also refer to Jesus himself; he is the one who is actually throwing the party. He is the host and bridegroom whose presence entails feasting, and only when he is removed from his disciples (ἀπαρθῇ ἀπ' αὐτῶν) will they fast. The metaphor further "points beyond Jesus' death to the continued existence of the disciples, who will then fast."³⁸

Some think that the inevitability of Jesus' departure derives from the will of the Father. Yet, that removal, in the context of these conflict stories, seems to indicate a violent action, hardly attributable to the Father.³⁹ Suffering and death are not the pre-ordained means for the attainment of glory,⁴⁰ either for Jesus or for his followers. Thus, when Jesus is arrested Mark looks beyond the disciples' flight to the possibility of their Galilean awakening. They are

36. Lindars, *Jesus the Son of Man,* 174.
37. See Crossan, *The Historical Jesus,* 261–64 on open commensality.
38. Dewey, *Markan Public Debate,* 122. Also 128: "The possibility or inevitability of death for Jesus is not an inevitability or necessity for the disciples. Indeed, in the central pericope of the concentric structure [of 2: 1–3: 6], the debate about fasting in which Jesus alludes to his coming death (2: 20), the disciples are explicitly excluded from the death which will overtake Jesus. They remain to fast after the bridegroom has been taken away."
39. Perrin, "The High Priest's Question and Jesus' Answer," 90, focuses on the son of Man being delivered up: "Twice in the Last Supper scene, 14: 21: 'the son of Man goes as it is written of him ... the Son of Man "is delivered up" (*paradidotai*),' and once in the Gethsemane scene, 14: 41: 'the Son of Man is "delivered up" (*paradidotai*).' These references pick up the use of *paradidotai* in 9: 31 and 10: 33, and they carefully set the stage for the passion of Jesus as the passion of the Son of Man and as ordained by God." Jesus' deliverance is then presented by Perrin as "itself an enthronement" (93). Yet, here in Chapter 2 Mark first presents the future course of Jesus as a violent removal, without any suggestion of divine inevitability. One should, perhaps, factor in this passage with its ἀπαρθῇ into the discussion about the sense of the verb παραδίδωμι.
40. Kolenkow, "Beyond Miracles, Suffering, and Eschatology," 160–165, and Dewey, *Disciples on the Way,* 81–94.

not expected to duplicate in their lives the very same passion and death of Jesus. They will drink the cup of suffering, as do all human beings. But it will be their cup, and then the time for feasting will have passed and they too will fast.

The Old and the New
2: 21–22

[21] *"No one sews a piece of unshrunken cloth on an old cloak; otherwise, the patch pulls away from it, the new from the old, and the tear gets worse.* [22]*And nobody puts new wine into old wineskins; otherwise, the wine will burst the skins, and the wine is lost and the skins too. No! New wine into fresh skins!"*

The metaphors of the patch and the new wine do not simply indicate the newness of Jesus' teaching over that of the old traditions. If Mark is recommending Jesus' new teaching over the old teachings of the Torah, he has done a singularly inept job of presenting just what is specifically new in those teachings. Nowhere does he outline Jesus' ideological position.

Rather, the obverse is intended. In order to patch an old garment, the patch first has to be shrunken, i.e., made old, so that it will not shrink on the cloak and rip it. Jesus' teachings, if they are to renew the minds and hearts of his hearers, must recover the depths of the Torah traditions. It is not the content of the traditions understood that Mark stresses, but the mind that understands those traditions, the mind converted from its frozen hardness to understanding and wisdom. Such a recovery itself constitutes something new. New wine, in contrast to old patches, needs new skins, so that as it expands, they will have the flexibility to expand with it.

In Mahāyāna terms, the point of these metaphors is that when one engages in practicing the middle path, all fixed forms, whether old or new, are seen as dependently co-arisen, and thus empty of final meaning. This is why Jesus' path is perceived as a threat, for it empties the norms of any absolute tradition, so as to reaffirm the conventional validity of traditions.[41] It is the practice of this middle path that Jesus embodies, both in his fasting and in his feasting. Such a spirituality cannot be contained either in the forms of a wilderness spirituality or in the rigor of the Pharisees' strict adherence. Jesus is free from both, and thus able both to feast and to fast.

---

41. Dewey, *Markan Public Debate*, 93: "The point seems to be stronger than that the old and new do not mix; rather the new is an active threat to the continued existence of the old, and may itself be harmed in the destruction of the old." Yet, it is also a reclaiming of the dependently co-arisen validity of the old, not an ideological substitution for the old. The first metaphor does, in fact, speak of patching an old garment, not of making a new one.

Sabbath Corn-Picking
2: 23–28

²³One Sabbath he was going through the grainfields; and as they made their way his disciples began to pluck ears of grain.[42] *²⁴And the Pharisees said to him, "Look, why are they doing something on the Sabbath day that is forbidden?" ²⁵And he replied, "Have you never read what David did in his time of need when he and his followers were hungry—²⁶how he went into the house of God when Abiathar was high priest, and ate the loaves of the offering which only the priests are allowed to eat, and how he also gave some to the men with him?"*

²⁷And he said to them, "The Sabbath was made for man, not man for the Sabbath." ²⁸So the son of man is master even of the Sabbath.[43]

This passage is a mind bender. When examined logically, Jesus gets it all wrong. The Pharisees' criticism is against the disciples' plucking of the corn on the sabbath, for such labor is proscribed on the sabbath. The Jewish philosopher Philo writes that "[the Sabbath] extends also to every kind of tree and plant; for it is not permitted to cut any shoot or branch, or even a leaf, or to pluck any fruit whatsoever."[44] The issue is much more serious than recommended fasting or asceticism, for "sabbath violation could be a serious charge, punishable by death (Exod 31: 14–15; M. Sanhedrin 7: 4)."[45] The issue here and the account of healing the man with a withered hand on the sabbath which follows (3: 16) seem to take on a serious, foreboding dimension.

Yet Jesus' answer is hardly to the point. He presents a case of David's men eating what is forbidden. But, their eating of the forbidden loaves is an emergency, while Jesus and his group are merely taking a walk! To add to the confusion, Jesus misidentifies the high priest as Abiathar, while *1 Samuel* 21: 1–6 identifies him as Ahimelech, Abiathar's father. David is fleeing from Saul and comes to Ahimelech, the priest at Nob. He asks the priests for bread, and is informed that Ahimelech has only consecrated bread, which *Leviticus* 24: 9 teaches is to be eaten only by the priests. Yet, Ahimelech does not refuse to give the bread to David. Rather, he seeks to ascertain if David's group "have kept themselves from women," i.e., are they ritually pure as the priests would be. Upon learning that "the soldiers' things are

---

42. Following the RSV translation. Malbon, *Narrative Space,* 183.39: "The phrase *hodon poiein* does not mean 'make a road' but 'go along a path.' Thus Jesus and the disciples are not trampling the grain down as they go across the field (as Schweizer, *Good News,* 72, assumes), but walking along a regular path through the field. The idiom is used comparably in the Septuagint text of Judges 17: 8. In classical Greek the 'expression would be *hodon poieishai*—'journey,' 'go along' (Taylor, *St. Mark,* 215; Bratcher and Nida, *Handbook,* 96–97)."

43. Following Fowler, *Let the Reader Understand,* 103–04, who argues that verse 28 is not a continuation of Jesus' utterance, but a comment by the narrator.

44. In Sheehan, *The First Coming,* 246.36. The citation is to Philo's *Life of Moses* II.iv.

45. Dewey, *Markan Public Debate,* 101.

clean, . . . the priest then gave him what had been consecrated." For this deed of assistance to David, Ahimelech and his family are killed by Saul, with only Abiathar escaping, to later join up with David. There does not appear to be much of a parallel between David's action and the disciples' plucking of grain.

However, the rule against plucking grain on the sabbath comes not from the Deuteronomic law, but from the Mishnah (Sabbath 7: 2). Jesus could have answered by differentiating the Mosaic law from the later traditions of the elders, as he does in 7: 1–13. But he does not!

An impartial judge, of whatever persuasion, would see the logical inappropriateness of Jesus' response. It seems unlikely then that Mark's point is the recording of logical argumentation. Perhaps it is significant that this passage follows immediately after the discussion of feasting and fasting, for it too relates to eating, a theme that takes on central importance in the gospel—as a test of whether the disciples really understand what Jesus is all about. Here, the eating of the grain on the sabbath leads into Jesus' pronouncement on the validity of the tradition of the sabbath itself. Jesus empties not only the tradition of the elders, but also the Mosaic law of any final, fixed validity. The Pharisees see both the traditions of the elders and the Mosaic law in imagined fixity, and so the Markan Jesus, ignoring the casuistry of introducing an inappropriate case, offers an example where even the high priest neglects a tradition. It is not a question of which traditions can at times be ignored, but of the validity of tradition itself, in all its forms. By raising the question of just when such tradition can be neglected, the point is made that there are such times. This question then leads directly to the saying about the Lord of the sabbath.

The sabbath is one of the central elements of Jesus' religion. *Exodus* 20: 11 explains that ". . . in six days Yahweh made the heavens and the earth and the sea and all that these hold, but on the seventh day he rested; that is why Yahweh has blessed the sabbath and made it sacred." The sabbath was a religious and cultural time of withdrawal from daily affairs and work, a time when the entire people were to rest in the quiet awareness of Yahweh. Jesus is hardly opposed to such withdrawal. Yet, here Jesus pronounces that the sabbath itself is a social convention, made sacred for human rest. He is reclaiming the depths of the traditional meaning of sabbath by emptying it of absolute significance.

The phrase, "son of man" (ὁ υἱὸς τοῦ ἀνθρώπου), included in the comment by the narrator,[46] has been taken to mean that Jesus, as the eschatological son of man is Lord also of the sabbath. Some take it to mean that Jesus is here somehow equated with Yahweh, for it is Yahweh who is truly the Lord of the sabbath. Yet, as above in 2: 10, the flow of meaning is the other

---

46. Fowler, *Let the Reader Understand*, 77: "The '*amēn*,' 'whoever,' and 'Son of man' statements are the clearest expressions we have of the norms and standards of judgment of the narrator of Mark's Gospel."

way: not upward by associating Jesus with the supernatural and sacred, but downward by associating the sacred traditions with humans. Having seen the emptiness of all traditions, one sees the sabbath too as a human construct (*vijñpti*), and thus it is made for humans. Any son of man is then lord even of the sabbath (ὥστε κύριός ἐστιν ὁ υἱὸς τοῦ ἀνθρώπου καὶ τοῦ σαββάτου), for, aware that even the most sacred traditions are empty, any imagined ultimacy is deconstructed. Not, however, discarded, for as lord of the sabbath, one observes its conventional validity. The middle path entails not only insight into the emptiness of all things, but also into the truth of their dependent co-arising.[47]

The conflict stories all relate to questions of conventional traditions and ultimate meaning.[48] Mark strives to differentiate ultimate meaning from those conventions, in order not only to point beyond convention to the otherness of ultimate meaning, but also to be able, as in the Jerusalem controversy stories in Chapters 11 and 12, to reclaim those very same traditions. That differential awareness is itself the middle path.[49]

---

47. Fowler, *Let the Reader Understand,* 129: "Ambiguity lingers in all of the Son of man sayings because no one explicitly says who the Son of man is in either the story or the discourse. Readers must come to understand the riddle of the Son of man on their own."

48. They are not then to be read as Christian-Jewish debate. See Kelber, *The Kingdom in Mark,* 22: "Instead of a Jewish-Christian struggle we might therefore better assume an internal Christian situation (reflected in the controversy stories 2–3:6). . . . Mark's opponents see their own argumentation and piety mirrored in that of the Scribes and Pharisees." And 23: "The Kingdom generates a radical alternative to a Jewish Christian way of life."

49. I differ from Hamerton-Kelly, *The Gospel and the Sacred,* 89, who interprets the Son of Man "as a symbol of human resistance to the sacred." The sacred is a polysemous notion that, once freed from any role as the justification of 'sacred violence' serves as the silent otherness of ultimate meaning. When frozen in imagined rigidity, then indeed the Markan Jesus is its antithesis.

3

The Practice of the Middle Path

Curing a Withered Hand
3: 1–6

¹Another time he went into the¹ synagogue, and there was a man present whose hand was withered. ²And they were watching him to see if he would cure him on the Sabbath day, hoping for something to charge him with. ³He said to the man with the withered hand, "Get up and stand in the middle!" ⁴Then he said to them, "Is it permitted on the Sabbath day to do good, or to do evil: to save life, or to kill?" But they said nothing. ⁵Then he looked angrily round at them, grieved to find them so obstinate, and said to the man, "Stretch out your hand." He stretched it out and the hand was restored. ⁶The Pharisees went out and at once began to plot with the Herodians against him, discussing how to destroy him.

The conflict over the conventional nature of religious traditions continues, for 3: 1–6 forms the ending to the unit of controversy stories begun in 2: 1. Jesus goes, directly from the walk through the grain fields, again into the synagogue, in Capernaum, for he has not abandoned conventional forms in favor of a wilderness spirituality. Mark joins the two scenes not only by a common theme, but by the connecting particle, "and" (καὶ). He describes the Pharisees as "watching" Jesus to find a legal charge against him, but the verb he uses (παρετήρουν) also signifies religious observance.² It seems then that Mark means to suggest not only that they were observing Jesus, but that that observing takes place within a fixed observance of the sabbath. They have framed Jesus' actions within a conventional norm, for it is not

---

1. Following the translation of εἰς τὴν συναγωγήν. Some texts omit τὴν.

2. Lane, *The Gospel According to Mark,* 121: "The healing of the man with the withered hand forms the last of this first series of five conflict narratives. It takes its place at this point naturally by topical association with the previous incident and demonstrates that Jesus is Lord of the Sabbath."

what he does that is significant to them, but how what he does impinges upon that conventional framework. On a day other than the Sabbath it is permissible to cure. Their intent is to lodge a charge against him of violating religious laws, but Jesus' answer hardly moves on legal grounds. "In the first place, the saying does not directly address the issue of legality on the sabbath. It was not legal to do harm or kill on any day of the week; saving life was permitted on the sabbath even if it violated the sabbath rest. The Pharisees would consider Jesus' answer irrelevant to the issue of sabbath observance."[3] Here, the silence of Jesus' opponents implies that they indeed consent to what he says. Their silence indicates that they can find no grounds for any accusation.[4] However, Mark moves the passage beyond legal questions of religious practices to issues of life and death.

The stage is set when Jesus tells the man with the withered hand to "stand up, out in the middle!" (ἔγειρε εἰς τὸ μέσον). The surface meaning is obvious: the man is to stand in the center of the scene. But there is more to it than that, for it also has a symbolic meaning. The verb ἔγειρε means not only "to stand up," but also "to raise up," or "to awaken." It is used frequently to refer to the resurrection or awakening of the dead, a meaning often found in Mark. In a Yogācāra reading, to be raised up from death is to be awakened to life. Resurrection is awakening to the new, converted consciousness Jesus has preached from the very beginning, a consciousness that moves freely both in the silent awareness of the wilderness presence of God and in the conventional world of religious practices and teachings. In Mahāyāna terms, such insight into the emptiness of all forms and thus into their dependently co-arisen validity is termed "the middle path" (*madhyama*), not in the Greek sense of a half way point between two extremes, but in the sense of living in the healthy tension between emptiness and dependent co-arising. Thus, the phrase can as well, if eisegetically, be translated as "Awaken to the middle!" See both the emptiness of sabbath observance and its dependently co-arisen and conventional validity. It is such wisdom that cures the man's withered hand, i.e., a hand that, having become desiccated or dried up (ξηράν), is useless. Just as the paralytic in the story at the beginning of chapter two reflects the paralysis of the scribes, so here, the withered hand symbolizes the dried-up consciousness of a merely formal religious practice on the part of the Pharisees. The phrase for their obstinacy (ἐπὶ τῇ πωρώσει τῆς καρδίας) literally means "because of their hardness of heart." Their hearts have dried up and withered because they discriminate and cling to conventional forms as if traditions constituted absolute truth. They function in an imagined pattern of consciousness, precluding the wisdom of the middle path by clinging to

---

3. Dewey, *Markan Public Debate,* 102.

4. Rhoads, *Mark and Method,* 137: "Why did the Pharisees not indict Jesus when he healed the man? The reason is that Jesus clearly evaded indictment by avoiding any real 'work.' He does not touch the man or command him to 'be healed' but only tells him to 'stretch out the hand.' No wonder the Pharisees went off in frustration to plot with Herod to destroy Jesus."

delusions.[5] By standing in the middle path such consciousness is healed. Yet, the Pharisees do not opt for the middle ground, but immediately leave and begin to plot with the Herodians, not only to find a religious charge to lodge against Jesus, but now to kill him. The natural and immediate (εὐθύς) outflow from reifying religious norms is plotting to destroy anyone who questions those laws.[6] Mark highlights the irony by having the Pharisees, devout upholders of the Jewish teachings, conspire with Herodians, those who want to temporize with the Roman authorities. It is a rather unlikely alliance, brought together not by shared ideology, but by shared delusion.[7] The response to Jesus' first healing in this collection of conflict stories is that the people glorify God (2: 12); here they begin to plot his death, for that is the natural result of the mind that grasps truth by an inner debate and a hardened heart.

By walking a middle path between wilderness spirituality and synagogue practice, Jesus engenders the hatred of the religiously deluded. It is perhaps reasonable to expect him to use his miraculous power to counter and subdue that hatred, and, in fact, that is what his disciples want him to do. Yet, that would be simply another form of appropriating conventional realities, beating the Pharisees at their own game.[8] Mark's point, however, is that Jesus

---

5. There are echoes of wisdom/delusion themes throughout the passage. Humphrey, *He Is Risen,* 33: "Their watching Jesus so as to be able to denounce him (3: 2) is not unlike the attitude of the 'ungodly men' (Wisdom 1: 16) who say, 'Let us be in wait for the righteous, because he is inconvenient to us and opposes our actions' (Wisdom 2: 12)." Robbins, *Jesus The Teacher,* 125, quotes a passage from Ryle much to the same point: "Learning *how* or improving in ability is not like learning *that* or acquiring information. . . . We learn *how* by practice. . . . often quite unaided by any lessons in the theory." See G. Ryle, *The Concept of Mind,* 59, 41. Robbins concludes that Jesus teaches "the system of understanding." I would rather speak of challenging one to change one's pattern of understanding, for no systematic teaching is discernible in Mark.

6. Dewey, *Markan Public Debate,* 118: "Further, the fact that the notices of opposition in 3: 1–6 are information given to the reader only and not to the internal audience of the story, indicates that a, if not the, major function of the Galilean controversy stories in the gospel of Mark is to make the reader aware of the opposition to Jesus. The emphasis in 2: 1–3: 6 is not upon Jesus' triumph over his opponents, but in their implacable hostility." So also Schweizer, "Mark's Theological Achievement," 48: "Overcoming the law, which will open the gospel to Gentiles, at once brings the cross into view (3: 5f). The world's blindness to God's revelation becomes visible. . . ."

7. Camery-Hoggatt, *Irony in Mark's Gospel,* 118: "Their subsequent collusion with the Herodians makes that irony especially poignant: it is on the *sabbath* that they hand down the decision that Jesus must be destroyed. Mark hardly needs to point out the irony of that decision. The second couplet of Jesus' unanswered question strains the irony almost to the breaking point: 'Is it lawful on the sabbath . . . to kill?' he asks."

8. On one level I agree with Camery-Hoggatt, *Irony in Mark's Gospel,* 119: ". . . Mark has indicted Jesus' accusers. In the process he has summoned the reader—as jury—to hand down a verdict which is far different from the one for which the accusers watched." On a yet further ironic level, the very assumption of the role of jury aligns such a reader with the Pharisees, adjudicating affairs in terms of respective viewpoints and arguments. When Mark's rhetoric distances readers from characters of the story, it maneuvers them into assuming the very same pattern of externalized consciousness expressed in the story through those characters, albeit with different views to expound.

negates the very framework of the imagined realities by which the game is defined.[9]

The Crowds and the Unclean Spirits
3: 7–12

[7]Jesus withdrew with his disciples to the sea, and great crowds from Galilee followed him. From Judaea, [8]and from Jerusalem, and from Idumaea and Transjordan and the region of Tyre and Sidon, great numbers who had heard of all he was doing came to him. [9]And he asked his disciples to have a boat ready for him because of the crowd, to keep him from being crushed. [10]For he had cured so many that all who were afflicted in any way were crowding forward to touch him. [11]And the unclean spirits, whenever they saw him, would fall down before him and shout, "You are the Son of God!" [12]But he warned them strongly not to make him known.

The initial action in this passage is that Jesus and his disciples withdrew (ἀνεχώρησεν), which term means not only "to go away," but also "to seek refuge." It is, perhaps, the key to the passage. Taking his disciples, Jesus seeks refuge from the delusion of those who want to kill him. He withdraws from the synagogue scene, hoping to recapture the peace and quiet of a lonely place. Yet his fame among the people dashes his hopes. Large crowds follow him. Mark exaggerates the crowds—a great multitude (πολὺ πλῆθος) from all over. The places he names are startling. One would expect that his fame had spread in Galilee; beginning with 1: 14, the action has all taken place there. Jesus was baptized in Judaea by John, and so he was known there. Jerusalem, however, the heart of Jewish cultic practice, has, to this point in the narrative, never been visited by Jesus. It seems unlikely that so many people from there would have noticed a Galilean preacher. But that is not Mark's point. The gospel has been discussing cultic and religious practices, and so Mark brings the issue right to the seat of religious authority. Moreover, some in the crowds come even from Idumaea, south of Judaea, the farthest reaches of Israel (where there were few towns), and from gentile places in the north in Tyre and Sidon in Syro-Phoenicia,

---

9. Dewey, *Markan Public Debate*, 121: "Opposition . . . arises because Jesus' basic ministry includes as prominent elements healing and eating behavior which could not be accommodated in the wine skins of the Judaism of his time." Dewey also argues, 119, that "the controversy section is not just a concatenation of miscellaneous acts of Jesus to which the opponents increasingly take exception. The effect of the literary unity of the section on the reader is to emphasize that the opponents objected to Jesus' activity as a whole, and to the messianic claim which was the basis of Jesus' action." Yet, to this point Jesus has made no messianic claim at all. Rather, the opposition grows "merely" from the threatened and hardened consciousness of those charged with the maintenance of the traditions. Jesus' only claim so far entails his human status as son of man, with power and authority on earth.

and to the east in the Transjordan. The point is not geographical accuracy, little of which is to be found in Mark in any event. Rather, in suggesting the broad extent of Jesus' reputation as a wonder-worker, Mark indicates the inclusivity of his subsequent teaching. "Before Jesus is reported to have traveled beyond Galilee teaching and healing, a multitude comes to him from Judea, Jerusalem, Idumea, beyond the Jordan, and Tyre and Sidon (3: 7–8). . . . Later, Jesus himself goes to each of these places (with the exception of Idumea) that have first come to him in a metaphorical way through their inhabitants: Tyre and Sidon (7: 24, 31), Judea (10: 1), beyond the Jordan (10: 1), Jerusalem (10: 32)."[10] All boundaries are collapsed in the compass of his Galilean teaching and healing activity.[11] The crowd has heard what he is doing ('ὅσα ἐποίει) and now everyone with any sickness hopes for a cure. They, like the woman with a hemorrhage hope only to touch him, believing that power flows from his very body.

The healings Mark does record, however, are not meant to portray Jesus simply as a powerful healer, as the "divine man" of Greek-Jewish thinking.[12] That misunderstanding of Jesus sees divine power breaking into the conventional framework of everyday living from a separate, distinct realm. This is what the unclean spirits recognize, for, in their delusion, they confess Jesus as "the son of God" (σὺ εἶ ὁ υἱὸς τοῦ θεοῦ), which, from their mouths, means one with divine powers. In 1: 1 Mark announced that Jesus indeed is "the son of God." Since Wrede, exegetes have often affirmed the ironic truth of this judg-

---

10. Malbon, *Narrative Space,* 29.

11. Malbon, *Narrative Space,* 43: "Furthermore, because Galilee is, within Mark's Gospel, the gathering place for the various multitudes (3: 7–8) as well as the home base for Jesus' foreign travels, Galilee itself, in a sense, mediates between JEWISH HOMELAND and FOREIGN LANDS. Galilee seems to have played a similar role in first-century history and culture. The name *Galilee* means 'ring, circle' and was likely given to the district 'in recognition of the circle of Gentile nations which had infiltrated the region' (Clark, "Galilee, Sea of," 348)."

12. Broadhead, *Teaching With Authority,* 90: "What is unacceptable to the narrative structure of the Gospel of Mark is not the description of Jesus as Son of God (1: 1; 15: 39), but the linkage of the title to miracle activity. The title is consistently suppressed within the narrative until it may be properly linked to the death of Jesus on the cross (15: 39)." That is to say, until it can be emptied of other-worldly connotations. I agree with Camery-Hoggatt, *Irony in Mark's Gospel,* 121, that Mark has elected to highlight Jesus' ministry of healing and exorcism because "these are two primary elements of the messianic expectation," but think it significant that at the same time Mark refuses to grant the validity of the title they signify. He describes Jesus in messianic terms and yet refuses to identify him as messiah, until all expectations can be emptied. Even in so describing Jesus, Mark provides the reader with a flash-forward to the emptying of all definition on the cross. So I read Broadhead, *Teaching With Authority,* 83: "The miracle story in Mark 3: 1–7a plays a decisive role in the larger characterization of Jesus. The image of Jesus as authoritative teacher/preacher was initiated in Mark 1. 14–15 and given graphic development throughout the first major section (1.1–3.7a). In the miracle story of 3.1–7a this authority of Jesus was brought into sharp conflict with the religious leadership of Israel. Jesus was first accused of blasphemy (2.7), and now becomes the object of a death plot (3.6). Both the accusation and the death plot are repeated in Jerusalem near the end of Jesus' life (14. 64; 11.18)."

ment of the unclean, arguing that Jesus prohibits them from making him known because he wants to guard the messianic secret.[13] This is a persuasive interpretation, for Jesus often prohibits both spirits and people from making him known. The point of that secret, however, is not, I think, that Jesus had to hide his true identity to avoid a premature confrontation with the authorities.[14] Such an interpretation assumes the possibility of a correct and valid identification of the person of Jesus, one that would define his true identity. I suggest that Mark's intent is different, that by repeating the initial description of Jesus in 1: 1 as christ and son of God on the lips of demoniacs, Mark is deconstructing even that identity. Even in 8: 29, Peter's identification of Jesus as christ finds no acceptance but rebuke from Jesus. There is no proper verbal identification for Jesus, for he moves in the tension of the two truths. No conventional title can depict his selfhood, for selfhood is a reality only to a deluded understanding, trying to fasten essences onto dependently co-arisen being. Even if the unclean spirits identify him correctly, they clearly are mistaken. Even a correct viewpoint (*samyagdṛṣṭi*) is still a viewpoint (*dṛṣṭi*), engendered by forgetfulness of emptiness.

It is not only that Jesus is not to be known as a "divine person, endowed with awesome powers, as a messiah who will deliver the people within the framework of imagined realities. He is also not a pre-ordained "suffering messiah," moving toward the divine inevitability of execution. The point is not correctly understood doctrine, but, as 1: 15 proclaims, a conversion of one's understanding, from clinging to essences to the practice of the middle path of reengaged wilderness wisdom. The crowds mistake Jesus for a conventional miracle-worker, while the demons see him as an other-worldly invader.

In Mahāyāna teaching deluded consciousness is unable to differentiate the two truths of ultimate meaning and worldly convention. Either one ignores ultimate meaning to focus on the truths one imagines to grasp in the world, or one denigrates this world in favor of a single-minded focus on ultimate meaning. It is the latter option that Nāgārjuna, the Mādhyamika philosopher, criticizes as "emptiness ineptly grasped," and pronounces as most difficult to cure. Emptiness is meant as a cure for adherence to viewpoints deemed to be absolute (*dṛṣṭi*), but to make emptiness itself the single-minded center of one's activity is to make emptiness itself yet another viewpoint. Nāgārjuna teaches that "the Victors have declared emptiness as the expeller of all views, but those who hold

---

13. Wrede, *The Messianic Secret,* sees the leitmotif of Mark as this messianic secret underlying Jesus' commands for silence addressed to demons, the parable theory, and the disciples' misunderstanding. See Räisanen, *The 'Messianic Secret' in Mark,* for a full discussion of the issue. Camery-Hoggatt, *Irony in Mark's Gospel,* 112 concurs: "It is a subtle touch that *demons* should be made agents of revelation."

14. Rhoads and Michie, *Mark as Story,* 75: "Jesus also keeps his identity a secret throughout the story until he is ready to complete his work by facing the consequences of acknowledging his identity," and again, 84: "The dilemma for Jesus is this: how can he inaugurate God's rule, yet evade the efforts of the authorities to trap him? Many aspects of the secrecy motif are related to this problem."

emptiness as a view they have pronounced incurable."[15] Any single-minded adherence to the emptiness of the wilderness is a spirituality without reengagement in the towns of conventional living.

The unclean spirits see that Jesus is not bound by the worldly and conventional. Indeed, that has been the point of the immediately preceding passages about the sabbath. They see Jesus as free from the confining structures of religion, while the authorities negate the very possibility that one can have access to Yahweh apart from those religious structures. In 1: 11 Jesus hears the voice of God proclaiming that he is "the beloved son" of God, and this immediately drives him into the wilderness. When he returns into Capernaum and cures a man possessed with an unclean spirit, the spirit recognizes him as "the holy one of God" (1: 25). In the present passage the unclean spirits not only recognize him as a divine being, but they prostrate themselves in worship before him. And they do so publicly. Nothing Mark says suggests that their confession is not heard by the crowds. They fall down before him and cry out (ἔκραζον)—hardly actions that one would expect to go unnoticed. Jesus is then hiding nothing, for their confession is already public. "Jesus' own strenuous . . . but apparently futile efforts to keep himself from being known,"[16] are far from historical reminiscences. Rather, Mark is negating all theological confession of Jesus' identity, all understandings of messiah.[17]

The wilderness spirituality places one beyond all conventional norms and all conventional definitions. That is why he charges the demons not to make him known.[18] Jesus is grounded in the immediate awareness of God, apart from all conventions in direct contact with ultimate meaning. Yet, if that contentless awareness of Yahweh is forced back within and identified with worldly conventions, it begins to parade as other-worldly power and prestige. When Mark envisages Jesus' direct experience of the ultimacy of God through the eyes of the demoniacs, who are themselves outside conventional norms, he suggests not truth, but misunderstanding. In their eyes Jesus is, like them, beyond the conventional. But Mark has Jesus reject their testimony with its implication of dispensing with reengagement in the dependently co-arisen world. Jesus forbids them to make him one of their lineage of "other-worldly" beings, focused simply on the emptiness of all forms. This point is reaffirmed

---

15. Nāgārjuna, *Mūlamadhyamakakārikā*, 13: 8.

16. Tolbert, *Sowing the Gospel*, 142.

17. Perrin, "The Christology of Mark," 99, remarks: "The christology of Mark may best be approached by assuming that he uses 'Christ' and 'Son of God' to establish rapport with his readers and then deliberately reinterprets and gives conceptual content to these terms by a use of 'Son of Man,' a designation which is not, properly speaking, a christological title but which to all intents and purposes becomes one as Mark uses it." I take "son of man" to be precisely an emptying of all titles, and this is why, as Perrin continues, the "son of man is never found in Mark except on the lips of Jesus," for it constitutes Mark's emptied christology.

18. Schweizer, "Mark's Theological Achievement," 57: "The fundamental hiddenness of God, which is disclosed only to the followers, is intended by Mark's messianic secret which he introduces four times with his characteristic word *diastellesthai* ('to charge')."

in the next section, where Jesus concretizes the conventional nature of his wisdom: he appoints the twelve to preach and have authority over demons. With his disciples he engages the world, redefining preaching, not any longer as a speaking in place of God, but as a guarding of the silence of God by recognizing the conventional nature of the preaching.

The Preaching of the Twelve
3: 13–19

¹³He now went up onto the mountain and summoned those he wanted. So they came to him ¹⁴and he appointed twelve: they were to be his companions and to be sent out to proclaim the message, ¹⁵with power to drive out devils. ¹⁶And so he appointed the twelve: Simon to whom he gave the name Peter, ¹⁷James the son of Zebedee and John the brother of James, to whom he gave the name Boanerges or "Sons of Thunder"; ¹⁸Andrew, Philip, Bartholomew, Matthew, Thomas, James the son of Alphaeus, Thaddaeus, Simon the Zealot, ¹⁹and Judas Iscariot, the man who was to betray him.

Jesus returns to the silence of a mountain, to the source of his wilderness spirituality of direct awareness. And he summons his new disciples to that experience, much as God summoned Moses to the mountain in *Exodus.*[19] Mark speaks of a single mountain (τὸ ὄρος), suggesting mountain epiphanies from the Hebrew Bible; there are strong overtones of the twelve tribes assembled at the Mount of the Covenant.[20] It is to be for them a time of silent revelation.[21] They are to immerse themselves in the silent emptiness of Yahweh, and then descend to the worldly tasks of preaching.[22] The unclean spirits also sometimes dwell in mountains and also see beyond conventional realities, but Jesus sends the disciples down to preach, to reengage in human discourse. And that reengagement in language and discourse is itself the power to cast out demons, to bring the realization of emptiness from its wilderness embodiment in devil consciousness into the world of men and women.

---

19. Malbon, *Narrative Space,* 84: ". . . when the narratives of Exodus and Mark are examined in parallel, Jesus plays not so much the role of Moses as the role of God. Jesus does the calling in Mark as God does the calling in Exodus. God calls only Moses to come up on the mountain (19: 20), and through Moses the people are called to the foot of the mountain; all those whom Jesus calls come up on the mountain."
20. Wrede, *The Messianic Secret,* 136: "The mountain is not to be sought on the map. . . . It is an ideal mountain."
21. Tolbert, *Sowing the Gospel,* 143.
22. Kelber, *Mark's Story of Jesus,* 26: "No sooner has the full ecumenical shape of the new community come into view than Jesus proceeds to appoint its leadership. He leaves the lakeside and goes up to a mountain. The mountain is a place of great significance: it is the site of revelation."

An old maxim claims that the mind of a theologian is most like that of a devil. Living as if above the world and in special communion with the ultimate, theologians at times fail to reengage in the world. In fact, we all live in the one, single cosmos. Devil consciousness, taking possession of men and women, pretends to live apart from conventions, and consequently is unable to function in the world at all. The authority to cast out devils flows directly from reengagement in human discourse, in preaching the kingdom. To be sent (ἀποστέλλη), to be an apostle, means to burn away one's delusions through insight into emptiness and then to reengage in the world of conventional action and words. It does not mean to take a position in isolated splendor above the world or in coercive authority within the world, but to be fully and totally engaged in the dependently co-arisen world. In the phrase of the *Gospel of John,* it is "to be in the world, but not of it." Not to be bound by the imagined pattern of clinging to putative realities, but freely to adopt and adapt worldly usages to the task of preaching the gospel. The twelve are to share this task with Jesus, they are to be his companions. Notice that at this juncture Mark does not describe their activity. We see them actually begin to preach and cast out devils only in 6: 7, where it will be noted just how inadequate their understanding has been, even though their preaching does indeed succeed in casting out some demons. But, at this juncture Mark's Jesus and his disciples simply return home.

Jesus gives new names to Simon and to James and John. Simon is to be Peter, rock-solid, an irony the reader cannot overlook in light of Peter's repeated denials of Jesus during the Passion narrative. James and John are called sons of thunder. In the Mahāyāna tradition, emptiness is said to have the sound of thunder. The Bodhisattva Vimalakīrti answers the deepest question about emptiness by maintaining his silence, and that silence in Mahāyāna devotion is heard thundering down the ages.[23] Yet, no thunder emerges from the disciples, except the thundering nonsense of their request to sit on Jesus' right and left in his glory (10: 37), for they have not understood how to live in the dynamic tension between ultimate meaning and worldly convention. In Mark, they will come to serve as examples of emptiness ineptly grasped, as persons who try to identify their own conventional lives with ultimate meaning, thus rendering themselves incapable of understanding Jesus as empty messiah.

Even beyond the failure of Peter, James, and John, Mark emphasizes the deluded nature of all Jesus' chosen disciples, stating starkly that Judas was

---

23. Thunder is traditionally associated with the silence of the layman Vimalakīrti in *The Holy Teachings of Vimalakīrti,* trans. Robert Thurman, 77: "Then [after all the bodhisattvas have given their explantions,] the crown prince Mañjuśri said to the Licchavi Vimalakīrti, 'We have all given our own teachings, noble sir. Now, may you elucidate the teaching of the entrance into the principle of nonduality!' Thereupon, the Licchavi Vimalakīrti kept his silence, saying nothing at all. The crown prince Mañjuśri applauded the Licchavi Vimalakīrti: 'Excellent! Excellent, noble sir! This is indeed the entrance into the nonduality of the bodhisattvas. Here there is no use for syllables, sounds, and ideas.' "

the one who betrayed Jesus.[24] The conflict is not simply between rival camps, Pharisees and followers, outsiders and insiders. Even insiders, failing to understand, stand opposed to Jesus' practice.

Jesus as Madman
3: 20–21

[20]*He went home again, and once more such a crowd collected that they could not even have a meal.* [21]*When his relations heard of this, they set out to take charge of him; they said, "He is out of his mind."*

From the summit of the mountain charge given to the twelve, Jesus returns home with his companions, to Capernaum.[25] They are again swamped by the expectations of the crowds. It does no good to have mountaintop experiences if one does not return to the world of men and women. The wilderness of the mountain abates all conventional distinctions, for therein one abides in the non-abiding of unmediated experience. Such a consciousness is beyond good and evil, is indeed a mark of emptiness, as Nietzsche knew so well. Conventional judgments about how to practice are constructed through discriminative thinking and cannot go beyond the conventional. Thus, to move beyond the conventional is in some sense a Zarathustra-like rejection of the norms of good and evil. The present passage is about how others perceive the emptying of normal conventions and traditions. His relatives[26] claim that

---

24. Fowler, *Let the Reader Understand,* 105: "Already we know the identity of the one—a disciple!—who will later deliver up Jesus. We should take care to observe that the verb in 3:19 is not in the future tense; the aorist indicative tense of the verb describes Judas' delivering up of Jesus not as an event that is forthcoming in the world of the story but as an event that lies in the past of the narrator's world and our own. This verse reminds us, when we stop to think about it, that the entire narrative is told from a retrospective point of view. . . . For all we know, the first Christian storyteller to cast Judas in the role of traitor was the author of Mark's Gospel."

25. Against Kelber, *Mark's Story of Jesus,* 26: "Jesus enters a house (the RSV rendering with 'and he went home' is inaccurate) . . ."

26. Literally οἱ παρ' αὐτοῦ, which is translated in RSV as family, but it may include friends, followers, and disciples, like the οἱ περὶ αὐτὸν of 4: 10. See Tolbert, *Sowing the Gospel,* 99.19. See Fowler, *Let the Reader Understand,* 200, on how Matthew and Luke clean up the ambiguity of Mark: "Sometimes rather than specifying the unstated subject, Matthew or Luke has resorted to the broader editorial stroke of cutting out the ambiguous word or phrase in Mark. One such example, Mark 3:21, says with artful ambiguity that Jesus' 'associates' (*hoi par'autou*) set out to seize him because they think he has gone crazy. The ambiguity of who these associates are creates suspense that engages the reader throughout the metaphor-filled debate over Jesus' exorcisms that follows in 3:22–30. When we reach Mark 3:31, Jesus' mother and brothers arrive to fetch him; it is *they* who think he is crazy and would seize him if they could! *They* are his 'associates.' Matthew and Luke, who hold Jesus' family in higher esteem than Mark, completely destroy this revelatory moment in the reading of Mark 3:31–35 by deleting Mark 3:21 altogether."

he has gone off his rocker, that he no longer can maintain a human balance to things. He is maddened by awareness of emptiness. They say that he has gone out of his mind (ἐξέστη), literally that he stands outside of his identity. The verb is the same as to be in ecstasy, but the sense here is totally negative, for they come to apprehend, seize, or forcefully take him away (ἐλῆθον κρατῆσαι αὐτὸν). They recognize that he has indeed seen beyond conventional definitions, that he is not attached even to his own self, that self fostered by the conventional and social factors that give us our identities. In Mahāyāna terms, the deepest and most tenacious attachment is to self (*ātman*), when we consider it to be an inner, permanent core of our personal being, immune to change and transience. Insight into emptiness negates such a self, for no one has such an inner, essential being. Thus, Zen people talk about the true self as being the self of emptiness, the self constructed in awareness of the conventional nature of all human existence.

Here, the complaint is that Jesus may well embody an unconventional awareness, but that he does not really engage in the everyday world. Rather, he is seen as disturbing the peace of the town, causing a ruckus. Their concern is "What will people say?" And so they come to take him away, to capture him, as one would take away a demoniac. Mark portrays Jesus' family as single-mindedly focused on the conventions of town, emphasizing the point in verses 31–35, while the immediately following scribal accusation that he is possessed by devils urges the same point: that Jesus has gone beyond all the conventions of Israel into realms of demonic madness.

Ultimate Meaning and Devil Consciousness
3: 22–30

²²*The scribes who had come down from Jerusalem were saying, "Beelzebul is in him," and "It is through the prince of devils that he drives devils out."* ²³*So he called them to him and spoke to them in parables,* ²⁴*"How can Satan drive out Satan? If a kingdom is divided against itself, that kingdom cannot last.* ²⁵*And if a household is divided against itself, that household can never last.* ²⁶*Now if Satan has rebelled against himself and is divided, he cannot last either—it is the end of him.* ²⁷*But no one can make his way into a strong man's house and plunder his property unless he has first tied up the strong man. Only then can he plunder his house.*

²⁸*"In truth I tell you, all human sins will be forgiven, and all the blasphemies ever uttered;* ²⁹*but anyone who blasphemes against the holy spirit will never be forgiven, but is guilty of an eternal sin."* ³⁰*This was because they were saying, "There is an unclean spirit in him."*

The scribes expand on the charge made by Jesus' relatives: Jesus is mad and possessed by the devil. The scribes are identified as from Jerusalem—they represent the conventional structures of religion which will eventually crush

Jesus under their oppresive weight.[27] They recognize that Jesus ignores the traditions and violates the norms, a recognition not ill-founded, for Jesus does indeed represent a danger to the traditional norms. Yet, if one simply overthrows traditions and violates order, the result is usually not wisdom or enlightenment, but chaos and anomie. The traditions of Israel, as of other peoples throughout the world, embody the wisdom of the ancestors in coping with and wisely living life. They may not be easily sloughed off just because they are man-made. Jesus does not recommend such a total rejection. What he is negating is servile attachment to traditions as if they captured absolute truth, not adherence to traditions as wise human constructs. His actions flow from beyond the traditions, for tradition itself cannot justify itself. It exists in virtue of deep experiences that both ground and transcend it. There are traditions about Moses on Mount Sinai, but the actual encounter of Moses with Yahweh on that august peak both founds the tradition and goes beyond anything the tradition may attempt to describe. Direct experiences with God are anomic, and if not reengaged back into the traditions of men and women, can wreak havoc on healthy, customary structures. This is why Jesus not only moves beyond the traditions,[28] but also discourses about the coming kingdom, i.e., about reengagement in the world in commitment to justice and peace.

Some interpreters say that Beelzebul was originally a divine title, meaning the Lord of the Mansion, or Lord of the Abode.[29] If this is the case, the present usage depicts a divinity localized in an abode separate from and thus opposed to the localized presence of Yahweh in the Jerusalem temple. Perhaps the Jerusalem scribes see Jesus as opposing the Temple presence with an alternate, demonic localization of Beelzebub, and thus a feared disrupter of the accepted order and tradition. The charge of the scribes is that Jesus has violated the cultural norms, that he ignores the conventions of the elders.

Jesus' response is expressed in down-to-earth parables, accessible to all. He does not here talk about the ultimacy of conversion to God or allude to

---

27. Malbon, *Narrative Space,* 30: "Jesus' journey to Jerusalem is anticipated. . . . Scribes come down (*katabantes*) from Jerusalem to confront Jesus (3: 22; 7: 1), and Jesus and his followers go up (*anabainontes,* 10: 32; *anabainomen,* 10: 33; *sunanabasai* 15: 41) to Jerusalem and to confrontation with the religious establishment."

28. Via, *The Ethics of Mark's Gospel,* 187: "Since Jesus does the unexpected and transgresses the principles of traditional piety (2: 1-3: 27), having faith is to see through the offense and to encounter in Jesus, not the presence of demons, but the Holy Spirit as the disrupter of human expectations."

29. Crossan, *The Historical Jesus,* 319: The term Beelzebub "preserves, as Joseph Fitzmyer notes, 'the name of an old Canaanite god, meaning "Baal, the Prince," or "Baal of the Exalted Abode" (*The Gospel According to Luke,* 920).' But that unique epithet is the voice, surely, of the Little Tradition, an attack that bespeaks a village environment." Also see Best, *The Temptation and the Passion,* 11.3, notes that "the most probable meaning appears to be 'Lord of the House,' " which ties in with the subsequent discussion about a divided house. Also see Grant, *The Interpreter's Bible,* 7: 690; and Mack, *A Myth of Innocence,* 198.

wilderness awareness. His answer both to the scribes and to his relatives is couched in parable as the most effective method to counter the deluded thinking of his critics.[30] Parables are tensive probings meant not to demonstrate a clear and logical idea, but to lead the hearer into awareness of the middle path of emptiness and dependent co-arising. Jesus does not admit a reified absolute in the traditions. His questioning is meant to lead the scribes into the middle path, awareness both of the complete otherness of ultimate meaning and the conventional validity of language-formed custom and practice. He is saying that there is no localized presence of God, just as, by switching the name of Beelzebub to Satan in his answer, he is suggesting that there is no localized presence of the devil. The place of God and of Satan is within the heart, either open to the Spirit or hardened in demonic opposition to God.

The rhetorical logic of Jesus' argument is not rigorous, but the point is not logical one-upmanship.[31] Jesus' reasoning rests on an analogy between the unity of kingdoms and households and the kingdom of Satan. The most usual interpretation of the strong man who is bound identifies that figure with Satan who cannot stand if his kingdom is divided. On the face of it, that is rather strange, for one does not picture devils as running a harmonious and well-ordered household. Rather, devils are seen as agents of chaos and disorder.

Perhaps Jesus himself is the bound strong man. Verse 3: 19 finished the listing of the disciples by noting that Judas was the one who would betray Jesus. Furthermore, 1: 7 has already depicted Jesus as the one stronger than John (ὁ ἰσχυρότερος). If the strong man of the present parable indicates Jesus himself, then it is the delusion of any localized containment of God, whether by the authorities or by Beelzebub, which binds (δήσῃ) Jesus in the either/or of a localized presence. The scribes' perspective that Jesus has misidentified God's presence with Satan's provides "the context for the denunciation of Jesus as a blasphemer by the chief priests at the trial (14: 61–64). Indeed, this whole section of Mark 3: 20 for the reader is filled with

30. Schweizer, "Mark's Theological Achievement," 49: "The redactional note in v. 23 that Jesus began to speak in parables follows on this double hardening in vv. 21 and 23. The framework at the end of the pericope corresponds to this: in v. 30 Mark relates the saying about the unforgivable sin explicitly to the hardening of the scribes in v. 22 and in vv. 31–5 he contrasts the true family of Jesus, which hears his word and does the will of God, with the hardened family of v. 21. So according to Mark the parable discourse is the response to the world being hardened, from the closest relations of Jesus to the leaders of Israel."

31. Fowler, *Let the Reader Understand,* 186: [Jesus'] "reply does not answer the question of 3:23 explicitly, but it does imply that if the scribes really believed what they were saying they would not oppose him; they would instead encourage and congratulate him for hastening the demise of the kingdom of Satan. Jesus demonstrates through the logic of his metaphors that the paradox of Satan casting out Satan leads to conclusions that those putting forward the paradox probably would not accept. This paradox does not make any sense; it is not a paradox at all, but nonsense."

chilling forebodings concerning what is coming."[32] Jesus' relatives have likewise just tried to bind (κρατῆσαι) and take him away. Both groups try to force upon Jesus an unmitigated adherence to the conventional religious tradition. His relatives want to seize him and drag him back apparently to his Nazareth home; the scribes want to exclude him from that tradition by placing him beyond it in the false otherness of the demonic. Both attempts to bind negate the middle path and its practice of abiding in a tensive and healthy differentiation of the two truths.

Having bound Jesus, his critics intend to plunder his property (τὰ σκεύη). But σκεύη does not mean simply disposable goods, but useful goods or instruments.[33] By binding Jesus within or apart from the tradition, the scribes want to rob him of his ability to reengage by skillful means (*upāya;* τὰ σκεύη) in furthering the kingdom and undermining those traditions. Having absolutized religion, they want to keep it for themselves by banishing Jesus to the irrelevance of a purely localized spirituality, which has no social impact.[34]

The parable, however, is followed by a solemn pronouncement on the unforgivable sin of attributing Jesus' exorcisms to an unclean spirit. The scribes fail to recognize the presence of God in Jesus because they have already reified ultimate truth in their Jerusalem conventions. This is the blasphemy that will never be forgiven, Jesus is saying, because it precludes insight into the ultimacy of God. It freezes one in deluded religion, thus rendering ineffective the Spirit meant to carry one beyond delusion. Mark is not concerned to show that in fact Jesus is not inhabited by a devil—all that he has assumed from the very first verse. Rather, the pronouncement aims at exposing a deluded pattern of consciousness, a pattern that gets things upside down.

The scribes, as well as Jesus' relatives, are examples of people attached to assured religious truth in primal ignorance (*avidyā*). They are the Jewish authorities only by accident and force of social context, in no way to be

---

32. Tolbert, *Sowing the Gospel,* 100.

33. Zerwick, *Analysis Philologica Novi Testamenti Graeci,* 85, defines it as *res utensilis, vas, instrumentum.* The term will occur significantly in Jesus' refusal to let people carry "anything" (11: 16) through the temple area.

34. Compare Best, *The Temptation and the Passion,* 10–14. Also compare Myers, *Binding the Strong Man,* 164–67, who sees 3: 20–35 as the campaign climax wherein Jesus declares ideological war. Following Theissen, he sees Satan as a symbolic accentuation of the negative experiences of earthly rule, and Jesus' mission as likened to "criminal breaking and entering." Thus, "Mark has come clean: Jesus (a.k.a. the 'stronger one' heralded by John, 1: 8) intends to overthrow the reign of the strong man (a.k.a. the scribal establishment represented by the demon of 1: 24)." In a Mahāyāna reading, Jesus indeed empties the ideological foundations of the traditions, but not to establish an alternate ideology. Rather, he teaches the emptiness of all ideologies, and thus their dependently co-arisen validity in particular circumstances. It is, I think, because of Myers' focus on social action that he tends almost to dismiss Mark's wilderness theme, as, for example, on 168: "And with those words, Jesus retreats to the sea to reflect upon the fortunes and future of his messianic mission (4:1)." The image is of a revolutionary taking a few moments of respite from the struggle.

distinguished from religious authorities elsewhere. Almost all of the characters in Mark's gospel are Jews. Having apprehended emptiness ineptly they reify it into yet another intellectual viewpoint, and the fire of the Spirit of wisdom meant to burn away sickness and delusion becomes a hot iron ball searing one's innards and consuming one's spirit. Notice that Jesus says that such a sin of attributing to the devil what comes from God will not be forgiven, i.e., the verb is in the passive voice. He does not say that God will not forgive such a sin, active voice. The grammar is important, for it is not that God regards such a sin as particularly horrendous. More horrendous things have been done, mass murders and genocides. The reality of the holocaust serves as the modern symbol for devilish evil unleashed upon the world. Of course, such sins are infinitely more horrendous than simply violating religious norms. The point, however, is that failure to discern the presence of the Spirit renders one incapable of being converted, for it places obstacles in the way of listening to true teaching. It is such hardness of heart that Mark contrasts to the mind of faith, for it chokes off insight into emptiness.[35]

In Yogācāra teaching there are two obstacles to awakening. The first is the obstacle of the passions that lead one astray in seeking life and happiness in images. The second is the obstacle to understanding, which is identified as the imagined pattern of consciousness that clings to such images as if they are real. This pattern, even if engaged outwardly in religion, filters out from one's hearing anything not congruent with already held views. Our very views on life get in the way of life, simply because they represent it so partially, in piecemeal fashion. In 2: 1–12 the scribes had already accused Jesus of blasphemy because he had said that the man's sins were forgiven. The son of man there had authority to pronounce forgiveness. Here, the sin of clinging to a false ultimate truth is a sin beyond forgiveness, for it occludes the liberating insight that would issue in gratitude and forgiveness. The scribes cannot forgive Jesus his reengagement into their religious world because he disrupts their lettered lives.

The reader sees all this, for she stands far removed from the plot action of the story.[36] The judgment of the scribes may indeed have been intended as a righteous judgment from their deluded perspective. "That it is ironic becomes clear when Jesus condemns it categorically as an act of blasphemy."[37]

---

35. Via, *The Ethics of Mark's Gospel*, 119: "Heart in Mark, as in the Old Testament, is the hidden inner core of the human being, and hardness of heart is religious and moral deformation."

36. Fowler, *Let the Reader Understand*, 76–77: "When we realize that the teaching of Jesus in Mark's Gospel has little effect upon his hearers at the story level, we understand that his teaching serves primarily as evaluative and interpretive commentary for the reader. The words of Jesus in Mark do not contribute so much to the story as to the discourse. This efficacy at the level of discourse is generally true of the words of Jesus in Mark but especially true of the frequent 'truly (*amēn*), I say to you . . .' phrases (3:28–29, . . .). In such statements Jesus is interpreting the significance of events of the story from a position within the story."

37. Camery-Hoggatt, *Irony in Mark's Gospel*, 125.

The reader knows that Jesus is the son of God and messiah. Yet, care should be exercised here: by so asserting the righteousness of the Messiah's judgment, one comes perilously close to concurring in the frequent "revelation" of Jesus' true identity and righteousness announced from the mouths of demons. Such a concurrence entails a viewpoint that the house of Satan is indeed divided, for Satan becomes both the source of chaos and sin, and the source of truth and revelation. The first Markan level of irony, in virtue of which the reader distances herself from the sorry disciples, maneuvers the reader into asserting the ironic truth of the confessing demons. Mark's rhetorical irony in his narrative discourse contradicts the messianic assertions in the story. Herein lies a deeper, second level irony, one that not only identifies the truth in the story reported, but also, by associating the reader with demons, challenges the reader to the very depths of her consciousness.

Family Problems
3: 31–35

[31]Now his mother and his brothers arrived and, standing outside, sent in a message asking for him. [32]A crowd was sitting round him at the time the message was passed to him, "Look, your mother and brothers and sisters are outside asking for you." [33]He replied, "Who are my mother and my brothers?" [34]And looking at those sitting in a circle round him, he said, "Here are my mother and my brothers. [35]Anyone who does the will of God, that person is my brother and sister and mother."

The criticism of the scribes is pressed once again by his own family. They come and stand outside (ἔξω στήκοντες) his house; the last location mentioned by Mark is in 3: 20, when Jesus was "at home." His relatives had accused him of being "out of his mind," because he acts beyond the traditions. Here his family stand outside the circle of his teaching and again call him back to the everyday life of primal ignorance. His mother, brothers, and sisters ask for him to leave the circle of his followers, for Jesus is depicted as sitting in the center of a maṇḍala, a circle of the common people (καὶ ἐκάθητο περὶ αὐτὸν ὄχλος), who were listening to his words of awakening. He is the teacher with authority, and thus the list of his family members leaves out any mention of his father, as will Jesus' description of the eschatological family in 10: 30, where those who give up father and family receive back only family. The patriarchial father figure is effaced.[38] His family,

---

38. Crossan, *The Historical Jesus*, 299: ". . . Mark, in keeping with his severe criticism of the family of Jesus, has made the encounter much more inimical by the intercalation of 3: 19b–21, 31–35 with 3: 22–30. He has also added in 'sister' in 3: 35 to connect with the following equally inimical encounter in 6: 3. But apart from that addition, both *Gospel of Thomas* 99 and Mark 3: 31–35 agree on 'brothers and mother' twice in the former case and on 'mother and brothers' three times, with 'brother . . . and mother' once, in the latter case. They agree on excluding the father. The exclusion might be interpreted

without authority, stays outside the circle (ἔξω στήκοντες), clinging to the supposed reality of outer things and requesting him to leave and come out to their more identifiable world.[39] The story looks forward to the parable discourse in 4: 10–12, where those outside hear only in parable and fail to understand. Thus, Jesus' answer is that his true family consists in all those who do the will of God (τὸ θέλημα τοῦ θεοῦ), thereby moving them within the circle of his followers.[40]

But what precisely that divine will in fact wills is not so easily identified, for doing the will of God is not a program to follow. It depends on discernment of the presence of God permeating our everyday lives. The point is the same as the last section about Beelzebul: how to experience the ultimate, non-localized meaning of God in the everyday activities of our conventional lives. In Mahāyāna terms, one first gains insight into emptiness and withdraws from the world and its delusions. But then one empties emptiness itself, for it provides no sure superworld for us to live in. To reify emptiness is to fail to understand emptiness. Having emptied emptiness, one engages in the conventional world of dependent co-arising with one's total attention and commitment. This is the ideal of the bodhisattva, the enlightened being, who rejects a static emptiness in favor of carrying out the tasks of compassion in the world. Dynamic insight into emptiness means moving freely in a world experienced as worldly convention-only (saṃvṛti-mātra) in order to perfect wisdom. One is then in the perfected pattern of wisdom consciousness engaged in the here and now without hankering after or trying to live in any superworld, content to benefit others in forgetfulness of the delusion of a personal self that constantly needs to be bolstered and supported by further delusions and viewpoints.

And yet, no program is provided, for determining the most appropriate action or practice is precisely the task of any concrete reengagement in the world, since conditions vary and cannot be predicted beforehand.

---

in many different ways: Joseph was busy that day, was already dead, or was omitted to protect either the virgin birth or God as Jesus' true father. I underline, therefore, less the father's exclusion as the mother's inclusion. Jesus declares his followers to be a replacement family. Notice, for example, that the dependent version of *2 Clement* 9:11 speaks only of 'my brethren,' a much less striking usage than 'my mother and brothers.' And, however we explain the absence of Jesus' father, his new metaphorical family lacks one as well."—as shown in Matthew 10: 34–36, Luke 12: 51–52, Mark 10: 28–31.

39. Brown, et al., *Mary in the New Testament,* 286: "Mary at this point (i.e., Mark chapter 3) stands outside of Jesus' 'eschatological' family."

40. Tolbert, *Sowing the Gospel,* 47: "Like others of his age [of increased mobility], Mark's constantly journeying Jesus is divided from his own family and hometown (Mark 3: 31–35; 6: 1–6), rejected by the traditional leaders of his religion, and thus leads the way to a new family and a new faith, based on a new word for all to hear." Yet it should be kept in mind that Jesus to this point has not left his native Galilee; moreover, before his passion and death Jesus himself predicts his return to Galilee(14: 28), and the young man in the tomb says that in fact Jesus is going before into Galilee (16: 7).

4

Parabolic Patterns of Understanding

The Parable of the Sower
4: 1–9

¹Again he began to teach them by the sea, but such a huge crowd gathered round him that he got into a boat and sat in it on the sea.¹ The whole crowd was beside the sea on the land.² ²He taught them many things in parables, and in the course of his teaching he said to them, ³"Listen! Imagine a sower going out to sow. ⁴Now it happened that, as he sowed, some of the seed fell on the edge of the path, and the birds came and ate it up. ⁵Some seed fell on rocky ground where it found little soil and at once sprang up, because there was no depth of earth; ⁶and when the sun came up it was scorched and, not having any roots, it withered away. ⁷Some seed fell into thorns, and the thorns grew up and choked it, and it produced no crop. ⁸And some seeds fell into rich soil and, growing tall and strong, produced a good crop; the yield was thirty, sixty, even a hundredfold." ⁹And he said, "Anyone who has ears for listening should listen!"

The image of the chaotic sea dominates the above passage. "Jesus sat in a boat on the sea (or, in the Greek, literally, 'sat on the sea' [καθῆσθαι ἐν τῇ θαλάσσῃ]."³ Jesus, just having come from hostile encounters with the

---

1. Following RSV.
2. Following RSV.
3. Malbon, *Narrative Space,* 32. Also, Malbon, *Mark and Method,* 36: "At the beginning of chapter 4, the Markan narrator takes considerable trouble to make sure the narratee locates Jesus at the sea. Within one verse the word *sea* occurs three times and the word *boat* once." Kelber, *The Kingdom in Mark,* 27: "Mark emphasizes not the sitting in the boat, but the sitting in the sea (*en tē thalassē*)! This is reminiscent of a motif from royal ideology according to which the king is enthroned at the center of the primeval flood (Ps 29: 10; Ezek. 28: 2)."

scribes and with his family, takes up a position right in the center of chaos. The sea parallels the wilderness as a symbol for that which is beyond all human conventions, outside all human control. Jesus has just been censured for going beyond the traditional conventions, accused of being himself possessed of a chaotic demon. Here, teaching the crowds of common people who remain safely on the land, he sits calmly on the very surface of the uncontrollable sea. Sitting on the sea of emptiness, he engages in teaching the crowd: his awareness of the wilderness immediacy of God enables him to engage in conventional tasks of compassion.

And he teaches in parables, tensive symbols that leave one wondering about the security of one's own life. At first glance, however, this parable of the sower is more of an allegory than a parable, for its meaning is discovered by identifying the respective referents for the different seeds. It invites the listener to question just what these different seeds represent. Shortly Jesus does take his disciples apart and interprets it for them, but the initial presentation of the parable takes place in public. Some scholars explain that the allegory was found in Mark's source, and that he added the later explanation in 4: 13–20 to flesh out its meaning, and that indeed seems reasonable. But even when the Markan Jesus offers that explanation, he prefaces it by criticizing his disciples for lack of faith: they should have been able to deal with the parable on their own.

Note that Mark says that Jesus "taught them many things in parables" (καὶ ἐδίδασκεν αὐτοὺς ἐν παραβολαῖς πολλά). Yet, Mark seldom details the content of that teaching. The other gospels, especially John, often break the flow of the action to give Jesus an opportunity to discourse at length.[4] Some think that Mark moves his narrative so quickly through the constant flow of actions of Jesus, his disciples, and his antagonists that he has no time to halt the flow for extended discourses. Yet, there is perhaps a deeper significance, for in the above sentence the important thing is not what the "many things" Jesus taught were, but that he taught them in parables. The gospel Mark presents is not a specific set of teachings to be learned, but an invitation to reverse the unconverted structure of the mind. The constant interplay between the actors highlights the difference between the converted consciousness of Jesus and the unconverted consciousness of the others.[5] Jesus has distanced

---

4. Kertledge, "The Epiphanies of Jesus in the Gospel," 84: "Alongside the narrative material the speeches and sayings of Jesus in Mark are very modest in scope. Apart from the parables chapter (4: 1–34) and the Markan apocalypse (Chapter 13) and to some extent the instruction in 7: 1–23, this Gospel contains no large discourses, only individual pieces of debate, parables and sayings of Jesus."

5. Schweizer, "Mark's Theological Achievement," 46: "Jesus' speaking in parables is thus for Mark not simply a more or less chance form. These illustrations are neither a pedagogical tool nor are they optional. On the contrary, pure communication of facts can be taken over and handed on without active participation. But the pictorial saying challenges the hearer, because it can only be understood by someone who opens himself personally to the speaker, as the pictorial language of love shows. For that reason parabolic speech withholds the meaning from those who do not allow their hardened hearts to be opened in existential confrontation with the one who addresses them."

himself from the crowd by getting into the boat and moving slightly offshore. They are on the land (ἐπὶ τῆς γῆς), for they are the ground upon which the seed word is sown.[6] None of the things Jesus taught have any importance apart from that interplay.

The surface meaning of the parable is not difficult to understand. The image of the sower was frequently used in the ancient world to represent the teacher, as in Plato and in *2 Esdras,*[7] and really needs no further explanation. All that is needed is for one to examine how the word has taken root in one's own consciousness. This is what Jesus means when he tells people to listen and hear with their ears, i.e., to hear directly without intellectualizing the parable. To hear (ἀκούειν) is a common Markan term and indicates more than verbal apprehension of ideas. Rather, it indicates a pattern of understanding open to the call to conversion.[8]

The same image of seeds implanted in the mind is a favored theme of the Yogācāra philosophers. Hearing the doctrine of awakening implants seeds (*śrutavāsanā*) in the mind which, countering the karmic seeds of passion and ignorance (*kleśajñeyāvaraṇabīja*), turn one toward a conversion of consciousness, toward awakening. Those seeds are not innate within the mind, but flow from hearing the doctrine of true awakening preached by buddhas, i.e., awakened persons. In permeating one's consciousness, such seed words transform the consciousness of the hearer, so that the very ground in which they are sown is gradually turned from passion and ignorance toward wisdom and awakening. The ground of consciousness is not set and unchangeable, for all conscious patterns are other-dependent, and thus empty of any set essence. What is in the first instance shallow, rocky, or entangled by passion can, in the second instance, break through those obstacles to become fertile ground for hearing, and thus for awakening.

Parable Teaching
4: 10–12

[10]*When he was alone, the Twelve, together with the others who formed his company, asked what the parable meant.* [11]*He told them, "To you is granted the secret of the kingdom of God, but to those who are outside everything comes in parables,*

---

6. Tolbert, *Sowing the Gospel,* 149: "In the parables that follow, those who hear the word that Jesus speaks may respond in one of the same four ways in which the four different types of earth (γῆ) respond to the seed sown in them. The huge crowds that listen to Jesus 'on the land' are types of the parabolic 'earth' about to be expounded."

7. Grant, *Interpreter's Bible,* 7: 695, "The figure of the sower scattering seed was frequently used in the ancient world for the teacher (Plato, *Laws* VI.777E; *II Esdras* 9: 31, 33)."

8. Tolbert, *Sowing the Gospel,* 150: "Forms of the verb 'to hear' (ἀκούειν) appear thirteen times in Mark 4: 1–34." Again, 45: 'To hear' means 'to understand'."

> *[12]so that they may look and look,*
>   *but not perceive;*
>   *listen and listen, but never understand;*
>   *to avoid changing their ways and being healed."*

The above sentence includes a quotation from *Isaiah* 6: 9–10, where it constitutes the Lord's charge to Isaiah: "Go, and say to this people, 'Listen and listen, but never understand; look and look, but never perceive.' Make the people's heart coarse, make their ears dull, shut their eyes tight, or they will use their eyes to see, use their ears to hear, use their hearts to understand, and change their ways and be healed." The charge both in *Isaiah* and in *Mark* is strange, that the Lord would desire people not to understand, that Jesus would use parables to conceal his meaning. Some think that Mark here adopts the gnostic idea of a select, inner circle who alone have access to the mysteries. Yet, this very notion requires interpretative gymnastics that twist and turn Mark's words, rather than admit the literal, apparently obvious sense.[9] One commentator says that "Mark's theory can only be described as perverse."[10] Attempts at interpretation often turn to redaction criticism, trying to ascertain the true Markan perspective from elements that preceded him, which he struggled to alter. Schweizer identifies verses 11–12 as coming from a pre-Markan tradition and not really compatible with the rest of Mark.[11] Such a critique contrasts Mark's source with his redacted treatment of that source, carried out in order both to identify Mark's opponents, the disciples who adhere to a "divine man" notion and think they have a special privileged position, as in verses 11–12, and to criticize that opinion, as Mark does the disciples throughout the gospel.[12] The problem with such redaction critiques is that they are too facile, for one can find pre-Markan material wherever the spirit moves one to find it.

If we base ourselves upon the narrative structure of the text as it stands, it soon becomes abundantly clear that even that inner circle of Jesus' company, although granted the secret of the kingdom, does not understand and in fact has no inner access to the mystery of the kingdom. They are the ones who do not understand the clear meaning of the parable of the sower and who immediately press Jesus to clarify it for them. They demand that the parable become a literal allegory, so that its meaning can be laid bare in objective

---

9. Taylor, *The Gospel According to St. Mark,* 257, describes the idea that Jesus' parables prevent understanding as "intolerable," while Schweitzer, *The Quest of the Historical Jesus,* 63, deems it "repellent." Matthew, apparently to soften the impact of Mark's phrase "so that" (ἵνα), substitutes "because" (ὅτι).

10. Grant, *Interpreter's Bible,* 7: 700.

11. Schweizer, "Zur Frage des Messiasgeheimnisses bei Markus," *Zeitschrift für die Neutestamentliche Wissenschaft* 56 (1965): 1–8. For a critique see Drury, "The Sower, the Vineyard, and the place of Allegory in the Interpretation of Mark's Parables," *Journal of Theological Studies,* 24 (1973): 367–79.

12. Weeden, *Mark—Traditions in Conflict,* 139–49.

terms without engaging their own deeper minds at all. They insist that the parable must have some decipherable inner meaning, an inner referent not apparent to all. If, in fact, the referent of the parable is their own minds, and not a separate meaning, they have indeed listened but missed the point. That point is both subtle and simple.[13] The lack of understanding manifested by Jesus' hearers results not from the verbally esoteric nature of the parables themselves, but from the fantasy patterns of the unconverted minds of the hearers/readers, focused on meaning as a property of a graspable external reality. This is why the disciples request a further explanation. Yet, when Jesus gives that explanation in 13–20, he merely describes the deluded quest of those who function in the imagined pattern of consciousness without internalizing its meaning.[14] The point relates not to revealed content, but to the very act and pattern of understanding revelation as the manifestation of that which remains beyond any verbal manifestation.[15] In Barth's words, "All true knowledge of God begins with the knowledge of the hiddenness of God."[16]

Mark's quotation from *Isaiah* follows *Isaiah's* use of irony,[17] for although the secret is given to them, the disciples themselves remain on the outside, searching for water in the midst of the river. The point is how one listens to the parables.[18] The disciples grapple with the verbal meaning of Jesus' teaching, while Jesus' intent is "to change a person at the core of his or her being,

---

13. Tolbert, *Sowing the Gospel,* 88, argues that "the story as a whole ought to be fairly obvious, straightforward, and repetitious rather than subtle and esoteric." Again, she argues, 96, that Mark permits "no moral ambiguity to enter the story." Again, 130 explains that parables "ought to be readily apparent in the narrative itself, for the very nature of popular literature is to be available to a broad spectrum of readers with greatly varying degrees of knowledge or sophistication." And 183 repeats the notion: "Popular literature must be broadly accessible; so, its main points ought to be obvious and repeated." So also Crossan, *The Historical Jesus,* 349: "The enigmatic injunction 9 *Who Has Ears* (1/ 5) should be interpreted in the simplest possible way. It means, on the lips of the historical Jesus, 'You have ears, use them; what I say is as clear and obvious as I can make it; all you have to do is listen. It is not cryptic, hidden, mysterious; it is obvious, maybe that is its problem, it is too obvious. Listen!' "

14. Kelber, *The Kingdom in Mark,* 32: ". . . the crucial point is that Jesus is not said to *speak in parables* to outsiders, rather that everything is or *occurs in riddles* to the outsiders *(ta panta ginetai)."* No matter how he speaks, their pattern of understanding turns everything into a riddle precisely because they cling to imagined *(parikalpita)* meanings.

15. Schweizer, "Mark's Theological Achievement," 50: ". . . at Mark 4: 12, it is the event of revelation, the gospel itself, which has to reveal the blindness of mankind and so bring the world under God's judgment."

16. Barth, *Church Dogmatics,* 2/1, 183.

17. Malbon, *Mark and Method,* 37: "This ironic allusion to Isaiah 6: 9–10, which is itself ironic, is an intertextual echo of the Septuagint." When irony is piled upon irony, one does indeed sense that in the deluded pattern of trying to grasp meaning, we are thrust into a hall of mirrors, all of which reflect only illusions.

18. Achtemeier, "Mark as Interpreter of the Jesus Traditions," *Interpretation,* 32/4 (1978): 345, "explains that the parable of the sower and this section of listening to parables have the same point, how one listens to and responds to Jesus." See Via, *The Ethics of Mark's Gospel,* 184.

to rewrite the heart (2 Cor 3:3). It is the power of this language, written or spoken, to remove the veil from the mind (2 Cor 3: 16–17),"[19] to soften the hardness of hearts of those who fix meanings in an external realm of supposed truths. That softening is itself a turning around or changing of one's way (ἐπιστρέψωσιν) that leads to healing the deluded mind.

What then is the secret or the mystery of the kingdom of God (τὸ μυστήριον . . . τῆς βασιλείας τοῦ θεοῦ)? This is the only instance where Mark employs the term "secret" or "mystery." And its meaning in context is not that of a special, messianic secret, but the clear and obvious significance of the parable itself: that the seed of God's word must take root in the depths of our minds. That rooting is the hidden mystery about the kingdom, not the status of Jesus as messiah, or any other piece of privileged information. It is hidden, because language itself can only cover it up in fabricated meaning, projecting its significance out there into a realm of detached truths. Kermode speaks of the simultaneous function of parable as proclamation and concealment: "Parable, it seems, may proclaim a truth as a herald does, and at the same time conceal truth like an oracle."[20] Such an understanding of parable parallels the Mahāyāna notion of conventional truth (*saṃvṛti*), which is interpreted to signify both a revelation (from the root *sam-vṛt*, to arise, the coming about of truth in the world) and a covering over and hiding (from the root *sam-vṛ*, to conceal).[21] Language in Mahāyāna reflects deluded misunderstandings and occludes truth to unawakened persons, yet at the same time reveals to the awakened that which can never be grasped by language. And so Jesus teaches in parables to break through language itself and reveal the deep mind of conversion. He talks a language of enigma so that the literal meanings of his words may be heard but not understood (ἀκούοντες ἀκούωσιν καὶ μὴ συνιῶσιν), for Jesus' teaching is not accessible to the imagined pattern of understanding (*parikalpita*).[22] The enigma simply highlights the impasse such attempts are bound to reach. The parable, for all its simplicity, is opaque for the mind that imagines meanings to be outer essences to be grasped. While functioning in such a deluded pattern, one cannot be converted, one cannot be healed or forgiven.

No revelation of the kingdom can be understood by this fantasy pattern of consciousness, for it immediately externalizes meanings and projects them into manipulative ideas. Thus, every revelation remains hidden and concealed. Mark 4: 1–34 is "the harshest and most extreme expression of the concealed

19. Via, *The Ethics of Mark's Gospel,* 17.
20. Kermode, *The Genesis of Secrecy,* 47.
21. Nagao, *The Foundational Standpoint of Mādhyamika Philosophy,* 39–42.
22. Schweizer, "Mark's Theological Achievement," 49: "Everything that Jesus has to say is a *mysterion* (a 'mystery' or 'secret,' 4: 11) as regards its significance, incomprehensible for mankind. . . . Matthew and Luke . . . changed the singular, *to mysterion,* which describes the mystery of revelation itself, namely the word of the cross, into a plural and so find all kinds of individual mysteries behind the parables, which we then unveil in allegorical fashion."

revelation motif."[23] Hidden, not as a privileged piece of special information, but as that which, in its bare simplicity, is beyond the understanding of the mind which is focused upon the unquestionable reality of the self and its patterns of understanding. Those who are outside (ἐκείνοις δὲ τοῖς ἔξω) do not then constitute a particular, identifiable group of people, but are those who externalize the meaning of the parables, and this includes, as becomes apparent, all of Jesus' inner circle of disciples. No matter how close they are physically to Jesus—whether his mother (3: 31) or his constant companions—to them, everything becomes muddled and opaque. Fowler explains, "What has not been grasped is that here is a moment of opacity in the discourse. It is the first time in the Gospel that any mention has been made of the giving of the secret of the Kingdom of God. Typically critics have flipped back through the early pages of the Gospel to seek when and where this might have taken place in the story. The thought has not occurred to such critics that the secret of the Kingdom of God might be intended to be a secret that excludes them. The notion that this episode is an intentionally opaque moment in the narrative has been unthinkable to many. . . . For the reader of the Gospel, the giving of this secret lies behind an opaque veil. We are not privy to it. Until 4: 11 we did not even know that the secret existed. Mark 4: 11 confronts us with our own blindness as readers, a blindness to which most critics have been blind. . . . troubling is the realization that must come to every reader at this juncture, if only unconsciously, that because the reader does not possess this touted 'secret of the Kingdom of God,' the reader must therefore be an outsider."[24] The parables are then presented in order to (ἵνα, 4: 12) counter that pattern of grasping after meaning, whether on the part of the story-level disciple or the discourse-level reader. They are presented so that one might not understand, and, not understanding, experience heightened tension between true and false patterns of understanding.[25]

---

23. Via, *The Ethics of Mark's Gospel*, 183.

24. Fowler, *Let the Reader Understand*, 168-69.

25. Thus I disagree with Tolbert, *Sowing the Gospel*, 163: "For the Gospel of Mark, it is simply the hard and painful truth that some people are in essence good and others are not." There is, I think, an essentialist philosophy at work in Tolbert's literary analysis that leads her to dichotomize the typology presented in the parable of the sower. She identifies the gospel as a concrete universal, explaining that "in ancient thought, the moral significance of literature was derived from its ability to indicate the universality of the types of events, responses, or experiences depicted in it. Thus, Aristotle, for example, argued that poetry was closely related to philosophy in its presentation of the probable and necessary in accordance with universal laws. And although Plato himself ultimately decided to banish poets from the ideal republic, the force of the Platonic view that the tactile world was only a pale copy of the spiritual realm of essences, which alone was real, was to define the serious didactic task of the writer as the revelation of universal, spiritual reality in seemingly particularized, individual experiences. . . . Mark not surprisingly would stand closest to Wimsatt's arguments about Aristotle: the particular action with agents that forms the story line of the Gospel illustrates universal principles" (129 and 129.7). The philosophy adopted in the present Mahāyāna commentary rejects essentialism and sees Mark not as a representative of ancient Greek essentialism, but as doubling

Note that 4: 1–20 is a chiastic structure, moving from the parable of the sower (1–9) on to the disciples' request for explanation (10), and then on to the high point of the ring structure about how parables prevent understanding (11–12). It turns again to a reproof of the disciples, implying that they should indeed understand the parable (13), and then ends with Jesus' exposition of the parable (14–20). Only in the middle passage is the parable characterized as a mystery, riddle, or enigma. Elsewhere the parable is meant to be understood, as Jesus insists to the disciples.[26] The middle passage is warning the reader not to allegorize the parable into a simple typology, for that information leads nowhere. A parable not only opens up its meaning to those who are able to hear, but also conceals meaning from those who externalize their consciousness in the cultural symbols and codes of understanding available to them.[27] "Mark . . . has taken what is essential to the parable, the double-meaning effect, and made it the starting point of a theological theme concerning the audience's resistance to hearing the word,"[28] and that audience includes everybody, even the skilled exegete.

---

back to question such a mind-set at many points in his narrative, just as Jesus returns again and again to the task of instructing the crowds and the disciples.

26. Dewey, *Markan Public Debate,* 149.

27. Against Camery-Hoggatt, *Irony in Mark's Gospel,* 129: "As the narrative later turns against the disciples, as the reader with Jesus is called upon to judge the disciples themselves for their blindness (cf 14–21), he becomes closer than the disciples, closer even than the inner circle." And 130: "Mark's rhetorical strategies therefore come close to the surface here. By use of the rather sharp word of judgment he has reinforced and deepened the reader's sense of superiority over the story's characters and has done so in such a way that the reader identifies his deeper insight with the 'mystery of the Kingdom of God'." In disagreement, I hold that Mark has brought to the surface the reader's blindness, for she also is without a clue about the kingdom, knowing only that the disciples in the story do not understand it either. Mark has, I think, snookered the reader into a forced identification with those disciples/characters by teasing her into adopting a reified viewpoint, much as the disciples request in the story. I agree with Fowler, *Let the Reader Understand,* 169: "In retrospect, the verses immediately preceding 4: 13 begin to take on a new tone. Jesus may now appear to have been toying with the disciples all along, playing a cat-and-mouse game with them, or perhaps more to the point, the narrator has been playing with us." One may have to reevaluate the rhetorical sphere open to a narrator in Gospel times, for although it is held that the "unreliable narrator" came into existence only in the sixteenth century and therefore can be read back into a gospel text only as an unfounded anachronism (Boomershine, *Mark, the Storyteller,* 4.7, quoted in Dowd, *Prayer, Power, and the Problem of Suffering,* 31), yet here the narrator is indeed a tricky fellow! Bowker, "Mystery and Parable," 302, asks, "Would Jesus trick his listeners?" In a Mahāyāna context, the Buddha preaches through the employment of skillful means (*upāya*), sometimes leading his listeners on by promises and explanations not literally "true," yet effective for encouraging the practice of the path to awakening. See the parables in Hurvitz, tr. *The Lotus Scripture.* An entire hermeneutic developed to deal with the doctrine of scriptural validity expressed by such sūtras, for which see Asaṅga, *The Summary of the Great Vehicle,* tr. John P. Keenan, 46–47, and more broadly the essays in *Buddhist Hermeneutics,* ed. Donald Lopez.

28. Boucher, *The Mysterious Parable,* 83.

Explaining the Obvious
4: 13–20

[13]He said to them, "Do you not understand this parable? Then how will you understand any of the parables? [14]What the sower is sowing is the word. [15]Those on the edge of the path where the word is sown are people who have no sooner heard it than Satan at once comes and carries away the word that was sown in them. [16]Similarly, those who are sown on patches of rock are people who, when first they hear the word, welcome it at once with joy. [17]But they have no root deep down and do not last; should some trial come, or some persecution on account of the word, at once they fall away. [18]Then there are others who are sown in thorns. These have heard the word, [19]but the worries of the world, the lure of riches and all the other passions come in to choke the word, and so it produces nothing. [20]And there are those who have been sown in rich soil; they hear the word and accept it and yield a harvest, thirty and sixty and a hundredfold."

Jesus begins by criticizing the disciples. He has just said that to them "is granted the secret of the kingdom," yet they refuse to interpret the parable within the context of their own lives. Jesus provides an interpretation that may assist them, but that does not excuse them from the task of appropriating it for themselves.[29]

In their defense, it can be noted that Jesus' criticism precedes his interpretation of the parable of the sower.[30] But Jesus' criticism is not simply that they do not have the proper interpretation. Rather, in their pattern of non-understanding—refusing to internalize the parable—how could they understand anything? In that pattern of looking for the objective meaning of words out there, apart from the inner mind, they will always avoid the import of the parable. This parable constitutes Mark's hermeneutical key,[31] for it insists

29. Fowler, *Let the Reader Understand,* 184: "In keeping with the rhetoric of indirection, note that the interpretation of the parable in 4: 14–20 is far from clear: it too needs to be interpreted. The sower is said to sow 'the word' (*ho logos*). What on earth is that? 'The word' figures very nicely both the teaching of Jesus at story level and the narrator's discourse, and therefore 'the sower' might be taken as a metaphor for Jesus, for both simultaneously, or for still other sowers of words. Interpreting the sower metaphor by saying that the sower sows 'the word' merely introduces another metaphor that requires yet another effort at interpretation. An interpretation requires its own interpretation, especially if metaphor is used to interpret metaphor. The move from the parable of 4:1–9 to the interpretation of it in 4:14–20 is a paradigm of an endless reading and rereading process."

30. Fowler, *Mark and Method,* 71–72: "We observe that 4: 11 reveals a gap in the discourse of the Gospel. There Jesus says that his followers have 'been given the secret of the kingdom of God,' but the giving of that secret was never narrated."

31. Tolbert, *Sowing the Gospel,* 129: "The Sower, coming first in the narrative [before the other major typology of the Tenants] and additionally tagged by the character Jesus as the guide to understanding all the other parables (4: 13), offers a fairly generalized and universal typology of four different responses to hearing the word."

that parables cannot be understood simply by decoding their language.[32] Rather, one must interiorize their meaning in concrete practice. The parable of the sower focuses not on the seed, which remains constant, but on the ground that receives that seed, i.e., on the consciousness that hears the word of the gospel.

This is what Jesus' exposition of the content of the parable of the sower emphasizes. In order to germinate, a seed must be planted in good and deep soil, and likewise, the word must be planted in the depths of the minds of Jesus' followers. The presence and activity of the seeds that flow from awakened discourse, one of the principal Yogācāra metaphors for the hearing of doctrine, counter a consciousness which is occluded by karmic seeds, sown in the mind through the performance of deluded activity (*karma*) and structuring the pattern of its misunderstanding. These karmic seeds constitute the two obstacles to awakening. One is the obstacle of the passions (*kleśāvaraṇa*), the worries of this world and the lure of passions and riches. The other is the obstacle to knowledge (*jñeyāvaraṇa*), which prevents one from understanding that all meaning is empty of essence and in the end unobtainable. If doctrine is clung to as a set of ideas deemed to be true, it can scarcely withstand the attacks of Satan or the trials of persecution, for it has taken root only in shallow soil. Yet, the imagined pattern can be converted into the perfected pattern. One can gain deep insight into the emptiness of all doctrine, and thus into its dependently co-arisen meaning. Such a conversion takes place upon hearing the teaching, which itself plants seeds of awakening within the mind. The Yogācāra master Asaṅga speaks of this seed as a hearing [of doctrine] that flows from the realm of reality (*dharmadhātu-niṣyanda-śruta-vāsanābīja*). Such a hearing permeates (*vāsanā*) consciousness, leads toward the practice of the middle path, and issues in wisdom (*prajñā*), with its fruitful harvest of compassion (*karuṇā*). It is this deep structure of consciousness that Mark presents in the parable of the sower, not a secret lore that can be known through imagined clinging to words, for the gospel is not a viewpoint (*dṛṣṭi*) gained by intellectual manipulation. One must hear and receive the word within oneself (ἀκούουσιν τόν λόγον καὶ παραδέχονται) for it to bear fruit.

Among the four types of people depicted, the first are those whose practice is marginal, for they are at the edge of the path (οἱ παρὰ τὴν ὁδόν). Examples

---

32. Against Hamerton-Kelly, *The Gospel and the Sacred*, 87: "The reason why three quarters of the hearers of the parable and readers of the Gospel do not understand and accept the word is that they are in thrall to the Sacred and its mythology, which can be decoded only in the light of the cross." To regard the sacred as an essentially fixed ideology serving only to justify scapegoating and violence leads one to imagine an opposing decoded ideology of the cross as only the rejection of that sacred violence. Violence is indeed to be rejected and any notion of the sacred that serves to justify it is to be abandoned. Yet, the tensive interplay is not between competing ideologies, but the dynamic tension of living in the middle path.

are perhaps Judas or the authorities. They indeed hear the word, but dismiss it forthwith, for they do not practice the path at all.

Those symbolized by the patches of rock welcome the word, but their minds are occluded by the obstacle to understanding. Their awareness of the implications of the word is shallow, because it is rooted only in their own defiled thinking. They believe in the word because it is a path toward glory and power. And so when that glory and power is threatened, they immediately fall away (εὐθὺς σκανδαλίζονται). Mark here alludes to Jesus' words in 14: 27 that all his disciples will fall away (πάντες σκανδαλισθήσεσθε) and Peter's boastful rebuttal that he at least will never fall away. Peter's underlying storehouse consciousness (ālaya-vijñāna), that "ground repository" of the seeds of all previous actions, remains unconverted and thus still habitually enmeshed in delusion, even though he is following Jesus' path. The word has permeated only his thoughts, not his basic orientations. He is the prime example of such rocky ground, even being nicknamed "Rocky" (3: 16).[33]

Those in whom the seed-word is strangled by thorns are those occluded by the obstacle of the passions, as the text itself says. They mistake things for meaning, and cling to outer objects as if they provided an inner stability. The word, by contrast, promises no stability at all. Rather, the practice of the path entails insight into the emptiness of all things and thus of all the passions for wealth, power, or pleasure.

By contrast, the good earth are those whose consciousness is thoroughly permeated by the seed of the gospel. Their deep minds are turned around and opened to the gospel word, as well as their thoughts and images. Not occluded by false images of power or passion, they nurture the seed and produce the fruits of awakening.

These typologies are not merely mnemonic devices so "the audience can interpret correctly the general point being illustrated in each episode or by each group of characters as the story progresses."[34] That would make their impact upon the implied reader a matter of personal unconcern. Rather, the Markan Jesus' point is to depict responses anyone can make, even those identified socially as disciples of Jesus' path. All four types represent Mark's audience.

A Parable of Light
4: 21–23

[21]*He also said to them, "Is a lamp brought in to be put under a tub or under the bed? Surely to be put on the lamp-stand?* [22]*For there is nothing hidden,*

---

33. Tolbert, *Sowing the Gospel,* 145: "The first disciple listed, Simon, whose name is additionally set off from the rest grammatically, is nicknamed 'Peter' (Πέτρος) by Jesus, but the narrator gives no further elaboration [here at 3: 16]. The explanation of the nickname will come in the parable of the Sower when the second type of ground upon which the seed is sown is described as πετρώδης (καὶ ἄλλο ἔπεσεν ἐπὶ τὸ πετρῶδες, 4: 5). Simon Πέτρος, Simon the 'Rock,' signals the basic relationship of the disciples to the πετρώδης, the 'rocky' ground."

34. Tolbert, *Sowing the Gospel,* 128.

but it must be disclosed, nothing kept secret except to be brought to light.
²³Anyone who has ears for listening should listen."

Jesus had ended the parable of the sower with the call for those who have
ears to listen. When asked what it meant, he responded with the enigmatic
words about using parables to occlude understanding. Here he repeats the
words about the people with ears, and claims that everything is perfectly
clear, for there are no secrets![35] There is no secret meaning that can be guarded
and preserved; that is why the actual giving of the secret to the disciples is
never recorded by Mark. There is no point to any mysterious knowledge that
remains mysterious. Everything is open and shining for all to see.

If one places a candle under a tub, a peck-measure, the light will go out.
If under the bed, the whole house will burn down. A light is to be placed
on the lamp-stand, where it will be of use. Verse 4: 12 spoke about parables
as intended (ἵνα) to prevent listeners from understanding. Here things are
kept secret only to be (ἵνα) revealed. Mark is doubling back upon the former
statement, to highlight the revelatory power of that which is secret: it reveals
inasmuch as it hides.[36] Yet, despite nothing being hidden, truth is occluded

---

35. Noting the chiastic structure of 4: 2b–20 (a: 2b–9, the parable of the sower; b: 10,
the disciples' question; c: 11–12, the sayings about the hidden mystery and the nature of
parable; b: reproof of the disciples' misunderstanding, and á: interpretation of the parable
of the sower), Dewey, *Markan Public Debate,* 149, notes: "This rhetorical structure brings
out the contrast between the idea presented in the center (c), that parables are a mystery
in need of explanation, and the idea in the remainder of this narrative (which reads
smoothly without the interposition of c), that parables are intended to be understood."
The point is stressed, as if to avoid any possible confusion, immediately after the chiastic
ring, in the present passage: nothing is hidden at all, and so nobody has to be excluded.
Looking back to 4: 11, breathing a sigh of relief, one can conclude with Fowler, *Mark
and Method,* 72 that 4: 11–12 is ironic: "Jesus uses parables with the express purpose of
keeping people from understanding them. Otherwise they would turn their lives around
and receive forgiveness, and we would not want that, would we? Of course we would!
If taken literally, however, this is the logic of 4: 12, and it strikes us as absurd. (Thus
step 1 in the process of reconstructing irony is invoked: the literal meaning of 4: 12 is
nonsense.) But maybe we should not take it literally (step 3—surely both Mark and his
protagonist Jesus want to have an impact on their respective audiences, so that they will
turn their lives around; see Mark 1: 1 and 1: 15). Could Jesus be speaking with tongue
in cheek throughout 4: 11–12, teasing his disciples (step 2)?"
36. Kermode, *The Genesis of Secrecy,* 28: "To perceive the radiance of the shrine (in
Kafka's *The Trial*) is not to gain access to it; the Law, or the Kingdom, may, to those
within, be powerful and beautiful, but to those outside they are merely terrible; absolutely
inexplicable, they torment the inquirer with legalisms. This is a mystery; Mark, and
Kafka's doorkeeper, protect it without understanding it, and those outside, like K, and
like us, see an uninterpretable radiance and die." To the point, Nagao, *The Foundational
Standpoint,* 66: "Thus, emptiness consists in a single, absolute denial and negation of the
entire worldly and conventional dimension of discourse that seeks to validate the reality
of countless competing truth claims." And 78: "The true path is the path that is originally
not a path. The path that is a path is not the true path, since ultimate meaning is truly
and ultimately meaningful only because all verbal, conditioned methods remain closed
to it. The destiny of one following the path consists in knocking repeatedly at a door that
remains eternally unopened, in waiting expectantly, even in despair, before that unopened

from the imagined pattern of understanding. Even when that imagined pattern is rejected in awakened wisdom, the ultimate truth cannot be expressed or manifested by any conventions whatsoever. Even here one is aware of the otherness of truth, marked by the veiling curtain of revelatory silence. Even to an awakened buddha, ultimate meaning remains completely other. The meaning of parables, then, is not to reveal ultimate truth, but simply (and profoundly) to illumine conventional practice of the path within the other-dependent pattern of understanding, to allow the gospel seeds to germinate within one's mind. The maturation of the gospel seeds refers to the ability to regain that other-dependent pattern, freed from clinging to imagined realities. This parable of the light is a parable on parables, for parabolic teaching takes on its meaning in the dependently co-arisen context of its hearers. Again the tension between imagined patterns and other-dependent patterns of consciousness is highlighted. The disciples expect that the meaning of parables will be imparted in a once-and-for-all manner to their karmically defiled consciousnesses, rather than in their concrete hearing of the simple word calling for conversion (1: 15). Faith understanding comes not from beholding in a vision the divine verities, but from listening with the ears, from regaining the original other-dependent pattern of understanding and personally appropriating the consciousness of Christ, both ultimate in its desert emptiness and conventional in its verbal presentations.[37]

A Parable on Standards
4: 24–25

[24]*He also said to them, "Take notice of what you are hearing. The standard you use will be used for you—and you will receive more besides;* [25]*anyone who has, will be given more; anyone who has not, will be deprived even of what he has."*

The initial phrase "Take notice of what you are hearing" entails a mixing of sense perceptions, for the text literally says "look at what you hear" (βλέπετε τί ἀκούετε). It is as if Jesus' advice is not to trust perceptions from any single sense which seem to reflect the way things actually are. Take notice of the way you hear parables. Do not only hear, but look. Do not only look, but listen.[38] The advice is to keep one's eyes open, to be consciously

---

door, in the pilgrimage of knocking again and again." The Japanese, too, it seems, are familiar with Kafka!

37. Kermode, *The Genesis of Secrecy,* 126: "What must not be looked for is some obvious public success. To see, even to perceive, to hear, even to understand, is not the same thing as to explain or even the same thing as to have access."

38. *Chuang Tzu,* Watson tr., 57–58: "Make your will one! Don't listen with your ears, listen with your mind. No, don't listen with your mind, but listen with your spirit. Listening stops with the ears, the mind stops with recognition, but spirit is empty and waits on all things. The Way gathers in emptiness alone. Emptiness is the fasting of the mind."

awake, not just to reify the words heard into their supposed referents. Later in the narrative, Mark's Jesus frequently enjoins watchfulness upon his drowsy disciples. They are to wake up and not sleep in the dreams of delusion. Here, Jesus is recommending that his disciples abandon the discriminative knowledge they employ to wrest "objective" meaning from his parables, employing it as a bulwark to prop up their "subjective" selves. They size up, measure out, and standardize (μετρεῖτε) that meaning in terms of imagined units (ἐν ᾧ μέτρῳ), and that is just what they get back (μετρηθήσεται). In computer language, garbage in, garbage out! Thus, their understanding is limited by their pattern of understanding, for that same pattern acts as a grid or standard which determines what they understand. "The measure one brings to hearing conditions the measure of understanding one gets."[39]

The entirety of Chapter Four is about how one is to understand revelation and doctrine, not about the content of what is understood. "The correlations of blindness and seeing, lack of hearing and full comprehension, an opaque life 'in parables' and enlightenment in private sessions move us into the theological orbit of hiddenness and revelation which is at the core of the messianic secret."[40] But that secret is not a special bit of knowledge, but the very minds of the listeners. One is to understand by listening with one's ears, with one's original other-dependent mind, to the parabolic discourse of Jesus about the hidden things that, while remaining hidden, are made manifest. One who listens with a mind opened to the meanings Jesus constructs in parable is not limited in what she will receive, while one not so open will lose even that which she thinks she has, for discriminative knowledge fails at every turn to understand Jesus' parabolic discourse.[41]

Spontaneous Growth
4: 26–29

[26]*He also said, "This is what the kingdom of God is like. A man scatters seed on the land.* [27]*Night and day, while he sleeps, when he is awake, the seed is sprouting and growing; how, he does not know.* [28]*Of its own accord the land produces first the shoot, then the ear, then the full grain in the ear.* [29]*And when the crop is ready, at once he starts to reap because the harvest has come."*

Jesus came out from the wilderness to preach the arrival of the kingdom of God. That is the content of his good news (1: 15). And yet, the kingdom

---

39. Via, *The Ethics of Mark's Gospel,* 185.
40. Kelber, *The Kingdom in Mark,* 35.
41. Kermode, *The Genesis of Secrecy,* 241: "Parables are stories, insofar as they *are* stories, which are not to be taken at face value, and bear various indications to make this condition plain to the interpreter; so the other scale is a measure of their darkness. Some are apparently almost entirely transparent; some are obscure." The measure of a true understanding entails a guarding of that darkness and obscurity, for parables take on concrete meaning only in the varied contexts of individual lives.

is not any specific viewpoint to which one must adhere. Rather, the kingdom refers to the transcendent, eschatological mystery of inner conversion that is both the source for conversion and faith and the frame for the above discourse about the sower. More immediately, the kingdom refers to the understanding of the three preceding parables, of the seed, the light, and the standard. The mind in which the kingdom grows is not engaged in minute observation and judgment about the meaning of the parables. Rather, while one is engaged in other things, awareness grows spontaneously (αὐτομάτη), from stage to stage, without the person's being aware of it at all (ὡς οὐκ οἶδεν αὐτός).[42] The awareness of the secret is not something that one can communicate verbally. As the seeds from hearing doctrine permeate the mind, awareness shifts. The attempt to capture reality is abandoned and emptiness is understood. Only then does one become aware of the mystery—that the mystery lies already present at the depth of our own consciousness.[43]

Yet, this does not mean that the mind is originally and already awakened. The seed comes from hearing doctrine and grows spontaneously, aiding in the recovery and restoration of the original dependently co-arisen structure of consciousness. That other-dependent pattern of consciousness is what has been present from the beginning of creation, albeit covered over and occluded by false imagining. Yet, by abandoning those delusions and emptying the mind of its cherished adherence to images and words, one becomes able both to maintain silence in the presence of Abba and to reengage in the world of conventional affairs and tasks.

The last sentence of the passage alludes to *Joel* 4: 12–13, where the prophet announces Yahweh's promise of renewal and salvation for all peoples, proclaiming that the Lord comes to render judgment upon the nations. That passage has Yahweh proclaim: "Let the nations rouse themselves and march to the Valley of Jehoshaphat, for there I shall sit in judgment on all the nations around. Ply the sickle, for the harvest is ripe." Mark's phrase for "at once he starts to reap because the harvest is come" is literally "he puts in the sickle (ἀποστέλλει τὸ δρέπανον) because the harvest is come." Yet, here the harvest of judgment does not come about because of the external pronouncement of the Lord, but spontaneously, from the inner growth of the seed activity beyond the limits of discriminative knowing. It is a process of growth, not merely of personal awakening, but of the growth of the kingdom itself.[44]

---

42. Tolbert, *Sowing the Gospel,* 161: "Productive earth, the good earth, produces on its own, as the repetitions of seed (σπόρος, vv. 26 and 27) and earth (γῆ, vv. 26 and 28) emphasize."

43. Via, *The Ethics of Mark's Gospel,* 186: "Where does this 'of itself' come from? Within Mark's frame of reference could it be other than a trace of the beginning of creation before hardness of heart set in (10: 5–9), a trace of the primordial nature which is now being restored eschatologically?"

44. Kee, *Community of the New Age,* 108: "The secret of the kingdom is not, however, the time when the consummation will take place; indeed the day of redemption is known only to God (13: 32). The kingdom . . . is a present reality as well as an event awaited in the future. It is characterized by growth and conflict; it must be entered or received

In the Pure Land tradition of Mahāyāna one must receive the mind of faith (*shinjin*) by abandoning any self-powered (*tariki*) attempt to calculate (*hakarai*) the nature of faith and its timing. Grace comes spontaneously in the abatement of all attempts to manipulate things. So, here "a seed has been sown, the inaugural program (1: 14–15) stands confirmed, and the Kingdom has indeed become a reality. But as the seed will yet have to grow to become the tree it was intended to be, so will likewise the Kingdom arrive at its prime time only after having accomplished the passage through the middle time."[45] That middle time is, in Mahāyāna, the practice of the middle path, focused not on grasping or attachment to religious ideals, but on the embodiment of compassion and kindness in society. This is a most ordinary kingdom that comes, without fanfare and without empirical verification. "After the farmer has sown the seed, he settles down to live the rhythm of an ordinary life (4: 27a). In the meantime the seed ripens, grows, and develops into a cornstalk without the farmer's agency. Not only does the farmer not intervene on behalf of the corn, but the whole development is said to elude his comprehension (4: 27b). He initiated a process which now runs 'of its own accord' (4: 28a: *automatē*)."[46] The return to the ordinary is, I think, a major theme of Mark, for Jesus after he rises, returns to the ordinary life of Galilee, inviting his disciples to join him there in that everyday practice of the kingdom.[47]

Mustard Seed Parable
4: 30–32

[30]*He also said, "What can we say the kingdom of God is like? What parable can we find for it?* [31]*It is like a mustard seed which, at the time of its sowing, is the smallest of all the seeds on earth.* [32]*Yet once it is sown it grows into the biggest shrub of them all and puts out big branches so that the birds of the air can shelter in its shade."*

The theme continues. How do we understand the mystery of the kingdom? Through comparisons and parables, not through imagined adherence to frozen images. There is no correct view on what constitutes the mystery, for that

---

(4: 26–30; 3: 24; 13: 8; 9: 47; 10: 23–25; 12: 34). In the parables of Mark 4—or rather, in the Markan interpretation of those parables—the kingdom is explicitly compared with growth phenomena, especially with seeds and plants in progress of maturation and productivity."

45. Kelber, *The Kingdom in Mark*, 41.
46. Kelber, *The Kingdom in Mark*, 39.
47. Kelber, *The Kingdom in Mark*, 46, remarks that "for all of the importance Mark attaches to Galilee, his full concept of Galilee, or 'all of Galilee' still remains strangely obscure." I take that obscurity to refer to the simple engagement in everyday life, awakened by Jesus' wilderness spirituality to reengage in the conventional world to perform the deeds of the compassionate kingdom.

mystery is known only when it is identified within the personal consciousnesses of its hearers. It evolves, as does the mustard seed, for it is not an
inner or outer essence waiting to be uncovered.

The mustard shrub recalls images of the grand establishment of God's
kingdom in the Hebrew scriptures, as in *Ezekiel* 17: 22–24.[48] But it refers
not to a grand cedar tree, but to edible garden herbs or vegetables. Crossan
comments: "The mustard seed can grow only into a bush or shrub, and, at
its very best, is hardly competition for the Lebanese cedar. When one starts
a parable with a mustard seed one cannot end it with a tree, much less the
great apocalyptic tree, unless of course one intends to lampoon . . . the whole
apocalyptic tradition. I am thus in complete agreement with Brandon Scott . . .
who thinks that this story 'calls into question and burlesques the expectation of
the kingdom under the symbol of the cedar or apocalyptic tree'."[49] The
Markan choice of the image of the mustard shrub suggests to the reader who
has ears to listen that the kingdom is a garden variety kingdom, an everyday
affair of cultivation and sweat. This image provides the context for subsequent
discourse about the kingdom, which warns the reader not to erect a glorified
imaginary kingdom where Jesus' followers always win and have the eschatological upper hand.

Although the seed grows spontaneously, it must be both planted and tended.
All the images about seeds and growth refer to the work of gardening and
farming, not to simply bumping into full grown awareness while sitting in
a forest dale. The seed word of the gospel will not grow unless it finds good
soil. That good soil is that consciousness which through hearing is permeated
by the meaning of doctrine and recovers its originally dependently co-
arisen nature.[50]

---

48. Heil, *The Gospel of Mark as a Model for Action,* 111: "The global and universal
significance of the full grown mustard plant is confirmed by its allusion to several Old
Testament passages in which a great tree symbolizes a kingdom which provides protection
for *all* the birds, *all* the beasts, *all* the peoples of the world. In Ezekiel 17: 23 the restored
kingdom of David is compared to a tree which has become so 'great' that 'under its
shade' (see 4: 32) 'every bird' will rest."

49. Crossan, *The Historical Jesus,* 277, repeating *In Parables,* 48. The reference is to
Scott, *Hear Then the Parable,* 386.

50. Tolbert, *Sowing the Gospel,* 162: "How does the mustard seed become the bushy
refuge of the birds of heaven? *By being sown in the earth.* The power of the earth makes
the difference. . . . the creative power of the earth. Such powerful earth is the kingdom
of God, and those who hear the word, accept it, and bear fruit are its human manifestations.
They are the ground of God. Jesus, in preaching the word, does not create them or convert
them; he *reveals* them." Again 163: "Hence, the sowing-earth or hearing-response typology,
as the Gospel of Mark defines it, is a typology of disclosure and interaction, rather than
conversion and dominance." If conversion is understood as dominance, then Tolbert's
interpretation is valid. Yet, the initial message of Jesus about the arrival of the kingdom
is indeed directed toward conversion (μετάνοια). This conversion is not acceptance of
the power of doctrine, but the manifestation and recovery of the occluded yet originally
present other-dependent mind. It is indeed a disclosure, one which occurs because of conversion.

Doctrine as Parable
4: 33–34

[33]*Using many parables like these, he spoke the word to them, so far as they were capable of understanding it.* [34]*He would not speak to them except in parables, but he unraveled*[51] *everything to his disciples when they were by themselves.*

Jesus spoke the word (ἐλάλει τὸν λόγον) to his disciples and the surrounding crowds. His teaching was not without content. That content of his word, however, is not presented as a viewpoint about reality or a perspective on life.[52] The Greeks differentiated between the inner word and the spoken word, the latter making the former manifest. Jesus' speaking brings the experience of the kingdom to manifesting speech, without presenting a verbal account of things.

Words have two functions in Mark. In the mouths of Jesus' disciples and his opponents, they are human constructs, although not recognized as such by their speakers. In the imagined pattern, words are taken as pictorial roadways to essences and placed as real over against the putative reality of the speaker. In the mouth of Jesus words are recognized as constructs only (*vijñapti-mātra*), and that is why he speaks in parables, trying again and again to express incisively what cannot be expressed at all: the experience of conversion and the silent awareness of the wilderness. His words spontaneously emerge from such awareness and lead others through the challenge and paradox of parable speech to like experiences and like awarenesses.

Jesus does not program his speech. Rather, he teaches in parable "so far as they were capable of understanding" (καθὼς ἠδύναντο ἀκούειν). "Jesus transmits his *logos* 'as they could hear' or 'in proportion to their capacity.'"[53] Because of the Mahāyāna doctrine of emptiness, all teaching is described as *upāya*, skillful methods of approaching sentient beings with doctrine that is fitted to their capabilities. Here, Jesus employs skillful methods, for he too moves within a world of experiences empty of any final essential identification. Yet because of that emptiness, he engages in constructing dependently co-arisen stories to elicit awakening on the part of those who listen.

---

51. Taking ἐπέλυεν in its literal sense, of "to loosen, set free, or unravel."

52. Fowler, *Let the Reader Understand,* 214: "Mark 4: 34 points to something else that happens frequently in the discourse of the Gospel. Not only are we regularly deprived of almost all of Jesus' (presumed) private interpretations of his parabolic teachings but also in the first half of the Gospel we are usually cut off from the content of the teaching itself. The scholarly literature notes this absence as a curiosity; referentially oriented critics are at a loss to know what to do with elements of the story that are alluded to in a narrative but not actually narrated."

53. Kelber, *The Kingdom in Mark,* 33.

There have been some scholars who think that Mark exaggerates about Jesus' teaching only in parable.[54] Yet, if we understand this to mean that Jesus models his words on the capacities of his hearers, i.e., that he teaches through skillful methods, then his parable style is indeed appropriate. If one conceives of words as a verbal presentation of truth, then Mark does indeed present problems, for he does not report Jesus as offering such presentations. Rather, he makes it a hermeneutical principle that, whatever Jesus teaches, he does so in parable.

Thus, the last sentence from verse 34b, "but he explained everything to his disciples when they were alone," must not be taken to counter Jesus' parable methods. Jesus does not, and indeed cannot, reduce parable teaching to a few clear words. Yet, neither his disciples nor the crowd understand, for his parable speaking counters imagined patterns of understanding. Thus the present section reinforces 4: 11–12, where parables are intended to prevent understanding. "So to speak the word to the crowd in parables as they were able to hear it means to speak to them what they could not understand."[55] Yet, that very obfuscation is in the service of bringing all secrets to light, for it is aimed at disenabling deluded thinking with its standards of objective reality.

Jesus does, however, unravel the inner sense of his teachings; the verb usually translated as "he explained" (ἐπέλυεν) in verse 34 literally means "to loosen, set free, or unravel." Here, it would seem, this meaning is most appropriate, for he attempts to set free their understanding by turning them away from objectifying speech to a careful listening to teaching and a personal appropriation of it. The content of these private sessions is not reported, for it is not a content that can be reported. Rather, Jesus' efforts were to further the purpose of the parable itself, to bring his disciples to moments of existential choice.

In a similar vein, the Yogācāra thinkers spoke the Buddha's twilight speech, the intent of which was not contained in the words themselves, but in their underlying intent. Thus one of the basic Yogācāra scriptures is entitled *The Explication of Underlying Meaning (Saṃdhinirmocana)*, for no literal reading is adequate to realize the meaning of the scriptures. Thus the Buddha is depicted as himself explicating or unraveling (*nirmocana*) the meaning of the scriptures, just as Jesus here must unravel everything for his disciples. Yet, even then, there is no guarantee that they will understand. In fact, they do not, and constantly counter his parable speech with their attachments to the putative realities of self-centered language. One "begins to doubt the perspicacity of the disciples,"[56] not because they are lacking in intelligence,

---

54. Grant, *Interpreter's Bible*, 7: 708, on verse 34: "*He did not speak to them without a parable* seems exaggerated, in view of the other traditions of Jesus' teaching."

55. Dewey, *Markan Public Debate*, 150–51. Kelber, *The Kingdom in Mark*, 34: "The *choris parabolēs* in 4: 34a will likewise point to the *logos'* being darkened by a film of incomprehensibility. . . ."

56. Tolbert, *Sowing the Gospel*, 101.

but because they have too much intelligence, functioning in patterns of deluded understanding.

The division between Jesus' wilderness awakening and the disciples' town-bound knowledge increases throughout the gospel. "The earth is divided into Satan's realm and God's."[57] Yet both realms, however mythically described, are located within the ground of human consciousness. Other-dependent consciousness is characterized by a twofold process: its initial proclivity to grasp images and ideas as it seeks security in a radically impermanent world and, upon awakened conversion, its recovery of the original purity of joy and zest in celebrating that very impermanence. What liberates is recognition that at the very base of our being, all is empty and nothing is solid, for thereupon one regains true human practice in the world just as it is.

A Calming Parable
4: 35–41

[35]*With the coming of evening that same day, he said to them, "Let us cross over to the other side." [36]And leaving the crowd behind they took him, just as he was, in the boat; and there were other boats with him. [37]Then it began to blow a gale and the waves were breaking into the boat so that it was almost swamped. [38]But he was in the stern, his head on a cushion, asleep. [39]They woke him and said to him, "Master, do you not care? We are lost!" And he woke up and rebuked the wind and said to the sea, "Quiet now! Be calm!" And the wind dropped, and there followed a great calm. [40]Then he said to them, "Why are you such cowards? Have you still no faith?" [41]They were frightened with a great fear [58]and said to one another, "Who can this be? Even the wind and the sea obey him."*

The parable discourse continues. The raging sea is a metaphor for the troubled mind,[59] the mind described in the Epistle of James as discriminative, being in two minds (*James* 1: 5–8).[60] The passage is modeled on *Psalm* 107: 23–25: "They cried to the Lord in their trouble, and he brought them out of their distress; he made the storm be still, and the waves of the sea were hushed." In Mark, however, that storming sea is the mind that cannot listen

---

57. Tolbert, *Sowing the Gospel*, 163.

58. Following Kelber's translation, *Mark's Story of Jesus*, 30–31.

59. Malbon, *Narrative Space*, 77: "As frequently depicted in the imagery of the Psalms, the sea, the wind, the storm are under the power of God. To still the storm and save those in danger is also the power of the Lord (Psalm 107: 23–32). But this is what Jesus does on the first crossing, rebuking the stormy sea as he earlier rebuked an unclean spirit (4: 39, paralleling 1: 25, *phimousthai*, 'to be silent,' cf Psalms 104: 7; 106: 9; 107: 29)." To be under the power of God means that this stormy sea is not under the control of the fishermen/disciples.

60. See Keenan, *The Meaning of Christ*, 34–35.

to parables, contrasted with the mind of faith, which can abide in the tension of parabolic consciousness, without the need to find firm footing in any imagined metaphysically solid land. Parables leave one at sea and deprive one of accustomed footings. They threaten the accustomed ordering of conventional life.[61] Thus, Jesus says "Let us cross over to the other side" (διέλθω-μεν εἰς τὸ πέραν), "pioneer(ing) the breakthrough journey toward new shores."[62] The expression here is fortuitously parallel to the Mahāyāna notion of the perfection of wisdom (*prajñā-pāramitā*), where perfection (*pāramitā*) literally means "the other shore." This Mahāyāna image is that wisdom passes beyond the conventional world to the far shore of emptiness, from whence it returns to engage in the conventional tasks of compassion, for even that far shore is empty of any solid and fixed meaning. Any security found on this side or imagined on the other side disappears into an abyss of nothingness.[63]

Jesus set out on his world journey, leaving behind all social identity markers and group definitions. This first of Jesus' sea crossings begins a series of crossings that depicts his activity through 5: 43, an activity which encompasses all kinds of people, Jews and Gentiles, men and women, within the purview of his compassionate preaching of the coming kingdom. His Galilean time in Capernaum comes to an end. But he does not withdraw, for the crossing to the other side is not merely a crossing to the transcendent wisdom of the wilderness, but an active engagement in another world of conventional reality.

Jesus is already sitting in the boat, for he has been teaching parables there from the beginning of the chapter. The disciples take him, just as he is (αὐτὸν ὡς ἦν), toward the other side, without going back to the shore. In Mahāyāna parlance, awakening is described as the realization of suchness *(tathatā)*, awareness of reality "just as it is." Here Jesus embodies suchness in his parabolic story telling, and, just as he is, begins his journeying not with a plan of action or a defined strategy.

Other boats are said to accompany him out onto the raging sea. The account is hardly historical report; no mention is made of the fate of the other boats. In a historical report one would want to know what Jesus did for these other boatloads of people. But Mark is not interested in reporting events. He is engaged in talking about parables, about how they calm the raging sea of discriminative consciousness. If indeed meaning is not a property of things, then the discriminative quest to find objects which will bring happiness cannot but invite the grief of failure. That kind of mind is described as the monkey mind, forever jumping from one thing to another, as the monkey moves incessantly from branch to branch.

The disciples react to the raging chaos not by calming their minds, for they lack faith insight. Rather, they are filled with a great fear (ἐφοβήθησαν

---

61. Via, *The Ethics of Mark's Gospel*, 107–08: "The sea symbolizes the chaos monster which Yahweh had to subdue in order to bring an orderly cosmos out of chaos." In Mark the parables create chaos to the deluded ordering of the disciples' understanding.

62. Kelber, *The Kingdom in Mark*, 50.

63. See Nishitani, "What is Religion?" in *Religion and Nothingness*, 1–45.

φόβον μέγαν) and try once again to fit Jesus, who himself is now the
parable, into their framework. They wonder just who he is. "The disciples
have not even begun to fathom the person whom they call 'teacher' in their
time of peril."[64] They cling to dysfunctional attempts at definition. Their final
question "must be viewed as a statement made in lack of faith. It is out of
fear and lack of understanding that they confess the lordship of Jesus over
nature."[65] They want to define Jesus as a miracle-worker, but any definition
is beside the point, even, as will become apparent, Mark's initial identification
of Jesus as the messiah. Here, after the storm is quieted, the disciples begin
to see him as a wondrously divine being, with power over the sea and wind.
"They treat him as an epiphany of the *mysterium augustum, tremendum, et
fascinans* rather than as a symbol of the wilderness wandering far from sacred
centers, and as a result their hearts are hardened."[66] Yet, it is simply Jesus,
just as he is, asking them why they are such cowards, why they yet have no
faith. The alternatives are fear and faith.[67] Their tempestuous minds seek a
solid and secure haven from the radical impermanence of life's journeying,
and they rebuke Jesus for being asleep and not joining in their efforts at self-
help. But the Markan Jesus again counters the disciples' standardized grasp
of reality, just as the earlier parables doubled back upon the patterns of their
understanding. The calming of the sea is yet another parable, suggesting that
faith affords one security over the sea of demonic chaos by abandoning
security.[68] It is a miracle story aimed at inner wisdom transformation.[69] "Mark

---

64. Fowler, *Loaves and Fishes,* 102. Also *Let the Reader Understand,* 133: " 'Who
then is this?' is a question that remains open for the reader and the disciples alike in the
course of the telling of the story (e.g., at 4:41), and it may still be open at story's end.
Mark's Gospel is designed to ask and to keep open this one all-important question; it
resists the temptation to answer the question once and for all. The Gospel seems to be
designed to present Jesus with question marks rather than with periods or exclamation
marks. Mark wants to acquaint us with a Jesus who defies familiarity; that is, Mark
'defamiliarizes' Jesus for us." In Mahāyāna terms, Mark empties Jesus of any set definition.
65. Kelber, *The Kingdom in Mark,* 50, which continues: "[The story] will have to be
considered not as a sea miracle which manifests the power of Jesus, but as a mysterious
crossing which is misunderstood by the disciples as a sea miracle."
66. Hamerton-Kelly, *The Gospel and the Sacred,* 63.
67. Camery-Hoggatt, *Irony in Mark's Gospel,* 130–31: "A careful reader can scarcely
avoid the ways Mark has underscored the befuddlement of the disciples in this pericope.
The fact that they are terrified by Jesus' power is paradoxical: they are more afraid of
the peace in the boat than they were of the storm in the sea. That the disciples do not
understand the power of the peace is evident from their final question: 'Who then is
this . . . ?' (v. 41). In this way Mark makes it clear that their reason for waking Jesus
in v. 38 reflected a purely practical urgency: they wanted him to bail water, or some
such thing."
68. Mauser, *Christ in the Wilderness,* "ἐπιτιμάφ ('rebuked' in 39) is used to express
Jesus' superior command to demons in 1.25, 3.12, and 9.25. The sea is enjoined to obey
in the words, 'silent, [be still]' (σιώπα, πεφίμωσο), again reminiscent of the terms in
a demon story (φιμώθητι, 1.25). The sea obeys as the demons obey and this results in
a great stillness (4.39)."
69. Heil, *The Gospel of Mark as a Model for Action,* 116: "In Wisdom 14:1–4, for

adapts and uses miracle stories to illustrate a theological program. The miraculous physical transformations of the healings are only the outward manifestations of a condition of the heart characterized as faith in the gospel and faith, as the parable of the Sower indicates, is an immediate response to hearing the word which results in mighty works."[70] That immediate response of faith is grounded in a recovery of the original mind that recognizes without fear the absence of any support for selfhood in a radically impermanent world. And that is what the disciples are loath to recognize. Their response is fear for their own well-being and, consequently, a view of Jesus as a messiah who might deliver them from such fear. And so the sea he is really trying to calm remains troubled by fear and self-clinging. The disciples want to be insiders, true disciples of Jesus.[71] Yet the only way to do that is to get inside one's own heart and realize the parabolic wisdom of the Markan Jesus. Although Mark says that Jesus habitually explains his parables to his disciples, in the story only rarely does that occur. "Jesus does not interpret many of his parables in Mark because the narrator wants that to become the narratee's 'response-ability.' "[72]

example, God's power to bring a boat safely through the raging waves shows that he 'can save from every danger.' "

70. Tolbert, *Sowing the Gospel,* 177.

71. Moore, *Mark and Method,* 88: "What distinguishes disciples from outsiders is that disciples long to be inside, to *be* the insiders they are said to be."

72. Fowler, *Let the Reader Understand,* 183.

5

The Differentiation of the Two Truths

¹They reached the territory of the Gerasenes on the other side of the sea, ²and when he disembarked, a man with an unclean spirit at once came out from the tombs towards him. ³The man lived in the tombs and no one could secure him any more, even with a chain; ⁴because he had often been secured with fetters and chains but had snapped the chains and broken the fetters, and no one had the strength to control him. ⁵All night and all day, among the tombs and in the mountains, he would howl and gash himself with stones. ⁶Catching sight of Jesus from a distance, he ran up and fell at his feet ⁷and shouted at the top of his voice, "What do you want with me, Jesus, son of the Most High God? In God's name do not torture me!" ⁸For Jesus had been saying to him, "Come out of the man, unclean spirit." ⁹Then he asked, "What is your name?" He answered, "My name is Legion, for there are many of us." ¹⁰And he begged him earnestly not to send them out of the district. ¹¹Now near the mountain¹ there was a great herd of pigs feeding, ¹²and the unclean spirits begged him, "Send us to the pigs, let us go into them." ¹³So he gave them leave. With that, the unclean spirits came out and went into the pigs, and the herd of about two thousand pigs charged down the cliff into the sea, and there they were drowned. ¹⁴The men looking after them ran off and told their story in the city and in the country round about; and the people came to see what had really happened. ¹⁵They came to Jesus and saw the demoniac sitting there—the man who had had the legion in him—properly dressed and in his full senses, and they were afraid. ¹⁶And those who had witnessed it

---

1. Following Malbon, *Narrative Space*, 84: "The demons are sent into a herd of swine 'near the mountain' (5:11, my translation of *pros tō orie*)." That seems more likely, since swine are not mountain animals.

reported what had happened to the demoniac and what had become of the pigs. [17]Then they began to implore Jesus to leave the neighborhood. [18]As he was getting into the boat, the man who had been possessed begged to be allowed to stay with him. [19]Jesus would not let him but said to him, "Go home to your people and tell them all that the Lord in his mercy has done for you." [20]So the man went off and proceeded to proclaim in the Decapolis all that Jesus had done for him. And everyone was amazed.

In the opening account of Jesus' public activity, he performed an exorcism in the Capernaum synagogue (1:·21–28). Here he moves into Gentile country, at least symbolically, on the eastern shore of the Sea of Galilee,[2] and repeats his action, for the same patterns of delusion and wisdom apply to all human beings.[3] His ministry is meant to be all-inclusive and not confined within the ethnic boundaries of Israel.

The demoniac is described as one who lived apart from the conventional world, living among the tombs and in the mountains. Buddhist texts often speak about meditating among the tombs, beholding decaying corpses to bring home a sense of human impermanence. Yet, if one becomes attached to such other-worldly practices, no reengagement ensues and Mahāyāna practice is aborted. Such an option is recognized within the tradition in the figure of the solitary enlightened person (*pratyekabuddha*), who, being awakened (*buddha*) to the causes (*pratyeka*) that result in worldly suffering (*saṃsāra*) and aware of emptiness apart from the world, chooses not to take any part in society.

The experience is not, I think, peculiar to Buddhists. The Mahāyāna philosopher Keiji Nishitani speaks of the vertigo that one experiences when faced with the abyss of nihility, what Western thinkers refer to as a privation of being. It is this nihility that he sees in the works of John Paul Sartre. He sharply distinguishes this meaningless nihility from absolute nothingness, the fecund source of everything beyond both being and nonbeing.[4] It is this absolute nothingness that the Chinese designated by the character *wu*, nothing, a Taoist influenced rendering of the notion of emptiness. It is beyond both the being and nonbeing that are perceived by the imagined pattern of understanding, and thus described as absolute in regard to that pattern. But it also

---

2. Kee, *Community of the New Age,* 103, notes that the reference to the eastern shore of the Galilean sea as the country of the Gerasenes is "patently inaccurate." It remains, however, that it is gentile territory, and that is sufficient for Mark's symbolism. See Malbon, *Mark and Method,* 38: "Historical interpreters, perhaps beginning with Matthew, who substitutes the name Gadarenes (Matt 8:28), have had difficulty locating such a place. From a narrative critical point of view, the country of the Gerasenes is gentile territory opposite Jewish Galilee."

3. Kelber, *Mark's Story of Jesus,* 32.

4. Nishitani, "What is Religion?", in *Religion and Nothingness,* 1–45.

entails the affirmation of dependently co-arisen being, and the basic insight of the practice of the middle path.[5]

The demoniac lived among the dead and dwelt in the solitude of mountain places. He was not bound by any of the customs or norms of town living, and so could not be held by chains or fetters. Knowing all that to be empty, he howled and gashed himself with stones. This is the madness of insight into emptiness unaccompanied by insight into dependent co-arising. He is possessed by the terror of realizing that nothing has any firm and permanent validity; that is why he lives among the dead.[6] He has attained a freedom from all conventions, but it is an unmitigated attachment to the wilderness, a "freedom for nihility."[7]

And that is why the man recognizes Jesus as one who also understands the empty wilderness. The disciples see Jesus solely within their conventional perspective; the demoniacs see him solely within their ultimate perspective. And so the demons begin to bargain with Jesus. They are not simply his archenemies but are opposing players in the unfolding of the gospel's differential awareness of ultimate meaning and worldly convention. Yet they are fixated on emptiness to the detriment of dependent co-arising. Emptiness ineptly grasped removes not only the deluded reliance upon falsely imagined essences, but also the conventional support of the dependently co-arisen world.[8] The emptiness of any essential and permanent selfhood is mistaken for the absence of any dependently co-arisen identity; as a result of this

5. This is the Yogācāra interpretation, as described in Nagao, *The Foundational Standpoint of Mādhyamika Philosophy*, 39–42, 61–65, 91–96.

6. Via, *The Ethics of Mark's Gospel*, 65, asserts that a conflict between life and death "is seen in the story of the demoniac in that he experienced Jesus' will to liberate him as a tormenting threat which he resists." Clinging to the viewpoint of emptiness is itself not insight into emptiness, but a perversion of emptiness, forcing it into the pattern of imagined understanding and imprisoning one in the torment of relative nothingness. And so Via, 109, sees the demoniac story as a "proleptic resurrection story." The man is awakened from his clinging to the imagined reality of emptiness to life in the dependently co-arisen world, clothed in his garments and in his right mind.

7. Kermode, *The Genesis of Secrecy*, 136, alluding to J. Starobinski: "From his freedom—a freedom to be naked among the tombs, and to scream, *une liberté pour rien*—he passes to the constraints of clothes, houses, and proclamation."

8. Nagao, *The Foundational Standpoint of Mādhyamika Philosophy*, 122: "Emptiness ineptly grasped . . . pays no heed to the differentiation of the worldly and conventional from ultimate meaning. In point of fact, the Buddha did articulate a doctrine. He did venture to bring the inconceivable and ineffable ultimate realm to speech, and thus to establish worldly convention from an awareness of essence-free emptiness. His teaching represents the development of a verbal and reasoned doctrine (*dharma-deśana*), and the structure of the two truths builds on this articulation to present the logical form of this single, all-emcompassing world. . . . Far from being an escape into ultimate meaning, emptiness is the only context in which conventional discourse can be validated. . . . Suffice it here to mention the eighth stanza [of Nāgārjuna's *Stanzas on the Middle*, chapter 24d], which states that 'all buddhas preach doctrine in reliance on the two truths,' and the tenth, which says that 'without relying on conventional truth, the highest, ultimate meaning cannot be realized.'"

misunderstanding one sinks into madness. The demoniac has deeply realized the emptiness of self (*ātman-śūnyatā*), and in dread has taken on multiple personalities, for the demons are legion. Jesus tries to lead his disciples into awareness of emptiness by breaking through their imagined grasp on reality. In contrast he heals the demoniac by restoring his everyday mind. The people saw that he was sitting, clothed, and restored to sanity (καθήμενον ἱματισμένον καὶ σωφρονοῦνται). He sends the man home, to his people, to once again live within the conventional world, there reporting on the Lord's mercy.

Fixated emptiness is destructive of human life. The Mahāyāna masters insisted that emptiness itself is not sufficient, that one must reengage. They did so in rejection of those solitary hermit figures who dwelt alone in the forest, meditating on the impermanence of life and seeking a final and absolute cessation (*nirvāṇa*). Such people were compared to the rhinoceros, living alone, useless to others. They were said to be lacking in the perfection of wisdom (*prajñāpāramitā:* literally, the wisdom of the other shore), since they clung to emptiness without compassion for others. They are the examples against which Mahāyānists contrast the fully awakened buddhas who empty even emptiness. In Mark, such solitary figures are often described as demoniacs, deranged by their insight into the emptiness of all things, and destructive of all social identity. Thus so the poor pigs drowned themselves in the sea.

Yet there is more to the multiple personalities of the demoniac than simply spiritual delusion. The possessing demons are named Legion (λεγιὼν ὄνομά μοι). Ched Myers comments on the term legion: "A Latinism, this term had only one meaning in Mark's social world: a division of Roman soldiers. Alerted by this clue, we discover that the rest of the story is filled with *military* imagery. The term used for 'herd' (*agelē,* 5: 11)—inappropriate for pigs, who do not travel in herds—often was used to refer to a band of military recruits (Derrett, "Contributions to the Study of the Gerasene Demoniac," 5). Derrett also points out that the phrase 'he dismissed them' (*epetrepsen*) connotes a military command, and the pigs' charge (*ōrmēsen*) into the lake suggests troops rushing into battle (5: 13)."[9] Jesus' victory over these demonic legionnaires is then a "brief performancial summary . . . of every Jewish revolutionary's dream."[10] In this reading, the demoniac had been driven mad because of his hatred of the Roman oppressors. He is caught in an inner conflict so intense the only option is withdrawal from society, raving among the tombs of his forebears.[11]

Jesus' cure, however, has little political impact, for he restores the man to his everyday mind and sends him home. The now-sane fellow wants to

---

9. Myers, *Binding the Strong Man,* 191.
10. Crossan, *The Historical Jesus,* 314.
11. Hollenbach, "Jesus, Demoniacs, and Public Authorities," 573: "The tension between his hatred for his oppressors and the necessity to repress this hatred in order to avoid dire recrimination drove him mad. . . . He retreated to an inner world where he could symbolically resist Roman domination." Cited in Myers, *Binding the Strong Man,* 192.

stay with Jesus (ἵνα μετ' αὐτοῦ ᾖ) and become a disciple.[12] But he is not allowed to do so; rather he is told to go back to his normal life in society and tell his friends what the Lord's compassion has done for him. No program of political resistance is recommended, simply that, reengaging in his everyday life, he announce the Lord's mercy. And so he begins to preach throughout the Decapolis (καὶ ἤρξατο κηρύσσειν ἐν τῇ Δεκαπόλει).[13] To preach usually refers to the proclamation of the gospel, yet the restored demoniac has been given no doctrine at all to communicate. Rather, he preaches what Jesus has done for him (ὅσα ἐποίησεν αὐτῷ ὁ Ἰησοῦς), i.e., that Jesus has resurrected for him the world of conventional living.[14] He preaches a contentless gospel, without any preset program. Jesus does not address the issue of how one is to cope with oppressors. That too is left to the insight and courage of all healed persons in their reengagement in the world. The account "presents a new understanding of discipleship. The disciple mold is broken and recast by the story in Mark 5.1–21b."[15] Those who evince faith or are healed the Markan Jesus sends home, while those who persist in misunderstanding accompany him throughout. To be a disciple is not then to accompany Jesus, but to return home and reengage in the world of everyday living by proclaiming how the Lord has had mercy on us (v. 19). The twelve do not go home throughout the narrative, but after the resurrection, they are to go to Galilee, their home; Jesus will precede them (14: 28; 16: 7).

Jesus preaches no ideological program. Yet the imagery of this passage does offer indications of the Markan Jesus' attitude. In the first place, Jesus has launched a mission beyond the borders of Israel into gentile lands.[16] There will be no ethnic boundaries between people in Jesus' kingdom, no fundamental distinction between gentile Romans in charge and gentile Gerasenes in torment. (Perhaps Mark, aware of the political danger of his story, has simply invented the unlocatable Gerasenes to serve as a symbol for oppressed gentiles.) Secondly, the destruction of the herd of swine indicates the destructiveness of all political oppression, of all ideology that subjugates

---

12. Broadhead, *Teaching With Authority,* 99–100: "The dialogues then narrow to the conversation between Jesus and the healed demoniac. . . . He asks Jesus that he might 'be with him' (ἵνα μετ' αυτοῦ ᾖ in 5.18). In Mk 3.14 Jesus appoints twelve who are to 'be with him' (ἵνα ὦσιν μετ' αὐτοῦ). This is the first task of discipleship. Thus the healed demoniac in 5.18 is asking to follow Jesus as his disciple."

13. Tolbert, *Sowing the Gospel,* 167 sees him as an example of the good earth, in which the seed of the word has yielded a harvest. Yet no word has been imparted to him at all, simply a restoration of his sanity.

14. Via, *The Ethics of Mark's Gospel,* 109, sees preaching as related to the preaching of the Gospel and ties the demoniac, who is seated and clothed (5: 15) with the young man at the empty tomb, who is also seated and clothed in a white robe (16: 5). Both evoke fear and amazement, and both are associated with tombs. Thus, he concludes that a resurrection symbolism is present.

15. Broadhead, *Teaching With Authority,* 101.

16. Kelber, *The Kingdom in Mark,* 51: "Mark corroborates the Gentile nature of the miracle by identifying the area as the Decapolis (5: 20)." And 52: ". . . the Gerasene exorcism in 5: 1–20 constitutes the crucial watershed of the mission to the Gentiles."

people, in Mahāyāna terms, of all ideology deemed to capture (i.e., compre-hend) the reality of affairs. From a Jewish perspective the pigs symbolize all that is unclean. "The desire of the demons to dwell in tombs and in swine magnifies the unclean, desperate, tormented image which they present. . . . The depth of their evil and the depth of their destruction is unsurpassed: unclean spirits flee into unclean swine and the demonic mob is swallowed into the depths of the mysterious, chaotic sea."[17] Jesus grants the request of the demons to enter the swine: let the legionnaires wreak their havoc on pigs, who, unable to internalize oppression and escape into madness, self-destruct in the cosmic chaos they represent in society.

When the townspeople learn of these events, their sense of a well-ordered world is threatened. They can allow that demons sometimes possess people and can drive those persons out of the world of men and women. But they cannot abide one who, aware of the ultimate meaning of the wilderness, can also reengage in the everyday world, for that upsets imagined patterns of conventional living.[18] This is why the people are amazed (καὶ πάντες ἐθαύμα-ζον), a reaction frequently elicited from those who sense the security of their conventional world being undermined by Jesus. And so they ask Jesus to leave their neighborhood.

Life and Death
5: 21–43

[21]When Jesus had crossed again in the boat to the other side, a large crowd gathered around him and he was beside the sea.[19] [22]Then the president of the synagogue came up, named Jairus, and seeing him, fell at his feet [23]and begged him earnestly, saying, "My little daughter is desperately sick. Do come and lay your hands on her that she may be saved and may live." [24]Jesus went with him and a large crowd followed him; they were pressing all round him.

[25]Now there was a woman who had suffered from a hemorrhage for twelve years; [26]after long and painful treatment under various doctors, she had spent all she had without being any the better for it; in fact, she was getting worse. [27]She had heard about Jesus, and she came up through the crowd and touched his cloak from behind, thinking, [28]"If I can just touch his clothes, I shall be saved." [29]And at once the source of the bleeding dried up, and she felt in

---

17. Broadhead, *Teaching With Authority,* 99. Also Heil, *The Gospel of Mark as a Model for Action,* 120: "Jesus has thus powerfully purged the land of the Gerasenes not only of a threatening legion of unclean spirits but of a herd of unclean swine (5: 13)." Yet, Jesus will soon (7: 14–23) declare that the Jewish rules of purity are invalid!

18. Camery-Hoggatt, *Irony in Mark's Gospel,* 135: "The calm of the demoniac parallels the calm of the sea. Here, too, the calm is met by expressions of terror, by a desperate effort to be rid of the one who can bring peace so readily (v. 17)."

19. Following RSV.

herself that she was cured of her complaint. [30]*And at once aware that power had gone out from him, Jesus turned round in the crowd and said, "Who touched my clothes?"* [31]*His disciples said to him, "You see how the crowd is pressing round you; how can you ask, 'Who touched my clothes?' "* [32]*But he continued to look all round to see who had done it.* [33]*Then the woman came forward, frightened and trembling because she knew what had happened to her, and she fell at his feet and told him the whole truth.* [34]*"My daughter," he said, "your faith has restored you to health; go in peace and be free from your complaint."*

[35]*While he was still speaking some people arrived from the house of the president of the synagogue to say, "Your daughter is dead; why put the Master to any further trouble?"* [36]*But Jesus overheard what they said and he said to the president of the synagogue, "Do not be afraid; only have faith."* [37]*And he allowed no one to go with him except Peter and James and John the brother of James.* [38]*So they came to the house of the president of the synagogue and Jesus noticed all the commotion, with people weeping and wailing unrestrainedly.* [39]*He went in and said to them, "Why all this commotion and crying? The child is not dead, but asleep."* [40]*But they ridiculed him. So he turned them all out and, taking with him the child's father and mother and his own companions, he went into the place where the child lay.* [41]*And taking the child by the hand he said to her, "Talitha, kum!" which means, "Little girl, I tell you to get up."* [42]*The little girl got up at once and began to walk about, for she was twelve years old. At once they were overcome with astonishment,* [43]*and he gave them strict orders not to let anyone know about it, and told them to give her something to eat.*

These stories of healings are meant to interpret one another, since the story of the woman with a hemorrhage is inserted in the middle of the story of Jairus' daughter.[20] Both women are addressed as daughter. The little girl is twelve years old, the exact time the woman had been suffering from her affliction. Her twelve years of suffering the social and cultural alienation consequent upon her defiled status is transformed by the resurrection of the young girl. Both stories are related to the restoration of womanhood, one to restored sexuality and one to life itself.[21]

The culture of the ancient world included miracles. People believed that great miracle-workers had power to heal and did indeed effect miraculous healings. The supernatural was brought within the sphere of the everyday

---

20. Malbon, *Mark and Method*, 39: "But Markan intercalation is always for interpretive purpose. The framing story is to be interpreted in light of the inside story, and vice versa."

21. Via, *The Ethics of Mark's Gospel*, 110. Note Heil, *The Gospel of Mark as a Model for Action*, 125: "The lowly social status of this woman as a nameless female whose financial resources have been depleted and who has no position in the community sharply contrasts the status of the named male, Jairus, who holds a prominent place in society as a synagogue official." Yet no distinction is drawn in the text of Mark: the same faith is demanded of all alike.

world in the form of strange and wondrous happenings. People are amazed and astonished, but the supernatural events are not without precedent. They are simply the most unexplained, and thus awesome, aspect of conventional living.[22] These events may appear to issue directly from an ultimate realm of power, but that would trivialize the ultimate by forcing it into conventional terms. Even the pinnacle of the conventional world remains conventional. In Mark such miracles issue always from faith, here the faith of the woman and the faith of the girl's father. "Faith, then, is the prerequisite of healing for the Gospel of Mark, not its result. . . . The miracles in Mark are not intended as signs to induce belief; they are, instead, the visible, tangible fruits of faith."[23]

In both cases in this passage the same demand for faith is made, for faith is the opposite of the fear which people have in the face of sickness and death. Mark has apparently enfolded the story of the woman into that of the child because they share the same theme: the opposing options of faith and fear (5: 32).[24] The story begins when Jesus has returned to Galilee from the gentile land of the Transjordan and is immediately surrounded by the now familiar crowds. He stays again by the seaside, perhaps telling more parables. The synagogue president, Jairus, comes with his earnest request and Jesus goes with him. Along the road Jesus feels "power go out of him" (ἐπιγνοὺς ἐν ἑαυτῷ τὴν ἐξ αὐτοῦ δύναμιν ἐξελθοῦσαν), and yet when he talks with the woman, he does not attribute her cure to his power, but to her faith: "your faith has restored you to health." Indeed, the insertion of this healing episode is structured to emphasize the central role of faith. The term "has restored you to health" (σου σέσωκέν σε) signifies not only physical healing, but also spiritual salvation.[25] That is perhaps why the disciples do not get the point and chide Jesus for asking who touched him in such a mob scene. They see only appearances, not the woman's faith, which draws the power out from an unaware Jesus.

This is not the ordinary portrait of a wonder-worker: the woman sneaks up behind him and, as it were, steals some power from him when he isn't looking. The scene is ironic, for then, feeling the exit of power, Jesus begins to look all around (ἐπιστραφεὶς . . . περιεβλέπετο), trying to identify the source of his power drain. Just as the blood has been flowing from the sick woman, so power has flowed from Jesus—beyond his control and without his volition. Mark constructs a portrait of a bewildered Jesus, searching around for the source of a problem not apparent to anyone else. Only when

22. See Crossan, *The Historical Jesus,* 320f, on event and process in miracle.
23. Tolbert, *Sowing the Gospel,* 159.
24. Tolbert, *Sowing the Gospel,* 171: "The four episodes of Mark 4: 35–5: 43 are designed primarily to clarify the distinction between the rocky ground and the good earth," and 181: "After Mark 5: 1–43, the audience should have identified the Gospel group illustrating the good earth type as those who are healed." Yet, they pass so quickly from the scene that one wonders if they even constitute a stable group in the gospel. Rather, as Jesus' disciples, they immediately disappear back into their ordinary lives.
25. Tolbert, *Sowing the Gospel,* 169.59.

the woman comes forth and Jesus begins to talk about faith does he again regain his composure. Faith is the actor here, not Jesus' power.

When Jesus overhears the report of Jairus' daughter's death, he reiterates his advice, telling the president not to be afraid, only to have faith (μὲ φοβοῦ, μόνον πίστευε). It is faith that gives life; fear and amazement are grounded in clinging to the imagined pattern of stable conventional realities. He takes Peter, James, and John with him, for they are his favored witnesses, both to his transfiguration and to his agony in the garden. Here, they are to understand the life-giving power of faith. When he enters the house of the official, he sees there a great commotion. Just as the sea had been raging, so here the people are in tumult. And Jesus tells them to calm down, for the girl is just asleep! The family members laugh at him, for, as the ones most concerned, they had been keeping watch over the sick child and know her to be dead.[26] Again Mark has portrayed Jesus in ironic terms. He fails to recognize what everyone knows. Yet, he merely goes in and tells her to get up, and she awakens at once. It seems that indeed she has just been sleeping.[27] To Jesus sleep and death seem here to be identified. Instead of a miraculous cure, Jesus winds up waking a sleeping child, who begins to walk around, for she was twelve years of age and apparently couldn't sit still. The woman was cured by her faith and the girl simply wakes up. The resurrection of Jairus' daughter is explicitly described as an awakening.[28]

In presenting the healings as miracle stories Mark's narrative undermines their miraculous character. Jesus appears silly in both, bewildered by the first and uninformed in the second. Yet the tables are turned and the sick are healed. The impression still remains among the people that it is Jesus' awesome power that has effected the cure. Mark's recording of the Aramaic words Jesus used, *Talitha kum,* seem to suggest they have some magical power.[29] The crowd

---

26. Camery-Hoggatt, *Irony in Mark's Gospel,* 139: "Of course the girl was 'dead,' the whole movement of the story depends upon it. Jesus is not rejecting that notion, but rather is superimposing upon it a secondary—or, as Mark sees it, a new primary—frame of reference. Death is not final, not ultimate."

27. Kealy, *Mark's Gospel,* 44, reports the words of Erasmus: "Such as are in a deep sleep cannot many times be awakened, although men call them oftentimes with a loud voice, and pinch them never so much: and when they be called up yet they do not by and by awake, but being half awake and drowsy, gape, stretch their arms, nod their heads, that many times the chin striketh the breast: and if a man call not still upon them, they fall asleep again. But this dead maiden arose forthwith and walked at the voice of Jesus."

28. Kermode, *The Genesis of Secrecy,* 133, remarks: "Jairus is said to mean 'the awakener' and it occurs in the Book of Esther, which Mark knew well, and on which he drew for the Salome episode. Esther contains the story of a beautiful girl who survives the danger of death by inducing a sleepless king to touch her within a golden scepter. Is the story of the little girl a transformation of that story?" Possibly, but it does seem interesting that the name Jairus comes from Hebrew roots meaning, "He (i.e., God) will enlighten, he will awaken" (Bauer, *Lexicon,* 367).

29. But perhaps they are simply a reminiscence of Jesus' words. See Meier, *A Marginal Jew,* 265: "In my view, however, Mark 5: 41 and the *'abbā'* prayer of Jesus (14: 36) are the best candidates for Aramaic words that go back to the historical Jesus."

still sees him as a wonder-worker, as the presence of supernatural reality breaking into the conventional world. That is why "he ordered them strictly not to let anyone know about it." On the face of it, that again is silly. How could all those people, who thought they knew that the girl was really dead, have failed to learn that now she was alive and having something to eat!

Notice that when the woman with the bleeding was cured inadvertently,[30] i.e., when Jesus himself performs no conscious act to cure her, he makes a public scene trying to identify her. His anger is directed not to muzzling those who would reveal him, but to finding out just who has been healed through him.[31] This seems to me to be the main contrast in the rhetorical structure of the two stories. Jesus does not hide the power that healed the woman, yet tries to hide the raising of the dead girl. Wrede saw Jesus' implausible commands to silence as indications of the messianic secret,[32] yet in the inner story Jesus makes quite a fuss. The point appears to be that the Markan Jesus directs the reader to ignore Jesus the wonder-worker, to hide that image, but to see in Jesus the power of God flowing freely, spontaneously, just as the seeds the farmer planted grow all by themselves (4:27).[33]

---

30. Broadhead, *Teaching With Authority,* 105: "The healing motif of 5: 29 is most unusual because it is inadvertent. Jesus is unaware of the need and he responds only to the result of the healing."

31. Broadhead, *Teaching With Authority,* 105: "Within the narrative grammar of the Gospel of Mark, anger is implied by Jesus 'turning' (ἐπιστρέφω in 5.30; 8.23) and by his 'looking about' (περιβλέπομαι in 3.5; 5.32)."

32. Malbon, *Mark and Method,* 39: "Narrative critics see [the messianic secret] as a plot device that calls attention to the complexity of the image of messiahship in the Markan Gospel. . . . At 5: 43 the implied reader knows more than Jairus knows, but not yet the whole truth." I think the point relates not to the amount of truth known, but to the pattern of understanding.

33. Broadhead, *Teaching With Authority,* 110–11: ". . . Mk 5.21–6.1a provides interpretive keys by which the miracle activity is to be read. The narrative does not exploit the full potential of the miracle stories. There is no public preparation in the healing of the woman with the issue of blood. Indeed, the healing is inadvertent, and there are no narrative witnesses. The focus of the account falls not on the act, but on its result—the woman bows in reverence before Jesus, she is honored for her faith, she is pronounced saved and whole, she is sent on her way in peace. In the same manner the narrative does not exploit the full value of the raising account. The raising creates the potential for widespread acclamation of Jesus as *Wundermann,* but the opportunity is bypassed. Instead, the potential for construction of a christological portrait of Jesus as one who raises the dead is blunted. Jesus limits the number of witnesses to the raising, and he commands even these witnesses to silence. Because of this distancing from the effect and the acclamation of the miracle stories, another interpretive perspective is given a significant place within the stories. Prior to the miracle activity Jesus is cast again in the image of a teacher with authority (5.21b). In the face of his most powerful opponent—death—Jesus is addressed as διδάσκαλος, 'teacher.' Thus, it is Jesus the teacher who heals and raises the dead." In Mahāyāna terms, a teacher is constituted by relationships with disciples. So Jesus is teacher first and foremost, and his identity is taken from the dependently co-arisen circumstances of his life and mission. There is no prior definition of who he is that would depart from discipleship. The silencing is a muting of such attempts at identification. Thus, if one reads the Markan silencing commands simply as a strategy to hide Jesus'

Some think that Mark was just clumsy in his construction of such stories.[34] In retelling the stories, they maintain, he got things somewhat mixed up, much as people get jokes wrong in retelling them. On the surface, this is indeed a plausible explanation for the incongruities. Yet, on a deeper level, Mark is weaning his readers away from imagined miraculous happenings, away from confusing the realms of ultimate meaning and worldly convention. What the people are not to make known is Jesus, the wonder-worker.[35] In the story line there is little hope that they will not so identify him. But, in the narrative Mark tells his readers not to follow their example. Peter, James, and John will later be called upon to witness to two connected events, Jesus' transfiguration into glory and his agony in the garden—his immediate contact with silent ultimate meaning and his complete immersion in the dependently co-arisen circumstances of his passion. Here in chapter five Mark begins to differentiate the two truths, holding them in healthy tension while suggesting that they are indeed completely separate and other.

---

true identity, known full well by the reader, she in fact refuses to be distanced from the miracle-seeking mind that seeks to identify Jesus' definition as beyond everything human.

34. Meagher's theme in, *Clumsy Construction in Mark's Gospel.*

35. Thus I agree with Weeden, *Mark—Traditions in Conflict,* that Mark does indeed undermine a notion of a "divine man" (68: those "enamored of what attracts man: the miracle-working capacity of Jesus."), although I do not follow his identification of the disciples as the sole representatives of that view, or with Weeden's stress on the absence of Jesus after the resurrection. Rather, I see that absence as the emptying of imagined expectations and the affirmation of the everyday, dependently co-arisen presence of Jesus in Galilee.

6

The Wisdom of Non-Discrimination

Faith and the Mind of Discrimination
6: 1–6

¹Leaving that district, he went to his home town, and his disciples accompanied him. ²With the coming of the Sabbath he began teaching in the synagogue, and most of them were astonished when they heard him. They said, "Where did this man get all this? What is this wisdom that has been granted him, and these miracles that are worked through him? ³This is the woodworker,¹ surely, the son of Mary, the brother of James and Joset and Jude and Simon? His sisters, too, are they not here with us?" And they would not accept him. ⁴And Jesus said to them, "A prophet is despised only in his own country, among his own relations and in his own house;" ⁵and he could work no miracle there, except that he cured a few sick people by laying hands on them. ⁶He was amazed at their lack of faith.

The key to this passage lies in the reaction of the people who were astonished at (ἐξεπλήσσοντο) Jesus' teaching, for that is what underlies the lack of faith that renders miracles impossible. In 3: 20–21, Jesus had already encountered relatives who thought him crazy, and in 3: 31–35 his family stands outside the circle of his teaching. Here Mark has Jesus come with his disciples to his home town of Nazareth and begin to teach in the synagogue. The synagogue is the natural place for his teaching, probably the place where Jesus himself had first learned the traditions.²

---

1. Following Meier, *A Marginal Jew,* 280: "I prefer to translate *tekton* as 'woodworker' rather than as the popular 'carpenter' because the latter term has acquired a somewhat restricted sense in the contemporary American workplace, with its ever increasing specialization."

2. Meier, *A Marginal Jew,* 277: "Apart from Joseph, the most likely conduit of an education would be the synagogue at Nazareth, which could also have served as a sort of religious 'elementary school.' If indeed Jesus did receive his first scriptural formation

Many who hear him are "astonished," for they know him as a fellow townsman and cannot conceive him apart from that context.[3] They cannot admit that he now plays a different role—they know and admit that wisdom and power have characterized prophets and wonder-workers, yet they separate that wisdom and power from their everyday lives, falsely differentiating the knowable supernatural realm of the prophets from their ordinary lives, thus blocking any recognition of how such realms can come together in the person of a mere woodworker, a man no different from them.

To counter such impressions, Mark presents Jesus as merely teaching in his home town; he recounts no miracle. To be a prophet is not a role beyond the conventional world, for what lies beyond is hidden in the abyss of silence. The manifestation of ultimate meaning is embodied in the simple act of Jesus' conventional teaching, a teaching that undermines not only the townspeoples' expectations but all expectations.[4] Again Mark does not report just what he taught; that does not seem to be of importance.[5] They take offense and are

---

in the Nazareth synagogue, one can well understand the emotionally charged atmosphere surrounding the return of the adult Jesus to that same synagogue to teach his peers and elders (Mark 6:1–6a parr.). The reaction of 'Who does he think *he* is?' becomes quite understandable."

3. Meier, *A Marginal Jew*, 317: "The extended family, and then the village or town as a whole, impose identity and social function on the individual in exchange for the communal security and defense the individual received from the family. The break Jesus made with these ties to his extended family and village, after so many years of an uneventful life in their midst, and his concomitant attempt to define a new identity and social role for himself, no doubt left deep scars that can still be seen in the Gospel narratives (see Mark 3: 21, 31–35; 6: 1–6 . . .)." It seems to me that the same point can be urged against those in his present day family who are insistent in presenting Jesus with a new theological identity. The village mentality is not merely an ancient phenomenon.

4. Via, *The Ethics of Mark's Gospel*, 187: ". . . the concealment of revelation will never be fully broken through . . ., faith will always be like looking through the veil. God's revelation as hidden beneath the surface of ordinary existence and faith as penetrating the surface are complementary sides of the same reality. Mark portrays the ministry of Jesus as the key to this correlation. Who Jesus really is, for Mark, is concealed beneath the fact that he is an ordinary carpenter, son, and brother who dies a cruel and ignominious death. So a disciple must be able to see through the veil and beneath the surface and acknowledge that it is the Son of God on the cross (15: 39) and to understand himself or herself as the follower of *this* Son of God." One may note that immediately before the centurion's confession at 15: 39, the temple veil is torn apart, manifesting the emptiness of God's presence, i.e., veiled no longer by the ritual covering, but by the death of Jesus.

5. Kee, *Community of the New Age*, 117: "Mark's favorite designation for Jesus is teacher. . . . Yet Jesus does not appear as a rabbinic interpreter of the scriptures, but as a charismatic, divinely authorized spokesman for God. That is implied in most of the controversy stories of Mark, but is expressly dealt with in 6:1–6. There the crucial verses are 6:4, where Jesus depicts himself as a prophet, and 6:2, where the substance of his role is epitomized: his wisdom and his δυνάμεις. Mark does not tell us the source of either, but by his much favored interrogative device (πόθεν τούτῳ ταῦτα . . .; 6:22a) he puts the responsibility on the reader to provide the answer." I think that Jesus' role of teacher is described so meagerly by Mark to suggest to that reader not a divinely authorized spokesperson, but simply a prophet who speaks—on his own authority (1:22) and thus

astonished because they have bifurcated the sacred from the profane, expecting that the supernatural comes only as an external irruption into their ordinary lives. In Mahāyāna terms, ultimate truth indeed is totally other, apart from the samsaric world of delusion. Yet, as Nāgārjuna insisted, it is not an identifiable other, a separate realm that either irrupts into life or governs it from above. Rather, it is the quiet and silent awareness of the emptiness of everyday living, going beyond every attempt at characterization. The ultimate remains immersed in the dependently co-arisen world as the trace image of that which always goes beyond, and therefore as not apart from this dependently co-arisen world.[6] The townspeople, even apparently Jesus' mother, brothers, and sisters,[7] live within such a bifurcated world, and to them Jesus belongs entirely within their image of the mundane realm.[8] They would not accept him, literally "they were scandalized at him" (ἐσκανδαλίζοντο ἐν αὐτῷ). To be scandalized means to be caused to fall or to be caught, to take offense at someone, to be shocked. Perhaps they react thus because by turning from them Jesus repudiates the brokerage privileges they may have expected as the intimates of a wonder-worker and healer.[9] But there is no bargaining with God, whose ultimate presence remains always immediately available within the conventional world and apart from any of its structures. Jesus challenged their assumption of the divine as a reality apart from the everyday and subject to brokerage. They were offended because their imagined discrimination between realms rendered them incapable of faith, for discrimination attempts to force faith within the defined boundaries of the conventional. It was not that the people of Nazareth did not believe in miracles or in prophets. The synagogue teachings are replete with accounts of miracles and prophets. It follows that, if faith consists in the notional acceptance of such imagined realities, they did have faith. But, Mark suggests that it does not, for even though miracles flowed through his hands, he could perform none for them, except for a few healings. Faith is the prerequisite for miracles, and thus

---

from God—everyday teachings, about seeds and the kingdom. The Markan Jesus empties all expectations, and that is why he is a prophet.

6. Nāgārjuna, *Stanzas on the Middle,* 13: 3: "If there were something not empty, there might be something termed empty. But there is nothing not empty, and so where might there be an empty something?" The transcendence of ultimate meaning, although completely other from worldly convention, is itself empty of identifiable content, and thus not a separate sphere apart from the realm of worldly convention.

7. Pesch, *Das Markusevangelium* 1: 322–25 argues that these are true siblings, for that is the natural sense of the terms. See Meier, *A Marginal Jew,* 331–32.

8. Via, *The Ethics of Mark's Gospel,* 178: "What the townspeople take offense at is that as a known and familiar family member he does extraordinary things; in their understanding, that ought not to be the case. In a sense they resent the mystery which they tacitly acknowledge: that the extraordinary (wisdom and miracle) occurs in the familiar."

9. Crossan, *The Historical Jesus,* 347: "Any Mediterranean peasant would expect an expanding ripple of patronage-clientage to go out from Jesus, through his family and his village, to the outside world. But what Jesus did, in turning his back on Nazareth and on his family, was repudiate such brokerage, and that, rather than belief or disbelief, was the heart of the problem."

even Jesus' performance of a few miracles in his home town was to no avail. The mind of false discrimination cannot attain the mirror wisdom that sees all things just as they are. It is incapable of the equality wisdom that gains insight into the equal emptiness of both heaven and earth, both the world and the beyond. Thus, Jesus for his part is amazed (ἐθαύμαζεν) at their lack of faith.

Mark soon characterizes their lack of faith (διὰ τὴν ἀπιστίαν αὐτῶν) as their "hardness of heart" (ἀλλ᾽ ἦν αὐτῶν ἡ καρδία πεπωρωμένη; 6: 52), for just as the scribes in 2: 6 occlude faith and understanding by "debating in their hearts" and thus becoming obstinate and hard-hearted (3: 5), so Jesus' home town people are rendered unfaithful because of their preconceived, fixed notions of a false worldly convention.

The Twelve Go on Mission
6: 7–13

He made a tour round the villages, teaching. [7]Then he summoned the twelve and began to send them out in pairs, giving them authority over unclean spirits. [8]And he instructed them to take nothing for the journey except a staff—no bread, no haversack, no coppers for their purses. [9]They were to wear sandals, but, he added, "Don't take a spare tunic." [10]And he said to them, "If you enter a house anywhere, stay there until you leave the district. [11]And if any place does not welcome you and people refuse to listen to you, as you walk away shake off the dust under your feet as evidence to them." [12]So they set off to proclaim repentance; [13]and they cast out many devils, and anointed many sick people with oil and cured them.

The disciples set off (ἐξελθόντες), apart from Jesus, to preach so that people might be converted (ἵνα μετανοῶσιν). The theme of the kingdom Jesus announced in 1: 15 is now realized in his disciples' proclamation (ἐκήρυξαν). Their effectiveness is signaled by the exorcisms and healings they perform, signs of the presence of the messianic kingdom.[10] One need not wait for a future coming of the eschatological kingdom; it is realized in the early stages of Jesus' career.

Mauser notes that the disciples' journey alludes to the exodus of the people of Israel from Egypt. There is a "striking similarity of Mark 6: 8f to *Exodus* 12.11 where the Israelites on the eve of the exodus from Egypt are commanded

---

10. Crossan, *The Historical Jesus,* 345: ". . . Mark 6: 12 must be read in the light of Jesus' inaugural message according to the summary of Mark 1: 14–15. . . . Its emphatically Markan theology presumes, as Werner Kelber has shown so well, that the Kingdom is here and now present but in a mode of hiddenness and humility that demands repentance before acceptance is possible (7–11). So, for Mark, with 1: 14–15 read in conjunction with 6: 12, the message is the gospel of the Kingdom's hidden presence, and the response is repentance and faith."

to eat the Passover in haste, 'your loins girded, your sandals on your feet, and your staff in your hand.' "[11] The disciples recapitulate Israel's wilderness experience, bereft of any support beyond the presence of Yahweh, not relying on any support, whether material or mental.[12] Without conventional support, they preach a wilderness conversion, modeled on that of Jesus' direct awareness of God. If their message is not heard, they are to treat those who refuse to listen by the symbolic action of shaking off the dust from their feet as evidence or warning against them. "Strict Jews performed the same symbolic action when they re-entered Palestine after journeying abroad; the idea was to avoid contaminating God's holy land and people even with the dust of profane places."[13]

There are, however, closer social paradigms for the practice Jesus enjoins upon them, for, during the time of Jesus, Cynic philosophers did wander on the margins of society, pronouncing their aphorisms and critiques of society, while relying on the good will of their listeners to provide for their needs. The Markan disciples adopt much of the life style of these Cynic philosophers, particularly their voluntary poverty. In comparing the two, Theissen says, "Both are to take no money; both are to expect local hospitality; both are to pronounce judgment on those who spurn their teaching. The only reward they may accept is food, drink, and lodging."[14]

Yet, there are differences. One ancient critic described the Cynic philosophers as follows: "These Cynics, posting themselves at street corners, in alleyways, and at temple gates, pass around the hat and play on the credulity of lads and sailors and crowds of that sort, stringing together rough jokes and much tittletattle and that low badinage that smacks of the market place."[15] The Cynics themselves defended their life style, arguing that one should not mistake the outer appearances for the internal poverty and freedom.[16] They were socially marginal critics, wandering on the periphery of the cities, attracting crowds with their irreverent social barbs, and living off whatever they could beg from their listeners. They typically did carry bags or purses (πήραν), which were "supposed to indicate their self-sufficiency. Signaled thereby was their abnegation of the conventional norms of social security."[17] By contrast, Jesus forbids his disciples to carry such a purse. They are not to beg for their sustenance but to enter the homes of the people and share

---

11. Mauser, *Christ in the Wilderness,* 133.

12. Schweizer, *The Good News,* 129–130: "The poverty of the messengers who travel without provisions, without money in their pockets, and without additional protective clothing is the sign of a life like that of the 'birds' and the 'wild flowers' (Matt. 6: 25–34), in which there is no reliance upon one's own means. Messengers who wish to provide for every emergency do not have faith."

13. Nineham, *Saint Mark,* 170.

14. Theissen, "Wanderradikalismus," 260, cited in Kee, *Community of the New Age,* 104.

15. From Dio Chrysostom, *Discourses* 32: 8–9, cited in Crossan, *The Historical Jesus,* 340.

16. See Crossan, *The Historical Jesus,* 72–88.

17. Vaage, *Q: The Ethos and Ethics of an Itinerant Intelligence,* 319–20.

their table. Their life style embodies "the heart of the original Jesus movement, a shared egalitarianism of spiritual and material resources."[18] If all resources, spiritual and material are shared, one lives in radical contingency, in a deep awareness of dependent co-arising, without false notions of a separate, independent self (*ātman*). Grounded on insight into emptiness, the disciples are to engage in the tasks of preaching.[19] The very life style that Jesus enjoins on his followers entails insight into the emptiness of self and of all the things that support self. They are to rely on the open hospitality of the common people.[20] Even the shaking off of the dust from their feet makes more sense if one envisages it not as a rejection or curse, but as a somewhat comic act performed outside a rural house where they have been refused hospitality. After all, the mission of the twelve was at this point confined to Jewish Galilee and involved no gentile lands.[21]

A further interesting point involves the paired sending of the disciples in 6: 7, a feature dropped by Matthew. Often we understand that Jesus' twelve men are to journey in pairs, perhaps for emotional support. Such a practice did characterize later rabbinical tradition. Yet, perhaps, as Crossan argues, it

---

18. Crossan, *The Historical Jesus,* 341. Crossan, 421–22, identifies Jesus as a peasant Jewish Cynic. "He was neither broker nor mediator but, somewhat paradoxically, the announcer that neither should exist between humanity and divinity or between humanity and itself. Miracle and parable, healing and eating were calculated to force individuals into unmediated physical and spiritual contact with God and unmediated physical and spiritual contact with one another. He announced, in other words, the brokerless kingdom of God. . . . Jesus, as a peasant Jewish Cynic, was aready moving, but on a popular level, within the ambience of inclusive Judaism's synthesis of Jewish and Greek tradition." Also see Mack, *A Myth of Innocence,* 67–74.

19. Kee, *Community of the New Age,* 89: "The radicality of discipleship as Mark pictures it is evident in the demand of Jesus that all ordinary human ties and obligations be set aside, not in a radical retreat into the desert, however, but to go out into the world-wide mission. . . . The instructions given in 6: 7–13 require them to abandon everything except the most basic equipment for their protection and efficiency in carrying out their urgent work of preaching and exorcism. They are allowed a single tunic, sandals, a staff, and, by implication, a girdle. Prohibited are bread, knapsack (or more likely beggar's bowl), money. The total list of items included and excluded clearly reflects the equipment employed by the Cynic-Stoic itinerant charismatic preachers reported by Diogenes Laertius (6.13, 33). In the case of these wandering philosopher-preachers, the begging bowl was an indispensable factor, since it was on charity alone that they substituted. But in the case of the Markan itinerants, charity was to be sought solely in the form of basic food and shelter."

20. Crossan, *The Historical Jesus,* 340, argues that, whereas the Cynics avoided rural areas and their meager prospects for support, Jesus, "Is establishing a rural rather than an urban mission. Call it, if you will, Jewish and rural Cynicism rather than Greco-Roman and urban Cynicism. And its destination also explains why there is no bag. It is deliberately made not self-sufficient but, rather, dependent in a very particular fashion on commensality with those it would heal."

21. Crossan, *The Historical Jesus,* 352: "I do not think, by the way, that such barefoot dust shaking need be read as solemn eschatological curse. 'Indeed,' as Leif Vaage said, 'it is rather an amusing, if not hilarious, gesture when literally imagined. Perhaps, the humour was not unintended' (*Q: The Ethos and Ethics,* 342)."

can indicate the presence of sister-wives, as in *1 Corinthians:* "Do we not have the right to be accompanied by a sister wife (ἀδελφὴν γυναῖκα), as the other apostles and the brothers of the Lord and Cephas?" Crossan proposes "that a 'sister wife' means exactly what it says: a female missionary who travels with a male missionary as if, for the world at large, she were his wife. The obvious function of such a tactic would be to furnish the best social protection for a traveling female missionary in a world of male power and violence. Was that the original purpose and focus of the 'two by two' practice, namely, to allow for and incorporate safely the possibility of female missionaries?"[22]

Herod's Fear
6: 14–16

[14]King Herod had heard about him, since by now his name was well-known. Some were saying, "John the baptist has risen from the dead, and that is why miraculous powers are at work in him." [15]Others said, "He is Elijah;" others again, "He is a prophet, like the prophets we used to have." [16]But when Herod heard this, he said, "It is John whose head I cut off; he has risen from the dead."

Mark inserts this account of Herod's fear and his subsequently related murder of the Baptist to highlight and contrast the mind of converted wisdom with the mind of delusion and fantasy. The conventional opinions about the identity of Jesus look forward to those repeated in 8: 27–30, where Jesus himself poses the question of his identity to the disciples. Here Herod is moving entirely in the conventional world of real politics.[23]

That conventional world does admit, however, miraculous happenings as breakthroughs of the beyond into this usually ordinary life. Mark records no skepticism about the miracles and powers that worked through Jesus. Herod assumes them to be true, and then accounts for them by imagining John the Baptist to have returned, perhaps to seek revenge. Herod's own actions, his *karma*, had engendered in him a deep-seated fear about the results of his deed,[24] which is recounted in the next passage. And so he thinks that John has arisen. In the Chinese translations of Mahāyāna scriptures, the deluded realm of transmigration (*saṃsāra*) is translated as life-and-death, the encircling world in which humans pass from one lifetime to another in constant delusion, and it is no great victory to be reintroduced back into *saṃsāra*.

---

22. Crossan, *The Historical Jesus,* 335.

23. Camery-Hoggatt, *Irony in Mark's Gospel,* 145: "Herod was no king, but a tetrarch. Is Mark intending ridicule? Josephus (*Antiquities* XVIII.vii.2) indicates that Herod was deposed by Caligula for monarchical pretensions."

24. Schweizer, *The Good News,* 134: "Herod . . . stands under the terrible pressures of the consequences of a wrong decision made previously."

Herod interprets John's return in this fashion, and, driven by his karmic past, imagines John to have actually come back to get him. His delusions will lead him to eliminate the imagined threat of the Baptist. "As John's death coincided with the sending out of the disciples-apostles, so will Jesus' death usher in the mission."[25] The very proclamation of the need for conversion, just undertaken by the twelve, engenders the hatred of the deluded. The sufferings of Jesus and his disciples do not proceed from any divine fiat or plan, but from the complex chain of the dependently co-arisen actions of those who hear and begin to fear and feel threatened.[26]

But Herod is wrong and John has not come back. Note that the verb used for rising from the dead (ἐγήγερται ἐκ νεκρῶν, ἠγέρθη) also means to awaken, to rise from sleep. Resurrection in Mark is not a literal reconstitution and revivification of inert bodily structure. In Mahāyāna Buddhism, transmigration is not a reclaiming of one's personal selfhood, but a sinking further into the delusions that follow upon any belief in such a personal selfhood. True resurrection is an awakening from the dead world of samsaric sleep into the final victory of awakening (*buddhatva*), sovereign over both life and death.

The Head of the Baptist
6: 17–29

[17]*Now it was this same Herod who had sent to have John arrested, and had had him chained up in prison because of Herodias, his brother Philip's wife, whom he had married.* [18]*For John had told Herod, "It is against the law for you to have your brother's wife."* [19]*As for Herodias, she was furious with him and wanted to kill him; but she was not able to,* [20]*because Herod was in awe of John, knowing him to be a good and upright man, and gave him his protection. When he had heard him speak he was greatly perplexed, and yet he liked to hear him speak.*

[21]*An opportunity came on Herod's birthday when he gave a banquet for the nobles of his court, for his army officers and for the leading figures in Galilee.* [22]*When the daughter of this same Herodias came in and danced, she delighted Herod and his guests; so the king said to the girl, "Ask me anything you like and I will give it to you."* [23]*And he swore an oath, "I will give you anything you ask, even half of my kingdom."* [24]*She went out and said to her mother, "What shall I ask for?" She replied, "The head of John the Baptist."* [25]*The girl at once rushed back to the king and made her request, "I want*

---

25. Kelber, *Mark's Story of Jesus*, 34.

26. Tolbert, *Sowing the Gospel*, 198: "The story of John's death in Herod's court is the most shocking, graphic, and frightening description of the deadly nature of tribulation on account of the *word* to be found anywhere in the Gospel except at the crucifixion itself." The content of that word, however, is not specified, for it urges not a teaching to be accepted, but a change of heart and orientation to be effected.

you to give me John the Baptist's head, immediately, on a dish." [26]*The king was deeply distressed but, thinking of the oaths he had sworn and of his guests, he was reluctant to break his word to her.* [27]*At once the king sent one of the bodyguard with orders to bring John's head.* [28]*The man went off and beheaded him in prison; then he brought the head on a dish and gave it to the girl, and the girl gave it to her mother.* [29]*When John's disciples heard about this, they came and took his body and laid it in a tomb.*

Mark here gives Herod's karmic past, describing in grisly detail how he kills the Baptist and why.[27] It paints Herod as saddened by the request but at the same time driven by his fear of appearing stingy to his assembled guests.[28] He was saddened, because he was evidently interested in what the Baptist had to say, since he believed in the supernatural world. When he listened to John, he was "greatly perplexed" (πολλὰ ἠπόρει), for John spoke of a repentance that would overturn the very world that gave Herod meaning. This is why he thought Jesus was John resuscitated and come back to preach repentance and trouble his world again. He is troubled by his actions of servility before the dancing girl and his newly acquired wife, and his cruelty in severing and presenting John's head on a dish. Jesus' disciples are to share table with the common people, Herod's guests are served the grisly head of a prophet on a platter. His grotesque table manners highlight his own personal mind-set, caught in lust, delusion, and anger, the three poisons that in Mahāyāna doctrine constitute *saṃsāra*. Poisoned in mind, he is gripped in fear about Jesus, for he sees Jesus, falsely, as a supernatural breaking-through into his world of power and control.

Mark also links this banquet account, with its assembled guests, to the first miracle of the loaves, to follow immediately, for he describes that banquet as similarly arranged in the style of a Roman banquet, with neatly arranged rows of men in order.[29]

Note also that Herod's gruesome party takes place in Galilee. The establishment opposition to John's and Jesus' calls for repentance are not confined

---

27. The description perhaps alludes to the story of Queen Esther (Esther 5: 3f), where the king over his wine says that he will give to Esther whatever she asks, even up to one half of his kingdom. See Kermode, *The Genesis of Secrecy*, 161.10. Also Anderson, "Feminist Criticism," *Mark and Method*, ed. Anderson and Moore, 128, who presents the parallels that King Artaxerxes offers one half of his kingdom to Esther, and that Esther is also referred to as κορασία, as is Herodias' daughter in v. 22. Anderson concludes that Herodias' daughter, "Salome (so identified by Josephus, not by the Bible) is the dark obverse of Esther—Esther's shadow sister."

28. Tolbert, *Sowing the Gospel*, 158, sees Herod as a type of that seed sown among thorns, for the cares and desires of the world lead him to murder the Baptist, whom he rather enjoyed spending time with, for Mark portrays him as somewhat interested in the Baptist's words.

29. Klosinski, *Meals in Mark*, 119: "Herod's banquet (6: 14–29) . . . can be understood as an anti-type of the subsequent feeding of the five thousand (6: 30–44). Herod's guests constitute three groups (6: 21), while Jesus divides his guests into three groups (6: 39–40). Only men attend each banquet (6: 21–22, 44)."

to Jerusalem. John "is arrested or handed over (1: 14 *paradothēnai*); he is killed at a gathering of persons from Galilee (6: 21)."[30] The undermining of spatial boundaries by Jesus' voyaging across the Sea of Galilee from his Jewish homeland to foreign gentile regions, as well as the collapse of defined boundaries between profane and holy land signaled by the disciples' shaking off the dust from their feet against Galilean towns, is repeated once again, for Jesus' Galilean homeland neither accepts him nor spares the head of the Baptist. Despite Jesus' promised return to Galilee after his resurrection, Galilee is hardly a privileged locale in Mark's portrayal of Jesus' life and career.

There is perhaps a further allusion here to the story of the raising of Jairus' daughter. She is addressed by Jesus in 5: 42 as "little girl" (τὸ κοράσιον), the same term used in 6: 22 when the king addresses the little girl (εἶπεν τῷ κορασίῳ) who will bewitch him. Jairus' daughter signals resurrected life and vitality, while Herodias' daughter is the agent of murder and mutilation.[31]

First Miracle of the Loaves and Fishes
6: 30–44

[30]*The apostles rejoined Jesus and told him all they had done and taught.* [31]*And he said to them, "Come away to some lonely place all by yourselves and rest a while;" for there were so many coming and going that there was no time for them even to eat.* [32]*So they went off in the boat to a lonely place where they could be by themselves.* [33]*But the people saw them going, and many recognized them; and from every town they all hurried to the place on foot and reached it before them.* [34]*So as he stepped ashore he saw a large crowd; and he took pity on them because they were like sheep without a shepherd, and he set himself to teach them at some length.* [35]*By now it was getting very late, and his disciples came up to him and said, "This is a lonely place and it is getting very late,* [36]*so send them away and they can go to the farms and villages round about, to buy themselves something to eat."* [37]*He*

---

30. Malbon, *Narrative Space,* 23.

31. Kermode, *The Genesis of Secrecy,* 132–33: "When Jesus approaches her supposed corpse she is called 'the child,' but in healing her he addresses her as 'little girl' (*korasion,* the same word used of Salome). The word is still a neuter, but it can only mean 'little girl,' the change distinguishes her as approaching, from the other side, the condition of the cured woman, a healthy sexual maturity. The name 'Jairus' (missing from some manuscripts) is said to mean 'awakener,' and it occurs in the book of Esther, which Mark knew well and on which he drew in the Salome episode." The name Jair occurs in Esther 2: 5: "Now in the citadel of Susa there lived a Jew called Mordecai son of Jair, son of Shumei, son of Kish, of the tribe of Benjamin." Mann, *Mark,* 283 concurs that "the sense of the name itself in Hebrew means 'he who enlightens.' " If these allusions are correct, then Mark weaves a contrast between the "awakened and enlightened" daughter of Jairus—he who awakens—and the death-dealing daughter of Herodias, within a context of allusions to the story of Esther.

replied, "Give them something to eat yourselves." They answered, "Are we to spend two hundred denarii on bread for them to eat?" ³⁸He asked, "How many loaves have you? Go and see." And when they had found out, they said, "Five, and two fish." ³⁹And he ordered them to get all the people to sit down in groups on the green grass, ⁴⁰and they sat down on the ground in squares of hundreds and fifties. ⁴¹Then he took the five loaves and the two fish, raised his eyes to heaven and said the blessing; then he broke the loaves and began handing them to his disciples to distribute among the people. He also shared out the two fish among them all. ⁴²They all ate as much as they wanted. ⁴³They collected twelve basketfuls of scraps of bread and pieces of fish. ⁴⁴Those who had eaten the loaves numbered five thousand men.

After breaking his account of the mission of the disciples with the story of John's murder, Mark takes up the thread, now referring to the twelve as the apostles, i.e., those who have been sent out. After their report, Jesus takes them apart into a wilderness place (κατ' ἰδίαν εἰς ἔρημον τόπον), away from the crowd. This is the only time Mark calls Jesus' followers apostles (οἱ ἀπόστολοι), perhaps contrasting them with Herod who sent (ἀποσ-τείλας) his emissaries to have John arrested.³² Earlier instances of such periods of solitude lasted for some period of time, yet here the pattern is broken, for the fame of Jesus' career now disallows such prolonged withdrawal.³³ Increasingly, the course of events draws them into the world of convention-only (saṃvṛti-mātra), with no separate time for quiet awareness of the ultimate presence of Abba. And yet, the very chain of conventional events begins to carry an awareness of Abba; Jesus is totally immersed in the world and yet fully aware of what goes beyond. It is not just the wisdom of emptiness functioning here, but also the engagement of compassion, for when Jesus comes up out of the boat and sees the expectant crowd he is filled with compassion for them, moved in his innards (σπλάγχνον). This is no detached awareness, but a grinding of the heart, a visceral feeling of their sad confusion about the path, for they are like sheep without a shepherd.³⁴

32. Fowler, *Loaves and Fishes,* 76.
33. Tolbert, *Sowing the Gospel,* 138: "Jesus retreats to a 'lonely place' (εἰς ἔρημον τόπον) to pray, as he will try to do occasionally in the Gospel (e.g., 6: 31, 35, 46–47; 8: 3–4), but Simon [in 1: 36] 'pursued him.' The Greek word καταδιώκω carries a very strong, often hostile sense: Simon and the others often harassed him or hunted him down." Just as the crowds do here. Yet, Tolbert apparently sees Jesus' retreat to lonely places only as an attempt at prayerful respite. I see the wilderness itself as one of Mark's central themes, constantly in tension with Jesus' reengagement in the conventional world of towns and cities. This withdrawal/reentry scheme is paradigmatic for Mark, who begins his text with Jesus' withdrawal into the wilderness and ends with Jesus' silent going before the disciples into Galilee.
34. Kelber, *The Kingdom in Mark,* 56: "According to the traditional miracle story, Jesus takes compassion on the people because they are hungry. But Mark, breaking the logic of the miracle, has Jesus take pity on the people because they live in a leaderless situation. . . . The motif of the sheep without a shepherd foreshadows the moment when the shepherd will be struck and the sheep scattered about (14:27)."

After Moses has been forbidden to lead the Israelites into the promised land, in *Numbers* 27: 15–16 he asks Yahweh to appoint a leader, "so that Yahweh's community will not be like sheep without a shepherd." Yahweh grants Moses' request by appointing Joshua to lead the people. Here Jesus, Joshua's name-sake, responds to the confusion of the people by beginning to teach them many things, although nothing of the particular content of the teaching is indicated.

In fact, Jesus teaches this crowd at such length, i.e., so many things (πολλά), that night begins to fall, eliciting objections from the disciples, for what kind of compassion is it to cause people to go without their dinner? Their suggestion is obviously sensible: send them away from that lonely place so they can find something to eat. Jesus' response to them is bewildering. Does he really mean that the disciples should empty their own treasury, shelling out as much as two hundred denarii? The crowd has robbed the disciples of their retreat time and now, so it would appear, they are about to deplete their treasury also![35] But Jesus tells them that they are to feed the crowd.[36] First they gather up what little food they can find, and then they are told to arrange the people in groups on the green grass, in squares of hundreds and fifties.[37] Why does Mark bother to report such a detail? Perhaps a clue is to be found in the final sentence, where the narrator informs us that five thousand men ('άνδρες) ate the loaves. This recalls the customs of Roman banquets from which women were excluded. This is why at Herod's banquet Herodias was standing outside the banquet hall and why her daughter had to go out to talk with her. Furthermore, the seating of the guests at these banquets was a matter of strict control and a clear pecking order was to be observed. By identifying the people as men ('άνδρες), whether that is taken to signify both genders or just men, Mark is directing the reader's attention to Herod's banquet and its structure. He parodies the power elite by having a company of rustics in the wilderness assume upper-class manners. Jesus, whom Herod mistakes for a resurrected John, gives a banquet that mimics the structure of Herod's blood feast!

---

35. Fowler, *Loaves and Fishes,* 81. Fowler also notes, 83, that the present fear on the disciples' part of spending two hundred denarii for food echoes later in the complaint about the three hundred denarii price of the ointment used on Jesus in 14: 5.

36. In the background of Mark's story lies *2 Kings* 5: 42–44: "A man came from Baal-Shalishah, bringing the man of God bread from the first-fruits, twenty barley loaves and fresh grain still in the husk. 'Give it to the company to eat,' Elisha said. But his servant replied, 'How can I serve this to a hundred men?' 'Give it to the company to eat,' he insisted, 'for Yahweh says this, "They will eat and have some left over." ' He served them; they ate and had some left over, as Yahweh had said."

37. Broadhead, *Teaching With Authority,* 120, sees the reclining in groups of hundreds and fifties on the green grass as a clear allusion to the shepherding imagery of Psalm 23. Heil, *The Gospel of Mark as a Model for Action,* 145, thinks that their ordering is reminiscent of the past salvific ordering of the people of Israel in *Exodus* 18: 21, 25. I follow Camery-Hoggatt, *Irony in Mark's Gospel,* 146, who sees a "paradigm of the messianic banquet," with eucharistic significance.

The location of Jesus' banquet is called a wilderness place (ἔρημός ἐστιν ὁ τόπος) in verse 35, but in Mark this refers not to an actual wilderness, dry and arid. Rather, it refers to a place of spiritual emptiness, where ultimate awareness can more easily break through the conventional structures which pattern human life. In this passage it is a grassy place, surrounded by villages and farms, right along the shore line. It sounds more like a picnic spot, if only they had brought enough food. This is the scene of conflict between the common sense advice of the disciples and Jesus' strange behavior.

The image of multiplying food is not, however, the central focus. Indeed, if one insists on a literal interpretation which stresses the power of Jesus, or of God miraculously to provide food for the hungry, then the obvious question is why so many in this world are allowed to starve. In a world of supernatural divine power, there is no reason for the inactivity of a supernatural and compassionate personage. Rather, as Malbon argues, the story "foreshadows for the implied reader the eucharistic meal. The four verbs *took, blessed, broke,* and *gave,* are repeated in the narrative of the last supper (14: 22)."[38] Jesus has the people eat of the blessed bread, as much as they want. And still there is a superabundance, twelve baskets of scraps left over. The point is not that Jesus has instituted the most wonderful meals-on-wheels program, that he has in fact fed a hungry crowd, for they could have found food in the surrounding farms and villages, as the disciples suggested. Rather, the point is that the blessed bread is superabundant, fully satisfying the needs of all the people. It was not that they came hungering for bread, and they could have left at any time to go buy some; the wilderness here is not a literal wilderness. The point is that they came confused and shepherdless.

The question then becomes: what does this blessed bread signify? To many interpreters it prefigures the Eucharistic liturgy, which involves similarly blessed bread, with its power to grant life to those who share it. To medieval theologians it teaches that the divine Jesus is not bound by the laws of nature and thus is able to transform the bread of the Eucharist into his body and blood. Yet in the pericope the only suggestion of this link to the Eucharist is that the bread is blessed by Jesus. Yet the fish are also blessed, and they have no eucharistic liturgical significance at all.

Rather, the feeding of the crowd should be seen as the culmination of Jesus' compassionate teaching. As Crossan holds, before the eucharistic meal of bread and wine were ritualized, a meal of bread and fish was also common. Both symbolize the open table-fellowship of Jesus.[39] The superabundance of his compassion is a direct outflow of his Abba awareness, flowing into the teachings of the path; the feeding follows directly upon his extended teaching. It is that teaching, contentless in Mark's account, that engenders a hunger in

---

38. Malbon, "Narrative Criticism," in *Mark and Method,* 41. So Klosinski, *Meals in Mark,* 165, who explains that the miracle "was allegorized by insertion of the eucharistic language borrowed from chapter 14."

39. Crossan, *The Historical Jesus,* 398–404.

the people, that is then satiated by the blessed openness of sharing everything
in awareness of the interdependence of one upon another. This is what is
depicted in the life style Jesus has just recommended for his disciples.[40] The
feeding of the crowd is another example of the presence of the kingdom,
open to all without intermediary. As Broadhead comments, "the distribution
of bread in the wilderness actuates the calling of the people of God, and the
miracle is subsumed by its own theological significance. This understanding
of the feeding has crucial soteriological and ecclesiological import: the
kingdom of God which was announced in Mark 1: 14–15 is now actuated
in the calling forth of a new community to be the people of God."[41]

This story of feeding has caused many headaches for biblical scholars,
because it is repeated in substantially identical terms at the beginning of
chapter 8. Scriptural scholars try to unearth the original account,[42] see the
two accounts as variations of the same cycle of pre-existing stories,[43] or
otherwise try to trace the origin of the two accounts in terms of Mark's felt
need to present his sources. Indeed, the two stories are variants of a single
story. Each is followed by a crossing of the Sea of Galilee (7: 1–23, 8:
11–12), another story dealing with bread or leaven (7: 24–30, 8: 13–21), and
a healing story (7: 31–37, 8: 22–26). They do appear to initiate two parallel
cycles of stories in chapters six and eight of Mark.[44] Yet, duplication and
doubling, both back and forward, are characteristics of Mark's style.[45] A

---

40. Broadhead, *Teaching With Authority*, 118–19: "By replacing the expected miracle
activity with emphasis on Jesus' teaching, the import of the story becomes clear: it is the
teaching of Jesus which properly satisfies the need of these shepherdless people. Thus,
the configuration of the unit around the teaching once again subsumes the miracles of
Jesus within a crucial interpretive context: they are demonstrations of the power and
mercy of Jesus the teacher."
41. Broadhead, *Teaching With Authority*, 122.
42. So Taylor, *The Gospel According to Saint Mark*, 631.
43. So Jenkins, "A Marcan Doublet," 87–111. See also Achtemeier, "Toward the
Isolation of Pre-Markan Miracle Catenae," and "The Origin and Function of the Pre-
Markan Miracle Catenae," which attempt to reconstruct parallel chains of miracle stories
underlying Mark 4–8.
44. Fowler, *Loaves and Fishes*, 5. Fowler rejects attempts to identify two pre-existing
cycles, 11: "Even though we must reject this hypothesis [of variant cycles in Mark 6:
30–7: 37 and 8: 1–26], we must admit that it is inspired by the valid perception of
parallelism in this material, primarily with the feeding stories, but also with the other
material in Mark 6–8."
45. Neirynck, *Duality in Mark*, 46, 50, 63: "As a result of the temporal and local
statements, double questions and antithetic parallelisms in the Gospel of Mark, it may be
suggested that the progressive double phrase be placed on the list of the characteristics
of Markan usage. Duality, however, is not restricted within the limits of these categories,
but it pervades the different parts and strata of the gospel." Again, on 71–72, Neirynck
explains that redundancies and repetitions have often been used to uncover and reconstruct
Mark's sources in the interest of source criticism. By contrast, he argues that they be
recognized as a dominant feature of Mark's style of composition. Fowler, *Loaves and
Fishes*, 33, argues that "this two-stepped construction is found also at the level of larger
units of material, perhaps of entire pericopes." And then indeed he argues that Mark has
doubled the feeding stories himself to prepare the reader for the second account in chapter 8.

persuasive explanation, offered by Fowler, is that Mark himself has created the present feeding story on the model of the account given in 8: 1–10 in order to stress the density of the disciples. When the second story occurs in chapter eight, the disciples still have no idea how to feed such a large crowd, although they have already witnessed Jesus doing precisely that in chapter 6. The point of the double stories is then to heighten the intensity of the confrontation between Jesus and his disciples.[46] "Mark takes special care to rework the innocent discussions of 8: 3–4, creating the antagonistic debate of 6: 36–38."[47]

Water Walking
6: 45–52

[45]*And at once he made his disciples get into the boat and go on ahead[48] to the other side near Bethsaida, while he himself sent the crowd away.* [46]*After saying goodbye to them he went off into the mountain[49] to pray.* [47]*When evening came, the boat was far out in the middle of the sea,[50] and he was alone on the land.* [48]*He could see they were distressed in rowing,[51] for the wind was against them; and about the fourth watch of the night he came towards them, walking on the sea. He was going to pass them by,* [49]*but when they saw him walking on the sea they thought it was a ghost and cried out;* [50]*for they had all seen him and were terrified. But at once he spoke to them and said, "Courage! It's me! Do not be afraid."* [51]*Then he got into the boat with them and the wind dropped. They were utterly and completely dumbfounded,* [52]*because they had not seen what the miracle of the loaves meant; their hearts were hardened.[52]*

The tumult of a raging sea is a frequent image for confusion and ignorance, both in Mahāyāna texts and in Christian writings. The present account of a

---

46. Fowler, *Loaves and Fishes,* 60–61. Note, however, that Crossan, *The Historical Jesus,* 401, holds just the opposite, that 6: 33–44 is pre-Markan and 8: 14–21 a Markan composition. Crossan's interpretation of Mark's purpose is similar to that of Fowler: ". . . Mark composed 8: 14–21 as a doublet whose presence greatly increased the culpable incomprehension of the disciples and emphasized their climactic failure in 8: 14–21."

47. Fowler, *Loaves and Fishes,* 92.

48. Malbon, *Narrative Space,* 54: "In fact, *proagein* (6: 45) may be translated 'lead the way.' " This suggests that the disciples were charged to take the lead in crossing the sea to proclaim the message in Gentile lands.

49. The Greek singular εἰς τὸ ὄρος is, I think, better translated in the singular (i.e., to the mountain) to maintain both its symbolic significance as a wilderness location and to preserve the contrast of Jesus, first on the mountain and then on the land, with the disciples in the middle of the sea.

50. Following Malbon's translation, *Narrative Space,* 79.

51. Following Malbon's translation, *Narrative Space,* 78.

52. I prefer the literal sense of the RSV rather than the Jerusalem Bible's rendition of "their minds were closed," because it is more than a question of having a mind open to the ideas of others. Rather, the hardening of hearts stands in contrast to faith and conversion. It is the imagined pattern of taking images to be realities.

distressful crossing of the sea recalls the first such story in 4: 35–41, when Jesus calmed the raging storm. Mahāyānists often compare the mind of enlightenment to the calm surface of the sea, reflecting reality without discrimination, as a mirror reflects whatever comes in front of it. By contrast the mind of delusion is troubled and disturbed, like the roiling waves in stormy waters.[53] *The Epistle of James,* likewise, talks of being in two minds, discriminating between things and causing the mind to be tossed about like waves on a troubled sea—against which it contrasts the mind of faith.[54] In the present Markan passage, Jesus sets the scene for the disciples. He makes them get into the boat and depart before he has taken his leave from the crowd.[55] He is forcing them to rely on their own resources, requiring them to return to their everyday skills as boatmen, just as he had forced the Gerasene madman to return home after he cast out the legion of devils. Jesus withdraws into the mountain, alone once again in silent prayer.[56] Mark's rhetoric suggests that, had the disciples not been distressed, they would have journeyed to the gentile shore before Jesus and carried out a mission similar to that recorded in Galilee (6: 12–13).

But they are harassed and distressed in making progress (βασανιζομένους ἐν τῷ ἐλαύνειν), struggling across the sea in the deepest part of the night. The passage, if taken literally, seems unintelligible. These are fishermen, accustomed to the sea (actually a lake), unlikely to be forced to set out into the teeth of a storm. It is as if Jesus forcibly sent them directly into the face of danger, as David sent Uriah into the front of the battle! Meanwhile, Jesus

---

53. *The Awakening of Faith,* trans. Hakeda, 41: "Ignorance does not exist apart from enlightenment; therefore it cannot be destroyed [because one cannot destroy something which does not really exist], and yet it cannot not be destroyed [in so far as it remains]. This is like the relationship that exists between the water of the ocean [i.e., enlightenment] and its waves [i.e., the modes of mind] stirred by the wind [of ignorance]. Water and wind are inseparable; but water is not mobile by nature, and if the wind stops the movement ceases. But the wet nature remains undestroyed. Likewise, man's mind, pure in its own nature, is stirred by the wind of ignorance." Note that this text is at variance with the teaching of emptiness presented by Nāgārjuna and stressed by the Yogācāra philosophers. It belongs to the tradition of Tathāgatagarbha thinking, for which see Keenan, *The Meaning of Christ,* 146–148.

54. Keenan, *The Meaning of Christ,* 34–35.

55. Malbon, *Narrative Space,* 28: "*Anagkazō,* used only here [in 6: 45], means 'force,' 'compel'; the 'word implies unwillingness on the part of the disciples.'" See Bratcher and Nida, *A Translator's Handbook,* 211. Also Kelber, *The Kingdom in Mark,* 57: ". . . the disciples are to be in the vanguard and truly lead the movement to the Gentiles. This is why Jesus exerts pressure (6:45a *ēnagkasen*), forcing the disciples to spearhead the move across the lake (6: 45a: *proagein eis to peran*)."

56. Against Kee, *Community of the New Age,* 161: "In the Markan tradition, prayer functions in two essential ways: as a mode of commitment and as a channel of power. In 1: 35 and 6: 46, Jesus is pictured in the context of Markan editorial material as withdrawing from the crowds for strengthening and renewal as he faces the next stage in his ministry." This is an instrumental understanding of prayer, always in service of something else. I understand prayer in Mark to be foremost a withdrawal from all instrumental activities, into the mystery and silence of Abba.

himself goes to the darkness of the mountain to pray, removing himself from the conventional concerns of his disciples. When he goes to pray, "in all cases Jesus is alone: in 1: 35 in the wilderness spot, in 6: 46 on the mountain, and in 14: 32–42 in the garden of Gethsemane. . . . The three passages are, furthermore, akin as the prayer always occurs during the night. . . . In 1: 35 this is expressly stated, in 6: 46 it is suggested by the following section as Jesus meets his disciples 'about the fourth watch of the night' (6: 48), and in the Gethsemane story it is indicated by the fact that the preceding meal with the disciples took place 'when it was evening' (14: 18). Night and solitude are the setting for Jesus' praying in Mark."[57]

Yet, while night is a time for Jesus' prayerful awareness of the Father, for the disciples darkness signifies their confused state of mind, entangled in mistaking images for realities. They have maintained their view of Jesus as a special kind of being, apart from them and supernatural in status. They cannot function apart from him, for they do not understand about the loaves: that the kingdom is shared by all without need for mediation, without the physical presence of Jesus. They are becoming outsiders, unable to penetrate the opacity of Jesus' parabolic appearance.[58] The passage contrasts their mental attachment to Jesus with the converted mind, for it ends with the explanation that "their hearts were hardened (ἀλλ' ἦν αὐτῶν ἡ καρδία πεπωρωμένη)", their inner understanding was petrified, hardened against any new insight or new way of understanding.[59]

The reader of Mark perhaps begins to distance herself from these fearful disciples, but caution should be exercised. After all, they are asked by Jesus, forced by Jesus, to undertake a mission outside their native land and culture: he tells them to go to the other side of the sea, near Bethsaida.[60] It is not just that they do not understand the import of that mission. Their fear derives not so much from the stormy sea, as from their clear understanding that they are once again to proclaim repentance and the presence of the kingdom to foreigners. What prospect does that have of success? How many gentiles are likely to repent at the urging of a bunch of Jewish fishermen? Their hearts are hardened not simply by obtuseness, but by fear. They are afraid that

---

57. Mauser, *Christ in the Wilderness,* 107–08. Taylor, *The Gospel According to Mark,* 328, notes Euthymius' maxim: "The mountain, night, and solitude are suitable for prayer."

58. Boucher, *The Mysterious Parable,* 80, notes that the feeding stories are similar to parables, having "more than one level of meaning and are thus subject to the same misunderstanding." Also Boobyer, "The Redaction of Mark IV.1–34," 63, says that Mark takes the term parable to include both Jesus' spoken words and his deeds. Kelber, *The Oral and Written Gospel,* 123–24 argues that the entire gospel is parabolic.

59. Tolbert, *Sowing the Gospel,* 199, comments on the line "their hearts were hardened" (ἡ καρδία πεπωρωμένη, 6: 52) as follows: "The gravity of this description is increased by the fact that the same words were used to describe the Pharisees and the Herodians who were plotting to destroy Jesus (ἐπὶ τῇ πωρώσει τῆς καρδίας αὐτῶν, 3: 5–6)."

60. Malbon, *Narrative Space,* 42: "Bethsaida is clearly marked in the text as being on 'the other side' of the sea (6: 45; 8: 13,22) from Galilee, that is, beyond the borders of Galilee."

Jesus' vision of a kingdom of total openness, one that forces people into direct contact with one another, is impractical. They have not understood about the loaves, the direct presence and availability of God to human beings, and of human beings to one another. Their hearts are hardened because they are not up to the task.[61]

The reader finds herself in a situation not unlike the disciples: how to make sense out of a text that sets up interpretive hurdles at every juncture. What is the connection of loaves to hardening of hearts? What has all that to do with the disciples' fear? and with Jesus' identity? "Not enough information has been supplied in the narrative up to this point to clarify the confusion and the reader is led, at a crucial point in the narrative, to *the same internal disposition that the disciples possess in the narrative: misunderstanding and confusion.*"[62] Their increasing lack of understanding forces the reader to disassociate herself with the disciples,[63] yet, possessed of a similar fear of the insecurity of the unknown shores, she is forced to repeat their confusion. Only those freed from all fear are enabled to embark on the passage of true discipleship, leaving the comfort of Jesus' presence behind in the mountain and crossing the sea to proclaim the kingdom.[64] How then can one be freed from fear while clinging to the preoccupations of selfhood?

When Jesus begins to pass the disciples by in the dark of the night, they take him to be a ghostly image, a phantasm (ἔδοξαν ὅτι φάντασμά ἐστιν)

---

61. Against Malbon, "Narrative Criticism," in *Mark and Method*, 41–42: "What do loaves have to do with the sea? And why are so many images from Exodus being stacked up here? Bread in the wilderness, walking on (through) the sea, 'I am'—and now hardened hearts. The passive voice (their hearts were hardened) suggests that the disciples' hearts, like Pharoah's, were hardened by God so that God's overall purpose for the people could be worked out." If the multiplied loaves signify the availability of Jesus' teachings to all, Jew and gentile, then their failure to understand about the loaves relates to their distress in rowing to the other side to share Jesus' teachings. The fearful hardening of their hearts frustrates Jesus' purpose, and thus God's purpose.

62. Bassler, "Parable of the Loaves," 165. I hold that such confusion is not relieved in the narrative grammar of Mark, but continues beyond into the lives of his readers. Also Fowler, *Let the Reader Understand,* 124: "Once we are told bluntly that the disciples did not understand statements or actions in the story because 'their hearts were hardened,' their minds clouded (6: 52; cf. 8: 17–21; 3: 5). Often, that is, inside views of knowledge inform us that characters in the story (usually the disciples) do not know something. In keeping with Mark's rhetoric of indirection, moreover, when the narrator tells us that the disciples did not understand something, he refrains from telling us exactly what they did not understand. We are then in a position of ignorance not unlike that of the uncomprehending disciples, with the difference that they often do not realize that they do not understand whereas we usually do."

63. Fowler, *Let the Reader Understand,* 68: "Rather than feeling empathy for the terror-stricken disciples, we cannot help judging them unfavorably. How could they not recognize who is coming to them? We, after all, know who it is; why do they not? Moreover, do they not remember, as we surely do, what happened in the previous sea incident back in Mark 4: 35–41, when Jesus calmed both wind and wave in their presence? How could they be so obtuse as not to recognize who this must be, 'that even wind and sea obey him'?"

64. See Moore, *Literary Criticism and the Gospels,* 81–84.

and are afraid. They experience the world in images (φάντασμα, i.e., *parikal-pita*) and envisage ghosts. The expression "passing by" denotes an epiphany, a manifestation of God that, being seen, immediately withdraws.[65] This recalls *Sirach* 24: 5–6, where the journey of Wisdom is described: "Alone, I have made the circuit of the heavens and walked through the depths of the abyss. Over the waves of the sea and over the whole earth, and over every people and nation I have held sway." The Markan epiphany of Jesus to his disciples does not, however, elicit any epiphanic wisdom; it is not a triumphant cosmic circuit at all. The disciples do not become aware of the wilderness silence of God or of the transient presence of Jesus. They simply see a ghost! They are captured within the imagined pattern of consciousness, and that is why their hearts are hardened and their minds closed. They cannot see without abandoning that pattern of supposed security, without emptying their minds of accustomed sureties.

Mark is not trying to demonstrate the reality of the supernatural. He is not insistent upon Jesus' ability to walk on the water, and the stilling of the sea "appears almost incidental, occurring without gesture or command."[66] During his cultural time, all great prophets were capable of such miracles. In the narrative event, the miracle of water-walking is to no real effect, for it does not lead the disciples to faith, but to a hardening of their hearts.[67] The real thrust of Mark's story is that, when the disciples cry out that there is a ghost meandering about the lake, Jesus speaks to them at once and identifies himself, "It's me! Do not be afraid." As long as he is seen as a supposed ghost, he passes them by (παρελθεῖν αὐτοὺς): that is what ghosts do best! Yet, the supernatural visage turns out to be simply Jesus. Jesus is not being elevated by attributing to him supernatural status. Rather, supernatural status is being emptied by being identified with Jesus, who calms the winds of delusion in the minds of humans. Jesus' answer, "It is I" echoes the "solemn words of

---

65. Broadhead, *Teaching With Authority*, 125.2: " 'Passing by' is an epiphanic imagery from the Old Testament. See God's passing by of Moses in Exod. 33.19,22; 34.5–7; and of Elijah in 1 Kgs 19.11." Against Heil, *The Gospel of Mark as a Model for Action*, 149: ". . . 'passing by' functions as a technical term to express not the withdrawing away but the drawing near of a divine being in order to show himself before human eyes (Exod 33: 18–34: 6; 1 Kgs 19: 11; Gen 32: 31–32; LXX Dan 12: 1)." One passes by not simply to reveal presence, but, in revealing presence, to immediately become absent. The entire tensive interplay between hiddenness and manifestation is at work here. See Via, *The Ethics of Mark's Gospel*, 176, who writes that "the strange motif, difficult to interpret that Jesus meant to pass by the struggling disciples (6: 48) would bring to bear on this story of revealed presence the related theme of concealment. . . . [This] suggests the mysterious, nonmanipulable hidden dimension of revelation." God and his kingdom are hidden from their imagined pattern of understanding, for this image does not reveal, but serves to occlude insight.

66. Broadhead, *Teaching With Authority*, 126.

67. Broadhead, *Teaching With Authority*, 127: "Ironically, Mark 6.47–53 employs a miracle story to narrate the failure of miracles to lead the followers of Jesus to faith and understanding. None of the miracles, even this epiphany, is sufficient to give them insight into the identity of Jesus."

the revelation formula spoken by Yahweh to Moses from the burning bush."[68] Yet, the revelation here is not of any numinous being, but, as the New Jerusalem Bible translates, just Jesus: "It's me!" Mark structures the account as an epiphany of the ordinary, for Jesus comes to the distressed disciples from the silence of the mountain into the ordinariness of their conventional fears about a gentile mission. The wind calms down and again they are dumbfounded (καὶ λίαν ἐκ περισσοῦ ἐν ἑαυτοῖς ἐξίσταντο), not just because they have seen somebody walking on the water, but because it is merely Jesus. Their continued expectations of a more than life-sized Jesus do not fit into the story, with Jesus again merely present in the boat with them. The same phrase "I am" will be used by Jesus in 14:62, where it is directed to the high priest's question, "Are you the Christ?" There, the New Jerusalem Bible translates more solemnly, "I am," echoing the revelatory formula of *Exodus*. Yet, Mark here gives the clue to how we are to understand such a pronouncement, as emptying the person of Jesus of any identifiable essence, as just Jesus in his naked humanity, for that dependently co-arisen being is the being of emptiness.[69]

Yet, it is a difficult point, for one has to let go of fixed ideas about religion, to abandon supernatural understandings of faith itself. Otherwise, no matter how intensely religious, one's heart will be frozen and petrified within the imagined pattern.

Gennesaret or Bethsaida
6: 53–56

[53]*Having made the crossing, they came to land at Gennesaret and moored there. *[54]*When they disembarked people at once recognized him, *[55]*and started hurrying all through the countryside and brought the sick on stretchers to wherever they heard he was. *[56]*And wherever he went, to village or town or farm, they laid down the sick in the open spaces, begging him to let them touch even the fringe of his cloak. And all those who touched him were saved.*

Notice that Mark appears to make major geographical mistakes throughout his gospel. In the immediately preceding passage Jesus tells his disciples to

---

68. Malbon, *Narrative Space*, 78. See also 85: Jesus' prayer "on the mountain" (16: 46) is followed immediately by the account of Jesus walking on the sea and saying to the disciples at 6: 50, *egō eimi*, 'I am' (RSV 'It is I'),. . . [This] recalls the proclamation of Yahweh to Moses from the burning bush on Mount Horeb: *egō eimi*, 'I am' (Ex 3: 14, LXX). In addition, the disciples to whom Jesus speaks, just as the Pharaoh to whom Moses spoke the words God gave, did not understand, 'for their hearts were hardened' (Mark 6: 52; cf. Exodus 10: 1 and passim)."

69. Fowler, *Loaves and Fishes*, 103: "The original epiphantic ἐγώ εἰμι is undermined— Jesus may reveal himself but the disciples do not perceive. We repeat: 'their hearts were hardened.' " There is no revelation within the imagined pattern of understanding, for attachment to images and ideas occludes the spontaneity and otherness of revelation.

go ahead to Bethsaida, yet here they arrive at Gennesaret. These errors about geography lead scholars to think he "has almost no concern for his geographical references."[70] Some have thought that this very confusion of places means that Mark, writing from Rome or some other distant place, simply did not know his geography. Yet, perhaps there is more than this to Mark's geographical inconsistencies. Bethsaida is on the eastern, foreign shore of the Sea of Galilee and in making his disciples head there, Jesus is directing them once again to gentile territory, now to preach the gospel of the kingdom. But they had once previously visited the country of the Gerasenes together with Jesus and were asked to leave (5: 17). The west side of the sea is the homeland of Jesus and the disciples. "Jesus, in asking his disciples to go before him to Bethsaida (6: 45) is asking them to move out to others, to move beyond his own people, their own religious tradition. . . . As commanded, the disciples set out in the boat, but they are 'distressed in rowing because of the wind' (6: 48), fearful at Jesus' appearance because they do not recognize him, and (as the Markan narrator adds) without understanding 'about the loaves' for 'their hearts were hardened' (6: 52). Are the disciples, according to Mark, also distressed, fearful, and without understanding about going to Bethsaida?"[71] The distress in their minds leads them back to the familiar western shore, to Gennesaret. They do not precede Jesus to the gentiles. Their mission is aborted and they land back in familiar territory.

Their intended goal of Bethsaida is reached only in 8: 22, in the company of Jesus! The intervening narrative highlights Jesus' freedom from spatial and ethnic boundaries. He argues against laws of ritual purity that separate Jew from gentile, he heals the Syro-Phoenician woman, and then, returning from Tyre by way of Sidon, north of Tyre—another Markan geographical puzzle, he arrives at the Decapolis, which is southeast of Galilee. He feeds the second multitude on the eastern, gentile shore, and then returns to Dalmanutha, the location of which is unknown! Jesus has taken his fearful disciples on a roundabout tour of gentile lands, inculcating in them the total inclusivity of the kingdom. Only after this prolonged excursion does the projected voyage to Bethsaida come to its deferred conclusion in 8: 22. This is more than mere authorial confusion about geography. Between the disciples' setting out for Bethsaida and their eventual arrival there, Mark consciously fractures geography to demonstate to the disciples (and the reader) the total compass of the kingdom. Already, by announcing at the very beginning of Jesus' ministry that the kingdom has arrived, Mark has fractured linear time frameworks, and this is accomplished with even greater intensity in the eschatological discourse of Chapter Thirteen.[72] No boundaries seem to apply anymore. "Jesus

---

70. Fowler, *Loaves and Fishes,* 66.

71. Malbon, *Narrative Space,* 28.

72. Fowler, *Loaves and Fishes,* 40, raises questions about whether Mark's gospel in fact has a denouement. What time notion is thereby assumed? Does recognizing Mark as literature really imply such a plot sequence? This contrasts sharply with Tolbert, *Sowing the Gospel,* who notes on 144 that by 6: 17, when the Baptist meets his cruel fate, one

seeks to break down and break open the exclusive categories of the sacred and the profane, which the scribes—and the entire religious establishment— seek to maintain."[73] Those boundaries are, however, also maintained by Jesus' disciples, for everyone wants to know "the lay of the land," and everybody finds foreign lands "not merely benign or indifferent, but threatening."[74]

Once more in Gennesaret Jesus again engages himself in the tasks of compassion. On the one hand, Mark accuses the disciples of having closed minds for not understanding about the loaves and for not recognizing Jesus on the water—in a word, for seeing Jesus only within their concept boundaries of supernatural reality. On the other hand, he insists that Jesus is not to be seen by opposing a concept of the supernatural to the concrete society of the "natural" world. He does perform very concrete miracles and heals all who but touch the fringe of his garment.

Nineham points out that this fringe "is probably a reference to the blue fringe or tassel every male Jew was required to have on the corners of his robe (see Num. 15: 38f and Deut. 22: 12). If so, and the tradition is good, it is a further indication of Jesus' loyalty to the religion of the Law."[75] Mark's rhetorical design would appear not to be simply to destroy the traditions or undermine their value but to empty them of absolute value and see them as conventional practices.

The movement of Mark's text is back and forth and up and down, trying to suggest that ultimate meaning will always remain beyond any conventions, and yet that all is worldly convention-only. Thus, Jesus moves through the open places, i.e., the market places (ἐν ταῖς ἀγοραῖς) without concern for ritual purity. When the woman with the hemorrhage had touched him in the crowd in 5: 27, Jesus had reacted by insistently asking who had touched him as if to object to ritual defilement. But, here any ritual hesitancy is absent. "Jesus' loyalty to religious law, to sacred distinctions, is illustrated. Yet, as Jesus allows himself, in the profane marketplace, to be touched by the sick— some of whom were probably women, many of whom must have been ritually 'unclean'—Jesus' overturning of the distinction between the sacred and the profane, the very foundation of the religious law, is dramatically portrayed."[76] Almost immediately in 7: 3–4, Mark notes that strict observers of the law regard the marketplace as ritually defiling, for, after returning from there, they have to ritually bathe (i.e., "sprinkle themselves" of 7: 4) before eating.

---

should recognize that the disciples will indeed fail. Thus 145: "The central tension in the Gospel of Mark, as in Xenophon's *An Ephesian Tale,* Chariton's *Chaereas and Callirhoe,* Homer's *Odyssey,* or Greek epic and drama generally, is not *what* is going to happen, *but how it will happen.*" Tolbert sees a clear plot in Mark, modeled after popular Hellenistic literature.

73. Malbon, *Narrative Space,* 30, commenting on 3: 22, where the scribes who accuse Jesus have, already at this early juncture in the narrative, come down from Jerusalem.

74. Malbon, *Narrative Space,* 43.

75. Nineham, *Saint Mark,* 186.

76. Malbon, *Narrative Space,* 92.

The path Jesus follows is the middle practice of differentiating ultimate meaning from worldly convention, maintaining both in dynamic tension. While destroying nothing of the traditions, he empties them all, thereby enabling one to reclaim their validity as dependently co-arisen. As Jesus' wilderness sojourns disappear from the narrative, he seems to become increasingly oblivious to the distinctions between sacred and profane space. The two truths of ultimate meaning and worldly convention are no longer expressed by Markan withdrawals into the lonely places of the wilderness, but in their place Mark depicts experiences of direct awareness by locating Jesus on mountains, at the transfiguration, on the Mount of Olives, and finally on the hill of Calvary.

7

Traditions

The Attempt to Capture Truth
7: 1–8

[1]The Pharisees and some of the scribes who had come from Jerusalem gathered round him, [2]and they noticed that some of his disciples were eating with unclean hands, that is, without washing them. [3]For the Pharisees, and all the Jews, follow the tradition of the elders and never eat without washing their arms as far as the elbow; [4]and on returning from the market place they never eat without first sprinkling themselves. There are also many other observances which have been handed down to them concerning the washing of cups and pots and bronze dishes. [5]So these Pharisees and scribes asked him, "Why do your disciples not respect the tradition of the elders but eat their food with unclean hands?" [6]He answered, "How rightly Isaiah prophesied about you hypocrites in the passage of scripture:

> *This people honors me*
> *only with lip service,*
> *while their hearts are far from me.*
> *[7]Their reverence of me is worthless,*
> *the lessons they teach*
> *are nothing but human commandments.*

[8]You put aside the commandment of God to observe human traditions."

Mark's overall theme of truth is here raised in terms of the validity of tradition. The tradition in question is not only the Jewish tradition, although that constitutes the specific context in which the question is raised. Furthermore, Jesus' critique of human traditions in 7:9-13 (τὴν παράδοσιν τῶν ἀνθρώπων) was not unique to him. The Jews of the Hellenistic Diaspora and Hellenistic Jewish Christians distinguished the primary law given to Moses on Sinai from secondary, post-Sinaitic, man-made laws, "which are also recorded in the Pentateuch and which Hellenistic Jews believed God gave Israel as an intolerable burden because of the hardness of their hearts (cf. Ezekiel 20:25–26). In Mark 7:3–8, which in this case reflects the views of Hellenistic Jewry, these laws are called 'the tradition of the elders' or 'the injunctions of men' (*paradosis tōn presbyterōn, entalmata tōn anthrōpōn*), as contrasted with 'the [authentic] commandment of God' (*hē entolē tou theou*), to which the Hellenist Jews sought to return."[1]

All human traditions are called into question, all forms which attempt to embody truth in human forms.[2] The disciples, who have been confused about how to differentiate ultimate meaning from worldly convention, here violate the traditions about eating, hungrily ignoring a tradition that Mark by way of exaggeration tells us, "all Jews follow."[3] Verses 3 and 4 give a brief summary of a Jewish practice, the function of which is described as a ritual washing upon returning from the market place (ἀπ᾽ ἀγορᾶς), lest one eat with profane, unclean hands (κοιναῖς χερσίν).[4] "The marketplace is a profane

---

1. Sheehan, *The First Coming*, 246.37.

2. Cohen, *From The Maccabees to the Mishnah*, 78: "And then there were Jews who integrated the new piety into their lives through the observance of the myriad rituals and observances but did not seek to sanctify their lives thereby. They ignored the meaning and purpose of the entire regimen, and the sanctification of life and the direction of one's thoughts to God and to God's revealed truth. These are the Jews whose 'legalism,' that is, reliance upon the mere external observance of the rituals to ensure them favor in God's eyes, has loomed so large in Christian polemics against Judaism. Such people are to be found in all religious communities (including Christian, as the sermons of the church fathers abundantly attest) in all ages, and we may assume that such Jews existed in ancient times, even if we disbelieve the jaundiced portrayal of the Pharisees in the Gospels. Jesus was not the only preacher to attack the hypocrisy and ostentatiousness of the self-righteous (cf. *Psalms of Solomon* 4, a text often attributed to a Pharisaic teacher!)." The notion of a new covenant is, I think, quite in harmony with Cohen's remarks. Kee, *Community of the New Age*, 114, notes that in: ". . . the controversy over the traditions of the leaders (Mark 7), a scriptural text is quoted (from the LXX of Isa. 29:13) to show that, although Israel's official interpreters of the Law of God claim to be obeying its commands, in fact their 'heart is far' from God. Here there is an implicit contrast with the new covenant as portrayed in Jer 31:33, where what is essential in the covenant relationship is not the written law but the law written 'upon their hearts.' " When in Mark 14: 24 Jesus offers his blood of the covenant, it is this inner covenant he has in mind.

3. The point is not good hygiene, nor proper moral purity, but the ritual purity entailed in daily life. Cohen, *From the Maccabees to the Mishnah*, 130, reports that: "According to Leviticus and Numbers, anyone and anything that enters the 'camp,' the abode of God, must be pure. That which is impure must be expelled from the camp. The camp includes all the children of Israel: the tabernacle, the priests and Levites, and the twelve tribes. It was not until the period of the second temple that the full implications of this conception were actualized. Priests and sectarians observed all the purity laws, because God was in the 'camp.' . . . For most Jews of the second temple period, however, the sanctification of daily life was not implemented to such a radical degree." As Cohen explains, 159, the very name, Pharisee, deriving from the Hebrew and Aramaic *perushim*, suggests "separation" from ritual impurity.

4. Via, *The Ethics of Mark's Gospel*, 89: "Mark 7 uses both the adjective *koinos* ('defiled' or 'unclean') (7: 2, 5) and the verb *koinoō* ('defile') (7 15, 18, 20, 23). In Judaism, *koinos* could mean common, as held in common; profane or given to general use as opposed to

space and any contact with it demands ritual purification (7: 3–4)."⁵ It is the tradition which serves to differentiate between the sacred and the profane, the clean and the unclean. The present question regards the validity of such a dichotomy and Mark has Jesus address this issue: how is truth embodied in human traditions?⁶

The Pharisees were indeed devoted to the traditions. They were recognized by their contemporaries as most zealous in religious observances and not, as Mark depicts them, simply as nitpickers or pettifogging lawyers.⁷ The traditions they follow were handed down from the elders, and are recorded in the Pentateuch. And yet Jesus here negates their attitude by quoting those same elders, for he cites passages both from Isaiah and from Moses to assert that the tradition itself is not sacrosanct, but itself a human creation. To observe the traditions of men (κρατεῖτε τήν παράδοσιν τῶν ἀνθρώπων) means to cling to and take firm hold of conventional truth as if it were itself ultimate. Yet, no matter how revered or sanctified by ancient warrants, traditions are but human fabrication (*saṃvṛti-mātra*) which, if regarded as of unchanging, divine validity, pretend to move beyond any cultural relativity and any dependent co-arising. It is this attitude of clinging to what one falsely regards as the fundamentals that constitutes the attitude Mark attributed to the Pharisees, not the actual content of their teachings. It is the clinging itself that disenables, not what is clung to.

The quotation from *Isaiah* 29:13 is apropos, for in its Isaiahan context it treats the closing of the eyes of the prophets and the veiling of the heads of seers.⁸ No longer can they see, for truth is veiled from them. This is false conventional truth (*mithyā-saṃvṛti*), false because one clings to images and ideas as if they represented reality itself. Thus, for Isaiah, vision is sealed off and truth cannot be discerned. Mark has Jesus use the passage with much the same intent, to criticize those who think they have captured the vision, who identify the human lessons they teach (διδάσκοντες διδασκαλίας) as "the teaching."

But such a verbal identification of truth and tradition is worthless and vain, empty of purpose (μάτην). Such a literal worship is vain because it pretends to have grasped God in teachings and traditions. To this false clinging to convention, Jesus counterposes the commandment of God (τήν ἐντολὴν

holy; and ritually or cultically unclean. In the sense of cultically unclean, *koinos* was virtually synonymous with *akathartos* ('impure,' 'unclean')."

5. Malbon, *Narrative Space,* 92, notes that whether one has to purify oneself or things bought in the market, "the separation of the sacred and the profane is presupposed."

6. See Malbon, *Narrative Space,* 131–32: "The Pharisaic opposition is ... between those persons, places, and things made sacred by Torah observance and all other—profane—persons, places, and things.... The Markan Jesus and the Markan narrative seem to move toward the opposite pole of disvaluing the sacred/profane distinction (See Mark 7—in its entirety)."

7. Mann's translation of ὑποκριτῶν, *Mark,* 313.

8. One could as well cite *Amos* 5: 21–24, where Yahweh scorns the ritual worship of vain sacrifices and oblations.

τοῦ θεοῦ). Here Jesus is not talking about a set of rules or commandments, for the term is in the singular. The primal commandment is the practice of love of God and compassion for human beings (Mark 12: 28–34). That is the practice of the kingdom. Yet, such a commandment offers no firm recipe for action. One has to decide what is compassionate in terms of the dependently co-arisen conditions of one's life. One loves only in the particular and cannot capture love in any set of traditions. Nevertheless, the traditions do provide guidance and can lead toward true practice, as will become clear in chapter twelve, so long as they are not mistaken for absolutely true norms governing each and every human situation. There are no such norms, whether from the Old or New Testament. We must write the endings of all our practices.

An Example of Being a Hypocrite
7: 9–13

⁹And he said to them, "How ingeniously you get round the commandment of God in order to preserve your own tradition! ¹⁰For Moses said, 'Honor your father and your mother,' and 'Anyone who curses father and mother must be put to death.' ¹¹But you say, 'If a man says to his father or mother: Anything I have that I might have used to help you is Korban (that is, dedicated to God),' ¹²then he is forbidden from that moment to do anything for his father or mother. ¹³In this way you make God's word ineffective for the sake of your tradition which you have handed down. And you do many other things like this."

Jesus ironically congratulates his critics to clarify just what he means about avoiding the Mosaic injunction of compassion for one's parents, the great commandment of God, by invoking the human tradition of pledging one's goods to the temple.[9] This is to erect tradition in the place of God's commandment of loving compassion. Note that the teaching is not peculiar to the New Testament. Rather, the commandment of God here comes from Moses, from the Torah itself (*Exodus* 20:12, 21:17, *Leviticus* 20:9, *Deuteronomy* 5:16), and Jesus is portrayed as a defender of the Mosaic tradition. Yet, traditions are all human constructs and never ultimately valid. Their practice is to be judged in terms of their harmony with the word of God's compassion. It is then a mistake to interpret the passage as if it recommends the priority of the word of God over the scribes and Pharisees' traditions. Those traditions themselves contain the word of God, the Mosaic word. Jesus' critique is against understanding tradition in an imagined pattern of consciousness, the

---

9. Fowler, "Reader-Response Criticism," *Mark and Method,* 68: ". . . Jesus himself speaks ironically. In Mark 7:9, for example, Jesus 'congratulates' the Pharisees and scribes for setting aside one of God's commandments: 'You have a fine way of rejecting the commandment of God in order to keep your tradition!' "

resultant delusion of which entails the distortion of the very practice the tradition is meant to promote. Jesus' critique of the tradition is that, by clinging to images, tradition annuls itself, and renders any worship offered to God worthless. To declare something *korban* meant to dedicate it to a sacred purpose.[10] Even though considered sacred, traditions remain traditions.[11]

On Being Clean
7: 14–23

[14]*He called the people to him again and said, "Listen to me, all of you, and understand.* [15]*Nothing that goes into someone from outside can make that person unclean; it is the things that come out of someone that make that person unclean.* [16]*Anyone who has ears for listening should listen!"*

[17]*When he had gone into the house, away from the crowd, his disciples questioned him about the parable.* [18]*He said to them, "Even you—don't you understand? Can't you see that nothing that goes into someone from outside can make that person unclean,* [19]*because it goes not into the heart but into the stomach and passes into the sewer?" (Thus he pronounced all foods clean.)* [20]*And he went on, "It is what comes out of someone that makes that person unclean.* [21]*For it is from within, from the heart, that evil intentions emerge: fornication, theft, murder,* [22]*adultery, avarice, malice, deceit, indecency, envy, slander, pride, folly.* [23]*All these evil things come from within and make a person unclean."*

The *Dhammapada,* one of the earliest of Buddhist texts, in its opening verses states: "All things are ruled by mind, take mind as lord, and come to be from mind. If a person speak or act with a defiled mind, then, like a cart wheel following the tracks of the animal pulling the cart, suffering will follow him. All things are ruled by mind, take mind as lord, and come to be from mind. If a person speak or act with a pure mind, then, like a shadow constantly

---

10. Nineham, *The Gospel According to Saint Mark,* 251: "The basic purpose of the [korban] formula was to place a ban on something, reserving it for sacred use and withdrawing it from profane use by another person. The vow creates a prohibition with regard to an object and fixes upon it the character of an offering dedicated to God." Fowler, *Let the Reader Understand,* 107, notes that the parenthetical explanation of *korban,* "that is, given to God" (ὅ ἐστιν δῶρον), makes sense only as a comment by the narrator to the reader.

11. Schweizer, *The Good News,* 149: " 'Corban' is what one says when he wants to dedicate an object to God, i.e., to withdraw it from ordinary use, but without handing it over directly to the temple treasury. This example, which is shockingly clear to every Gentile, does not settle the question of the law, because in this case, at least, the later Jewish teachers are fully in agreement with Jesus. The only thing important about it is Jesus' attitude, which is continually and unconditionally oriented toward the needs of man (3: 4)."

following a person, joy will follow him."[12] The point of Jesus' remark is likewise that all depends on mind, on the inner heart of a person. That is where purity or defilement occurs, not in anything external. Scholars detect the remnants of a scatological aphorism here, about not being defiled by human waste, but rather by what comes out of the heart.[13] A famed Zen kōan from *The Gateless Barrier* reports: "A monk asked Unmon, 'What is Buddha?' Unmon said, 'A shit-stick!' " The shit-stick, kept in the latrine, was used in place of toilet paper. Zenkei Shibayama's commentary explains that Unmon's "reply would root out any possible preoccupation in the student's mind such as 'virtuous Buddha, inviolate holiness' and the like."[14]

Notice that the disciples ask Jesus about the meaning of this "parable." The saying about what comes from within and what comes from without remains enigmatic to them. The point seems obvious enough, yet they refuse to think out its implications. It is enigmatic because the disciples constantly try to "get it right." Their eating with unclean hands was apparently not a conscious rejection of the traditions, but merely an inadvertent act, serving as the occasion for the discourse on the sacred and the profane. Their question is casuistic: just what is included in Jesus' talk about inside and outside? Jesus' answer is clear: no physiological process defiles, neither the eating nor the evacuating of food matters for purity. What does matter are one's inner thoughts, the mind of awakening or the mind of delusion. This answer echoes 4:11, where Jesus says that to those who externalize meaning, everything seems parabolic and enigmatic ("to those outside everything comes in parables"). The mind is not a mere recorder of external realities, but itself engenders purity of insight or defilement of ignorance.

The list of the things which defile a person is not simply a catalogue of unclean acts that defile. Rather, it is a list of the actions of an unclean mind, of the inner consciousness which leads to such action. The actions and the

---

12. *Dhammapada,* Yamakavagga, 1–2.

13. Mack, *A Myth of Innocence,* 189: "The original retort was not lost in this process [whereby the original chreia or anecdote was domesticated]. . . . Scholars have frequently noted that verse 15 is odd and enigmatic, and that much of what follows it appears to be an attempt to tone down an otherwise risqué rejoinder. By putting this saying together with the original objection about eating with unwashed hands, a fine chreia can be reconstructed. The original chreia can be given in paraphrase: When asked why he ate with hands defiled, Jesus replied, 'It is not what goes in, but what comes out that makes unclean.' The humor is scatological, typically Cynic, but should not detract from the clever logic employed. The issue is, again, the matter of clean/unclean. The topic is table manners. The objection registered in verse 2 is that Jesus and his disciples are violating the ritual laws of purity. The response shifts the order of discourse about things unclean from table manners to what happens to the food one eats. The usual confusion of categories occurs. For a moment the thought is allowed that it doesn't matter whether one washes one's hands or not, since putting food into the mouth is not where uncleanness resides. In the process of domestication the saying was too risqué to use for the thesis, but too good to dismiss altogether. A later scribe, afraid that it might be buried in the elaboration, knowingly added a scholion: 'If anyone has ears to hear, let that one hear' (vs 16)."

14. Shibayama, *Zen Comments on the Mumonkan,* 156.

mind that engenders them are held in mutual dependency, each leading to the other. In a constant karmic conditioning, the unclean mind brings forth an unclean act, which in its turn implants its seeds (*vāsanā-bīja*) in that mind, leading to the germination of ever new unclean acts. The last items Jesus mentions, pride (ὑπερηφανία) and folly (ἀφροσύνη), sum up the entire list of "evil things," for they constitute an all-encompassing ignorance which mistakes images for realities and leads one down the garden path. Pride and folly are directly counter to the humility and insight that in wisdom sees things just as they are (*tathatā*), and that, so seeing, can both affirm and engage tradition with purity and zest.

Jesus and the Little Girl's Mother
7: 24–30

[24]He left that place and set out for the territory of Tyre. There he went into a house and did not want anyone to know he was there, but he could not pass unrecognized. [25]At once a woman whose little daughter had an unclean spirit heard about him and came and fell at his feet. [26]Now the woman was a gentile, by birth a Syro-Phoenician, and she begged him to drive the devil out of her daughter. [27]And he said to her, "The children should be fed first, because it is not fair to take the children's food and throw it to the little dogs." [28]But she spoke up: "Ah yes, sir," she replied, "but the little dogs under the table eat the scraps from the children." [29]And he said to her, "For saying this, you may go home happy; the devil has gone out of your daughter." [30]So she went off home and found the child lying on the bed and the devil gone.

This account follows upon the discourse on the value of traditions, and contrasts the response of the gentile woman with the Jewish disciples. They constantly refuse to interpret what Jesus says and have to ask for further explanations, while she grabs the bull by the horns, wresting a cure from Jesus by her reasoning.

What has been at issue are the boundaries defined by tradition between what is sacred and what is profane, and now also between who is sacred and who is profane.[15] Is there a holy people, a people of God, in contrast to whom others are deemed little dogs (κυνάρια)? Not even wild dogs, who have something of the nobility of self-sufficiency about them, but dogs, servile and whining.[16] Jesus' answer is yes, there is indeed a chosen people, and they are the children to whom the food of his ministry is directed.

---

15. Kelber, *Mark's Story of Jesus,* 37: "Before acceptance of Gentiles is formalized, this legal issue has to be settled. This is the function of the abolition of ritual taboos (7: 1–23)."

16. Broadhead, *Teaching With Authority,* 130: "Here Jesus addresses the woman and the need of her daughter with a proverbial command: 'Permit first the children to be satisfied, for it is not good to take the bread of the children and to throw it to the dogs.' This saying is terse and harsh on the lips of Jesus (the use of the diminutive [κυναρίοις]

His response is somewhat of an enigma. Why is Jesus traveling to Tyre, a pagan city, and there encountering a pagan woman who probably does not even believe in the God of Israel, only to stress that she is like a dog? The people of Tyre had a reputation among the Jews. "Tyre . . . traditionally represented a Gentile people who have achieved a proud power and superior wealth by harshly oppressing their Jewish neighbors (Isa 23; Joel 4:4–8; Zech 9:2–4)."[17] Jesus travels right into the heart of unfriendly territory and proceeds to insult its inhabitants! His disciples abort their sea journey into gentile lands for fear of an unfriendly outcome; and they were all asked to depart from the land of the Gerasenes. Now, Jesus calls the Syro-Phoenician woman a dog and she proceeds to bark at his heels, to test the cultural limits of Jesus' teaching.

The brief discussion between Jesus and the woman is not an irenic broadening of cultural boundaries. It resembles more the kind of ironic, caustic confrontation reported in Zen "interviews" (*dokusan*) or *kōan* repartee, intended not to communicate any verbal teaching but to test the authenticity of the disciple's experience.[18] "Kōans can also be used as the focus of a rapid fire question and answer session, reminiscent of the Tibetan debate, called 'Dharma Combat' (*shuso hosen*)."[19] At issue is not a correct answer, but the very depth of one's experience of life.[20] In a similar fashion, Jesus' interview with the Syro-Phoenician woman is a testing. The discussion is "irony of a special kind. Clavier called it 'ironie d'épreuve.' In English it is peirastic irony. Peirastic irony—from πειράζειν (to test)—is a form of verbal challenge

---

does not always soften the command. For example, the 'little' in 'little witch' makes the slur no less offensive. Indeed, the diminutive may be the more derisive term), and probably represents a typical Jewish response to Gentiles and their religion." Tolbert, *Sowing the Gospel,* 185.15: "In likening the Gentile woman to a little dog (κυνάριον), the author may be playing on another common type in Hellenistic society, the Cynic philosopher. . . . Diogenes of Sinope, the founder (fourth century B.C.E.) was called 'the dog' (κύων) for his rudeness and impudence, thus naming the κυνική φιλοσοφία (Cynic philosophy) school." On Jesus' similarity to Cynic wisdom practice (*mētis*), see Mack, *A Myth of Innocence,* 67–74.

17. Heil, *The Gospel of Mark as a Model for Action,* 160.

18. Rhoads, "The Syrophoenician Woman," 360: ". . . Markan faith has little to do with beliefs about Jesus. For example none of the suppliants know that Jesus is the Messiah. Many in the crowds think he is John the Baptist or Elijah or one of the prophets (6:14). Bartimaeus inappropriately calls him 'son of David' (10:47–48). In regard to the Syrophoenician woman, it is irrelevant to the narrative whether she believes in the Jewish God. The focus of faith in Mark is 'trust that a request will be granted.' "

19. Corless, *The Vision of Buddhism,* 233.

20. Robert Aitken, *The Gateless Barrier,* 197, commenting on kōan 31, "Chao-chou Investigates the Old Woman," reports a story: "When Anne Aitken and I were studying with Yamada Rōshi in Kamakura in the 1970s, the rōshi heard about a layman in a nearby town who was teaching as a Zen master. His curiosity was aroused and he went to see him for an interview. He told us afterwards that he sat before the would-be teacher and said, 'Now I will examine you!' His verdict: 'That fellow is quite a roughneck!' Chao-chou and Yamada Rōshi were not just trying to expose a charlatan. For the Zen Master, nothing is more interesting than an encounter with someone who has creative insight."

intended to test the other's response. It may in fact declare the opposite of the speaker's actual intention."[21]

Unlike the disciples, who need private sessions to get it all straight, the woman "speaks up" and bests Jesus in verbal repartee.[22] "Two can play at metaphors. 'Sir, even the dogs under the table eat the children's crumbs.' She has him. She has risked a second rebuke and won her daugher's health."[23]

"An outsider asked the World-Honored One (i.e., Buddha), 'I do not ask for the spoken; I do not ask for the unspoken.' The World-Honored One just sat still. The outsider praised him, saying: 'The World-Honored One with his great compassion and mercy has opened the clouds of my delusion and enabled me to enter the Way.' He then made bows and took his leave. Ānanda asked, 'What did that outsider realize to make him praise you?' The World-Honored One said, 'He is like the fine horse who runs even at the shadow of the ship.' "[24] So the outsider gentile runs with Jesus' testing words and goes home happy. Like all the others who get the point of what Jesus says, she disappears from the Markan story. Her daughter (τό θυγάτριον αὐτῆς), although she is a gentile outsider, is purified from the unclean devil, just as the daughter (τὸ θυγάτριόν μου) of Jairus (5: 23), the president of the synagogue, was awakened from her deathly sleep.

There is also a connection here between the word of the woman and the word of God in verse 13. There Jesus accused the Pharisees of nullifying the word of God by their traditions about korban. Here Jesus says that, "for saying this" (διὰ τοῦτον τὸν λόγον), by daring to speak out of her compassion, her daughter is healed. The connection is that in both cases the word uttered is a word of compassion. In contrast to the hypocrite who nullifies the law by following human tradition, the gentile woman fulfills the true tradition by embodying the compassionate love of God for others, even in

21. Camery-Hoggatt, *Irony in Mark's Gospel,* 150. Rhoads, "The Syrophoenician Woman," 361, argues: "Some commentators deal with Jesus' refusal by arguing that his initial response to the woman is merely a put-on statement by which Jesus is testing the woman's faith. I would argue, instead, that Jesus has a genuine change of mind here. He begins the scene by assuming that the kingdom is for the Jews now and only later for the Gentiles. He ends the scene with a willingness for gentiles to benefit significantly from the kingdom even now."
22. Similarly, Rhoads, "The Syrophoenician Woman," 347: "The story of the Syrophoenician woman intersects with that of the disciples. On the one hand, the disciples have failed to understand a riddle of Jesus (as narrated in the preceding episode). On the other hand, the Syrophoenician woman understands Jesus' riddle and even responds with a riddle of her own." Bryan, *A Preface to Mark,* 97: ". . . this is the one occasion in Mark where Jesus is shown losing an argument, and that to a woman and a foreigner."
23. Malbon, "Narrative Criticism," *Mark and Method,* 44. Also Fowler, *Let the Reader Understand,* 117: "The woman takes up the figures of speech Jesus uses and turns them against him. In this instance he who lives by the metaphor dies by the metaphor. Bested in this contest of wits and words, Jesus relents from his initial reluctance to help the woman and pronounces her daughter free of the demon."
24. Aitken, *The Gateless Barrier,* 199.

the face of the harsh rejection of Jesus, who utters such gruff words because he is evidently sick and tired of being bothered so much.

A Deaf Person
7: 31–37

³¹Returning from the district of Tyre, he went by way of Sidon towards the Sea of Galilee, right through the Decapolis territory. ³²And they brought him a deaf man who had an impediment in his speech; and they asked him to lay his hand on him. ³³He took him aside to be by themselves, away from the crowd, put his fingers into the man's ears and touched his tongue with spittle. ³⁴Then looking up to heaven he sighed; and he said to him, "Ephphatha," that is, "Be opened." ³⁵And his ears were opened and at once the impediment of his tongue was loosened and he spoke clearly. ³⁶And Jesus ordered them to tell no one about it, but the more he insisted, the more widely they proclaimed it. ³⁷Their admiration was unbounded, and they said, "Everything he does is good, he makes the deaf hear and the dumb speak."

Mark's geography beggars the imagination. Chapter seven began in a Jewish setting where Jesus is confronted by the Pharisees and scribes who have come from Jerusalem. Jesus then travels northward to gentile territory of Tyre. Now, according to Mark, he comes back south to the Sea of Galilee by journeying further north to Sidon, on the way passing through the Decapolis region, which in fact is southeast of the Sea of Galilee.[25] Interpreters often dismiss the confusion by noting that Mark simply did not know his geography.[26] Yet perhaps there is more involved than a faulty sense of direction. What Mark's text does accomplish rhetorically here is utter confusion about boundaries, and this has been his theme throughout the entire section. One is no longer quite sure where this deaf man lives or to what gentile group he belongs. The only certain direction in the passage is upward, when Jesus looks up to heaven.[27] Other boundaries simply do not matter,[28] and Mark is

---

25. Schweizer, *The Good News,* 154: "The impossibility of this route of travel must be illustrated by an example from closer to home, e.g., going from New York to Washington by way of Boston down the Mohawk Valley."

26. For example Schweizer himself, *The Good News,* 113.

27. Malbon, *Narrative Space,* 83: "In healing a deaf man Jesus also looked up to heaven (7: 34), from where the Spirit had come down (1: 10). And when Jesus said, 'Be opened,' the man's 'ears were opened . . . and he spoke plainly.' (7: 34–35), just as the voice from heaven would later speak plainly to the disciples, 'listen to him' (9: 7), let your ears be opened (cf. 4: 9; 4: 23; 8: 18). Jesus' action in turning toward heaven contrasts with the failure of the Pharisees to orient themselves to heaven or to recognize that heaven had been opened to the earth through Jesus."

28. Kelber, *The Kingdom in Mark,* 58: "The whole area of Tyre, Sidon, and the Decapolis is with the aid of the prepositional connections *ek, dia,* and *ana* drawn together into one Galilee domain which borders on . . . the Lake of Galilee. . . . the Kingdom's drive to cover 'all of Galilee' is consummated." And 62: ". . . the boat trips are designed to

"less concerned with the logic of the travel route and more concerned with the nature of the destinations: Tyre, Sidon, the Decapolis. Gentile place-names are accumulated, the deaf-mute who is healed is also a Gentile."[29]

The miracle here is one of hearing and speaking. Jesus has stressed earlier the need to listen. He has invited those who have ears to listen to the discourse about traditions. He has just granted the request of the woman who spoke up. Now, in the presence of his mute disciples, he restores this fellow's hearing and speech. The miracle provides both ears with which to hear and speech with which to respond to that hearing. The image is one of recovering insight and wisdom. "And in Wisdom 10:21, a verse that surely influenced Mark 7:37, the imagery says that: 'Wisdom opened the mouth of the dumb, and made the tongues of babies speak clearly.' "[30]

Jesus then orders the crowd (αὐτοῖς) to tell no one about it! About what? How could they hide the cure? It is public knowledge. Obviously the Markan Jesus is not trying to keep secret the fact that the man has been cured. They, i.e., the crowd, had brought the man to Jesus and were waiting to see what happened. Mark describes Jesus' healing activity by citing Jesus' use of the Aramaic word: "Ephphatha," as if to stress to his audience, who did not speak Aramaic, its magical character.[31] Then he directs attention away from Jesus as wonder-worker, focusing it upon the result of the miracle: the regaining of hearing and speech, the regaining of the wisdom of original dependent co-arising. That is how Mark's readers are to interpret Jesus: not as a wonder-worker, but as one who enables such wisdom to occur. Time and again people are astonished and amazed. Here their admiration is unbounded (ὑπερπερισσῶς ἐξεπλήσσοντο), they have passed out of their everyday minds and beyond normal measure. They tend to see Jesus himself as a sacred personage, thus removing him from their ordinary lives. It is this

---

dramatize, not a centrifugal course of action, spinning out from the Galilean center to ever more distant lands, but a unitive movement, alternating between the two sides of the sea."

29. Malbon, "Narrative Criticism," 44.

30. Humphrey, *He Is Risen,* 63. Broadhead, *Teaching With Authority,* 133, also sees imagery from the Hebrew scriptures: "In addition, the Old Testament provides the backdrop for the story. Indeed, the unusual description of the man as 'speaking with difficulty' (μογιλάλον) draws directly upon Isa. 35.6. The acclamation of 7.37 reflects Isa. 35.5–10, where the opening of deaf ears and the loosing of silent tongues will accompany the regathering of Israel. Mk 7.31–37 employs this eschatological imagery to tell of the healing of the deaf and silent man."

31. Fowler, *Let the Reader Understand,* 108: "First, Aramaic or Hebrew words stand out in a narrative written in Hellenistic Greek. They lend an exotic flavor to the narrative, especially in the two episodes in which Jesus utters Aramaic words in the manner of magical spells, once to effect the resuscitation of a dead girl (5:41) and once to heal a deaf-mute (7:34). In this Greek narrative, the Palestinian Aramaic once familiar to Jesus and his disciples has become a mysterious and sometimes magical foreign tongue. The offering of Aramaic or Hebrew words accompanied by a Greek translation allows the narratee both to experience the exotic strangeness of the words and to go beyond the strangeness into understanding."

superabundant abandonment of their everyday minds that Jesus seeks to prohibit; that is the point of the so-called messianic secret. It is not that Mark tries to hide a precious piece of information, that indeed Jesus is messiah, until the characters of the narrative are ready to assent to it properly. Rather, Mark counters any attempt to construct a numinous understanding of Jesus.

But, alas, Jesus' efforts are thwarted, for the crowd broadcasts his good news and is beside itself with religious wonder. They see Jesus in terms of a dichotomized ultimate meaning, for he, unlike all of them, has done everything well. Mark's point, however, is that his readers are not to emulate the crowd, not to lose their everyday minds in an excess of devotional astonishment. The rejection of a power christology is not just the denial of a set of ideas, but, more basically, the abandonment of an emotional commitment to Jesus as a falsely imagined hero figure. Joseph Campbell has written about the hero with a thousand faces, and masterfully delineated the contours of the many parallel mythic figures he sees in different cultures.[32] Mark, however, does not want his readers to see Jesus as a hero. He is in fact no superstar, either theological or theatrical. He is not the once and for all embodiment of ultimate truth, precisely because there is no conventional embodiment of ultimate meaning, The two truths of ultimate meaning and worldly convention, each empty of any defining essence, remain forever disparate and completely other.[33]

---

32. Campbell, *The Hero With a Thousand Faces*, vii, sets out to "uncover some of the truths disguised for us under the figures of religion and mythology by bringing together a multitude of not-too-difficult examples and letting the ancient meaning become apparent of itself. The old teachers knew what they were saying." It soon becomes clear that these old teachers are, in fact, Vedantists. Campbell's hope, viii, "is that a comparative elucidation may contribute to the perhaps not-quite-desperate cause of those forces that are working in the present world for unification, not in the name of some ecclesiastical or political empire, but in the sense of human understanding. As we are told in the Vedas: 'Truth is one, the sages speak of it by many names.'" Yet, as his *The Masks of God: Oriental Mythology*, 12–13, points out, those many names do include those of Western monotheism, which, understood simplistically as God over against human beings, is said to be a "fundamental betrayal of the human cause, . . . normal and even required in the Levant. (32)" In a similar vein, Gandhi was quite willing to accept the incarnation of Christ, questioning only why that need have been a unique phenomenon, for in Hindu thought many avatars manifest the ultimate reality of brahman. That is all good Vedanta, and to be respected as such. But it is not Mark's vision or Mark's christology, which stresses that Jesus, although cheered as a heroic wonder-worker, himself always dampens that enthusiasm and deconstructs his own superstar status.

33. For the christological implications, see Keenan, *The Meaning of Christ*, 50–57, 221–239, and "The Emptiness of Christ: A Mahāyāna Christology."

8

Awakening

Bread in the Wilderness
8: 1–10

¹And now once again a great crowd had gathered, and they had nothing to eat. So he called his disciples to him and said to them, ² "I feel sorry for all these people; they have been with me for three days now and have nothing to eat. ³If I send them off home hungry they will collapse on the way; some have come a great distance." ⁴His disciples replied, "Where could anyone get these people enough bread to eat in a deserted place?" ⁵He asked them, "How many loaves have you?" And they said to him "Seven." ⁶Then he instructed the crowd to sit down on the ground, and he took the seven loaves, and after giving thanks he broke them and began handing them to his disciples to distribute; and they distributed them among the crowd. ⁷They had a few small fish as well, and over these he said a blessing and ordered them to be distributed too. ⁸They ate as much as they wanted, and they collected seven basketfuls of the scraps left over. ⁹Now there had been about four thousand people. He sent them away ¹⁰and at once, getting into the boat with his disciples, went to the region of Dalmanutha.

Mark has already told a story of Jesus feeding a crowd of people in 6:30–44. He retells (πάλιν) another version of the same account in Chapter 8. Here, Mark's narrative places Jesus in a perplexing situation, one he should not have gotten into in the first place. He has not addressed the problem before it became grave. If moved by feelings of compassion, why did he let the crowd remain for three days before anyone noticed that there is no bread in the desert (ὧδε χορτάσαι ἄρτων ἐπ’ ἐρημίας)? Before the people are on the point of collapse? And, unlike the story in Chapter 6, this is indeed a deserted place, where there are no villages or farms round about to which one might send a hungry crowd for lunch. In the earlier instance, the disciples' advice to send the crowd to these villages (6: 36) was reasonable, and although Jesus did otherwise, he did not reject that advice as impracticable. Here that

184

option does not exist. Mark has so constructed the passage as to preclude any rational response, for there are no possible solutions.[1] Mark highlights the isolation of the location. The people can't stay, and they can't go. Jesus presents his disciples and Mark his readers with a conundrum, a kōan, a story without a rational resolution.

The situation recalls that of Psalm 78: 19, where the Israelites "blasphemed against God, 'Is it likely' they said 'that God can give a banquet in the wilderness?' " The grammar of this passage implies a negative answer, for the Israelites did not believe such a thing possible.[2] Similarly the disciples have no expectation of any miracle.[3] They are at sixes and sevens, for the task of feeding a crowd is simply impossible in such a wilderness. Not rooted in Jesus' wilderness spirituality, they are unable to draw sustenance from the wilderness. "The disciples preach, heal and exorcise, but they are impatient with prayer and respond to difficulties with anxiety instead of faith in God who does the impossible. Jesus calms the storm for them in spite of their unbelief and continues to involve them (e.g., in the feeding miracles), in spite of their failures."[4]

The story relates to the differentiation between ultimate truth and worldly convention. The wilderness plays the narrative role of the ultimate, where all conventional solutions disappear. Bread signifies the conventional world and its needs. The issue is: How can one be aware of the ultimate, and at the same time engaged in the conventional? What path is one to follow? The Mahāyāna teachings find an answer in the practice of the middle way, the tensive and dynamic practice of differentiating ultimate meaning and worldly convention. And "it is fair to say that Mark has structured the central part of the Gospel with the way motif."[5] The way of the Markan Jesus is not simply a geographical journey, but a process that begins with the opening up of the heavens at Jesus' baptism and ends with the splitting of the temple veil at Jesus' death—to reveal in the course of Jesus' career the ultimate embodied in the everyday.

---

1. Thus I would qualify Schweizer, *The Good News,* 156: "The fact that after the experience described in 6: 32–44 the disciples now (vs. 4) have no idea whatever about what can be done cannot be explained psychologically. This very impossibility is what is important to Mark, who was the first to put the two variant accounts side by side. He wants to use this means to show how absolutely and unimaginably blind man is to the activity of God." The advice of the disciples remains worldly and conventional in both stories, the only difference being that the isolation in the present account renders any practical advice impossible.

2. Dowd, *Prayer, Power, and the Problem of Suffering,* 102.

3. Dowd, *Prayer, Power, and the Problem of Suffering,* 110, notes that, while many of Jesus' miracles demand faith on the part of the beneficiary, "in other miracle stories no one evidences any confidence in Jesus' power or any expectation of his help prior to a miracle. This is the case in both the feeding accounts (6: 35–44, 8: 1–10)."

4. Dowd, *Prayer, Power, and the Problem of Suffering,* 121.

5. Kelber, *Mark's Story of Jesus,* 44.

Yet, the story-level problem here is that, if the people are sent back to the conventional world (καὶ ἐὰν ἀπολύσω αὐτοὺς νήστεις εἰς οἶκον αὐτῶν) without being fed, they will grow weary and collapse in their practice of the way (ἐκλυθήσονται ἐν τῇ ὁδῷ). Where is there bread in the desert?

The rhetorical point of Mark's narrative is that the common sense perspectives of the disciples do not work. They apparently should now know that the wilderness itself can supply the people with bread and fish, for they have witnessed the earlier feeding. Yet, they are still in the dark and respond in character only with common sense advice, or, in this case, with the lack of any such advice. They are not, however, to be faulted for failing to suggest another miracle. "Ah, Jesus, couldn't you do a repeat of that other multiplication, please! That would solve our problem nicely." Jesus has asked them a practical question, and they respond with the practical observation that they have no idea of what can now be done,[6] and they do not presume to request divine assistance.[7] In the absence of villages and farms, they have no advice to offer at all. The point is that the common sense viewpoints that make our worlds livable do not work here, that worldly perspectives must first be abandoned in a direct awakening to the power of silence and Abba. Yet, once that awakening has occurred, its impact on the worldly and conventional problems of life is great, for such problems then become the focus for compassionate action. The conventional as the occlusion and hiding of truth becomes the conventional as the veiling of the wondrous silence of ultimate emptiness.

Yet a problem remains with this interpretation. Although it is good Mahāyāna thinking, does not the passage itself suggest the direct action of a supernatural agent to solve a conventional problem? In Mahāyāna the realms

---

6. Thus I differ from Tolbert, *Sowing the Gospel,* 102: "The story [of the first feeding in 6: 35–44] provides the disciples and the audience with another example of Jesus' amazing power. A little later, in Mark 8: 1–9, Jesus is again (πάλιν) faced with a large hungry crowd ('four thousand people') in a deserted place. The narrator uses the πάλιν in 8: 1 to remind the audience that this type of situation has occurred before. When Jesus broaches the issue of feeding the multitude, the disciples, rather than remembering what Jesus has done before and responding willingly, ask, 'How can one feed these (people) with bread here in the desert?' For the audience the answer is shockingly plain: the same way he did in the past. Indeed, Jesus then proceeds to repeat his earlier feat. . . . The irony is manifest: Jesus had more food and a smaller crowd, but still the disciples, who *distributed* the food in the earlier episode, professed ignorance about how the crowd could be fed." Fowler, *Loaves and Fishes,* 36, similarly argues that Mark has created the first feeding story in 6: 30–44 in order to stress the unawareness of the disciples. These arguments presuppose that the disciples should have learned the supernatural abilities of Jesus and should have expected he would work another similar miracle. Rather, the heightening of rhetorical tension is found, I believe, in the impossibility of any practical solution in the present account, not in hopes for more miracles, for the seeking of signs is negated in the immediately subsequent account in 8: 11–13.

7. Lane, *The Gospel According to Mark,* 272: "It would have been presumptuous for the disciples to have assumed that Jesus would, as a matter of course, multiply a few loaves as he had done on an earlier occasion."

of ultimate meaning and worldly convention remain disjunctive and other. There is no reaching from worldly convention to ultimate meaning, as if one could climb up on or descend from a spiritual ladder. There are no incursions from ultimate meaning into worldly convention, for ultimate meaning remains silent. It has no commodity or use value. There is no linear continuity between the two truths, no direct interplay between one and the other. Rather, when one becomes awakened to ultimate meaning, that very awakening both empties the pretensions of convention to be absolute and totally reengages one in the dependently co-arisen world, for bodhisattva wisdom cannot abide in a non-compassionate silence. Yet, by contrast, the gospels present many examples of intercourse between the divine and the human. Here, as so often interpreted, Jesus solves a human problem by miraculous means.[8]

It is precisely such a supernaturalist reading that is avoided by a Mahāyāna interpretation. I read Mark as struggling by his use of a spiraling sense of comic irony to demolish any supernaturalism, to wean his readers away from the perspective of the unconverted disciples, to reinterpret miracles. Most all societies, early Palestine as much as early India and China, did in fact function within such a supernatural perspective, whether naive, mythic, or metaphysical. Yet, such a supernatural perspective, simply by being a perspective *(dṛṣṭl)*, remains worldly and conventional. The Mahāyāna thinkers developed their critique of emptiness as a medicine for such deluded strivings to capture the ultimate and bring it into linear continuity with everyday life. If the ultimate meaning of God needs to be so brought into continuity with everyday life, then ordinarily and for the greater part, God is absent from life. The relevance of faith does not mean to make everything consonant with the unconverted mind of miraculous expectations. Neither does it mean resting in the false surety of a supposedly absolutely true view of things, expecting to see one's view validated by signs. Mark is not trying to convince his readers that we can expect Jesus miraculously to feed the hungry. That thought is absurd, for, although hungry crowds abound, there are only two feeding miracles performed during the course of the gospel. In sum, a mere nine thousand people have one free lunch, and then they must go home to rely on their own larders.

Mark's task is double: to demolish an exclusively worldly and common sense view of things, and then to demolish an exclusively other-worldly view of things. From episode to episode the focus shifts from the one to the other. Here the first is in evidence: the disciples cling to their common sense view of the possible. But, right away in the next passage the second task will come

---

8. For example, Mann, *Mark,* 299: "It is plain from our gospels that the miracles were treated as signs of the incoming reign of God, but also as the instruments through which the Reign of God came." Schweizer, *The Good News,* 157: "The story was told first as a miracle-story designed to extol the unlimited divine power of Jesus." Nineham, *Saint Mark,* 208: "8: 14–21 suggests that St. Mark may have included both stories because he attached a very special significance to the scenes they depicted, with their obviously supernatural character. . . ."

into view, when Jesus refuses to provide any supernatural, self-validating sign to the Pharisees. The overall intent is to lead the reader to see that faith consciousness is not itself any absolutely true view at all, whether worldly or other-worldly.[9] Rather, it is wilderness stillness rebounding in town engagement. Jesus is again collapsing the boundaries between the sacred and the profane: there is no dichotomy between the supernatural and the natural such that a miracle would be a breaking in of God to the natural world. No boundaries, for Abba is immediately available to all.

Miracles are not incursions from the divine, but pointers to what is already present among all peoples: the kingdom of God announced in Jesus' initial preaching. To those who have ears to hear and eyes to see, the very existence of the world is already the kingdom of God. A sense of the extraordinary impact of miracles appeals to the unconverted consciousness of the crowds who lack awareness of the presence of the kingdom, yet the unfolding of the Gospel leads one to distance oneself from such expectations. Although many are healed and delivered from their distress, Jesus himself, despite his Gethsemane prayer, receives no miraculous deliverance.

With this second feeding account, Mark is also breaking down the barriers between Jews and gentiles, for it occurs in gentile territory. "After a massive exorcism (5: 1–20) and a vast number of healings (6: 53–56) among Gentiles, an individual exorcism (7: 24–30) and an individual healing (7: 32–37) in Gentile land, the time has come for the formal ratification of the Gentile part of the community. The feeding of the four thousand (8: 1–9), the expected counterpart to the earlier feeding of the five thousand, constitutes this Gentile confirmation."[10] Malbon notes that the number of baskets left over after everyone has eaten perhaps symbolizes the different ethnic locations of the two feedings, for in the Chapter 6 account twelve baskets are mentioned, while here only seven are left over. "As twelve is a number symbolic of the Jews, so seven is a number symbolic of 'the nations,' the Gentiles."[11]

The feeding itself points to the fecundity of the wilderness, for the disciples provide the food by gathering up the seven loaves already present. Similarly in 6: 37 Mark's Jesus is not described as multiplying anything. Jesus tells

---

9. Thus I agree with Schmithals, *Wunder und Glaube,* 90, that faith in Mark's gospel does not involve "holding something to be true," and differ from Dowd, 103: "In Mark 11: 22–24, 'to believe' or 'to have faith' *does* mean to 'hold to be true' the world-view that asserts God's power to affect events in the world in ways that are impossible for humans or other natural agents."

10. Kelber, *Mark's Story of Jesus,* 39. Also Malbon, *Narrative Space,* 29, who identifies the unknown Dalmanutha as a Galilean site, and sees the crossing in 8: 13 as a return from Gentile territory.

11. Malbon, "Narrative Criticism," 45. But see Broadhead, *Teaching With Authority,* "For the first feeding story this setting is thoroughly Jewish; for the second feeding the setting is thoroughly Gentile. This narrative distinction may clarify the contrasting elements in the stories. The differing numbers, blessings and baskets do not appear to hide deep symbolism. On the contrary, these elements are the only internal differences between the two units, and that is their message: the stories are alike but they are different."

his disciples themselves to give the people something to eat. Neither account mentions any magical increase: that is a later interpretation of exegetical mathematicians who thereby lessen the narrative's attack on common sense by appeal to a higher mathematics. The stories themselves retain their narrative character as polemics against any version of common sense. Jesus merely says the blessing and has the disciples distribute the loaves and the few fish to the people. It is the wilderness itself which has provided the food, and Mark does not say that Jesus has multiplied any loaves or fishes. The superabundant food flows from the wilderness itself. There are such resources in the wilderness.

The imagery of this account, as well as of the previous feeding, has been seen by many scholars to reflect early Eucharistic practice. "At 8: 6 Jesus commands the crowd *anapesein epi tēs gēs,* that is, literally, 'to recline' (as at table) on the earth. . . . Along with many of the details of the miraculous feeding, the use of *anapesein,* appropriate to a formal meal or banquet, rather than *kethēsthai* ('sit'), appropriate to an outdoor meal or picnic, points to the Church's celebration of the Eucharist and to the imagery of the Messianic Banquet (cf Mark 6: 39–40 and 14: 22–25)."[12] If this reading is correct, the answer to Jesus' kōan is not an answer at all. Rather, it is participation in the eucharistic feeding of the liturgy, known not conceptually but only by participation. Both feeding stories begin with an extended teaching period. In 6:35 Jesus teaches late into the evening. In 8:2 the crowd has been with Jesus "three days." They must indeed have been hungry! In 8:31, Jesus predicts that he will rise "after three days," signifying not chronological time, but the eschatological saving act of God, the coming of the kingdom announced to be at hand. So here the presence of the listening crowd for

---

12. Malbon, *Narrative Space,* 79, drawing, among others, on Nineham, *Saint Mark,* 178: "In St. Mark's account of the feeding, the actions of Jesus are precisely those of a host entertaining guests. Here perhaps we come near the original significance of the incident; it may have been intended by Jesus as an anticipation, more or less sacramental in character, for the Messianic Banquet. . . ." And on Schweizer, *The Good News,* 157, who queries: "Did the church which handed down this narrative perhaps employ this as a liturgy for the Lord's Supper, and did the church which handed down 6: 32–44 employ a somewhat different liturgy?" See Juel, *Augsburg Commentary: Mark,* 112, on the repetition of the feeding stories: "The story is the same, the numbers slightly different. Rather than blessing the bread, Jesus gives thanks *(eucharisteō).* The same variation in terminology between 'blessing' and 'giving thanks' occurs in accounts of Jesus' Last Supper. In Mark 14: 22 and in Matt. 26: 26, Jesus 'blesses' the bread; in Luke 22: 19 and in 1 Cor. 11: 24, Jesus 'gives thanks.' As noted above, it seems likely that the feeding of the crowds anticipates Jesus' last meal while at the same time it reflects the church's special 'breaking of bread' that had become a regular feature of corporate life long before Mark's Gospel." See also Robbins, "Last Meal," 21, who interprets the last meal as the completion of the feeding stories, the purpose of which is "to diffuse a view that Jesus' miraculous powers are the basis for belief and to link the Christian meal with Jesus' suffering and death and resurrection into heaven." Klosinski, *The Meals in Mark,* 176: "The language which allegorizes the bread miracle in terms of the eucharist invests the miracle with a certain metaphorical quality. This accounts for its parabolic nature for the readers of the gospel."

three days suggests that, once again, the kingdom has come in the sharing of the blessed food of the messianic banquet.

Another puzzling point in the story is the destination for which Jesus and his disciples depart in the boat at the end, for nobody today knows anything about any Dalmanutha. Either Mark had geographical knowledge beyond our present sources, which given his demonstrated geographical naiveté seems unlikely,[13] or he is confused, which is possible. On the other hand, perhaps he simply made up a place name, which is puzzling. Yet, if Mark consciously constructed the unlikely itinerary of 7: 31, he may well have simply invented an unidentifiable place here, in order to break down all spatial boundaries.

Heavenly Signs
8: 11–13

[11]The Pharisees came up and began to argue[14] with him; they demanded of him a sign from heaven, to put him to the test. [12]And with a profound sigh he said, "Why does this generation demand a sign? In truth, I tell you, no sign shall be given to this generation." [13]And leaving them again and re-embarking he went away to the other shore.

Jesus has just performed a stupendous miracle, reminiscent of the manna from heaven which fed the wandering Israelites in the wilderness. Yet here Mark depicts Jesus as refusing to give any sign at all. Mark is strange, for he first gives signs and then immediately takes them away; now you see it, now you don't. Throughout the narrative, Jesus performs miracles that indicate the presence of the kingdom. "The healings and exorcisms of Jesus have evoked the response among the people that he is a prophet (6:15; cf. 8:28). These mighty deeds *(dymaneis)* are not enough for the Pharisees. Such could be accomplished by a common magician or deceiver. Therefore they demand a sign *(sēmeion)* from heaven . . . that Jesus is a true prophet."[15] Their request is, I think, reasonable. Jesus was not the only healer or wonder-worker around. And there was great similarity between miraculous events, regardless of who performed them.[16] If the point of miracles were that God is the supernatural

---

13. Although it is possible. In Vermont, a state of nothing but small towns, there are crossroads and hamlets that, appearing on the occasional map, are yet unknown to people living even a few miles away.

14. Following Malbon's translation, *Narrative Space,* 83.

15. Collins, *The Beginning of the Gospel,* 62.

16. Dowd, *Prayer, Power, and the Problem of Suffering,* 148: "The author of Mark may have been well aware that the healing and exorcistic practices of his community differed little, if at all, from those of outsiders." Note 64 continues the point: "Judah Goldin ('The Magic of Magic and Superstition,' 121–22, citing the *Peskita de Rav Kahana* 74f) provides an example of the issue of magic vs. religion in Jewish apologetic. When confronted with great similarity . . . between Jewish ritual and pagan witchcraft, Yahanan ben Zakkai responds by saying that the difference is that the Jewish ritual has been commanded by God. Therefore, the Jewish ritual is done in obedience to the will of God,

agent working through Jesus, then it would be most reasonable for Jesus to provide the requested sign. He could then have validated his identity as God's spokesperson and avoided the conflict that led to his arrest and death. By not doing so, he is not clinging to a death wish, as is clear from the Gethsemane scene. Nor is he simply refusing the test of the unbelieving Pharisees, for he has just worked a miracle for his unbelieving disciples; faith is not an absolute condition for miracles in Mark.[17] Rather, no sign can validate anything. All human occurrences, even miracles and signs, remain conventional. The reporting of miracles in Mark is structured precisely to avoid seeing them as sure and dependable signs of God's power. The Markan focus is turned away from the event of the actual happening to its significance in the narrative unfolding of the Kingdom.[18]

The Pharisees tempt Jesus, they put him to the test (πειράζοντες). Evidently they want to see if he has divine approval for his teachings and actions. They want a miracle to prove to them his validity. Not only has he just performed one, but the Pharisees witness many such miracles throughout the gospel. Christian theologians have frequently employed the miracle accounts as such proofs for Jesus' divine status. They demonstrate, so it is argued, that God was with and in Jesus, that Jesus is himself divine. And yet Jesus here says that no such sign will be given. Within the imagined pattern of deluded understanding, there is no clear indication of divine power or potency. No miracle could convince a mind already attached to its preset images and ideas.[19] The miracles remain ambiguous and no hermeneutical sign of their significance is provided. Jesus performs miracles (δυνάμεις) but does not perform signs (σημεῖα) to validate his identity.[20]

In chapter 1: 13 Jesus was similarly tempted (ἦν . . . πειραζόμενος) in the wilderness by Satan. There the testing was directed to Jesus' wilderness experience of the ultimacy of God. Here, the Pharisees want to test the validity of his unfolding career in the world. Both tests try to bring the

---

however much it may resemble magic in practice. The Markan position is similar in that the evangelist does not attempt to differentiate Christian practice from magic on the level of details, but on the level of the stance of the practitioner in relationship to the will of God."

17. Dowd, *Prayer, Power, and the Problem of Suffering,* 109.

18. See Crossan, *The Historical Jesus,* 320–21.

19. Fowler, *Let the Reader Understand,* 195–96: "Modern readers tend to regard this passage [about the Pharisees' request for a sign] as a brief sketch of the Pharisees' opposition to Jesus at story level or as a throwaway transition in the narrator's discourse, an interlude in which the narrator can catch his breath. However, considering the passage more seriously, primarily at the level of discourse, is worthwhile. Mark 8:11 is a request for certainty, resolution, and clear referential ('sign') meaning. The Pharisees ask Jesus for an escape from uncertainty, and he turns them down. This passage demonstrates clearly to the reader that this narrative will not strive for clarity at any price. Clarity is not always its highest priority."

20. Malbon, "Narrative Criticism," 45: "In Mark's Gospel Jesus performs mighty deeds *(dynameis)* but not signs *(sēmeia).* (Contrast John's Gospel.) To ask for a sign is to demand that divine power be present on one's own terms rather than to perceive it wherever it manifests itself."

ultimate silence of the wilderness and the affairs of the world of religion into continuity. And that is why no sign will be given, for there is no such continuity. In the imagined pattern of consciousness one demands demonstrations of heavenly power, signs from heaven. Yet, any sign given remains from the world and conventional. Thus Mark deconstructs all heavenly signs, thus emptying even the prior miracle accounts of their imagined significance. The miracle of the superabundant loaves and fishes is valid only as a conventional sign to the unconverted mind-set of the disciples, not as a sign of Jesus' ultimacy. Here the representatives of an intense and dedicated religious practice, the Pharisees, become examples to show that clinging even to religious images is no less deluded than clinging to irreligious perspectives. Unlike the disciples in the last episode, they do expect a miracle-sign, yet because of their set ideas about the miraculous they also are deluded. What is needed is a conversion of consciousness (μετάνοια), not a new content to be understood. It is a subtle point, for both converted and unconverted consciousness may affirm the same doctrines and see the same things, albeit in different modes of awareness. This is why Jesus sighs profoundly (τῷ πνεύματι αὐτοῦ, i.e., in his spirit). There is no answer within the imagined pattern *(parikalpita)* of their questioning, only a call to convert that consciousness into the full perfection of insight into the emptiness of any signs *(parinispanna)*. Their incipient debating (καὶ ʼήρξαντο συνζητεῖν αὐτῷ) indicates their reliance on discriminative thought *(vikalpa),* and finds a doctrinal parallel in Matthew 11: 25–27, where revelation is hidden from the wise and the intelligent (ʽότι ʼέκρυψας ταῦτα ἀπὸ σοφῶν καὶ συνετῶν), but manifested to mere children.[21] Yet both Matthew and Luke were apparently ill at ease with Mark's account, and append the phrase, "except for the sign of Jonah," who was in the belly of the whale for three days, just as Jesus would be in the belly of the tomb for three days. Mark, however, does not see even the resurrection as a heavenly sign, so he has no sign at all to give to "this generation" who seek signs (ζητεῖ σημεῖον).

Bread and Yeast
8: 14–21

[14]*The disciples had forgotten to take any loaves of bread[22] and they had only one loaf with them in the boat.* [15]*Then he gave them this warning, "Keep your eyes open; look out for the yeast of the Pharisees and the yeast of Herod."* [16]*And they were arguing with one another,[23] "It is because we have*

21. See Keenan, *The Meaning of Christ,* 32.

22. Following Kelber, *Mark's Story of Jesus,* 40, who argues that the plural "loaves" (ʼάρτους) must be reflected in the translation, for he sees it as contrasted with the disciples' "one loaf," which symbolizes the oneness of Jew and Gentile.

23. I think the *New Jerusalem Bible's* "and they said to one another" fails to bring out the strength of διελογίζοντο πρὸς ἀλλήλους, which denotes a more spirited and contentious interchange.

no loaves of bread." [17]And Jesus knew it, and he said to them, "Why are you arguing about having no loaves of bread? Do you not yet understand, still not realise? Are your hearts hardened?[24] [18]Have you eyes and do not see, ears and do not hear? Or do you not remember? [19]When I broke the five loaves for the five thousand, how many baskets full of scraps did you collect?" They answered, "Twelve." [20]And when I broke the seven loaves for the four thousand, how many baskets full of scraps did you collect?" And they answered, "Seven." [21]Then he said to them, "Do you still not realise?"

The disciples are again reasoning and pondering (διελογίζοντο) their breadless situation. Inexplicably they have forgotten to bring enough bread with them in the boat, even after the previous two occasions when Jesus had to supply the hungry crowds. Perhaps they had by now come to depend on Jesus to do so again. What a bonanza, never to have to worry about bringing lunch anymore! But, Jesus, having just rejected the sign-seeking understanding of the Pharisees, now accuses his disciples of failing to understand, because they too have closed and hardened their hearts. "The tables are now turned. The language initially used to describe outsiders and opponents is now employed to characterize insiders and friends: seeing, hearing (4:12) and hardness of hearts (3:15, cf 6:52 where it is applied to the disciples). All the boundary markers are destroyed."[25] The disciples, like the Pharisees and Herod, have reified their understanding and are driven to see reality in terms of images mistaken for truth. Images do indeed drive people; they sell cars and shampoo.

I prefer the more literal translation of a hardened heart (πεπωρωμένην ἔχετε τὴν καρδίαν ὑμῶν) over the *New Jerusalem Bible's* rendering of a closed mind, for the point is not that one excludes new images or insights, but that one clings to and reifies images, whether old or new. Hardening of the heart is the externalization of meaning into images and ideas, as if they were cages of reality. The contrast is between the disciples' hardened hearts, engaged in inner debate and argumentation, and the need for understanding and realization (οὔπω νοεῖτε οὐδὲ συνίετε).[26] Such harsh criticism of the disciples causes a strain on the expectations of the reader, who has been drawn to identify with Jesus' disciples. Now, she has to distance herself from them, for "the implied criticism of the disciples threatens to become criticism of the reader."[27] This, it seems, is Mark's rhetorical intent. Mark's narrative

---

24. Following Bratcher and Nida, *Handbook,* 254.

25. Klosinski, *The Meals in Mark,* 125.

26. Kee, *Community of the New Age,* 160: "The most frequently repeated advice to Mark's readers is that they are to watch and pray. Mark uses three terms: προσεύχειν, γηγορεῖν, βλέπειν. The latter is used in some important passages in the sense of 'perceiving.' Actually in 4:11 and 8:18 it describes the inability of the non-elect to discern the truth about Jesus even when they observe it."

27. Tannehill, "The Gospel of Mark as Narrative Christology," 70. See Dowd, *Prayer, Power, and the Problem of Suffering,* 154.

discourse is not designed so that the reader will attain the correct perspective by means of privileged information unavailable to the story-level characters, but that, thrown into confusion by the criticism of the model-disciples, she might begin to question herself. The disciples remain models for all of Jesus' followers, in all their confusion and failings. "The conclusion of a large section of Mark (4: 1–8: 21) with Jesus' questioning of the disciples (8: 14–21) suggests that Jesus' disciples are distinguished from his opponents not by possessing the right answers but by being possessed by the right questions: not 'Why does he not perform a sign from heaven?' (see 8: 11), but 'Who then is this . . . ?' (4: 41)."[28]

Thus, Jesus warns them about the yeast or leaven of the Pharisees and of Herod. He is talking not about bread at all, but about the consciousness that demands signs, that sees miracles as incursions from the other world. Yeast permeates the dough and causes it to rise into a corrupt mass.[29] In a similar fashion the Yogācāra thinkers talked about the defiled seeds of consciousness *(vijñāna-bīja)* that are planted in consciousness by past actions and that permeate *(vāsanā)* its mode of understanding, causing it to arise in the imagined pattern of understanding. Jesus warns not to insert the Pharisees' yeast into the dough of consciousness to gain assurance of the absolute truth of one's traditions, not to insert the yeast of Herod to be so assured on the correctness of political choices. The more one clings to traditions or to political necessities as absolute, the more one's consciousness is hardened. In such a leavened consciousness, the richness of the dependently co-arising world is seen not as other-dependent conventional reality, but as in the frozen solidity of an occluded vision. The sacred is dichotomized from the profane and the everyday world is falsely viewed as corrupt and evil.[30]

The disciples have already been described as having hardened hearts in 6:52, where it was said that they did not understand about the loaves.[31] So

28. Malbon, "Narrative Criticism," 46, which continues: "To hear only the silence of the disciples [to Jesus' critique] and not also the rhetoric of the implied author is to try to read the story without the discourse." It is that discourse that challenges, not the disciples, but the reader.

29. Camery-Hoggatt, *Irony in Mark's Gospel,* 153: "In the ancient world, leaven is a universal metaphor for evil and corruptive influences. The concern of the Pharisees is for liturgical precision, and the OT proscriptions against leaven in ritually prepared food (Ex. 12.18; 13.6f; Num.28.16f), together give this warning its particularly sharp bite."

30. Crossan, *The Historical Jesus,* 280: "The essential point is 'that leaven in the ancient world was a symbol of moral corruption,' according to Brandon Scott, since it was 'made by taking a piece of bread and storing it in a damp, dark place until mold forms. The bread rots and decays. . . . modern yeast . . . is domesticated.' Furthermore, 'in Israel there is an equation that leaven is the unholy everyday, and unleaven the holy, the sacred, the feast' (Scott, *Hear Then the Parable,* 324)."

31. Via, *The Ethics of Mark's Gospel,* 119: Hardness of heart "is the opposite of faith and is illumined by the meaning of faith in Mark. Heart in Mark, as in the Old Testament, is the hidden inner core of the human being, and hardness of heart is its religious and moral deformation. The heart that is the inner core is made clear in 7: 14–23, where the

Jesus recounts the events of the previous bread miracles, but he does not make any more bread, for the point of those miracles in Mark is the call to break through deluded worldly convention, not to supply bread lines! All along, in the feeding stories and here in the boat, the issue is not about the amount of bread available. They have only the one loaf (καὶ εἰ μὴ ἕνα ἄρτον οὐκ εἶχον). That is clearly not enough if we are really talking about baked bread. But, if the reference again is to the messianic bread of the kingdom which includes all, Jews and gentiles, then that one loaf is enough to be shared among all.

Notice that Mark specifies no content to what it is that the disciples are to understand. Scholars debate just what that content might be.[32] But I do not think that it is a something that they fail to understand. Rather, the issue is their understanding, not what they have understood. Realization is directed first and foremost to the wilderness presence of God apart from all content, and subsequently to engagement in all the conventional affairs of the world—the kingdom, Jesus' passion, the traditions—whatever. The only identifiable content of the disciples' hoped-for realization is worldly and conventional, in all of its variety and complexity, and that is what they do not understand, for their minds are imbued with false expectations and they have not allowed themselves the risk of moving beyond attachment to convention to insight into emptiness. Thus they are unable to understand conventional reality just as it is (*tathatā*).[33] What is needed is a change of the *way* one understands,

---

heart (7: 19,21) is explicitly the inside (*esōthen*, 7: 21, 23), as contrasted with the outside (*exōthen*, 7: 15, 18)."

32. Via summarizes the debate in *The Ethics of Mark's Gospel,* 189: ". . . the disciples are accused of hardness of heart because they do not understand about the loaves multiplied in the feedings of the multitudes. What exactly should they have understood? According to Kelber, what they fail to grasp is the meaning of the 'one loaf' (8:14)—Jesus as the unifier of Jew and Gentile in one community [*The Kingdom in Mark,* 53, 57–58, 62]. For Howard Kee, the mystery is not that Jesus is the Messiah but the nature of his messiahship. It is the insight that contrary to appearances there is no hopeless incongruity between Jesus' eschatological claims and the death he died [*Community of the New Age,* 96, 173]. In the judgment of Quentin Quesnell the mystery of the kingdom, knowledge of the parables, freedom from the purity laws, and the understanding of the loaves all belong together; and Quesnell assumes that this comprehensive mystery is something that can be identified and understood. . . . The mystery is the content of the Gospel, what is revealed as an object of faith. Or it is the theme of the resurrection . . . [*The Mind of Mark,* 125, 161, 188–89, 219–20, 232, 257]. There are other interpreters of Mark who think that when we arrive at 8: 14–21 the disciples are expected to understand something about the kingdom of God but have never been told in a straightforward way what it is. We do not know what it is they are to understand. The mystery is impenetrable, and its content cannot be identified. . . . Kermode also sees the mystery as impenetrable, to the disciples, to Mark, and to us [*The Genesis of Secrecy,* 28, 47, 143]."

33. Via, *The Ethics of Mark's Gospel,* 190: "The meaning of the kingdom of God and the suffering-death-resurrection of the Son of man (-mystery) can never be exhausted and is subject to endless interpretation, but that which can never be exhausted is named and qualified." Yet, even here the content they are to understand is a mysterious "something," rather like the Taoist concept of the unnameable Tao, which, though called Tao, is beyond

a realization of the originally other-dependent character of all understanding.[34] This point is central, for the narrative is building up to Peter's confession that Jesus is the Christ, the supposed main point of Mark's Jesus.

Blindness and Sight
8: 22–26

[22]They came to Bethsaida, and some people brought to him a blind man whom they begged him to touch. [23]He took the blind man by the hand and led him outside the village. Then, putting spittle on his eyes and laying his hands on him, he asked, "Can you see anything?" [24]The man, who was beginning to see, replied, "I can see people; they look like trees as they walk around." [25]Then he laid his hands on the man's eyes again and he saw clearly; he was cured, and he could see everything plainly and distinctly. [26]And Jesus sent him home, saying, "Do not even go into the village."

It was announced in 6:45 that the disciples were to go ahead to Bethsaida, but their journey was interrupted, not only by their seeing the ghostly image of Jesus walking on the sea, but by a number of stories about breaking down the barriers between sacred and profane. Here, at last, that projected journey is completed and they come to Bethsaida, a city on the gentile side of the Sea of Galilee.

Directly after accusing his own disciples of blindness, Jesus cures a blind man: there is hope for them yet! Through the healing spittle of Jesus one

---

all definition. The point at issue is *noesis,* not *noeta,* the pattern of conscious understanding, not that which is understood. Via continues, 192: "It is these disciples who do not and cannot understand what the dying and rising of the Son means for them (8: 32–37; 9: 32–37; 10: 35–41)." Here, irony does not, as Tolbert argues, merely distance the reader from the disciples, but, since we readers are also confused, identifies us with their perplexity. Thus Tannehill, "The Disciples in Mark," 142: "The more clearly the reader sees that the disciples represent himself, the more clearly the necessary rejection of the disciples' behavior becomes a negation of one's past self."

34. Kermode, *The Genesis of Secrecy,* 46: "The sign given them by the Feedings is lost on them. . . . So he takes them once more, slowly, through the story of the Feedings. Five thousand were fed with five loaves, how many baskets were left over? Twelve, they correctly reply. Four thousand at the second Feeding were served with seven loaves: how many baskets of fragments were left over? Seven. Well then, don't you see the point? Silence. Perhaps the disciples mistook the riddle as we do the one about the elephants: there is a strong suggestion that the answer has to do with number, but it probably doesn't." The riddle about the elephants is: how do you fit five elephants into a Volkswagen? Focusing on the number of these huge animals makes one question its possibility, yet if one switches to baby elephants, the answer becomes obvious: two in the front seat and three in the back. Yet Mark's riddle is, I think, subtler, about how to untie the knots of consciousness that prevent one from realization. In Mahāyāna, that is the function and purpose of insight into emptiness. Don't just get smaller elephants, but a Volkswagen as big as the universe!

passes gradually from fixed images to insightful vision.[35] The man comes from outside the village. He is brought to Jesus after the latter's arrival in Bethsaida. Jesus then takes him outside the village, outside the conventional world, for only by removing oneself from the occlusion of conventional truth can one see things as they really are. There is a sequence to this cure: the man first sees men (βλέπτω τοὺς ἀνθρώπους), but misinterprets his images: they look like trees walking.[36] He sees, but not clearly and not truly. Only when Jesus lays his hands on a second time is the man able to see clearly—perhaps when Jesus is done curing them, the disciples too will see? Sight entails not simply vision, but also interpretive insight. Thus the full restoration of sight involves not only regaining one's visual acuity, but the ability to interpret what is seen as well. This also is demanded of the disciples: they are not merely to see, but to interpret and understand.

After restoring his sight, Jesus tells the man not even to go into the village, lest he lose his sight again and begin his false interpretations. Rather, he sends him home (εἰς οἶκον αὐτοῦ). Those who regain their sight have no further need to accompany Jesus. They are sent back to their everyday lives, away from the fanfare of the village or town. Only the still-struggling disciples continue on as Jesus' companions.

The blind man's enlightenment is not here a once and for all event, but grows out of and needs to be perfected, by constant discipline. One cannot be enlightened and immediately return to the old haunts and old habits, for the residual yeast of delusion may again assert its influence. Reengagement demands a firm grounding in awareness of emptiness, not merely in recently acquired sight, nor in verbal assertions of insight.

Peter's Profession
8: 27–30

[27]*Jesus and his disciples left for the villages round Caesarea Philippi. On the way he put this question to his disciples, "Who do people say I am?"* [28]*And they told him, "John the Baptist, others, Elijah, others again, one of the prophets."* [29]*"But you," he asked them, "who do you say I am?" Peter*

---

35. Crossan, *The Historical Jesus,* 325: "The Markan story was not accepted by either Matthew or Luke. They also refused to accept 238 *Deaf Mute Cured* [2/1]. Since both miracles mention Jesus' use of his spittle, in Mark 7:33 and 8:23, that seems the most likely reason for their avoidance. Morton Smith mentions spittle as an instance of how 'the miracle stories in the Gospels show a great many of the minor traits of magical procedures' (*Clement of Alexandria:* 233) and David Aune places it among 'techniques . . . well-known to both Jewish and Graeco-Roman magical practitioners' ("Magic in Early Christianity," 1537)."

36. Broadhead, *Teaching With Authority,* 138: "The victim's response indicates that his healing is only half accomplished. In a pattern that is unusual among healing stories, the healing and the response are repeated."

spoke up and said to him, "You are the Christ." ³⁰And he gave them strict orders not to tell anyone about him.

Where is Jesus going and why? Caesarea Philippi is north of Galilee in Trachonitis, beyond Jewish land and ideas. And it is there, where it would have little impact, that Peter confesses Jesus to be messiah. This passage is often seen as the turning point in Mark's Gospel.³⁷ Here, it is claimed, Peter sees and confesses the truth about Jesus: that he is the christ, the messiah.³⁸ Wrede saw in Peter's confession the heart of the messianic secret, the truth about Jesus that is hidden until revealed in the events of his passion and death.³⁹ It was to be hidden lest people see Jesus as the glorious messiah king come to bring about a golden age of power and prestige.⁴⁰

Yet, another interpretation is possible. Peter's confession plays a part in the ongoing discourse about the deep structure of the two truths of worldly convention and ultimate meaning, about emptiness and dependent co-arising. The answer to Jesus' question is double-tiered. The first tier identifies Jesus as a special, numinous being. Harkening back to the reports circulated to Herod in 6: 14–16, the disciples answer that he is John the Baptist or Elijah come back to life. Or at least, he is a prophet, like the prophets of old (see 6: 14–16). Jesus, however, does not accept these identifications but presses the question. Then Peter, taking clue from Jesus' further questioning, identifies Jesus as the messiah. Some have thought that such a truth assertion could only have been uttered under the influence of some divine grace. Yet, in point of historical fact, there were many claimants to the title of messiah in and about the time of Jesus. And the significance of messiah was not clear and fixed. "So manifold was the messianic idea in Judaism during the period

---

37. Tolbert, *Sowing the Gospel,* 114: "Since those anticipations of the Passion (e.g., 8: 31; 9: 31; 10: 32–33) begin immediately after the incident at Caesarea Philippi where Peter identifies Jesus as 'the Christ' (8: 27–30), that incident, occurring so near the physical center of the narrative, easily qualifies as the central turning point of the story (peripeteia), because at that point the momentum turns in a different direction."

38. Tolbert, *Sowing the Gospel,* 201: "Consequently, by 8: 29 the audience knows that Jesus is indeed ὁ Χριστός, the Son of God, and would recognize Peter's assertion as correct. Peter now understands what the audience has known from the beginning about Jesus." In 1: 1 Mark has identified Jesus as the christ. Yet, Peter's confession, since it is almost immediately rejected by Jesus, should call into question its correctness. For he misunderstands what it means to be christ.

39. Wrede, *The Messianic Secret,* 80–81, 113–114, 124–129. For an insightful discussion on Wrede's thesis, see Kingsbury, *The Christology of Mark's Gospel,* 1–23.

40. Weeden, *Mark—Traditions in Conflict,* 52–69. Especially, 54: "If the Gospel is so read [the way the first readers approached it without preconceived ideas], when the reader arrives at the point of Peter's confession he has no recourse but to assume that whatever insights dawned upon Peter must have grown out of a recognition of the nature of Jesus revealed to the disciples (and to the reader) prior to the confession. What, then, is the picture of Jesus revealed to the reader? . . . [It is] drawn in the tradition of the Hellenistic *theios aner* (divine man). In such a perspective Jesus is characterized as the epiphany of God, the divine savior in human form, who intervenes in human affairs to work miracles in behalf of man. He is not a deity, but superhuman—a combination of the divine and human."

from Daniel to Akiba that one has not said much when one states that Jesus was the messiah. What kind of messiah? A prophet, a teacher of the Law, a bearer of angelic power, a priest-king (as in Test. Levi) or a political-national king?"[41] Moreover, Jesus does not accept Peter's identification. Rather, he "warns" the disciples not to say anything about him to anyone (καὶ ἐπετίμη-σεν αὐτοῖς ἵνα μηδενὶ λέγωσιν περὶ αὐτοῦ). That warning (ἐπετίμησεν) is more than a mild piece of advice. It is the same word used in the next passage, where Peter rebukes Jesus and is in turn rebuked as Satan by Jesus. "The threefold rebuking (in 8: 27–33) conjures up a demonic milieu and suggests that each of the protagonists treats the other as a satanic personality."[42] It would seem that indeed Jesus does not accept Peter's confession. The point does not lie in identifying who Jesus is, and so he neither accepts nor rejects Peter's statement because it does not mean very much.[43] Who Jesus is comes clear only in the unfolding events of his dependently co-arisen course, in the events of his passion, death, and resurrection, and, even then, it has no fixable definition. In Mark the point is "Jesus' own positive repudiation of this category as inadequate or even misleading,"[44] for Jesus rebukes his disciples and tells them to say nothing about him. He has elicited their ideas, and proceeds to reject each one.

The point is that a verbal confession that Jesus is the christ doesn't say anything about the consciousness that utters it. Saints and murderers have likewise confessed Jesus as christ. It is not enough just to step forward and accept Jesus as your savior, for that can mean many different things, from true faith to utter hypocrisy. The constant theme of Mark is that it is conversion which Jesus came to preach (1: 15). Peter's confession is indeed a central turning point in the narrative, because it calls into question the very need for definitions. The imagined pattern of understanding, being uncomfortable with the need for constant conversion, constructs categories of truth and attributes essences to images and ideas which are seen not as dependent upon their context, but as beyond culture and time, as absolutely true. Revelation, conceived as communication of truth statements that are essentially and unalterably true, becomes a refuge from humanness and transience. That is the "divine man heresy" which Mark opposes.[45] The Prajñāpāramitā Scriptures would have declared, "Christ, Christ, there is no Christ, and that is why

---

41. Kee, *Community of the New Age,* 116, quoting from Volz, *Jüdische Eschatologie,* 196.
42. Kelber, *Mark's Story of Jesus,* 48.
43. Fowler, *Let the Reader Understand,* 106: "Jesus . . . is also called 'Christ' and 'King of the Jews,' but these acclamations turn out to be either insincere (e.g., Mark 15:2, 12, 18, 32) or shallow (8:29)."
44. Grant, *The Interpreter's Bible,* 7: 767.
45. See reference in note 21 of this chapter and Weeden, "The Heresy That Necessitated Mark's Gospel." Similarly, Perrin, "The Christology of Mark": ". . . there would also be general agreement that a major aspect of the Marcan purpose is christological: he is concerned with correcting a false christology prevalent in his Church and to teach both a true christology and its consequences for Christian discipleship." I agree with Weeden and Perrin, but see that christological distortion not as a formal heresy, but as the human tendency to cling to images.

Jesus is Christ." There is no ready-made essence of christ, no imagined understanding of who Jesus is. Only then, in the emptiness of all essence, can one confess that Jesus is Christ.

Passion Talk
8: 31–33

[31]Then he began to teach them that the Son of man was destined to suffer grievously, and to be rejected by the elders and the chief priests and the scribes, and to be put to death, and after three days to rise again; [32]and he said all this quite openly. Then, taking him aside, Peter tried to rebuke him. [33]But, turning and seeing his disciples, he rebuked Peter and said to him, "Get behind me, Satan! You are thinking not as God thinks, but as human beings do."

"Mark set it (8: 27–33) up in such a way that the reader almost instinctively identifies with Peter and his Christ confession. He teases the reader, as it were, into accepting Peter's confession at face value."[46] But then Jesus begins to present his own description of himself, as the son of man,[47] not glorious as in the popular imagination, but simply as a man caught in his given social context.[48] He must (δεῖ) undergo sufferings, be judged useless (ἀποδοκιμα-σθῆναι) by the religious authorities, and finally killed. Jesus empties Peter's confession of its expected correctness: no messianic glory will ever ensue.[49]

There have been arguments aplenty about the nature of the necessity for Jesus' suffering and death. One scholar writes, "There is nowadays a gathering consensus among Marcan scholars that the emphasis by the evangelist on

---

46. Kelber, *Mark's Story of Jesus*, 48.

47. Crossan, *The Historical Jesus*, 255–59, argues Mark first created the title son of man and applied it to Jesus as the suffering and rising son of man.

48. Collins, *The Beginning of the Gospel*, 64: "The use of 'Son of Man' as a name for Jesus in Mark thus served to tie together his earthly activity and his exalted, heavenly status. Because of its connotations of ordinary humanity and its association with the heavenly figure of Daniel 7, the epithet was well suited to the Markan project of reinterpreting the meaning and function of the Messiah." Geza Vermes, in his *Jesus the Jew*, argues that son of man is a circumlocution for "I."

49. Camery-Hoggatt, *Irony in Mark's Gospel*, 157: "Peter's confession is accurate only in its vocabulary. . . . As Peter intends it, the confession—'You are the Christ'—is a shadow of the truth. He is dazzled by visions of splendor, apparently, is blinded by a flash of false light." Again, 155: "It is strange and significant that the necessity for Jesus' death has never yet become a matter of Mark's sustained focus. Peter does not yet see it, and neither does the reader. Jesus *will* die. That the reader knows. But does he understand that this death is *necessary*, that it is itself messianic? Perhaps it is that the reader, like the disciples, is being set up for a dramatic reversal which is fully portrayed only in the figure of the immolated victim on the cross. As he reads further he will discover that impaled on the cross along with Jesus are all the fondest aspirations he might attach to the figure of a Messiah."

the divine necessity of Jesus' sufferings and death ('the way of the cross') represents a major thrust of his christological presentation."[50] Some, like Telford in the citation above, think that we are dealing with a divine necessity for Jesus' sufferings and death.[51] Others, more insightfully, see only the necessity that comes from the course of evil human actions. Tolbert comments that Herod's killing of John "provides an important clue to why such suffering must be expected. By failing to note the connection between this first Passion prediction and the episode of Herod and John the Baptist, established narratively through the exact repetition and allusion (the putative identities for Jesus: Elijah, John revivified, a prophet are identical in 6: 14–16 and 8:28), many commentators have assumed that the Markan δεῖ like δεῖ in much apocalyptic literature, refers primarily to divine necessity. God, thus, ordains the suffering of Jesus and those who follow him. While for Mark, God is certainly sovereign over all creation, the direct cause of suffering for Jesus is the current dominance of 'this adulterous and sinful generation.' It is not God's will but the evil will of the present authorities and powers that makes suffering inevitable."[52] Jesus is as immersed in the dependently co-arisen events of human history as anyone. "What is involved is nothing less than the acceptance of a submission to the events of history as an expression of the will of God; one's essential status is not the point."[53]

---

50. Telford, "Introduction: The Gospel of Mark," 18.

51. For example, Nineham, *Saint Mark,* 225: ". . . when Jesus said must in v. 31 he meant this. He used the word in a sense in which it was often used in contemporary apocalyptic literature, as showing that certain future events were part of the firmly decreed will of God. Thus, to persuade Jesus to shrink from those events was to tempt him to disobey the will of God, as Satan had done in the wilderness." Weeden, *Mark—Traditions in Conflict,* 52–3, comes close to this: "There is no particular problem in identifying Jesus' christological position. Authentic messiahship is suffering messiahship which leads inevitably to crucifixion. . . . Mark seeks to convince the reader that Jesus' role as a suffering servant was not only the central and most important element in his messiahship but was the role specifically ordained by God and by which he was finally accurately identified by man." Kermode, *The Genesis of Secrecy,* 155 (translating Marin, *Sémiotique de la Passion,* 106f): "The death of God is necessary and impossible; someone must make it necessary, possible: how? By the random act of treachery. . . . The traitor is the necessity of a logic of narrative that has to solve an impossible problem." Kelber, *The Kingdom in Mark,* 70: "But despite the divinely ordained necessity of Jesus' passion and resurrection, the realm of freedom and personal decision remains untouched. Jesus himself takes the initiative and wills his fate." Such a decision, however, seems more akin to a Stoic's acceptance of unalterable fate. See the argument in Dowd, *Prayer, Power, and the Problem of Suffering,* that Jesus' acceptance is not a Stoic resignation. Dowd herself, 134, accepts the notion of divine necessity: "That their plot will succeed is made clear by three passion predictions, the first of which (8:31) emphasizes the divine will behind the passion by the use of δεῖ: 'It is necessary for the Son of Man to suffer many things . . .' "

52. Tolbert, *Sowing the Gospel,* 202.

53. Humphrey, *He Is Risen,* 4. Also Robbins, *Jesus the Teacher,* 211: "In contrast to the gospels of Matthew and Luke, the Gospel of Mark accepts rejection, suffering, and death from the inside. The members of early Christianity do not presuppose that they will be able to overcome this experience while on earth, nor do they presuppose that those who reject them will be destroyed in an eternal punishment. Rejection, suffering, and

For the reader the impact of the necessity of Jesus' suffering and death is stark. Mark is not, I think, simply attempting to deal with the problem of theodicy: how could a kind and omnipotent God allow Jesus to suffer and die?[54] Rather, the rhetorical impact derives from Mark's maneuvering the implied reader into a very uncomfortable situation. Mark snookers his implied reader, unawakened and entangled in the cycle of sin and delusion, into an awareness that only an awakened person can maintain. Jesus' passion predictions orient that reader toward an acceptance of the inevitability of suffering, while Peter's comforting advice to Jesus reflects the reader's wistful feelings and counters that inevitability. Is it possible, as Jesus asserts in Gethsemane (14:36, "Father, all things are possible to you"), to avoid the cup of suffering? The reader indeed hopes to avoid suffering in her own life! But the thrust of Mark's narrative is toward inner conflict, engendered by knowing that one has (δεῖ) to reject what in fact one feels. "Through the course of these verses [about suffering], the reader stands observing the scene, seeing things now from the perspective of the disciples, now from Jesus' perspective, and so on, back and forth. When we arrive at verse 33, however, no one can vacillate; the reader must choose. Will the reader side with Jesus and God or with Peter and humankind? Clearly the author wants the reader to choose the former."[55] Just as clearly any unawakened reader is impelled to choose the latter. In such a reading the referent of the Markan δεῖ (the inevitability of suffering) is not the objective divine command, but the dependently co-arisen inevitability in every life that, like Jesus, the reader must accept the inevitability of suffering and death.[56]

---

death are accepted without pronouncement of curses upon those who cause the rejection, suffering, and death." Suffering and dying are not strange events calling for a special explanation. Rather, they are the most universal facts of human living, constituting the first of the four noble truths of Buddhism: that all life entails suffering (*duḥkha-satya*).

54. Dowd, *Prayer, Power, and the Problem of Suffering,* 160–52, argues that in fact Mark can offer no solution to the problem, but a "way to cope with the tension that pervades their existence as empowered sufferers. That tension, which may not be relaxed, is to be integrated into the community's prayers."

55. Fowler, *Let the Reader Understand,* 71. Yet perhaps Mark's rhetorical intent is different, focusing not on an intellectual choice of sides, but on the engendering of tension within one's own life. See Bassler, "Parable of the Loaves," 165–66: "It is with some surprise and consternation that the reader suddenly finds the [Markan] disciples the object of stern criticism in chapters 6 to 8. . . . Now the reader would like to dissociate from the disciples, but the gaps in the text at this point render this impossible. Thus the identification with the disciples initially undertaken quite willingly by the reader, continues—but now unwittingly. . . . By 8: 21 the position of the disciples has become quite desperate, but this desperation is shared by the reader. . . . The primary emotion the implied reader experiences at this point is confusion." Passage cited by Moore, *Literary Criticism and the Gospels,* 82 and 97. Emotional confusion is often this writer-reader's state of mind when reading Mark.

56. See Hamerton-Kelly, *The Gospel and the Sacred,* 48: "Jesus' impending death, unadorned by the pretense that it is a good thing, will remove him as a sacred object and subvert the possibility of Jesusolatry. In order for Jesus to remain a sacred hero, his death must be heroic—either in its courage or in its suffering—rather than ignominious, and

Mark's Jesus speaks openly and plainly (παρρησίᾳ), for what he says is now no great secret. The life course of every person, especially one set against the religious or political establishment, is characterized by suffering and dying.[57] Suffering indeed is the lot of all human beings. Yet, for Jesus, suffering and death are not the end of it all. The complete acceptance of his conventional reality—not the glorious career of an imagined messiah—is the path to resurrection and life.[58] But Peter has his own agenda and his confession evidently did not envisage this kind of christ. "Jesus' teaching about his upcoming suffering in Jerusalem is either ignored, misunderstood, or rejected by his disciples."[59] They reject the realm of dependent co-arising, characterized by the universality of suffering *(duḥkha-satya),* and imagine a future life free from all pain and trouble.[60] They have failed to recognize that Jesus also is subject to the human inevitability of suffering and dying.[61] So Peter rebukes Jesus.[62] Jesus, however, rejects such an imagined understanding of

his followers should stand fast to the end, showing either great courage or willingness to suffer. In this way, his death would qualify as a sacrifice or a noble death for the sake of a higher morality or patrician community, and that community would come into being properly, by loyalty and self-sacrifice. Instead, Jesus dies ignominiously and his community humiliates itself by cowardice." Again, 50: "[His disciples] have not understood that Jesus is no sacred hero, religious virtuoso, or saint, but simply a victim of violence in need of moral support."

57. Via, *The Ethics of Mark's Gospel,* 54: "Thus the really new thing beginning at 8: 31–32 is a deepening or doubling of the irony: the explanations did not really explain and the open teaching was not really open. This directs us to read 8: 32 in the light of 4: 34 [i.e., Jesus' talking in parables]. However 'open' Jesus' words, they are still parables, enigmas." Yet, the enigmatic part of Jesus' first passion prediction—that he will rise, is hardly mentioned. Peter seems to focus merely on the prospect of suffering, no enigma at all, but the common condition of all human beings.

58. Sheehan, *The First Coming,* 112: "As regards the 'time' of the resurrection, the phrase 'on the third day' is *not a chronological designation but an apocalyptic symbol* for God's eschatological saving act, which strictly speaking has no date in history." Also Fuller, *The Formation of the Resurrection Narratives,* 25: The third day is "not a chronological datum, but a dogmatic assertion: Christ's resurrection marked the dawn of the end-time, the beginning of the cosmic eschatological process of resurrection." Yet that beginning of the eschatological kingdom is already announced in Mark 1: 15–16.

59. Tolbert, *Sowing the Gospel,* 200.

60. Tolbert, *Sowing the Gospel,* 202: "The teaching to which Peter has the presumption to object concerns the necessity (δεῖ, 8: 31) of suffering not only for Jesus but, as Jesus explains to the multitude (8: 34), for all who wish to follow him as well. Suffering, the cross, and death are the inevitable results of walking the way of Jesus 'in this adulterous and sinful generation' (8: 38). . . ." It should be noted that not only Jesus' followers suffer and die, but that all human beings share the same condition. Suffering and dying are inevitable for everybody.

61. Kelber, *Mark's Story of Jesus,* 46: "That Jesus is going to Jerusalem in order to die and be resurrected is what the disciples and above all the reader, have to learn on the way to Jerusalem."

62. Sheehan, *The First Coming,* 123–24, on Peter's confession and subsequent flight: "The point was clear: The only way to save Jesus was to let him die, and then go on living the kind of life that Jesus had led, a life set entirely on the present-future, on God-with-man." Thus Peter's sin was that he followed a Jesus/hero right into the high priest's

christ and rebukes Peter, describing him as Satan, who had tempted him in the wilderness.[63] Peter plays the part of Satan, trying to confuse the ultimate meaning Abba with a glorious reign of the messiah. "Peter is the only human being who is identified, and identified by Jesus, as a satanic personality."[64] Illusory dreams are hard to abandon. Peter has his mind set on the things of man, not of God (ὅτι οὐ φρονεῖς τὰ τοῦ θεοῦ ἀλλὰ τὰ τῶν ἀνθρώπων), i.e., Peter clings (φρονεῖς) to his human ideas without insight into their emptiness. The problem lies not in his confession, but in his way of thinking, affixed on the imagined realities of his religious world and not on God, who empties all things in the depths of silence. No titles, not even christ, provide a clear identification of Jesus.[65] And so, unaware of emptiness, Peter would have Jesus abandon his awareness of dependent co-arising and substitute the images of a deluded clinging to superstar dreams. In 1: 17 Jesus had called Peter to come behind him (δεῦτε ὀπίσω μου), now he tells him to get behind him (ὕπαγε ὀπίσω μου).[66]

The Practice of No-self
8: 34–9: 1

[34]*He called the people and his disciples to him and said, "If anyone wants to be a follower of mine, let him renounce himself and take up his cross and follow me.* [35]*Anyone who wants to save his life will lose it; but anyone who loses his life for my sake, and for the sake of the gospel, will save it.* [36]*What gain, then, is it for anyone to win the whole world and forfeit his life?* [37]*And indeed what can anyone offer in exchange for his life?* [38]*For if anyone in*

---

courtyard, clinging to the kingdom as a separate, empirical reality. "He was turning Jesus into the last thing the prophet wanted to be: a hero and an idol, an obstacle to God-with-man. . . . Simon erred not in abandoning Jesus but in not abandoning him enough."

63. Mauser, *Christ in the Wilderness*, 123: "The basic cause of their disbelief is their determination to run away from the desert."

64. Kelber, *Mark's Story of Jesus*, 48. Camery-Hoggatt, *Irony in Mark's Gospel*, 202.101, reports with reservations that: "In a recent article ("Peter: Stumblingblock and Satan," 187–90), B. A. E. Osborne has argued that there is a subtle play on words underlying this condemnation of Peter: Peter is said to have aligned himself with the 'thoughts of men' (8.33). But the thoughts of men are themselves under the influence of the evil *yetzer*, and it is for that reason that they are set over against the 'thoughts' of God. In *TB. Sukkoth* 52a, one of the seven names of the evil *yetzer* is 'stumblingblock', and in Pesikta 165a, the *yetzer* is a rock which causes travelers to stumble at a crossroads. If this sort of thinking is in view in Mark 8.31–33, there is a subtle play on Peter's name: a moment ago Peter—the *petros*—was the cornerstone, here he has become a stumblingblock."

65. Tromcé, in *Christ and the Spirit in the New Testament*, cited by Kealy, *Mark's Gospel*, 182: "None of the titles in Mark is used as a vehicle for his Christology. Neither Son of God, Son of Man nor teacher is used to give expression to a new image of Jesus. For Mark the right Christology is primarily an acceptance of suffering for the sake of Christ."

66. Tolbert, *Sowing the Gospel*, 202.44.

*this sinful and adulterous generation is ashamed of me and my words, the
Son of man will also be ashamed of him when he comes in the glory of his
Father with the holy angels."*
*¹And he said to them, "In truth I tell you, there are some standing here
who will not taste death before they see the kingdom of God come with power."*

Peter has just been told to get behind Jesus. Now Jesus calls a crowd
together and invites people to follow behind him (εἴ τις θέλει ὀπίσω μου
ἀκολουθεῖν), and demands that they renounce all self and self-definition
(ἀπαρνησάσθω ἑαυτὸν).[67] Without the realization of no-self *(anātman)*, no
salvation is possible.[68] This means much more than not being selfish. It means
that one must abandon the final validity of all the definitions of self which
we construct in our coping with the world.[69] Personality is a construct, socially
fabricated upon the dependently co-arisen basis of heredity and environment.
It is not, as the Greeks thought, an inner essence of a person, an unalterable
core of personal being. Such a definition is affixing one's mind to the things
of man, to a convention deemed beyond convention. The Buddhists stress
this notion in the doctrine of no-self *(anātman)*, that there is no inner core
to anything. We live moment to moment in a radical contingency, fearing to
let go and live. And so Jesus says that to live, we must lose our lives. The
emptying and abandoning of an imagined inner core to our lives frees one
to engage in the true dependently co-arisen beauty and joy of human being.[70]
Yet, this also means engaging in the world with an awareness of the silence
of ultimate truth, and thus it means the cross, for all life involves suffering.[71]

67. Via, *The Ethics of Mark's Gospel*, 177: "Each indication of failure to understand
who Jesus is is followed by a teaching on suffering discipleship and being servant of all
(8: 34–37; 9: 35–50; 10: 42–45)."
68. Fowler, *Let the Reader Understand*, 189–90: "Note that the paradox is not 'Whoever
would save his life will lose it; whoever loses his life will save it.' Apparently, for Mark
saving one's life invariably means losing it . . .'" In Mahāyāna terms, without the realization
of *anātman*, no salvation is attained, for awakening is blocked. It is not, however, that
the path of Jesus is based on suffering as "the central and dominant feature of discipleship
in Mark" (as Dowd, *Prayer, Power, and the Problem of Suffering*, 135, notes that some
think), but that awakening to a consciousness of no-self transforms the mind into the
mirror of the will of God.
69. Schweizer, "Mark's Theological Achievement," 53: "Only in following is that
discipleship possible in which one becomes free from oneself, finds one's true life in no
longer having to worry tensely about one's own life, and is able to find it truly in self-
abandonment and self-giving (8: 35)."
70. Via, *The Ethics of Mark's Gospel*, 70: "The archetypal idea of fullness through
emptiness comes to expression in Mark in the principle that one can find life only by
passing through death . . . (8: 34–37). But he does not just teach it; he enacts it for them
(8: 31; 9: 31; 10: 33–34, 45; 14:21), and this pattern of existence also takes on the specific
content of an ethical demand."
71. Epictetus, *Discourses* 2.2.20: "If you want to be crucified, just wait. The cross will
come. If it seems reasonable to comply, and the circumstances are right, then it's to be
carried through, and your integrity maintained." Cited by Crossan, *The Historical Jesus*,
353, who remarks: "There is, therefore, no need to take Jesus' saying as either retrojected

No one ever escapes the suffering that is entailed in simply being human, although we all try our best to do so. Jesus' recommendation is that, if one would be his follower, one must face life concretely, one must carry the cross of human transience and suffering. This is not meant to be a nihilistic despair, for nihilism occurs only when false dreams are frustrated. No delusions of wealth and power, even if realized, are worth the ruin of one's life.

The words about Jesus being ashamed of those who are ashamed of his words are directed against Peter-like refusals to hear about Jesus' suffering, about our cross. They are directed against those who imagine a life free from the struggle that is entailed in reengagement and who become disillusioned when their false hopes are emptied.[72] It is difficult to accept no-self and impermanence, for the world constantly solicits us toward delusion, toward self-definitions of ourselves, our groups, our nations. That is why Jesus shocks his hearers. Jesus' saying in verse 35 "must shake our deep assurance that we know what saving life and losing life mean. It attempts this by taking the meaning of our words away from us . . . Only this shaking of our deep, largely unconscious convictions can do this. On the other hand, if the saying fits within our lives as something reasonable, the possibility of bringing about significant change would be lost."[73] So also Jesus speaks of this adulterous and sinful generation, for the term adulterous (μοιχαλίδι) refers not merely to sexual transgression, but to the power of the world to entice and solicit one away from insight into no-self. In a world where everyone is protecting self, there can be no peace, but only mutual competition and struggle.[74] But such is not the struggle of the cross, which offers no resistance precisely because one has realized no-self. And in that realization, one realizes resurrection.

---

or projected prophecy [about his actual crucifixion]. Jesus 'was discussing,' as Leif Vaage put it about Epictetus, 'the . . . cost of adopting a particular way of life.' " The reference to Vaage is to "Q1 and the Historical Jesus," 173.

72. See Kee, *Community of the New Age,* 133–34, where he argues that 'to be embarrassed' (ἐπαισχυνθῇ, v. 38) has the sense of 'to become disillusioned.' "

73. Tannehill, *The Sword of His Mouth,* 195.

74. Reps, *Zen Flesh, Zen Bones,* 7, offers a story about no-self: "The Zen Master Hakuin was praised by his neighbors as one living a pure life. A beautiful Japanese girl whose parents owned a food store lived near him. Suddenly, without any warning, her parents discovered she was with child. This made her parents angry. She would not confess who the man was, but after much harassment at last named Hakuin. In great anger the parents went to the master. 'Is that so?' was all he would say. After the child was born it was brought to Hakuin. By this time he had lost his reputation, which did not trouble him, but he took very good care of the child. He obtained milk from his neighbors and everything else the little one needed. A year later the girl-mother could stand it no longer. She told her parents the truth—that the real father of the child was a young man who worked in the fishmarket. The mother and father of the girl at once went to Hakuin to ask his forgiveness, to apologize at length, and to get the child back again. Hakuin was willing. In yielding the child, all he said was: 'Is that so?' "

Jesus talks not only about the cross, but in verse 38 also about his coming in the glory of the Father.[75] The last sentence, the first of chapter 9, follows logically upon Jesus' reference to his coming in the glory of the Father with the angels. What does he mean by his coming in the glory of the Father? Does he really mean that the kingdom of God is to come in the lifetime of some of his hearers? That is its obvious sense: that Jesus, and Paul after him, does indeed expect the end of the world to happen soon. There was such an expectancy at the time.[76]

Yet, perhaps, another interpretation is possible and the reference is not to a coming of the kingdom in the linear future. Jesus has just been speaking about losing one's life and thereby gaining life. The life so gained is not merely physical continuity, but the life of the kingdom. When he speaks about the kingdom of God coming in power, it is not the power that conquers the world, for that has been rejected. Rather, the power is the paradoxical power of abandonment, and the kingdom is seen even now, during one's life span, by those who do in fact lose their lives, by those awakened to the truth of no-self. Jesus identifies himself both as the one who has to take the cross and the one who is exalted in glory. He is the conventional manifestation of ultimate truth, transparently mirroring the empty awareness of Abba in the dependently co-arisen conditions of life. In such a life and such a death, the kingdom comes in glory.

---

75. Kelber, *The Kingdom in Mark,* 74: "8:38 is the first explicit announcement of the parousia."

76. Donahue, *Are You the Christ?* 166: "Prior to 8:27 the kingdom is proclaimed as a present reality manifested in the ministry of Jesus (1: 15; 4: 11; 4: 26; 4: 30), after 8: 27 the kingdom takes on a future dimension: 9: 1, it is coming in power; all these sayings on entering the kingdom come after 8: 27 (9: 47; 10: 23–25)."

9

The Epiphany of Just Jesus

Jesus Transfigured
9: 2–8

²Six days later, Jesus took with him Peter and James and John and led them up a high mountain on their own by themselves. There in their presence he was transfigured; ³his clothes became brilliantly white, whiter than any earthly bleacher could make them. ⁴Elijah appeared to them with Moses; and they were talking with Jesus. ⁵Then Peter spoke to Jesus, "Rabbi," he said, "It is wonderful for us to be here; so let us make three shelters, one for you, one for Moses and one for Elijah." ⁶He did not know what to say; they were so frightened. ⁷And a cloud came, covering them in shadow; and from the cloud there came a voice, "This is my Son, the Beloved. Listen to him." ⁸Then, suddenly, when they looked around, they saw no one with them any more but only Jesus.

Mark's Jesus had just said that some (τινες) of his contemporaries will see the kingdom of God before they die. Here, the Markan Jesus takes Peter and James and John up a high mountain to experience that very kingdom.[1] The transfiguration here recounted is a transitory event, in contrast to the more usual idea, both among Jesus' contemporaries and among modern scholars, of the kingdom of God as the definitive establishment of the rule of God on earth.[2]

---

1. Tolbert, *Sowing the Gospel,* 173: "Before Jesus, the kingdom is present in potential; with Jesus, it is revealed with power. Jesus' saying to the crowds and the disciples in 9: 1 functions perfectly well on the level of second degree narrative." Also Crossan, *The Historical Jesus,* 396, speaks of "the Transfiguration, a foretaste not of resurrection but of parousia according to 9: 9–10." Crossan argues that the account was rewritten by Mark and relocated from the *Cross Gospel's* resurrectional apparition back to the earthly life of Jesus, for which see *The Cross That Spoke.*

2. Via, *The Ethics of Mark's Gospel,* 49: "The coming down of the Spirit on Jesus in the beginning (1: 10) corresponds to the rising up of Jesus presupposed in the end (16: 1–8), and the coming down of Moses and Elijah in the middle (9: 2–8) corresponds to

Jesus takes the three disciples apart to the very top of a mountain (εἰς ὄρος ὑψηλὸν), alone and away from the crowd and its false conventions.[3] The scene is a high point in Mark's narrative. "All indications point to the transfiguration as the true scene of recognition. Structurally, its place is precisely at mid-point in the gospel. Theologically it marks God's only intervention outside baptism. Dramatically, it stages God's attestation of his Son in opposition to Peter's vainglorious christos."[4] Throughout the gospel, Jesus invites his disciples to break through their imaginings to the numinous silence of Abba. There in the silent awareness of ultimate meaning, all is transformed and things no longer have their accustomed definitions or limitations. The images are all other-worldly. Jesus' garments take on an apocalyptic, revelatory whiteness beyond anything possible on earth.[5] And he appears together with Elijah and Moses; previously some had thought Jesus was Elijah or one of the prophets. Here he is associated with the founders of the Jewish traditions, and symbols of the end-time.[6] His garments shine bright, as did Moses' face on Mt. Sinai and as perhaps did Elijah as he was whooshed up into heaven by the whirlwind. Both are figures of

---

both. . . . Beginning, middle, and end interpenetrate each other in the middle." Just as Mark collapses the spatial boundaries between Jew and gentile, between sacred and profane, so also he collapses ordinary notions of linear time. The middle time brings to the present moment both the very beginning and the end time. Via at times seems to be thinking in parallel to Mahāyāna philosophers. The interpenetration of all things (*shih shih wu ai*) is a major theme of Hua-yen thought, for which see Cook, *Hua-yen Buddhism,* 36–38. Dōgen takes up the construction and deconstruction of time as the linear form of being in his "The Time-Being" (*uji*) in *Moon in a Dewdrop,* ed. Tanahashi, 76–83. And Nishitani presents existentialist essays, "Śūnyatā and Time," and "Śūnyatā and History" in his *Religion and Nothingness,* 168–285. See also the essays by Langdon Gilkey, Thomas J. J. Altizer, and Gordon D. Kaufman in *The Religious Philosophy of Nishitani Keiji,* ed. Taitetsu Unno.

3. Mauser, *Christ in the Wilderness,* 109: The mountain is "associated with moments of ultimate revelation." Malbon, *Narrative Space,* 85: "The biblical tradition of the mountain as the place of divine revelation and meeting, manifested in the Law (Moses) and the Prophets (Elijah), is woven into the fabric of Mark's Gospel."

4. Kelber, *The Kingdom in Mark,* 84–85. See also 78: "The mountain of transfiguration, however, is an exceptional mountain, for it is the only 'high mountain' (9: 2 *oros hypsēlon*) in the gospel. Towering above all other peaks of revelation, it designates the transfiguration as the epiphany of all epiphanies."

5. Kelber, *The Kingdom in Mark,* 79: "The whiteness of Jesus' garments . . . portrays the transfiguration in Mark. White, the apocalyptic color par excellence, lends the quality of end time to the mountain epiphany."

6. Heil, *The Gospel of Mark as a Model for Action,* 186: "The epiphany thus portrays Jesus in close association with two revered prophetic figures of old who are now in heavenly glory. Elijah went up by a whirlwind into heaven without dying (2 Kgs 2: 1–11); and because the place of Moses' burial was unknown (Deut 34: 5–8), various Jewish traditions arose about his ascension into heaven possibly without dying. Although the epiphany indicated that Jesus is destined to join Elijah and Moses in the glory of the heavenly realm, Jesus has already announced that, unlike Elijah and Moses who may have arrived at glory without dying, he will arrive at heavenly glory through the divine necessity of suffering, rejection and death (8:31, 38)."

ultimate meaning. Therefore, even though they speak with Jesus, no words
are given. In Mahāyāna terms, silent emptiness is said to have the voice of
thunder. This is indeed an experience of power, the power of the otherness
of ultimate meaning, threatening always to break through whatever limitations
we set on our lives.

Peter, not knowing what to say, yet cannot maintain his silence. He wants to
capture and domesticate the epiphany, by erecting three shelters (ποιήσωμεν
τρεῖς σκηνὰς)—to bring its silent otherness back within the sphere of human
fabrication (*prapañca*).[7] One might find refuge and make the divine presence
geographically defined, for he is frightened by the manifestation of power,
power that goes beyond self-definitions.[8]

It is in this epiphany that Jesus is defined, not in Peter's confession of
Jesus as christ.[9] Following directly Jesus' rejection of his disciple's confession,
this mountaintop transfiguration defines Jesus by the undefinable brightness
of his person, i.e., he has no ordinary definition. Peter, terrified, wants to
localize and delimit that presence by circumscribing it within accustomed
images, just as he wanted to identify Jesus as the expected messiah. Yet, at
this very moment, all further knowing is cut off by the overshadowing of
the cloud (καὶ ἐγένετο νεφέλη ἐπισκιάζουσα αὐτοῖς), from which the
voice identifies Jesus not in terms of his own selfhood, but in terms of his
relationship to Abba as the beloved son.[10] That is then who Jesus is: a mirror
of the Father, both during this mountaintop experience and afterward when
things return to normal.

This account harkens back both to the wilderness experience of Israel
when Moses ascended Mount Sinai and was covered by the cloud for six

---

7. Peter's shelters may allude to the tent of meeting in *Exodus* 27: 21, but more likely
to the tent of testimony in *Numbers* 9: 15, which says: "On the day the Dwelling was
erected, the cloud covered the Dwelling, the tent of the Testimony. From nightfall until
morning it remained over the Dwelling looking like fire. So the cloud covered it all the
time, and at night it looked like fire." Peter's tenting desire is then to bring the experience
within the scope of the traditional understandings, thus to handle it just as he imagined
his forefathers had handled Yahweh's presence in times of old. Malbon, *Narrative Space,*
83, notes that "the biblical cloud both conceals and reveals the divine presence. And this
motif also finds expression in Mark."

8. Tolbert, *Sowing the Gospel,* 200, speaks of "the amazing episode known as the
transfiguration (9: 2–8), all of which the narrator uses to begin to sketch the disciples'
desire for very human glory, status, and power in contrast to the 'glory' of suffering, the
'status' of servanthood, and the 'power' of new life associated with the kingdom of God
as Jesus reveals it." Yet, it seems the account also has a further function—the contrast of
the disciples' attachment to convention in the face of the otherness of ultimate meaning.

9. Broadhead, *Teaching With Authority,* 151: "The first focus of the divine voice is the
identity of Jesus: he is the beloved Son of God. First narrated to Jesus alone in 1.11, the
identity of Jesus is now conveyed to the inner circle of three."

10. These themes are developed in the apophatic tradition of mystic thought. See
Keenan, *The Meaning of Christ,* 86–119, on Gregory of Nyssa and Pseudo-Dionysius.

days (*Exodus* 24: 12–18) and to the experiences of Jesus in the wilderness,[11] alone on the mountain praying to Abba. Now, however, that experience is shared with the three disciples. The voice does not identify the content of Jesus' words to which we are to listen, but says only that we are to listen.[12] This is strange business, for the entire gospel is insistent that we are indeed to listen, but is meager on just what it is to which we must listen.[13]

However, if we attend to the twin stories of Jesus' identity, between the story of Peter's identification and Jesus' rejection of that identification (8: 27–32) and the story of God's identification (9: 2–8) lies the teaching of Jesus on the losing of selfhood. Therein lies the central teaching about Jesus' identity, as to all identities: having lost identity, Jesus shines with the brightness of the end-time when God's kingdom is realized through the experience of conversion (μετάνοια).

Jesus came preaching conversion, "The time has come," he said, "and the kingdom of God is close at hand. Repent and believe the Good News!" (1: 15). Mark reports the coming of the kingdom and conversion as the content of Jesus' preaching and that is what we are to listen to. These two aspects are not unrelated, two factors only accidentally joined together. Rather conversion itself entails the awakening to emptiness and ultimate meaning that is necessary for constructing the kingdom. The kingdom comes then in power not as a future apocalyptic incursion from beyond, a star-wars scenario, but from the power of awakening, to the brightness of ultimate meaning and to bringing about the kingdom in the world. Mark is redefining the kingdom, not as a definitive external event in history, but as the power of awakening. In the present passage, the kingdom comes not only temporarily during the clouded experience, but more permanently when three disciples look up and see no one with them anymore but only Jesus (οὐκέτι εἶδον ἀλλὰ τὸν Ἰησοῦν μονον μεθ᾽ ἑαυτοῶν). This is not the end of the experience, but its culmina-

---

11. Mauser, *Christ in the Wilderness*, 111: "Every main feature of the transfiguration story finds its counterpart in the wilderness tradition of the Old Testament."

12. Tolbert, *Sowing the Gospel*, 200: "Being divinely required to listen to Jesus when he is not talking but glistening in the whitest of garments turns the whole episode on its ear." In a Mahāyāna context, one would recognize another kōan, something like the demand to hear the sound of one hand clapping, i.e., the silence of emptiness.

13. The demand of the clouded voice that we listen to him (ἀκούετε αὐτοῦ) perhaps alludes to *Deuteronomy* 18: 15, which reports Moses as telling the people that "Yahweh your God will raise up a prophet like me; you will listen to him" (αὐτοῦ ἀκούσεσθε). Tolbert, *Sowing the Gospel*, 204 relates the present passage to Jesus' comment in 8: 38 about the son of man coming in the glory of his Father with the holy angels, for here he comes surrounded not only by God's messengers, Moses and Elijah, but validated by the Father's voice. Tolbert's remark that "to the authorial audience the episode for all its dramatic force presents little new information: they already know that Jesus is God's beloved Son." If indeed it is an epiphany signaling the realm of ultimate meaning, perhaps one should expect no information.

tion, an awareness of ultimate meaning expressed and embodied only in the presence of the everyday Jesus.[14]

The Yogācāra philosophers talk about worldly convention-only (*saṃvṛti-mātra*), meaning that the bodhisattva empties even emptiness, returning to the realm of suffering and becoming totally engrossed therein. This is perhaps similar to the Ignatian ideal of *contemplatio in actione:* an awareness of the ultimacy of God immersed in the concrete practices of constructing the kingdom in the world. Here there are no religion and no religious considerations. The carrying out of compassion is not a function of a spiritual elite coming down to pick up the bedraggled world. That is but a religious version of delusion, religious imagination. It is in the mere conventional presence of Jesus in the world that the kingdom has come in power and has been witnessed by Peter and James and John. Jesus, the beloved Son of God, is just Jesus ('Ιησοῦν μονον; *Yesu-mātra*).

Elijah's Coming
9: 9–13

[9]*As they came down from the mountain he warned them to tell no one what they had seen, until after the son of man had risen from the dead.* [10]*They observed the warning faithfully, though among themselves they discussed what "rising from the dead" could mean.* [11]*And they put this question to him, "Why do the scribes say that Elijah must come first?"* [12]*He said to them, "Elijah is indeed first coming to set everything right again; yet how is it that the scriptures say about the Son of man that he must suffer grievously and be treated with contempt?* [13]*But I tell you that Elijah has come and they have treated him as they pleased, just as the scriptures say about him."*

As they return from the mountaintop, Jesus warns the three disciples not to tell anyone what they had seen, and for the first time in Mark's narrative this advice is followed. Everywhere else, those who are so warned rush off to tell the entire world. But here the disciples keep their silence, although Peter had not been able to hold his tongue during the epiphany itself.

Their silence, perhaps, derives not just from their obedience to Jesus' warning. Rather, they do not understand what they have seen and do not know just how to tell anyone about it. What would they say? That they had seen Jesus whitened and talking with Elijah and Moses? But that experience was soon emptied when the cloud overshadowed them. Any glory they

---

14. Against Kelber, *The Kingdom in Mark,* 84: "Peter's eyes are on the present. He mistakes the future for the present and takes the now for the answer,. . . guilty of a mistaken realization of eschatology." Kelber sees the end of the story simply as the finish of the epiphany, not as its paradoxical culmination. I think Peter's fault is that, not understanding the presence of the kingdom in the mere presence of Jesus, he attempts to make an imagined future permanently present by building the tents.

witnessed was immediately taken away. They could say that they heard a voice from the cloud saying that they were to listen, but then that voice fell quiet and, suddenly looking around (verse 8: καὶ ἐξάπινα περιβλεψάμενοι), they saw nothing but Jesus. When Jesus tells the disciples not to tell what they have seen (verse 9: ἃ εἶδον), that points directly to the disciples' seeing only Jesus. They have had Jesus identified for them by a clouded voice as the son of God in glory, and it turns out to be just Jesus. The expected encampment of God's glory, symbolized by Peter's desire to erect tents, has not happened. How are they to tell anybody that? They would be able to understand that the Jesus of glory is simply Jesus only if they understood the witnessless resurrection of the son of man,[15] and his return to the everyday world of Galilee.[16]

Mark reports that the three disciples question what the rising from the dead could mean,[17] for they have just encountered not only two resurrected

---

15. Kee, *Community of the New Age,* 130, notes that the 'son of man' has connotations from Psalm 8: 4–7, "not to mankind as an abstraction or to a randomly selected individual, but to Man, the Son of Man—that is, to the descendants of Primal Man—who has been chosen to exercise authority over the creation on God's behalf." Thus, Jesus' prediction of the sufferings and the resurrection of the son of man extends beyond the story level self-reference to include all the sons and daughters of Adam and Eve.

16. Via, *The Ethics of Mark's Gospel,* 52–53 notes the irony of the passage, since the disciples do not in fact witness Jesus' resurrection: "Revelation, then, is ineffective, not only because it is refused by the disciples but because the revelation which is given is *concealed* by the revealer." This ineffectiveness of revelation "is a function of eschatology and of the mysterious personal nature of God." Even revealed, ultimate meaning remains completely other.

17. Against Tolbert, *Sowing the Gospel,* 207, who sees the disciples' questioning about the meaning of the rising from the dead to be "especially preposterous coming from the disciples and the multitudes who were permitted to accompany Jesus to Jairus' house and see him *raise Jairus' daughter from death* (5: 37–42)." Yet, in 5: 39 Jesus explicitly says that she is not dead, but asleep, despite common appearances. On 253–54 Tolbert builds her case that the disciples have evidence for an unquestioning faith in resurrection: "For the Gospel of Mark, then, resurrection is presented as a normally accepted view. . . . in Mark God's activity of raising the dead extends back at least to Abraham, Isaac, Jacob, Moses, and Elijah, is currently visible through Jesus in Jairus' daughter, and will continue in the future for Jesus and his followers. Hence Jesus' resurrection is not a unique event, nor does it really distinguish him from messengers God has sent to the vineyard in the past. For the Gospel of Mark, Jesus' *death,* as the death of the final messenger, the son, which provokes the coming of the Lord of the vineyard, *is what makes Jesus distinctive and vitally important,* while his resurrection is depicted as simply an assured aspect of God's abiding practice. That Mark ends with just an announcement that Jesus has risen and an empty tomb (16: 1–8), rather than the glorious appearances of the resurrected Jesus that close the Gospels of Matthew and Luke, accords well with this understanding. It is not Jesus' resurrection but his death—and what that death inevitably stimulates—that makes Jesus unique. Resurrection is part of God's long-standing procedure, as proved by Scripture and argued enthymematically by Jesus to the detriment of the Sadducees." Tolbert's argument is well taken in regard to the lack of the specific uniqueness of Jesus' resurrection. Yet even though one may expect the disciples to accept such a doctrine of resurrection, that hardly precludes their wondering about what it means. Furthermore, if the coming of the kingdom has already arrived with the mere coming of Jesus to begin

figures, Elijah and Moses, but have also seen the mere presence of the living Jesus who still talks about his resurrection. The ping-pong reverberations from epiphany to everydayness are confusing. If Jesus is son of God, then would resurrection not be a powerful manifestation of God's might? But if Jesus, just like any other human, godly son, has to suffer, what does that imply about God's might and mean for their hopes? Elijah, just seen in glory, did not have to suffer and die, and he must (δεῖ) come first. What need is there for suffering then? Cannot one simply await the arrival of the eschatological kingdom and share it with the deathless Moses, Elijah, and Jesus?[18]

The disciples' questioning relates to the understanding of the two truths, how ultimate meaning and worldly convention are related, for the discussion occurs while they are coming down from the mountaintop back into the conventional world. Perhaps for Mark it is only when Jesus has risen from the dead that he is no longer in danger of becoming an imagined hero figure, for then, in Mark's account, he is no longer physically present. Not being present, his meaning, transfigured or everyday, cannot be reified in terms of the disciples' eschatological expectancies.

But the question about resurrection is merely raised here, not answered. The imagery is present: when they are coming down (καταβαινόντων) from the mountaintop experience of ultimate meaning, Jesus talks about being once again raised up (ἀναστῇ). One ascends to such an experience only to return to the everyday; yet even so, there is no dimensional continuity between the ascent and ultimate meaning. No matter how high one ascends, ultimate meaning remains other and beyond grasp. Even when Jesus is risen, no explanation of resurrection is given, beyond the return to the ordinary world of Galilee. The descent of Jesus and the disciples from the mountaintop is thus not in a linear coming down from ultimate meaning, but signals an awareness of the total otherness of that ultimate. And this is why one should usually mistrust people who talk a lot about religion. The authorities Jesus criticizes really think they have reached the ultimate truth and are confident

---

his preaching career, it is not a future event generated by Jesus' unique death. Jesus also signals its arrival in the announcement that the eschatological figure of Elijah has already come. Therefore, one cannot validly argue that Jesus is unique because of his death, since the kingdom has already come—in a context of an emptied eschatology. Moreover, arguments about Christ's or Christianity's uniqueness function most often within a philosophical framework of essences, as does Tolbert, 129. Such a framework is negated in a Mahāyāna reading.

18. Heil, *The Gospel of Mark as a Model for Action,* 189–90: "The implication is that suffering and rising from the dead is not part of God's plan for final-age salvation and entrance into heavenly glory (9: 11)." But, ". . . Jesus shocks his disciples by announcing that not only has the expected return of the prophet Elijah already taken place with the coming of John the Baptist as the messenger-Elijah (1: 4–8) but, moreover, he has already suffered a very humiliating death, when 'they did to him whatever they pleased' (6: 14–29), in accord with God's scriptural plan of salvation 'as it is written of him' (see 1 Kgs 19: 2, 10, 14)." Here God's plan is equated with the concrete course of human affairs. The necessity of Elijah's coming is not a supernatural event to be awaited, but the inevitability of the unfolding of dependently co-arisen events.

they have gathered it within their netting ideas. And that, in Mark, is also the common attitude of the disciples, caught in the net of their own delusions. But they at least question. As it turns out in Mark's narrative, the Christian community begins not with those in the know, but with confused people who continue to question.

Although the three discuss the question of the meaning of the resurrection, they soon shift their focus to questions about Elijah, for he is a figure of heavenly life. There was a scenario about Elijah coming first to restore all things in preparation for the coming of the messiah, probably alluding to *Malachi* 4: 5–6 which declares that Elijah will come before the great and illustrious day of the Lord to restore the hearts (ἀποκαταστήσει καρδίαν) of fathers to their sons and the hearts of human beings to their neighbors.[19] The disciples ask Jesus about this notion of projected history. Jesus does not reject the idea, but, as is his wont, reinterprets it in terms of concrete experience. Yes, he says, Elijah is to come first, but in fact he already has. Now that must have been a surprise to the disciples. Here they were expecting Elijah to come in some glorious eschatological future—which they have just glimpsed for a transient moment—and now they learn that he has already snuck in the back door. Jesus doesn't really mean Elijah, of course, but John the Baptist, who plays in Mark the role of a precursor. Jesus accepts the religious notions current within his context, empties them of their imagined meanings, and reaffirms them in the other-dependent pattern: the great day of the Lord has already come. Jesus, not Bultmann, is the first Christian demythologizer. The heavens might have hung low in those days, as Bultmann observes, yet there is only the one world we live in, no ethereal realm. Cities of God are nothing but conventional images standing in for the silence of ultimate meaning and do not exist as such. By the very fact of calling it a city, it is a human construct. So the true founder of Augustine's city of God is obviously Augustine, not God.

Further insisting on the dependently co-arising context of human life, Jesus questions the disciples about the suffering son of man.[20] For if the messiah is to suffer, this certainly negates grand ideas about the kingdom of God

---

19. Tolbert, *Sowing the Gospel,* 208. Against Kee, *Community of the New Age,* 87, who describes Elijah as "the prophetic-apocalyptic figure whose coming heralds and even precipitates the breakdown of the family and other basic structures. The end is at hand; there is no time to lose: all human obligations and ties must give way before the urgent demand of preparing God's elect people for the last day." That day has already come, witnessed by Jesus' fractured ties with his family and village, and the urgency of the mission he preaches to be at hand.

20. Note also that the conjunction of the title 'son of man' with the suffering servant of Isaiah is a Markan innovation, with, as Sandmel, " 'Son of Man' in Mark," 177, explains, "only the dimmest echoes of the antecedent Jewish use." Also see Crossan, *The Historical Jesus,* 238–59. Furthermore, no one knows just which scriptures say that the son of man had to suffer, or what scriptures treat the events that happened to the Baptist. See Fowler, *Let the Reader Understand,* 112; Dowd, *Prayer, Power, and the Problem of Suffering,* 134.

coming in power. And that is the function of the stress on suffering—to counter ideas of imagined glory. The son of man is not only going to suffer, but he is also to "be treated with contempt," or "to be set at naught" (ἐξουδεν-ηθῇ).[21] And it is only when Jesus has been set at naught, emptied of expected imaginings that he confesses to being the christ. His predictions of suffering are not meant to construct a new set of grand ideas about the inscrutable necessity of suffering and pain, but to empty ideas about the messiah as the grand winner.[22]

But, if Elijah sets all right, then how come the world remains immersed in suffering? If John the Baptist prepared the way before Jesus, then why is Jesus the suffering servant? Jesus does not accept the title of messiah Peter suggests and then apply it to himself. Rather, in his transfiguration, his identity as son of God is established by the clouded voice and manifested in the simple presence of just Jesus (*Yesu-mātra*). The title of messiah that he finally applies to himself in 14: 62 has already been emptied of all imagined meaning. He is then no otherworldly messiah, but, if one may say so, *just* the messiah (lower, not upper case). And this entails the suffering and dying that accompany everything that is *just* human (*duḥkha-satya*).

Argument and Amazement
9: 14–15

[14]When they rejoined the disciples they saw a large crowd around them and some scribes arguing with them. [15]At once, when they saw him, the whole crowd were struck with amazement and ran to greet him.

---

21. Zerwick, *Analysis Philologica,* 102 defines ἐξουδενηθῇ as *nihili facio*. Also Perrin, "The Christology of Mark," 103: "9: 12b, where the Son of Man *polla pathē kai exoude-nēthē* ('must suffer many things and be set at naught') shatters the tight-knit structure of 9: 9–13 so obviously that many commentators have argued that it is a post-Marcan gloss that crept into the text of the Gospel, and I can only agree. It can and indeed must be ignored as far as the use of the Son of Man by Mark is concerned." In a Mahāyāna reading, however, it is quite to the point of the narrative, emptying the notions of messiah and son of man so that Jesus can later affirm them.

22. Altizer, "Emptiness and God," 81: "So it is that Nishitani is opening contemporary Christianity to a modern Christian prophecy, and doing so as a Buddhist thinker, and a Buddhist thinker who understands what Christian dogmatics has forgotten. And that quite simply is the Crucified God, the kenotic God of absolute self-negation, and an absolute self-negation which a Buddhist thinker can know as absolute nothingness. This is a nothingness which has long been present in the deeper expressions of Christian mysticism, just as it has been present again and again in Christian apocalypticism, and just as it has ever more fully come to dominate the Christian imagination. But it is a Buddhism which is now most clearly naming a Christian nothingness, and perhaps it has ever done so, for it knows absolute nothingness as absolute compassion, and therein knows in its original form and identity what the Christian has named as Christ. Not even if Christianity has always deeply known Christ as the Crucified God, its own theology has again and again evaded and refused this absolute Christian ground. Clearly such a ground is present in Buddhism, and today is more fully present in Nishitani than in any Christian thinker, a presence which the Christian theologian can greet only as a wholly unmerited grace."

There are three groups present: the disciples with their accepted notions of who the messiah is; the apparently gentile crowd, for the last geographical marker is in 8:27 where Jesus and his band are on the way to Caesarea Philippi; and the scribes, heretofore representatives of Jewish orthodoxy, who have evidently wandered rhetorically into gentile lands! Everybody is on the scene. They are engaged in argument (συζητοῦντας), just as on the way down the mountain the disciples have been arguing (συζητοῦντες). The scribes and the disciples have often engaged Jesus in argument, yet here everyone is amazed (ἐξεθαμβήθησαν) at seeing Jesus approach. Why, if it is just Jesus and the three disciples? What is so amazing about that?

Perhaps Mark alludes to the *Exodus* account of Moses coming down from Mt. Sinai. When Moses ascends Sinai, he encounters Yahweh within a dense cloud (Ex 19: 16). "The cloud covered the mountain, and the glory of Yahweh settled on the mountain of Sinai; for six days the cloud covered it, and on the seventh day Yahweh called to Moses from inside the cloud" (Ex 24: 16). Moses shuttles back and forth between the people, who are forbidden to ascend the mountain, and Yahweh who dwells there in the cloud. He talks with Yahweh and at times cajoles Yahweh. But even Moses can catch a glimpse only of Yahweh's back, "for man cannot see me and live" (Ex 33: 19). When he comes down from the mountain with the tablets of the law, the people are unable to venture near him.

When Moses came down from the mountain of Sinai . . . he did not know that the skin on his face was radiant after speaking with Yahweh. When Aaron and all the sons of Israel saw Moses, the skin on his face shone so much that they would not venture near him. But Moses called to them, and Aaron with all the leaders of the community came back to him; and he spoke to them. Then all the sons of Israel came closer, and he passed on to them all the orders that Yahweh had given him on the mountain of Sinai. And when Moses had finished speaking to them, he put a veil over his face. Whenever he went into Yahweh's presence to speak with him, Moses would remove the veil until he came out again. And when he came out he would tell the sons of Israel what he had been ordered to pass on to them, and the sons of Israel would see the face of Moses radiant. Then Moses would put the veil back over his face until he returned to speak with Yahweh (Ex. 34: 29–35).

Together with his three disciples, Jesus has likewise just encountered Yahweh on the mountain and heard the voice from the cloud. Jesus' clothes have become radiant and whiter than any earthly bleacher can make them. And when he descends the mountain and meets the people, they too are amazed. It does seem that Mark is forcing his implied reader to remember the glory of Moses' face and the amazement his presence engendered among the

Israelites. With that in mind, the reader might well expect a similar response from the crowds on seeing the recently transfigured Jesus.[23]

Yet in Mark Jesus requires no veil over his face. The three disciples have seen just Jesus alone in his simple humanity. The crowd likewise sees just Jesus, not the brilliance of the transfiguration. The point seems to be that in Mark it is precisely this simple Jesus who is the manifestation of ultimate meaning. His conventional being is itself the veil, pointing to the otherness of Yahweh. In Mark this is what is amazing, just the simple Jesus who is a manifestation of Yahweh. Rather than run away, as did Aaron and the sons of Israel, the people all run *to* Jesus. Mark is constructing theological variations on ancient themes.

The Spirit of Dumbness
9: 16–29

[16]*And he asked them, "What are you arguing about with them?"* [17]*A man answered him from the crowd, "Master, I have brought my son to you; there is a spirit of dumbness in him,* [18]*and when it takes hold of him it throws him to the ground, and he foams at the mouth and grinds his teeth and goes rigid. And I asked your disciples to drive it out and they were unable to."* [19]*In reply he said to them, "You faithless generation, how much longer must I be among you? How much longer must I put up with you? Bring him to me."* [20]*They brought the boy to him, and at once the spirit of dumbness threw the boy into convulsions, and he fell to the ground and lay writhing there, foaming at the mouth.* [21]*Jesus asked the father, "How long has this been happening to him?" "From childhood," he said,* [22]*"and it has often thrown him into fire and into water, in order to destroy him.* [23]*But if you can do anything, have pity on us and help us."* [24]*"If you can?" retorted Jesus. "Everything is possible for one who has faith." At once the father of the boy cried out, "I have faith. Help my lack of faith!"* [25]*And when Jesus saw that a crowd was gathering, he rebuked the unclean spirit. "Deaf and dumb spirit," he said, "I command you: come out of him and never enter him again."* [26]*Then it threw the boy into violent convulsions and came out shouting, and the boy lay there so like a corpse that most of them said, "He is dead."* [27]*But Jesus took him by the hand and helped him up, and he was able to stand.* [28]*When he had gone indoors, his disciples asked him when they were by themselves, "Why were we unable to drive it out?"* [29]*He replied, "This is the kind that can only be driven out by prayer."*

---

23. Kee, *Community of the New Age,* 132: "Fittingly, the biblical background of the Transfiguration scene is from Daniel 10, where the revelatory agent, Daniel, on receiving a communication about the end time from the throne of God, is himself transformed, so that his garments glow with radiant light (Dan 10: 8), while his companions flounder in awe, confusion, and incomprehension."

The boy's spirit is initially described as a spirit of dumbness, rendering him incapable of sharing in human speech. That contrasts immediately with the verbal argumentations that had been going on earlier among the disciples and now among the crowd. The spirit grabs the boy and makes him foam at the mouth and grind his teeth (ἀφρίζει καὶ τρίζει τοὺς ὀδόντας), an apt description not only of possessed boys, but also of frustrated debaters. Such an experience renders the boy rigid (καὶ ξηραίνεται), the root meaning of which term is to dry up, become dessicated. To become rigid recalls the phrase about hardening of the heart, closing one's mind off from concrete experience; in both instances one becomes fixated. Just after Jesus' three disciples have silently listened to Jesus' teaching about suffering, they encounter a boy with a dumb spirit, who is just as rigid in body as they are in mind.

The content of the debate with the scribes is not given, but they are apparently arguing about how to cure the boy. The debaters are caught in the net of verbal fabrication (*prapañca*), and thus Jesus criticizes the group as a faithless generation, for they rely not on the wordless faith of prayer but on argumentation. The translation "How much longer must I be among you?" can perhaps be rendered as "How much longer do I have to listen to (ἀνέξομαι) you?"[24] The point is that Jesus is weary of listening to such arguments, for discriminative thought occludes faith. It substitutes the verbal clinging to words and ideas for the awareness of faith, which involves first the direct, immediate awareness of silence and then the ability to mediate that awareness in words—both silence and speech. Faith is the absence of fabrication and the presence of a childlike consciousness to which the secrets of the kingdom are revealed. The arguing crowd relies solely on conventional reasoning, the boy's father confesses to his lack of faith, and the disciples are rendered incapable of casting out the dumb spirit because they themselves do not know enough to maintain silent prayer.[25] "The disciples still have blame in the Markan version, but their fault is not lack of faith, but prayerlessness. The narrative as it stands gives two reasons for the failed exorcism: The father lacked faith and the disciples neglected prayer."[26]

In contrast to the disciples and their fixation on avoiding human suffering, the dumb boy is fixated by a demonic spirit on silence, as if mere insight

---

24. Bauer, *A Greek-English Lexicon,* 66, give as a meaning for ἀνέχω: *to endure,* in the sense of *hear* or *listen to willingly.*

25. Tolbert, *Sowing the Gospel,* 188: "If such exorcisms require prayer, and the disciples failed, the obvious implication is that the disciples do not pray." Mack, *A Myth of Innocence,* 232: "Only two more miracles are performed after Caesarea Philippi. They were used to heighten the tensions created by this section of the story. The first is the exorcism of the unclean spirit from the deaf and dumb boy. Mark placed it after the private instruction to Peter, James, and John about Jesus' true nature and destiny (transfiguration, resurrection, Mark 9: 2–13). The point of the miracle story is that the disciples left behind were still trying their hands at casting out demons, but failed. This was especially embarrassing, because the scribes were looking into the matter. Jesus casts the unclean spirit out in order to set the contrast...."

26. Dowd, *Prayer, Power, and the Problem of Suffering,* 117–18.

into the emptiness of ultimate meaning were sufficient. Demonic spirits move outside the realm of common discourse; they are wilderness dwellers apart from all convention, like the Gerasene demoniac who dwelt among the tombs (5: 3). The boy's condition is parallel to that of the Gerasene fellow, who was raving and breaking chains and such. Thus when the spirit sees Jesus, engaged in the world again after his mountain experience of radiance, he causes the boy to fall down in convulsions. We are told that the boy from his childhood has been so afflicted, often driven to the point of death, either in water or in fire. Emptiness ineptly grasped leads to an early and useless cessation (*nirvāṇa*), a seeking for final peace and rest. It is insight into emptiness without the wisdom of dependent co-arising. It kills one's ability to understand, keeping one aloof from the swirling arguments of men and women, reacting angrily to any suggestion of reengagement in human affairs. The cure is faith, not as the acceptance of doctrine, for no doctrine is mentioned here at all. Rather, here faith is engagement in the dependently co-arisen being of emptiness, derived from silent prayer in the otherness of Abba.[27] Faith is a practice, not a position—the practice of the middle path, awakened

---

27. Against Dowd, *Prayer, Power, and the Problem of Suffering,* 95: "We will argue that in the Markan miracle stories and prayer teaching, faith means confidence in the power of God to do the impossible on behalf of the community." Dowd distinguishes such faith from the total response to Jesus, which is called "following." Referring to the faith of the boy's father, she writes: "Faith is a condition for miracle in Mark in the sense that maintenance of the world-view [that God can do even the impossible, i.e., ἀδύνατον] is essential for the ongoing experience of the community." In the context of the then current Hellenistic dispute over miracles and whether God can do the impossible (see Dowd, 78–93), Dowd's argument seems a perfect hermeneutical grid for the Markan teachings on prayer and miracle, for he does use "the same categories to express the polarities [as did his contemporaries]: the category of will and the category of power (159)." Nevertheless, I do not think that Mark "understands the problem in the same way as his contemporaries, (159)," for I see Mark not only moving within the rhetorical options of that debate, but as undercutting those options. Mark does say that all things are possible to God, that faith can move mountains, but, as it turns out, Jesus cannot avoid suffering, despite his plea to do so in Gethsemane, where he explicitly confesses that all is possible to the Father. It is not adequate to leave the issue of Jesus' suffering and death unexplained by alluding to the will of God. The very silence of God at Jesus' death indicates not a prayer unanswered for some divine reason, but rather that faith is not a viewpoint which takes anyone beyond the dependently co-arisen world. The key, I think, is Jesus' teachings about no-self, in virtue of which the entire issue is undermined and emptied of urgency, for if there is no self, there is no self to be anxious about. Thus, I agree with Dowd that "the author of Mark does not offer his community a solution to the problem of theodicy, but he does give them a way of coping with the tension that pervades their existence as empowered sufferers (162)." That tension between the power of God to do anything and the persecution and suffering of humans is indeed heightened by Mark's narrative, yet not merely to leave one with prayer as a means of coping. Rather, prayer itself leads to the wilderness experience of the immediacy of God in which all concerns of self are negated. Thus, "Whoever loses his life for Jesus' sake and for the sake of the gospel will ultimately save it (162)." I see then no reason to criticize interpreters such as Schreiber (163), who asserts that "the prayer of faith does not look for its own salvation."

to the foundational wisdom of emptiness and thus to the subsequent wisdom of skillfully engaging in words and actions.

When the father asks Jesus to take pity and cure the boy, Jesus repeats the father's words ironically: "If you can? (τὸ εἰ δύνῃ)" It is not a question of Jesus himself coming into the dichotomized context of either argument or silence, but, as shown in the next phrase, of the faith of the father. For one with faith anything is possible (πάντα δυνατὰ τῷ πιστεύοντι), he says. It is thus the faith of Jesus that informs his command, not his awesome power. Such faith and power, however, are available to anyone.[28]

The spirit is further described as unclean, being both deaf and dumb, completely apart from human communication. Jesus rebukes (ἐπετίμησεν) the unclean spirit and the cure renders the boy death-like, thrown down inert on the ground.[29] Then Jesus raises him again to life. This is an image of resurrection into the conventional world.[30] Only one so awakened, so full of faith, is capable of such a cure. That is why prayer is essential, for without silent awareness of Abba, no power avails for anything. The disciples are unable to effect the cure because their faith remains caught in false, conventional patterns of verbal consciousness apart from prayer, while the unclean spirit dwells only in silence apart from the conventional world.

An alternate, later reading of this text says that such a spirit can only be cast out by prayer *and fasting*.[31] On the surface level, this would appear to

---

28. Collins, *The Beginning of the Gospel*, 61: "Not only are the twelve sent out to preach, heal, and exorcise, but the Gospel implies that anyone who has faith may exorcise through prayer (9: 23, 29). . . . Similarly, the resurrection of Jesus is not a special privilege given to him as one like, or greater than, Elijah. On the contrary, faithful disciples will share in the resurrected life (8: 34–38; cf (: 42–48)." Also note Dowd, *Prayer, Power, and the Problem of Suffering*, 110–11: "The sense of the second part of Jesus' response is much debated, because of the ambiguity of the phrase πάντα δυνατὰ τῷ πιστεύοντι. Is Jesus demanding faith from the father, or is he saying that his own ability to exorcise the boy comes from his faith? . . . The question of whether miracle-workers or patients or both must have faith is resolved when we remember that from the evangelist's point of view the healer and the patient have the same status with respect to miraculous power. It is not the case that one human is the worker of the miracle and another the recipient. Rather, both are recipients. The miracle is always, so the author of Mark thinks, done by God."

29. Kee, *Community of the New Age*, 169: "Among those elements that have nothing to do with secrecy about the kingdom or about Jesus' messiahship are the exorcism stories. Cf. 1: 23–26; 9: 14–29, and the stilling of the storm in 4: 36–41. In each of these three cases, the command (a form of ἐπιτιμάω) is a technical term by which Jewish and Christian exorcists brought demons under control and expelled them from the person or object in which they had set up operations. What is at stake is a struggle for dominance, not a lack of secret information." Yet, if the coming of the kingdom is the overcoming of the demonic, the binding of the strong man, then exorcism stories are very much related to that kingdom, which is witnessed by the very healings, not as secret information, but in the clear light of day, for all to see.

30. Broadhead, *Teaching With Authority*, 155: "Here, the exorcism imagery gives way to the imagery of resurrection."

31. Achtemeier, "Miracles and the Historical Jesus," 476.

mean that prayer and fasting from food render one more effective in curing people. But on the deep Mahāyāna level, perhaps another interpretation is possible. The Taoist Chuang Tzu talks about the fasting of the mind, not fasting from food: "Make your mind one! Don't listen with your ears, listen with your mind. No, don't listen with your mind, but listen with your spirit. Listening stops with the ears, the mind stops with recognition, but spirit is empty and waits on all things. The Way gathers in emptiness alone. Emptiness is the fasting of the mind."[32]

Perhaps this is what Jesus means by watching and listening. The disciples, however, listen only with their minds and cannot understand the spirit-affliction of the dumb boy. Jesus is looking for faithful persons who can practice the fasting of the mind. Then he would not be so weary with this generation. Yet such faith is not easily attained. The father first begs Jesus to have mercy on him and help him if he can (ἀλλ' εἴ τι δύνῃ, βοήθησον ἡμῖν σπλαγχνισθεὶς ἐφ' ἡμᾶς)) and then, when Jesus answers, "If I can" (τὸ εἰ δύνῃ), he cries out not only for Jesus to help his lack of faith, but that he already has faith (πιστεύω, βοήθει μου τῇ ἀπιστίᾳ). In its originally present dependently co-arisen structure, the mind is open to faith, sees things both in their contextuality and in their emptiness. Yet that mind is overlaid with attachments to images and ideas which occlude that original structure. In Mahāyāna terms, faith comes from the permeations within the mind resultant on hearing the doctrine (*śruta-vāsanā*). Here the father needs support to counter his lack of faith. After all he has just experienced the failure of Jesus' own disciples to help his boy. Yet Jesus, seeing the gathering crowd, does nothing for him at all! No advice, no doctrine. Only the restoration of the boy to conventional living, for that restoration is itself the character of faith.

The Second Passion Prediction
9: 30–32

[30]*After leaving that place they made their way through Galilee; and he did not want anyone to know,* [31]*because he was instructing his disciples; he was telling them, "The Son of man will be delivered into the hands of men; they will put him to death; and three days after he has been put to death he will rise again."* [32]*But they did not understand what he said and were afraid to ask him.*

Mark follows up the account of the death and resurrection of the spirit-filled boy by having Jesus talk about his own death and resurrection. He too will be thrown to the ground, only to rise again. Jesus consistently avoids playing the role of the long-expected messiah. In fact, he deconstructs that role in favor of the practice of the middle path. That is to say, he empties

---

32. Watson, tr., *Chuang Tzu*, 57–58.

the role of messiah and reinterprets it as reengagement in the predictable dependently co-arisen conditions of his life. That is what messiah means to him: engagement despite the suffering and death which are clearly foreseen. The disciples, with their set ideas about who the messiah is to be, do not understand him. They do not see why he has to suffer, nor what it means to rise after three days. They are ignorant (ἠγνόουν) and afraid (ἐφοβοῦντο) to ask him. In the face of words which threaten to break through their imagined pattern of consciousness, they hold on to their ignorance (*avidyā*), that primal ignorance which clings to self and to ideas which protect self.[33] Thus they are afraid not of Jesus' anger, but of the emptiness that lies behind their delusions, and, as will become apparent, at the emptiness of Jesus' tomb. When Mark's gospel ends in chapter 16, the women at the tomb are likewise afraid, and rendered mute (16: 8, καὶ οὐδενὶ οὐδὲν εἶπαν. ἐφο-βοῦντο γάρ). Here, the silent disciples are unable to break through their ignorance. Their lack of perception is starkly confirmed in the next passage, when they begin to debate among themselves who is the greatest.

With the disciples silent and mute, no one in the story seems to have learned anything from Jesus' predictions (see Mark 8: 22–33; 9: 31–34, 38–39; 10: 32, 35–45). The reader, by contrast, cannot help but be alerted by these signposts to the future course of the narrative."[34] Yet these signposts create crises for the reader about her own identity, for the gospel is not just about the identity of Jesus, but about discipleship, i.e., about who we are. And this—as much as a definition of Jesus—remains an enigma. Werner Kelber explains: "Jesus announces the Kingdom but opts for the cross; he is King of the Jews but condemned by the Jewish establishment; he asks for followers but speaks in riddles; he is identified as Nazarene but rejected in Nazareth; he makes public pronouncements but also hides behind a screen of secrecy; he saves others but not himself; he promises return but has not returned; he performs miracles but suffers a non-miraculous death; he is a successful exorciser but dies overcome by demonic forces; he is appointed by God in power but dies abandoned by God in powerlessness; he dies but rises from death. His beginning is nebulous and his future status is indefinite, and at the moment of Messianic disclosure he still speaks enigmatically of himself in the third person (14: 62; cf. 8: 31; 9: 31; 10: 33–34). If there is one single feature which characterizes the [Markan] Jesus it is contradiction or paradox. It might therefore be argued that '[Mark] presents not two conflicting views of Jesus' but one complex 'paradoxical view' ([Kim] Dewey)."[35] One might say that the Markan portrayal of Jesus is an emptying of all views of Jesus.

---

33. Kelber, *Mark's Story of Jesus,* 49: "While in the wake of the first prediction Peter is exposed as Satan, it is after the second prediction that the disciples are convicted of nonperception."

34. Fowler, "Reader-Response Criticism," 60.

35. Kelber, "From Passion Narrative to Gospel," 79.

The Greatest
9: 33–37

[33]They came to Capernaum, and when he got into the house he asked them, "What were you arguing about on the road?"[34]They said nothing because on the road they had been arguing which of them was the greatest. [35]So he sat down, called the Twelve to him and said, "If anyone wants to be first, he must make himself last of all and servant of all." [36]He then took a little child whom he set among them and embraced, and he said to them, [37]"Anyone who welcomes a little child such as this in my name, welcomes me; and anyone who welcomes me, welcomes not me but the one who sent me."

Jesus' disciples have returned to his home in Capernaum, ending their extended journey. On the way to Caesarea Philippi Jesus had questioned the disciples about his identity. Here, on the way back home, the disciples are engaged in dispute and argumentation (διαλογίζεσθε) about their own self-images. Questioned by Jesus, they fall silent (ἐσιώπων), not in the prayerful silence of wonder but in embarrassment for they have been disputing over the preeminence of self (*ātman*), over who is the greatest. The path they travel is not the path of differentiating the two truths, of realizing the emptiness of all absolute statements and the emptiness of an inner self, in the light of which one dedicates effort to dependently co-arisen and valued teaching, to the course of authentic living. Rather, their path is one of fabricating verbal argumentation (*prapañca*), of imagining a self exalted above all others, at the center of the world. Their trip with Jesus has not awakened them. Rather, more than ever, they see Jesus as their ticket to glory, to selfhood exalted, because of their imagined pattern of seeing miracles and cures as tokens of self-glory.

Jesus' sayings on discipleship have sometimes been seen as a collation of disconnected pronouncements,[36] but in fact they flow from the above context, for they are consistently directed against the disciples' notion of discipleship as assuring preeminence of position. To make oneself last is to negate the absolute stature of one's self, of one's own persona (*anātman*).[37] That is

---

36. Grant, *The Interpreter's Bible*, 7: 785–86.

37. Humphrey, *He is Risen*, 87: " 'If anyone wants to be first, let him be last.' *This* is the meaning of the Son of Man's having to die; there can be no resurrection without that obedient giving up of the self, even to the point of death." See Nagao, *The Foundational Standpoint*, 28: "The Buddhist doctrine of no-self (*nairātmya*) is a negation of self as an absolute reality that is mistakenly supposed to be the pride of an ultimately meaningful existence. It is not a negation of the worldly and conventional reality of selfhood. The self cannot be real in any ultimate sense; as existence constantly subject to change, it is simply empty." Also Kelber, *Mark's Story of Jesus*, 50: "Jesus tells the Twelve that the first must be last. It is noteworthy that Jesus does not sound the well-known reversal theme: that the first shall be last and the last shall be first. Rather, verse 9: 35, spoken to the Twelve, states simply that the first must be the last and serve. The term first suggests the issue of priority, power, and authority. What is under attack is the concept of authority as it was entertained by the Twelve." It is not about being first in any sense at all.

why receiving Jesus and the one who sent him here and elsewhere is often exemplified as the receiving of a little child, of one who has not yet developed a strong self-image, one who has no rank or particular importance. It is Jesus who approaches the disciples and the readers as a child, with no rank or importance whatsoever.[38] It is God, who sent Jesus, who approaches as a child, not as the romanticized image of sweet innocence, but as the weakest of the weak.[39]

The response of the reader is to disassociate herself from these egotistical disciples. Jesus has just been speaking about the inevitability of his suffering and dying. Their "insensitivity to Jesus' fate, combined with crass egotism, is not a stance that the reader is likely to embrace. . . . In this setting Jesus embraces a child as an object lesson for the self-seeking, self-glorifying disciples (9: 33–35)."[40] By rhetorical slight of hand, the Markan Jesus directly addresses the reader through a "whoever" statement: "whoever would be great must be your servant." In speaking about losing one's life, he used the same sentence form: "Whoever would save his life will lose it" (8: 35). Similarly, "If any person would come after me, let him deny self and take up his cross" (8: 34).[41] In these statements, the Markan Jesus is addressing himself to all people: Anyone who would practice the path of Jesus must reverse the patterns of imagined expectations and plunge into the paradoxical world of Jesus' doubling back discourse, and therein find the presence of the kingdom of nobodies.[42] Mark's irony seems on the one hand to assure the reader of having gained a viewpoint superior to the story's characters, but at the same time contains endless paradoxes. "Verbal paradoxes in Mark are oxymoronic turns of phrase, and thus they give the reader an experience different from that of irony or metaphor. Whereas irony invites the reader to see and to see through an incongruity and metaphor invites an exploration of the hitherto unexplored similarities in acknowledged dissimilars, the experience of paradox is the experience of being bracketed between seemingly incompatible but nevertheless coexisting polar opposites. Of all Mark's indirect moves, incongruity is at its sharpest in paradox."[43] And that, in Mahāyāna terms, describes the tension between the two truths of worldly convention and ultimate meaning. The polarity of the two is not simply apparent, however, for they never come together in any centripetal synthesis, but always spin apart within the same awakened consciousness.[44]

---

38. Fowler, *Let the Reader Understand,* 172–73, notes that Matthew has altered the issue from receiving a child, i.e., one who has no greatness at all, to becoming child-like.

39. See Myers, *Binding the Strong Man,* 266–71, citing the work of Alice Miller on the status of children argues that one should not idealize childhood, but see in Jesus' image of the child an oppressed human, without adult rights or privileges: the least of the least. One receives Jesus only in receiving the oppressed.

40. Fowler, *Let the Reader Understand,* 72.

41. See Fowler, *Let the Reader Understand,* 187–91.

42. Crossan, *The Historical Jesus,* 266–75.

43. Fowler, *Let the Reader Understand,* 184–85.

44. Nagao, *The Foundational Standpoint,* 45–55, 65–72.

Even God is not an ultimate self standing over against worldly selves. "If there were such a final reality in the form of a self—*ātman*—. . . this would amount to the Indian teaching that the world was created by the Almighty Īśvara, from whom all things come, and that I am saved by becoming *ātman* through vision of or union with the Almighty. The doctrine of no-self in Buddhism rejects the idea of a God who, as *ātman,* is obliged to leave the divine realms and engage in the world, and it does so precisely because of its notion of no-self."[45] Who is it then that sent Jesus? Why does Mark not even identify God as Jesus' source and sender? The Markan Jesus simply says that to receive the weakest of the weak is to receive him and "him who sent me" (τὸν ἀποστείλαντά με). In the same way, when the voice of God speaks from the heavens at Jesus' baptism in 1: 11 (καὶ φωνὴ ἐγένετο ἐκ τῶν οὐρανῶν), and again from the cloud at his transfiguration in 9: 7 (καὶ ἐγένετο φωνὴ ἐκ τῆς νεφέλης), Mark fails to mention just whose voice is speaking. Being clouded and from on high, we assume that it is the voice of God. Yet, when the Markan Jesus directly addresses his Father in Gethsemane in 14: 36, no voice is heard at all and no rescue implemented. But Jesus is the son of God and our assumption that the voices Mark allows us to hear are from God is not mistaken. What is mistaken is the notion that we know what that means.[46] Not only is Jesus impossible to identify in clear definitions, God is too. What then could it mean to be great?

Sectarian Feelings
9: 38–40

[38]*John said to him, "Master, we saw a man who is not one of us driving out devils in your name; and because he was not one of us we tried to stop him." [39]But Jesus said, "You must not stop him: no one who works a miracle in my name could soon afterwards speak evil of me. [40]Anyone who is not against us is for us."*

John does not follow up on Jesus' theme of receiving rankless children, but latches onto the name of Jesus to bring up the issue of just who can be said to belong to Jesus' circle. After all, throughout the narrative, Jesus harshly criticizes various groups of people, scribes, Pharisees, etc. Who could blame John for concluding that Jesus' disciples constitute a well-defined group, over against those others? Indeed, social identity was most probably a burning issue for the early church.[47] Nevertheless, party spirit comes not

---

45. Nagao, *The Foundational Standpoint,* 28.
46. See the essays by Masao Abe, Thomas Altizer, Eugene Borowitz, John Cobb, Catherine Keller, Jürgen Moltmann, Schubert Ogden, and David Tracy in *The Emptying God,* ed. John Cobb and Christopher Ives.
47. See Mack, *A Myth of Innocence,* 78–131.

from receiving Jesus and God as one would receive a child, but from the discriminative mind that would draw boundaries around peoples and ideas, the very boundaries Jesus has been at pains to undermine. It was this kind of party spirit that Paul had to counter in Corinth.[48] Like Paul, Jesus does not recommend party identity, but opens up the group to anyone who is not against him. In 9: 23, in the context of an exorcism, Jesus has stated that all things are possible to anyone who has faith. Here, he goes further, saying that anyone who is not against him (ὅς γὰρ οὐκ ἔστιν καθ' ἡμῶν), by that very fact, is for him (ὑπὲρ ἡμῶν ἐστιν). There are no fixed criteria for membership in the group—beyond the obvious rule that one not be against it. There is no imagined pattern of being Christian, no gold card of membership. These inclusive words of Jesus would apply to all those who do not go against Jesus, not only the various Christian groups, but also non-Christian groups. Buddhists who revere Christ as an awakened person, i.e., a buddha.[49] Muslims, who revere Jesus as one of the greatest prophets. Jews, who see Jesus as a reformer calling people to a renewed practice of the covenant. These non-Christian groups, of course, do not accept Christian ideas *about* Jesus, about his ontological status. Yet the words here recorded in Mark make no such stipulation. To be for Jesus does not necessarily mean to accept ideas about Jesus. Ideas, even doctrinal ideas, flow from conventional wisdom and are tied to historical contexts. Notions of essence and being, for example, take on their meaning only when one is conversant with the Greek intellectual climate that gave them birth. They are, I would argue, no longer functional terms today, even in the West. Certainly modern American culture seems as distant from Greek ontology as it is from Asian cultural patterns. It is perhaps driven more by a shallow social Darwinian insistence on winners and losers. Be that as it may, doctrinal criteria are themselves all dependently co-arisen, functioning only in terms of particular cultures and particular times,[50] empty of any essence of their own. Mark himself gives no clear definitions. His Jesus shies away from self-definition, reinterpreting traditional themes in terms of the concrete actuality of his lived life. The messiah is not the glory figure of his disciples' imagination, but the one who undergoes the sufferings

---

48. See Keenan, *The Meaning of Christ,* 30–34, 40–43.

49. Reps, *Zen Flesh, Zen Bones,* 20: "A university student while visiting Gasan asked him: 'Have you ever read the Christian Bible?' 'No, read it to me,' said Gasan. The student opened the Bible and read from St. Matthew: 'And why take ye thought for raiment? Consider the lilies of the field, how they grow. They toil not, neither do they spin, and yet I say unto you that even Solomon in all his glory was not arrayed as one of these. . . . Take therefore no thought for the morrow, for the morrow shall take thought for the things of itself.' Gasan said, 'Whoever uttered those words I consider an enlightened man.' "

50. See Knitter, *No Other Name?* for a culturally sensitive discussion of the theology of world religions and the evaluation of truth claims. Among the rapidly increasing volume of literature, see also Hick and Knitter, *The Myth of Christian Uniqueness,* and Raimundo Panikkar, *The Silence of God: The Answer of the Buddha,* and his most recent *The Cosmotheandric Experience.*

of a lived life. Jesus is not the messiah. Rather, the messiah is Jesus. In typically Mahāyāna terms, "Jesus is not the messiah, not the messiah, and that is why Jesus is the messiah." One ends up with the "being of emptiness," not a defensible position about the person of Jesus. So the follower of Jesus is not the one who belongs to the proper group (ὃς οὐκ ἀκολουθεῖ ἡμῖν). Rather, anyone who is not against Jesus is included. A very all-inclusive group indeed.

Belonging
9: 41–42

[41] "If anyone gives you a cup of water to drink because you belong to Christ, then in truth I tell you, he will most certainly not lose his reward. [42] But anyone who is the downfall of one of these little ones who have faith, would be better thrown into the sea with a great millstone around his neck."

Despite the all-inclusive compass of Jesus' teachings, there are groups and one does have to belong somewhere. Not belonging anywhere, in Mark, characterizes only the unclean spirits and demons. Emptiness must be concretized in the dependently co-arising world. To belong to Christ (ὅτι χριστοῦ ἐστε) is to follow the path of concrete community living that Jesus talks about, to be converted to the presence of the kingdom, although as just explained, it is not to belong to an exclusive group. Such inclusivity does not negate the formation of a Christian community, a very specific kind of group. It must be remembered, however, that the Church is not a supernatural society set down among mere humans, but is itself a dependently co-arisen gathering of the faithful. At its best it is aware of the otherness of Abba and of the historical and cultural conditioning of its own history, for there is no other kind of history apart from dependently co-arising history.

Interestingly, rather than instructing his followers to act kindly toward others, Jesus characterizes them as being in the position of receiving assistance from others, just as the disciples in 6: 7–13 are told to rely on the hospitality of others. The Markan community is on the receiving end, not the giving end, for it has no status and no resources. That it is then a worthy and meritorious deed for anyone to assist a Christ-follower entails that they too, in receiving a poor, thirsty disciple, receive also Jesus and his kingdom.[51]

---

51. Fowler, *Let the Reader Understand,* 99, notes that ". . . who is supposed to be speaking in the *hoti* clause in 9: 41 is not immediately clear. The clause is undoubtedly parenthetical, tucked into a collection of 'whoever' and '*amēn*' sayings by Jesus: 'For whoever gives you a cup of water for a name's sake'—*because you are of Christ*—'truly, I say to you that he certainly will not lose his reward' (RMF). Granted, my translation and especially my punctuation are slanted toward the way I read this *hoti* clause. The second-person plural form of the verb *este* ('you are') allows us to read the parenthesis either as a comment by Jesus to his intranarrative audience or as a comment by the narrator to his extranarrative audience (cf. Mark 13). The aspect of the parenthetical

One must remember, too, that anyone who places obstacles (σκανδαλίσῃ) in the path of "one of these little ones who have faith" is in for trouble: to be drowned in the sea just like the Gerasene pigs. In context such a placing of obstacles refers to sectarian blockages, circumscribing entrance into the community and supposedly into the kingdom, which in reality is available to all. It is possible that the man who was actually casting out demons in Jesus' name, in contrast to the ineffectual efforts of Jesus' own inner group, is an example of these little ones who have faith, sandwiched as he is between the immediately preceding reference in verse 37 about receiving children (ὃς ἂν ἓν τῶν τοιούτων παιδίων δέξηται) and the immediately following one in verse 42 about any of the little ones who believe (ἕνα τῶν μικρῶν τούτων τῶν πιστευόντων).[52] Although not a known member of the group around Jesus, he evidently had faith enough to invoke the name of Jesus and to effect exorcisms. Thus to place obstacles in his path, to entrap him, would be to demand that he cease his activity until official approval and validation are assured, and this is just what the disciples attempt to do. They then are the ones who had better watch their necks while passing by millstones at the seashore!

Cutting Off Bodily Parts
9: 43–50

[43]*"And if your hand should be your downfall, cut it off; it is better for you to enter into life crippled, than to have two hands and go to hell, into the fire that cannot be put out.* [45]*And if your foot should be your downfall, cut it off; it is better for you to enter into life lame, than to have two feet and be thrown into hell.* [47]*And if your eye should be your downfall, tear it out; it is better for you to enter into the kingdom of God with one eye, than to have two eyes and be thrown into hell where their worm will never die nor their fire be put out.* [49]*For everyone will be salted with fire.* [50]*Salt is a good thing, but if salt has become insipid, how can you make it salty again? Have salt in yourselves and be at peace with one another."*[53]

This passage from Mark had great influence on the first-century theologian Origen. It was not his hand or foot that led him toward sin, however, but his

comment that makes it problematic as a statement of Jesus at the story level is the use of the term 'Christ.' Nowhere else in Mark does Jesus so casually use so weighty a title to refer to himself. Here we are probably hearing the narrator speaking, interjecting his own parenthetical comment into a speech otherwise supposedly by Jesus."

52. Schweizer, *The Good News*, 197: "The 'little ones' are Jesus' disciples. This expression properly designates those who are 'spiritually poor' (Matt. 5: 3; cf. the men of lowly, i.e., humble, spirit in Qumran). This expression had become unintelligible, so Mark explained it with the phrase 'who believe.' "

53. Following *The New Jerusalem Bible*, verses 44 and 46 (and part of 49) are omitted as repetitions of 48, in accordance with the best manuscript evidence.

sexual organ. So, if the tradition be true, he castrated himself with a clam shell and went through life "a eunuch for the sake of the kingdom." One hopes he indeed did "enter into life," although the attitude of the tradition toward him has been somewhat ambiguous. Note that the opposite of hell, a reference to the refuse dump for Jerusalem,[54] is twice described simply as entry into life (εἰσελθεῖν εἰς τὴν ζωὴν), and once as entry into the kingdom of God (εἰσελθεῖν εἰς τὴν βασιλείαν τοῦ θεοῦ). The opposite of hell here is not a question of a heaven after death, or of entering any grand eschatological realm, but simply of being able to enter into life itself, to live a rich and full life and to follow the eschatological rule of God's justice and peace in life. Indeed, Jesus began his preaching with the proclamation that the kingdom of God is close at hand, right here in the everyday mind. The Ch'an practitioners have a saying: "The Way is your everyday mind." In other words, the practice of enlightenment is not a wow affair to be experienced in a different dimension, but just the simple, true nature of one's everyday living. It is, I think, such an everyday life that Mark is talking about here. In order to enter into life, one must accept human brokenness and live, rather than to insist on wholeness and be thrown into hell, the final rejection and torment of the self-enclosed. There is a notion, now more popular than ever, that true living means for the individual to be whole, integral, fulfilled in every human potential. That is a nice idea, but it certainly is not Markan. Nor is it true. Origen probably understood human limitation more profoundly, although the action he took was indeed extreme. Origen was in many ways an unusual fellow. He not only watched but encouraged his father to seek martyrdom, while he himself was restrained from following old dad's footsteps only because his mother hid his clothing. Too modest to venture out improperly dressed, he was unable to accompany dad into the final victory.[55] Now, that may sound suspicious, as though he had a lot of unresolved feelings about his father—and his mother. It fits nicely into the Freudian pattern of Oedipal angst. Perhaps Origen was psychologically awry and did only what he was driven to do. He did enter life a cripple, yet enter life he did. Because of his physical imperfection he has never been acclaimed a saint, and yet he was the most creative of first-century theologians, blending Christian faith with the gnostic ideas of his age.

---

54. Nineham, *Saint Mark,* 258: "Hell: a word with so many irrelevant associations that it is probably better to keep to the original word: *Gehenna.* This was a valley west of Jerusalem where at one time children were sacrificed to Moloch (2 Kings 23: 10; Jer. 7: 31; 19: 5f; 32: 35); after being desecrated by Josiah it came to be used as a refuse dump for Jerusalem, a fact which explains the imagery of worm and fire borrowed from Isa. 66: 24 in v. 48. The suggestion is of maggots preying on offal and fires perpetually smouldering for the destruction of refuse. Because of all its bad connotations, the Jewish imagination had come to picture *Gehenna* as the place of future torment for the wicked—cf. e.g., 2 Esdras 7: 36."

55. Greer, tr., *Origen: An Exhortation to Martyrdom,* Introduction.

However one regards Origen and his eccentricities, the point is to accept the dependently co-arisen world where the self has no entitlement to integral wholeness, nor to strive complainingly to measure up to some image of wholeness or perfection.

This interpretation applies to celibacy as well. For a celibate to whine and grumble about remaining sexually unfulfilled is beside the point. A celibate is obviously sexually unfulfilled. So perhaps are the playboy boys, no matter what their age. Full human sexual growth is a complex business, and not always achievable. Accepting human limitation, accepting the absence of growth in one facet of life, can and does enable one to enter life and practice the path of the kingdom. By contrast, to strive diligently to unravel one's psyche toward full sexual fulfillment may indeed prevent one from entering into life at all. It is possible to live entirely on the psychological margins, forever a patient, and never a participant.[56]

The sentence about the undying worms and unquenchable fire is drawn from *Isaiah* 66: 24, the final passage of that book, and the conclusion to an eschatological discourse. Verses 23 and 24 read: "From new moon to new moon, from sabbath to sabbath, all mankind will come to bow down in my presence, says Yahweh. And on their way out they will see the corpses of men who have rebelled against me. Their worm will not die nor their fire go out; they will be loathsome to all mankind." Here the worm and fire are reserved for those who rebel against God and are thus excluded from the eschatological kingdom. Yet, in Mark, that kingdom is simply the entry into life, while the worm and fire are the result of pretending that dependently co-arisen limitations do not exist, and that one can be securely fulfilled within the enclosure of an inner self. The permanence of the fire and the worm are metaphors signifying the illusory permanence of the imagined self. Desiring to be a permanent self and to be at the center, one achieves only the permanence of worm and fire, and is thus excluded from living within the dependently co-arisen world—which is the only world we have in which to live.

The phrase about being salted with fire ($\pi\nu\rho\grave{\iota}\ \dot{\alpha}\lambda\iota\sigma\theta\dot{\eta}\sigma\epsilon\tau\alpha\iota$) is hard to interpret. Bratcher and Nida mention that at least fifteen different explanations have been proposed, and remark that "the real problem with this verse is that we do not know exactly what it means."[57] According to one, to be salted with fire is a symbol of sacrifice, which used both salt and fire.[58] If this be the case, it may mean simply to sacrifice, to give up the striving for wholeness for the sake of entering into life. In this context, sacrifice is not some heroic deed looking forward to a future reward. Rather, it is recognition of no-self,

56. See Crossan, *The Historical Jesus,* 267, on the notion in the Gospel of Thomas of a return to the asexual, primordial moment before the gender-splitting of Adam and Eve.

57. Bratcher and Nida, *Handbook,* 304.

58. Lane, *The Gospel According to Mark,* 349: "In the OT the Temple sacrifices had to be accompanied by salt (Lev. 2: 13; Ezek. 43: 24; cf. Ex. 30: 35). Also see Cullman, *Revue d'Historie et de Philosophie religieuses* 37 (1957), 36–43 on salt as a symbol of sacrifice; and Hamerton-Kelly, *The Gospel and the Sacred,* 109.

of human transience and fragility. There is no one who can maintain a permanent self, independent of and apart from others. It is this illusion that must be sacrificed, that must be salted with the purifying fire. In Buddhist liturgies, fire is always a purifying agent, burning away delusion and passion.

Another interpretation adds to that image, suggesting that to " 'have salt' is parallel to 'be at peace.' In the Old Testament salt is a symbol of the covenant. One of the clearest texts is Leviticus 2: 13b: 'Do not let the salt of the covenant of your God be lacking from your cereal offering.' In Numbers 18: 19 an everlasting covenant is called a 'covenant of salt' (see also 2 Chr 13: 5). The background of this idea probably lies in the sharing of salt in a meal (Ezr 4: 14). To share salt with someone is to share fellowship with him, to be in covenant with him. The discourse began with two situations of conflict and strife, the self-seeking arguing of the disciples about rank and the conflict with the stranger exorcist. It went on to discuss the problem of scandal in the community. To all of this Mark opposes the peace of covenant fellowship."[59] The sacrifice of selfhood is the requisite for the ability to share in the fellowship of the covenant. Jesus would then be saying that to live the ancient covenant between God and the people, and between one person and another, one has to enter the purifying fire of sacrifice and share one's salt with others.

The concluding phrase refers back to the preceding sections, addressed throughout to the disciples. The experience of the transfiguration has left them with images of glory, with hopes of sharing in the wondrous future of the Christ. They do not get the point about the suffering of the messiah, about the limitations of a messiah who lives in the dependently co-arisen world and is thus himself immersed in its contradictions and limitations. And so they argue about who is the greatest, about how to establish a permanent position for selfhood. They do not understand about the little child, about being the servant of all, but think they have the right to exclude others from the in-group of Christ's followers. Jesus speaks to them first about obstructing others from the practice of the path, and then about placing obstacles to their own practice. All along, the main obstacle is adherence to selfhood, to deluded ideas about who one really is, or should be recognized to be. The advice about sacrificing parts of one's very body suggests the final sacrifice of self, the abandonment of the imagined pattern of clinging to consciousness as a permanent self.[60] To be salted with fire is to abandon the obstacles to under-

---

59. Fleddermann, "The Discipleship Discourse," 73.

60. Via, *The Ethics of Mark's Gospel*, 18: "Mark 9: 43–48 displays this interaction [between character and action]. Here Jesus tells his disciples: if your hand, foot, or eye causes *you* to stumble or sin, *you* cut it off or pluck it out. It is better for you to enter life maimed than to be thrown into hell with all your members. Character, the dimension of coherence and continuity, is represented by the personal 'you,' manifested in both the second person pronoun and in the verb endings of the second person imperative. Specific actions or directions are represented by the parts of the body—hand, foot, eye. The self is comprised of both character and act, but character comes closer to manifesting the whole self than does act, for character finally has more power. Thus I tend to use 'character' and 'self' interchangeably." Although the terminology differs, in the basic meaning of

standing and the obstacles of the passions (*jñeya-kleśa-avaraṇa*). The obstacle to understanding is the adherence to the idea of self as if it were a permanent and unchanging essence apart from the dependently co-arisen world. It is a failure to see the emptiness of self. The obstacle of the passions comprises all the emotional attachments whereby one vainly tries to realize that falsely exalted position of selfhood. To be free from such obstacles means to abandon, ever more fully, the false view of self (*satkāya-dṛṣṭi*) and to enter life—even if crippled or lame or half-blind—with both the understanding of emptiness and the emotional resonance of compassionate practice.

The image of salting indicates consciousness permeated with the flavor of converted wisdom. Insipid salt is life without the conversion of consciousness from deluded imagination to insight into emptiness. The Yogācāra philosophers teach that consciousness is an interplay between the latent store consciousness (*ālaya-vijñāna*) and the active consciousnesses (*pravṛtti-vijñāna*) of thinking, perceiving and sensing. The store consciousness is a seminal consciousness in that it contains seeds planted by the force of previous actions (*karman*), which permeate (*vāsanā*) the active levels of mental functioning and establish the mental habits of the imagined pattern of awareness. Our minds are not inner cameras simply taking snapshots of the world, but inner processes that construct our worlds, in either the deluded pattern of the fixed idea of a permanent self dealing with permanent entities out there, or in the perfected pattern of living within the healthy tension of transcendent insight into emptiness and reengagement into the dependently co-arisen world. Mark's image of insipid salt means that the mind becomes caught in the grasp of fixed ideas, of an almost innate attachment to so-called basic ideas of an essential self which copes with an essential world. Such a self is insipid because it lacks the very flavor of experience, fleeing from the transience of that experience to the bastion of false imagination. One seasons that consciousness through conversion, through a change of consciousness (μετ-άνοια, i.e. *āsraya-parivṛtti*) from delusion into wisdom. And that is what Jesus is talking about, how the disciples might change their consciousness, abandoning discussions about who is greatest and becoming the servants of all. To have salt in oneself and live at peace with one another means to live compassionately in the dependently co-arisen world, in awareness of emptiness and committed to loving one another.

---

character as a seal or impression that co-arises from conditions, Via's interpretation seems to parallel Mahāyāna notions. See Nagao, "Buddhist Subjectivity," 7–12, on the notion of the Buddhist negation of self as essential, but not as existential, i.e., as dependently co-arising.

10

Insight into No-Self

Tricky Questions about Marriage
10: 1–12

[1]After leaving there, he came into the territory of Judea and Transjordan. And again crowds gathered around him, and again he taught them, as his custom was. [2]Some Pharisees approached him and asked, "Is it lawful for a man to divorce his wife?" They were putting him to the test. [3]He answered them, "What did Moses command you?" [4]They replied, "Moses allowed us to draw up a writ of dismissal in cases of divorce." [5]Then Jesus said to them, "It was because you were so hard hearted that he wrote this commandment for you. [6]But from the beginning of creation he made them male and female. [7]This is why a man leaves his father and mother,[8] and the two become one flesh. They are no longer two, therefore, but one flesh. [9]So then, what God has united, human beings must not divide." [10]Back in the house the disciples questioned him again about this, [11]and he said to them, "Whoever divorces his wife and marries another is guilty of adultery against her. [12]And if a woman divorces her husband and marries another she is guilty of adultery too."

There is a marked transition from Jesus' activity in and around Galilee to his journey to Jerusalem. He leaves "there," his home ground around Capernaum, as last mentioned in 9: 33. The crowds accompany him, for his fame as a popular preacher goes with him. The drama continues, however, for even his disciples still do not understand what is unfolding through his movement toward the center of Jewish religious life.[1]

---

1. Via, *The Ethics of Mark's Gospel,* 78, describes Mark 10 as a relatively self-contained unit: "It is the transition between Galilee and Jerusalem, beginning with Jesus' departure (10: 1) from Capernaum (9: 33) and ending with his arrival near Jerusalem (10: 52–11: 1), beginning with the activity of Jesus' powerful teaching (10: 1) and ending with the actualized effect of that power in bringing man to follow in his way with sight, that is, understanding (10: 52). I have tried to show that Mark 10 contains a concentration of ethical and other related materials which make it a microcosm of the Gospel. It narrates an in-between time, so it is not a completed story, since more comes after it."

There was among the Pharisees a dispute about divorce. The followers of Shammai rejected easy divorce. Jesus' questioners perhaps wanted to know Jesus' position. They wanted to know where he fit in the framework of current religious debate. But Jesus hardly passes the test, for his answer undercuts the assumptions of the debate: the apparently obvious notion that marriage is a coming together of two individuals. What Jesus questions is the very idea of an individual self who might enter into or leave a marital relationship with another individual self. Rather, as *Genesis* teaches, God from the very beginning made them male and female, so that, leaving father and mother, the two become one flesh (εἰς σάρκα μίαν). Above, Jesus has recommended severing an offending part of one's body. Here, he refuses to sever the one common body of a married pair.[2] In the Jewish androcentric context, a man moves away from his parents and attaches himself to, adheres to, and is faithful to (προσκολληθήσεται) his wife, overcoming the separateness of self. They should not then be again divided (μὴ χωριζέτω), as if the individual could establish a fixed identity apart from human relationships. The oneness of the flesh exists from the beginning, before the onset of sclerosis of the heart, before the advent of fixed notions about an individual self. Thus Jesus recommends a recovery of that primordial relationship by an abandonment of hardened fixations upon self-definitions.

Divorce has been allowed, Jesus asserts, because people were unteachable, i.e., because their hearts were hardened (πρὸς τὴν σκληροκαρδίαν ὑμῶν).[3] A hardened heart characterizes actions performed from an attachment to

---

2. Via, *The Ethics of Mark's Gospel*, 101–02: "Jesus answers the Pharisees in what had to be a surprising and unexpected way, and Mark apparently wants to say that Jesus dominated them, overcame their appeal to the law, by using Scripture against Scripture. The intention of God expressed in Gen. 1: 27 and 2: 24 forbids divorce in Jesus' view, while the divorce law in Deut. 24: 1–4 allows it, and in so doing, the latter text expresses hardness of heart; Mark's Jesus sets God's primordial-eschatological will (Gen. 1: 27; 2: 24; Mark 10: 6–9) against a particular commandment of Moses and thus clearly questions the authority of a certain portion of scripture. . . . Marriage is a union between a man and a woman which takes precedence over other relationships, and it joins the two as one flesh. In the Old Testament, which Mark is quoting here, flesh sometimes represents the weakness of humankind in contrast with God. But it also has positive meanings. It can mean either a part of the human body or the whole body. It then moves in the direction of the personal pronoun, and, like *nephesh,* can mean humankind per se, but in the bodily aspect. Flesh binds people together and implies relationship. The one flesh in Gen. 2: 24 suggests a common body, and whether or not the Old Testament writer drew the conclusion that this meant fellowship for life, that is the meaning which Mark saw in it. Observe that Mark does not base the indissolubility of marriage on a oneness of heart or spirit but bases it on the oneness of flesh. The term may well have the connotation of the whole person on its perimeter, but its focal center is physical."

3. Via, *The Ethics of Mark's Gospel*, 45: "Mark sees hardness of heart as the condition of humanity throughout the course of world history. He does not speak explicitly of a fall but implies that hardness of heart, which has obtained since before the time of Moses, was not there at the beginning when marriage was established. But it is now, and it still qualifies the human condition."

images and ideas of an independent self.[4] In such an imagined pattern of consciousness, one is hardly united to one's spouse as one body, and so Moses allowed divorce, much as we modern Christians usually do, to recognize that marriages in fact do fail. Yet the source of that failure is the false view of self.[5] Marriage is not a partnership or an agreement between consenting adults, but an evolution from selfhood into the intimacy of a life-affirming and shared, other-dependent (not co-dependent in the psychological sense of individuals living off of one another) life together.[6] The Pharisees talk about the legal questions of divorce. Jesus talks about what constitutes a person.

Verses 10–12 expand the point into a gentile context. The case of a woman divorcing her husband reflects Graeco-Roman, not Jewish, practice and was unknown in Jewish law. But in Mark's "gentile" context, it apparently was of some concern. Jesus' response in verse 11 is apparently stringent in the extreme. Not only is divorce not allowed; it also amounts to committing adultery. In the discourse on following Christ by losing one's life in order to find it in 8: 38, Jesus had spoken of "this adulterous and sinful generation" (ἐν τῇ γενεᾷ ταύτῃ τῇ μοιχαλίδι καὶ ἁμαρτωλῷ). In chapter 9: 19 he speaks about "a faithless generation" (ὦ γενεὰ 'ἄπιστος). Here he describes divorce as itself adulterous (μοιχᾶται). In the first instance "adulterous" means clinging to one's life so as not to lose it, and that is the basic sin. This is the same sense as in the second usage in 9:19, for to be faithless means to cling to accepted definitions of life. The present usage is also similar, for adultery means more than simply the act of taking another spouse. Rather, it signifies the all-devouring craving of the deluded pattern of con-

---

4. Via, *The Ethics of Mark's Gospel,* 120: "Mark must have thought that specific acts of rejection produced a general condition, a habit of mind." This parallels Mahāyāna notions of the cumulative effect of actions *(karman)* in engendering the imagined pattern of misunderstanding and delusion.

5. Via, *The Ethics of Mark's Gospel,* 116–17: "We have observed that divorce in our text is an expression of hardness of heart. Whether the *pros* ('for') in *pros tēn sklērokardian* (10: 5, 'for your hardness of heart') means 'against' (as a curb upon), or 'in view of,' or 'in accordance with' (as an expression of), the point is still that there would be no divorce apart from hardness of heart; and that this term may be Mark's characterization for the fundamental fallenness of the human condition. . . . From this quick overview [of Old Testament passages] we might surmise that hardness of heart will be a deformation and impairment of the very wellsprings (Prov. 4: 23) of understanding, including the understanding of God or faith, and of decisive action. One classical Old Testament portrayal of this theme is Isa. 6: 9–10, which is not only quoted in Mark 4: 12 but in other New Testament writers as well (Matt. 13 14–15; 2 Cor. 3: 14; 4: 4). Isaiah saw or came to see that his proclamation produced a hearing without understanding and a seeing without perception. This failure of understanding is represented as a fat heart. . . . It is a manifestation of self-exaltation (Exod. 9: 17)."

6. Via, *The Ethics of Mark's Gospel,* 104, argues against a totally futuristic and eschatological reading: "Why should marriage be sustained if historical existence in the world may not have a positive value and dimension? And the eschatological per se, in its wholly futuristic aspect, *will* spell the end of marriage: there will be no marriage in the resurrection (12: 25). We see again that the permanence of marriage presupposes an ongoing history which is eschatologically revitalized."

sciousness, seeking support for self wherever one desires. Jesus is not giving a legal judgment, but describing the pattern of hardened hearts searching for happiness.

Furthermore, the Jewish legal dispute was envisaged from the viewpoint of the male. "The formulation of the divorce law in Deuteronomy 24: 1–4 is strictly androcentric: 'when a man takes . . . marries . . . writes . . . puts . . . sends . . .' It concerns how a husband divorces a wife and says nothing whatsoever about how a wife divorces a husband. It does not have to do so because the law does not allow it. Unlike, say, Greek, Roman, or Egyptian law at the time of Jesus, Jewish law did not allow the wife to initiate divorce proceedings. Adultery, furthermore, was also androcentric . . . Seen against such a cultural situation, the texts against divorce . . . are strikingly anomalous."[7] Thus, as Crossan explains, the term "adultery" takes its meaning from within an androcentric and even phallocentric honor and shame ideology. "By saying that the *male* who disembeds his wife and remarries commits adultery *against her* . . . Jesus implies that honour is not (only?) *androcentric*—I use the term descriptively rather than pejoratively—but (also or equally) *gynecentric*. Honour is still understood as a pseudo-commodity but it belongs as much to a woman as to a man. Hence a man can 'steal' his own wife's honour by divorcing her and remarrying. . . . In the Palestine of Jesus' day, which did not permit women to initiate a divorce, the dignity of women was not . . . easily guarded. It is for this reason that Jesus uses the dramatic term 'adultery' in so surprising a way. He thus brought sharply into focus the wife's honour. It is as much to be protected and respected as the husband's honour and the woman is as vulnerable to damage as the male." Thus, Jesus' attack against divorce is not simply a pronouncement that all divorce is illegal, but, as Kloppenborg rightly points out, is actually against "androcentric honour whose debilitating effects went far beyond the situation of divorce. It was also the basis for the dehumanization of women, children and non-dominant males."[8] The logic of the Mahāyāna notion of emptiness takes the critique a step further, depriving gender itself of any static, abiding essence. Marriage is not merely an agreement that protects the commodity-honor of the consenting parties, but the primal, from the beginning, example of a dependently co-arisen relationship that defines who we are.

Throughout the Gospel of Mark Jesus again and again questions common assumptions about who we are, about what a person is. He is unconcerned about the current opinions that would identify who he is, not even accepting Peter's confession that he is the christ. His identity will be manifested through the concrete course of his life, and death. It is then an inversion of the Gospel to read it as providing information about the person of Christ, apart from any grappling with the question of who we are.

7. Crossan, *The Historical Jesus,* 301.
8. Kloppenborg, "Alms, Debt, and Divorce," 195–96, quoted in Crossan, *The Historical Jesus,* 301–02.

The Child-like Mind
10: 13–16

[13]People were bringing little children to him, for him to touch them. The disciples scolded them, [14]but when Jesus saw this he was indignant and said to them, "Let the little children come to me; do not stop them; for it is to such as these that the kingdom of God belongs. [15]In truth I tell you, anyone who does not welcome the kingdom of God like a little child will never enter it." [16]Then he embraced them, laid his hands on them, and gave them his blessing.

At the end of chapter 9: 42 Jesus warns his disciples not to be one of those who obstruct the way of the little ones (ὅς ’ἄν σκάδαλίσῃ ’ἕνα τῶν μικρῶν τούτων τῶν πιστευόντων). Yet, immediately they scold and hinder (ἐπετίμησαν) the children from coming to him. Jesus is indignant and angry, telling them not to stop or impede the children (μὴ κωλύετε αὐτά). Just as the disciples had tried to prohibit the fellow who was throwing out demons, so here they again stand in the way. Again the struggle is between the disciples' sense of personal ownership over Jesus and his unconcern about personal stature or definition. In Chapter 9, Jesus talked about maimed and imperfect humans who nevertheless enter into life, into the kingdom of God (9: 47). Here he returns to the theme, telling the disciples that that kingdom is not the preserve of any privileged group, but a kingdom of humble children.[9] God does not play theological favorites, bringing some in and leaving others out. Thus, Jesus brings the children into contact (ἄψηται) and embraces them, here as above in 9: 36. Bringing one into such contact signifies something more than that Jesus likes small children. Rather, it "connotes contact with Jesus in faith, as is evident from 1:41; 3:10; 5:27, 28, 30, 31; 6:56; 7:33; 8:22; 10:13."[10] The same metaphor is used by the Yogācāra philosophers to indicate the way one realizes awakening, i.e., Dharma Body. Asaṅga explains in a rather detailed and scholarly way that the Dharma Body of awakening is acquired through contact *(sparśa)* inasmuch as it is realized through the wisdom of emptiness and the wisdom of dependent co-arising.[11] The Markan narrative image is more concrete and personal: Jesus touches those who enter the kingdom.

Early and late medieval theologies talked about divine election, but their theories do appear to be based on metaphysical favoritism, wistfully conclud-

---

9. Crossan, *The Historical Jesus*, 269: ". . . but still to be a child was to be a nobody, with the possibility of becoming a somebody absolutely dependent on parental discretion and parental standing in the community. That, I think, is the heart of the matter with all other allusions or further interpretations clustering around that central and shocking metaphor. A kingdom of the humble, of the celibate, or of the baptized comes later. This comes first: a kingdom of children is a kingdom of nobodies."

10. Kee, *Community of the New Age*, 91.

11. See Griffiths et al, *The Realm of Awakening*, 93–97 for Asaṅga's text and the commentaries.

ing that strange as it might seem, God of his own sovereign will has elected Christians, while not so freely supplying grace to others. That is not Mark's theology. Here little children are those who receive (δέξηται) the kingdom of God. The point is not that little children are always particularly pleasant or docile. Rather, it is that they receive things given without questioning their qualifications to so receive.[12] "In the [Jungian] archetype of itself, the child as potential for the future moves through the abandonment of a secure origin, through risk and danger toward adulthood. In the Gospel of Mark the adult is called on tacitly to become a child. If the adult does so, he or she must retrace the steps that the child takes in becoming an adult. That is, the adult must take risks and abandon security in order to move back to childhood. Of course, the inescapable implication of Mark's theology is that the adult has not really taken the dangerous way. He or she has, rather, held onto false securities (4: 19) and has become fixed, hardened in a dependence on something that cannot really sustain life (8: 36–37). The adult has become hardened in heart, so that the inner center of life is not open to a different future. Thus if one is to have life, one must make the move that one had not made before. One must move back to childhood and begin again. This entails renouncing the shape of one's present existence in order to recover an abandoned potential. Life must be lost in order to be found (8: 34–35)."[13] One cannot enter heaven unless such a child-like mind of wisdom receives and welcomes it.[14]

The Mahāyāna thinkers often talk about recovering a pristine state, wherein consciousness is purified from the adult delusions and ignorances that lead to evil actions and suffering. That pristine condition, however, is not an abstraction, but the recovery of what had been there all along, the reclamation of the world as originally dependently co-arisen in all its dynamism and creativity. The child-like condition which precedes hardness of heart is that which has been present from the beginning, in virtue of which Jesus has just declared that divorce is not possible. Thus the eschatological kingdom that Jesus proclaims is not merely a future expectancy. "Clearly for Mark, then, life in his community is seen as more than merely preparation for a heavenly kingdom or even for a kingdom in a new age from which the present is

---

12. Kee, *Community of the New Age,* 108: "Entrance [into the kingdom of God] can only be received as a gift, like the mystery of the kingdom itself (4:11). Although the particular quality of children implied in 10:15 is not directly stated, the context seems to require that it is receptivity (δέξηται . . . ὡς παιδίον). But the notion is excluded that it can only be received in the future; rather it can be entered now."

13. Via, *The Ethics of Mark's Gospel,* 130. See Myers' critique of Via's interpretation, *Binding the Strong Man,* 266–71.

14. Note Fowler, *Let the Reader Understand,* 172–73, who argues that the point is not to receive the kingdom as a child would, but to receive it "when it approaches in the form of a child." I follow him above in 9:37, but here the phrase in verse 14, "for it is to such as these that the kingdom of God belongs" (τῶν γὰρ τοιούτων ἐστιν ἡ βασιλεία τοῦ θεοῦ) differentiates between children and the kingdom and implies that the point is indeed how one enters the kingdom, i.e., as a child.

somehow radically disjunct."[15] Eschatological discourse in Mark moves beyond linear time to announce definitive judgment on the expectancies of linear time. It is the narrative analogue to the Mahāyāna discourse on ultimate meaning, declaring all structures and all putative realities empty of any final meaning. "Because the fulfillment of time is the leitmotif of the whole Gospel (1: 14–15), it must be assumed that the call for the permanence of marriage is grounded on the belief that the kingdom—a new kind of situation—is a present reality."[16] The eschatological kingdom itself is a recovery of the primordial time in which selfhood no longer holds sway.

The kingdom here consists in those who do so receive it as a gift, who are aware of the weakness and transience of human living. That is why Jesus returns again and again to the theme of his sufferings and passion, trying to disabuse his disciples, and thus Mark's readers, from any notion of power or status. Powerful people do not gracefully receive gifts, for to receive implies lack. The deluded quest for position and power, by contrast, is based on imagining a self without lack, an enclosed and independent inner individuality. That precludes insight into emptiness and thus entrance into the kingdom of God.

Good and Evil
10: 17–22

[17]*He was setting out on the way[17] when a man ran up, knelt before him and put this question to him, "Good master, what must I do to inherit eternal life?" [18]Jesus said to him, "Why do you call me good? No one is good but God alone. [19]You know the commandments: You shall not kill; you shall not commit adultery; You shall not steal; You shall not bear false witness; You shall not defraud; Honor your father and mother." [20]And he said to him, "Master, I have kept all these from my earliest days." [21]Jesus looked steadily at him and he was filled with love for him, and he said, "You need to do one thing more. Go and sell what you own and give the money to the poor, and you will have treasure in heaven; then come, follow me." [22]But his face fell at these words and he went away sad, for he was a man of great wealth.*

Mark joins this account to what has immediately preceded it to contextualize the fellow's question. Jesus has just been talking about receiving the kingdom of God as a child. The man was listening and, realizing that he

15. Kee, *Community of the New Age,* 109. Also 141: "Clearly, for the Markan tradition, 'kingdom' is not only the eschatological reality about to be consummated in the future (9:1), but it is also the colony of the new age in the present time."

16. Via, *The Ethics of Mark's Gospel,* 47.

17. Following Malbon's translation, *Narrative Space,* 70. The underlying theme treats Jesus' practice of the way. He is on the way to Jerusalem. Chapter 10 ends with the now sighted Bartimaeus following along the way.

indeed did lack that consciousness of the kingdom, he runs up to ask his question, lest Jesus' departure leave him in the lurch. He reverences Jesus and addresses him as good master (διδάσκαλε ἀγαθέ), as if Jesus has captured the good he was seeking, the answer of just how to inherit or possess (κληρονομήσω) eternal life. He was a rich man who had many possessions, yet his "real concern is to make himself secure,"[18] and so he sets out in quest[19] of the one possession he lacks: eternal life.[20]

Jesus answers strangely by questioning what the man means by calling him good master. Once again, like a Zen master, he challenges the assumption of the question: that one can possess eternal life by being good. The fellow had indeed been good, for Mark tells us that he had from his youth kept the commandments and followed the path laid out in the scriptures and the traditions. In the tradition it had often been taught that a good, virtuous life issues in happiness, long life, and abundant possessions. This indeed is the question posed in the Book of Job—how can one live a just and faithful life, and yet experience suffering and poverty? This man, no Job he, still enjoys the benefits of a prosperous life; he is a man of great wealth. Yet he knows his life will sometime come to an end in death. Something more is needed. Matthew (19:22) describes the man as young, but here the image is rather of one who, having been successful in life, now faces the question of death. He is a rich man, willing and committed to being good, but not willing to give up his self-image about who he is: a good rich man. He is caught in the trap of selfhood, desiring to have his self validated not only here and now, but forever.

That is why Jesus tells him that he must abandon his self, give away all his possessions to the poor, to beggars (τοῖς πτωχοῖς). Having constant difficulty in training the disciples who are with him, Jesus offers this man the opportunity to become a true disciple, abandoning self and the possessions of self *(ātman-ātmya)*. The cured and the saved Jesus sends home, but those who are still enmeshed in their delusions he invites to be his disciples. But Jesus' offer is too much for the man; he is not for abandoning self but for assuring the continuance of that self. Treasures in heaven appear particularly empty and distant, so the prospect of abandoning the wealth that defines his person brings only sadness, dismay, and rejection.[21]

---

18. Via, *The Ethics of Mark's Gospel*, 134.

19. The story is identified as a quest story by Tannehill; see Mack, *A Myth of Innocence*, Appendix I, 382.

20. Via, *The Ethics of Mark's Gospel*, 136: "But the self-interest [motivating the rich man] which is served by gaining eternal life is a paradoxical one, for eternal life here as interpreted by the story, is the freedom from the self, from self-interest, which enables one to give all to the poor."

21. Via, *The Ethics of Mark's Gospel*, 138: "The episode (Mark 10: 17–22) dramatizes the theme stated earlier in 4: 19 that the deceitfulness of riches or possessions chokes the word of the gospel. Here the desire to retain his wealth has deflected this man from his pursuit of eternal life. According to Fernando Belo, the man 'who has' is unfruitful because he lives in a class society, a society in which desires are bewitched by the dominant

The Mahāyāna theologians teach that the wisdom of awakening transcends conventional distinctions between good and evil. There are, they explain, mundane good states that are indeed valuable in the practice of the path, and they outline numerous rules to follow. Yet they recognize that the mere practice of mundane good leads only to a mundane result—clinging to one's goodness in religious illusion. Jesus' questioning of why the man calls him good is meant to overturn such a delusion. Only God is good, for transcendent good is realized only in the abandonment of all selfhood, only in insight into the emptiness of everything we call good or evil. To possess eternal life is to abandon all attempts to possess anything. It is that insight into emptiness that allows one to follow the commandments, not as a means to earn eternal life, but as conventional paths of practice which point beyond those paths to the silent mystery of God. One can only be good by abandoning goodness. Not to embrace evil, but to embrace emptiness.

The Impossibility of Entering the Kingdom
10: 23–27

[23]Jesus looked round and said to his disciples, "How hard it is for those who have riches to enter the kingdom of God!" [24]The disciples were astounded by these words, but Jesus insisted, "My children," he said to them, "how hard it is to enter the kingdom of God! [25]It is easier for a camel to pass through the eye of a needle than for someone rich to enter the kingdom of God." [26]They were more astonished than ever, saying to one another, "In that case, who can be saved?" [27]Jesus gazed at them and said, "By human resources it is impossible, but not for God: because for God everything is possible."

To enter the kingdom is to abandon self.[22] That is why it is difficult for a rich man to do so, for riches are often recognized support for selfhood. The

---

codes, in this case the desire for material wealth. One may doubt that it is only or peculiarly in a class society, a non-Marxist society, that material wealth is a spiritual problem in which one's desires are bewitched. Surely Mark understands himself to be dealing with a fundamentally human problem, the problem of how human beings deal with, and are dealt with by, material wealth in the middle of time when hardness of heart is endemic. Deceit is an element—perhaps both weapon and symbol—of hardness of heart. Riches and possessions deceive in the precise sense that they seduce one into believing that life can in fact be found in them (8: 36) rather than in following Jesus. And yet one *knows* that he is letting himself be deceived, otherwise why would the man have gone away sorrowful?" The reference is to Belo's *A Materialist Reading of the Gospel of Mark,* 172. The same critique can, I think, be leveled, *mutatis mutandis,* to Myers' *Binding the Strong Man,* a socio-political reading of Mark, in which Jesus is waging a war of ideologies and proclaiming a program of political liberation.

22. Via, *The Ethics of Mark's Gospel,* 96: "Faith (believing) is, in the light [of 9: 24-*panta gar dynata tō theō*], the freedom from self-interest which is eternal life and which enables radical obedience from the heart and the giving up of all security for the other—the poor."

tradition saw riches as a reward from God for good living, and so the disciples' attitude is in context understandable. "If the author of Mark rejects the solution which blames suffering on the victim's lack of faith, he is equally disdainful of the Deuteronomistic equation of suffering with disobedience to God. This is the understanding which lies behind the disciples' astonishment in 10:23–31 at the notion that prosperity is not an indicator of righteousness. Entry into the kingdom is not earned but given by the God who does that which is impossible for humans."[23] Thus they are astounded (ἐθαμβοῦντο) and more astonished than ever (περισσῶς ἐξεπλήσσοντο). Their repeated astonishment derives from Jesus' negation of their assumptions, from his shifting of the context in which life is understood. Here he has generalized the admonition to the rich man. It is not merely a question about being rich though, but about striving for security.[24] Indeed, Jesus is not merely a good teacher outlining moral maxims and encouraging people to uphold a more plausible morality.[25] He is an overthrower of morality itself, in favor of morality.

---

23. Dowd, *Prayer, Power, and the Problem of Suffering,* 161. See Via, *The Ethics of Mark's Gospel,* 140. See also Belo, *A Materialist Reading of the Gospel of Mark,* 173.

24. Via, *The Ethics of Mark's Gospel,* 141: "The motif that it is hard for the rich to enter the kingdom of God in 10: 23 is enforced in 10: 25 by the metaphorical statement that it is easier for a camel to go through the eye of a needle. But in the statement about the difficulty of entering the kingdom in 10: 24b the reference to riches is omitted, which makes the assertion of difficulty/impossibility apply generally to anyone. This ties in with the hint in 10: 17–22 that holding on to security in the world (8: 36), any security, is the real problem. The recognition that everyone has something to hold on to produces the shocked question, 'Then who can be saved?' . . . There is no indication in Mark that evil arises fundamentally from wealth! But the text does clearly say that *pleonexia* (the grasping desire for advantage) comes from within, from the heart (7: 21–22); and *pleonexia* attaches itself to possessions." See Cranfield, *St. Mark,* 241: "πλεονεξίαι: 'acts of covering', or perhaps 'deeds of lustfulness'; for the word is quite often (as here) associated with words denoting sexual sin." In a broad sense, it parallels the Buddhist use of *trsna,* the "thirst" to possess life itself, which in some texts is the beginning of the chain of karmic transmigration, i.e., the beginning of delusion. See also Kelber, *The Kingdom in Mark,* 88: "A Kingdom saying warning the rich (10: 23b) is almost literally repeated as a warning to the disciples (10: 24c). The focus lies in the intervening 10: 24ab, which reports the disciples' amazed reaction and Jesus' specific reply to them. The disciples were astounded because what seemed to be a concern to the rich alone, Jesus applies to them. Far from being guaranteed a free passage, their entrance into the Kingdom is a most difficult achievement."

25. Against Dowd, *Prayer, Power, and the Problem of Suffering,* 93: Noting that "the Alexandrian Jews (as reported by Philo) provided for their adherents a 'plausibility structure'—a world—in which the members of the religious community lived and by means of which they interpreted their experiences," she writes that "the gospel functions as the narrative version of the plausibility structure within which the Markan community must live and interpret its experiences." In Mahāyāna terms, such a structure is indeed needed and constructed for each and every community, yet it remains dependently co-arisen, not a matter simply of having the proper viewpoint, for all viewpoints or plausibility structures must first pass through the fire of emptiness. I think, that such a Mahāyāna framework, itself dependently co-arisen and conventional, addresses Dowd's concerns about suffering and the power of God to do even the impossible through its dialectic of emptiness: losing life to save it.

Remember that in verse 19 he outlines the practice of the path for the rich man, and that path retains its conventional validity. Yet, even keeping all the commandments does not make one a follower of Jesus, nor does it lead to salvation, for the ultimate meaning of God always goes beyond any human practice. Only when the path is emptied of guaranteed success can it be engaged in wisely and profitably. But, regarded as a sure entryway into eternal life it remains ineffectual. It is impossible for one who clings to enter the needle's eye.

In the fifteenth century the needle's eye was read to refer to a night-time gate through which, only with difficulty and on its knees, a camel might enter the city. But Mark seems to mean not that one must try harder, but that one must give up all attempts so to enter. The phrase is a "reverse ἀδύνατον," in Dowd's insightful analysis, a rhetorical assertion of the possibility of something quite impossible in any common sense context.[26] However, the point of Mark's usage is not, I think, to assert an alternate viewpoint in which camels do pass through needles, but to empty the common sense viewpoint that adjudges things possible or impossible. It seems impossible to the disciples that anyone can be saved, if even the rich find it impossible. Yet, no viewpoint adjudicates who is saved and who is not.

The Zen masters employed such rhetorical devices in telling their stories. "Wu-tu said, 'It is like a buffalo that passes through a latticed window. Its head, horns, and all four legs all pass through. Why can't its tail pass through as well?' " Wu-men challenges the reader to "get upside down with this one, discern it clearly, and give a turning word. . . ."[27] No matter how one attempts to interpret such a crazy case story *(kōan),* it defies all common sense and turns one's accustomed world upside down. To get upside down with it entails the emptying of all plausible world structures. "The Priest Shih-shuang said, 'How do you step from the top of a hundred-foot pole?' " To which Wu-men comments, "Stepping forward, turning back—is there anything to reject as ignoble or unworthy? Be that as it may, how do you step from the top of a hundred-foot pole? Sah!"[28] In the common-sense world, some are worthy and some ignoble, some righteous and some depraved, some blessedly rich and some deservedly poor. The Markan Jesus undercuts that by a direct and frontal attack on the deluded assumptions that underlie such ideas.

It is not valid to psychologize this passage away. "The words of this verse are clear and precise in their meaning. . . . The camel was the largest animal in Palestine and the eye of a needle the smallest opening: the metaphor of a camel going through the eye of a needle vividly defines an impossibility."[29]

26. Dowd, *Prayer, Power, and the Problem of Suffering,* 71: "Instead of using ἀδύνατον to emphasize how impossible it is that something should happen, the figure is used to assert that an impossible action *can* be performed or has been performed by a deity or by a human assisted by divine powers."

27. Aitken, *The Gateless Barrier,* 231.

28. Aitken, *The Gateless Barrier,* 272.

29. Bratcher and Nida, *A Translator's Handbook,* 323.

It is impossible for humans to enter the kingdom, for attachment to self in fear of human transience occludes that possibility.

Yet Mark's Jesus says that all things are possible for God (πάντα γὰρ δυνατὰ παρὰ τῷ θεῷ), the same phrase he will use in his Gethsemane prayer. The sentence alludes to passages from the Tanach. *Genesis* 18:14 has Yahweh scold Abraham because his wife Sarah laughed when she heard that she was to conceive a child in her old age: "Is there anything too wonderful for Yahweh?" *Job* 42: 2 has that longsuffering man address Yahweh: "I know that you are all-powerful: what you conceive, you can perform." Nevertheless, it is still not possible for a camel to pass through the eye of a needle, nor for that buffalo to slip through the latticed window. I do not think, however, that Mark's use of such "impossibility cases" (ἀδύνατον, *kōan*) is meant to assert their literal possibility. The Mādhyamika logicians in their disputes with more realistic philosophers, claimed that they were presenting "nonimplicative negations," negations that do not entail the assertion of their opposites.[30] I read Mark as undermining assumed viewpoints in much the same manner. He empties the assumptions of the disciples by means of a nonimplicative use of impossible cases.[31] He does not affirm that camels actually do pass through needles' eyes: what would be left of any camel that did?

The point is that with God anyone can be saved, for salvation is not something done by any human efforts.[32] Rather, entering the transcendent

---

30. Huntington, *The Emptiness of Emptiness,* 58: "Indian philosophers traditionally define two distinct types of negation: (1) Negation which indirectly affirms the existence of something else *(paryudāsa),* (2) Negation which leaves nothing in its place *(prasajya).* The Mādhyamika has assigned a particular significance to each of these. The first type of negation is 'relative,' 'implicative,' or 'presuppositional' negation. Taken as a philosophical principle, it leads to the opposed ontological positions of nihilism and absolutism. The second type, 'nonimplicative' or 'nonpresuppositional' negation, is used by Mādhyamika to express the radical, deconstructive negation effected through application of the concept of emptiness. When one negates the reality of a reflection he necessarily affirms the reality of the reflected entity, but when the Mādhyamika philosopher negates the reality of the world, he affirms neither a 'something' nor a 'nothing' in its place. . . . in order to know and accept the world as it is both in its everyday appearance and in the paradox and mystery of this appearance, he steps entirely outside the language game that can be played only by holding onto positions *(pratijñās)* and views *(dṛṣṭi).*" Such a step outside language games is indeed itself a language game, but one that undermines the very rules of any language game.

31. Thus my reading differs from Dowd, *Prayer, Power, and the Problem of Suffering,* 75–78, where she sees the assertion that God can do the impossible as a claim grounded in the omnipotence of God. "It is clear that the evangelist regards the affirmation of divine omnipotence as essential to his view of prayer. To affirm God's power to act in the world in response to the prayers of the community, the author of Mark employs a formula with a rich heritage in the Greek religious and philosophical traditions: πάντα δυνατὰ παρὰ τῷ θεῷ."

32. This is a central theme of Pure Land Mahāyāna: that self-power *(jiriki)* cannot effect salvation, which comes only from entrusting or faith *(shinjin)* in the other-power *(tariki)* of the Awakened One of Infinite Light and Life (Amida). Thus Shinran can say, "Even a good person can attain birth in the Pure Land, how much more so the evil person. But the people of this world constantly say, even the evil person attains birth, how much more so the good person. Although this appears to be sound at first glance, it goes against

insight into the emptiness of all things, one immediately and spontaneously receives the kingdom. In verse 24 Jesus calls his disciples "children," for that is the key: not to achieve the kingdom, but to receive it directly as a free gift, for it is immediately available and at hand and not some distant goal reached only by incessant implementation of rules and commandments or by special insight into a communicable secret.[33] It's not there for the taking, but it is there for the receiving.

Note that Jesus speaks of the difficulty of "entering the kingdom of God" in the context of having just offered to a rich man he loved the possibility of following him and entering that kingdom by abandoning all self-support *(ātmya).* Entrance into the eschatological kingdom is a present possibility, awaiting no cosmic events and no coming of the son of man on the clouds of heaven. The Markan Jesus has just presented the story-level character, and thus the readers, with a moment of abandonment of all linear expectations, and that is the eschatological import of the kingdom.

Abandonment
10: 28–31

[28]*Peter took this up. "Look," he said to him, "we have left everything and followed you." [29]Jesus said, "In truth I tell you, there is no one who has left*

---

the intention of the Primal Vow of Other Power [to save all beings]. The reason is that since the person of self-power, being conscious of doing good, lacks the thought of entrusting himself completely to Other Power, he is not the focus of the Primal Vow of Amida. But when he turns over self-power and entrusts himself to Other Power, he attains birth in the land of True Fulfillment." (Unno, tr., *Tannishō: A Shin Buddhist Classic,* tr. 8).

33. Aitken, *The Gateless Barrier,* 231, presents a parallel about conversion and awakening that also deals with dividing people into good and evil and about secrets. Hui-neng, an illiterate lay-brother, had been given the Dharma robe, a sign that he was the Dharma heir of the Fifth Patriarch and told to leave the monastery at night to avoid the jealousy of the monks: "The Sixth Ancestor [Hui-neng] was pursued by Ming the head monk as far as Ta-yü Peak. The teacher, seeing Ming coming, laid the robe and bowl on a rock and said, 'This robe represents the Dharma (i.e., the true teaching). There should be no fighting over it. You may take it back with you.' Ming tried to lift it up, but it was as immovable as a mountain. Shivering and trembling, he said, 'I came for the Dharma, not for the robe. I beg you, lay brother, please open the Way for me.' The teacher said, 'Don't think good; don't think evil. At this very moment, what is the original face of Ming the head monk?' In that instant Ming had great satori (enlightenment). Sweat ran from his entire body. In tears he made his bows saying, 'Beside these secret words and secret meanings, is there anything of further significance?' The teacher said, 'What I have just conveyed to you is not secret. If you reflect on your own face, whatever is secret will be right there with you.' Ming said, 'Though I practiced at Huang-mei [temple] with the assembly, I could not truly realize my original face. Now, thanks to your pointed instruction, I am like someone who drinks water and knows personally whether it is cold or warm. Lay brother, you are now my teacher.' The teacher said, 'If you can say that, then let us both call Huang-mei our teacher. Maintain your realization carefully.' " So Crossan, *The Historical Jesus,* 349, speaks of the open secret of Jesus teaching: "It means on the lips of the historical Jesus, 'You all have ears, use them; what I say is as clear and obvious

house, brothers, sisters, mother, father, children or land for my sake and for the sake of this gospel [30]*who will not receive a hundred times as much, houses, brothers, sisters, mothers, children, and land—and persecution too—now in this present time and, in the world to come, eternal life.* [31]*Many who are first will be last, and the last, first."*

Peter, who wanted Jesus to avoid all suffering and all persecution, wants to know what all this talk of abandoning riches means to him. "What about us" (ἰδοὺ ἡμεῖς)? What are we going to get out of following you? Jesus does not answer directly and tell Peter what he will get. Rather, speaking to the reader, he says that anyone who has left his possessions, even the most prized possessions of family and home, will receive (λάβῃ) richly, both goods in this present life and eternal life in the world to come.[34] This seems a strange answer, for Jesus has just disabused the rich man of his assumption that living a good life results in permanent attainment of the good life.

But here Jesus demands a first stage of abandoning, of emptying all self-support, and then one will receive, when one has ceased to focus on receiving, a hundredfold. Such a superabundance points to an eschatological fulfillment.[35] Only if one abandons self for my sake and for the sake of the good

---

as I can make it; all you have to do is listen. It is not cryptic, hidden, mysterious; it is obvious, maybe that is its problem, it is too obvious. Listen!' " Such a cry for listening ill accords with the imparting of any viewpoint. What is clear and obvious is the presence of one's original face, the already available kingdom of nobodies. Yet, as with head monk Ming, even after realizing its presence, one still has to maintain that realizationn carefully. Awakening to the kingdom is not a fixed and unmoving status, but an ongoing process.

34. Kee, *Community of the New Age,* 110: "Yet their (i.e., the disciples') destiny is not limited to the joy in suffering that awaits them in the present age; rather they are called to look beyond νῦν ἐν τῷ καιρῷ τούτῳ (now in this age) to eternal life in the coming age (10:30). Eschatological existence for Mark involves acceptance of present opportunities and obligations towards the present as a transitional epoch." In a Mahāyāna reading all epochs are transitional *(anitya)* and the kingdom a process grounded in the breaking of linear time expectations.

35. Via, *The Ethics of Mark's Gospel,* 144–45: "An essential part of eschatological salvation is the restructuring of social relationships on a material basis. And in what kind of time? The community exists explicitly now in *this* time *(nun en tō kairō toutō),* the time of suffering and persecution (10: 30; 13: 9–13), which is clearly distinguished from the age to come, which is the time of eternal life. How, then, can the community be called new or eschatological? It can be, because for Mark, the coming kingdom has already dawned in this age and overlaps it. And the imagery of this passage shows that the community in particular is qualified by the eschatological newness. The disciple will receive brothers and sisters, houses and lands, now a hundredfold; and hundredfoldness is the mark of eschatological fulfillment. This derives from its employment in the parable of the sower (4: 8) and in the interpretation of that parable (4: 20)." Tolbert, *Sowing the Gospel,* would seem to agree, 161: "The kingdom of God is a mystery (τό μυστήριον, 4: 11), and as such, it cannot be defined or explained in propositional language. It can, however, be illustrated by comparison with actions more commonly experienced, like the growth of seeds in the earth." Again, 164: "Jesus' task is to sow the good news throughout the nations, and that good news is the announcement that the kingdom of God has already come (Mark 1: 15). Those who hear this gospel and believe it reveal themselves to be

news, will one then receive those rewards, i.e., only if one abandons the very hope of rewards and commits oneself to Jesus' gospel of eschatological awareness of the kingdom. Only if one is converted to the horizon of that kingdom.[36] There is not quid pro quo here, as if one earns the result by the performance of an act of renunciation. To abandon things in the context of self is merely to strengthen one's sense of self and will in no wise avoid self-clinging. That is why those who think themselves to be first, to be already disciples and followers of Christ, will be last. Peter and the disciples, as is shortly apparent in the request of James and John, do indeed think that they should be first, but have they abandoned everything for the sake of the gospel?[37] In Mark, what they finally abandon is Jesus himself.

The shape of that eschatological horizon is here fleshed out somewhat, for, although one abandons family and receives a new community, that community is without fathers, not included in the listing in verse 30. One leaves fathers, but does not receive them back! In 9: 35 the norm servanthood is recommended, and shortly in 10: 41–45 power relationships are rejected in the new Christian community. The role of fathers, conceived in terms of the paterfamilias, entailed the exercise of power, however wisely that may have been exercised. Yet here, no fathers are present in the eschatological community at all and the patriarchial assumptions of Jesus' day are negated.[38] In 3: 20–21 and 31–35 Jesus questioned the very identity of his family.[39] In the new community, one is still to honor parents, as shown in 7: 9–13 where Jesus rejects the dodge of declaring one's goods korban, and in 10: 19, where Jesus reiterates the commandment to honor one's father and mother.[40] Yet,

---

part of the kingdom and, further, are transformed by such a disclosure into producing abundant fruit."

36. Via, *The Ethics of Mark's Gospel*, 142: "The affirmation that there should be . . . a community [based on the renunciation of family and personal wealth (10: 28–29)] is the social horizon which makes conceivable the imperative to sell all one has and give to the poor (10: 17–22)."

37. Best, "Mark's Preservation of the Tradition," 122: "Had Peter in fact left house and family as this implies and as 1: 16–18 probably does also? In 1: 29 we find that Peter still maintains a home to which he goes back and 3: 9; 4: 1, 36 show that the disciples as a whole still have a boat at their disposal."

38. See Crossan, *The Historical Jesus*, "Against the Patriarchial Family," 299–302.

39. Via, *The Ethics of Mark's Gospel*, 149–50: "Stanley Hauerwas has observed that the family becomes demonic if it is the only thing there is to protect people from death. . . . We could say that an institution is demonic when it exerts destructive power over us because we have inflated it with more value than it can bear. Mark's understanding of the relationship between the new Christian community and the family speaks to this problem." In line with this, the social critique of Ivan Illich against the institutional usurpation and alienation of basic human functions—praying, learning, healing—is much to the point. I would argue that Illich's critique in such books, as *Celebrations of Awareness, Deschooling Society, Energy and Equity,* and *Medical Nemesis* presents a more incisive appraisal of social structures in the light of Mark's gospel than do those of Belo or Myers, for Illich rejects the construction of a rival ideology as the counterbalance to the oppressive ideological fetters of the present.

40. Kee, *Community of the New Age*, 89–90: ". . . in response to Peter's mingled boast

no patriarchal relationships will obtain in the new kingdom. "Patriarchal, autocratic authority has been removed."[41] However, in Mark, wives and husbands are not abandoned in 10: 29 and so they are not shared in 10: 30,[42] for their union is from the beginning, the time recapitulated by the arrival of the eschatological community. Their oneness signals the oneness of the community itself, just as the one loaf of bread in 8: 14 signals the oneness of Jew and gentile.

Jesus further qualifies his promise by adding that there will also be persecution (μετὰ διωγμῶν). This is not part of the traditional theory of exact retribution, such as forms the assumption behind the *Book of Job*. Rather, Jesus, familiar with the story of Job, makes no such promise. He states the opposite, that there will be such persecution. That seriously alters the context of the promise. No longer can one expect to abide at ease among one's new possessions and family circle, for persecution will accompany one's commitment to the gospel. The family and goods promised are not then personal possessions that support the security of selfhood, but the context of one's participation in the broad community of men and women.[43] The martyrs who went to their death for the sake of the gospel were rich in the goods of the kingdom, supported by the prayers of the community and bolstered by whatever concrete goods that community could provide. There is then no guarantee of just how one's life will turn out. No great expectation that one will turn out to be the hero of one's

---

and complaint about having left all to follow Jesus, he is promised that those who abandon family and property ('fields') for the sake of the ministry will in the present age receive a hundredfold new equivalents of these, 'with persecution,' and in the age to come eternal life. Obviously this cannot be intended literally, since marriage to more than one wife is expressly prohibited in the Markan form of the tradition (10:1–12) in the wider context of our present passage. The aim of the saying is equivalent compensation in the new community: the roles filled by literal wives and children and worldly possessions are served by new realities in the new covenant people." Yet wives are not in fact mentioned at all! The point seems to have more to do with breaking from one's family of origin, and recovering a new family with siblings, mothers, children, and lands, for that appears to be the pattern set in the depiction of the Markan Jesus' relationship with his original family in Nazareth.

41. Via, *The Ethics of Mark's Gospel*, 146. "According to James M. Robinson [in *The Problem of History in Mark*, 81], the omission of the father in 10: 30 is intentional, as it is in 3: 31–32, 33–35; and 6: 3, because for Mark, God is the father of Jesus absolutely (8: 38; 14: 36); he is also the father of the disciples (11: 25). The gap in the spiritual family is filled by God. He is the only father in the Christian situation."

42. Via, *The Ethics of Mark's Gospel*, 151–52. Note that Luke 14: 26 both strengthens the rejection of family and includes wives: "Anyone who comes to me without hating father, mother, wife, children, brothers, sisters, yes and his own life too, cannot be my disciple." Again Luke 18: 29 has: "In truth, I tell you, there is no one who has left house, wife, brothers, parents, or children for the sake of the kingdom of God who will not receive many times as much in this present age and, in the world to come, eternal life."

43. Kelber, *The Kingdom in Mark*, 90: "As the arrival of the Kingdom was tantamount to the fulfillment of the *kairos* (1: 15), so is the replacement for the loss of the old way of life granted *nyn en tō kairō toutō* (10: 30a). The fact that this new fellowship will have to exist *meta diōgmōn* (10: 30a) is in keeping with Mark's theology of the hidden kingdom."

life. Yet, even if one loses one's life for the gospel, both present eschatological fullness and eternal life in the world to come remain.

A Third Prediction about Suffering
10: 32–34

³²They were on the road, going up to Jerusalem; Jesus was walking on ahead of them; they were in a daze, and those who followed were apprehensive. Once more taking the twelve aside he began to tell them what was going to happen to him: ³³"Now we are going up to Jerusalem, and the Son of man is about to be handed over to the chief priests and scribes. They will condemn him to death and will hand him over to the gentiles, ³⁴who will mock him and spit at him and scourge him and put him to death; and after three days he will rise again."

Jesus is leading the way (προάγων) now, just as he will lead the way (16: 7, προάγει) to Galilee after his resurrection. At that time the women are filled with fear (16: 8, ἐφοβοῦντο) and do not relay the message to his disciples to follow him to Galilee. Here too his followers are dazed (ἐθαμ- βοῦτο) and fearful or apprehensive (ἐφοβοῦντο) about what they have just heard: their hopes for the good life have been seriously undermined.[44] They are perhaps unwilling to remonstrate again with Jesus, for Peter has been called a satan for doing that. Yet, they still cling to the imagined pattern of consciousness, in which good works lead to salvation and giving up one thing issues in the possession of another, better thing. They do not get the point, and are indeed afraid of getting the point: that there is no self to cling to, no self to protect. The kingdom is not the good life. Jesus, going up to Jerusalem, does not mince words. He again takes the twelve apart and tells them about suffering and death. Mark and his readers, of course, already know the final outcome of Jesus' life. Mark is not trying to depict Jesus' fortune-telling ability. It was not then, nor perhaps now, unusual for prophets to be persecuted and killed. Mark employs Jesus' prediction of suffering and death to heighten the disciples' dilemma of just how that could constitute

---

44. Malbon, *Narrative Space*, 70: "These concerns [about discipleship] are made con- crete 'on the road, going up to Jerusalem' (10: 32a). Jesus leads the way (*proagein*, 10: 32b) and following is shown to entail amazement and fear, for the way leads to suffering and death for the Son of man." Kelber, *The Kingdom in Mark*, 71: "Jesus leads the way (10: 32b: *kai ēn proagōn autous*) and the disciples are to follow him (10: 32d: *hoi de akolouthountes*). Jesus not merely teaches the way, but he literally shows the way. If they follow after Jesus' *proagōn,* they will not only learn their leader's identity, but in the process find themselves and their own calling." Via, *The Ethics of Mark's Gospel*, 156, explains that the central theme of 10: 32–52 is following the Jesus path, for that frames the pericopes in 10: 32 and 10: 52: "This section discloses what is really entailed in following and thereby deepens, by contrast, the falsity of Peter's claim that the disciples have given up all and followed."

their course, their reward. Suffering is a mark of life itself, and especially of life committed to the gospel, for that commitment always challenges the assumptions of the unconverted power brokers of any society. Jesus offers no escape from the humanness of our being human. Only resurrection.

Another Request for Self-Validation
10: 35–40

[35]James and John, the sons of Zebedee, approached him. "Master," they said to him, "we want you to do us a favor." [36]He said to them, "What is it you want me to do for you?" [37]They said to him, "Allow us to sit one at your right hand and the other at your left in your glory." [38]But Jesus said to them, "You do not know what you are asking. Can you drink the cup that I shall drink, or be baptized with the baptism with which I shall be baptized?" [39]They replied, "We can." Jesus said to them, "The cup that I shall drink you shall drink, and with the baptism with which I shall be baptized you shall be baptized, [40]but as for the seats at my right hand or my left, these are not mine to grant; they belong to those to whom they have been allotted."

Each time Jesus tries to break through the *ātman* consciousness of his disciples, they become fearful and retrench themselves in their imagined truths, here asking for assurances that when Jesus achieves his empirical victory they will be his principal officials, sharing in his power. Mark has them make this request immediately after Jesus' prediction of his sufferings. "With methodical precision the evangelist has each passion-resurrection prediction evolve into a clear case of discipleship misconception."[45] He has not been talking about his attainment of power and glory, but about being handed over and killed by the gentiles. And so he asks them if they can share in those sufferings and be initiated into life through suffering and dying.[46] They say, "Sure, we can," and Jesus allows that they indeed will, for that is simply to be human.[47]

---

45. Kelber, *Mark's Story of Jesus,* 52. Again 53: "Whenever the disciples, the Twelve, or members of the triumvirate make an appearance in the midsection of the Gospel, they appear almost always without exception either in overt or in covert conflict with Jesus."
46. Delling, "βάπτισμα βαπτισθῆναι," explains that this term, "the baptism with which I am to be baptized," is an Old Testament term, indicating Yahweh's wrath, not restricted solely to Jesus' sufferings and death.
47. Kolenkow, "Beyond Miracles," 163: "Mark portrays the disciples as seeking a power in glory like Jesus'. Mark shows James and John as assuming that Jesus will have endtime power and seeking the same for themselves. Thus, they all desire endtime power." Their willingness to accept suffering is thus deluded, for it is oriented toward a glorious future of self-empowerment over others in a reified vision of the eschatological kingdom. They do indeed accept the need for suffering, as Kolenkow, 161, explains: "The problem, however, with saying that the disciples-opponents do not accept suffering [as do Kelber and Weeden] is that Mark presents the disciples as accepting a demand for suffering. The second of the disciples seeking-for-power stories (10:35ff) hinges on the issue of suffering

No promises are made about future renown or glory.[48]

The very fact that we are born entails suffering, growing old, sick, or fragile. The mental suffering of meaninglessness, as well as the physical suffering of illness. That is why Jesus tells his disciples that they shall drink the cup of suffering.[49] Yet that does not guarantee any future positioning. Where we wind up depends on the complex course of human action, on all the interweaving lines of individual actions. This the Buddhists call *karma,* human action, the polymorphous interconnections of which occur in such

---

as the basis for power. James and John ask to sit beside Jesus in his glory. Jesus effectively asks whether they are able to suffer as he does. They say yes. Thus Mark presents the disciples as acknowledging the necessity of suffering as prerequisite for power. Mark portrays Peter's (and others') willingness to die (14:31)." Indeed, James and John do say they are able to suffer, yet I do not think that that implies they are willing to abandon their very selves to the dependently co-arisen course of events that lies in store for Jesus (and for them). Their version of suffering is that of accepting trials and pains before eventual triumph, the hero who has to pass through sufferings to attain the final victory. It is that victory that Jesus refuses to promise them, for he is no hero and when the opportunity presents itself for them to share in Jesus' sufferings, they flee—that was not what they meant! Again, Kolenkow, 163, sees Mark as countering the view that "would argue that reward will follow the suffering undergone on earth and that this reward will be through the witness of the Son of Man. This is what Mark disagrees with." No eschatological victory within the context of selfhood!

48. Tolbert, *Sowing the Gospel,* 227–28: "Understanding the disciples' desire for glory and renown as a foil to Jesus' actions suggests a different construction [from that of Wrede's] for secrecy: Jesus' commands for silence and his attempts to stay hidden define his steadfast rejection of personal renown and glory. . . . Hence the author's intention in fashioning the secrecy passages is not to propose that Jesus remained unknown and did not attract crowds but rather to verify that Jesus did not seek for himself renown or glory, although the spread of his fame and the growth of multitudes around him was inescapable, given who he was and what he did." Secrecy thus serves to stress Jesus' rejection of the imagined pattern in which he was understood and to undermine both the highfalutin titles and expectancies projected upon him. This the disciples never grasp, for, as Tolbert says, 229: "Their path to eternal life in the kingdom has gone astray through their desire for self-aggrandizement."

49. Against Fowler, *Let the Reader Understand,* 139.26: "I do not think that Jesus 'predicts' a postresurrection meeting with his disciples (my reading of 14:28 and 16:7). But I am unsure how to read 10:39. If this is part of Mark's plot of contingency, then by story's end James and John have failed to live up to the ideal of dying for one's commitments, making this one prediction by Jesus that is not fulfilled in the story, because of human obtuseness. If, however, this is part of Mark's plot of predestination, then Jesus' prediction must yet come to pass beyond the bounds of the narrated story. In other words, Jesus' predictions are usually in the service of the plot of predestination, but 10:39 may instead be part of the plot of contingency, and thus may not be destined for fulfillment." Rather I read the necessity for suffering as always dependently co-arisen, arising from the course of human karmic actions. That James and John will drink the cup of suffering is their lot simply as humans. The Western theological arguments over freedom versus predestination never occurred in Buddhist doctrinal development, for it was taught from the very beginning that humans are free within the constraints of karmic conditioning to choose the path of practice that leads to awakening. Thus the necessity of suffering issues not from a divine will but from the accumulated evil actions that humans do: all is radical contingency.

complexity that they cannot be plotted in advance. Rather, collectively we reap the results of our individual actions. Jesus cannot predetermine where one is to wind up, for positions, even in the kingdom, belong to those to whom they have been allotted, or for whom they have been prepared (οἷς ἡτοίμασται). In fact, those who do attain to those positions on Jesus' right and left are the two bandits in 15: 27, while James and John run away.

Lorditis
10: 41–45

[41] *When the other ten heard this they began to feel indignant with James and John,* [42] *so Jesus called them to him and said to them, "You know that among the gentiles those they call their rulers lord it over them, and their great men make their authority felt.* [43] *Among you this is not to happen. No; anyone who wants to become great among you must be your servant,* [44] *and anyone who wants to be first among you must be slave to all.* [45] *For the Son of man himself did not come to be served but to serve, and to give his life as a ransom for many."*

The Yogācāra philosophers talk of the world as conscious construction only (*vijñapti-mātratā*), by which they mean that we live within a world constructed through our own fabrication.[50] They are not (usually) suggesting a form of epistemological idealism, wherein no reality exists apart from inner thought, for they reject the absolute status of both outer reality and inner reality: all is dependently co-arisen and without any firm hold on being. This is why it is silly to pretend that one controls one's existence, to lord it over others, i.e. to dominate (κατακυριεύουσιν) others. Manipulative behavior is based on primal ignorance (*avidyā*), ignorance of the human condition that all is transient and nothing stable enough to rely on. So Jesus calls the powerful "those they call their rulers," i.e., those who appear or seem to rule (οἱ δοκοῦντες ἄρχειν), not to suggest any lack of worldly power, but to signify the deluded nature of the entire power enterprise of human manipulation and dominance.

The practice Jesus recommends is counter to such power playing, such lording it over others.[51] In 9: 35 James and John are preoccupied with being great, thereby engendering the anger of the other ten disciples. Here Jesus rejects the "self-deception in the ten's implied moral claim."[52] Being the

50. A thesis parallel to that of Peter Berger, *The Sacred Canopy*.

51. Cranfield, *St. Mark*, 341: "κατακυριεύουσιν. In the LXX the verb is nearly always used of the rule of an alien. The κατα- gives it the sense of using lordship over people to their disadvantage and to one's own advantage."

52. Via, *The Ethics of Mark's Gospel*, 158. Again, 70–71: "The teacher leads into emptiness, into the death or forgetfulness of the ego's ideas and values, so that the depth of truth (fullness) might become manifest. One need not strain to find echoes of this in Mark. Jesus eats with sinners and is known for his feasting rather than fasting (2: 15–17,

servant to others precludes lording it over them. Being a slave counters any sense of being important at all.[53] Mark has Jesus use the term, "son of man," for Jesus does not claim a power title over humans. In this context "son of man" has little futuristic import, for he has come to serve concrete people in the world. Its eschatological significance has been collapsed into engagement in the service of others, just as emptiness becomes embodied only in the realm of dependently co-arisen bodhisattva reengagement. For the Markan Jesus, the son of man is simply a man, come not to win a prime position for self, but to serve all and even to abandon all the structures of self, to die so that others might live. And that is why Jesus is the eschatological bearer of the kingdom.

What on earth does that mean? How does Jesus' death cause others to live? Jewish martyrs are often described as dying for the people. Judas Maccabeus and his brothers were killed by Antiochus Epiphanes one after the other. In *2 Maccabees* 7: 37–38, the last of the seven brothers died after the following confession: "I too, like my brothers, surrender my body and life for the laws of my ancestors, calling on God to show his kindness to our nation and that soon, and by trials and afflictions to bring you to confess that he alone is God, so that with my brothers and myself there may be an end to the wrath of the Almighty, rightly let loose on our whole nation." Here the scripture sees the trials and persecution of the Hellenistic rulers as trials derived from God, who in his wrath is punishing Israel for its unending infidelities. This indeed is a frequent pattern of ancient and modern thinking: ascribing the evil we experience not to our own delusion or attachment to idols, but to God who punishes that delusion and idolatry. Thus, one dies to assuage God's wrath.

But Mark makes no such claim. He merely has Jesus say that he will suffer and then give his life as a ransom for many, literally, as a ransom in place of, in behalf of many (λύτρον ἀντὶ πολλῶν). This verse about Jesus giving

---

18–19). He also teaches the necessity of dying (8: 34–37). The archetypal idea of fullness through emptiness comes to expression in Mark in the principle that one can find life only by passing through death. Jesus teaches this principle to his disciples (8: 34–37). But he does not just teach it; he enacts it for them (8: 31; 9: 31; 10: 33-34; 45; 14: 24). And this pattern of existence also takes on the specific content of an ethical demand (10: 42–44)." The only Mahāyāna note would be to stress that the necessity of dying is not a supernaturally empirical enigma, but the common, although denied, lot of all human beings.

53. Kolenkow, *Beyond Miracles,* understands the son of man in 33 and 45 as the eschatological figure, and then demythologizes such eschatology, see 164: "Mark 10: 44 [about being first by being a slave to others] is one more in the group of presentations where Mark uses eschatology for ethics. Mark has been shown to take the accepted motifs of following Jesus in suffering and being rewarded by the Son of Man in the endtime (eschatological-martyr motifs) and turn these motifs into the idea of a suffering-dying Son of Man idea which is useful in the Markan ethics of service. It will also be argued below that the presentation of the future given in 13 actually also carries the paraenetic intent of showing the claiming of earthly power as an evil. Thus eschatology is a point which Mark relies on himself and his audience having in common. It, as miracles and suffering, is not the major point of Mark's argument, but is one more point used by Mark for the purpose of paraenesis."

his life as a ransom "is the clearest such statement [about the meaning of Jesus' death] in Mark, but that does not imply that it is actually clear! This saying is even more of a mystery than the predictions of the passion of the Son of Man."[54]

To whom does Jesus pay such a ransom? Who has captured humanity so that it need be ransomed? In Mark there is no suggestion that humanity is under the control of Satan, as Anselm seems to have thought. Jesus' death is not a sacrifice demanded directly by God. Rather, "Jesus' suffering and death are the inescapable results of challenging the authority of the present tenants. . . . Jesus' crucifixion is the act that will finally prompt the coming of the kingdom in all its glory and wrath. [And the ransom is] "the price required to sow the word abroad, to awaken the good earth into abundant fruitfulness."[55] That prompting of the kingdom issues from Jesus' abandonment of any divine plan to wrest an empirical victory over his enemies. If the characters in Mark's gospel had awakened, then perhaps there would have been no necessity for Jesus' dying. If the world was not in the grasp of primal ignorance (*avidyā*), sufferings would not be engendered. Yet, selfhood and its karmic expressions render one hard of heart, in need of the transformation of child-like wisdom and compassion. Indeed, "the cross saves by giving insight. But obviously this is not a matter of information. . . . Therefore a change of understanding is a change in the *person*."[56] The eschatological kingdom is constituted by such transformed, awakened persons. Mark emphasizes the disciples' attachment to their own self-glory as he does, for that apparently reflected his own experience of Christian community, bound by its imagined patterns of consciousness, caught in the net of its own false fabrications, so that one mistakes power for service, manipulation for living. The ransom is paid not to some power lord; they are after all only so-called, apparent lords. Rather, Jesus' dying is meant to finally break through that tenacious self-attachment which renders the disciples incapable of understanding Jesus' message of conversion, of the kingdom at hand.[57] It is a price paid

---

54. Collins, *The Beginning of the Gospel*, 68.

55. Tolbert, *Sowing the Gospel*, 262. See also Hamerton-Kelly, *The Gospel and the Sacred*, 71–72 for a parallel interpretation based on the Girardian theory of a generative mimetic scapegoating mechanism, according to which Jesus does not die as a sacrifice to a vengeful God, but as a victim of mimetic rivalry in order to expose the underlying structures whereby competition issues in the violence of scapegoating.

56. Via, *The Ethics of Mark's Gospel*, 142.

57. The ransom phrase perhaps alludes to the suffering servant of *Isaiah* 53: 11–12: "After the ordeal he has endured, he will see the light and be content. By his knowledge, the upright one, my servant will justify many by taking their guilt on himself. Hence I shall give him a portion with the many, and he will share the booty with the mighty, for having exposed himself to death and for being counted as one of the rebellious, whereas he was bearing the sin of many and interceding for the rebellious." Isaiah is thus used to support the notion that Jesus' death was an atonement for sins of others. Yet Kee, *The Community of the New Age*, 47–48, warns: "In spite of efforts to read Isa. 53 into Mark, especially at 10:45, the controlling factors in Mark's portrayal of the events leading to Jesus' death and his portrayal of the struggle within himself reflected in the scenes in Gethsemane and on the cross is not a theory or even an image of atonement, but the

to selfhood, so that, shocked by the deconstruction of all imagined hope, one might break through and be freed from bondage.

But why the image of a ransom in the first place? In context, the term indicates various transactions, all of which connote some kind of return to a pristine, prior condition.[58] The ransom of Jesus' death ushers in a now present eschatological kingdom that is itself a recovery of the pristine condition that obtained "from the beginning." It is a return not merely to an awareness of the emptiness before creation, but also to the originally present realm of dependent co-arising, in which compassionate action, after the pattern of Jesus' miracles and exorcisms, abound. In the Zen phrase, it is the attainment of one's original face, one's true humanness. Ransomed means recovery of our pristine human condition.

All three of Jesus' predictions of his passion are followed by a discourse on being a disciple or servant. Indeed, his passion occurs from his commitment to such service, from his reengagement in the conventional world of men and women. By contrast, Buddhist monks sometimes tended to remain apart, secure in their Indian monasteries and focused on solitary meditation practices. I think it true that often they did not actively engage in the world. For example, Buddhist rules forbid injury to any living thing. But, until modern ecological awareness made its impact, that never became much of an active attempt in Buddhist countries to protect animals from suffering.[59] Yet Mahā-

suffering of Jesus is portrayed by Mark, therefore, in keeping with the biblical and extrabiblical tradition of the faithful messenger of God." Again on 135: "Scholarly attempts to demonstrate that Jesus' sense of mission combined with messiahship a role as the suffering servant of Isa. 53 fail to carry persuasion, both because of a lack of New Testament exegetical evidence in support of it and because of the absence for this synthesis in pre-Christian Jewish interpretation of Isa 53 or of other messianic titles. Both the Lord's supper tradition in Mark (14:24) and 10:45 manifest the same concern to interpret the death of Jesus in terms of Isa 53, but there is here no developed doctrine of atonement; rather, the main intent is to demonstrate that the death of Jesus was in accord with the scriptures. Both 10:45 and 9:12 are presented by Mark in contexts in which the problem is the necessity for Jesus to suffer." The classical statements of this atonement theology are found in Otto, *The Kingdom of God and the Son of Man;* Cullmann, *Christology of the New Testament;* and Fuller, *Mission and Achievement of Jesus,* although Fuller has abandoned this position in *Foundations of New Testament Christology.*

58. Collins, *The Beginning of the Gospel,* 69, gives various examples: freedom for slaves (*Leviticus* 25: 51–52), money for war prisoners (*Isaiah* 45: 13), compensation for damages (*Exodus* 21: 28–32; *Numbers* 35: 31–32; *Proverbs* 6: 35), and the buying back of ancestral lands (*Leviticus* 25: 24–28).

59. See Schmithausen, *Buddhism and Nature,* 12: "It has become fashionable to reject the view that Buddhism is escapist. This may be fully justified in the case of Mahāyāna, or village Buddhism, or socially involved currents in modern Buddhism. But it is highly problematic to deny the existence and even predominance of detachment from the world in early monastic Buddhism. There can hardly be any doubt that in the canonical texts of Early Buddhism all mundane existence is regarded as unsatisfactory, either because suffering prevails or because, even when this is not the case, existence is inevitably impermanent. Therefore, the only goal ultimately worth striving for is Nirvāṇa, which, however one may have to understand it, was at any rate conceived of as entirely beyond mundane existence, and hence beyond death and impermanence." Mahāyāna emptied even

yāna thought countered that aloofness by demanding a reengagement in the world, intelligently to practice the deeds of compassion, to be of use to others. Such practice is the only true sign of bodhisattva activity. So here, Mark associates suffering not with some preordained plan, but with the committed practice of servanthood and discipleship.[60]

Who's Blind?
10: 46–52

[46]*They reached Jericho; and as he left Jericho with his disciples and a large crowd, Bartimaeus—that is, the son of Timaeus—a blind beggar, was sitting at the side of the road.* [47]*When he heard that it was Jesus of Nazareth, he began to shout and to cry out, "Son of David, Jesus, have pity on me."* [48]*And many of them scolded him and told him to keep quiet, but he only shouted all the louder, "Son of David, have pity on me."* [49]*Jesus stopped and said, "Call him here." So they called the blind man over. "Courage," they said, "get up; he is calling you."* [50]*So throwing off his cloak, he jumped up and went to Jesus.* [51]*Then Jesus spoke, "What do you want me to do for you?" The blind man said to him, "Rabbuni, let me see again."* [52]*Jesus said to him, "Go; your faith has saved you." And at once his sight returned and he followed him along the road.*

In 8: 22–26 Jesus healed a blind man, right after his disciples had failed to understand about the loaves. So here another blind man is sighted, right after the disciples have again failed to understand that being first means to be slave to all. Each restoration of sight is followed by an important turning point in the narrative: in 8:27, on the way to Caesarea Philippi, the issue of Jesus' identity as messiah is broached, while immediately after healing blind Bartimaeus, Jesus draws near to Jerusalem.[61] It is as if Mark offers the reader a restoration of the insight the disciples lack, so as to be ready for what follows.

---

that notion of nirvāna, and today modern Mahāyāna thinkers like Schmithausen are at work developing a Buddhist environmental ethics.

60. Malbon, *Mark and Method,* 34: "After each misunderstanding, Jesus renews his teaching on this topic [of suffering] (8: 34–35; 9: 35–37, 39–50; 10: 42–45). Of course, each time Jesus teaches the disciples, the implied author teaches the implied reader. Repetition adds clarity and force." The readers are typed in the story by Jesus' followers, the disciples, and then brought to extra-textual crises through the ironic, unpleasant awareness that they too, despite Jesus' reiterated teaching, are similarly enmeshed in misunderstanding and hardness of heart, in virtue of which they allow divorce and reject child-like receptivity.

61. See Kee, *Community of the New Age,* 57. Also Mack, *A Myth of Innocence,* 233: "This story . . . clearly forms a doublet with the healing of the blind man at the beginning of the journey to Jerusalem. Many scholars have remarked on this, the consensus being that the two stories were intended to bracket the section on the way to Jerusalem with sight miracles to contrast the blindness of the disciples. The consensus is undoubtedly correct, for the conclusion of the story has it that 'he received his sight and followed him

This story is linked to the earlier story of the children in that the recipient of Jesus' attention is first hindered from coming to him. When, in 10: 14 the children come to Jesus, the disciples "turned them away," that is, they scold them (ἐπετίμησαν αὐτοῖς). Here the crowd tries to do the same, for they scold the blind man (ἐπετίμων αὐτῷ) to hush him, limiting his access to Jesus, just as the disciples had tried to limit the children's access. Mark has structured his narrative so as to suggest that the blind man is reprimanded by the exclusive consciousness of the discriminative mind of the crowd, just as the children were by the disciples.

This is also linked to the request of James and John. When the blind man does come before Jesus, Jesus asks him "What do you want me to do for you?" (τί σοι θέλεις ποιήσω;), the same phrase he uses when he asks James and John what favor they want from him (τί θέλετε ποιῆσαί με ἡμῖν;) in verse 10: 36. Mark contrasts the request of the blind man for healing with the request of James and John for power. Thinking themselves whole, his disciples never think to ask for healing.

Furthermore, the man's sight is restored not because of something Jesus does, but "his faith has saved him" (ἡ πίστις σου σέσωκέν σε), just as Jesus says faith has saved the woman with the hemorrhage in 5: 34 (ἡ πίστις σου σέσωκέν σε). Those who have faith and are not concerned with power positioning are free from the imaginative pattern (*parikalpita-lakṣaṇa*) and thus can regain their original sight. In Mahāyāna terms, this is the recovery and resurrection of dependently co-arisen life and understanding (*paratantra-lakṣaṇa*) from its bondage to false imaginings. The man is told to get up, to arise (ἔγειρε), and so he throws off his cloak, his accustomed protective covering, to regain what was originally his: the ability to see clearly. And that is the point: the ability to regain the humanness that we are born with, but which has been covered over by the manipulative pattern of trying to be first, trying to always be the winner. That way lies only illusion, and finally failure, as the disciples experience when they flee from the death of Jesus.

The blind man calls Jesus Son of David, a title that is called into question in 12: 35–37.[62] The crowd tries to silence him from so crying out, recalling Jesus' desire not to be identified, either by demons or by those he has healed. Again Mark evinces a vagueness about identifying titles, a lack of concern with proper definitions and status. Rather he portrays Jesus as a model of eschatological service, for he answers the blind man's call for mercy and

---

on the way' (Mark 10: 52), as if to remind the reader that the discipleship theme of 'following' should not be forgotten just because the disciples were doing such a poor job of it."

62. Against Meier, *A Marginal Jew*, 240: "Mark certainly takes the cry of Bartimaeus in 10: 47 ('Son of David, Jesus, have mercy on me') in a positive sense, and so he probably does not mean 12: 35–37 . . . to be a rejection of Jesus' Davidic sonship, but rather simply an indication that it is of less importance than Jesus' status as Lord and Son of God." It seems to me that Mark's point is not to cling to any title or identity for Jesus, and titles are accepted only after being emptied of their accustomed content.

compassion (ἐλέησόν με) with the last recorded healing miracle, with the result that thereafter the newly sighted man follows Jesus along the path (καὶ ἠκολούθει αὐτῷ ἐν τῇ ὁδῷ) of compassionate practice. "Although Jesus delivers the normal command for the healed, 'Go,' the narrative reports that Bartimaeus 'followed him along the way' (ἐν τῇ ὁδῷ) (10: 52). Following Jesus on the way, though often with fear rather than faith, has been the function of the disciples (e.g., 1: 18, 20; 2: 14; 6: 1; 10: 28, 32)."[63]

Although Jesus has refused the requests of his own disciples to be placed in privileged positions, he grants the request of a perfect stranger, who has his sight restored and follows him rejoicing. The disciples, struggling with their tenacious sense of self-value, always seem to ask things that elicit Jesus' rebuke or refusal. You'd think that they would get the point. Mark's rhetorical discourse indeed revolves around the disciples and discipleship.

And the reader cannot help but distance herself from the egoistical disciples. "Thus, when at the end of this section, blind Bartimaeus receives his sight (10:46–52), the reader has a new figure with whom to identify. It has always been puzzling that this unit would close with a miracle clearly symbolizing the achievement of insight, since the disciples appear as blind as ever. Yet if the text has 'worked,' the disciples and the reader are no longer one. The disciples continue their blind way through the narrative, but the newly enlightened reader can now identify with the newly sighted Bartimaeus and has, like him, the potential of following Jesus."[64] But I wonder about this identification. Mark's rhetoric has a double whammy effect, I think. Indeed, "as the disciples' lack of understanding intensifies, each repetition of Jesus' passion prediction being followed by a clear indication of the disciples' inability to comprehend, light finally begins to dawn for the reader. Acquiring the understanding so elusive to the disciples, he or she finally begins to draw away from them."[65] But just how enlightened or how understanding is the reader? Mark's rhetoric has maneuvered her away from the disciples, but is a literary construct really the vehicle for enlightenment? Now sighted Bartimaeus, ignoring Jesus' advice to go home (52, ὕπαγε), does follow him. Yet he hardly serves as a new story character to identify with, for in fact he, like all the others who have been made whole by their faith (ἡ πίστις σου σέσωκέν σε), now disappears from the narrative altogether. Only the unenlightened need to follow Jesus through the rest of the story; the enlightened go home to the tasks of announcing the good news, as the healed Gerasene has done, vanishing from the story altogether. The reader, willy-

---

63. Tolbert, *Sowing the Gospel,* 190. Note that faith cannot relate to doctrinal assent, for no teaching has been given to Bartimaeus, and he even refers to Jesus as the son of David, a title Jesus himself will apparently call into question in 12: 35–37. See Via, *The Ethics of Mark's Gospel,* 162. Rather, as Via says on 60: it is "this seeking of Jesus [that] is interpreted as faith (5: 34; 10: 47), a faith to which Jesus' story has brought [the woman with the haemorrhage and the blind Bartimaeus]."

64. Bassler, "Parable of the Loaves," 167.

65. Moore, *Literary Criticism and the Gospels,* 82.

nilly, must follow Jesus through the remaining narrative in the company of the unenlightened disciples. It is a forced, perhaps distasteful association, but there is no other option. Perhaps the reader is not yet enlightened? Has she, like the disciples, failed to attain insight into the emptiness of self-status, or not yet experienced the healing of the blinding nighttime experience of Jesus' wilderness prayer contact with Abba? Mark's reader is never coddled along as "dear reader." She is thrown off balance and, as in a bad movie, coerced to identify with unsavory characters. Until and unless she can identify with Jesus and, forgetting self, be servant to all.

11

Prayer and Traditions

Entry into Jerusalem
11: 1–11

¹When they were approaching Jerusalem, at Bethphage and Bethany, close by the Mount of Olives, he sent two of his disciples ²and said to them, "Go to the village facing you, and as you enter it you will at once find a tethered colt that no one has yet ridden. Untie it and bring it here. ³If anyone says to you, 'What are you doing?' say, 'The Master needs it and will send it back here at once.'" ⁴They went off and found a colt tethered near a door in the open street. As they untied it, ⁵some men standing there said, "What are you doing, untying that colt?" ⁶They gave the answer Jesus had told them, and the men let them go. ⁷Then they took the colt to Jesus and threw their cloaks on its back, and he mounted it. ⁸Many people spread their cloaks on the road, and others greenery which they had cut in the fields. ⁹And those who went in front and those who followed were all shouting, "Hosanna! Blessed is he who comes in the name of the Lord! ¹⁰Blessed is the coming kingdom of our father David! Hosanna in the highest heavens!" ¹¹He entered Jerusalem and went into the Temple, and when he had looked around at everything,[1] as it was late by now, he went out to Bethany with the Twelve.

Jesus, who began by proclaiming that the kingdom has arrived (ἤγγικεν ἡ βασιλεία τοῦ θεοῦ, 1: 15) is now drawing near to Jerusalem (ἐγγίζουσιν εἰς Ἱεροσόλυμα), the seat of religious authority for all the Jews, to experience the eschatological hour of his suffering, when the kingdom is fully manifested.[2] The geographical sites are somewhat muddled,[3] but Jesus is pictured

---

1. Following the RSV translation.
2. Tolbert, *Sowing the Gospel,* 118, notes that 11: 1—ἐγγίζουσιν εἰς Ἱεροσόλυμα εἰς . . . βηθανίαν and 11: 11—εἰς Ἱεροσόλυμα . . . εἰς βηθανίαν constitute an inclusion that aims at reinterpreting the theme of the apocalyptic messiah. It also seems to double back to the initial proclamation of the arrival of the eschatological kingdom in 1: 15, for that is the context in which all apocalyptic themes in Mark are to be read.
3. Malbon, *Narrative Space,* 31: "The order in which the names of the outlying villages

a little outside the city, gazing at it in the distance, in sight of the garden where his passion will begin.

The focus of the entire section from 11: 1–13: 37 is on "Jesus' dealings with the temple" and its religious practice.[4] The present passage, which announces the predominant activity of Jesus in Jerusalem,[5] is replete with theological symbols from the Hebrew scriptures. The colt on which Jesus rides alludes to a passage from *Zechariah* (9: 9–10). There, the prophet presents an oracle of entry into the new promised land and describes the entry of the messiah as follows: "Rejoice heart and soul, daughter of Zion! Shout with gladness, daughter of Jerusalem! See now, your king comes to you; he is victorious, he is triumphant, humble and riding on a donkey, on a colt, the foal of a donkey. He will banish chariots from Ephraim and horses from Jerusalem; the bow of war will be banished. He will proclaim peace for the nations. His empire will stretch from sea to sea, from the River to the ends of the earth."

Zechariah has here recast the traditional images of victorious kings, resplendent with war horses and chariots. *Jeremiah* (17: 24–27) had described an entry into Jerusalem as follows: "But if you listen carefully to me, Yahweh declares, and bring no burden in through the gates of this city on the Sabbath day, if you keep the Sabbath holy and do no work on that day, then, through the gates of this city, kings and princes occupying the throne of David will continue to make their entry, riding in chariots and on horseback, they, their chief men, the people of Judah and all the inhabitants of Jerusalem, from the territory of Benjamin, from the lowlands, from the highlands, from the Negeb, to offer burnt offerings and sacrifice, and cereal offerings and incense, to offer thanksgiving in the Temple of Yahweh. But if you do not listen to me to keep the Sabbath day holy, and to refrain from entering the gates of Jerusalem with burdens on the Sabbath day, then I shall set fire to its gates; fire will devour the palaces of Jerusalem and not be quenched."[6]

---

are mentioned is somewhat peculiar since Bethphage is closer to Jerusalem than Bethany." Perhaps there is a play on words, for Bauer, *A Greek-English Lexicon,* 140, explains Bethphage as "house of unripe figs," and Jesus will shortly curse an unripe fig tree.

4. Kelber, *Mark's Story of Jesus,* 57. Dewey, *Markan Public Debate,* 152–53, explains that chapters 11 and 12 "contain the second major block of public debate material in the gospel." In 11: 11 Jesus leaves the temple on the first day, while in 13: 1 Jesus leaves for the last time. These parameters form "the narrative frame for Jesus' public ministry in the temple of days two and three." Also Hamerton-Kelly, *The Gospel and the Sacred,* 17: "The statement, 'Into Jerusalem into Bethphage' (11:1), links the city and the temple because, according to the Talmud, Bethphage was the outermost limit of the sacred precinct. The consecration of showbread there was valid, up to but not beyond Bethphage. The closing statement, 'And he went into Jerusalem into the temple' (11:11), is parallel to 11:1, and summarizes the aim of locating Jesus within sacred space."

5. Tolbert, *Sowing the Gospel,* 114.

6. Similarly *Jeremiah* 22: 4–5 repeats the refrain: "For if you are scrupulous in obeying this command [to act uprightly and justly], then kings occupying the throne of David will continue to make their entry through the gates of this palace riding in chariots or on horseback, they, their officials and their people. But if you do not listen to these words, then I swear by myself, Yahweh declares, this place shall become a ruin!"

In *Zechariah* the king is humble, riding only on the traditional mount of princes, a colt, while *Jeremiah* presents a glorious entry of the rulers of Jerusalem. Mark adopts *Zechariah's* imagery to depict Jesus' entry into the holy city of Jerusalem, suggesting that indeed Jerusalem has not been faithful to Yahweh. He contrasts the glorious triumph of the king's victorious panoply with Jesus' modest entry. Furthermore, Mark uses such messianic imagery only eventually to deconstruct the messianic adulation of the crowd.[7] Jesus is the promised messiah, but not quite as imagined. The messianic imagery is intensified when Jesus arrives at the Mount of Olives, for it is "from there that the Messiah was supposed to enter Jerusalem."[8]

Jesus tells two of his followers to go into the nearby town, where they will immediately or at once (εὐθὺς) find a colt tied up and waiting for them. The term "immediately" here signals that we are not dealing with any literally historical narrative, but with a theological discourse. Things happen "immediately" not in the historical world, but in the rhetorical realm of theological discourse.

Although many scholars argue otherwise, there seems to be little room here for Christian ideas of displacing the Jewish traditions. Mark aligns himself with *Zechariah* and writes his gospel so as to emphasize even more strongly the lowly entry of the messiah Jesus into the city. The colt is described as set aside, apart from ordinary conventional use. It is sacred, for no one has yet ridden it (ὅν οὐδεὶς οὕτω ἀνθρώπων ἐκάθισεν). In *1 Samuel* 6: 6, the Philistines are told to "take and fit out a new cart, and two milch cows that have never borne the yoke" to carry the ark of the covenant away. They must use the new cart and the unworked beasts because they are to be employed for a sacred purpose.[9] Mark is not talking about an historical occurrence, but about Jesus' messiahship. Jesus rides on the newly found and never used colt in a symbolic story, identifying the triumphant entry of the messiah into Jerusalem with the lowly and concrete conditions of his life as the earthly son of man.[10] It is ordinary life that is sacred, not the glorious imagery of power and victory. His kingdom is one in which power and war

---

7. Camery-Hoggatt, *Irony in Mark's Gospel,* 170: "It is an irony which borders on the paradoxical. In the sense in which we find it here, the acclamation of the crowds is a kind of counter-point to the mockery of the soldiers. Either one is a parody of the truth. But they are so in different ways, and to different rhetorical effect." Both the admiring crowd and the soldiers who mock Jesus during his passion are bounded by imagined realities, one overtly religious and expectant, the other anti-religious and dismissive of all expectancies.

8. Mauser, *Christ in the Wilderness,* 57.1.

9. Similarly see *2 Kings* 2: 20 for Elisha's new bowl, *Numbers* 19: 2 for the heifer that has never borne the yoke; and *Deuteronomy* 21: 3 for the unworked heifer to be used in a sacrifice of truth telling.

10. Crossan, *The Cross That Spoke,* 76–82, discusses the passion account of Jesus presented by 'Abd al-Jabbār, in which the imagery of the colt is deepened in anti-Christian imagery when Jesus is placed on a donkey and his face is turned to its backside in mockery and then provided with the crown of thorns. Such an image functions only by deepening what is already an anti-victorious image in the Christian sources.

are under eschatological judgment. And so, upon going into the town the disciples find the colt in a very public place, "outside in the open street, or at the middle of a crossroads" (ἔξω ἐπὶ τοῦ ἀμφόδου), i.e., a most common and profane space. They are given the use of the colt by the bystanders because "the Lord has need of it," that is, because, profane as it is, it must serve a sacred purpose. The bystanders send the colt to Jesus, for that is the only action proper in view of its sacred use. It is being moved symbolically out of the conventional realm into the ultimate. Yet any ultimate falls far short of being itself ultimate, and remains conventional.[11]

Then the disciples and the crowd take off their cloaks and throw them both onto the back of the colt and on the roadway where Jesus will pass. In the last episode of chapter 10, the blind man threw off his cloak and jumped up to meet Jesus. Here all the crowd does the same, but they do not have the same faith as did the blind man. Rather, they spread their cloaks in hopes of witnessing the final triumph of the messiah as he enters the holy city. Yet, Jesus has not in fact entered the city itself but remains on the outskirts where there is greenery from country fields that may be cut.[12] Mark has excised all triumphant aspects from the messianic imagery.[13]

The imagery of the entry itself is heightened by Psalm 118, which is a processional hymn for the Feast of Tabernacles. It is a victory song about how Israel defeats its enemies. Israel is the stone that the builders rejected, but Yahweh has come to the rescue and granted victory to his people, while wreaking havoc on all Israel's enemies. Verses 25–27 declare: "We beg you (i.e., hosanna), Yahweh, save us. We beg you, Yahweh, give us victory! Blessed in the name of Yahweh is he who is coming! We bless you from the house of Yahweh. Yahweh is God, he gives us light. Link your processions, branches in hand, up to the horns of the altar."

The branches are of myrtle or palm, and to be waved in the procession as it circles the altar. Mark adopts this imagery and depicts Jesus' entry as a joyous triumph. The crowd shouts, "Blessed is the coming of our father

---

11. Tolbert, *Sowing the Gospel,* 119: "The detailed instructions to the two disciples concerning where to find the colt, what to do with it, and what to say (vv. 2–3) and the narrated confirmation of every element (vv. 4–6) are reminiscent of scenes from the Hebrew Scriptures in which God has given explicit instructions to an individual that are then meticulously followed (e.g. Exod 4: 1–31; 7: 8–13, 14–24; 8: 1–7, 16–19; Gen 24: 10–21; 35: 1–4). From Mark 11 until the end, all of Jesus' predictions become focused on closely impending or immediate events and are matched by scenes indicating exact fulfillment (e.g., 14: 13–16; 14: 30, 72)." The narrative implication is that Jesus, close by the eschatological Mount of Olives, enunciates the prophetic voice of Yahweh.

12. Kelber, *The Kingdom in Mark,* 93: "The acclamation is schemed in such a way that it does in fact not concur with the entry into the city. Mark, and Mark alone, has Jesus' companions cut leafy branches 'from the fields' (11: 8b), which adverts to a rural location. It is only *after* Jesus has been hailed that he enters the temple, by himself (11: 11a: *eisēlthen*), unobserved and unapplauded."

13. Kelber, *Mark's Story of Jesus,* 58, notes that the people are not the people of Jerusalem, but "primarily the disciples and those who joined on the way to Jerusalem."

David," the coming of the victorious kingdom that will reverse all suffering and attain universal triumph. "The figure of David was an image embodying the aspirations of the covenant people for renewal and vindication, . . . David was regarded as the instrument through whom the light of the knowledge of God would go out to the nations; . . . through him there would be a renovation of the worship of God and the defeat of the powers of evil."[14] Yet such an image is made only after they have welcomed Jesus as "he who comes in the name of the Lord." In Psalm 118, that is not the victorious king David, but simply a participant in the procession. "In Psalm 118.26 the one who comes in the name of the Lord is the worshiper. . . . Is Jesus merely an honored pilgrim, or is he acclaimed as messiah? Mark intends the reader to discern the hidden meaning behind the outward phenomenon. There is no word in this passage which sets Jesus apart from the others, and nothing which points to his messiahship. The esoteric flavor of the narrative is heightened by the peculiar preparations to have the ass ready for his ride into the city. . . . Just as in the blind Bartimaeus incident (10:47,48), so here Jesus does not accept the designation as Son of David, although he is certainly associated with the fulfillment of the promise of David and his descendants about the eschatological kingdom. But the concept of the Davidic kingdom is being revised."[15] The victory Jesus ushers in will prove to be no victory, and that is the eschatological victory. There is renewal, but no vindication, the triumph only of a pilgrim traveler. Jesus enters only to face his passion and death. Even the resurrection will not serve as empirical validation of the imagined hopes of both his disciples and the crowd. Jesus is rejected, and Yahweh does not come to save him. The sacred imagery of the colt and the victory parade is emptied of any final significance. The conventional manifestation (*udbhāvanā-saṃvṛti*) is itself conventional, nothing but conventional (*saṃvṛti-mātra*), and that is the point of Mark's account of Jesus' entry into Jerusalem.[16]

---

14. Kee, *Community of the New Age*, 126.

15. Kee, *Community of the New Age*, 127.

16. Against Tolbert, *Sowing the Gospel*, who offers a different interpretation, 248: "By stocking the episode of the triumphal entry with allusions to messianic and kingship texts (e.g., the king's prerogative to take animals, Mark 11: 2–3, in 1 Sam. 8: 10–11, 17; the messiah riding a colt, Mark 11: 7, in Zech. 9: 9; the spreading of garments before the king, Mark 11: 8, in 2 Kings 9: 13), Mark presents Jesus as the Davidic Messiah-King." In *1 Samuel,* the prophet is presenting the disadvantages of having any king, pointing out that kings "will take your sons and direct them to his chariotry and cavalry, and they will run in front of his chariot" (1 Kings 11). *Zechariah* 9: 9–10, given above, seems to be downplaying the royal panoply of Jeremiah. *2 Kings* 9: 13 speaks of the officers of Jehu's army, "who took off their cloaks and spread them under him on the bare steps; they sounded the trumpet and shouted, 'Jehu is king!' " The imagery is indeed found in Mark, yet the location of Jesus' acclamation outside the city and the undermining of the very concept of Davidic lineage in Mark 12: 35–37 suggest that Mark is, as usual, ill at ease with any title for Jesus. Kingsbury, *The Christology of Mark's Gospel,* 107–08 parallels Tolbert's analysis. Both scholars themselves tone down the royal imagery, Tolbert in deriving Jesus' authority from God rather than from David, and Kingsbury by noting the

The last verse of the passage stresses the point. Sometimes it is taken to be merely an editorial verse, marking the transition for the cleansing of the temple in verses 15–18.[17] Yet in a Mahāyāna analysis it has significance. Immediately after his triumphant entry into Jerusalem, heralded as king, Jesus goes straight to the Temple, the very center of religious authority, looks around, and then goes right home! What a disappointment that is. *Pariuntur montes, nascitur ridiculus mus!* Victory, victory, there is no victory, and that is why there is victory. All Jesus does is to look around (περιβλεψάμενος πάντα).[18] In going back to Bethany with the Twelve,[19] Mark has Jesus turn his back on the prospects of replacing the Jewish institutions.

And if Jesus does not attempt to replace those institutions, then what on earth would justify Christians claiming that they have indeed replaced Judaism? Displacement theology is based on readings insensitive to Mark's use of irony and paradox. The point is not that Jesus brings a new and better religion, but that he calls for a conversion away from the deluded pattern of false imaginings, whatever religion those imaginings might appeal to. In the strongest terms yet, Mark empties the hopes of Jesus' followers. But that emptying is not meant merely to negate the particular institution of the Temple, but also to reaffirm, to resurrect the meaning of faith from the frozen and fixed notions of primal ignorance, whether common sense or theological, into the conventional validity of dependently co-arisen understandings. The theme remains valid: withdrawal into the silent wonder of ultimate meaning, followed by and held in dynamic tension with reengagement in conventional words and deeds.[20]

---

insufficiency of the title in light of 12: 35–37. I would go further and assert that in Mark it is only because Jesus is no king whatsoever that he may be called king. Mark uses kingly imagery to foreshadow the official charge of the crucified Jesus and thus empty any notion of empirical kingship. I agree with Kelber, *Mark's Story of Jesus*, 58: "The acclamation story is one of supreme irony. . . . Those who acclaim Jesus' Davidic messiahship perpetuate an attitude shown earlier by the refusal to listen to the passion-resurrection predictions."

17. Grant, *The Interpreter's Bible*, 7: 827.

18. Kelber, *The Kingdom in Mark*, 98: "During his first day in the sanctuary he is said to have 'looked around at everything.' The Markan *periblepsesthai* intimates a critical or even judgmental look by Jesus." Also see Broadhead, *Teaching With Authority*, 175: "Looking around (περιβλέπομαι) already carries a sense of foreboding in the Gospel of Mark," and a sense of anger (105). The term is found in 3: 5, 34; 5: 32; 9: 8; 10: 23, and 11: 1. Even though it may have been a withering look, yet that is all Jesus does.

19. Kelber, *Mark's Story of Jesus*, 58: "The Twelve are made to witness his solitary inspection of the temple. What they observe is hardly a triumphal entry. Jesus is neither recognized nor installed in the temple as Davidic Messiah." Again, 62: "Far from living up to expectations associated with the temple, Jesus makes 'his place' at the Mount of Olives, opposite the temple mount, and journeys back and forth."

20. Tolbert, *Sowing the Gospel*, 119, writes: From 11: 1–11, "Jesus initiates public recognition . . . secrecy, hiddenness, lonely places, commands to silence are all things of the past." Yet, Jesus does enter into the loneliness of Gethsemane, is silent before Pilate, and arises from the tomb to an unaware world.

The Fig Tree
11: 12–14

[12]Next day as they were leaving Bethany, he felt hungry. [13]Seeing a fig tree in leaf some distance away, he went to see if he could find any fruit on it, but when he came up to it he found nothing but leaves; for it was not the season for figs. [14]And he addressed the fig tree. "May no one ever eat fruit from you again," he said. And his disciples heard him say this.

This is a very strange story—about appearances and reality. Right after his triumphant entry into the holy city, Jesus leaves, sleeps, and the very next day tries to assuage his hunger by looking for figs in the off-season. The narrator knows full well that there are no figs. But the story is not really about figs. It makes no sense that way. If one insists on taking it literally, then Jesus becomes a rather stupid fellow who, piqued, takes his revenge on a poor fig tree that is just following its biological rhythms.[21]

Rather, this is a parabolic evaluation of Jesus' acclaimed entry into the Temple and the accompanying messianic hopes.[22] Just as one might seek for figs and find only leaves (φύλλα), so the acclamation of the crowd provided merely leafy greenery (στιβάδας, 11: 8)[23] but no inner fruit, no inner reality. It is not the time for figs (ὁ γὰρ καιρὸς οὐκ ἦν σύκων), for the kingdom announced by Jesus in 1: 15, present and available at every moment, has no linear time reference. At the beginning of his career Jesus proclaims that the

---

21. Camery-Hoggatt, *Irony in Mark's Gospel,* 69, remarks that the story "depends upon the knowledge that *taqsh* appear on the tree as edible precursors of real figs; if they are missing it means that there will be no figs when the time is ripe." Thus, that Jesus could find no fruit on it means that he could find no *taqsh.* Yet, that ill accords with Mark's aside to the reader that the reason for its fruitlessness was that it was "not the season for figs." I agree with Broadhead, *Teaching with Authority,* 169: "The simple informational note—'for it was not the season for figs'—creates a deconstructive break in the logic of the narrative. This deconstruction of the narrative logic is consummated in Jesus' harsh, prophetic condemnation of the fig tree—'never again through eternity shall anyone eat of your fruit' (11. 14a). The curse is followed by the second intrusion of the narrator (11. 14b). This intrusion intimately links the disciples to the curse—'and the disciples were hearing him.' Following this explosive deconstruction of the initial narrative logic, the plot action diverts to the scene in Jerusalem, leaving the implied reader to ponder the incoherence of the events of the story."

22. Tolbert, *Sowing the Gospel,* 192–93: "The cursing of the fig tree, with the story of Jesus' cleansing of the temple inserted in the midst of it (11: 15–19), is a miracle illustrative of the unfruitfulness, hard-heartedness, and opposition now poised to engulf Jesus." Mark's observation that it is not the time for figs is meant to encourage "the audience to perceive the symbolic rather than the mundane character of Jesus' action." Mark's intercalation of Jesus' Temple action between the accounts about the fig tree indeed follows his established rhetorical pattern, yet Jesus' so-called triumphal entry is directly tied to the Temple and its practices.

23. Cranfield, *St. Mark,* 350: "στιβάδας. The word στιβάς denotes a '*bed of straw, rushes,* or *leaves,* whether strewn loose or stuffed into a mattress.' So here perhaps translate 'foliage'."

time has already been fulfilled (πεπλήρωται ὁ καιρὸς), so one need not try to identify it in the future.[24] So here Jesus says that no one will eat of the fruit of the tree until the end of the age (εἰς τὸν αἰῶνα).[25] The barren tree is a sign of the fall of Adam in rabbinical and Midrashic texts.[26] "By contrast the Messianic Age, the Age of Blessings, will cause the earth to produce abundantly and beyond human expectation. . . . Fruit out of season may be looked for, or expected, only by one entering upon the New Age. . . ."[27] When the Markan Jesus goes to look for figs out of season, he signals his expectancy that the eschatological kingdom has indeed arrived. The absence of fruit means that Temple-like institutions abort the eschatological kingdom and, in light of 13: 28, where Jesus compares the leafing of a fig tree that informs one of the coming of summer with the events that accompany the end time, no summer follows from its barrenness.[28]

---

24. Kelber, *Mark's Story of Jesus*, 59–60: "The difficulty comes with the last clause of 11: 13. Jesus finds no fruit 'because it was not the right time for figs.' That does not seem to make sense. Why condemn the tree if it is not the proper time for bearing fruit? The term inadequately translated in the RSV with 'season' gives the clue to the puzzle. It is not a botanical term indicating the season for figs but a religious term denoting the time of the Kingdom of God. Indeed it is precisely the term Mark had used in Jesus' programmatic message announcing the 'right time' of the Kingdom of God (1: 14–15). By introducing this loaded term into the fig tree story Mark gives it a religious dimension. Jesus' encounter with the fig tree signifies more than the barrenness of the tree. The absence of 'the right time for figs . . . suggests the absence of the right time for the Kingdom." That time will arrive only when Jesus is handed up to suffering and death (14: 41), for that is the time Jesus has foretold three times to his disciples. Again Kelber, *The Kingdom in Mark*, 99: "But why condemn the fig tree for what it could in the nature of the case not possibly have produced? At this point, scholars resort to the world of fig trees in hope of turning up a natural explanation for the tree's failure. But Mark the theologian does not share the scholars' enthusiasm for the tree life of Israel. If 11: 13c breaks the cogency of the plot, in it may well be the clue to the whole. *Ho gar kairos ouk ēn sykōn*, the very clause which disrupts the logic of the story, is one of Mark's *gar* clauses which invite the reader 'to understand the context in the light of something outside the data explicitly presented to us' (See C.H. Bird, "Some *gar* Clauses in St. Mark's Gospel," 173)." Nineham, *St. Mark*, 112, draws an explicitly replacement conclusion from the cursing of the fig tree: "The manner and the place of its insertion strongly suggests that the story was intended to make a didactic point, the fate of the fig tree symbolizes the fate that awaited Jerusalem and the Jewish people and religion."

25. Hiers, "Not the Season for Figs," and Derrett, "Figtrees," quoted in Mann, *Mark*, 440.

26. Mann, *Mark*, 454.26, notes the rabbinic suggestion that the forbidden fruit in the Garden of Eden was a fig, not the apple of later European artists.

27. Mann, *Mark*, 441.

28. See Mann, *Mark*, 439, where he critiques Telford's thesis that the pericope is focused on the Temple. He "tries to prove altogether too much. Mark is remarkably little interested in the temple (as compared, for example, with Luke and John), and though Mark's community may initially have been bewildered by the conflicts which resulted in the destruction of the temple, contemporary Judaism was of such diverse complexion, and so heavily weighted numerically in favor of the diaspora, that we may ourselves be in danger of giving the temple a centrality which it may not have enjoyed. . . . Mark's concerns in the direction of impending judgment may have included the temple, but it was by no means paramount."

In any event, seeking for figs when it is not the proper time is not a rational thing to do. It recalls the famous Ch'an kōan about Nansen killing a cat: "Once the monks of the Eastern Hall and the Western Hall were disputing about a cat. Nansen, holding up the cat, said, 'Monks, if you can say a word of Zen, I will spare the cat. If you cannot, I will kill it!' No monk could answer. Nansen finally killed the cat. In the evening, when Joshu came back, Nansen told him of the incident. Joshu took off his sandals, put them on his head, and walked off. Nansen said, 'If you had been there, I could have saved the cat!' "[29] Perhaps the monks were arguing over the much disputed point of whether animals had Buddha nature, whether they too were originally enlightened. Shibayama's interpretation reports that one master says, "What Nansen killed was not only the cat concerned, but cats called Buddhas, cats called Patriarchs, are all cut away." Buddhas and patriarchs signal the sacred realm of enlightenment, yet they too must be cut away, for the sacred is not a dichotomized realm apart from the everyday. It is in the everyday that one lives, suffers, dies, and rises again. Shibayama continues: "It is said that Jesus Christ rose from death after his crucifixion. As I am not a Christian, I do not know the orthodox interpretation of the resurrection in Christianity. I myself believe, however, that Jesus' resurrection means to die in human flesh, and to revive as the Son of God transcending life and death. His resurrection means the advent of the Kingdom of God. It is the mysterious work of God to create the new and true world. There everybody, everything, lives in God, and all the provisional names and defilements of this earth are never found in the least. . . . In other words [Nansen] tells us to appreciate the wonder of resurrection in the face of the Great Death." Here, Jesus says that no one will ever eat (φάγοι) of the eschatological fruit of the fig tree, just as Jesus is about to wreak havoc in the Temple and proclaim it a house of prayer for all the peoples. And his disciples heard (καὶ ἤκουον οἱ μαθηταὶ αὐτοῦ). Jesus has been asking them to listen. Just what did they hear? What did they understand? Stayed tuned!

Jesus and the Temple Tradition
11: 15–19

[15]*So they reached Jerusalem and he went into the Temple and began driving out the men who were selling and buying there; he upset the tables of the money changers and the seats of the dove sellers. [16]Nor would he allow anyone to carry anything through the Temple. [17]And he taught them and said, "Does not scripture say: My house will be called a house of prayer for all peoples? But you have turned it into a bandits' den." [18]This came to the ears of the chief priests and the scribes, and they tried to find some way of doing*

---

29. Shibayama, *Zen Comments on the Mumonkan,* 107–113.

away with him; they were afraid of him because the people were carried away by his teaching. *[19]And when evening came he went out of the city.*

For the first time after his entry on the colt's back and his looking around, Jesus returns to Jerusalem and goes straight to the Temple area. He begins to throw out the vendors, overturning tables and chairs in the process. Mark only says that he began to throw (ἤρξατο ἐκβάλλειν) them out, however, not that he succeeded in finishing the job. Jesus is then undermining the temple, but not in light of his new teaching, or on his own authority.[30] Rather, he alludes to and draws his authority from *Isaiah* 56: 7, which describes the Temple as the Lord Yahweh's "house of prayer, . . . for my house will be called a house of prayer for all the peoples,"[31] and to *Jeremiah* 7: 11, in which Yahweh warns that humans must not "take this Temple that bears my name for a robbers' den."

The cultic practices in the Temple were supported by the availability of animals for sacrifice and the convenience of money exchangers to facilitate the purchase of such necessary elements for the cult. Jesus' action signifies that those cultic practices are all appearance, that those holocausts and sacrifices are not in fact acceptable on the altar of Yahweh, as in Isaiah 56: 7. Just as the fig tree is all appearance, with many attractive leaves but no reality, so the cult is all outward observance with no inner conversion. Jesus is here upholding the authenticity of the Temple traditions and castigating those who have reduced them to formal observances.[32] He is not trying

---

30. I think Tolbert, *Sowing the Gospel,* 249, overstates the case: "In driving out the merchants and money-changers, Jesus publicly asserts his jurisdiction over the center of Jewish religion, the temple." Public indeed are Jesus' actions, yet their source is identified in the text as deriving from Isaiah.

31. Mark alone includes the Septuagint phrase "for all the people" (πᾶσιν τοῖς ἔθνεσιν), while Matthew 21: 13 and Luke 19: 45 omit it. John 2: 14–16 recasts the episode by omitting the reference to Isaiah altogether, attributing Jesus' authority to Jesus himself. Kelber, *Mark's Story of Jesus,* 61, notes that "there exists an unshakeable connection between the ecumenical community in the north and Jesus' vision of the 'house of prayer for all the nations'." I agree that the ecumenical kingdom is to include all peoples, but interpret the north, that is, Galilee, not as a physical location, but as the return to the everyday life of Christian practice.

32. Against Crossan, *The Historical Jesus,* 357: ". . . Mark 11:15–19 . . . is often and quite incorrectly called the purification of the Temple. It is not at all a purification but rather a symbolic destruction. First of all, and in general, there was absolutely nothing wrong with any of the buying, selling, or money-changing operations conducted in the outer courts of the Temple. Nobody was stealing or defrauding or contaminating the sacred precincts. Those activities were the absolutely necessary concomitants of the fiscal basis and sacrificial purpose of the Temple. Second, Mark himself knows that Jesus was not just purifying but symbolically destroying the Temple because he carefully framed his action with the fruitless fig tree's cursing in 11:12–14 and withering in 11:20." I agree that the Temple activities are normal and necessary concomitants to the liturgical practices of the Temple but think the fig tree symbolizes inefficacious appearances (that is, deluded attachment to any localized and circumscribed presence of Yahweh) in a narrative aimed at emptying any structure in eschatological reversal. Once emptied, however, any tradition, Jewish or Christian, can reclaim a dependently co-arisen validity. The so-called purification of the temple is not then a physical cleansing, but a purification of the mind of the

physically to clean up the Temple area, to actually drive out all the vendors. Rather, he is demanding a change of consciousness. Jeremiah had railed against the same thing. *Jeremiah* 7: 1–15 treats the vanity of the cultic observance and the text climaxes when God rejects the Temple because of the hypocrisy of those who pray therein, trusting that their practices will be validated because "this is the Temple of the Lord."

Jesus "would not allow anyone to carry anything through the temple." One interpretation holds that what Jesus is doing is prohibiting the use of the temple area as a shortcut, for in point of fact such a prohibition was made in the Talmud.[33] Yet the term "anything" ($\sigma\kappa\epsilon\hat{\upsilon}o\varsigma$) probably refers to the liturgical utensils necessary for cultic practices in the Temple.[34] If this is Mark's meaning, then Jesus is obstructing the cultic functions of the Temple.[35] In prohibiting its liturgical functioning, Jesus is emptying the Temple of any

---

practitioner-reader from attachment to absolute structures to a reengagement in the traditions. Furthermore, the Markan perspective on the validity of the temple is altered by the destruction of that august edifice, whether just past, or imminent. In a similar vein Hamerton-Kelly, *The Gospel and the Sacred,* 2, writes: "The 'cleansing' of the temple is a symbol of the rejection of the sacred and the denial of its place at the center of significance. *Significance from now on is eccentric; there is no holy city, no holy land, and, by implication, no chosen people.* In Christ all are chosen for salvation and so no one is especially chosen. The rending of the sanctuary's veil at the moment of Jesus' death confirms this symbolic message. It shows that the sanctuary is empty—'there is no there there'—and prompts the centurion's confession that God is present on the cross and accessible to the Gentiles, even to a Roman executioner (15:38–39). The tension between Jesus and the temple, therefore, is the central relationship in the narrative. It is the tension between the Gospel and the sacred and in order to understand the Gospel of Mark we need a theory of the Sacred that will help us to interpret its poetics." Hamerton-Kelly provides just that with his adaptation of Girard's theory on scapegoating. I find much with which to agree, yet I would argue that a better framework for interpretation lies in Mahāyāna thought with its tension, not between the particular institution of the temple, but between the two truths and against any usurpation by worldly convention of an ultimate status, whether on the part of the institutional symbols or on the part of Jesus' own followers. I am in full agreement that Jesus' actions empty any supposed sacred realm of central significance, for the sacred remains within the realm of worldly and conventional truth.

33. *Berakoth* 9: 5.

34. Bauer, *A Greek-English Lexicon,* 754, defines it as thing or object used for any purpose, but notes that "by an added statement or through the context $\sigma\kappa\epsilon\hat{\upsilon}o\varsigma$ can become an object of a specific kind: $\tau\grave{\alpha}\ \sigma\kappa\epsilon\acute{\upsilon}\eta\ \tau\hat{\eta}\varsigma\ \lambda\epsilon\iota\tau o\upsilon\rho\gamma\acute{\iota}\alpha\varsigma$ the equipment used in the services in Hb 9: 21."

35. Thus Kelber, *Mark's Story of Jesus,* 60: "The second action undertaken by Jesus in the temple is to prohibit people from carrying 'anything' through the temple (11: 16). The original Greek word for 'anything' (mistranslated in the RSV) is *vessel.* Jesus would not allow anyone to carry a vessel through the temple. The reference to vessel in a temple story suggests a cultic dimension, Jesus puts an end to the religious practices of the temple. To sum up, Jesus' two actions [of disrupting the tradespeople and prohibiting the carrying] are tantamount to the shutting down of the business and religious functions of the temple. One must wonder whether this can truly be called a cleansing of the temple." Again, *The Kingdom in Mark,* 101: "Understood in a religious sense, the obstruction of the vessel's transport effects the cessation of the temple's cultic function." Malbon concurs, *Narrative Space,* 121.

sacred status. Yahweh/Abba cannot be circumscribed in any place. "Jesus' actions, however, do not really function as a 'cleansing,' despite the traditional caption of the pericope, and no new temple is anticipated here as in Ezekiel [40–48]. The final chapters of Zechariah, alluded to elsewhere in Mark, present a more exact interpretive clue. On the day of the Lord, reads Zechariah 14:21, 'there shall no longer be a trader in the house of the Lord.' There shall be no need of traders to provide sacred materials for sacrifices, for 'every pot in Jerusalem and Judah shall be sacred to the Lord of hosts, so that all who sacrifice may come and take of them and boil the flesh of the sacrifice in them' (Zechariah 14:21). The distinction between sacred and profane will be invalid because 'on that day' all shall be 'Holy to the Lord' (Zechariah 14:20). Jesus experiences the overcoming of the distinction between sacred and profane and so perceives no further need of traders in the temple or of the consequent carrying of any utensil (*skeuos,* 11:16) through the temple. For the Markan Jesus, 'that day' is this day."[36] Such an attitude was not specific to Jesus. Pagan and Jewish writers express a similar critique.[37] "The critique of temples 'made with hands' (χειροποίητος), in Acts 7:48 and found implicitly in Mark 14:58, as well as other New Testament passages, draws upon a much older Greek tradition that was critical of images and temples as loci for the presence of deity."[38] In the then mobile culture, sacred places became less important and access to the divine transcended any particular place.[39] Even "if the temple had not been destroyed, it would have had to be neglected. For it represented a locative religious situation no longer perceived as effective in a new, utopian religious situation with a concomitant shift from a cosmological to an anthropological viewpoint."[40]

In a Mahāyāna reading, however, the overcoming of the dichotomy between sacred and profane, between cessation (*nirvāṇa*) and the suffering world (*saṃsāra*), does not entail a rejection of the conventional world in favor of an overly-stressed emptiness. In Mark, Jesus' temple actions embody a middle way, affirming the emptiness of what is dependently co-arisen. Thus perhaps we can coax forth another interpretation. If *Jeremiah* 17 indeed lies in the background of Jesus' acclamation and entry into the Temple city, then perhaps its admonition against bringing any burden into the gates of the city on the Sabbath day and working on that day (LXX 17: 24: τοῦ μή εἰσφέρειν βαστάγματα διὰ τῶν πυλῶν τῆς πόλεως ταύτης ἐν τῇ ἡμέρᾳ τῶν

---

36. Malbon, *Narrative Space,* 122.

37. Dowd, *Prayer, Power, and the Problem of Sacrifice,* 45–53.

38. Dowd, *Prayer,* 51.

39. Dowd, *Prayer,* 52: "Sacred places became relatively less important and religious associations became the individual's protection against external hostile powers. The devaluation of temples was accompanied by emphasis on religious community, not only in diaspora Judaism, in Christianity and at Qumran, but in other Hellenistic religions as well." Also 50: "The change of emphasis from sacrifice to prayer and the focus on the synagogues and the houses of study as replacements for the destroyed temple represent the success of rabbinic Judaism in coping with the loss of temple and cult."

40. J. Smith, *Map Is Not Territory,* 128.

σαββάτων καὶ ἀγιάζειν τὴν ἡμέραν τῶν σαββάτων, τοῦ μὴ ποιεῖν πᾶν ἔργον) serves as the key for Jesus' prohibition in Mark. Just as Jeremiah speaks only of burdens, i.e., anything carried, so Mark suggests that the work carried out in the temple defiles its holy status. Jeremiah has proclaimed that if his words are not heeded, destruction and ruin will result to the holy city and its temple. Indeed, if Mark writes from knowledge either of the imminent or the recently occurred destruction of the second temple, Jesus' action takes on the force of Jeremiah's prediction against the surety of the first temple. It is not that Jesus totally invalidates the temple practices,[41] for that may well have been a moot point. Rather, he rejects the usurpation of the open availability of Abba in any form. Mark explains that he, like Jeremiah before him, stands for the sanctity of the temple and sees its profanation as the cause for its ruin, as at the opening of chapter 13, Jesus is fully aware of its imminent destruction. The prohibition is not then against one form of cultic worship, but against the usurpation of ultimate meaning by a fixed notion of the sacred.[42]

Jesus had often negated the cultic concerns of the Pharisees, who "by their concern with purity . . . ritualized life by imposing the Temple's cultic rules

---

41. Dowd, *Prayer,* 53.84, notes that "the notion of the community as replacement for the temple presupposes the *rejection* of the temple but not necessarily its *destruction.* Cf. Neusner, "Judaism in a Time of Crisis," 319: 'Christians experienced the end of the old cult and the old Temple before it actually took place, much like the Qumran sectarians. . . . Whether the essays on that central problem were done before or after 70 C.E. is of no consequence.' " Lightfoot, *The Gospel Message of St. Mark,* is more sanguine, 63: "No attempt is made to interfere with the existing Jewish ritual or worship, and the Lord confines himself entirely to the removal, from the court of the Gentiles, of all that made prayer or worship difficult or impossible for Gentiles, in that one and only part of the temple to which they had already the privilege of access."

42. Mack, *A Myth of Innocence,* 291: Jesus' temple "act is contrived. Some gesture was required that could symbolize both casting out and taking charge with some semblance of legitimacy. Demons would be too much, since Jesus is about to be taken. It would, in any case, have been implausible. But filthy lucre would do just fine. Taxes and the temple treasury had been hot political issues underlying much of the history of the conflict between Jerusalem and Rome. The citations from Isaiah and Jeremiah could put Jesus on the safe side of the conflict, motivated by righteous indignation. Jewish authorities (scripture) could be used against Jewish practice. The subtheme of temple robbery, moreover, given with the citation from Jeremiah, was also most convenient. Temple robbery was a stock image of degradation in the popular imagination, combining criminal activity with impiety. The first use of the theme in Mark is Jesus' application of Jeremiah's charge to those who bought and sold in the temple (that is, animals for offerings and money at foreign rates of exchange). This subtheme recurs at the arrest where Jesus chides the arresters for coming after him as though he, not the money changers, were the temple robber (Mark 14: 48). This develops the theme somewhat, playing on the symbolic significance of the temple act and putting the countercharge in the opponents' mouth. At the trial the question of Jesus' authority is the more important theme, but the temple act has not been forgotten. . . . The hearsay about destroying the temple pushes the symbolism of the act in the direction of an exorcism (casting out as destroying). And underlying the charge of blasphemy is the notion of desecration, also related allusively to the temple act. When Jesus is crucified, then, he is positioned between two robbers, that is, as one who desecrated the temple (Mark 15: 27)."

of purity on it."[43] Now the chief priests and scribes are challenged on their own turf. They have frequently sent emissaries to test him. Now Jesus comes right into their preserve and accuses the temple cult of being a mere show. He is acting like a prophet, and his teachings here reflect the depths of the Hebrew traditions. But the authorities fear the people, for they are overwhelmed and carried away (ἐξεπλήσσετο) by his teaching. It is not just that the people are pleased by that teaching. They are confused and bewildered by it, for Jesus has taken Isaiah and Jeremiah seriously, thus removing the surety that traditional religious observances afford. It is not a competition pitting Jesus and his crowd on the one side against the authorities on the other. The crowd, who ironically has just hailed Jesus with hosannas, is now itself dismayed, and thus unpredictable. The priests are now concerned—as priests often are—about disturbing the people's minds and want to comfort them by assuring them that the Temple is indeed a secure place for worship. This is why they want to remove Jesus.[44]

Curse and Prayer
11: 20–25

[20]*Next morning as they passed by, they saw the fig tree withered to the roots.* [21]*Peter remembered, "Look, Rabbi," he said to Jesus, "the fig tree that you cursed has withered away."* [22]*Jesus answered, "Have faith in God.* [23]*In truth I tell you, if anyone says to this mountain, 'Be pulled up and thrown into*

---

43. Klosinski, *Meals in Mark,* 89.

44. Kelber, *The Kingdom in Mark,* 101, describes the reaction of the Jerusalem leaders in plotting Jesus' death: "It is solely the view of Mark that Jesus' temple 'cleansing' precipitates the plot against his life." So also, Lightfoot, *The Gospel Message of St. Mark,* 61. Hamerton-Kelly, *The Gospel and the Sacred,* 21, insightfully writes: "We meet 'the chief priests and the scribes' (11:18), that is, the administrative and legal managers of the temple. We also meet that source of all authority, the crowd (ὄχλος) (11:18). We are told that the authorities were afraid of Jesus because the crowd was hypnotized (ἐξεπλήσσετο) by his teaching (11:18). This revealing statement is usually taken to mean that the crowd was on his side; but that is a misunderstanding and it causes a further misunderstanding when later the crowd turns on him. The crowd is not on his side; for the most part, it is on the side of the leaders, and only wavers from time to time in response to Jesus' teaching and miraculous power. Even in its waverings, it remains essentially on the side of the leaders, within the order of sacred violence. The leaders fear Jesus because his teaching has enthralled the crowd and, for the moment, removed it from their control. It is not positively on Jesus' side but only unavailable at the moment to the temple managers. The term ἐκπλήσσω means, literally, 'to strike out, to drive away from, to expel' and here seems to bear the metaphorical meaning of 'to strike out of one's senses, to be overwhelmed with desire.' The teaching and actions of Jesus have caused the crowd to be overwhelmed with desire, because he has impugned the sacral institution that channels desire. The teaching has expelled them from the womb of sacred violence and they are on the verge of chaos. No wonder the chief priests and the scribes fear Jesus!"

the sea,' with no doubt in his heart, but believing that what he says will happen, it will be done for him. ²⁴I tell you therefore, everything you ask and pray for, believe that you have it already, and it will be yours. ²⁵And when you stand in prayer, forgive whatever you have against anyone, so that your Father in heaven may forgive your failings too."

It is Peter who, the narrator tells us, remembers about the fig tree, although Jesus' encounter with it had occurred only the day before.[45] "Peter interpreted Jesus' words as a curse, but . . . this was not necessarily so . . . the words in v. 14 do not imply this. The tree was dying, if not dead, and it was *withered all the way down to the roots.*"[46] Jesus has pronounced on the fruitlessness of the tree; Peter sees Jesus as effecting that fruitlessness. Again one suspects that Peter has heard, but not understood.[47]

Jesus answers Peter by talking about faith and prayer—another apparent non sequitur, if we are simply talking about curses and trees.[48] But Jesus has not been talking about curses, or figs, or even about the tree, but about the eschatological fruit of awareness of the presence of the kingdom. And that is what he continues to discuss: eschatological faith and the mountain.

Some scholars argue that the mountain is not just any mountain. Rather, Jesus refers to "this" mountain: "if anyone says to this mountain" (τῷ ὄρει τούτῳ). This mountain is the Temple mount, the high seat of religious author- ity.[49] That is where Jesus and his disciples have just come from. That is where they were going when Jesus cursed the fig tree. It is the figless fig tree of the metaphor. It should have figs, but its season is over and it is barren because it has usurped the place of ultimate meaning. To this barrenness Jesus contrasts the faith in God which consists in not hesitating in one's heart (μὴ διακριθῇ ἐν τῇ καρδίᾳ).

But again more is involved than simply Jesus' repudiation of the Temple cult. The prayer sayings represent another Markan employment of "impossible

---

45. Tolbert, *Sowing the Gospel,* 194: "This miracle of destruction and death is actually called to Jesus' attention by—most appropriately—the epitome of the rocky ground itself, Peter (11: 21). Furthermore, the narrator heightens the association of the unfruitful tree with Peter and the disciples by describing the tree, 'withered away to its roots (ἐξηραμμένην ἐκ ῥιζῶν)' (11: 20), in words that echo the problem of the seed on rocky ground that withered away because it had no root (διὰ τὸ μὴ ἔχειν ῥίζαν ἐξηράνθη, 4: 6)."

46. Mann, *Mark,* 451 and 441.

47. Dowd, *Prayer,* 58: "This tells the audience much more about the narrator's character- ization of Peter than about the narrator's own view of what happened."

48. Also Broadhead, *Teaching With Authority,* 171:"The disciples' role intensifies when they initiate the unraveling of the enigma of the fig tree (11. 21). In this manner the story returns to the plot line shattered by the deconstruction of the expected narrative logic. Significantly, Jesus addresses the enigma through teaching activity (11. 22–26). Jesus' teaching on faith, authority, prayer and forgiveness provides the key to the withering of the fig tree."

49. Kelber, *The Kingdom in Mark,* 104: "It is the temple mount against which this saying is addressed." Also Dodd, *The Parables of the Kingdom,* 45, Lightfoot, *The Gospel Message of St. Mark,* 78, and Telford, *The Barren Temple,* 119.

276   *Commentary on the Gospel of Mark*

causes" (ἀδύνατον). "The command to the mountain . . . is a figure of speech that is common in Mark's environment, and represents something thought to be impossible."⁵⁰ As in chapter 10: 25 about the camel strained through the needle's eye, the point is to undercut all common assumptions and all viewpoints.⁵¹

Mark identifies faith with the absence of doubt. The verb "to doubt" (διακρίνω) "is concerned with judgment, decision, and in the New Testament in the middle and passive voices it means 'to hesitate' or 'to doubt.' "⁵² Mahāyāna thinkers regarded such judgmental hesitation to be discrimination (*kalpanā, parikalpa*), the inner source for delusions, for humans tend to cling to images and differentiate ideas as if these do in fact represent fixed and solid realities. Such discrimination creates the common-sense worlds in which one is indeed enabled to know when to expect figs from a fig tree. But, when seen as itself the criterion for truth, discrimination filters out from experience whatever cannot be accepted by an unawakened mind, a hardened heart. It mis-takes the conventional to be absolute, and tries to capture faith realities in linguistic definitions. This is the charge which Jesus lays to the Temple authorities—that they treasure the traditions of men over the things of God, that they confuse conventional truth, expressed in words and images, for the ultimate meaning, silent and apart from any image. Faith which does not hesitatingly discriminate overturns the mountain of judgmental doubt and throws it into the sea of silent awareness. The depths of the sea symbolize the complete absence of human constructs, the emptiness of all supports for conventional language. Out there one can neither speak words nor listen to them. The faith which abandons words and images is not thereby rendered contentless; its content is not verbal. Rather, it is emptiness itself, in the positive sense of that which absence indicates. Thus, when the Markan Jesus talks about faith as not hesitating or doubting (μὴ διακριθῇ ἐν τῇ καρδίᾳ αὐτοῦ ἀλλὰ πιστεύῃ), he is not simply recommending that one have strong confidence in the truth of the view that God is indeed omnipotent.

Yet Mark's text does specify the content of such undoubting faith: one can expect "that what he says will happen" (23, ὅτι ὃ λαλεῖ γίνεται)—that when you pray, "you have it already" (24, ὅτι ἐλάβετε). The first statement of the content of undoubting faith promises that if one says something with faith, it will indeed happen. And this does express the viewpoint, shared with

---

50. Dowd, *Prayer,* 64.

51. Against Dowd, *Prayer,* 71: "When the saying about the mountain in Mark 11:23 is understood as an ἀδύνατον, it must be read as a claim that the power of God to do the impossible is available to the believing community through prayer (11:24)." The use of "impossible cases" is not meant, I think, to recommend one alternative over another within the accepted viewpoints: whether God can or cannot do the impossible, but to empty notions that any viewpoints capture the heart of the matter, i.e., prayerful engagement. Thus, I agree with Schmithals, *Wunder und Glaube,* 90, (cited by Dowd) that faith in Mark does not involve "holding something to be true," and against Dowd, 103, that faith entails accepting the opinion (δόγμα) that everything is possible to God.

52. Mann, *Mark,* 453.

other Hellenistic thinkers, that God can do the impossible, like removing mountains to the sea.[53] However, such a faith is not yet, in the Markan text, associated with prayer, only with saying (λαλεῖ) something in faith. When Jesus actually recommends that one pray without hesitating discrimination, he switches the verb tenses from the present in verse 23 (used to refer to the future), "it will happen" (γίνεται) to the aorist of "you have it already" (ἐλάβετε).[54] The impossible eschatological fruit to be asked for in prayer has already been given, for the kingdom has come and is immediately available, despite the withered cultus of any temple or tradition. If one enters into a prayerful state, modeled on Jesus' wilderness contact with Abba, then the kingdom will become a reality (καὶ ἔσται ὑμῖν). In Jesus' version, one does not simply ask for future benefits, but in prayer asks and seeks (προσεύχεσθε καὶ αἰτεῖσθε) for awakening to the presence of the kingdom.

Yet it is not enough just to pray. One cannot simply focus on wilderness prayer and ignore conventional truth. One must be in harmony with others, and one must forgive others in order to attain harmony with the Father in heaven. "The forgiveness of the sins of the praying community is made dependent upon their forgiveness of each other. Both are necessary in order for the community to receive everything they pray and ask for."[55] It is not a quid pro quo, where the Father will forgive us once he sees we have forgiven others. Rather, again Jesus insists upon abandoning the mind of deluded discrimination, which offends against others in service of self. One cannot become aware of the Father as a separate and sacred personage apart from the dependently co-arisen community in which one lives. If the sacred has been emptied by Jesus' temple action, so a sacral God is emptied by his immediate presence to the community. Thus, a prayer that harbors resentment against others occludes the silent awareness of Abba, and renders one incapable of awakening. So one cannot truly pray at all. Here prayer with forgiveness embodies understanding both of the emptiness of the wilderness God and

---

53. Thus I agree with Dowd, *Prayer*, 64, that this first ὅτι clause recommends faith in the impossible.

54. Bratcher and Nida, *A Translator's Handbook*, 357: "*pisteuete hoti elabete* 'believe that you received it': ASV and RSV 'you receive it' is obscure because of the tense forms. Most translations accurately give the sense of the aorist *elabete;* cf. especially Moffatt and Manson 'you have got it'." Also Dowd, *Prayer*, 65: The aorist reading "is to be preferred both because it is extremely unlikely that the present or the future [variants in some manuscripts] would have been changed to an aorist and because the aorist is attested by Sinaiticus, Vaticanus, and other important witnesses. The value of the variants is that they indicate that this aorist was understood by early readers of the gospel as a past tense and regarded as erroneous or offensive. The contrast in the original tenses is emphasized in the proposed translation . . . by translating the tenses progressively: 'Keep on believing that you have received everything that you are praying and asking for, and it will be done for you.' " I think that does not make much sense, for why continue to ask for what one has in fact already received? The point of the final "it will be yours," or "it will be done for you" is that by prayer one may realize what has been available all along, i.e., the kingdom.

55. Dowd, *Prayer*, 65.

the dependently co-arisen embodiment of that awareness in communities of men and women. Both need to be present, for Christian practice is a practice that holds these two truths of the ultimate and the conventional in dynamic tension, differentiating them but not dichotomizing them.

There is, moreover, a connection between Jesus' sayings on prayer and the temple episode. As Dowd points out, "the temple has been rejected as a failure long before the Romans destroyed it, but because of its traditional role as the guarantor of the efficacy of prayer, [this rejection] required a reassertion of the importance of community prayer and the power available to it. The evangelist has arranged his materials in chapter 11 so as to follow the proleptic destruction of the temple with the necessary assurances about the efficacy of prayer, and he has used the fig tree pericope as a metaphorical clamp to hold the two ideas together."[56] Having emptied any localized and circumscribed presence of God, Jesus reaffirms God's availability to anyone who engages in the conventional practice of prayer with unhesitating faith in his presence.

At the end of the gospel, the risen Jesus is promised to be present back in Galilee, where he had earlier set up home. So Mark's Christians gather and go home: to that which has been present all along. Where did Christians in fact pray? They could emulate Jesus and pray in the solitude of wilderness places. But, where else could they gather but at home? Malbon observes, ". . . may it not be that the house, which replaces the synagogue and stands in opposition to the doomed temple in Mark, does suggest the early Christian community? With the destruction of the temple (13:2) and the rejection in the synagogue (13:9), the Christian community must come together in 'house churches.'"[57] Like all those healed by Jesus, in the final journey one goes home realizing that she has already received all that she has asked for.

The Validation of Truth
11: 27–33

[27]They came to Jerusalem again, and as Jesus was walking in the Temple, the chief priests and the scribes and the elders came to him, [28]and they said to him, "What authority have you for acting like this? Or who gave you authority to act like this?" [29]Jesus said to them, "I will ask you a question, just one; answer me and I will tell you my authority for acting like this. [30]John's baptism: what was its origin, heavenly or human? Answer me that." [31]And they argued this way among themselves: "If we say heavenly, he will say, 'Then why did you refuse to believe him?' [32]But dare we say human?"— they had the people to fear, for everyone held that John had been a real

---

56. Dowd, *Prayer,* 53.
57. Malbon, *Narrative Space,* 135. See 113–120, 130–136, and "Tē Oikia Autou: Mark 2: 15 in Context."

prophet. [33]So their reply to Jesus was, "We do not know." And Jesus said to them, "Nor will I tell you my authority for acting like this."

On his third trip into the Temple Jesus is accosted and questioned by Temple officials. But he does not answer their questions directly. The obvious answer would be that God is the source of all authority. Prophets do their speaking because of God. But Jesus refuses to so identify his role as a prophet or to claim God as the source of his authority, for within the imagined pattern of consciousness, that would result only in their mistaking the conventional validity of what he does for the absolute presence of God. Yet, to say that God is not the source of his authority would be to invite the misunderstanding that he had no valid authority whatsoever, for no one could enter the temple and overturn the vendors' tables and chairs merely on a human whim. The authorities want to know just whence this Jesus derives his authority.

Mark constructs this passage not so much to highlight their concern, as to focus on the interplay between the two truths. Jesus poses a parallel question to the men about the source for the Baptist's authority. And they argue the point among themselves (διελογίζοντο πρὸς ἑαυτούς). An alternate reading says that they reasoned the point (ἐλογίζοντο). Because they argue when the only answer is to abandon argument, they are caught in the net of verbal fabrication (*prapañca*) and finally rendered mute. Their lack of knowledge renders them without authority,[58] and thus they cannot press the issue. They have no way out of the dilemma, as the narrator makes sure the reader knows by the insertion of the phrase, "they were afraid of the crowd, for everyone held that John had been a real prophet."[59] They are unable to differentiate the two truths that might identify the authority of Jesus' actions as purely human (*saṃvṛti-mātra*) and therefore fully divine. This controversy over Jesus' authority leads directly into the beginning of chapter 12 and the parable of the wicked tenants.

---

58. Tolbert, *Sowing the Gospel*, 234.
59. See Fowler, *Let the Reader Understand*, 115–16.

12

Social Practice

The Tenant Authorities
12: 1–12

¹He went on to speak to them in parables, "A man planted a vineyard; he fenced it round, dug out a trough for the winepress and built a tower; then he leased it to tenants and went abroad. ²When the time came, he sent a servant to the tenants to collect from them his share of the produce from the vineyard. ³But they seized the man, thrashed him and sent him away empty-handed. ⁴Next he sent another servant to them; him they beat about the head and treated shamefully. ⁵And he sent another and him they killed; then a number of others, and they thrashed some and killed the rest. ⁶He had still someone left: his beloved son. He sent him to them last of all, thinking, 'They will respect my son.' ⁷But those tenants said to each other, 'This is the heir. Come on, let us kill him, and the inheritance will be ours.' ⁸So they seized him and killed him and threw him out of the vineyard. ⁹Now what will the owner of the vineyard do? He will come and make an end of the tenants and give the vineyard to others. ¹⁰Have you not read the text of this scripture:

> *The stone rejected by the builders*
> *has become the cornerstone;*
> *¹¹this is the Lord's doing*
> *and we marvel at it?"*

¹²And they would have liked to arrest him, because they realized that the parable was aimed at them, but they were afraid of the crowds. So they left him alone and went away.

Jesus has just refused to identify his authority to the Temple authorities. Now he draws on the Hebrew Bible to present a story about authority and its validation. The story of the vineyard draws from *Isaiah* 5: 1–7: "Let me sing my beloved the song of my friend for his vineyard. My beloved had a vineyard on a fertile hillside. He dug it, cleared it of stones, and planted it with red grapes. In the middle he built a tower, he hewed a press there too.

He expected it to yield fine grapes, wild grapes were all it yielded." The story goes on to identify this vineyard with the House of Israel.[1] Its destruction is brought about by Yahweh, who lays it waste because of its unproductivity.

In a similar fashion *Hosea* 10: 1–2 speaks of Israel as a luxuriant vine, with plenty of fruit, but as having divided hearts (LXX ἐμέρισαν καρδίας αὐτῶν), because of which they set up altars to other gods and erect stone pillars (ᾠκοδόμησε στήλας): "Israel was a luxuriant vine yielding plenty of fruit. The more his fruit increased, the more altars he built; the richer his land became, the richer he made the sacred pillars. Theirs is a divided heart; now they will have to pay for it. He himself will hack down their altars and wreck their sacred pillars." Here the unfaithfulness of Israel comes from a consciousness whose single focus on Yahweh becomes divided, just as in Mark the authorities insist on discriminative consciousness, distinguishing their absolutely valid traditions from the profane lives of the people.

Jeremiah 12: 1–17 speaks of Yahweh's favorite estate becoming a wilderness because of the treachery of the people's shepherds: "Many shepherds have laid my vineyard waste, have trampled over my plot of land, the plot of land which was my joy, reducing my favorite estate to a deserted wilderness." Yahweh's choice vine becoming a degenerate, bastard plant, as in *Jeremiah* 2: 20–21, reiterates this theme: "It is long ago now since you broke your yoke, burst your bonds and said, 'I will not serve!' Yet on every high hill and under every green tree you have sprawled and played the whore. Yet I had planted you, a red vine of completely sound stock. How is it that you have turned into seedlings of a vine that is alien to me?"

No Jew could have failed to get Jesus' reference, and the Temple authorities exhibit no particular discernment in seeing that the parable was aimed at them.[2] Mark keeps to the point—the vineyard of Israel is but leased to Israel, to the people, by Yahweh, who is not present in the day to day running of affairs. That is up to the people and, most especially, to the tenants, the authorities. In Mahāyāna terms, ultimate meaning remains completely other from worldly convention—God does not intervene within the conventional world, for that would imply that normally God is absent. Rather, God is present always, as that which remains hidden and absent, that which is encountered only in the silence of withdrawal and in the midst of the forgiving community. Thus, the Mahāyāna affirmation that all is only worldly conven-

1. See Kee, *Community of the New Age*, 83.

2. Tolbert, *Sowing the Gospel*, on the parable of the sower in 4: 1–9 and this account of the tenants, 104: "These parables were *not* intended to be confusing, misleading, or obscure to the reader—at least to the authorial reader." Similarly, Mack, *A Myth of Innocence*, 232: "To guide the audience through the material, another parable plot synopsis is supplied close to the beginning of the segment: the parable of the Vineyard and the Tenants." Indeed, the point is so clear even to the characters in the story that this is the only occasion in Mark where the point is explicitly stated to have been understood; Schweizer, "Mark's Theological Achievement," 60.26: "It is only once said that they all understood the parable (12: 12), but this leads only to hardening and judgment." See Ambrozic, "Mark's Concept of the Parable," 220–27.

tion (*saṃvṛti-mātra*) is meant to deny the sometime incursion of ultimate reality into worldly convention, and to affirm its constant presence as that which is covered by and thus signified by everyday affairs.

Yet, despite the wholly conventional operation of this vineyard, one does not get to keep all the fruit, for the vineyard of Israel is received as a gift, and one must make an eschatological return to its creator on the last day. The workers are farm hands (γεωργοὺς) meant to tend that vineyard and bring forth the fruit of compassion and justice. They must not cling to the results of their labor as if they were fully responsible. Nevertheless, the workers confine themselves to a conventional viewpoint and hoard the fruit of the vineyard.[3] They try to assert the primacy of worldly convention over ultimate meaning, rejecting any eschatological claim from the distant owner.

Note that the image of the owner is that of an absentee-landlord, never a figure to inspire warm feelings.[4] And workers who have to do all the work often harbor feelings of resentment. But Mark's point here is not simply about social justice. Rather it is about the closing off of ultimate meaning by the narrow perspective of an enclosing selfhood, the root cause of the injustices men inflict upon one another. Self-clinging is a denial of the nearness of the eschatological kingdom announced by Jesus (1: 15) and embodied in his compassionate miracles and exorcisms.

Mark, i.e., Mahāyāna Mark, wants to differentiate the two truths, and so there is a play on the verb "to send." The master sends his servant (ἀπέστειλεν ... δοῦλον), much as Jesus sends his disciples out to announce the coming eschatological kingdom (6: 7–13), the judgment of ultimate meaning that empties all conventional traditions and activity. The workers receive that servant but send him back empty handed (ἀπέστειλαν κενόν), asserting the primacy of their conventional ownership. And this not once but a number of times.[5] They take the final action of killing the messengers, even the

---

3. Hengel, *Judaism and Hellenism,* 1:56–57, describes how the aristocratic exploitation by the upper class served "to exacerbate the situation of the lower strata of the population. It prepared the ground for apocalyptic speculation and the later revolts, which had increasingly strong social elements, right up to the time of the Bar Kochba rebellion." The social situation presupposed by Mark included great landowners, tax farmers, administrators, moneylenders, day-laborers, speculation in grain, and slavery for debts, as Kee, *Community of the New Age,* 79, explains.

4. Kermode, *The Genesis of Secrecy,* 44: "Jeremias and Dodd say that [the parable of the tenants] reflects the resentment felt by Galilean tenant farmers toward their absentee landlords; such landlords might, when all else failed, send their sons to collect, and the tenants might kill them in the hope of benefiting from a law that assigned ownerless property to the first claimant. They were wrong to do so, of course, and God would give the vineyard not to them, but to the poor (Jeremias, *Parables,* 70f; Dodd, *Parables,* 96f). But this is only a more rationalistic allegory; it denies that the parable was originally what it certainly later became, a prophecy of the crucifixion, and turns it into a somewhat ridiculous fable about current affairs."

5. Fowler, *Let the Reader Understand,* 95, suggests a possible parallel between this servant who was beat about the head and treated shamefully with John the Baptist, whose wound shamefully severed his head. That seems likely as the previous encounter has left the chief priests and scribes mute about the authority of the Baptist.

beloved son, who has already been identified by the voice from heaven as Jesus himself (1: 11).[6] They insist on seeing the son as within the realm of their imagined pattern of consciousness, as a threat against their possession of authority. He becomes an unwelcome intruder, for any hint of that which breaks through worldly convention threatens the absoluteness of that conventional perspective. Yet, the messengers keep coming, for worldly convention is never independently self-sufficient.

The owner sends his beloved son unprotected. That in itself seems strange, for one would expect a wise master to take cognizance of how the servants and messengers he sent earlier have been treated.[7] But no defending army accompanies the beloved son. The narrative point of the sending of the son is to elicit recognition in the reader of the otherness of ultimate meaning, not to mount a story-level invasion into the conventional from the realm of ultimate meaning. The tenants not only kill him, but throw his body out of the vineyard, hoping thereby to claim the inheritance for themselves.

By calling the last messenger, Jesus himself, "the beloved son," Mark does imply that he had a close, intimate relationship with God. But he does not say that Jesus is qualitatively different from the other messengers. He is not recommending a replacement theology, whereby the new religion of Jesus takes over from the outmoded religion of the Jews.[8] All the imagery of the vineyard, including the evil tenants, is derived from the prophets of Israel, and the present story draws upon that narrative tradition of prophetic, eschatological judgment. The beloved son is the last in a long line of messengers. Mark is not arguing for the superiority of Christianity over Judaism. The point concerns not the relative validity of religions, but the recognition of the otherness of ultimate meaning, of the falsity of clinging to any tradition, whether Jewish or Christian. Such clinging, no matter what its content, collapses any dynamic tension between conventional practice and that which is other. The workers repeat the pattern of *Genesis*, where Adam and Eve want to be in firm and full control of the garden, determining whether they get to eat all of the fruit of the garden. The result is similar: they are expelled from the garden, for it was never theirs in the first place. To identify oneself within a tradition does not imply that that tradition is one's possession. To claim that is but a subtle form of self-clinging, of attachment to me and mine (*ātma-ātmya*).

Above, Jesus "cursed" the fig tree, even though it was not the time for it to bear fruit (ὁ γὰρ καιρὸς οὐκ ἦν σύκων). Here, the owner sends his son

---

6. Kermode, *The Genesis of Secrecy*, 43: "And when Mark describes the last messenger as the *huios agapētos* (beloved or only son) of the Lord, he cannot be forgetting that he makes God use exactly these words of Jesus at the opening of his book [*Su ei ho huios mou ho agapētos*], 1: 11)." It also perhaps alludes to the passage from Isaiah above.

7. Tolbert, *Sowing the Gospel*, 236: "This act defies common sense and surpasses human compassion."

8. Against Kelber, *Mark's Story of Jesus*, 63: "With this parable Jesus has set himself up as the cornerstone of the new temple, the Kingdom of God, which however is not synonymous with the old temple but antithetical to it."

when it is the time (τῷ κιρῷ) for him to receive his share in the fruit of the vineyard (ἵνα . . . λάβῃ ἀπὸ τῶν καρπῶν τοῦ ἀμπελῶνος). The time for finding fruit is envisaged as having come; it is not a future hope. Thus, in the story, Mark describes the landlord not as simply killing the workers, giving them, as it were, their comeuppance. Rather, he comes and "makes an end" to the tenants (ἐλεύσεται καὶ ἀπολέσει τοὺς γεωργούς) and gives the vineyard to others.[9] For them the end time has arrived. They murder his servant, thus bringing the linear expectancies, both their own and those of the owner, to an end, while he renders their efforts totally inefficacious. The verb used of their actions is "they murdered" (ἀπέκτιναν), while the action of the owner is "to bring them to naught" (ἀπολέσει), since no effort to absolutize worldly convention can lead to any other result. All human endeavors are empty, without firm and abiding essence. The tenants' failure to realize that emptiness is what has led to their violent clinging to the illusion that they own the vineyard.

Mark ends the passage by quoting the section about the rejected cornerstone from *Psalm* 118: 22–23, the section immediately preceding the quotation found in the Palm Procession in 11: 9, where the people cry out, "Hosanna! Blessed is he who is coming in the name of the Lord!" *Acts* 4: 11 quotes the same passage as a judgment against those who crucified Jesus, in whom alone salvation is possible. Yet it is not within the deluded pattern of clinging to imagined realities that Jesus saves. In that pattern, it simply does not matter whose name one invokes.[10] Rather, Jesus, the worldly and conventional presence of the otherness of ultimate meaning, coming in the name of the Lord as a pilgrim worshiper, leads people to salvation precisely out of deluded ignorance and all the passionate violence that entails. Christ is the cornerstone rejected by the authorities, and that very rejection exposes the falsity of every tradition that is deemed more than conventionally valid. Just as the stone of the temple edifice at the opening of Chapter 13 will be destroyed, so Jesus himself is destroyed.[11] His transience, his passing from the linear story, is even more stark than the stones of the temple. He is the cornerstone that is no cornerstone, and that is why he is the cornerstone.

---

9. Bauer, *A Greek-English Lexicon,* 95, does indeed give the meaning of ἀπόλλυμι as to ruin, to destroy, and, when used of persons, to kill or put to death. Yet Lampe, *A Patristic Greek Lexicon,* 200, from his patristic sources refers particularly to spiritual ruin or loss: "*Destroy, ruin,* of spiritual ruin in the present life, or *lose,* of spiritual loss." It seems to me that Mark is contrasting ἀπολέσει, the action of the owner, with the murder (ἀπέκτειναν) of the son. Also see Kee, *Community of the New Age,* 83: "Those who have given up all human security in their fidelity to God will be given the roles of power in the kingdom of God (Dan 7:27). The deprivation they have voluntarily accepted will be compensated for in their day of vindication when they receive the everlasting kingdom (Dan 7:14)." That sums up the request of James and John to sit on Jesus' right and left in positions of power(10:35–40), but hardly the anticlimactic ending of Mark, where everybody is to go home to Galilee.

10. For a theological treatment, see Knitter, *No Other Name?*

11. Tolbert, *Sowing the Gospel,* 237: "The parable's closing stress on the stone (λίθον)

Perhaps another interpretive model may be employed here, that of the *Bhagavadgita,* where the message is that humans are to engage in their cosmic duty without becoming attached to the fruits of that duty (*karmaphalā-saṇga*). Ārjuna, the main character in that ancient Hindu drama, must fulfill his allotted role of warrior in an inter-clan war, despite his attachment to his friends and kinsmen. In Gandhi's famous reading of the *Gita,* the text is not recommending warlike actions, but rather complete detachment from all action, while demanding the fulfillment of one's allotted role. One must work as if all depended upon oneself, while realizing that in fact all depends on God. That is how transient vineyard workers are to act, and, so acting, transform any vineyard into the kingdom.

The last paragraph of the parable of the tenants refers back to 11: 27, where the authorities question Jesus' authority. In the present parable the chief priests, scribes, and elders (11: 27) play the role of the tenant farmers. Perceiving that the parable indeed applies to them, that—as in the parable—they do not own the vineyard, they want to arrest Jesus but are afraid of the crowd, just as they were in 11:32. The crowd, usually the champion of poor workers against rich landlords, here apparently enjoys the ironic reversal of roles. They take the side of the wronged owner, against the tenant-bosses who will be brought to naught.

Mark has opened this episode by saying that Jesus is continuing to teach in parables (καὶ ἤρξατο αὐτοῖς ἐν παραβολαῖς λαλεῖν), leading one to recall the parable discourse in Chapter 4: 10–12 and its theme on the inscrutability of parables to outsiders. Yet the only parable cited here is the one about the vineyard, the point of which is obvious to the Jerusalem authorities who have come to question Jesus (11: 27). But perhaps the parable is easy to misread, not for the intra-story authorities, but for the extra-story reader. The authorities get the point that Jesus threatens any conventional ownership of traditions, but Christian readers have all too often read into it justification for their own Christian arrogance and superiority. Mark is not simply writing a Christian apologetic against the Jewish tradition. He quotes the Hebrew scriptures as his authority, reiterating their teachings about conversion, about work and attachment to the fruits of one's labor. The authorities' perception that the parable applies to them is the reason that it does apply to them. Had they not clung to the absolute status of their traditions, they would not have been threatened by Jesus. The surface point is crystal clear, and so the tenant farmers throw the heir out of the vineyard. One wonders if modern readers do not repeat the pattern of the tenants described in the parable, clinging to their traditions and trivializing Jesus as their embodiment of an ownership of orthodoxy.

---

rejected by the builders (οἱ οἰκοδομοῦντες) in Mark 12: 10 will guide the audience's understanding of Jesus' extended response to the disciple who marvels at the 'wonderful stones' (λίθοι) and 'wonderful buildings' (οἰκοδομαί) of the temple in Mark 13: 1–2, which is often called the Apocalyptic Discourse."

This episode opens a second Jerusalem controversy section, paralleling the Galilean controversy section in 2: 1–3:6.[12] This debate cycle, however, affirms his broad agreement with the Pharisees' and the scribes' position on basic issues, while excoriating only their false practice. Those among them who desire to arrest him have misconstrued his parable in light of their fixed religious ideology. Were it not for that primal ignorance, there would be no necessity for Jesus' arrest or his death. Again, this parable hides more than it reveals, for its point relates not only to its allegorical impact, but also to the inner minds of its hearers. Indeed, shortly one of the scribes, impressed with what he hears, shares a moment of deep agreement with Jesus on the theme of loving God and neighbor. Even beyond the intra-story hearers, Mark's rhetoric maneuvers the extra-story reader into a position parallel to that of the evil tenants, clinging to the truth of one's accepted tradition above all other options. Interpreters also "see but do not understand" (4: 12).

There is further irony in the assumed support of the crowd, for it is that crowd who will support Jesus only to the limit of their false conventional horizon. They too fail to discern the wondrous reality of working in the vineyard, i.e., in the world, without coveting the fruits of that world. The debate on how to differentiate these two truths of worldly convention and ultimate meaning continues immediately in the next section on tribute to Caesar, and shortly into the Passion narrative, for that narrative is the focal description of Jesus' manner of worldly and conventional engagement. How does one both engage in the dependently co-arisen world in awareness of its eschatological emptiness, and still not let that world slide away into blank nothingness? Jesus will die for the sake of his world-work in leading others to resurrection, while not absolutizing that work into a static truth for all to mimic. All engagement, even Jesus', is dependently co-arisen and not immediately transferable apart from the complex of conditions that contextualize his life and the lives of his followers.

God and Caesar
12: 13–17

[13]Next they sent to him some Pharisees and some Herodians to catch him out in what he said. [14]These came and said to him, "Master, we know you are an honest man, that you are not afraid of anyone, because human rank

---

12. Dewey, *Markan Public Debate,* 162: "First, Jesus in direct teaching attacks the behavior of the Jewish leaders, prophesies their destruction, and their rejection of the one whom God will establish (A,B 12: 1–12). Then in three interwoven debates, Jesus answers questions on basic issues of Judaism, showing his agreement with the Pharisaic scribal position on the political issues of taxation, on the hope of resurrection, and on the fundamental demand of God (C, D, C'). Then once again in direct teaching, Jesus attacks the scribes' understanding of christology, warns against their behavior, and prophesies their condemnation. (B', A', 12: 35–40)."

means nothing to you, and that you teach the way of God in all honesty. Is it permissible to pay taxes to Caesar or not? Should we pay or not?" [15]Recognizing their hypocrisy he said to them, "Why are you putting me to the test? Hand me a denarius and let me see." [16]They handed him one and he said, "Whose portrait is this? Whose title?" They said to him, "Caesar's." [17]Jesus said to them, "Pay Caesar what belongs to Caesar—and God what belongs to God." And they were amazed at him.

In the story of the tenant farmers, they, and by implication the Jerusalem authorities, focus only on their conventional work, on the fruits of their vineyard. Here the Pharisees and Herodians turn the tables and accuse Jesus of focusing only on the ultimate meaning of God, while denigrating worldly convention altogether. Any person in authority in any institution must prudently guide that institution within the world. Otherwise, the institution will most certainly be short-lived. Such prudence demands an analytic understanding of the concrete conditions that institutions face. The Pharisees and Herodians are here concerned about the relationships between the Jewish Temple cult and the Roman authorities. In fact, "it was by refusing to pay the imperial taxation that Israel later entered into the revolutionary war against Rome which resulted in the Jewish defeat and the destruction of the Temple."[13] Their strategy was to cooperate where needed so as to ensure that the Roman powers would not disrupt or interfere with religious practice. A prudent strategy, to be sure. Basing themselves on the clear need for political understanding, they see Jesus as bereft of such understanding, and thus think they can easily catch him up in words (ἀγρεύσωσιν λόγῳ), i.e., in his inability to think in conventional terms. They accuse him of being honest (ἀληθής) and of teaching the path in honesty (ἀληθείας), i.e., in truth. Here truth or honesty seems to signify an awareness apart from conventional considerations. That is what they say: Jesus is unconcerned about anyone else (οὐ μέλει σοι περὶ οὐδενός), i.e., he does not fear anyone. He is not a respecter of outward appearances (οὐ γὰρ βλέπεις εἰς πρόσωπον ἀνθώπων), i.e. human rank means nothing to him. In a word, they think that Jesus is so focused on ultimate matters that he has lost sight of conventional realities. Such a path of disengagement cannot, they deem, be truly the path, for it ignores the concrete situations in which people find themselves. This is the

---

13. Kelber, *Mark's Story of Jesus*, 64. Kee, *Community of the New Age*, 97–100, describes four options for first-century Jews in their encounter with Hellenism and the Roman establishment: collaboration, exemplified by Herod and the Herodians, passive acquiescence, practiced by the Pharisees, complete withdrawal, opted for by the Essenes, and insurrection, the choice of the Zealots and others. But the Markan Jesus fits none of the above options. "In a time when not only Jews but Jewishness were suspect, the Markan community which had put forward these prophetic claims [about their covenant, 14:24] and yet refused to identify itself with any of the wholly Jewish groups of that epoch would find itself a radically alienated social group that could expect little but suspicion and alienation from Jew and Gentile alike."

import of their question about paying the tax to Caesar, to the Roman occupiers. Can one who is focused on ultimate truth compromise with unjust civil authorities? They attempt to place Jesus on the horns of a dilemma, where he will be forced either to affirm or deny the conventional necessity of paying the tax.

Again Mark has Jesus overturn his questioners' assumption that one has to choose between ultimate and conventional truth. It is not a question of which to choose, but of living in the differential tension between the two truths. Jesus sees through their hypocrisy, their pretense of capturing the ultimate in conventional forms. Indeed, the constant temptation of institutional advocates is precisely to reduce the ultimate meaning of tradition into the conventional framework of obvious necessities. Jesus asks them why they are again testing (πειράζετε) him. The same verb "to test" is used in 8: 11, where the Pharisees question him about a validating sign, and again in 10: 2 about divorce. All allude back to Jesus' wilderness testing (πειραζόμενος) by Satan in 1: 13, whether he can translate that wilderness encounter into conventional living. Thus, they test him to see if he comes up to their conventional standards.

Jesus' answer clearly differentiates between worldly convention and ultimate meaning. Worldly convention is the realm of concrete, political judgment, and so, in the circumstances, one should render to Caesar what is Caesar's. Yet, one must also render to God what is God's, for God's image is on no one's coinage. God must be served by rendering to him the fruits of our endeavors, for all human endeavors are in fact empty of any supporting essence. The Pharisees, as his own disciples so frequently are, are amazed (ἐξεθαύμαζον ἐπ' αὐτῷ), for Jesus agrees with their position on the issue.[14] Yet he still does not fit into their framework, for he affirms the hegemony neither of worldly convention nor of ultimate meaning.

The story has its funny side also, for, although the Pharisees and scribes do upon request hand Jesus a denarius, Mark neglects to mention whether Jesus ever gives it back to them. After all, it was not their portrait that was on the coin!

Conventional Life and the Ultimate Resurrection
12: 18–27

[18]Then some Sadducees—who deny that there is a resurrection—came to him and they put this question to him, [19]"Master, Moses prescribed for us that if

---

14. Kelber, *Mark's Story of Jesus,* 64: "Jesus' well-known answer rejects any violent Zealotic insinuations: one may serve God as well as Caesar." Dewey, *Markan Public Debate,* 157, sees 12: 13–14 as a rhetorical subunit of "variants of debate form in which Jesus engaged in no objectionable act." In all three issues "Jesus and the Pharisaic scribal faction of Judaism are on common ground."

a man's brother dies leaving a wife but no child, the man must marry the widow to raise up children for his brother. [20]*Now there were seven brothers; the first married a wife and then died leaving no children.* [21]*The second married the widow, and then he too died leaving no children; with the third it was the same,* [22]*and none of the seven left any children. Last of all the woman herself died.* [23]*Now at the resurrection, when they rise again, whose wife will she be, since she has been married to all seven?"*

[24]*Jesus said to them, "Surely the reason why you are wrong is that you understand neither the scriptures nor the power of God.* [25]*For when they rise from the dead, men and women do not marry; no, they are like the angels in heaven.* [26]*Now about the dead rising again, have you never read in the Book of Moses, in the passage about the bush, how God spoke to him and said, 'I am the God of Abraham, the God of Isaac and the God of Jacob'?* [27]*He is God not of the dead, but of the living. You are very much mistaken."*

This passage flows from the immediately preceding one, introduced by the paratactic conjunctive, "and (καὶ)." It too is about transcendence and religion, about the ultimate state and conventional reality. The Sadducees follow the ancient tradition and refuse to admit a resurrection (ἀνάστασιν μὴ εἶναι) from the dead. Their argument about the potentially polyandrous woman shows that in fact what they refuse to affirm is a parallel between the present life and the resurrected life, which their reasoning clearly invalidates. The only raising up they talk about is the raising up of children (ἐξαναστήσῃ σπέρμα), a somewhat risqué—perhaps funny—interpretation of the resurrection, offered in contrast to the literal interpretation they oppose. They suggest the only resurrection warranted by Moses is that of the brother's penis, in fulfilling the need to maintain the brother's family line. Thus we have a contrast between a literal reading of resurrection, the absurdity of which is expressed by the case example, and a very this-worldly interpretation that sees things most concretely indeed. Between a falsely imagined supernaturalism, wherein this life simply is restored later on, and an absolutized worldly convention, in which one imagines that what counts is clear and obvious. Their case example does refute a literal version of resurrection as a restored continuity of worldly and conventional living. If indeed one arose in continuance with conventional life, if ultimate meaning were continuous with worldly convention, then the married state would still maintain. And then the poor woman would most certainly be a heavenly polyandrist! Apparently, the Sadducees expect Jesus to hold to a literal view and thus to be unable to reply to their question.

Jesus, however, affirms both the conventional validity, indeed, the indissolubility of marriage (10: 1–12), and the ultimate falling away of marital relationships in the silence of ultimate meaning.[15] Jesus' reply is stark, "You

---

15. Via, *The Ethics of Mark's Gospel*, 104–15: "We have to recognize that Mark as a unified whole story has, by means of his dual realized and futuristic eschatology, fused the eschatological attitude [that would dispense with marriage] with an intensified concern

do not understand the scriptures!" This is harsh in the extreme.[16] The Sadducees are people who cling to scripture in a fundamentalist version: they deny
the resurrection because it is not clearly taught in the Hebrew scriptures. In
this, of course, they are correct; the Hebrew scriptures do not teach life after
death. The first appearance of the notion of eternal life beyond death is the
Book of Wisdom, written in Alexandria in the Greek language.[17] Even Jesus'
quotation from *Exodus* 3: 6 about the God of Abraham, Isaac, and Jacob
does not directly teach that there is a resurrection. Jesus has to interpret that
text, bringing out its significance—that God is a God of the living, not the
dead.[18] The power of God stands for what is beyond worldly convention, an

---

about the quality of the believer's personal family and communal life in the world. Mark
has thus established one paradoxical position which is the norm for all disciples. Let us
say hypothetically that in the pre-Markan tradition the belief in the near end promotes
the abandonment of marriage (at least in principle), while world concern promotes the
permanence of marriage. Mark then, by making *realized* eschatology the ground for
revitalized life in the historical world, has reversed the way in which the tradition dealt
with the issue of the permanence of marriage. No longer does the expectation of the end
call for the abandonment of marriage. Rather, the actualized anticipation of the eschatological new creation is the basis for its indissolubility, as is the tacit continuation of primordial
unfallenness. And world concern or compromise with the world is not the ground for the
permanence of marriage but is rather an expression of the hardness of heart that undermines
marriage. But Mark has also retained the position that has been transcended. Why should
marriage be sustained if historical existence in the world may not have a positive value
and dimension? And the eschatological per se, in its wholly futuristic aspect, *will* spell
the end of marriage: there will be no marriage in the resurrection (12: 25). We see again
that the permanence of marriage presupposes an ongoing history which is eschatologically
revitalized." Rather than a dual eschatology, I suggest that Mark has an emptied eschatology, i.e., an end time that is the end of time. The falling away of marriage is not the
result of a future moment of continuity, but of the discontinuous resurrection, in the light
of which the conventional and worldly validity of marriage is affirmed as a recovery of
the beginning.

16. Meier, *A Marginal Jew,* 346: ". . . the Synoptic Jesus engages in debate with the
Sadducees (made up mostly of the priests and lay aristocracy in Jerusalem) only once,
namely, in the dispute over belief in the resurrection of the dead on the last day (Mark
12: 18–27 par.). The encounter is marked by hostility on both sides. . . . [Jesus' response
that they are ignorant of the scriptures and of God's power] is a remarkably pointed barb
aimed at the priestly guardians of divine revelation and divine power, supposedly centered
in the Jerusalem temple."

17. See Schillebeeckx, *Jesus,* 518–23; Keenan, *The Meaning of Christ,* 25–27.

18. Kee, *Community of the New Age,* 156: "The difficulty lies in the fact that there are
a number of apparent logical gaps in the second part of the argument which seeks to
prove the resurrection by appeal to Ex. 3:6. As Haenchen has shown, the thrust of the
psalms and prophets is to declare that man can serve and honour God only during life.
When man is in the grave, that relationship of honour and dependence comes to an end.
(Haenchen, *Der Weg Jesu,* 410f.) What seems to be implied is that Yahweh did not say,
"I was the God of Abraham, of Isaac, and of Jacob, and I *now am* your God,' but that
on the same plane of being God says to Moses at a point of time chronologically remote
from the days of any of these patriarchial figures, 'I *am* the God of Abraham, of Isaac,
and of Jacob.' This point could not be made at all on the basis of the Hebrew text, which
contains no form of the verb 'to be,' but it makes a kind of sense in the LXX, where the
passage opens with the solemn declaratory self-identification, ἐγώ εἰμι. But curiously,

awareness of which is necessary for an understanding of scripture. The words of scripture are not signs encapsulating the final truth, but expressions of experiences of insights and understandings that go beyond those words. The Sadducees are misled (πλανᾶσθε) by their imagined pattern of understanding, for there is no continuity between this life, with its marriages and children, and the resurrected life. The verb "to be misled" admits not only the passive sense reflected in the translation, but also a middle sense, i.e., "you have misled yourselves," through the deluded pattern of your own consciousness. Jesus does not go on to describe that resurrected life. He only says that we will be like the angels, who do not marry. And thus the Sadducees' objection does not hold.

The passage about the bush to which Jesus refers is from *Exodus* 3: 1–6. It describes Moses' silent sojourn in the wilderness of Mount Horeb, where he encounters the strange and numinous presence of Yahweh in the burning bush. The sacred presence is indicated when Yahweh tells Moses to take off his shoes, "for the place on which you stand is holy ground." This is a breakthrough experience for Moses, going beyond any worldly and conventional form. Thus, Jesus implies that the resurrection too is a breakthrough experience, going beyond any conventional life form. It is the failure of the Sadducees to differentiate such ultimate meaning that often leads them astray (πολὺ πλανᾶσθε), for by trying to fit resurrected life into conventional forms, they fail to recognize the complete otherness of ultimate meaning. Nevertheless, God is not apart from human living. His otherness is expressed by indirection in conventional language; that is the only language there is. God is the God of Abraham, Isaac, and Jacob, the God who is the beginning and the end of the path presented by the traditions. Traditional descriptions are not, however, exact explanations, but merely conventional terms (*saṃvṛti-mātra*) that manifest the otherness of God (*saṃvṛti-udbhāvanā*). The traditions point to God, without literally spelling out the content of their descriptions.

εἰμι is not found in the text of Mark either, so that one can only conclude that it is understood implicitly and that what is being asserted is the identity of relationship between God on the one hand and the succession of patriarchial figures on the other. That this relationship is described, by implication at least, in the present time, is presumably understood by Mark as affirming that God's association with his people is an ongoing reality, rather than merely a memory from an irrecoverable past. In a way that stands on its head the despair and finality of the psalms concerning death, the Markan tradition here argues that since God is not the God of the dead (12: 27a), these persons are alive and he is their God. An explicit doctrine of the resurrection is not taught, but both the mistaken notion that life in the age to come must be defined in terms of present limits and patterns, and the excluding of a continued relationship to God beyond death in an age to come are combated." I am not sure what to make of the logic of Jesus' argument, but understand resurrection in a Mahāyāna fashion as beyond both being and nonbeing, for which see the writings of Nishitani, also Waldenfels, *Absolute Nothingness,* 159–62.

Practicing the Differentiation of the Two Truths
12: 28–34

²⁸One of the scribes who had listened to them debating appreciated that Jesus had given a good answer and put a further question to him, "Which is the first of all the commandments?" ²⁹Jesus replied, "This is the first: Hear, Israel, the Lord our God is the one, only Lord, ³⁰and you must love the Lord your God with all your heart, with all your soul, with all your mind and with all your strength. ³¹The second is this: You must love your neighbor as yourself. There is no commandment greater than these." ³²The scribe said to him, "Well spoken, Master, what you have said is true, that he is one and that there is no other. ³³To love him with all your heart, with all your understanding and strength, and to love your neighbor as yourself, this is far more important than any burnt offering or sacrifice."³⁴ Jesus, seeing how wisely he had spoken, said, "You are not far from the kingdom of God." And after that no one dared to question him any more.

Jesus has been disputing matters with the Temple emissaries. The central focus has been the difference between ultimate meaning and worldly convention, in other words, on the practice of the middle path. The barren fig tree stands for desiccated forms of worship. The expulsion of the temple traders says that worldly convention has usurped the role of ultimate meaning. But the authority of Jesus, as the beloved son of the vineyard's owner, is not justified in terms of worldly convention. The ultimate meaning from which Jesus derives his authority does not intrusively enter the realm of worldly convention. One should still pay taxes to the Romans. One should still raise up children to deceased brothers. The present passage continues the dialogue, the dialogue Mark constructs with his readers about the differentiation of the two truths, about the differentiation of true worship from formal cultic practice, about the greatest of the commandments.

The scribe who has been listening to this dialogue is impressed. Jesus has answered well, for he has insisted on the discontinuity of ultimate meaning from all conventional forms. Jesus points away from religious fabrication (*prapañca*) and from the imagined pattern of religious attachment (*parikalpita*). Understanding the import of Jesus' sayings, the scribe seeks to elicit a more positive response from him. Just what is really important?

Jesus answers as any good Jew would answer, by quoting the Torah. The first half of his response is for the Jews the most basic statement of faith in Yahweh, from *Deuteronomy* 6: 4–5. The Shema (Hear, O Israel) is the hallmark of Judaism. It insists, as Jesus has been insisting, on the uniqueness of the Lord, God. God is not one among other gods. God is not one being, no matter how powerful, among other beings. Rather, God abides as the only member of the class God, which is to say, there is no class God. Jesus reaffirms this traditional faith. The later Christian conceit that Jesus proffers a religion of love in contrast to the ancient faith of Israel is simply hogwash.

The Hebrew Bible is not simply a dispensation of laws, for here Jesus himself, following the example of pious Jews everywhere, encapsulates all Torah into these two commandments about love.

It is not enough just to love the Lord; one must also love one's neighbor as oneself. Mark has Jesus quote from *Leviticus* 19: 18, again affirming the traditional faith of Israel against any formal cult such as that of the Temple authorities. But it is not that these are two separate commandments, for they stand together. Neither is possible to fulfill without the other. One cannot love the Lord while hating one's neighbor. Nor can one love one's neighbor without grounding that in the silent mystery of God, of ultimate truth, for if human beings do not share in a deeper mystery, there is no reason why we should not simply use one another. Thus, while the scribe asks Jesus for the first of all commandments, Jesus answers by giving two.

Nāgārjuna teaches that one cannot approach ultimate meaning without worldly convention, for the teaching must be expressed in words and concepts. Likewise, worldly convention cannot be understood apart from ultimate meaning. If one has no insight into the silence of emptiness and ultimate meaning, worldly and conventional statements and actions are falsely imagined to be themselves absolute, the proverbial bottom line of the short-sighted.

The scribe says that Jesus indeed speaks truly, just as the Pharisees and Herodians in 12: 14 said that Jesus spoke in truth and honesty. Their praise may have been disingenuous, but the scribe does recognize that Jesus in fact speaks from the truth of ultimate meaning. In 12: 13–17, on the question of tax and here too, perhaps, the concern is whether that truth is relevant to concrete living. After all, there have been many people whose higher level of discourse may have expressed a deep truth, but who remain aloof from human concerns and problems. Yet, by his speaking, Jesus here insists that there is no higher discourse, no talk that is beyond talk. One must hold the two truths in dynamic tension, and love both God and neighbor in the one fulfillment of Torah.

The scribe and Jesus are in total agreement. Indeed, in the entire Gospel of Mark this scribe receives the most positive treatment: he is not far (οὐ μακρὰν) from the eschatological kingdom of God, which is already at the door (1: 15).[19] He gets the point. His thoughts harmonize with those of Jesus. He is pronounced to be not far from the kingdom of God, i.e., not far from

---

19. Mann, *Mark,* 481–82: "Jesus' reply brings us once again to an enigmatic statement about the Kingdom of God. The idea is certainly that of a realm in which the sovereign will of God will be unquestioned and his reign unchallenged. But in this context, is *You are not far from the Kingdom of God* being understood in some future eschatological sense, or does Jesus mean it to be understood as a present or almost present reality? It appears somewhat odd to suggest that the man is well on the way to being found acceptable and ready when the Reign of God dawns, and the present writer finds it impossible to resist the conclusion that the Reign of God is presented by Jesus as a present reality. . . . We are therefore faced with yet another saying which carries the plain implications of 'realized' eschatology." Again I prefer to say that it is a realized eschatology because emptied of any content apart from the dependently co-arisen content of human living.

practicing the rule of God on earth. He has learned how to practice the differentiation of the two truths, how to love God and one's neighbor. This contrasts sharply with all of Jesus' disciples, family, and friends, none of whom ever do get the point, who always distort Jesus' teachings through their own preconceived ideas, and who all desert Jesus at the end. But, the scribe is not asked to follow Jesus, as was the rich man. Evidently the scribe had no such desire. Lagrange opines that "he almost has the necessary disposition to receive the Gospel."[20] Yet, that does not fit the text, for in Mark the disciples who do ostensibly receive the Gospel are described pejoratively, while this scribe is described by Jesus in a very positive light.

At this passage the questioning about the two truths ceases for the moment, for Jesus and the scribe have come together, and in so doing, have met the concerns of Mark's readers. It is not a question of the superiority of Christian belief over Jewish—on the most important level they are identical, for the first and foremost commandment is the very same.[21] Mark's readers, who apparently identify themselves as Christians, are again maneuvered into the position of admiring a Jewish scribe who shows no interest in following their path. The point is not to stress the differences between the two traditions. Many scholars think that Mark reflects the polemic of the early Jewish Christians against the religious establishment that has ousted them. Yet even if this is the case, he does not reject the foundational faith of Israel and one need not repeat the anti-Jewish polemic of first-century Christians in interpreting Mark.

Jesus' Casuistry
12: 35–37

[35]*While teaching in the Temple, by way of response*[22] *Jesus said, "How can the scribes maintain that the Christ is the son of David?* [36]*David himself, moved by the Holy Spirit, said:*

---

20. Quoted in Bratcher and Nida, *A Translator's Handbook,* 387.

21. Dewey, *Markan Public Debate,* 166: "As a prophet, Jesus may not be dismissed by the Jewish leaders out of hand, as Jeremiah could not be killed outright when he predicted the fall of the first temple (Jer. 7: 26). The Jewish establishment must first show Jesus to be a false prophet, not speaking for God. In the ensuing public debates, however, Jesus demonstrates that he stands on the ground of true Judaism. The agreement between Jesus and the Jewish belief is made explicit in the scribe's and Jesus' approval of each other's answer to the question of God's fundamental command (12: 32–34). Jesus' opponents' attempts to discredit him have instead served to establish Jesus as an orthodox Jew." There are then no valid grounds for arresting Jesus at all and thus no absolute necessity to do so.

22. Dewey, *Markan Public Debate,* 159, notes that 12: 35 begins with καὶ ἀποκριθεὶς ὁ Ἰησοῦς ἔλεγεν, the only instance in Mark where ἀποκρίνομαι occurs at the beginning of a unit and the only instance where it occurs without obvious referent. Dewey refers it to the previous debate. *The New Jerusalem Bible* leaves it untranslated. The immediate context suggests that Jesus' response was not to the scribe, for his conversation with that

> *The Lord declared to my Lord,*
> *take your seat at my right hand*
> *till I have made your enemies*
> *your footstool.*
> [37]*David himself calls him Lord; in what way then can he be his son?"* And
> *the great crowd listened to him with delight.*

A messiah of Davidic lineage was expected by many to be the deliverer
of the oppressed people, with all the revolutionary violence that entails.[23]
Here that notion is rejected, for, in Jesus' reading of Psalm 110: 1, David
himself refers to the messiah not as his son, but as his lord or master.[24]
"Because fathers do not call their sons masters, David's reference to the
Christ as my master (in 'my Lord') proves that the Christ cannot be David's
son in any traditional sense."[25] Mark does not have the infancy narratives of
Matthew or Luke. Like John, he seems not to know of these traditions, which
place Jesus within the Davidic lineage (John 7: 40–42, 52).[26] Rather, Mark

---

person has reached a most amicable conclusion and needs no further response. Perhaps
it refers to the silence that ensued after that conversation, perhaps to an implied notion
that Jesus, who had just pronounced the scribe near to the Kingdom, was himself the
Davidic messiah who would usher in that Kingdom.

23. Crossan, *The Cross That Spoke,* 55: "In discussing 'royal pretenders and messianic
movements' in the first century of the common era, Horsley and Hanson note, first, that
'in the royal psalms . . . the "anointed of Yahweh," who was always the established
Davidic monarch, was understood as secured in his position by divine adoption as "son
of God" ' (Horsley and Hanson, *Bandits, Prophets, and Messiahs: Popular Movements
in the Time of Jesus,* 97), but that, second, 'because of the special interest that attaches
to Jesus and his movement, it is worth noting . . . that there were several mass movements
composed of Jewish peasants from villages or towns such as Emmaus, Bethlehem, Sepphoris—people rallying around the leadership of charismatic figures viewed as *anointed
kings* of the Jews. These movements occurred in all three principal areas of Jewish
settlement in Palestine (Galilee, Perea, Judea), and just at the time when Jesus of Nazareth
was presumably born' (Horsley and Hanson, 117)." Also Hamerton-Kelly, *The Gospel
and the Sacred,* 33: "The violent political dreams of the messianic age, measured by the
memory of the Davidic kingdom, are replaced by the nonviolent kingdom of the victim
vindicated by resurrection."

24. Tolbert, *Sowing the Gospel,* 245.25, understands the title κύριος in the second
instance to be a term of respect: "The 'my Lord' of the Scripture quotation at Mark 12:
36 should probably be understood in this respectful manner to distinguish it from 'the
Lord': so, The Lord said to my master."

25. Tolbert, *Sowing the Gospel,* 255. Also Kee, *Community of the New Age,* 129:
"Mark's tradition [in regard to 12: 35–37] is therefore subtly bringing together three
strands: Son of God, Son of David, Lord (κύριος), all of which connote for Mark the
kingly role for which Jesus is destined, not in simple fulfillment of Jewish expectations,
but in transformation of them." In Mahāyāna parlance, in emptying them.

26. The passage from John reads: "Some of the crowd who had been listening said,
'He is indeed the prophet,' and some said, 'He is the Christ,' but others said, 'Would the
Christ come from Galilee? Does not scripture say that the Christ must be descended from
David and come from Bethlehem, the village where David was?' The passage goes on
to report that the guards who are sent to arrest Jesus, impressed by his speech, return
empty handed to the Pharisees, who are then upset with the guards. Nicodemus then

says that such a thing is unnecessary. Jesus does not here claim the title messiah, but he does deconstruct it so that it might be so applied.[27] It is not that Jesus is that august Davidic figure, but rather, that, once deconstructed, that august Davidic figure is simply Jesus.

Jesus draws his authority for undermining Davidic expectations from the Tanach. Jesus says that David spoke in the Holy Spirit (ἐν τῷ πνεύματι τῷ ἁγίῳ). This introductory formula is unique in the Synoptic gospels, conforming with the rabbinical formula that sees the scriptures as manifestations of the Spirit.[28] At the beginning of Mark's gospel, Jesus saw the descent of the Spirit after his baptism and was then driven by the Spirit into the wilderness. Here, just after his agreement with the scribe, Jesus both recognizes and draws his authority from the Spirit-filled Hebrew tradition, in order to empty the imagined expectations of that tradition. It is, however, the same Spirit that is found both in the wilderness and in the text of the scripture.

Phony Scribes
12: 38–40

[38]*In his teaching he said, "Beware of the scribes who like to walk about in long robes, to be greeted respectfully in the market squares, [39]to take the front seats in the synagogues and the places of honor at banquets; [40]these are the men who devour the property of widows and for show offer long prayers. The more severe will be the sentence they receive."*

speaks a word of prudence and justice, pointing out that Jesus must have a hearing before he is judged. Whereupon, in verse 52, the Pharisees reply, "Are you a Galilean too? Go into the matter, and see for yourself: prophets do not arise in Galilee." John's text, which has no infancy narrative, presents no response to their identification of Jesus as simply a Galilean, leaving the question of whether John intended the passage to be read ironically, knowing full well that Jesus was born in Bethlehem, or simply was unaware of any such tradition. See Brown, *The Gospel According to John,* 330, who argues that John is being ironic, and Schillebeeckx, *Christ,* 312–21, who argues that John sees Jesus as the Mosaic eschatological messiah, not the Judaic Davidic messiah.

27. Dewey, *Markan Public Debate,* 166: The "narrative . . . returns to Jesus' offensive against the Jewish leaders, challenging their Davidic messianic hopes and prophesying their eschatological doom (12: 35–40)." Again Kelber, *Mark's Story of Jesus,* 65: "The Davidic issue is resolved, Jesus has not come to ordain the kingdom of David on Mount Zion in Jerusalem but to proclaim the Kingdom of God 'to all the nations.' "

28. Schweizer, *The Good News,* 256: "The introduction to the quotation is unique within the Synoptics; the only other places where similar introductions are found are Hebrews 3: 7 and 10: 15. It conforms to the rabbinical formula, i.e., a kind of theology which restricts the activity of the Holy Spirit to salvation history in the distant past so that in the present the Holy Spirit can only be found 'packaged and preserved' in the Scriptures. The uncommon formula . . . emphasizes the special significance of the quotation which follows." The "packaging" of the Spirit, however, is hardly to be restricted to the rabbinical tradition; it refers to all who would imagine the words of scripture to encapsulate ultimate meaning, whether Jew or Christian. Furthermore, on Jesus' lips it signals a recognition of the dynamic presence of the Spirit in the Hebrew tradition.

This is the first instance in Mark where Jesus is explicitly described as having his own teaching (ἐν τῇ διδαχῇ αὐτοῦ). But, as it turns out, this teaching is not about doctrine, but about practice, for it relates to the behavior of phony scribes. They are accused of denigrating both ultimate meaning and reengagement in worldly convention, for they collapse the sacred into the profane. Their long robes[29] were garments "properly to be worn at prayer and while performing certain other scribal duties. Thus the garments served as signs of the scribes' sacral character, and the scribes depicted at 12: 38 were wearing them inappropriately in public and profane places to distinguish themselves, as members of the sacred realm, from the profane."[30] In 7: 3–4, Mark has explained that the Pharisees and some of the scribes regarded the market place as a profane place, for they had to perform ritual ablutions after returning therefrom.

To the Markan Jesus there are no separately identifiable realms of the sacred and the profane. In 5: 27 Jesus himself is insistent on identifying who among the pressing crowd has touched his clothes. When the woman, now cured of her bleeding, comes forward, however, issues of ritual impurity that would censure her as unfit for human contact are bypassed in favor of healing faith. And in 6: 56 it is reported that the Gennesaret sick, who had been brought and laid down in the open market spaces, begged Jesus to let them touch the fringe of his cloak. As many as did were saved. Jesus has emptied the sacred from its august position. Yet, once emptied, the sacred takes on its dependently co-arisen validity as a marker of the ultimate. In the Mahāyāna phrase, to an awakened person the very realm of suffering (*saṃsāra*) is identified with the realm of ultimate cessation (*nirvāṇa*). In the Markan passage, by contrast, the scribes cling to an imagined sacred status, while devouring the property of widows. Their lengthy prayers mock ultimate meaning while negating any compassionate reengagement in worldly convention. One is reminded of Jesus' attack on the practice of korban, treated in chapter 7: 12–13.

But in Jesus' teaching no doctrine precedes his criticism of the practice of the scribes. Practice is not a subsequent step to be taken only after one has understood the teaching. Rather, as the great Japanese Sōtō Zen Master Dōgen teaches, practice itself is enlightenment, for that alone provides the understanding of doctrine. It matters hardly at all if one has a correct conceptual understanding but omits or postpones practice. This leads only to a pattern of religious attachment wherein one is solicited by notions of selfhood and self-importance. This delusion, both here in Mark, and in Buddhist thought, matures into future sufferings, for the sentence of such religious scribes will indeed be greater. They will reap the reward of what they sow— they will be enclosed within those pretentious selves.

---

29. Nineham, *Saint Mark,* 333: "The reference to 'long robes' (*stolai*) is to the Jewish outer garment known as *tallith,* of which the scribes wore a distinctively large version."
30. Malbon, *Narrative Space,* 93.

About Devoured Widows
12: 41–44

[41]He sat down opposite the treasury and watched the people putting money into the treasury, and many of the rich put in a great deal. [42]A poor widow came and put in two small coins, the equivalent of a penny. [43]Then he called his disciples and said to them, "In truth I tell you, this poor widow has put more in than all who have contributed to the treasury; [44]for they have all put in money they could spare, but she in her poverty has put in everything she possessed, all she had to live on."

Jesus has just talked about the scribes who swallow up the possessions of widows. He now focuses on one such widow, rendered poor by their oppression, and she becomes the model for true practice. There is here no explicit recommendation to lift the political oppression of the poor. Yet Jesus does not acquiesce in unjust social practices. He condemns the scribes who cheat widows. Nevertheless, the present point is not directly about social policy, but about the patterns of consciousness that lead either to oppressive or to converted practice. If one clings to the control of things, then, no matter how much one gives, one is controlled by things. There is no continuity between ultimate meaning and conventional practice. One cannot "get there" by doing one's duty.[31] Only if one empties oneself (*ātmagrāha*) of all things, of all clinging to things (*dharmagrāha*) is one freed to practice the dynamically conventional forms of religion. The widow gives up her entire means of livelihood ('όλον τὸν βίον αὐτῆς), not just the amount she can afford.[32] Only in awareness of their discontinuity can one truly appreciate the validity of conventional forms of religious practice. The widow has put in more than all because she has emptied herself of everything, even the very support of her life. The point is theological, not a recommendation for increased penury or imprudent abandonment of the world in favor of an imagined absolute reality. Here the widow who gives to the point of having nothing left is no longer identified as one devoured by the scribes, but as one who gives more than the scribes.

---

31. See Nagao, *The Foundational Standpoint,* 77–80, on the character of the path as the negation of any continuous road map to awakening.
32. See Kee, *Community of the New Age,* 90.

13

The Eschatological Discourse about Awakening

The Fall of the Temple
13: 1–2

[1]As he was leaving the Temple one of his disciples said to him, "Master, look at the size of those stones! Look at the size of those buildings!" [2]And Jesus said to him, "You see these great buildings? Not a single stone will be left on another; everything will be pulled down."

The primary insight of the Buddha Śākyamuni was probably insight into the impermanence (*anitya*) of all things.[1] There is nothing that remains stable and apart from the constant flow of change. No abiding self, and, in the Mahāyāna, no abiding substance to anything else either. The history of Buddhist doctrinal development is a commentary on impermanence, on what to do in a world that affords but meager stability and thus little comfort. In the West, Heraclitus saw that all things flow ($\pi\acute{\alpha}\nu\tau\alpha$ '$\rho\epsilon\grave{\iota}$), but the main currents of classical Western thought followed a more "positive" notion of being. If not the unchanging being recommended by Parmenides, then certainly the rather stable being of Aristotle's essences. In a word, the West adopted a Greek metaphysic of being, in which framework the early Church Fathers, themselves culturally and ethnically Greek, interpreted the Gospel messages of Jesus. Mark writes for a culturally Greek audience, perhaps in one of the great Hellenistic cities, such as Rome or Antioch. He did not directly challenge the philosophic assumptions of his day—indeed he was not a philosopher. But the eschatological discourse in Mark 13 presents Jesus' eschatological discourse as an undermining of the stable and comforting view of life.

Mark lived in a time rife with expectations for a radical and definitive reversal of affairs. In the year 66 the Romans had been driven out, only to

---

1. See Hakamaya, "Kūshō rikai no mondaiten, [Issues in Understanding Emptiness]", *Risō* 610 (1984): 50–64.

return in force and destroy the temple in 70. The present eschatological discourse presents Mark's understanding and critique of these expectations. "We can see how Mark wrote this story in part to reveal what he considered to be the destructive attitudes in Israel that led to the Roman-Jewish war."[2] His discourse is the narrative parallel to the Mahāyāna notion of impermanence, though it is much more dramatic and its images much more forceful and frightful. Yet, in its core meaning eschatology denotes the passing of structures and identities deemed to be stable and unchanging.

The temple is more than just a building. It is the traditional center of and symbol for the religious cult of Israel. Of all institutions the temple was the

---

2. Rhoads, *Mark and Method,* 138. Most scholars, it seems, link this "little apocalypse" with the events of the temple destruction and its concomitant social upheavals. There are various views about this *Sitz im Leben,* however. Kelber thinks that it was written after the fall of Jerusalem in 70 for disoriented Christians; see *The Kingdom in Mark,* 1: "What they needed was a new place and a new time. To meet the present crisis, a system was required which could create a new configuration of time and space, and provide a sense of continuity and stability." Also Kelber, *Mark's Story of Jesus,* 67–68, notes: "The reason Jesus' biography ruptures, and ruptures at this moment [at chapter 13], is that he has reached a point where it touches on problems in Mark's lifetime and that of his readers. . . . [There is] a particular anxiety some forty years after the life and death of Jesus." Hartmann, *Prophecy Interpreted,* 44–45, shows that Mark 13 is "a coherent exposition of or meditation on" the Book of Daniel, especially Daniel 7; 11; 12, "with passages borrowed from other Old Testament apocalyptic-type prophetic utterances." It is, in a word, a midrash on Daniel, which is quoted in every chapter of Mark. But he does not believe it was written specifically in light of the conditions surrounding the destruction of the temple, for such a discourse appears earlier in Paul; See 211: "If we assume that the basic 'midrash' was a borrowed Jewish parenetic (!) apocalypse, this 'midrash' is evidenced by the examinations of First and Second Thessalonians as having been christianized a few years before 50 A.D., i.e., it must at any rate have had a Christian *Sitz im Leben* for at least two decades before Mark's Gospel was written down." Gaston, *No Stone Upon Another,* 61f, sees it as an attempt to specify the nature of Christian hopes in the context of Jewish nationalism and the execution of Jesus as an insurrectionist within a prophetic interpretation of those swiftly changing events. Drawing upon the style and content of Daniel, the author uses his Christian tradition to understand the political crisis and encourage the faithful (457). Kee, *Community of the New Age,* 6, sees Mark's apocalyptic strategy moving through linear time to an eschatological denouement in the creation of a new Christian community, seeing Jesus' prediction of the destruction of the Jerusalem Temple in terms of a struggle between Jerusalem and Galilean communities of Christian believers. Conzelmann, "Geschichte und Eschaton nach Mc 13," *Zeitschrift für die neutestamentliche Wissenschaft* 50 (1959): 210–21, sees Mark's community as eschatologically oriented and eagerly awaiting the final eschaton, before which the Lord remains absent. Weeden, "The Heresy That Necessitated Mark's Gospel," 71–72, in support of the thesis that Mark was combating a *theios anēr* christology, remarks that in such a context, "how devastating would be the arrival of *theios anēr* Christians." Feeling intrigued by but unconvinced of the validity of suppositional contextualizations, the present attempt aims at reading the text, chapter 13 included, in terms of meanings not attributed to Mark's original community, whatever that may have been. To be noted is Tolbert's contention, *Sowing the Gospel,* 304, "that the Gospel of Mark was *not* written in response to the problems of a specific, local community but was instead intended, as were the ancient erotic novels, for a wide readership. . . . Mark's rhetorical goals are exhortation and proselytizing."

most stable, for it was founded by Yahweh and was his holy place. "In the first century, the Jewish nation was a temple state under the control of the Roman Empire. For Jews living there, religious, political and economic life centered around the Temple in Jerusalem. This Temple was a huge complex that dominated the city. It housed more than two thousand priests at a time. During religious festivals the Temple teemed with tens of hundreds of Jews from all over the known world."[3] The Maccabees died one after the other rather than defile that temple, for the temple was the locus of the presence of Yahweh, the central sign of the holiness that constituted Israel as Yahweh's elect. "Holiness was a core value of the society. It was the major concept by which the nation-culture structured and classified everything in the world—people, places, objects, and times."[4]

Eschatological language stood over against such sureties and emptied the accepted structures, all in the very name of Yahweh himself. It is not, I think, that the final days represent an alternate structure, but, in Mark at least, that they depict the collapse of all structure in the nakedness of Yahweh's non-structuring presence. If rules of purity and pollution order society and give shape to the holiness of Israel,[5] the breaking of such boundaries threatens such order and dislocates holiness.[6] If the temple-embodied holiness is not emptied, then the very presence of Yahweh is circumscribed and becomes unavailable apart from its protective boundaries. When Jesus comes preaching that the kingdom is at hand, he is freeing Yahweh from all cultural boundaries, in the tradition of the ancient prophets. "The prophecy of verse 2 tacitly

---

3. Rhoads, *Mark and Method*, 144–45. But see Mann, *Mark*, 439, who is not as convinced about the centrality of the temple for Mark because of the diverse complexion of diaspora Judaism. That may well have been the case. Nevertheless, the temple as the central symbol of Judaism seems to have been more important than its function as a working institution, so that its destruction would have been devastating even for diaspora Jews who seldom if ever could visit the temple. If the Vatican were destroyed by the Mediterranean fleet, Roman Catholics in Davenport, Iowa, would be very, very upset. Hamerton-Kelly, *The Gospel and the Sacred*, 1, writes: "The temple is the central symbol [of the sacred] in the Gospel of Mark because it is the focal point of the passion." This evaluation of the centrality of the temple is also found in Juel, *Messiah and Temple*, and Elliott, "Social Scientific Criticism," cited by Hamerton-Kelly. I agree with his appraisal that Jesus' life and death emptied all symbols of an absolutely sacred realm.

4. Rhoads, *Mark and Method*, 146.

5. Rhoads, *Mark and Method*, 150–51: "The ancient Hebrew culture as reflected in Leviticus is a purity-pollution system based on 'holiness.' "

6. Thus, although Mark 13 borrows heavily from the images of Daniel, there are contrasts. Kee, *Community of the New Age*, 81: "It is in the Book of Daniel, however, that the contours of the Hasidic movement become clear and that the features of an apocalyptic community are unambiguously apparent for the first time. The values enjoined by Daniel are maintenance of purity (Dan. 1) and persistence in piety (Dan. 6), even in the face of martyrdom at the hands of the state. To those who thus persevere God grants insight into his future purposes, including foreknowledge of the defeat of their enemies and of their own vindication (Dan. 7–12)." In Mark, by contrast, there is a sustained polemic against the maintenance of purity, no foreknowledge of the defeat of enemies is promised.

locates Jesus within a tradition of prophets who announce the temple's dissolution (Mic 3.10–12; Jer 7.14; 26.6,18; I Enoch 90.28; . . .). While seemingly detached from the proclamation of a singular catastrophe, the query in verse 4 (πότε ταῦτα ἔσται . . . ὅταν μέλλῃ ταῦτα συντελεῖσθαι πάντα) echoes the eschatological phraseology of Dan 12.7 (LXX, συντελεσθήσεται πάντα ταῦτα).[7] From the very beginning of the Gospel, Jesus is placed in the prophetic company of John the Baptist and all the prophets, even to the point where many mistake him for Moses, Elijah or one of the prophets. Jesus' own prophetic actions (11.12–21) and his disregard for the authority of the established religious leaders (11: 27–44) reinforce the point: he proclaims freedom from cultural boundaries which circumscribe the holiness of Yahweh and divide people one from another. There are no boundaries between God and people, or between one class of people and another.[8] His location on the Mount of Olives echoes *Zechariah* 14: 4, which declares that "the Lord's feet shall stand on the Mount of Olives on the day of the Lord; from that point the earth-shaking events of the end time will radiate outward."[9]

In such a context, Mark develops the eschatological discourse of chapter 13 to contrast his understanding with current expectancies. "The linguistic milieu in which the evangelists worked was heavily invested with literary and oral traditions—personal convictions given expression in stories, and national aspirations given voice in apocalyptic visions."[10] Those national aspirations were indeed of intense political and cultural significance. The religious authorities constantly had to guard against any disruption of the social order, because of the very real and soon realized fear that the Roman forces would disrupt or interfere with their administration of the Temple. But even the Temple is not stable. It too will be pulled down, not a stone left upon a stone. There is no realm apart from emptiness, no cultural essence anywhere that one might rely upon. If then any institution or any teaching is elevated above emptiness, it usurps the role of ultimate meaning, which in itself is no role whatsoever. No matter how much the disciples want to feel secure in their religious affiliation, it remains worldly and conventional.

---

7. Black, "An Oration at Olivet," 70.
8. Rhoads, *Mark and Method*, 155: "At the death of Jesus, God rips apart the curtain of the sanctuary and breaks out of the confines of the sanctuary (15: 38). . . . Mark eliminates the cosmological boundaries that would identify people or things as unclean in and of themselves. For example, Mark eliminates the notion that animals might be unclean in and of themselves, for the Markan Jesus declares all foods clean (7: 19). Also, Mark eliminates the notion that Gentiles are unclean in and of themselves. Mark rejects the boundary line distinguishing pure Jews from impure Gentiles. In Mark's view, any Jew or Gentile may be on God's side or against God based on faith and moral behavior rather than on ritual purity (3: 29; 7: 29). Also gentile territory is not unclean in and of itself (4: 1–20; 7: 24–8: 10)." That is to say, all boundaries remain merely conventional without any essence *in and of themselves* that might afford them more than cultural significance.
9. Malbon, *Narrative Space*, 86.
10. Camery-Hoggatt, *Irony in Mark's Gospel*, 71.

Thus, it too will be dissolved (καταλυθῇ), for it too is conventional (*saṃvṛti*).

The initial two verses set the stage for the entire following discourse. The Markan Jesus expresses insight into the emptiness of all conventional forms in apocalyptic rhetoric, the appropriate vehicle for doing so in his cultural context. He takes skillful advantage of common images of reversal, a reversal of the present order of things to a new age and a new temple where God will indeed reign, where the kingdom will be fully realized. Instead of philosophic terms about emptiness and ultimate meaning, he adopts the social, political terms of his tradition. Everything will fall apart, for radical impermanence is the character of all things.

There is also an implicit doubling back from the image of the temple stones to 12: 10–11, where in the parable of the evil tenants, Jesus is depicted as himself the cornerstone rejected by the builders, quoted from Psalm 188: 22–23.[11] It also reaches forward, alluding to 14: 58, where the false witnesses accuse Jesus of saying that he will replace the Temple made with hands with one not so made. In fact, Mark has described Jesus as the cornerstone, and as having declared the destruction of the stones of the Temple.

Facing the Temple
13: 3–4

³And while he was sitting on the Mount of Olives, facing the Temple, Peter, James, John and Andrew questioned him when they were by themselves, ⁴"Tell us, when is this going to happen, and what sign will there be that it is all about to take place?"

Jesus is sitting over against the temple (κατέναντι τοῦ ἱεροῦ).[12] This is more than a geographic location, for Jesus has put himself on a collision course with the Temple in that he negates the absolute validity of any religious form. Ultimate truth is always apart from and beyond any conventional form. The experience of Abba cannot be channeled within human traditions. It remains as empty as the vastness of the wilderness places. The authorities, then and now, tend to adhere to the traditions as if they did indeed capture the emptiness of ultimate meaning, and thus in practice they tend to negate the emptiness of all forms.

Yet it is only by emptying all traditions that one can reclaim tradition. To cling to tradition as absolute truth is a religious pattern of false imagination

---

11. Tolbert, *Sowing the Gospel,* 259: "In structuring the opening exchange of the Apocalyptic Discourse with a chiastic repetition of the key words 'stones' (λίθοι) and 'buildings' (οἰκοδομαί), the implied author signals the authorial audience that the discussion to follow will explain how the rejected stone becomes 'the head of the corner.' "

12. Malbon, *Narrative Space,* 32: "The seat of the Markan Jesus' authority is not the temple, but the mountain (13: 3). . . . ."

(*parikalpita*) which ill serves tradition. On the other hand, to see tradition
as empty of meaning is merely to make emptiness yet another viewpoint;
this is to deconstruct tradition in favor of a false view of emptiness. The
middle path, recommended by Mahāyāna philosophy, is not to sketch some
midway position, halfway between two extremes. Rather, it is to gain insight
into the emptiness of tradition, and then to reaffirm the conventional validity
of tradition as dependently co-arisen. It is to value intensely one's tradition
without having to make exaggerated claims for its superiority over all other
traditions. The eschatological judgment is aimed not merely against the Jewish
tradition, as if one could validly and effectively cling to a Christian tradition.
Rather it deconstructs all traditions that would usurp the unidentifiable and
immediate availability of Yahweh. Here in Mark Chapter 13, Jesus focuses
on the emptying of the religious traditions of his day. And so he is located
over against the temple.

Furthermore, Jesus is seated in eschatological judgment on the Mount of
Olives (καθημένου αὐτοῦ εἰς τὸ ὄρος τῶν ἐλαιῶν), the site where shortly
he will experience intense suffering.[13] The sufferings entailed by the dissolution of the Temple are not separate from the sufferings of devout Jewish
practitioners, Jesus included. Jesus was indeed a Jew and, though he did not
cling to the traditions, he did adhere to them. The son of man is lord over
the Sabbath, but he does not dispense with the Sabbath. So here, he sits over
against the temple at the site of his personal sufferings. The entire chapter
"is placed before the passion story, at least in part as preparation for the
events in chapter 14," for it depicts situations the disciples will soon encounter
when Jesus is arrested and warns them to stay awake and not be caught asleep
(13: 33–37).[14] This eschatological discourse frames the passion narrative and

13. Malbon, *Narrative Space*, 32–33: "The Mount of Olives was, from ancient times,
a place of prayer (2 Samuel 15: 30,32) and the scene of Ezekiel's vision of the glory of
the Lord (Ezekiel 11: 23). Later the Mount of Olives was associated by the rabbis with
the resurrection of the righteous dead and the coming of the Messiah. Most dramatically,
the Mount of Olives was the destined place of the initiation of the end of this age, the
eschatological judgment, the day of the Lord: 'On that day his (the Lord's) feet shall
stand on the Mount of Olives which lies before Jerusalem on the east; and the Mount of
Olives shall be split in two from east to west by a very wide valley; so that one half of
the Mount of Olives shall withdraw northward, and the other half southward' (Zechariah
14: 4)."

14. Tannehill, "The Disciples in Mark," 150. Broadhead, *Teaching With Authority,* 175:
"The conflict between Jesus and the religious leadership of Israel dominates the extended
unit of Mark 11.1–13.37. The conflict was prominent in Mark 1–3, but almost absent from
Mark 4–10. The stories of Mark 11.1–13.37 re-introduce this tension as the background for
Jesus' suffering and death in Jerusalem." Again he notes, 179: "The narrative [11.1–13.37]
thus addresses the potential christological dichotomy between the glorious deeds of Jesus
and his ignominious death. As the passion predictions (8.31; 9.31; 10.33–34) have shown,
the authoritative ministry of proclamation—demonstrated through words and deeds of
power—is inseparably linked to the destiny of Jesus in Jerusalem." Note Donahue, *Are
You the Christ?* 169 (quoting from Lloyd Gaston, *No Stone Upon Another*): Chapter 13
has "no explicit reference to the suffering of Jesus or the Son of Man. This is explained

prepares the reader to understand the final events of Jesus' life, for "the story does not end even there. It continues into the reader's own time. Mark 13 links the fate of the disciples to the situation of the reader in the continuing story. The time between the resurrection and the parousia will be one of trial and testimony, of endurance or apostasy. And so failure is a continuing possibility, for the reader no less than the disciples."[15]

When things are about to go out of control, when one is threatened by dissolution, one tries to maintain the conventional forms in continuity. That is why the four disciples come to Jesus and try to get a handle on things. They want a sign, a special piece of information that will enable them to cope. They want to know how things will turn out in the last analysis (τί τὸ σημεῖον ὅταν μέλλη ταῦτα συντελεῖσθαι παντα).[16] James and John, concerned about being great, want to be in on God's plan for the future.[17]

---

by the function of the whole discourse which is not to make an explicit Christological statement, but to be an eschatological paraenesis to the believers."

15. Moore, *Literary Criticism,* 75, giving a synopsis of the Tannehill article mentioned above.

16. Hartmann, *Prophecy Interpreted,* 145, explains that μέλλη ταῦτα συντελεῖσθαι πάντα is a conscious allusion to Daniel 12: 7, where the angel says that "when the dispersion is ended they shall know all these things" (ἐν τῷ συντελεσθῆναι διασκορπισμὸν γνώσονται πάντα ταῦτα). Again, in more detail, 221: "This question in 13: 4 joins the saying about the fall of the Temple with the eschatological discourse: ταῦτα . . . πάντα clearly alludes, linguistically speaking, to the preceding prophecy [about the fall of the Temple]. Does the question apply to the eschatology at the same time? It consists of two parallel clauses. This parallelism means that it cannot be divided up into two separate questions, one on the Temple and one on the consummation, but it also means that the two clauses do not necessarily express the same things. The second clause may be expansive or explanatory. The decisive factor is then the nuance of meaning which is to be read in συντελεῖσθαι. If it has no eschatological reference, the sentence means that the first step has been taken towards 'de-eschatologizing' the discourse, which in that case is made to deal with the fall of Jerusalem as a divine punishment. However, this particular phraseological similarity to Dan 12: 7 indicates that συντελεῖσθαι here really alludes to 'the close of the age.' This means that the destruction of the Temple and the events of the last days are linked by this framework and that the eschatology then also includes sayings about this catastrophe." Eliade, *Sacred and Profane,* 73–76, similarly speaks about the linkage between temple and time ("Templum and Tempus") in such fashion that one sees the destruction of the Temple as the dissolution of time itself, the rupture of linear time flow. See 75: "We find a similar temporal symbolism as part of the cosmological symbolism of the Temple at Jerusalem. According to Flavius Josephus (*Ant. Jud.* III, 7, 7), the twelve loaves of bread on the table signified the twelve months of the year and the candelabrum with seventy branches represented the decans (the zodiacal division of the seven planets into tens). The Temple was an *imago mundi;* being at the Center of the World, at Jerusalem, it sanctified not only the entire cosmos but also cosmic life—that is, its time. . . . *Templum* designates the spatial, *tempus* the temporal aspect of the motion of the horizon in space and time." Thus, the Temple was not only the symbolic center of the cosmos, but sacred structure in which cosmic time itself was given birth and renewed. The fall of the Temple meant not only the disruption of spatial categories, but the very collapse of time itself. The eschatological end time is then the end of linear time, no longer capable of being mythically reconstructed at the center of the cosmos.

17. Kee, *Community of the New Age,* 84: "Miracles are regarded in apocalyptic circles, therefore, as signs of divine approbation toward the faithful community, and as signs of

But there is no way to cope. One can only flee, for the eschatological dissolution of the temple is not a matter of conventional continuity. Rather, it is the emptying of that entire conventional continuity, the collapse of all normal linear expectations.

The disciples' questions structure the answers which follow. Their "second query, τί τὸ σημεῖον [what sign will there be?], is addressed by roughly the first three quarters of the *narratio* (vv 6–27); the remainder, vv 28–36, takes up their first question, πότε ταῦτα ᾿έσται [when is this going to happen?]."[18] The answers build in crescendo, being amplified from the more immediate and familiar images that are described as the beginnings of the birthpangs in verses 6–8, to the more intensely personal sufferings in 9–13, and culminating in the cosmic turbulence of 24–27.[19]

Beware about Signs
13: 5–8

⁵Then Jesus began to tell them, "Take care that no one deceives you. ⁶Many will come using my name and saying, 'I am he,' and they will deceive many. ⁷When you hear of wars and rumors of wars, do not be alarmed, this is something that must happen, but the end will not be yet. ⁸For nation will fight against nation, and kingdom against kingdom. There will be earthquakes in various places; there will be famines. This is the beginning of the birthpangs."

The disciples seek to know the sign that will presage the fall of the temple, just as the Pharisees in 8: 11 have demanded "a sign from heaven."[20] Jesus' answer is contained in the very first sentence: beware lest anyone deceive you. Lest anyone cause you to meander around, to wander away (πλανήσῃ).[21] Jesus is concerned that by seeking a sign his disciples will be

---

the kingdom of God which is about to be established. The signs will take place on earth, yet they have implications for the powers of heaven as well (6: 27)." James and John envisage a future kingdom in which they will have positions of power.

18. Black, "An Oration at Olivet," 74–75.

19. Black, "An Oration at Olivet," 76.

20. This supports Dowd, *Prayer, Power, and the Problem of Suffering,* 118.109: "In Mark 8: 38 the 'adulterous and sinful generation' are those who reject Jesus. In Mark 8:12 the Pharisees who argue with Jesus (συζητεῖν) are meant: 'this generation seeks a sign.' Mark does not include the disciples in 'this generation.' " Yet the sign they receive in Chapter 13 is neither a miraculous sign, as the Pharisees requested, nor information on the timing of the eschatological future.

21. Kelber, *The Kingdom in Mark,* 16, "notes that the phrase μὴ θροεῖσθε ("do not be alarmed") occurs only here and in *2 Thessalonians* 2: 2, sounding a note of eschatological caution. All the more so since 13: 7 rejects the assumption of the End: ἀλλ᾿ οὔπω τὸ τέλος."

deceived and led astray, and the tone of this entire discourse is admonitory.[22] The danger is that his disciples might go on an intellectual journey trying to determine signs of the future. But the point of the Gospel is not to provide a psychological defense against transience and change, against the destruction of temples, or churches. Rather, it is aimed at the dissolution of absolute values and recommends that one take care and see to (βλέπετε) the present moment of practice. The present eschatological discourse follows closely the preceding maxims: focus on love and sacrifice, not on trying to maintain conventional forms. Yet the rhetorical style reflects the drama of common millenarian hopes and fears. "Much of the material in these verses [5b–8] is widespread eschatological tradition, deriving ultimately from the Old Testament."[23]

Many will come to satisfy the disciples' deluded quest for surety.[24] The exigency of the imagined pattern of consciousness for security engenders such claims as "I am the One, I am he," the expected messiah.[25] The point is not to identify who in fact is the messiah, but to abandon clinging altogether, even to messiah. Only then will one encounter the messiah. Thus, Jesus deconstructs the very notion of messiah, for in claiming it he first empties it of supernatural significance.[26] That messiah, that is merely (*mātra*) me! The easiest way to find false security is to live off a supposed parental figure. Then one is led astray, wandering through time without being able to live in the present.

Jesus says not to fear the flow of time. When you hear about wars, do not be surprised, for human beings constantly perform inhuman acts. Jesus alludes to *Isaiah* 19: 2–3, which says: "And I shall stir up Egypt against Egypt, they will fight one another, brother against brother, friend against friend, city against city, kingdom against kingdom. Egypt's spirit will fail within her and I shall confound her deliberations." This oracle was pronounced by Isaiah somewhere around 710 BCE and is aimed against Sibo, the envoy of the Pharaoh Tephnakt, who was attempting to rally the Near East against

---

22. Lightfoot, *The Gospel Message of St. Mark,* 50: "A remarkable feature of the discourse is that it contains at least as much counsel and warning as apocalyptic revelation."

23. Collins, *The Beginning of the Gospel,* 81. Also Donahue, *Are You the Christ?* 236: "Since the world was for the Marcan community a world of dissolution of structures and of eschatological expectations, the Marcan narrative has many of the qualities of apocalyptic literature which flourishes in times of persecution and crisis."

24. Collins, *The Beginning of the Gospel,* 82: "The most likely historical allusion here is to the Jewish messianic pretenders who came forward during the Jewish war with Rome, beginning with Menachem in 66 CE." Thus she interprets the phrase ἐπὶ τῷ ὀνόματί μου to mean "requisitioning or claiming my name, i.e., messiah."

25. Hartmann, *Prophecy Interpreted,* 160, notes that "Εγώ εἰμι is . . . a LXX form of the Old Testament revelation framework." The claim in Mark 13: 6 is then a usurpation of the revelatory identity of God.

26. Kelber, *The Kingdom in Mark,* 122: "In the first section of the apocalypse (13: 5b–23) Mark rewrites a period of history in repudiation of Christian parousia prophets. He de-eschatologizes the time of the Jewish-Roman War. . . ."

Assyria.[27] In Jesus' mouth it refers not to Egypt, but more generally to wars expected to occur during the time of Mark and his community, the Roman war in particular. The oracle is no longer limited to Yahweh's enemies, but also includes the people of Israel. Indeed, Mark's passage was written from the perspective of one who had witnessed the series of wars and rebellions that led up to and followed the destruction of the Temple in 70 CE and thus the reference is most concretely to the events of Mark's time. In that light, it counsels that one should not think that any of the wars of rebellion would themselves lead to a reversal of the conventional realities of life. Just as Yahweh will empty out the spirit of the Egyptians, so he will empty out the false eschatological expectancies of those who try to reach the end time through military means. A parallel passage is found in 2 *Chronicles* 15: 5–7, which states that "in those times there was no security for people as they went about their business, but great unrest afflicting the inhabitants of all countries, nation being crushed by nation and city by city, since God caused confusion among them by every kind of distress. So be strong, do not be discouraged, for your deeds will be rewarded." Here, the prophet Azariah promises final victory to the people of Israel. By contrast Mark mentions no final victory, announcing only the beginning of birthpangs. Wars of liberation, even when politically necessary, issue most often not in a bright new age, but only in the beginnings of birthpangs. Being conventional, they cannot effect the end time (τέλος), but result only in the beginning of more suffering (ἀρχὴ ὠδίνων). The contrast is between the end and the beginning, and the message is that any conventional act leads only to the beginning of another conventional act, not to the end of convention, nor to the recovery of the primal beginning.

Dan Via has offered an insightful interpretation based on the assertion that "apocalyptic thinking writes history from a mythological standpoint."[28] Thus Mark creates a new middle time by connecting it with the primal beginning (1: 1) and the final end (Chapter 13), in the middle of which one recovers and actualizes the harmony of the beginning. "The end is,. . . in mythological terms, the re-actualization of the beginning. But . . . Mark . . . creates a new beginning and end for the world of the reader. By connecting the middle to both the beginning and the end it also creates a new middle. . . . The good news is that the vitality and newness of the beginning can overcome the repetitiousness of habit in the middle."[29] In this context, Jesus' negation that the end will be effected by false messiahs means that no conventional endeavors can bring about that which lies beyond conventional time. Such hopes are but another example of imagined delusion, and lead only to the beginning of more sufferings. By contrast, Jesus' advice is to live in the middle time, i.e., in the present. Indeed, one cannot live in the future because it does not

27. *Jerusalem Bible,* 1171, note 19a.
28. Via, *The Ethics of Mark's Gospel,* 30.
29. Via, *The Ethics of Mark's Gospel,* 30.

exist. Thus the future orientation of the present discourse is meant not as a recommendation to cling to images of victory and glory, but to empty the structures and traditions of the present. The mythic force of eschatology in Mark, expressed in images of the future, stands in judgment over the present reality of the Temple establishment.[30] Even future hope, however, is exercised in the present, and the thrust of Mark is not toward clinging to an imagined future, as if hope were some kind of guarantee. Rather, future hope is radical openness to a future as dependently co-arisen as any other conventional reality.[31]

The beginning of birthpangs (ἀρχὴ ὠδίων) is taken to refer to "the terrors and torments traditionally viewed as a prelude to the coming of the messianic age."[32] They seem to signify that the trials Jesus talks of are merely the

---

30. Donahue, *Are You the Christ?* 233: "Therefore Mark uses apocalyptic motifs to give a radically future orientation to his gospel. These elements enable him to complete his time scheme by integrating past, present, and future into one unity. The past of Jesus is relived in the present experience of the community, but, as in the case of Jesus, so too in the case of the believer the ultimate meaning of his existence is determined by future hope." Note the impact of the last sentence: if the ultimate meaning of Jesus is future hope, then one can hardly construct a present definition of his identity.

31. Sheehan, *The First Coming,* 125: "In Jesus' preaching, eschatology had been removed from the mythical context of apocalypse and had become a simple but radical appeal to be as merciful as the Father was. Therefore, for Jesus' disciples to preach the nearness of the kingdom did not mean to pass along information about an imminent end of the world, but to live an exemplary life 'worthy of God, who calls you into his own kingdom' (1 Thessalonians 2: 12). It meant dissolving eschatology into ethics." I think eschatology retains its rhetorical impact only as long as it is not collapsed into an identifiable present content, whether ethical or cosmic, for it is meant to undercut all such content. Ethics can be tied to an imagined (*parikalpita*) image as much as any millennarian schema. See Perrin, *Jesus and the Language of the Kingdom,* 44–45: "The apocalyptic practice of 'sign seeking' was dependent upon a view of myth as allegory, and upon the treatment of symbols as steno-symbols. Typically the apocalyptic seer told the story of the history of his people in symbols where,... for the most part each symbol bore a one-to-one relationship to that which it depicted. This thing was Antiochus Epiphanes, that thing was Judas Maccabee, the other thing was the coming of the Romans, and so on.... Jesus categorically rejected the seeking after 'signs to be observed' [see Mark 8: 11–12] and in so doing necessarily equally categorically rejected the treatment of the [apocalyptic] myth as allegory and its symbols as steno-symbols. In the message of Jesus the myth is true myth and the symbols of God's redemptive activity are tensive symbols.... the symbol of the kingly activity of God on behalf of his people confronts the hearers of Jesus as a true tensive symbol with its evocation of a whole set of meanings, and ... the myth is, in the message of Jesus, true myth with its power to mediate the experience of existential reality." Similarly Perrin notes in *Rediscovery of Apocalyptic,* 302 that the words attributed to Jesus concerning the future are to be regarded, not as "temporal" but as "exisential." But see also *Jesus and the Language of the Kingdom,* 77–80, where Perrin critiques Bultmann for taking apocalyptic imagery as steno-symbols (through which "Jesus envisaged the inauguration of the Kingdom of God as a tremendous cosmic drama"), necessitating a demythologizing into existential categories. Rather, from the first, the eschatological kingdom functions as a tensive symbol, enticing the reader to realize its presence in the present.

32. Bauer, *A Greek-English Lexicon,* 895.

accompanying birth throes that will issue in the new age. Yet, Jesus does not say that in fact the end time will come at any identifiable time. Rather, in a Mahāyāna perspective, intense suffering leads not to the realm of ultimate truth, but, when insight into emptiness occurs, to the collapse of all conventional support. That itself is an awakening, for one must then cease to rely on conventional realities. And that is the import of Jesus' discourse, for the experience of war and disaster should lead to the emptying of the combative spirit among peoples, just as Isaiah's oracle speaks about the emptying out or the failing of the spirit of the Egyptians (ταραχθήσεται τὸ πνεῦμα τῶν Αἰγυπτίων), i.e., to the unsettling of their spirit, to the breaking of their reliance on their own resources.

It is also to be noted that Jesus says that wars and rumors of war must occur (δεὶ γὰρ γενέσθαι). In the reference passages from *Isaiah* and *2 Chronicles,* these wars are brought about by Yahweh, to fulfill his designs. They parallel Jesus' predictions of the inevitability and necessity of his own passion. But that too is a mythic reading of history, discerning some divine purpose in the sad events that unfold.[33] The inevitability of war is not a literal divine necessity, but rather the maturation of complexes of human actions that are driven by self-clinging and group bias. Few scriptural scholars or theologians would care to lay the blame for warfare on Yahweh and his designs, yet the notion is still prevalent that God directly, if inexplicably, wills the necessity of Jesus' sufferings and execution.[34] Rather, just as wars occur because of human actions, so Jesus' passion and execution occur because of the grand plan of the authorities, not because of any divine program for Jesus.

Focus on Preaching the Gospel
13: 9–10

[9]*"Be on your guard: you will be handed over to sanhedrins; you will be beaten in synagogues; and you will be brought before governors and kings for my sake, as evidence to them,* [10]*and before all the nations."*

---

33. Kelber, *The Kingdom in Mark,* 177: "Wars come to pass in dire times and in accord with preordained necessity (13: 7c). . . . *Dei* in an eschatological context (13: 7c) is frequently indicative of a retrospection of history. . . . The Son of Man must suffer, die, and rise (8: 31: *dei*), but from Mark's own perspective he has already suffered, died, and risen. Elijah must come first (9: 11: *dei elthein*), but according to Mark's concept of history, he has already appeared in the person of John the Baptist." Thus the entire focus of future necessities for suffering treat present understanding of past events.

34. But see Mack, *A Myth of Innocence,* 353: "It was Mark's fiction of a fantastic infringement on human history that created Christianity's charter." Mack does hold that, 355: "According to Mark, Jesus' appearance in Galilee was a dazzling entrance of God's Son into the world with the power and authority to set things right. The world was wrong, set against the rule of God and in league with the powers under the control of Satan. Ultimately, these forces could be no match for the rightful rule of God. . . . Those who understood the secret [of the final triumph of God's kingdom] and endured until the end belonged and would belong to the new and perfect order of things." Such a view is indeed

To be on guard literally means "See to yourself!" (βλέπετε δὲ ὑμεῖς ἑαυτοῖς). It is not that one must guard against the times, but that, practicing the middle path, one need not worry about those times. Have no concern about the signs, about the grand eschatological plan! The dependently co-arisen horrors of wars and betrayals will be quite enough to worry about without trying to espy a secret underlying meaning to events. Indeed, the reader herself shares in the sufferings. Although circumstances differ, no one escapes the radical contingency of being human.[35]

Mark from his perspective alludes both to the events of Jesus' passion, when he appeared before the sanhedrin and stood before the governor, and to the trials of the early Christians in the face of persecution.[36] There is no

---

naive, and open to the criticism Mack levels on 368–76. One wonders, however, if he has not, as Perrin notes in regard to Bultmann, confused tensive symbols with steno-symbols and presented the eschatological discourses of Mark as a linear allegory, rather than as tensive, open-ended symbols of the collapse of all time. It does not seem to me that the Markan Jesus enters the scene in so dazzling a manner.

35. Camery-Hoggatt, *Irony in Mark's Gospel,* 167: "A second source of overcoding will also have influenced the reader: his own experience of suffering and catastrophe will find particular resonances here, especially in the Olivet Discourse in Chapter 13." This eschatological discourse provides the reader with a framework—the radical contingency of all human life—for understanding chapters 14 and 15. Fowler, *Let the Reader Understand,* 85–86, notes that "One linguistic signal of the dramatic nature of Mark 13 is the profusion of second-person plural pronouns in the discourse. In a highly inflected language such as Greek, the use of pronouns, at least in the nominative case, is semantically redundant. Therefore, the use of such superfluous pronouns serves as a way of adding unusual emphasis to an utterance. Mark 13 contains a number of such emphatic second-person plural pronouns (e.g., 'Now you look out for yourselves' [13: 9; R&M]). Ostensibly these pronouns engage the four disciples on the stage, but they are too emphatic to do only that. Rather, they raise the intensity of Jesus' language to such a pitch that the story level is all but transcended. Jesus' words in the story function primarily at the discourse level, and the second-person plural pronouns point primarily at Mark's, not Jesus', audience. If this intent were not clear enough in the midst of the chapter, the last verse of the chapter spells out explicitly at whom the whole speech is really aimed: 'And what I say to you I say to all: Watch' (13: 37). What Jesus says to 'you'—ostensibly the four disciples—is really aimed at 'all'—the audience of the Gospel drama. This statement is about as close as an ancient author can come to direct address by a character within the story to the audience outside the story. Another sign that all of Mark 13 functions as a discourse aimed primarily at Mark's audience is the framing of the entire chapter as a discourse about the future. Ostensibly, again, Jesus is describing the future of the disciples, but clear reference to their own personal roles in this future is oddly absent, if the apocalyptic discourse is intended for them. Rather, the future referred to in Mark 13 concerns primarily the time of the Gospel's implied audience. The future that the story level of Mark seems to be concerned about is actually the present for the reader, indeed, the present moment of the reading experience."

36. Fowler, *Let the Reader Understand,* 118: "Although verses 9 and 11 supposedly refer to future events in the story world, verse 10 drops this pretense of speaking about the future altogether in order to address explicitly the present moment of the implied reader's reading experience, which is a moment that anticipates the imminent 'preaching of the gospel to all nations.' Moreover, the reflexive term *gospel* is used. A reader of this narrative cannot help associating somehow 'the gospel preached to the nations' with the very story he or she is reading. Is not 13: 10 fulfilled as it is read? When a reader,

hint that somehow Christians will be immune to these sufferings. Rather, one should expect sufferings, for that is the constant outcome of primal ignorance. All life entails suffering (*duḥkha-satya*), as the earliest Buddhist scriptures claim.[37] It comes as it will, inevitably (δεῖ) as a part of every life, but as Crossan said somewhere, there is suffering and death and then there is lunch. The important thing (πρῶτον) is the necessity of preaching the Good News, the news about a conversion of consciousness that abandons the imagined pattern of clinging to any fixed idea or image.

Jesus is not giving a scenario of future events, according to which one can map out the events to be expected. Rather, he is saying that the important thing is to witness to the Gospel, no matter what events occur. Just as Jesus uses the messianic hopes of his disciples to empty them of imagined content, so here he is using their eschatological expectations to deconstruct those expectations, not to further them. First and foremost, see to the preaching of the Gospel, and then, if and when they bring you to trial, there is no cause for regret or worry.[38] The apocalyptic imagery presents a vision, in the light of which the events and sureties of the present stand under God's judgment and are emptied of any final validity. It would then be a mistake, I think, for interpreters, embarrassed by the millennarian enthusiasm of the text, to demythologize the eschatological speeches of the scriptures into a more manageable teaching, just as it is a mistake to erect that mythic vision into a roadmap for the future.[39]

---

especially a non-Jewish one, reads Mark 13, the Gospel/gospel is being promulgated 'to the nations.' "

37. Donahue, *Are You the Christ?* 234, remarks that apocalyptic is fundamentally "persecution literature," and on 213, that "Mark has in mind actual persecutions which his Church has undergone in the turmoil of A.D. 66–70." Also see 217–21, where the the events Mark predicts are those Josephus pictures the inhabitants of Jerusalem undergoing. One does wonder about Mark's Church, whether it is supported by the text to picture it as a clearly delineated community with its own social boundaries and defined identity. Mark does not mention a church (*ekklesia*) nor talk about any sociological structure. Rather, Mark talks about those who have faith in Jesus and set no boundaries, either on Yahweh's presence or between human beings.

38. Hartmann, *Prophecy Interpreted,* 150, comments on the background of verse 9, "They will deliver you up" as follows: "παραδώσουσιν may have been influenced by Daniel 7: 25, which says that the saints 'shall be given' into the hands of the last blasphemous king. . . ." Also see Perrin, "The Use of (Para)didonai," who sees the term as a technical term for the passion of Jesus.

39. See Hartmann, *Prophecy Interpreted,* 16: "This traditional meaning of the word [eschatological] has faded under the influence of the existentialist philosophy, so that 'eschatology' is no longer used to describe a saying on the 'last things' in the way mentioned above but is used instead of what is characterized by the existential decision (Entscheidung). In this process the time aspect disappears." I agree that an existentialist reading, embarrassed by the literal sense of apocalyptic speech, takes over the themes of eschatological discourse in favor of a modern philosophy, but think that such discourse, in its original writing, is itself open to many interpretations, for it embodies tensive symbols available to the creative interpretations of later thinkers. Bultmann's existentialist understandings are then not Mark's understandings. Neither are Mahāyāna categories.

The Chinese Taoist sage, Chuang Tzu, talks about hiding the world within the world, for so hidden, there is nothing that can be lost.[40] In Mark 8: 12 Jesus has refused to give any sign (σημεῖον) to this generation. Here he does not really reverse that refusal. There is no sign and no grand plan. It is not that once the Gospel has been preached to the nations, the end will come, for later Jesus explicitly says that nobody knows that time (13: 32).[41] In Mark's context, no one had ever written an apocalyptic history. "Apocalyptic never wrote a history of the heavenly Son of man because when the Son of man is manifest on earth that will be the end of history and cosmos. To write a connected story of the Son of Man as having already appeared and then to proclaim this as the gospel means the abolition of a totally future oriented apocalyptic."[42] Mark's apocalyptic discourse in Chapter 13 is, because embedded in the ongoing story of Jesus, a reinterpretation of apocalyptic in terms not of linear time, but of Jesus' life and death.

There is also here a strong suggestion that Jesus' disciples, to whom this discourse is addressed, will indeed be handed over to the authorities and suffer for his sake. "During the plot the disciples did not understand Jesus and they abandoned him when he was arrested. But in the situation that Jesus projects into the future, Peter, Andrew, James, and John represent the believing community. They are the ones who will suffer for Jesus' name. (13: 3–5, 9–11, 13)"[43] Although they all fail when Jesus is betrayed and Peter denies Jesus, the present passages suggest that they move beyond the elliptical

---

40. Watson, tr., *Chuang Tzu,* 80–81: "You hide your boat in the ravine and your fish net in the swamp and tell yourself that they will be safe. But in the middle of the night a strong man shoulders them and carries them off, and in your stupidity you don't know why it happened. You think you do right to hide little things in big ones, and yet they get away from you. But if you were to hide the world in the world, so that nothing could get away, this would be the final reality of the constancy of things." To hide the world in the world means to follow and harmonize with the Way (*tao*) in its permutations, without trying to counter it by intellectually ascertaining its structure or design.

41. Thus I disagree with Tolbert, *Sowing the Gospel,* 265: "Hence, sowing the gospel abroad becomes the one human act that can expedite the demise of this present evil, oppressive, and suffering-filled existence." If the final eschaton is not itself part of the conventional measuring of time, then nothing within that conventional time flow can bring it about.

42. Schulz, "Mark's Significance for the Theology of Early Christianity," 160. But see Collins, *The Beginning of the Gospel,* 27, who states that "Mark is an apocalyptic history." Again on 30, she writes: "Classical apocalypticism involves both a horizontal and a vertical dimension; that is, the apocalyptic mentality includes a perspective on history, especially regarding the destiny of the individual and the world, as well as the notion that earthly events are controlled by heavenly or spiritual powers." It seems to me that such an apocalyptic history affords only a mythic perspective, from which the earthly events are judged and emptied of final truth. Only if one transmutes that mythic vision of the eschaton into an ultimate viewpoint can one see earthly events as controlled by heavenly powers.

43. Via, *The Ethics of Mark's Gospel,* 56.

ending of 16: 8 finally to practice the middle path Jesus preaches, for the fulfillment of Jesus' eschatological descriptions lies outside the Gospel narrative.[44]

Negation of Selfhood
13: 10–11

[10]*"The most important thing is that the Good News must be preached.[45]* [11]*And when you are taken to be handed over, do not worry beforehand about what to say; no, say whatever is given to you when the time comes, because it is not you who will be speaking; it is the Holy Spirit."*

One is not to worry ($\mu\grave{\eta}$ $\pi\rho o\mu\epsilon\rho\iota\mu\nu\hat{\alpha}\tau\epsilon$), despite the dire situations which are described. The reason is that by bearing witness to the Gospel, one no longer functions in terms of self. Indeed that witness ($\epsilon\grave{\iota}\varsigma$ $\mu\alpha\rho\tau\acute{\upsilon}\rho\iota o\nu$ $\alpha\grave{\upsilon}\tau o\hat{\iota}\varsigma$) presupposes a conversion from self-focused illusion to insight into emptiness, and thus dependently co-arisen witness to the conventional validity of the Jesus path. So it is not you who speak ($o\grave{\upsilon}$ $\gamma\acute{\alpha}\rho$ $\grave{\epsilon}\sigma\tau\epsilon$ $\grave{\upsilon}\mu\epsilon\hat{\iota}\varsigma$ $o\grave{\iota}$ $\lambda\alpha\lambda o\hat{\upsilon}\nu\tau\epsilon\varsigma$)— there is no inner essence that has to perform or that has to be protected. Metaphysical notions of an inner self are fabricated in virtue of the flesh, the flesh that makes it difficult in the Garden of Olives for the disciples to be awake to their original selflessness. There is no self and thus no need to plan for how that self is to conduct itself. No need for a special insight into the eschatological design. Rather, Jesus negates that anyone has a handle on the plan, or, behind such plans, on the self who plans. God is not a transcendent self concocting overarching plans about what is to happen in the world. Ultimate meaning does not make incursions into the realm of worldly convention. God never directly enters into and alters the unfolding events of Mark's narrative. God is not a character in the Markan plot, for God appears only numinously at Jesus' baptism and at his transfiguration. Neither is God a stage manager behind the scenes.

---

44. Tolbert, *Sowing the Gospel,* 257. For Tolbert, such unfulfilled predictions refer not to the disciples, but to Mark's readers. 259: "Although the unfulfilled prophecies are delivered to the disciples (13: 1–5; 14: 28), the Jerusalem council (14: 62), and the women (16: 7), since their subject is the apocalyptic coming of the Son of man and the events that will precede it, their import concerns the audience and not the characters in the story world." If, however, the apocalyptic hour is itself the death/resurrection of Jesus, then one need not move outside the story's structure to see beyond its ending.

45. The above translation departs from *The New Jerusalem Bible* ("since the gospel must first be proclaimed to all nations"), for I have followed those scholars (Manson, Synodale, Lagrange, Kilpatrick, Bratcher and Nida, *A Translator's Handbook,* 400) who take verse 10 not with verse 9, but with verse 11. Furthermore, I take the term "first" ($\pi\rho\hat{\omega}\tau o\nu$) not to refer to time, but to importance, i.e., to the first thing, the most important thing.

It is not one's inner self who speaks, but the holy spirit who will speak for you. This holy spirit has been identified by later Christian thinkers as the Holy Spirit, God himself as transforming human consciousness. The Spirit is the mind of wisdom, realized by practicing the path of the Gospel, and speaking as needed. Yet, there still is no guarantee that even the spirit will speak well, confound the authorities, or carry the day. Perhaps, as with many thousands of martyrs, the spirit will merely babble—or remain silent, as did Jesus during most of his trial. Perhaps the spirit will express eschatological visions that undermine the assumed structures of reality. Yet, the point is not to win, but to follow the path and preach the Gospel. What the spirit gives may be nothing very much, but that nothing is quite sufficient.

The entire passage is a Markan counterpart to the Matthean passage about the lilies of the field, who do not labor or toil, but are nevertheless arrayed in beauty, despite the fact that tomorrow they will wither and die. Mark parallels the Japanese kōans,[46] which suggest hidden depths in everyday occurrences, and Shinran's insistence on abandoning the contrivance and calculation (*hakarai*) of self-power (*jiriki*) to practice the Pure Land path of faith (*shinjin*) in the other power (*tariki*) of Amida Buddha.[47] Yet in most Buddhist traditions such abandonment takes place in the balance and serenity of quiet meditation. Here, by contrast, it occurs under duress and persecution. The legendary Zen Master Bodhidharma retreats from the presence of Emperor Wu of the Liang dynasty, whom he has just informed that there is no merit in performing good deeds.[48] Christians in the time of Mark did not always so escape. Nevertheless, they too function in awareness of no-self, for the holy spirit centers their activity in practicing and witnessing the Jesus

---

46. Meier, *A Marginal Jew,* has little understanding of what a kōan (or a parable) is; he writes, 177: "A tweedy poetaster who spent his time spinning out parables and Japanese koans, a literary aesthete who toyed with first century deconstruction, or a bland Jesus who simply told people to look at the lilies of the field—such a Jesus would threaten no one, just as the university professors who create him threaten no one." Meier insultingly dismisses kōans without a notion of their doctrinal history or their impact within the tradition: to engender the great doubt that indeed threatens one's sense of the reality of selfhood in all its permutations. One wonders whence his animus derives and to whom it is directed.

47. On the analogous structure of faith in Pure Land Buddhism, see Unno, tr., *Tannishō: A Shin Buddhist Classic,* 49–51.

48. Dumoulin, *Zen Buddhism: A History, India and China,* 91: "According to the legend, the following conversation took place at Bodhidharma's first meeting with Emperor Wu of the Liang dynasty: The Emperor said, 'Since ascending to the throne, I have had temples built, sūtras translated, and monks ordained. What merit have I gained?' The master replied, 'No merit at all.' The emperor replied, 'Why no merit at all?' The master said, 'All these are but impure motives for merit; they mature that paltry fruit of rebirth as a human being or a deva (a god). They are like shadows that follow the form, having no reality of their own.' The emperor said, 'Then of what kind is true merit?' He answered, 'It is pure knowing, wonderful and perfect. Its essence is emptiness. One cannot gain such merit by worldly means.' Thereupon the emperor asked, 'What is the sacred truth's first principle?' The master replied, 'Vast emptiness, nothing sacred.' The emperor said, 'Who is this who faces me?' The master replied, 'I don't know.' "

path. In Mark it is the holy spirit who provides authentic continuity in the absence of the empirical Jesus.[49]

The Scenario
13: 12–13

[12] *"Brother will betray brother to death, and the father his child; children will come forward against their parents and have them put to death. [13]You will be universally hated on account of my name; but anyone who stands firm to the end will be saved."*

This section concludes the first part of chapter 13, which describes the birthpangs that will accompany the end time, warning that one cannot control the future by scoping the signs of its coming and gaining control over one's response to events. Indeed, the events described are not simply cosmic images of a supernatural event, but accurate portrayals of what in fact Jesus' followers are to experience shortly in Jesus' arrest and execution. "The situation depicted in the first stage is not only the ugly condition of the world faced by the later followers of Jesus but is likewise the precise situation now confronting Jesus and his disciples in Jerusalem."[50] Mark is not depicting a future scenario. He draws from past images of distress and trial, from Micah 7: 6–7, which states: "For son insults father, . . . a person's enemies come from within the household itself. But I shall look to Yahweh, my hope is in the God who will save me, my God will hear me." Like Micah, Jesus envisages such happenings, but he does not promise that God will actually deliver one from distress. Rather, the one who perseveres to the end will be delivered, who remains a selfless witness to the Gospel. There is no salvation of self, for there is no self to be saved. The end (τέλος) is not here a cosmic event, but one's death at the hand of the persecutors. One is saved not by knowing the eschatological story, but by abiding in love and service throughout life. Mark employs the common eschatological imagery to admit that distress will indeed be intense, but all things pass, even the very stones of the temple.

---

49. Weeden, "The Heresy That Necessitated Mark's Gospel," 74: "In Mark the Holy Spirit . . . controls what is said and done in the name of God. In 1: 10 the Spirit is bestowed. . . . The Spirit, however, . . . manifests complete control over the individual who has received it and directs his whole course of action (1: 12). . . . In Mark's argument it is the Holy Spirit that provides the authentic continuity between the pre-resurrected time of the historical Jesus and the post-resurrection period of the Church." In Mahāyāna terms, it might be better to describe the action of the Spirit as the attainment of one's original face, rather than as control of one's individuality. The action of the Spirit is not a losing of one's real, original self, but a regaining of its true reality as empty, and thus free.

50. Tolbert, *Sowing the Gospel,* 261.

Idolatry
13: 14–20

[14]"When you see the desolating sacrilege set up where it ought not to be (let the reader understand), then those in Judea must escape to the mountains; [15]if a man is on the housetop, he must not come down or go inside to collect anything from his house; [16]if a man is in the fields, he must not turn back to fetch his cloak. [17]Alas for those with child, or with babies at the breast, when those days come! [18]Pray that this may not be in winter. [19]For in those days there will be great distress, unparalleled since God created the world, and such as will never be again. [20]And if the Lord had not shortened that time, no human being would have survived; but he did shorten the time, for the sake of the elect whom he chose."

The interpretation of this passage depends on just how one understands "the sacrilege that desolates" (τὸ βδέλυγμα τῆς ἐρημώσεως). The phrase comes from *Daniel*, where it signifies both sacrilege and the persecutions consequent therefrom.[51] There are numerous references in the Hebrew Bible, all referring to idolatry. In describing his vision of the loathsome things practiced by the House of Israel, which drives God from his sanctuary, *Ezekiel* 8: 3 talks about an idol of jealousy standing in Jerusalem, which issues in violence throughout the country (Ezk 8: 17). This idol is perhaps the statue of Astarte set up in the Temple by Manasseh, described in 2 Kings 21: 7. *Daniel* 11: 31 says: "Forces of his [i.e., Antiochus Epiphanes'] will come and profane the Citadel-Sanctuary; they will abolish the perpetual sacrifice and install the appalling abomination (LXX, καὶ δώσουσι βδέλυγμα ἠφανισμένον) there." Here the reference is to the statue of Zeus set up in the Temple by Antiochus Epiphanes in 168 BCE, right before the composition of *Daniel*.

Yet another passage, *Daniel* 12: 5–13, is perhaps more germane to Mark, for it presents the very phrase Mark employs: τὸ βδέλυγμα ἐρημώσεως: "I, Daniel, then looked and saw two other people standing (LXX εἱστήκεισαν), one on the near bank of the river, the other on the far. One of them

---

51. Collins, *The Beginning of the Gospel,* 85–86: "The variety of opinions expressed indicates the difficulty of the problem. If we take the admonition to the reader in v 14 as an aside written by the evangelist, the implication is that the 'desolating sacrilege' of Daniel is an element of high importance at the final stage of the composition of the Gospel. Its importance is also indicated by the fact that it is the primary answer to the disciples' question about a sign (v 4)." The phrase certainly alludes to *Daniel;* see Hartmann, *Prophecy Interpreted,* 152: "We encounter 'the abomination of desolation' in Daniel in passages dealing with persecution and oppression. . . ." Also Kolenkow, "Beyond Miracles," 177: "As in several forecasts of the future (cf. IV Ez. 11, 12, II Bar. 37–40, 53), Mark's major model for a structure of prophetic history is Daniel. In 13:14, Mark alludes specifically to the abomination of desolation (from Dan. 11) and Dan 11–12 serves as his reference for an answer to the question which brings forth the prophecy of 13, when will the great buildings fall. . . ."

said to the man dressed in linen (τῷ 'ἁδρὶ τῷ ἐνδεδυμένῳ τὰ βαδδὶν) who was standing further up the stream, 'How long until these wonders take place?' I heard the man speak who was dressed in linen, standing farther up the stream: he raised his right hand and his left to heaven and swore by him who lives forever, 'A time and two times, and half a time; and all these things will come true, once the crushing of the holy people's power is over.' I listened but did not understand. I then said, 'My lord, what is to be the outcome?' 'Go, Daniel,' he said. 'These words are to remain secret and sealed until the time of the End. Many will be cleansed, made white and purged; the wicked will persist in doing wrong; the wicked will never understand; those who are wise will understand. From the moment that the perpetual sacrifice is abolished and the appalling abomination set up (καὶ δοθήσεται τὸ βδέλυγμα ἐρημώσεως): a thousand two hundred and ninety days. Blessed is he who perseveres and attains a thousand three hundred and thirty-five days. But you go away and rest; and you will rise for your reward at the end of time."[52]

It is this passage that lies directly behind Mark's usage. It speaks of the desolation caused by the sacrilege which invades the Temple sanctuary. It refers to a prophecy given by a man dressed in linen, a figure who appears twice in Mark, both times at moments of eschatological import. First briefly and cowardly in Mark 14: 50–52 as the fellow robed only in a linen cloth who follows the arrested Jesus but then escapes capture by wriggling out of his linen and running away. Second, in 16:5, where a young man dressed in a white robe announces Jesus' resurrection to the women at the tomb. The passage from *Daniel* also refers to those who persevere (ὁ ὑπομένων), echoing the immediately preceding sentence in verse 13 of Mark that anyone who stands firm (ὁ δὲ ὑπομείνας) to the end will be saved. Mark has left enough clues to identify the background of his use of the phrase.

Yet Mark does not merely follow the sense of Daniel. Rather, he adds the surprising and unique hermeneutical advice that it is to be interpreted by the reader, i.e., as the reader sees fit in present circumstances.[53] Let one apply the lesson to the present situation and see where the idol is now to be found.

---

52. *1 Maccabees* 1: 54, presents another reference, bringing the issue nearer Mark's time: "On the fifteenth day of Chislev in the year one hundred and forty-five (167 BCE) the king erected the abomination of desolation (βδέλυγμα ἐρημώσεως) above the altar. . . ."

53. Fowler, *Let the Reader Understand*, 83–84: "Once alerted to the ubiquitous narrator, we can more easily see that 13:14 is far from unique. What distinguishes it from other commentary by the narrator is the word *reader*. It is the only place in the Gospel that the storyteller calls the recipient of the story by that name. The word *reader* makes the parenthetical remark impossible as a statement by Jesus at the story level because the characters within the story do not address 'the reader' outside the story, at least not in ancient literature. . . . Therefore, the Gospel of Mark was probably written to be read aloud to an assembled audience, and the one possibility for identifying 'the reader' of 13:14 would be to take the parenthesis as a kind of wink or stage direction to an *anagnostes*, a professional reader reciting the Gospel of Mark before an assembled audience."

In Mark's context, that desolating abomination was probably the fall of the Temple itself, with all of the symbolic chaos that entailed.[54] "In the Septuagint ἐρημώσεως ['desolating'] refers almost exclusively to the destruction of Jerusalem, its temple, or the royal palace."[55] Jesus emptied the temple of its accustomed purpose; indeed, in light of its actual destruction, his words comfort those whose symbolic worldviews have been completely undermined. "Thus in chapter 13 the temple itself becomes part of Jesus' past, and its desecration and destruction part of the disciples' future and, apparently, (13:14), part of the reader's present. The 'sacrilege' (13:14) is not projected to destroy the temple but to make it 'desolate [*erēmōseōs,* from *erēmos,* 'wilderness'] by causing pious worshippers to avoid it because of the abomination, and thus depriving it of any meaning or purpose.' Jesus, however, abandons the temple not because its sacrality has been profaned but because he experiences a breakdown of the sacred/profane distinction. Thus the temple loses its meaning with Jesus' actions (11: 15–17; 13: 1–3); the loss of meaning at the time of the 'desolating sacrilege' is merely confirmatory (13: 14), as is the total destruction of the temple (13: 2)."[56] Jesus has rendered the temple empty of its sacral character, for the presence of Abba is immediately available to everybody without distinction.

In a broader context (as readers are directed to construct), the idol that renders desolate (*śūnya,* τῆς ἐρημώσεως) is more than just one religious statue. Rather, it is the surety of knowing the apocalyptic plan itself. The time allotted to the "one who perseveres" is not, as in *Daniel,* a fixed span of linear time; rather one who abides until the death of Jesus will hear the words of the white-robed young man about Jesus' eschatological resurrection.

---

54. Joel Marcus, "The Jewish War," argues that the pervasive influence of the Jewish revolt forms the context for Mark, for then the temple was occupied by various religious groups beginning in AD 67–68. These rebels precipitated the subsequent destruction of the temple by Titus in the year 70. He writes, 461–62: "Mark himself is a Jewish Christian from Judea who thinks that the presence of Gentiles within the church is a momentous sign of the eschatological fulfillment and who reads the handwriting on the wall when the Zealots occupy the temple to purify it of Gentile influence in the winter of 67–68. He and other like-minded Jewish Christians flee therefore to one of the Transjordan Hellenistic cities (Pella?), where they join a predominantly Gentile Christian community that has recently experienced its own difficulties at the hands of the Jewish revolutionaries." Thus Marcus interprets the abomination as the occupation of the Temple by Eleazar Son of Simon in 67–68, for the masculine participle (desolating) suggests a reference to a person (454).

55. Kelber, *The Kingdom in Mark,* 120.30, where he refers to Pesch, *Naherwartungen,* 143. See also Kolenkow, "Beyond Miracles," 177–78: "The problem which Mark seems to be answering by his use of the Daniel 11–12 model is the relation between the fall of the temple and the endtime." Thus, "Daniel provides a structure which allows Mark by saying that the fall of Jerusalem is what is referred to by the abomination of desolation (Daniel 11:31), to set up a distance between the time of the fall of Jerusalem and the endtime."

56. Malbon, *Narrative Space,* 124, citing Kittel, *Theological Dictionary of the New Testament,* 660.

Further, the sacrilege that makes desolate (ἐρημώσεως) is cognate with the recurring Markan theme of the wilderness (ἔρημος), signifying the emptying of the Temple cult. Yet, in neither Jesus' time nor Mark's is there any concrete reference to what that sacrilege might be.[57] Caligula indeed wanted to erect his image in the temple, but the uproar among the Jewish populace and authorities caused the Romans to postpone that deed until after Caligula's death when it was forgotten.[58] Mark's passage is further strange in that there is an apparent grammatical mistake. He modifies the neuter noun, sacrilege (τὸ βδέλυγμα) with a masculine participle, "set up, standing" (ἑστηκότα).[59] Perhaps more than an error in grammar is involved.

The interpretative key, I think, is found in the symbolism of the words "wilderness" and "desolating." The wilderness is the symbolic presence of ultimate meaning, emptying all conventional realities of any final meaning. Likewise, the sacrilege set up where it should not be empties the Temple of any final significance, for that is the theme of this eschatological discourse. Not a stone will be left upon a stone, all will be rendered desolate. Mark is doubling back to the emptiness of the wilderness to empty the Temple itself of its claim to finality. However, the eschatological event that brings this emptying about is not simply a pagan incursion into the temple precincts, but the very crucifixion of Jesus. It is he who is "set up" (ἑστηκότα) on the cross, and who is taunted with the request that he come down and save himself (15: 30), and thus the masculine form of ἑστηκότα refers to Jesus on the cross. He takes over the role of Daniel's linen-robed oracle who stands on the side of the river, for to all appearances he is lifted up (ἑστηκότα) in death and judgment. "Because the Son of man who suffers, dies, and rises is the eschatological Son of man who has authority to forgive sins (2: 28) and who will come at the end as judge and savior (8: 38; 13: 26–27), his death and resurrection is the eschatological event."[60] The sacrilege is executing Jesus to defend the absoluteness of worldly conventions, for that very act renders those conventions, however valid and precious, empty of final mean-

---

57. Thus I disagree with views such as Kelber's, *Mark's Story of Jesus,* 69, which sees the desolating sacrilege as a "coded reference to the Roman general Titus who commanded the final assault on the temple and took possession of the ruined site." But I would agree with Tolbert, *Sowing the Gospel,* 263, who sees the desolating sacrilege as "an esoteric image, the proper interpretation of which depends on knowledge supplied, not by the story, but by information obtained from some external, initiated group."

58. Myers, *Binding the Strong Man,* 60.

59. Tolbert, *Sowing the Gospel,* 263: "Mark, oddly, modifies the singular neuter noun, τὸ βδέλυγμα, with a masculine participle, ἑστηκότα ('set up'), suggesting perhaps a personal agent rather than an object behind this new 'desolating sacrilege." Fowler, *Let the Reader Understand,* 92: "Such liberties taken with syntax are inexcusable in a polished, literate text, but they can be effective and therefore acceptable in an oral presentation. The abundance of anacolutha is yet another characteristic of Mark's narrative that suggests that it was intended for oral performance."

60. Via, *The Ethics of Mark's Gospel,* 164.

ing.[61] At his death, the Temple veil will be torn from top to bottom (15: 38); once the presence of Yahweh is unveiled, there is no longer any locally circumscribed presence of Yahweh. The Temple is empty of Yahweh—the divine is present only as that which is covered (*saṃvṛta*).

The deluded quest to know beforehand the grand eschatological plan functions within the pattern of false imagination, clinging to the essence of events so as to protect oneself from distress. But, when events actually happen, the only course a Christian may take is empty-handed flight into the mountain wildernesses, flight from deluded understanding to insight into the emptiness of all plans and all constructs. In fact, the advice that those in Judea are to flee to the mountains is not advice on what to do at the end time, since its impact is limited to those in Judea, i.e., those who witness the desolating sacrilege of Jesus' death on the cross.[62] They are to seek out once again the wilderness where the presence of Yahweh is immediately available apart from any conventional support, i.e., their houses and fields. Any construct regarded as absolute becomes by that very fact an idol. Flee immediately, without hankering after the old patterns of mistaken attachment.

In the narrative event, that is exactly what most of the disciples in fact do when Jesus is arrested. They follow his advice and flee, all except Peter who, foolishly confident of his resolve, bravely enters the high priest's courtyard and puts himself in the situation of having to deny Jesus in order to save himself. The passage about women pregnant or with nursing children alludes back to the birthpangs mentioned in verse 8. There the apocalyptic vision talks about the beginning of birthpangs that bring forth the new creation. "The Gospel of Mark has, as it were, a double ending, the passion of Jesus (chaps. 14–16) and the passion of the community (chap. 13). In the one ending, women flee from the tomb (16: 8) and in the other 'those who are in Judea [are warned to] flee to the mountains' (13: 14). In the Markan context the mountains suggest revelation, new order, in the midst of chaos, just as the shattering of the chaos of the tomb [by the risen Jesus] offers

---

61. Mauser, *Christ in the Wilderness,* 142, notes that the wilderness passages are restricted to the first half of the gospel, their place being taken by the passion predictions from chapter 8 onward. Yet, here in chapter 13 there does seem to be a textual linkage to the wilderness theme in the sacrilege that makes desolate, i.e., that turns the Temple itself into a wilderness by freeing Yahweh from its confines.

62. Malbon, *Narrative Space,* 88: "The Markan text, however, does not command fleeing *from* Judea but fleeing *in* Judea; only 'those who are in Judea' need be concerned with fleeing, and they are to flee from where they live and work (13: 15, 'house;' 13: 16 'field') to the uninhabited mountains." Schweizer, *The Good News,* 273: "Above all, the construction of the Gospel contradicts the idea that this passage was drawn up as a document dealing with flight in the last days before the end of the world and that it was intended to appeal to men to conduct themselves properly in the last hour." Hartmann, *Prophecy Interpreted,* 241, notes an allusion to I *Maccabees* 2, where, after the abomination of desolation has been set up, Mattathias and his sons offer resistance, and then flee to the mountains (29, καὶ ἔφυγ αὐτὸς καὶ οἱ υἱοὶ αὐτοῦ εἰς τὰ ὄρη), leaving their property in the city (2 Mac 2:28)."

revelation, the new order of resurrection."[63] Thus, woe to those who are attached to the old order, the order of primal ignorance and delusion. The passage is replete with metaphor and figures of speech. Like Jesus' parable teachings, it is about the usurpation of ultimate meaning by conventional clinging to religious forms, the clinging both of the authorities who unwittingly establish idolatry by localizing the presence of Yahweh in the Temple and the clinging of those who would counter those authorities by learning from Jesus the exact time and sequence of future events. Mark plays on such expectancies to wean people away from them by describing the trials of the end time: idolatry will expose everyone to the desolate cold of winter which freezes young children at the breast and aborts the newborn.

To describe those trials further, Jesus again borrows from *Daniel* 12: 1, which states: "That will be a time of great distress, unparalleled since nations came into existence." Jesus, however, places this in a different context, signifying that at the end time when all conventional forms will collapse and be emptied, no flesh (σάρξ) can survive unless the Lord had shortened (εἰ μὴ ἐκολόβωσεν) those days. The flesh is conventional consciousness in its imagined pattern. The tense of the verb "had shortened" is past, in accordance with the Hebrew prophetic style of utterance.[64] Yet it clearly suggests that God has already "shortened" those days. The verb itself means not only to shorten, but also to collapse or curtail. If indeed the final eschatological, revelatory event is Jesus' death and resurrection, then the time of eschatological trial has been curtailed to the three days Jesus remains in the tomb.[65] The issue is not about how to follow the eschatological plan, but how to respond to Jesus' manifestation of Yahweh in the collapse of all imagined hopes and ideas, in his execution. The verb ἐκολόβωσεν ("to shorten") has an added sense of "to amputate," "to mutilate."[66] In this meaning, what is intended is a complete collapse of the idolators' time frame in which idols are fabricated. The elect are then those who are chosen not to follow the path of imagined

---

63. Malbon, *Narrative Space,* 164.

64. Bratcher and Nida, *A Translator's Handbook,* 410.

65. Crossan, "The Empty Tomb," 137, notes that in the passion predictions, " 'the third day' was not intended as historical chronology but as prophetic and/or eschatological symbolism." *Hosea* 6: 1–2 sets the theme: "Come, let us return to Yahweh. He has rent us and he will heal us; he has struck us and he will bind up our wounds; after two days he will revive us, and on the third day he will raise us up and we shall live in his presence." Mark's "shortening of the time" alludes then to these eschatological themes of returning to the immediately available presence of Yahweh in the wilderness of silent ultimate meaning.

66. Hartmann, *Prophecy Interpreted,* 163–64: "In the Greek phrase the actual main word κολοβοῦν is really somewhat peculiar. It has a concrete meaning, 'to mutilate,' 'to cut short,' 'to curtail,' and is used, for instance, of tree trunks or dog's tails. When the large lexica give a figurative meaning, 'to shorten' (of time), the only example quoted is the present passage. A survey of several concordances gives the same negative result. We should then at least be able to conclude that the figurative use is, if not unique, then somewhat original, and this originality must attract some attention." Hartmann suggests a scribal miscopy, but I conclude that the prime meaning of the term is indeed "to mutilate" days/time, i.e., to under- *cut* all linear time frameworks.

idols, not those who choose to cling to idolatrous hopes for a temporal and empirical vindication. The elect are those who love and serve until their end, for the entire passage is a preparation for the passion narrative to follow, a narrative which presents the Jesus paradigm (ἑστηκότα) of trials, sufferings, and death that renders all conventional usurpations of ultimate meaning (βδέλυγμα) empty (ἐρημώσεως).

Imagined Christs and the Inner Mind
13: 21–23

²¹ "And if anyone says to you then, 'Look, here is the Christ' or, 'Look, he is there', do not believe it; ²²for false Christs and false prophets will arise and produce signs and portents to deceive the elect, if that were possible. ²³You, therefore, must be on your guard. I have given you full warning."

Jesus alludes to *Deuteronomy* 13: 2–4, which contrasts the wondrous, empirical signs of false prophets with the great commandment to love God. The text says: "If a prophet or a dreamer of dreams arises among you, offering you some sign or wonder, and the sign or wonder comes about, and if he then says to you, 'Let us follow other gods (hitherto unknown to you) and serve them,' you must not listen to that prophet's words or to that dreamer's dreams. Yahweh your God is testing you to know if you love Yahweh your God with all your heart and all your soul." Jesus extends the idea to include not only prophets but messiahs, christs. In so doing he tells the disciples not to go looking for eschatological messiahs of the end time, for there is no end time messiah as imagined by those who would identify his coming as an empirical advent. This entire discourse began with the disciples asking Jesus what will be the sign of the coming eschatological end time. Jesus here identifies such signs (σημεῖα) as false, as leading one to idolatry and vitiating one's love of God. Take care that no one leads you astray, causes you to meander through the delusions of imagined realities. The present passage harkens back to the advice presented in 13: 5–6, with its warnings about false deceivers. Such framing identifies the intervening text as expatiating on the nature of such deception.[67] The message is clear: watch out and do

---

67. Kelber, *Mark's Story of Jesus*, 68: "The speech proper opens with a warning against certain persons who appear in the name of Jesus saying, 'I am he!' (13: 5–6). They are people who claim messianic power and announce the presence of the Kingdom. A similar situation is reflected in 13: 21–22. Prophetic personalities make an appearance saying, 'Look, here is the Christ!' and 'Look, there he is!' The experienced reader will recognize in 13: 5–6 and 13: 21–22 yet another instance of Markan framing composition. Both passages relate to one and the same kind of messianic prophets. By enclosing the first part of Jesus' speech (13: 5–23) with reference to these prophets, Mark suggests a connection between their activities and the events described in 13: 7–20." Kelber, *The Kingdom in Mark*, 137, sees the passage referring to "ecstatically aroused prophets" from the Jewish-Christian Jerusalem church, whose "unadulterated *theologia gloriae* did not attach any soteriological significance to the death and resurrection of Jesus. Not the

not be misled by imagined indications. Jesus has not answered the original request of verse 4, "What will be the sign?" Rather, he has already predicted everything and forewarned of everything, precisely in identifyng such signs as delusory. He does not say that he will reveal these signs, but that he has already given full warning (προείρηκα ὑμῖν πάντα), for there is no conventional plan that one can count on. Therefore, he repeats the advice: "See to yourself" (ὑμεῖς δὲ βλέπετε), echoing verses 5 and 9. Do not rely on signs imagined to be outer realities, but look within to your own minds and hearts. That is the best way to be on guard.

Note also that it is these false witnesses who will identify the location of the false christs (ψευδόχριστοι), saying "Here (ὧδε) he is," or "There (ἐκεῖ) he is!"[68]

Seeing in the Dark
13: 24–27

[24]*"But in those days, after that time of distress, the sun will be darkened, the moon will not give its light,* [25]*the stars will come falling out of the sky and the powers in the heavens will be shaken.* [26]*And then they will see the Son of man coming in the clouds with great power and glory.* [27]*And then too he will send the angels to gather his chosen from the four winds, from the ends of the world to the ends of the sky."*

Again the allusion is to the Hebrew Bible, to *Isaiah* 13: 9–10, which says: "Look, the day of Yahweh is coming, merciless, with wrath and burning anger, to reduce the country to a desert (ἔρημον) and root out sinners from it. For in the sky the stars and Orion will shed their light no longer; the sun will be dark when it rises, and the moon will no longer give its light." Such a day of the Lord is apart from linear time expectations, for it makes empty and desolate all imagined hopes. Isaiah talks about the Lord making the earth desolate, paralleling Jesus' words about the sacrilege that brings desolation. Idolatry in all its forms freezes ultimate meaning within conventional forms, and thus stands in need of being emptied and rendered desolate. Mark, however, speaks about the time after the eschatological sufferings of the community, after that distress (μετὰ τὴν φλῖψιν ἐκείνην), i.e., a time that is not time, that has gone beyond all conventional reckoning of time. "It is

---

crucified and resurrected Jesus of the past, but the Son of Man in his eschatological power and glory was to fulfill the messianic promise of deliverance."

68. Kelber, *The Kingdom in Mark,* 116: "The two local adverbs *hōde* and *ekei* raise the issue of place. The parousia prophets pointing to a 'here' and to a 'there' seem to have associated their eschatology with a specific site." Hartmann, *Prophecy Interpreted,* 194, notes that the term παρουσία is used in the Gospels only in Matthew 24. Is this because false prophets have usurped the term with their all too empirical version of the presence of Christ?

certainly true that the ultimate beginning and the end of apocalyptic world time cannot be contained in history. But it is not more an 'illusion' to project the experience of the eternal backward and forward than it is to speak of the source of eternity as depth or height. Both the temporal and the spatial terms are symbols of the transcendent on which the world depends, and the images of unspoiled primordial time and redeemed eschatological time are natural for a people who experience divine activity in history as purposeful."[69]

In this context Mark borrows Isaiah's imagery of the sun, moon, and stars failing to shine anymore. Only then, when conventional time is no more, when all the lights of heaven go out,[70] and when one has no light in which to see anything, can one see the coming of the son of man.[71] This seeing is not the ordinary seeing of imagined understanding, but a transcendent non-seeing that sees all. Seeing the Christ, seeing the Christ, is not a seeing of any Christ, and that is why it is a seeing of the Christ. His power and glory are not ever empirically visible, for they occur only in the darkening of ordinary understanding, of that discriminative thought that attempts to capture reality in its images and ideas. Note that Jesus is said to come after all the light from the heavenly bodies is darkened, *in* the clouds (ἐν νεφέλαις), not *on* the clouds. He is not riding the clouds in full view, but shrouded within their opacity. All revelations of ultimate meaning come veiled in conventional

---

69. Via, *The Ethics of Mark's Gospel,* 40.

70. Kelber, *The Kingdom in Mark,* 123, notes that the imagery is considerably muted from that of Isaiah: "The darkening of the sun, the absence of moonlight, the trembling of the heavens are apocalyptic metaphors traditionally associated with judgment in 'the great and terrible day' (Isaiah 13:10; 34:4; Joel 2:10; 3:15–16; Zephaniah 1:15). What is absent, however, are the more expressly stated features of judgment, such as the trembling of the earth and the fear of the people, the wrath of the Lord and the doom of sinners, the slaughter of the wicked and the overthrow of evil. In Mark the Son of Man does not arrive to execute judgment." On the development of the son of man traditions from Daniel, see Crossan, *The Historical Jesus,* 245–259, which concludes: "It was Mark, therefore, and Mark alone, who created the suffering and rising son of man and placed all those units in 240 *Passion-Resurrection Prophecy* [2/1] on the lips of Jesus, whence they were accepted and expanded by both Matthew and Luke."

71. Via, *The Ethics of Mark's Gospel,* 30: "In other than a literal reading of transcendent events these ultimate terminal points (of creative beginning and apocalyptic end) ought not to be thought of as happening in time." Tödt, *The Son of Man in the Synoptic Tradition,* 33, speaks of verse 26 as the closest to the sphere of Jewish apocalyptic, with its radical sense of the future. Von Rad, *Old Testament Theology,* 2: 119–125, 137, 289, describes Yahweh as coming "unexpectedly," bringing judgment upon the godless and salvation to those who fear God. One concludes that this radical sense of the eschatological future stands beyond time and comes beyond any expectancy within linear, historical time. It is rather the emptying of time as the assured mode of reality. It is an epiphany of the Lord. Donahue, *Are You the Christ?,* 170, remarks: "The vindication and salvation of the community comes with the arrival of the Son of Man. . . . the future of the verbs of 'seeing' in Mark shows a special concern of Mark for the parousia and characterizes it as a manifestation or epiphany." In Mark, the son of man comes in the very first chapter when Jesus announces that the kingdom is at hand, and he is manifested in his passion, death, and resurrection.

forms. Manifestation marks the presence of ultimate meaning by veiling and hiding its presence. This is why Jesus comes in the darkening of all common expectancies, and not in the broad daylight of the full sun (13: 35). *Daniel* 7: 13 also has the theme of the nighttime coming of the son of man: "I was gazing into the visions of the night, when I saw, coming *on* the clouds of heaven (μετὰ τῶν νεφελῶν τοῦ οὐρανοῦ), as it were a son of man." Here, the son of man comes on the clouds, which Mark has changed to "in the clouds," (ἐν νεφέλαις) for in Mark the stress is on a coming that is not visible to ordinary looking. The moon and the stars provide no nighttime illumination, and the Son of man comes hidden, even in his manifestation.[72]

It is in this context that Mark describes the cosmic, eschatological community, calling the elect together from the four corners of the earth. Here the elect are those who, having loved God and been of service to human beings, witness to that time after the end time, and break through temporal expectations. They enter a timeless time where ultimate meaning abides in silence, beyond the light of sun and moon. Jesus is transmuting eschatological language into kōans, conundrums that call into question one's deepest intimations and one's deepest experiences.

The When of the End Time
13: 28–32

[28]*"Take the fig tree as a parable: as soon as its twigs grow supple and its leaves come out, you know that summer is near.* [29]*So with you when you see these things happening: know that he is near, right at the gates.* [30]*In truth I tell you, before this generation has passed away all these things will have taken place.* [31]*Sky and earth will pass away, but my words will not pass away.* [32]*But as for that day or hour, nobody knows it, neither the angels in heaven, nor the Son; no one but the Father."*

The parable of the fig tree clarifies the preceding eschatological discourse. One is to learn from the fig tree ('Απὸ δὲ τῆς συκῆς), i.e., one is to compare the greening of the fig tree to the coming of the end time. The parable of the fig tree itself does not, however, offer any clues as to when the end time will come. Rather, it emphasizes themes already presented, that the earth produces the fruits of the kingdom of itself in the parable of the sower (4: 1–9). "The agricultural pattern [sower and tenants] clarifies the role of Jesus in relation to the kingdom. Jesus does not bring the kingdom, for the kingdom,

---

72. See Weeden, *Mark—Traditions in Conflict,* 129–131, for a refutation that this passage, considered the *locus classicus* for the descent of the son of man to earth for judgment at the final eschatological event, is in fact an enthronement of Jesus as the final eschatological event. If indeed, the death/resurrection of Jesus is the eschatological event, then his "enthronement" on the cross is itself a rendering desolate of all eschatological expectancies and his coming veiled in the clouds of faith.

like the good earth, already exists before the sower begins to sow. The use of the perfect tense in Mark 1: 15 (the time *has been fulfilled,* the kingdom of God *has come near*) reflects the sense that the kingdom began in the past and continues into the present."[73] This passage says that you will know that he is near, right at the gates (ἐγγὺς ἐστιν ἐπὶ θύραις), when you see these things happening. But the reader has already been told in 1: 15 that the time is fulfilled and the kingdom of God is at hand (πεπλήρωται ὁ καιρὸς καὶ ἤγγικεν ἡ βασιλεία τοῦ θεοῦ). The coming of the son of man is then not to be interpreted as a future empirical event, but as night-vision of the already come son of man, occurring only when the mind that clings to imagined realities has been totally darkened in eschatological silence.[74]

Thus, when one sees these things happen (ταῦτα γινόμενα), i.e., when the sun and the moon of illusory discrimination become darkened, then know that the birth pangs of awareness of ultimate meaning have begun to occur. When the discriminative mind-set that captured meaning in illumined images has been darkened, then one can see in the dark, one can see the glory of the coming Lord. That darkening is further symbolized in Jesus' cursing of the fig tree in 11: 12–14, 20–25, where it signified the barrenness and desolation of the Temple cult that defined the holiness of Israel. Not just cosmic light has been eclipsed, but also the liturgical presence of Yahweh in his Holy of Holies. Time has been collapsed (ἐκολόβωσεν) so that linear expectations are useless.[75]

Space too has been collapsed. Verse 31 about heaven and earth passing away "is a flash forward of narrative action concerning the poles of all spatial

---

73. Tolbert, *Sowing the Gospel,* 173.

74. I find Nishitani's account of solemn and privileged moments of time in Christianity in his "What Is Religion?" somewhat mistaken. As cited by Waldenfels, *Absolute Nothingness,* 113, "On this 'Bodhisattva Path,' every historical 'time'-point which penetrates into the field of emptiness, is to be an infinitely grave and solemn time. In Christianity, the most solemn moments are, no doubt, the moment that God created the world, the moment that Adam committed his sin, the moment of Christ's birth and resurrection, and the moment of the end of the world when the trumpets will sound and Christ will come again. Or, one may say perhaps that the moment wherein the self is brought to conversion is the solemn moment that truly realizes the solemnity of these moments. From the viewpoint of the Bodhisattva Path, every single moment of infinite time has the solemn gravity that these privileged moments possess in Christianity." Where is there time for lunch? Or for liturgy? Although Nishitani was familiar with Western existentialist philosophers, he could have profited from reading Bultmann, who in his 1957 Gifford lectures, *History and Eschatology,* as quoted in Kee, *Community of the New Age,* 121, said that "every moment is an eschatological moment."

75. Kee, *Community of the New Age,* 82: "One might suppose that the non-fulfillment of the events predicted on the eschatological timetable would discredit not only the particular set of prophecies but the apocalyptic approach as a whole. This was not the case, however, as is evident in Daniel's reversions of Jeremiah ([i.e., Dan 9:2; Jer 25:11; 29:10—reinterpreted] in the shifts of *termini* included in the present ending(s) of Daniel 12:11, 12) and in the continued use of Daniel, both at Qumran and in early Christianity." Perhaps the point was never the exact linear time framework, but the mythic deconstruction of each and every present age.

location. Something is projected to happen not so much *in* heaven and earth, as *to* heaven and earth. . . . Heaven and earth as spatial locations will cease to exist; spatial location will be invalidated at its very foundation."[76] When freed from the conventional confines of time and space in eschatological vision, even this generation can indeed experience the things Jesus has described.[77] Not that they will empirically see the cosmic cataclysm, but that their minds may be darkened so that they too might see that final hour in Jesus' crucifixion.[78] The text does not say that the world will shortly pass away during the life span of Mark's generation,[79] but that these things (ταῦτα πάντα) will occur, i.e., the darkening of light in which one might see a glorious Jesus. In a timeless time the mind of delusion will be abandoned

---

76. Malbon, *Narrative Space,* 57–58. Again, 82: ". . . all spatial location will be disestablished at its very foundation. Orientation in space will be replaced by orientation to Jesus' 'words' (13: 31)." Also 111, treating the spatial, architectural space of the text, notes: "At 13:29 Jesus says, as part of his eschatological discourse, 'So also, when you see these things coming to pass, you know that he [the Son of man] is near, at the door [*thurais*]' [my translation]. As the door marks the transition space between inside and outside, so the appearance of the Son of man 'at the door' signals the transition time between the present age and the eschatological age. Jesus' eschatological discourse closes with the parable of the doorkeeper." What she says in spatial terms, it seems to me Via says in temporal terms, collapsing the distinctions between inner-outer, then-now.

77. Kelber, *The Kingdom in Mark,* 125, on the phrase about "this generation," observes: "The assurance is directed to the present generations of Christians who will not (entirely) pass away before *tauta panta,* the eschaton, arrives. This is fully consistent with 9:1." Especially if the eschaton has already arrived. Dodd, *The Parables of the Kingdom,* 46f, speaks about a "realized eschatology," but in his *The Interpretation of the Fourth Gospel,* 447, he holds that "realized eschatology" is "not altogether a felicitous term," preferring "an eschatology which is being realized," as in E. Haenchen and J. Jeremias. In any event, Dodd stresses that the kingdom has already come and is available in the immediacy of the present.

78. Tolbert, *Sowing the Gospel,* 246: "While Jesus confesses that no one knows exactly when the coming will take place except God (13: 32), evidently for Mark it looms closely on the horizon, for the death of the son is its trigger. The imminence of the eschaton is mitigated in Matthew and Luke, and they both work to disassociate Jesus from the predominantly apocalyptic role that Mark fashions for him; so, for them Isa. 40: 3 is not an appropriate description of Jesus' message. For Mark, it is." Isaiah 40: 3 is the passage about the voice crying in the wilderness to make straight the highway for God, which Tolbert interprets as referring to Jesus, not to John. Its import is eschatological, and in Matthew and Luke it is clearly referred to John the Baptist. Yet, the eschatological role of Jesus in Mark is not the final empirical victory of Jesus coming to right all things, and thus Mack's critique of the Markan eschatology, *A Myth of Innocence,* 353–376, is, I think, misplaced.

79. Tolbert, *Sowing the Gospel,* 268, identifies this generation not with the disciples or followers of Jesus, but with the evil tenants who control the vineyard, i.e., the religious authorities. In this she agrees with Dowd, *Prayer, Power, and the Problem of Suffering,* 118.109, cited above, but differs somewhat from Kelber, *The Kingdom in Mark,* 125, who sees this generation as comprising Mark's present generation of Christians. In any event, if the eschaton in Mark is not the end of linear time, but the collapse of linear time in the revelatory moment of Jesus' death/resurrection, it is available for anyone in any generation.

and the revelation will have taken place, for everything that one prays for without hesitating has already been given (11: 24).

Everything passes away, so there is nothing to cling to in hope of avoiding impermanence. Yet, the words of Jesus will not pass away. This clearly cannot mean that all of Jesus' words are permanent; indeed it is quite a task to identify the very words (*ipsissima verba*) of Jesus.[80] No word in itself has an inner essence that could hold it in eternal being; rather words that flow from ultimate meaning share in that meaning, inasmuch as they flow directly from it. They may change and take on other forms and other languages, yet their outflowing from insight into silent ultimacy does not pass away, as long as there are those who repeat in themselves the converted consciousness embodied in Christ. The Yogācāra philosophers argue that the perfected pattern of consciousness, the pattern that has abandoned the imagined delusions of primal ignorance, not only opens up onto the silence of ultimate meaning, but also reengages in the dependently co-arisen world, both as a purified path (*mārga-vyāvadāna*) and as the purified content of doctrinal understanding (*ālambana-vyāvadāna*), which is then described as an outflow from the pure realm of reality (*dharmadhātu-niṣyanda*). This is not the eternal abiding of an unchanging essence, but the dependently co-arisen presence of an awakened practice of the middle path, in virtue of which the Mahāyāna philosophers describe the Dharma teaching as indefectible.[81]

Just as one learns from the parable of the sower that the good earth produces its fruit, the Markan Jesus recommends that the disciples/readers know from the blooming of the fig that the practice of the eschatological middle path, even at the end time, is of itself fruitful. "The kingdom of God for Mark is also future (9: 1; 13: 32–36). Therefore to enter the kingdom is to be placed in a new story which moves toward a redemptive future. It is to be walking on the way, the way to Jerusalem."[82] So long as there are minds, there will be awakened minds. Awakened practitioners (i.e., buddhas) are innumerable.

The last sentence clearly states that Jesus has not been producing a schema foretelling the stages of the forthcoming eschatological age. He says that no conventional judgment is applicable. Only the Father knows, and the Father dwells in silence. The end time is emptied time as ultimately meaningful, not any ascertainable period of linear time. That is why that present generation can experience it as ultimate, as that which is completely other, as that which is hidden (*saṃvṛta*) by the conventions (*saṃvṛta*) of temporal reckoning. Yet it is imminent, for "the references to a 'day' and an 'hour,' rather than to a month or a year, even if rhetorical, indicate imminent expectation."[83] The end time is not some planned and realizable future, but an always-receding and never-grasped point of reference that in fact is no point of reference at

---

80. That has been the project of the Jesus Seminar of the Society of Biblical Literature, from which such works as Crossan's *The Historical Jesus* flow.

81. See Keenan, *The Meaning of Christ*, 174–81.

82. Via, *The Ethics of Mark's Gospel*, 131.

83. Collins, *The Beginning of the Gospel*, 87.

all. That is why it is most appropriately expressed in the mythic terms of eschatology and apocalyptic. It is a narrative myth for the ultimate meaning that overturns all structures, both social and cosmic.[84]

Awakening
13: 33–37

[33] *"Be on your guard, stay awake, because you never know when the time will come. [34]It is like a man travelling abroad: he has gone from his home, and left his servants in charge, each with his own work to do; and he has told the doorkeeper to stay awake. [35]So stay awake, because you do not know when the master of the house is coming, evening, midnight, cockcrow, or dawn; [36]if he comes unexpectedly, he must not find you asleep. [37]And what I say to you I say to all: stay awake!"*

The final eschatological advice given by Jesus is again to look to oneself (βλέπετε) and to wake up (ἀγρυπνεῖτε) to the presence of ultimate meaning as completely other, as apart from any notion of a grand plan indicated by wondrous signs and foretold in clear terms. One cannot know the time (οὐκ οἴδατε γὰρ πότε ὁ καιρός ἐστιν), for such a time is not within time at all. Rather, it is the collapse of all time into a revelatory present moment. The kingdom has come and one must awaken to that kingdom, which is always at hand. Jesus has called his disciples from their native Galilee to be now pilgrims in Jerusalem, yet he tells them to imitate servants, staying at home and awaiting their master. They are to stay awake (γρηγορεῖτε), be awakened from the sleep of imagination and delusion to the presence of ultimate truth beneath all worldly convention, for the return of the master will come sud-

---

84. Camery-Hoggatt, *Irony in Mark's Gospel*, 32: "... the *telos* of the story may represent a kind of judgment on its parts. In theological terms, the eschatological judgment toward which history is leading significantly shapes what we make of events as they unfold; eschatology is not only the study of 'end times,' but is also the study of 'the way all things relate to the end.'" In Mahāyāna terms, the eschatological myth of the end time points to the silent realm of ultimate meaning, always in tension with conventional values and events, always emptying them of final significance, only then to reaffirm their deep significance as the field for awakened and compassionate bodhisattva activity. Note also Collins, *The Beginning of the Gospel*, 58: "A comprehensive framework, like the apocalyptic framework of meaning in which the miracles are set in Mark and Q, may rightly be emphasized as their main interpretive framework and function in texts in which it appears. If Jesus healed and exorcized people, however, those people did experience personal benefit. ... If the historical Jesus linked the healing activity to the rule of God, then this activity expresses what the rule of God is about. It includes compassion for those suffering physical, emotional, mental, and spiritual distress." In Mahāyāna terms, the eschatological end time is embodied in awakened, compassionate reengagement in the conventional world, and that is why the kindgom is at hand in every moment and every time.

denly, unexpectedly (ἐξαίφνης), when perhaps they will be asleep, as indeed were his intended companions in the garden of Gethsemane.[85]

His disciples are to be doorkeepers, awaiting at the door (34, καὶ τῷ θυρωρῷ ἐνετείλατο ἵνα γρηγορῇ) of ultimate meaning, not knocking to have it opened as in the Gospel of Luke, but maintaining their vigil before that which, in the Gospel of Mark, remains closed, always beyond discriminative sight. Yet that kingdom is always present, at the gates (29, ἐπὶ θύραις). The point is not to grow impatient at the lack of empirical vindication, but rather to practice the middle path in the context of worldly convention-only, where the total focus of the bodhisattva is on reengagement in building a world of justice and compassion. Take care of one's own tasks (34, ἑκάστῳ τὸ ἔργον αὐτοῦ) of compassion, for that is but the practice of awakened wisdom.[86] Note also that the final verbal phrase, "Stay awake" (ἵνα γρηγορῇ) means not only to awaken, but also to rise up, alluding to the resurrected life of Christ to be treated at the end of the passion narrative.[87] This term, to be awake, is repeatedly stressed in the above discourse. One must awaken (*buddha*) to ultimate meaning, for there are no conventional guarantees. We do not know when the master who is in charge of the household will return. Only that he will come suddenly or unexpectedly, as a breaking through of conventional expectancies. Let him not find us asleep (verse 37 is an aside directed not to the disciples, but to the readers of Mark's gospel) in the delusions of clinging to the imagined. Such an awakening, so described by Mark in the last chapter before the passion narrative, becomes a requisite for understanding what that passion, death, and resurrection are all about. They are not accounts of empirical defeat or victory. That is why there will be no resurrection appearances in Mark, for such a resurrection has no conventional witness, since it is not an imagined proof of anything.

The entirety of chapter 13 presents the context in which to read the passion narrative. In particular, verse 35 is linked to that narrative. It describes the master of the house coming in the evening (ὀψὲ) or at midnight (μεσονύκτιον)

---

85. Hartmann, *Prophecy Interpreted*, 176: "If we compare the content of the admonition within the 'midrash' [that is Mark 13] with that of the concluding admonition, we see that the great theme of the latter is 'to watch,' for the day will come 'suddenly.' While the interwoven paranesis warns the disciples against 'Antichrist' occurrences and against being led astray during the travail."

86. Tolbert, *Sowing the Gospel*, 269: "Since the servants do not know when the lord of the house will come, they must pursue their tasks conscientiously and faithfully in order to be ready at any moment for the return." Any moment can then be the final eschatological moment for those who await Jesus' coming, for at any moment they may share in the revelatory power of Jesus' death and resurrection, emptying their minds of any imagined patterns and reengaging in the dependently co-arisen world to practice the middle path that holds in healthy tension awareness of the complete otherness of ultimate meaning and the contextual validity of conventional traditions and tasks.

87. Malbon, *Narrative Space*, 152: " 'Watch' (*grēgoreite*, from *grēgoreō*) and 'risen' (*ēgerthē*, from *egeirō*) have a linguistic root in common and thus, perhaps, have some elements of meaning in common. *Grēgoreō* was a new formation in Hellenistic Greek from *egrēgora*, the perfect of *egeirō*; their shared significance is 'to be awake.' "

or at cockcrow (ἀλεκτοροφωνίας) or in the dawn (πρωΐ). These time periods are picked up in the same sequence as the ensuing narrative, for in 14: 17 Jesus comes to share the Passover at evening (ὀψίας γενομένης), in 14: 43–50 Jesus' arrest takes place during the middle of the night, in 14: 72 Peter remembers Jesus' prediction of his denial at cockcrow (ἀλέκτωρ ἐφώνησεν), and in 15: 1 the women come to the tomb as soon as it was morning (εὐθὺς πρωΐ). The passion narrative is structured around the times of the eschatological warnings to awaken, serving to contextualize both its structure and its interpretation.[88] Mark directs his readers to continue reading with care and watchfulness, and not to fall asleep like the disciples in the now foreshadowed Gethsemane scene (14: 32–42), where they cannot stay awake, but sleep through the inception of Jesus' eschatological hour.[89] Mark ends the eschatological discourse starkly, with the reader's attention riveted on the upcoming passion narrative, for Mark's gospel "dramatically leaves its audience at the threshold of decision."[90] It is as if he is preparing us all for the abruptness of the ending at 16: 8.

---

88. From Lightfoot, *The Gospel Message of St. Mark,* 53.

89. Tolbert, *Sowing the Gospel,* 269: "By employing the images of the Lord of the House for the Gethsemane passage, the implied author also adds another dimension of meaning to this hour that the faithful must watch for: it represents not only the consummate hour when the Father sends the Son of man with the angels to gather the elect but it also represents that individual hour of suffering, persecution, and tribulation, which will inevitably come to test the faith of each follower, just as it does Jesus and the disciples, and which will best be endured by imitating Jesus' advice and example to watch and pray while avoiding the disciples' tendency to sleep." Indeed, suffering is inevitable in all human living, but the inevitability of persecution comes only from a too literal reading of Mark's references to what must come about and functions through a kind of sympathetic magic that supposedly links the dependently co-arisen life courses of Jesus' followers with the dependently co-arisen events of his life. Indeed, Tolbert, 237, writes: "The author has Jesus present the material as a prediction of future events, but by reference to the parable of the Tenants the audience understands that these future events are the consequences of killing Jesus, not simply the ineluctable working out of some cosmic plan set from the origins of the universe. Unrepentant human evil, climax[es] in the murder of the heir." Here there is no cosmic inevitability, but rather the working out and maturing of evil actions taken by human beings. That indeed may happen to anybody, but there is no cosmic necessity about it at all.

90. Black, "An Oration at Olivet," 77.

14

The Passion Narrative

The Beginning of the End
14: 1–2

¹It was two days before the Passover and the feast of the Unleavened Bread, and the chief priests and the scribes were looking for a way to arrest Jesus by some trick and have him put to death. ²For they said, "It must not be during the festivities, or there will be a disturbance among the people."

Just as the eschatological discourse in Chapter 13 intertwines themes of the beginning and end times, so the imagery of Mark's passion story is replete with beginnings and endings. Here, the Passover is the remembrance of the originating event of Jewish faith, when the angel of the Lord delivered the people from Pharaoh's oppression. Long since it had been combined with the immemorial springtime agricultural festival of Mazzoth, which continued for a week. Mark begins his story of Jesus' end on the feast that celebrates the beginning, for the events to be narrated concern the new eschatological beginning of awakening to the kingdom.[1]

---

1. Tolbert, *Sowing the Gospel,* 262: "Since the author of Mark uses so many of the images and admonitions from the Apocalyptic Discourse [of chapter 13] to portray the willing obedience of Jesus through his arrest, trials, beatings, mockings, and death on the cross as well as the failure of the disciples at Gethsemane (13: 32–37//14: 37–41), the reason for positioning the Discourse immediately before the events of the Passion is quite obvious. The audience is encouraged to understand the Passion not only as the death of the heir that will trigger the coming of the lord of the vineyard but also as an example of how the inevitable persecutions perpetrated by this evil generation on the followers of Jesus are to be endured faithfully—or how they may fail to be endured through fear. Moreover, that Jesus' tomb is found empty and the young man proclaims that he is risen, 'as he told you' (16: 7), stands as a final reassurance of Jesus' promise that one who endures to the end *will be saved* (13: 13). Further, it is from this double perspective on Jesus' death, as both trigger and example, that his earlier saying, 'For the Son of man also came not to be served but to serve, and to give his life as a ransom for many' (10: 45), should be viewed. For Mark, Jesus' death is *not* the innocent sacrifice demanded by a righteous and angry God to atone for the sinful state of humankind [in agreement with

The chief priests and scribes, being literalists, are the enemies who seek stealthily to arrest and execute Jesus, yet they fear causing a tumult or disturbance (θόρυβος) among the crowd. The crowd plays an ambiguous role in Mark. Here they seem to support Jesus against the authorities, yet shortly the same crowd calls for his crucifixion. They, like the disciples, are fickle and, even when they support Jesus, do so for the wrong reason.[2] They do not understand what his messiahship is all about, hoping merely to follow a hero figure into an imagined future. Jesus does not trust himself to the crowd, nor does he pander to their religious delusions. The structure of the passion narrative brings events to their final stage. From the very beginning it is placed in a liturgical context, beginning with the feast of Israel's beginnings. The subsequent account of the Eucharist is not then a separate section inserted into an account to which it bears little relationship. Rather, it is part and parcel of the overall liturgy of Jesus' dying and rising.

If this is true, then one should not expect Mark to focus on historical events. Rather, Mark and the early community he writes in and for, see behind the events a meaning for their lives. There are many discrepancies between the events reported in the Gospel narratives of Christ's passion and Jewish laws and regulations about the trial practices of the Sanhedrin. Mark is not concerned, however, with the historical truth of his account, but with the inner meaning of the events he has heard or his community has remembered.[3]

Kee, *Community of the New Age,* 47–48, 135–36]; instead, Jesus' suffering and death are the inescapable results of challenging the authority of the present tenants of the vineyard in order to sow the good news of the nearness of God's kingdom to the nations. . . . Jesus' life is given as a ransom to the murderous authorities of this generation, the price required to sow the seed abroad, to awaken the good earth into abundant fruitfulness."

2. See Hamerton-Kelly, *The Gospel and the Sacred,* 25.

3. The passion narrative has received much scholarly attention of late. The historicity of the account had been traditionally presupposed, to the point where some saw the gospels as passion accounts with appended materials pasted in front. Yet internal inconsistencies make it difficult to see it as history. Samuel Sandmel, "The Trial of Jesus," 74, after trying to unravel the historical contours of the text, concluded: "In short, I give up." Donahue, *Are You the Christ?,* 239 comments: "What Sandmel gives up on, in effect, is the attempt to find history where history is not intended." Kelber, *The Passion in Mark,* presents a number of essays that treat Mark 14–16 not as recorded history but as rhetorical theology. More fully developed arguments can be found in Crossan, *The Cross That Spoke* and *The Historical Jesus.* Although Crossan's reconstruction of the literary history is speculative and open to criticism, for the most part I find his reconstructions plausible— although the entailed issues of the doctrinal and textual development fall beyond the scope of this Mahāyāna commentary. Crossan, *The Historical Jesus,* 375–76, sums up his conclusion: "I propose that, first of all, Jesus' followers knew nothing more about the passion than the fact of the crucifixion, that they had fled and later had no available witnesses for its details, and that they were concerned, in any case, with far more serious matters, such as whether that death negated all that Jesus had said and done, all that they had accepted and believed. Second, what followed *in one very literate and highly*

sophisticated stream of tradition was an intense search of the Scriptures, similar to that at Qumran. It discovered verses and images each of which could be applied to the passion as a whole but not, of course, to its individual details, for no such details existed in their memories. Third, those individual scriptural connections and specific prophetic fulfillments could be organized into a coherent and sequential story. But, for this, some overarching form, shape, pattern, or genre had to be conceived or adopted. Finally, once such a narrative had been achieved, its historicity could be improved by more accurate versimilitude and refined by more precise detail. The process developed, in other words, over these primary steps. First the *historical passion,* composed of minimal knowledge, was known only in general terms recorded by, say, Josephus or Tacitus. Next, the *prophetic passion,* composed of multiple and discrete biblical allusions and seen most clearly in works like the *Epistle of Barnabas,* developed biblical applications over, under, around, and through that open framework. Finally, those multiple and discrete exercises were combined into the *narrative passion* as a single sequential story. I propose, furthermore, that the narrative passion is but a single stream flowing from the *Cross Gospel,* now embedded within the *Gospel of Peter,* into Mark, thence together into Matthew and Luke, and thence, all together, into John. Other reconstructions are certainly possible, but that seems to be the most economical one to explain all the data." The theme used to organize the insights into discrete prophetic allusions is explained on 385: "I propose, still following my earlier study (*The Cross That Spoke,* 297–334), that the first model applied to organize all those discrete prophetic applications to a full passion narrative was that of *innocence rescued.* But that process not only 'historicized' the prophetic passion, it allowed the 'historicization' of *passion and resurrection* so that resurrection, which was of course taken absolutely for granted in earlier dyadic *passion and parousia* prophecies, could now become part of the story and receive full focus in its own right. This is the model used to present what I call the *Cross Gospel,* the original passion narrative now found in . . . the *Gospel of Peter.*" Crossan continues, 389: "The first writer to use and develop the *Cross Gospel* composition was, in my judgment on the extant texts, the evangelist Mark himself. I see no convincing evidence that Mark has any other basis for his passion narrative than that source and his own theological creativity, But in following it, he made three profound changes. The first and most basic one was to change the overarching model from *innocence rescued* to *martyrdom vindicated.* No salvific miracle *seen here below* would save Jesus before, during, or after death. Only at the parousia would the resurrectional victory become visible according to Mark 13:26 and 14: 62. . . . The second major change was the duplication of the trial process from a single, composite, and general one in *Gospel of Peter* 1: 1–2, based on Psalm 2: 1, to distinct religious and political ones before, respectively, the Jewish Sanhedrin and the Roman governor. That explains how the trial's responsibility moves between Pilate and Antipas. . . . I do not believe, once again, that Jesus' followers knew anything about such details beyond what they could extrapolate from general expectations and prophetic texts such as Psalm 2: 1. And I am very unsure what level of Roman bureaucracy was empowered to eradicate a peasant nuisance like Jesus. I doubt that the 'trial' is even a good description of that process even when taken at its most minimal connotation. It is difficult for the Christian imagination, then or now, to accept the brutal informality with which Jesus was probably condemned and crucified. But, in any case, Mark was very interested in how Christians should behave before both religious and political persecution, as we know from Mark 13: 9, and in Jesus' passion he gave them a model for both situations. It is impossible, in my mind, to overestimate the creativity of Mark, but those twin trials must be emphasized for what they are, consummate theological fictions. It is also impossible, to my mind, to overestimate the terrible consequences of relocating such abuses as spitting, striking, and goading from an original situation involving Jesus as the Day of Atonement's scapegoat in *Barnabas* 7: 8–9, to Jesus with the people in *Gospel of Peter* 2: 5b–3: 9, to Jesus under separate Jewish and Roman trial in Mark

Anointing for Death
14: 3–9

³Jesus was at Bethany in the house of Simon, a man who had suffered from a virulent skin disease; he was at table when a woman came in with an alabaster jar of very costly ointment, pure nard. She broke the jar and poured the ointment on his head. ⁴Some who were there said to one another indignantly, "Why this waste of ointment? ⁵Ointment like this could have been sold for over three hundred denarii and the money given to the poor," and they were angry with her. ⁶But Jesus said, "Leave her alone. Why are you upsetting her? What she has done for me is a good work. ⁷You have the poor with you always, and you can be kind to them whenever you wish, but you will not always have me. ⁸She has done what she could: she has anointed my body beforehand for its burial. ⁹In truth I tell you, wherever throughout all the world the gospel is proclaimed, what she has done will be told as well, in remembrance of her."

This story is unusual. Jesus is resting, as was his custom (see 11: 10) in the house of Simon the leper in Bethany, a place of familiar refuge from the

---

14: 65 and 15: 19. It is magnificent theological fiction, to be sure, but entailing a dreadful price for Judaism. The third change made by Mark was a better 'historicization' of the *Cross Gospel's* account. Herod Antipas is removed completely from the story, and Pontius Pilate is now in full charge. And soldiers, not people, conduct the crucifixion. But that raises a problem, since Mark wants to have it both ways. Pilate must be in charge, since nothing else is historically plausible, but he must also be innocent of any wrongdoing in the unjust sentencing of Jesus. Mark's solution is to create the Barabbas incident in 15: 6–15. I do not believe for a second that it actually happened, that there ever was or ever could be any such open and preset Passover amnesty, or that Pilate deviated on this occasion from his normal [brutal] crowd control tactics. . . . But the Passover amnesty is a magnificent solution, since, for Mark, it symbolically sums up the events of the preceding decades. The people were asked to choose between a bandit or Jesus. They chose the bandit. They chose the leadership of the violent revolutionary over the pacific Jesus, and thereby, for Mark, came the war of 66 C.E. against Rome." Crossan follows (391–94) with discussions of the Markan creation of Joseph of Arimathea, for Jesus' followers, who had fled before his arrest and knew nothing about his burial, were horrified that he might not even have received a decent burial, and concludes, 394: "But all those industrious reductions set out to solve one simple problem. *Nobody knew what had happened to Jesus' body.* And the best his followers could initially hope for was that he had been buried out of Jewish piety toward Deuteronomy 21: 22–23. If you turn from the burier to the tomb, exactly the same phenomenon occurs. In Mark 15: 46 it was 'a tomb which had been hewn out of the rock.' In Matthew 27: 60 it is Joseph's 'own new tomb,' In Luke 23: 53 it is 'a rock-hewn tomb, where no one had ever been laid.' In John 19: 41 it is 'a garden, and in the garden a new tomb where no one had ever been laid.' But no amount of damage control can conceal what its intensity only confirms. With regard to the body of Jesus, by Easter Sunday morning, those who cared did not know where it was, and those who knew did not care. Why should even the soldiers themselves remember the death and disposal of a nobody? Still, Matthew 27: 19 records, in a unit taken possibly from the *Cross Gospel's* lost opening, that Pilate's wife had troubled dreams the previous night. That never happened, of course, but it was true nonetheless. It was a most propitious time for the Roman Empire to start having nightmares."

hostility of the authorities.[4] An unidentified woman comes in with the alabaster jar of very costly ointment, pure nard. She breaks the jar and pours the ointment on Jesus' head. Strangely some of the bystanders begin to complain that this is a waste. Their complaint seems contrived: "There must have been something about the woman's action that was objectionable. . . ."[5] Something was also objectionable about the woman herself, for Luke 7: 37 makes her into "a woman of the city, a sinner" (γυνὴ ἥτις ἦν ἐν τῇ πόλει ἁμαρτωλός) and her critic a Pharisee who thinks Jesus should know better than to touch such a defiled person, while John 11: 3 turns it around and transforms her into the more familiar and approved Mary, the sister of Martha. The Markan Jesus defends the woman and says that she has anointed him for his burial. That seems to be the climax of the passage, with Mark playing on the meaning of anointing. The contrast is between anointing of a king and anointing for burial. Jesus accepts anointing from the woman for his burial, but not for his kingship, for he has rejected that kind of messiahship.[6] Mark undermines the royal glory of king-making: Jesus is anointed almost by accident and by an unidentified woman.

This reading, however, leaves uninterpreted all the rich detail about the woman's precious ointment. The jar of alabaster or of oriental onyx,[7] is described as "a vessel with a rather long neck which was broken off (συντρίψασα) when the contents were used."[8] The ointment is spikenard (μύρου νάρδου), a plant native to India.[9] Yet it is not just a preciously-perfumed nard, for it is further described as πιστικῆς, a term that "defies all attempts to trace its deriva-

---

4. Malbon, *Narrative Space*, 46–47: "Refuge from the opposition of religious leaders in Jerusalem is provided Jesus and his disciples in Bethany. There Jesus stays in a private home, presumably the home of a friend, Simon the Leper (14: 3), where he is treated kindly—anointed by a woman." Also see 120.

5. Mack, *Myth*, 200: "J. D. Derrett is the only scholar who has noticed that the objection raised against the woman's action is contrived. There must have been something else about the woman's action that was objectionable in an earlier version of the story. He noted that the companion story in Luke 7: 36–50 shares the scene, but enters an entirely different objection. He concluded that both stories were versions of an originally shorter one in which Jesus responded directly to the challenge of some embarrassment created by the deed. The deed, he thought, would probably have been considered risque by most social codes of the first century." Reference is to Derrett, "The Anointing at Bethany."

6. Kelber, *Mark's Story of Jesus,* 72: "Anointment, the pouring of oil over the head, was the central act by which the kings of Israel were appointed and installed into the royal office." Yet the scene here is "in defiance of the traditional Davidic anointment."

7. Bratcher and Nida, *A Translator's Handbook,* 427, reports this as the interpretation of Lagrange.

8. Bauer, *A Greek-English Lexicon,* 34b.

9. Bratcher and Nida, *A Translator's Handbook,* 427. *Harper's Bible Dictionary,* 978, defines spikenard as: "a scented ointment or perfume imported from the Himalayas in alabaster boxes and opened on special occasions (Song of Sol 1: 12; 4: 13, 14)." Lane, *Mark,* 492: "The costly perfume is identified as nard, the aromatic oil extracted from a root native to India. To retain the fragrance of nard, enough ointment for one application was sealed in small alabaster flasks. The long neck of the flask had to be broken to release the aroma."

tion."[10] There are hypotheses. Some think it refers to the oil of the pistachio nut,[11] and interpret πιστικῆς as pure or unadulterated, on analogy with πιστικός, also perhaps deriving from πιστάκια, "pistachio tree."[12] Yet this term refers not simply to its purity, but to the specific plant source for the ointment. πιστικῆς is a phonetic rendering of the Sanskrit term *pishtaka,* which refers to the perfumed powder or dust used by Hindus to sprinkle over one another during the spring festival of Holākā.[13] This Indian festival is held at the approach of the vernal equinox and is associated with the boy Krishna and his dalliance with the Gopīs, the cow-herdesses. During the festival, even to this day, the people sprinkle the red powder from the *pishtaka* plant over one another to suggest the fertility of the springtime and of Lord Krishna.[14] In Mark, then, the unidentified woman, perhaps the Lukan "woman of the streets," was using the alien custom of sprinkling such a powder over Jesus' head as a sign of springtime life and love, and that is why it made some of his companions indignant (ἀγανακτοῦντες), not the waste on Jesus of a precious substance. In the familiar house of a friend, Jesus encounters a figure who performs an alien liturgy upon him, one that suggests spring life and fertility. It would not be very surprising for an Indian custom to be used in Judea, standing as it did astride the trade routes. Jesus accepts the woman's action, yet undercuts its significance by referring it to his burial. In Mark this passage announces the death of Jesus, for it has been intercalated between the account of the plot to kill Jesus in 14: 1–2 and 14: 10–11.

It is not altogether unreasonable for the bystanders in Mark to complain about the woman's action. The precious substance might well have been sold and the proceeds used for the poor. After all, Jesus in 10: 21 has told the rich fellow to sell all he has and give the proceeds to the poor. So here the bystanders, probably the disciples, were indignant and angry both at the waste and at the significance of the action. If it were an anointing of a messiah, they would hardly be so indignant, for that role was close to their hearts. But they scold (ἐνεβριμῶντο) the woman for the waste (ἀπώλεια), for they see that her action has no kingly significance at all.

Jesus' answer is a reference to *Deuteronomy* 15: 11, "Of course, there will never cease to be poor people in the country, and that is why I am giving you this command: Always be open handed with your brother, and with anyone in your country who is in need and poor." That is to say, Jesus agrees with the need not to waste, but to give to the poor. Still he defends the woman, for she has done a good deed (καλὸν ἔργον) in that she has anointed (μυρίσαι) Jesus beforehand for his burial (εἰς τὸν ἐνταφιασμόν). Note, again in support of the Lukan view that she was a sinner, that in Indian culture the act of anointing was done both for harlots and flute girls (which

---

10. Mann, *Mark,* 556.
11. Mann, *Mark,* 556; Black, *An Aramaic Approach to the Gospels and Acts,* 159–61.
12. Bauer, *Lexicon,* 662a.
13. Monier-Williams, *A Sanskrit-English Dictionary,* 629a.
14. Monier-Williams, *A Sanskrit-English Dictionary,* 498b.

suggest the Gōpis, associated with flutes in the *Gītagovinda,*)[15] to increase their allure, and for corpses, to decrease their repugnancy.[16] But Mark takes the action to refer not to spring life and sexuality, but to Jesus' death. From the inception of the passion narrative then, the contrast is between life and death, between the imminent death of Jesus and the springtime rising of life. The woman's action becomes a sign of life arising from death. Just as he is being anointed for fertility, Jesus predicts again his death, while the chief priests and scribes are plotting to kill him.

And so her deed will always be remembered wherever the Gospel is preached, for it presages to its hearers the resurrection itself. Yet her name is not recorded and she remains a cameo character in the narrative.[17]

Mark constructs the passage to serve as an introduction to the passion narrative, for it is the key for interpreting what follows: the arising of life from death. The anointing has entered into the liturgical progression of the narrative, and should not be forgotten in subsequent readings of the Jesus story. The narrative now moves directly from a story of Jesus' anointing by a woman of questionable repute to the story of the plot to betray him by one of his disciples.

Judas
14: 10–11

[10]*Judas Iscariot, one of the Twelve, approached the chief priests with an offer to hand Jesus over to them. [11]They were delighted to hear it, and promised to give him money; and he looked for a way of betraying him when the opportunity should occur.*

Mark has throughout his narrative focused on the theme of discipleship. Here, "Mark's concern with the betrayal of Judas and the failure of discipleship accounts for the form of his material."[18] Judas' character is never described by Mark; he stands exclusively as a cipher of failed discipleship. Just as

---

15. See Stoler Miller, *The Love Song of the Dark Lord, Jayadeva's Gītagovinda,* 76.
16. Arndt and Gingrich, *A Greek-English Lexicon,* 529.
17. Donahue, *Are You the Christ?,* 231: "The actions and destinies of the characters in the narrative become [the readers'] actions and destinies. The world of narrative is re-presented to them. In the Passion narrative Jesus himself suggests this function when in 14: 9 he says that wherever the gospel story is told the deed of the woman will be recounted in remembrance, *mnēmosunon,* of her. Marxsen (*Mark,* 101) says that the meaning here is that where the act is proclaimed, the act is present, so that the past of Jesus becomes part of the present of the reader." The Markan cameo appearances of "cipher characters" who are healed, usually, or do a good deed (cf. 15: 21, where Simon of Cyrene actually carries Jesus' cross) become transparent mirrors in which the reader can see her reflection. Thus, they all, having embodied compassion, drop from the narrative, back into everyday life.
18. Klosinski, *Meals in Mark,* 198.

those healed by Jesus pop into the story only to be immediately removed, so Judas is brought forward only as an example of failure. Our only prior introduction to him is at 3: 19, where the narrator informs us that he is Jesus' betrayer (ὅς καὶ παρέδωκεν αὐτόν). Now, without any intervening description of his state of mind, we are starkly informed that Judas Iscariot, one of the original twelve, "went to the chief priests in order to betray him to them" (ἀπῆλθεν πρὸς τοὺς ἀρχιερεῖς ἵνα αὐτὸν παραδοῖ αὐτοῖς). One may imagine that he was offended by Jesus' previous acceptance of anointing for his burial, but the narrator is unconcerned whether we know that or not. The text says that the chief priests promised him money (καὶ ἐπηγγείλαντο αὐτῷ ἀργύριον) but does not disclose whether he wanted the money, or accepted it. It only says that Judas "sought an opportunity to betray him."[19]

The other evangelists are apparently embarrassed at Mark's bare bones image of Judas and fill in the picture considerably. Matthew introduces Judas (10: 4) just as Mark does, as "he who betrayed him," but then presents an entire passage outlining Judas' motives (26: 14–15), where we learn that Judas is driven by greed ("What will you give me?") and makes a bargain to betray Jesus for thirty pieces of silver. Later Judas repents his betrayal, tries to return the blood money, and goes out and hangs himself (27: 3–7). In John (12: 4) it is Judas who complains about the waste of expensive nard, suggesting to the reader that he is greedy, an image expanded by John's aside identifying Judas as a thief who steals from the money box (τὸ γλωσσόκομον), of which he has charge. For Mark this is not a possible scenario, for in 6: 8 Jesus tells his disciples not to carry money in their purses (μὴ πήραν, μὴ εἰς τὴν ζώνην χαλκόν), but rather to rely on the hospitality of those who receive them. John has no such advice for the disciples. Luke does have Jesus give similar advice in 10: 4: "Carry no purse, no bag" (μὴ βαστάζετε βαλλάντιον, μὴ πήραν, but see 22:35–36), yet he is equally reticent of Judas' character, telling the reader only that "Satan entered Judas called Iscariot" (22:3).

Mark, however, never fills out Judas' intrastory character at all. Although one of the twelve, he remains a cameo character. If we have the other Gospels in mind, he seems to exemplify the seed that falls among thorns, in whom the lure of riches takes over (4:18). But Mark does not provide much support for this later interpretation. The only Markan indication of his character is the offer, unfulfilled in the narrative, from the priests to pay him. Judas is simply Jesus' betrayer. Even when he plants the identifying kiss on Jesus'

---

19. Both phrases of intention, ἵνα αὐτὸν παραδοῖ ("in order to betray him") and ἐξήτει πῶς αὐτὸν εὐκαίρως παραδοῖ ("he sought an opportunity to betray him") focus on Judas' act of betrayal, i.e., handing over, not his inner state of mind. The offer of money comes spontaneously from the elation of the chief priests (οἱ δὲ ἀκούσαντες ἐχάρησαν καὶ ἐπηγγείλαντο αὐτῷ ἀργύριον δοῦναι). Mark does not describe Judas as seeking the cash. See Perrin, "The Use of (Para)didonai in Connection with the Passion of Jesus."

cheek, no response is made either by Jesus or by the disciples. The other Gospel writers at least suggest why Judas betrays Jesus. Mark leaves him transparent. Perhaps Judas cannot understand how the ending that is death can be an opening to life, how an alien spring festival custom can substitute for kingly anointing. But Mark's passage is blunt in the extreme, stating simply that Judas sets his mind on betraying Jesus. It is sufficient that Judas simply cannot enter into the mind that finds life by abandoning life. Although he has shared in Jesus' table fellowship,[20] he appears only as a negative example of discipleship, an option open to all of Mark's readers.[21]

Preparations for a Passover Supper
14: 12–16

[12]*On the first day of the Unleavened Bread, when the Passover lamb was sacrificed, his disciples said to him, "Where do you want us to go and make the preparations for you to eat the Passover?"* [13]*So he sent two of his disciples, saying to them, "Go into the city and you will meet a man carrying a pitcher of water. Follow him,* [14]*and say to the owner of the house which he enters, 'The teacher*[22] *says: Where is the room for me to eat the Passover with my disciples?'* [15]*He will show you a large upper room furnished with couches, all prepared. Make the preparations for us there."* [16]*The disciples set out and went to the city and found everything as he had told them, and prepared the Passover.*

These preparations for the Passover closely parallel the preparations for Jesus' entry into the environs of Jerusalem in chapter 11: 1–6. There he is acclaimed as a pilgrim, addressed as "the one who comes in the name of the Lord," who somehow embodies the kingdom. Now he sets about finding a pilgrim's right to lodging. The description appears to present a portrait of

---

20. Klosinski, *Meals in Mark,* 140: "When the Lord's Supper truly is seen as the last supper in a series of suppers which Mark narrates, its significance differs from traditional interpretations of it. Its significance is not found in the words of institution or in the institution of the eucharistic practice of the early Church. It is not a cultic etiology. Its significance is found in its relationship to the entire gospel narrative. It is the culmination of the meals which Mark narrates. As such it is precisely the point where a number of Markan concerns and themes converge. It represents a narrative climax of the gospel, for at it table fellowship, discipleship and betrayal all come together. In terms of table fellowship, it is the last meal and the only meal with Jesus and the twelve together by themselves. In terms of discipleship, it is here that the disciples' final failure to understand and follow Jesus is revealed. And in terms of betrayal, immediately before Jesus hands over to his disciples the bread which is his body, the identity of the one who is to hand him over to the chief priests and scribes is exposed."
21. Kermode, *The Genesis of Secrecy,* 85: "All the Twelve, and especially Peter, are Betrayers and Deserters (*prodotēs,* a traitor, one who abandons in danger)."
22. Following RSV translation of ὁ διδάσκαλος.

one who has foreknowledge of the future. Its point, however, is not Jesus' miraculous foreknowledge, but rather his status as a pilgrim. "It was a Jewish custom that Passover pilgrims might ask any householder for the use of a room for the occasion."[23] The city teemed with diaspora Jews come "home" to Jerusalem during the great feasts.[24] "The citizens [of Jerusalem] had to entertain foreign pilgrims for nothing, for Jerusalem is the possession of all Israel. One of the ten miracles of God in the sanctuary, i.e., while the temple still stood, was that no one in Jerusalem ever said to another that there was no room to put him up for the night."[25] Thus, Jesus, in his capacity as pilgrim, could have his disciples ask anyone for a room with the sure expectation that one would be granted. He tells his disciples to go into the city and find the first person who has a servant, i.e., one who is carrying a jar of water back to the owner of the house. All the disciples had to do was go to the well and wait for the first likely person. No supernatural foreknowledge seems needed. Note that the disciples are instructed to tell that owner that "the teacher" asks for room to eat the Passover meal. Here, upon their arrival in Jerusalem, is the first time in the narrative that Jesus identifies himself as "teacher" (ὁ διδάσκαλος), another indication that Jesus comes to Jerusalem not as the Davidic deliverer, but simply as a pilgrim teacher,[26] and this is why he is the deliverer of his people.

Furthermore, why indeed did he have to go into the city at all? Did not the people in Bethany eat the Passover meal in their homes?[27] Jesus comes to the holy city as a pilgrim. That is the import of the passage and that is why he had no prior need to make preparations, for he could rely on the custom of easily finding such a room. He comes not as an inhabitant of the city, but as a visitor.

He tells his disciples to request from the owner of the house a room, and he receives "a large upper room" (ἀνάγαιον μέγα) all prepared and in waiting for a pilgrim's use. The "upper room" alludes to Elijah who resurrected

---

23. Grant, *The Interpreter's Bible*, 7: 873.
24. See Malbon, *Narrative Space*, 47.
25. Wrede, *The Messianic Secret*, 142.
26. Heil, *The Gospel of Mark as a Model for Action*, 283–84: "Whereas many have addressed Jesus as 'teacher' throughout the narrative, this is the first time Jesus refers to himself as 'teacher,' that is, 'the Teacher,' the one who 'teaches' a 'new teaching' with divine 'authority' and 'not as the scribes' (see 1: 21–28). By identifying himself for the first time as 'the Teacher,' Jesus not only brings to a climax the previous references to him as 'teacher' but recalls and confirms the powerful divine authority of all his previous 'teachings' throughout the narrative." All well and good, except that authority derives, not as with the scribes, from a supposed viewpoint into the mind of God, but from the powerful reclamation of the kingdom as dependently co-arisen and always at hand. More simply, Broadhead, *Teaching With Authority*, 186: "Most significantly, the passion account advances the portrait of Jesus as a powerful teacher (14: 14; 14: 45, 49)."
27. Malbon, *Narrative Space*, 47: "Because, at Passover, pilgrims often outnumbered inhabitants, the city limits of Jerusalem were extended to include Bethphage (less than a mile from the city) to accommodate them all 'in Jerusalem.' But the Markan Jesus stays *about two miles outside the city, in Bethany.*"

the widow's son in such an "upper room."[28] The setting itself then suggests the sharing not only of the festive meal, but also of the life-giving presence of the eschatological banquet.

It is clear, however, that the meal Mark describes bears little resemblance to the traditional Passover celebration.[29] Identification of the meal as such is further confused by Mark's reference to the eating of the Passover meal on the first day of the Feast of Unleavened Bread, contrary to the majority of Jewish traditions which place it on the following day.[30] Perhaps Mark's interest lies in contrasting this eating of unleavened bread with the previous warnings about the leaven of the Pharisees and of Herod (8: 15),[31] so as to highlight Jesus' rejection of false notions and images of the messiah, for that is not what his eschatological banquet is about.

Intimate Betrayal
14: 17–21

[17]When evening came he arrived with the Twelve. [18]And while they were at table eating, Jesus said, "In truth I tell you, one of you is about to betray me, one of you eating with me." [19]They were distressed and said to him, one after the other, "Not me, surely?" [20]He said to them. "It is one of the Twelve, one who is dipping into the same dish with me. [21]Yes, the Son of man is going to his fate, as the scriptures say he will, but alas for that man by whom the Son of man is betrayed! Better for that man if he had never been born!"

---

28. Malbon, *Narrative Space,* 120: "In the upper room in Jerusalem (*anagaion* is stated at 14: 15 and assumed at 14: 17–25), Jesus offers wine as his 'blood of the covenant' with the promise to 'drink it new in the kingdom of God' (14: 24–25). Both Elijah (1 Kings 17: 19, 23) and Elisha (2 Kings 4: 10, 11) were associated with death and 'resurrection' in an 'upper room' (LXX *huperōon*). Elijah carried out the resuscitation of the widow's son there, and there Elisha prophesied the birth of the wealthy woman's son, whom he later resuscitated in that space. Covenant, kingdom, messiahship involve not only a new future, a new life, but present death and burial."

29. Kelber, *Mark's Story of Jesus,* 74: "This last meal is as little a traditional Passover as the Kingdom of God is like the kingdom of father David, or the anointment at Bethany was like the expected royal investiture. Whatever they are eating, their meal is not centered around the paschal lamb and Jesus' words do not commemorate the Exodus event." Robbins, "Last Meal," 25: "The eating scenes which stand at 14: 17–21 and 14: 22–25 do not recount passover activities for two major reasons: (a) no bitter herbs are mentioned, and (b) there is no recitation of liturgy related to eating the passover lamb."

30. Robbins, "Last Meal," 26. But see Mann, *Mark,* 563, on the Markan dating of the meal: "*On the first day of Unleavened Bread:* This is not a clear indication of date, since the surface meaning is 15 Nisan, but the following temporal clause (*when it was customary* . . .) demonstrates that Mark means to indicate 14 Nisan. This use of temporal clauses is in fact common in Mark, with the second clause limiting the first (cf. 1:32,35; 4:35; 14:30; 15:42; 16:2)." However, the issue of the dating of the Last Supper is much disputed.

31. This is Robbins' thesis in "Last Meal."

The scene is intimate, a shared festival meal, with Jesus and his disciples dipping bread into the same dish.[32] Yet Jesus mentions his imminent betrayal, alluding to Psalm 41: 9–10, which says: "Even my trusted friend on whom I relied, who shared my table, takes advantage of me. But you, Yahweh, take pity on me! Put me on my feet and I will give them their due." The Psalmist is bemoaning a similar betrayal. Yet his prayer is aimed at redress, that the Lord would raise him up (ἀνάστησόν με) to requite his betrayer, much as the leaven of the Pharisees and of Herod raises one up in the service of selfhood. Mark draws the contrast between that triumphant raising up and Jesus' immersion in the unleavened, dependently co-arisen circumstances of his confrontation with those who absolutize conventions, both the authorities and here Judas, one of the Twelve. The contrast is between Jesus, who does not cling to self, and those who try to maintain conventions as a support for self. So the disciples become sorrowful and distressed (ἤρξαντο λυπεῖσθαι), for each individually cannot imagine himself as a betrayer. Self-clinging (*ātmagrāha*) is the source in Mahāyāna for the sufferings and sorrows we all experience. The request for self-assurance the disciples echo one after the other, "Is it I? (μήτι ἐγώ)" foreshadows Jesus' answer to the high priest in 14:62, "I am!" (ἐγώ εἰμι).[33] Yet their question has none of the revelatory force of Jesus' reply, signifying merely that they are unaware of what Jesus is all about, and see their future only in terms of rising up to requite their opponents. They envisage future roles for themselves in Jesus' eschatological kingdom, so they are upset with the role Jesus predicts for one of them.

Jesus does not identify his betrayer. And indeed, it is not that only one betrays him while the other eleven remain faithful. All twelve turn tail and run. In the light of that outcome, the reader recognizes that any one of Jesus' disciples, then or now, could play the role of betrayer, filling out the briefly sketched contours of Judas. Even at this farewell meal, self-clinging keeps them closed to ultimate meaning, and thus blind to the conventional course

---

32. But see Mann, *Mark,* 567–68: "Apart from noting the bewilderment manifested by the disciples that any one of their number should break the bonds of table fellowship by treachery, we are liable to pass by *one of you eating with me* and simply place it alongside *one who is dipping bread in the same dish.* However, an article on this very subject suggests a far deeper meaning than is apparent on the surface. F. C. Fensham ("Judas' Hand in the Bowl and Qumran," . . . 259–61) suggests that there is some important parallel material from Qumran. *The Rule of the Community* (1QS vi.1–8) prescribes, when food has been prepared, a hierarchical order in the reaching out of hands for food. In the author's view, the definitive *with me* may indicate that Judas, by not waiting his turn, deliberately denied the leadership of Jesus, and hence—to Jesus—marked himself as being in rebellion." To me that seems overly interpretive, especially in light of the breaking down of hierarchical order and boundary in Mark's Gospel, whereby Jesus' disciples even on occasion omitted the ritual washing of hands. Note Klosinski, *Meals in Mark,* 88: "Prior to 70 C.E. the Pharisees were a Jewish sect characterized by two principal postures: careful observance of tithes and agricultural taboos due to priests, and observance in one's own home at one's own table of the state of purity required of priests in the Temple service." That hardly characterizes Jesus and his band.

33. Kermode, *The Genesis of Secrecy,* 85.

of events that are unfolding. The disciples do not know if they will turn out to be betrayers because they still function as selves in quest of a deluded security, hoping to be the heroes of the drama. The scene is one of sorrow, for even here at Jesus' last supper, the mode is mournful, and Jesus speaks about the sufferings that such clinging to self will entail for his betrayer, for the betrayer of truth, and for himself, the teacher of truth. It is not a curse, but a statement of the karmic results of clinging to convention as if it were ultimate.

Jesus continues on his course, he goes to his fate. That fate is not a preset plan that he must follow, but the very living of his life as it unfolds day to day. The text does not use the term "fate," but merely says that "the son of man goes forth (ὅτι ὁ μὲν υἱὸς τοῦ ἀνθρώπου ὑπάγει), as is written about him." What has been written about him? In fact, although the formula "as it is written" usually points to the Hebrew scriptures, there is no specific text to be found.[34] What in point of literary fact has been written about his sufferings is found, not in the Hebrew prophets, but in the very prophetic, eschatological text of Mark himself: in the three passion predictions of 8:31–33; 9:30–32, and 10:32–34, all of which treat of the inevitability (δεῖ) of Jesus' suffering and death. Verse 8:31 spoke of the necessity (δεῖ) for those events. Verse 9:31 simply has Jesus tell the disciples that he will be delivered up (παραδίδοται), and in 10:32 Jesus informs them of what will happen to him (τὰ μέλλοντα αὐτῷ συμβαίνειν). The present verse 21 speaks of the son of man simply as "going as it has been written about him" (ὑπάγει καθὼς γέγραπται περὶ αὐτοῦ). The first prediction speaks of an all-encompassing inevitability, while the second and third express themselves in the future. Here, however, the verb "going" (ὑπάγει) is present tense: Jesus is now engaged in following the course he has already predicted in the past, the summation of the eschatological role of the son of man.[35]

---

34. Tolbert, *Sowing the Gospel,* 257. See Dowd, *Prayer, Power, and the Problem of Suffering,* 134: "Similarly, the Markan Jesus claims that 'it is written of the Son of man, that he should suffer many things and be treated with contempt' (9:12) and 'the Son of man goes as it is written of him' (14:21). Although the author does not specify where he found it 'written' that Jesus must suffer and die, his use of the formula indicating an appeal to prophecy shows that he understands Jesus' suffering and death as the will of God." One must ask: if Jesus' death is the will of God, how can Jesus say it is written in the prophets, when no such idea is contained therein?

35. Note Hamerton-Kelly, *The Gospel and the Sacred,* 40: "It is remarkable that among all the apocalyptic imagery of this discourse there is not one claim that the tribulations to befall humanity in the messianic apocalyptic history and the ultimate eschaton are expressions of the vengeance of God. Rather, the suffering is to be caused by wars, frauds, charlatans, natural catastrophes, misunderstandings, and persecutions. These are the sadly predictable human failings that cause human misery without any divine intervention. In fact, the one clear reference to divine intervention has God shortening the tribulations for the sake of the elect. There is, therefore, a significant omission of the divine vengeance from a traditionally apocalyptic styled passage. . . ."

The Markan predictions about the son of man, always on the lips of Jesus (as in 8:31, 9: 31, 10: 32–34), point to suffering and death.[36] Jesus is the son of man whose eschatological manifestation consists in embodying the kingdom by following his dependently co-arisen course. In fact, nobody comes to raise him up to victory over his betrayers. Even his resurrection is not an empirical event to demonstrate the rightness of his life. And that is why he is confessed as the christ.

A Last Supper
14: 22–25

[22]*And as they were eating he took bread, and when he had said the blessing he broke it and gave it to them. "Take it," he said, "this is my body." [23]Then he took a cup, and when he had given thanks he handed it to them, and all drank from it, [24]and he said to them, "This is my blood, the blood of the covenant, poured out for many. [25]In truth I tell you, I shall never drink wine any more until the day I drink the new wine in the kingdom of God."*

The Markan meal is the antidote to the self-clinging of the disciples, wherein Jesus redefines who he is.[37] The themes of discipleship and shared

---

36. Perrin, "The Christology of Mark," 99–106.

37. Crossan, *The Historical Jesus,* 360–67, outlines five developmental states of Christian Eucharistic practice. The first simply relates to the symbolic interrelationships between those who share food. The second is the open commensality practiced by Jesus, with its radical demands for social egalitarianism. The third is found in the two separate eucharistic celebrations in the *Didache.* Up to this point "there is absolutely no connection with Passover meal, Last Supper, or even the death of Jesus in general." The fourth stage (not unilinear) was Paul's use of the pre-Pauline tradition in 1 Corinthians, where the body and blood become symbols of Jesus' martyrdom. "We have now moved from, first, open commensality during the lifetime of Jesus through, second, general eucharistic meal without and then with a bread and wine(cup) emphasis and on, third, to a specific passion remembrance, celebration, and participation. And this later specification is given as Jesus' direct and explicit institution on, appropriately, the eve of his death. The fifth and final stage in Mark 14:22–25, which is copied into Matthew 26:26–29 and into Luke 22:15–19a, but with some textual conflation from 1 Corinthians 11:23–26 in Luke 22:19b–20. . . . What is most striking, however, is that Mark has no double command for repetition and remembrance but instead that terminal and emphatic 'truly, I say to you,' with its apocalyptic reference. What we are actually dealing with is, for Mark, almost an anti- or de-institutionalization of the eucharistic meal, as Burton Mack (*A Myth of Innocence,* 298–306) and his doctoral student Lee Edward Klosinski (*Meals in Mark,* 193–213) have shown so clearly. . . . I conclude that Mark is opposing an institutionalized eucharistic ritual that does not allow for Jews and Gentiles at the same table (Kelber, *The Kingdom in Mark,* 45–65) and that emphasizes the presence of Jesus *now* rather than the coming of Jesus *soon* within that liturgy. We have come, as it were, full circle. 'Mark is caught,' as Klosinski summarizes his doctoral dissertation, 'between two understandings of Christian commensality. One understanding envisions commensality as a continuation of the type of table-fellowship remembered from the time of Jesus. Another understands commensality in terms of the eucharistic elements of the Christ cult. Mark employs the language of the

commensality converge here.[38] He is not the body anointed for burial (τὸ σῶμά μου εἰς τὸν ἐνταφιασμόν) of verse 9. Rather, the shared sustenance of the unleavened bread, blessed in thanksgiving, is who he is, that is his body (τοῦτό ἐστιν τὸ σῶμά μου), and that is available immediately, during the very meal that signals Jesus' eschatological finale. Earlier the disciples, worried about having only one loaf of bread, were castigated by Jesus for having hardness of heart (8:14, 17). Now they share in the one loaf that is identified with Jesus, who is setting out on his final journey of martyrdom.[39] It is not just any bread, but the bread of thanksgiving, the bread that has been blessed. Such thankfulness is the primal movement of conscious life, grateful simply for being, anterior to all attempts to capture life and protect self. So here Jesus shares his very being, the being of emptiness, as a remedy (10:45, "as a ransom for many," λύτρον ἀντὶ πολλῶν) for the self-clinging of the disciples. This is the covenant he speaks of, alluding to passages from the Hebrew Bible. *Exodus* 24: 8 states: "This is the blood of the covenant which Yahweh has made with you," referring to the sacrificial blood used

---

Christ cult, but subverts its earlier meaning' (*Meals in Mark*, 203)." See Mack, *A Myth of Innocence*, 302–03: "Scholars have thought that Mark's attention to the cup word revealed an interest in sacrificial soteriology. Exactly the opposite must have been the case. The shift from Paul's text [in 1 Corinthians 11:23–26] is a shift away from the Christ cult and toward a more primitive notion of martyrdom. Blood is exactly what martyrs give, so that a martyrological significance could be retained for Jesus' death by signifying the wine as well as the bread. With the bread symbol so laden with Hellenistic connotations, Mark deemphasized bread and accentuated the symbolism of the cup. . . . All of the differences between the Markan text and the Pauline tradition point toward the same conclusion. Mark toned down the cultic nuances of the Hellenistic meal tradition [of Paul], just as he had reduced the Christ myth, by allowing the martyrological identifications basic to the Christ event to show through again."

38. Klosinski, *Meals in Mark*, 133: "Mark has structured his narrative in such a way that the Lord's Supper (14:17–25) is the point where the food and discipleship themes converge." Again, 137: "The importance of the Last Supper for Mark requires a certain rethinking. Given its relationship to other themes in the gospel, it is no longer possible simply to understand it as the institution of the Lord's Supper in the last of a series of suppers. At it, two favorite Markan themes, food and discipleship, converge." It is difficult to read the account of the Last Supper in such terms. Crossan, *The Historical Jesus*, 360, notes that "even to hear this case demands that you hold in abeyance two thousand years of eucharistic theology and a similar amount of Last Supper iconography."

39. Bassler, "Parable of the Loaves," 168: With "the blessing, breaking, and distributing of the eucharistic bread, which is Jesus' body, the reader's quest for consistency is finally rewarded. For these words recall the language of the feeding miracles where the loaves were also blessed, broken, and distributed. Thus the reader can now recognize what was opaque at that point in the narrative: that on some inchoate level the loaves referred to Jesus' broken body on the cross. But this insight is clear only in retrospect. And on further retrospection it also becomes clear that the discussion of the passion in chapters 8–10 *did* address the question of the loaves, and the understanding that the reader reached in those chapters was not only understanding of the significance of Jesus' suffering but also, ultimately, insight into the enigma of these loaves." (Cited in Moore, *Literary Criticism*, 82–83.) For the reflection of the language of 6:41 in 14:22, see Crossan, *The Historical Jesus*, 403.

to ratify the covenant. *Zechariah* 9: 11, says: "As for you, because of the blood of your covenant, I have released your prisoners from the pit in which there is no water." Here Jesus' blood, identified with the wine of thanksgiving (εὐχαριστήσας), is a source for liberation from the waterless pit of self.[40] The imagery is clear—only the bread that is broken can be shared, only the wine that is poured out and abandoned (ἐκχυννόμενον) can be drunk by many. So likewise, only the self that is handed over in eschatological abandonment can be the body of Christ.

The promise that ends the passage shows that Jesus no longer shares in conventional concerns. He moves toward the ultimate in that he has abandoned his body and his blood and shares in the eschatological kingdom of God, i.e., the practice of worldly convention-only, with the awareness of the complete otherness of ultimate meaning. "Mark offers his own unique eschatological formulation in 14:25. It serves to extend the emphasis on the cup, now connected with the soon-to-be absent Jesus. Thus, this saying ('In truth I tell you, I shall never drink wine any more until the day I drink the new wine in the kingdom of God.') serves Mark as a convenient way to interject his apocalyptic agenda into the narrative."[41] To drink the new wine in that kingdom is not to experience a wonderful victory, for, as soon becomes apparent, the cup that Jesus must drink is the cup of sufferings.[42]

Peter's Self-Resolve
14: 26–31

[26]*After psalms had been sung they left for the Mount of Olives.* [27]*And Jesus said to them, "You will all fall away, for the scripture says: I shall strike the*

---

40. Heil, *The Gospel of Mark as a Model for Action,* 291: "By referring to his blood as 'my blood of the covenant,' Jesus indicates that the blood of his death will effect the fulfillment of *the* covenant." Also Mauser, *Christ in the Wilderness,* 138: "While the version prescribed by Paul clearly refers to the new covenant in the words, 'this cup is the new covenant in my blood' (1 Cor 11:25), the Marcan version instead speaks of 'the blood of the covenant, which is poured out for many' (14:24)—an equally clear reference to the establishment of the Mosaic covenant in the wilderness (Ex 24:8). This is in keeping with the opinion of Mark that the last supper is to be understood in analogy to the establishment of the covenant with Moses." It seems to me more straightforward to read Mark as written: that Jesus' blood reaffirms that ancient and unabrogated covenant, embodied in the great commandment to love God and neighbor.

41. Klosinski, *Meals in Mark,* 201. Again, 203: "The Last Supper scene is also important for the construction of the gospel as an apocalypse. The emphasis on the cup highlights the theme of suffering." And 208: "The significance of the Last Supper is that it is a coda: it sums up all of the significant Marcan themes: discipleship, misunderstanding, betrayal, denial, suffering."

42. Fowler, *Loaves and Fishes,* 135: "When we take care to read the account of the last meal of Jesus and his disciples in light of the previous meals in Mark, we are struck by the recurrence of the dominant theme of discipleship failure in this account. To be sure, we are by now accustomed to portrayals of the disciples' ineptness and misunderstanding at the dinner table, but here [14:18, 30, 31–37] their failure assumes shocking proportions."

shepherd and the sheep will be scattered; [28]*however, after my resurrection I shall go before you to Galilee."* [29]*Peter said, "Even if all fall away, I will not."* [30]*And Jesus said to him, "In truth I tell you, this day, this very night, before the cock crows twice, you will have disowned me three times."* [31]*But he repeated still more earnestly, "If I have to die with you, I will never disown you." And they all said the same.*

Jesus' prediction that all his disciples will fail him (σκανδαλισθήσεσθε) is replete with the meanings from the scriptural passage he cites. *Zechariah* 13: 7 says: " 'Awake, sword, against my shepherd, against the man who is close to me,' declared Yahweh Sabaoth! Strike the shepherd, scatter the sheep." Here the passage is against idolatry and false prophets, and the sword that scatters the sheep is that of Yahweh. In the Markan narrative, by contrast, by crucifying him the authorities will remove any hope from the disciples that Jesus is a hero who might smite his enemies, and so his followers will be scandalized, obstructed from understanding. They still practice inner idolatry, clinging to an image of the messiah which in delusion they impute onto Jesus. Jesus himself becomes the sword that scatters his disciples, by disappointing their hopes. Yet the real obstacle (σκάνδαλον) is their clinging to the imagined pattern of consciousness. That pattern of false imaginings precludes understanding (*jñeya-avaraṇa*, the obstacle to knowing) and leads to passionate clinging (*kleśa-avaraṇa*, the obstacle of the passions). They are bound to fail, because they are bound by mistaking the conventional for the real.[43]

Verse 28 comes as a surprise, for here Jesus offers true hope, that he will be raised up (μετὰ τὸ ἐγερθῆναί με) and go before (προάξω) his disciples into Galilee (εἰς τὴν Γαλιλαίαν).[44] Psalm 41:10 had talked about being raised up to vanquish one's betrayers. Yet here although Jesus will be raised

---

43. Hamerton-Kelly, *The Gospel and the Sacred*, 47–48, observes: "The point the Gospel makes here is very difficult to grasp for a Christianity that has sold out to secularism. Pathetic Christianity, so eager to be of service in the world, sells itself as solidarity with victims for the sake of Jesus, or a way to psychological 'meaning' through identification with the crucified. 'Even if I must die with you I shall not forsake you.' And so say all of us; but the Gospel exposes the fallacy of such spiritual heroics. Not one of those heroes stood by Jesus."

44. Malbon, "Narrative Criticism," 33: "The Markan Jesus' prediction, echoed by the young man at the empty tomb (14:28; 16:7), that he will go before his disciples to Galilee, points proleptically to an event that is not narrated within the story-as-discoursed. . . . This narrative technique contributes to the often noted open ending of Mark's Gospel." Again, Malbon, *Narrative Space*, 23: "Thus the narrative sequence seems to end in Judea. The close of the geopolitical (i.e., journeys) sequence, however, turns the reader's attention away from Judea and back to Galilee. From the Mount of Olives Jesus informs his disciples that after he is raised up he will go before them to Galilee (14:28). At the cross the reader is given a flashback to Galilee in the description of the women 'who, when he was in Galilee, followed him, and ministered to him'(15:41). At the empty tomb, the women and the reader are given a flash-forward to Galilee where Jesus is going and where 'you will see him as he told you' (16:7)."

up, he will not even remain in the neighborhood. Just as he went forth (ὑπάγει) toward his course in verse 21, so here he will go before his disciples back into the ordinary life of Galilee. He will lead them back to conventional reality, back from the drama of the Jerusalem conflicts to the everyday mind of their normal living. Yet, that life will then be lived in the context of the resurrection, of the resurrection of the conventional kingdom from its imagined delusions. But that most certainly is not what the disciples expected. "In keeping with Mark's understanding of faith as a matter of insight, not merely information, he includes in his gospel—in addition to the three uncomprehended predictions in 8:31; 9:31; and 10:33—a simple pair of promises to Peter (14:27f; 16:7) that the fellowship shattered by Jesus' death will be restored when they 'see' him again in Galilee, risen from the dead. In characteristic Markan fashion, that event is merely pointed to in his narrative rather than being described, as it is in various forms in the other gospels. By his account of their flight in terror, Mark lets his readers know that the resurrection [and, I might add, the return to Galilee], in spite of predictions, was not expected, nor did the disciples even understand what it would involve (9:10) until after it had taken place."[45] What it would involve most concretely is that return to Galilee. No post-resurrection appearances either in Judea or in Galilee are promised; only that they will "see" him there in their ordinary lives, where they had failed to see him before because of their imagined projections. There is no supernaturally splendid ending, only the mature wisdom of worldly convention-only.

Peter boasts of his resolve not to fail, relying on himself to cope. Yet that self-boasting is the very obstacle that assures his denial. When Jesus cites *Zechariah* about the scattered sheep, no one in the story seems to hear at all. No uptake is evinced from anybody, except perhaps a reader who tumbles to the fact that Peter's courage, as real as it probably was, avails for nothing.[46] Peter does not fail simply because of a lack of courage. Rather, when his identity is emptied of clear and understandable content, in clinging to Jesus' assumed identity, Peter's courage evaporates. The self has no power to cope with paradoxical conditions, no matter how much one might protest to the contrary, no matter how much courage one has. Like the seed sown on the rocky ground, Peter at once falls away.[47] Not just Peter, for all the disciples make the same boast. Thus they deny Jesus (με ἀπαρνήσῃ), they negate his emptiness, as shown in the next passage in the garden, and they negate his dependent co-arising, as shown in the events of the passion narrative to follow. It is not merely that they do not acknowledge knowing him, but that

---

45. Kee, *Community of the New Age,* 172.
46. Fowler, *Let the Reader Understand,* 89.
47. Tolbert, *Sowing the Gospel,* 212: "Peter vigorously refutes this double authoritative dictum [14: 18 and 14: 27, "you will all fall away," σκανδαλισθήσεσθε], repeating again the key word "fall away" (σκανδαλισθήσονται, 14: 29) to confirm the allusion to the parable of the Sower ("immediately they fall away," εὐθὺς σκανδαλίζονται, 4: 17)."

they have long refused to see the emptiness of all things, Jesus included. Their denial is in fact already accomplished.

Even for the reader there is little to help in understanding what it means "to see Jesus back in Galilee." Mark provides no tools to aid in the interpretation. At the end of the story "the distance is total. To fret about this distance, however, and especially to play the game of trying to guess the rest of the disciples' story beyond Mark 16:8 is to fixate on the story level to the neglect of the discourse. The future of the disciples beyond Mark 16:8 is quite irrelevant to the chief aim of the Gospel. The Gospel is designed not to say something about the disciples or even to say something about Jesus, but to do something to the reader."[48] By disqualifying all of the disciples on the story level, Mark's discourse clears the way for a dependently co-arisen awakening and seeing on the part of his readers.[49] All appropriate model characters are whisked off the scene and the reader is left to herself to return to Galilee and see Jesus there.

The Emptiness of Jesus
14: 32–42

[32]*They came to a plot of land called Gethsemane, and he said to his disciples, "Stay here while I pray." [33]Then he took Peter and James and John with him. [34]And he began to feel terror and anguish. And he said to them, "My soul is sorrowful to the point of death. Wait here, and stay awake." [35]And going on a little further he threw himself on the ground and prayed that, if it were possible, this hour might pass him by. [36]"Abba, Father!" he said, "For you everything is possible. Take this cup away from me. But let it be as you, not I, would have it." [37]He came back and found them sleeping, and he said to Peter, "Simon, are you asleep? Had you not the strength to stay awake one hour? [38]Stay awake, and pray not to be put to the test. The spirit is willing enough, but human nature is weak." [39]Again he went away and*

---

48. Fowler, *Let the Reader Understand,* 79.

49. Against Camery-Hoggatt, *Irony in Mark's Gospel,* 59: "As he writes a narrator is able to assume an enormous variety of competencies on the part of his 'Model Reader'— . . . the ability to recognize and respond appropriately to the narrative's implicit points of view. . . . From what we have seen the entire narrative exchange may be understood as an oscillating interaction between two different sources of what we shall call 'competencies': competencies *assumed* by the text, and competencies *generated* by the text." I think that Mark is even craftier, bringing his reader to intellectual gridlock by presenting notions about which one has neither assumed nor generated competencies. He does this by maneuvering the reader to identify with Jesus against the disciples—the natural models if only they were a little more gracious—by asserting notions against which the very self of the reader rebels. Mark's text generates no ability to cope with such a direct challenge upon the bastions of selfhood, only, as with Peter, an invitation to the breakdown of one's functional selfhood (flee to the mountains). This is perhaps why people with an already weak sense of self should read one of the other gospels.

prayed, saying the same words. ⁴⁰And once more he came back and found
them sleeping, their eyes were so heavy; and they could find no answer for
him. ⁴¹He came back a third time and said to them, "You can sleep on now
and take your rest. It is all over. The hour has come. Now the Son of man
is to be betrayed into the hands of sinners. ⁴²Get up! Let us go! My betrayer
is not far away!"

This passage is loaded with allusions to eschatological symbols from the
Hebrew scriptures. The cup that Jesus is to drink recalls the cup of Yahweh's
wrath. *Isaiah* 51: 17 says: "Awake, awake! To your feet, Jerusalem! You
who from Yahweh's hand have drunk the cup of his wrath. The chalice, the
stupefying cup, you have drunk to the dregs." This cup of wrath is a favorite
eschatological symbol. *Jeremiah* 25: 15–16 parallels Jesus' prayer: "For
Yahweh, the God of Israel, said this to me, 'Take this cup of the wine of
wrath and make all the nations to whom I send you drink it; they will drink
and reel and lose their wits, because of the sword I am sending among
them.' " *Jeremiah* continues in verse 27: "You will say to them, 'Yahweh
Sabaoth, the God of Israel, says this: Drink! Get drunk! Vomit! Fall, never
to rise again, before the sword I am sending among you.' " The cup of
suffering is a metaphor for the truth that all living entails suffering
(*duḥkha-satya*), the basic fact of human experience announced by Śākyamuni.
Likewise, in the Hebrew scriptures suffering is elicited as the result of sinful
human actions, for Yahweh sends the cup because of Israel's unfaithfulness.
Yet he can also reverse that situation, and remove the cup from his people.
But here it is Jesus who drinks the cup of wrath and suffering, not the
enemies of Israel. Suffering is not reversed, but accepted. Still, that eschatological cup of suffering is said to be consumed in shame and drunkenness,
in staggering and vomit. This is why Jesus is terror stricken at the prospect.
The eschatology of Chapter 13 is fulfilled in Jesus' drinking of that cup. Yet
he prays that the degradation be removed, just as Yahweh in *Isaiah* 51: 22
removed the cup from Israel: "Look, I am taking the stupefying cup from
your hand, the chalice, the cup of my wrath, you will not have to drink it
again. I shall hand it to your tormentors." It is the prospect of that cup of
suffering that causes Jesus to be fearful and distraught. This is the hour (ἡ
ὥρα) that he wants to pass him by, for it is the very eschatological hour of
13: 32 which only the Father knows. The final eschatological trial has come,
but not in the way expected. Rather, it comes in Jesus' abandonment of his
own self to Abba, to the silent emptiness of Abba. At the end of the passage
Jesus says explicitly that the hour has come (ἦλθεν ἡ ὥρα), that his betrayer
is close at hand (ἤγγικεν), echoing 1: 15 where Mark says that the eschatological kingdom is near at hand (ἤγγικεν).⁵⁰
And the disciples sleep through it all, unaware that they too soon will
experience that same eschatological trial (38, πειρασμόν). James and John
had asked to sit on either side of Jesus in his kingdom and had affirmed that

50. See Kelber, "The Hour of the Son of Man," 45.

they too could drink his cup. Peter has just voiced his commitment never to abandon Jesus. Yet they are not awakened to Abba, nor aware of the course of events about to occur. They need more than resolve, they need to be awakened (γρηγορεῖτε), i.e., to be raised up with Jesus. Note that Jesus' fear and bewilderment occurs after he has prayed. Prayer does not change the dependently co-arisen web of human actions into a sweet security net, but, as here, ushers one into the awareness of the terrible otherness of God, apart from all conventional supports for selfhood. The disciples do not pray, for that is beyond them.[51] Self-clinging precludes prayer.

Prayer does not alter the course of events. The passion narrative is not a divine program and that is why Jesus becomes distraught. If it were simply the unfolding of a preset divine will, there would be no point in praying to avoid suffering and death.[52] A samurai attitude of stoically accepting one's fate would be quite sufficient. Jesus' prayer here is not a meditative state divorced from ordinary living, but is immersed in the complexities of ordinary living at its worst. In his previous prayers, usually in wilderness places, Jesus was detached from "the announcements of his impending suffering," and thus in Mark the reader "avoided a direct collision between the two conflicting themes of power and suffering."[53] But now these periods of peaceful prayer and contemplation are forgotten and Jesus is emotionally distraught.[54]

---

51. Tolbert, *Sowing the Gospel,* 189: "The audience should be surprised neither at the disciples' failure to exorcise a demon that requires prayer nor at their coming utter incapacity to watch and pray with Jesus in Gethsemane. Prayer in the Gospel of Mark is consistently outside the disciples' range of understanding or participation."

52. Against Dowd, *Prayer, Power, and the Problem of Suffering,* 133: "The author of the gospel explains the discrepancy between Jesus' teaching on prayer [that everything is possible to God] and the negative result of Jesus' own prayer in Gethsemane by his use of the concept 'will of God.' In 14:36 the Markan Jesus ends his prayer, 'Not what I want, but what you will' (οὐ τί ἐγὼ θέλω ἀλλὰ τί σύ). Since the Gethsemane scene is followed by the arrest, trial and crucifixion of Jesus, the audience is forced to conclude that the reason that Jesus' petition to be delivered from suffering was not answered was because the passion was the will of God." Again, 157: "So when the Markan Jesus repeats the omnipotence formula in his prayer and follows it with a request that the δεῖ of 8:31 be reversed, the audience understands this prayer as one which meets all the criteria for efficacious petition which have preceded it. The narrative up to this point has emphasized God's power and willingness to eliminate suffering no less than the necessity for Jesus' suffering and death. It is the real possibility of divine rescue at this point in the narrative that makes the scene in Gethsemane so terrible. The fact that the audience already knows that Jesus will die does not diminish the narrative tension, any more than the familiarity of Greek audiences with the mythological traditions prevented their experiencing the catharsis that the tragedies evoked." If, as Dowd explains on 120, "the portrayal of the praying Jesus is intended by the evangelist as a model to his community," then it seems to me mistaken to see the prayer in Gethsemane as a possible escape route from the dependently co-arisen factors that have been operative throughout Jesus' career in Mark. The only escape for Jesus would have been simple flight. Furthermore, I disagree with Dowd's interpretation of the efficaciousness of prayer, for which see Mark 11:23–24.

53. Dowd, *Prayer, Power, and the Problem of Suffering,* 154.

54. Dowd, *Prayer, Power, and the Problem of Suffering,* 153: "The verbs used in 33b to describe Jesus' emotional state (ἤρξατο ἐκθαμβεῖσθαι καὶ ἀδημονεῖν) express deep anguish. Reports of Jesus' emotions are rare in the Markan narrative, and never up to

The paradox is deeper than doctrinal; it rends Jesus to his very marrow.[55] Everything is possible for God (πάντα δυνατά σοι), but not as the Hellenistic philosophers imagined in their assertions that indeed God can accomplish the impossible. The realm of divine possibility is not one of a supernal actor on the stage of conventional realities. Rather, the action of God overturns all expected norms and patterns and is empty of all conventional constraints. It leaves one hanging without support before the otherness of Abba, not in servile submission to an imagined will of God. Jesus' prayers have to this point been generally effective. "We are thus surprised to step back from our reading experience and recollect that the only prayer actually presented in the Gospel is Jesus' agonizing prayer in Gethsemane (14:36). The effect upon the reader of withholding the words of all but the last of Jesus' prayers is not difficult to fathom. By presenting Jesus as a faithful man of prayer but withholding the prayers themselves, the narrator repeatedly carves out gaps in the discourse that the narratee hungers to have filled. If the prayer in 14:36 does not satisfy our hunger, nothing in Mark's narrative will. Of course, thinking that the narrative must necessarily satisfy all the hungers it arouses would be presumptuous. We have no guarantee that narrative will fill the emptiness to which it awakens us."[56] The sword of emptiness cuts away all hope and plunges both Jesus and the reader into a bottomless, absolute nothingness, leaving them in a tensive no-man's land where alone one may realize awakening not as an impossible dream, but in the very circumstances of our dependently co-arisen, everyday lives.

And this is the conflict Jesus experiences in the garden: to renounce the dependently co-arisen world and seek refuge in a solitary ultimate realm, to flee to the mountains, as he recommended in 13:14. Yet, in the dependently co-arisen realm of men and women, there is no escape from the maturation of our deeds and their effects on others. Jesus' abandonment of himself to the will of the Father is not the acceptance of a divine plan, for that not only makes God the punisher of Jesus, but it also trivializes the realm of ultimate meaning by confining it within a conventionally-constructed program.[57]

---

this point has the audience had any indication that Jesus felt distress about his own situation. . . . Here he is described as being in agony over his own situation and the picture is immediately reinforced by direct discourse: 'My grief is enough to kill me' (14:34a)."

55. Collins, *The Beginning of the Gospel,* 40: "In the Gospel of Mark, however, there is a sharp tension—one could say a paradox—between the God who gives Jesus power to heal and exorcize and power over the forces of nature and the God who wills that the Son of Man must suffer and die."

56. Fowler, *Let the Reader Understand,* 215.

57. Kelber, "The Hour of the Son of Man," 57, note 40: "In a deeper sense for Mark the cross is both the will of God and the fault of man. Human weakness and divine necessity belong together in inscrutable logic." Such a logic is called for only if one reads literally and sees Jesus' course as a divine plan set by the Father. In note 43 Kelber criticizes structuralism for taking "us back to a priori generalizations and into the [quoting Hirsch] 'magic land of meanings outside human consciousness.' " Yet is not an inscrutable logic also a magic land of meanings?

Rather, Jesus abandons selfhood to the concrete events of this hour, to the internalization of all eschatological hopes and fears. Jesus through his anguish in the Garden of Gethsemane brings eschatology down into his own concrete life, and thus into the lives of his followers.[58] The kingdom is at hand, purchased with the blood of the martyr Jesus.

Yet he comes and finds his disciples asleep. In the eschatological discourse of 13: 36, Jesus tells his disciples that they must be awake because they do not know the hour, for it may come unexpectedly (ἐξαίφνης). And here he finds them asleep. Jesus, the eschatological master, comes and finds Peter failing to stay awake. The one hour they cannot keep awake contrasts with the hour that is near at hand. Drowsy, they do not notice the approach of the final revelatory hour, when the son of man will be delivered up to the plans of sinners. Only with awareness of the otherness of God can they reengage in the conventional events of the passion. Thus they must pray, relate themselves to Abba in silence and sometimes in anguish. When all accustomed support is demolished, the spirit may be willing, but human nature is unable to cope. Personal images of identity die hard. The spirit is eager to be put to the test, but when no coping is possible, our very humanness shrinks away in horror. There is no escape from human transience and dying. Jesus' course will be to drink the cup of suffering, to be completely immersed in the dependently co-arisen plots of sinners. Yet there will be no reversal: no God will take the cup from his hands and make his enemies drink it. That is Jesus' deconstruction of expected hopes, as well as his emptying of the notion of an omnipotent *deus ex machina*.[59] No victories, only awakening and resurrection.

Yet the disciples sleep on. Mark is not talking about physical sleep.[60] It is not that Jesus wants their companionship, for he moves away from them to pray at a distance, leaving them to their own silent prayer. Rather, they themselves must be personally awakened, for they too will soon be immersed in sufferings, in the destruction of all their hopes. The three times Jesus finds them asleep parallels Peter's three denials. Perhaps it also ties in with Peter's wish at Jesus' transfiguration to construct three tents to house the numinous experience, for the sleeping disciples' inability to respond to Jesus in the

---

58. Malbon, *Narrative Space*, 34: "*Gethsemane* is generally taken to mean 'an oil press,' that is, a press for olives, and is thus linked with the Mount of Olives." This suggests that the eschatological concerns surrounding the Mount of Olives, from which Jesus delivered his "Little Apocalypse" of chapter 13, are again in the background here.

59. Against Robbins, *Jesus the Teacher,* 212: "In Mark the desire for integrity has led to the internalization of rejection, suffering, and death. Jesus' authoritative acceptance of rejection, suffering, and death stands as a model for this system of thought and action. This mode of understanding goes beyond the prophetic-apocalyptic tradition by portraying Jesus' internalized authority interacting with the external authority of God (14:36). His death is not simply imposed upon him by God. It is internally accepted as a benefit to others through insight into the will of God." Not accepting Mark as a system of thought, Robbins seems to teeter between an external deity who wills Jesus' death and a somewhat masochistic Jesus who internalizes that will.

60. Kelber, "The Hour of the Son of Man," 49.

garden recalls Peter's bafflement after the transfiguration (9: 6). Yet still they sleep while the kingdom arrives, when the hour is at hand.

And so Jesus announces that "It is all over. The hour has come." Jesus has withdrawn before into prayer, but with a more pleasing result. "Three times in the narrative the audience is informed that Jesus withdrew for solitary prayer. The first, 1:35–39, precedes the expansion of his ministry of teaching, healing and exorcism beyond Capernaum into 'all Galilee' indicating that both the direction and the power of Jesus' ministry are given by God in prayer. The second prayer scene, 6:46, follows the first feeding miracle and precedes the dramatic epiphany scene of 6:47–52. The third prayer scene takes place in Gethsemane (14:32–42)."[61] Thus the reader is alerted that when Jesus prays, something important is about to take place. But no expanded power ministry occurs, no further epiphany. Simply an arrest. It is all over, the power days are finished, the account settled (ἀπέχει).[62] The phrase is stark—no more miracles, the miracle book is closed and finished.[63] What account is he talking about? The term ἀπέχει literally denotes the closing of an account, the payment of a bill. The only earlier point of reference is found in 10:45, where Jesus talks of his blood as a ransom for many. Ransom (λύτρον) signifies the price of release, "in *koiné* Greek signifying the money paid for the release of slaves."[64] Thus when Jesus says ἀπέχει, he means that the account has been paid and by his eschatological passion and death, he has paid the debt to the authorities that will liberate his disciples to go and see him in Galilee.[65]

The Arrest
14: 43–52

[43]*And at once, while he was still speaking, Judas, one of the Twelve, came up and with him a number of men armed with swords and clubs, sent by the*

61. Dowd, *Prayer, Power, and the Problem of Suffering,* 118. See also 152.

62. Bratcher and Nida, *Handbook,* 452: "The form *apechai* is normally used of receipting bills, with the meaning 'paid in full.' " The term is troublesome and various interpretations and emendations are offered.

63. Collins, *The Beginning of the Gospel,* 96, notes: "In 1970 Eta Linnemann (*Studien zur Passionsgeschichte,* 24–28) . . . like Bultmann, . . . concluded that the Gethsemane pericope was originally independent. She translated *apechei* (14:41) as 'the account is closed' and took this as an expression of Jesus' acceptance of God's will. On this basis she was able to conclude that the story does not report a phase of Jesus' passion; it interprets the entire event of the passion."

64. Bratcher and Nida, *Handbook,* 336.

65. Kee, *Community of the New Age,* 172: "The resurrection is a private event: ἐκεῖ αὐτὸν 'ὄψεσθε. By implication, you alone, as his once faithful, recently scattered flock, will see him risen from the dead. That is explicit in 14:28: μετὰ τὸ ἐγερθῆναί με, the flock will be reconstituted by the once smitten shepherd. They *have* seen him risen from the dead, Mark is telling his reader. Not only is that their secret experience, but it is the secret solution to all the enigmas with which they were confronted by his life and death.

*chief priests and the scribes and the elders. ⁴⁴Now the traitor had arranged
a signal with them, saying, "The one I kiss, he is the man. Arrest him, and
see he is well guarded when you lead him away." ⁴⁵So when the traitor came,
he went up to Jesus at once and said, "Rabbi!" and kissed him. ⁴⁶The others
seized him and arrested him. ⁴⁷Then one of the bystanders drew his sword
and struck out at the high priest's servant and cut off his ear.*
　*⁴⁸Then Jesus spoke. "Am I a bandit," he said, "that you had to set out to
capture me with swords and clubs? ⁴⁹I was among you teaching in the Temple
day after day and you never laid a hand on me. But this is to fulfill the
scriptures." ⁵⁰And they all deserted him and ran away. ⁵¹A young man followed
with nothing on but a linen cloth. They caught hold of him, ⁵²but he left the
cloth in their hands and ran away naked.*

Even while Jesus was still speaking (καὶ εὐθὺς ἔτι αὐτοῦ λαλοῦντος),
the hour arrives. The account, for the most part, is straightforward: they come
and arrest Jesus. The account of his passion and death traditionally has been
taken by later Christians to be straight historical narrative. From later Christian
perspectives it was difficult to imagine that anybody was not aware of what
had gone on at that time. Indeed, Luke in 24: 18 emphasizes this point, for
when the disciples on the way to Emmaus say to the yet unrecognized Jesus:
"You must be the only person staying in Jerusalem who does not know the
things that have been happening there these last few days." Yet in Mark
Judas has to arrange a signal so that the armed men will know just whom
to arrest, despite the fact that Jesus was teaching daily in the temple. In
Mark's view, Jesus was not universally recognizable.
　Here the hour has indeed come, for he is handed over to the authorities.
The eschatological hour has come, not as a supernatural occurrence, but as
an arresting posse sent out by the religious authorities, here subsumed as the
chief priests and the scribes and the elders. The religious authorities are out
in full force, and thus the action of one of the bystanders (εἷς δέ τις τῶν
παρεστηκότων), identified in John 18: 10 as Peter, to fight against such a
show of force is indeed brave, even foolhardy. He cuts off the servant's ear.
Jesus rebukes him in Matthew 26: 52–53 and in John 18: 11, while Luke
22: 51 cleans up the scene by having Jesus heal the fellow's ear. But Mark
merely reports the attack, to suggest that what the disciples lack is not courage,
but awareness. They are ready to fight alongside Jesus, but not to be arrested.
As bystanders, they are merely observers of surface events (*mythā-saṃvṛti*)
and fail to see their inner import. Yet a more crucial function of the incident
is to disassociate Jesus from such behavior, for immediately after the ear-
severing sword strike, Jesus asserts that he is no bandit (λῃστήν). In 15:7

To change the figure, the event to which Mark only points but which he does not depict
is the key to the meaning of his entire account." In a Mahāyāna reading, that is the
awakening of his community to the presence of the kingdom in awareness of the risen
Christ.

Jesus is lined up with Barabbas, a rebel in an insurrection against the political authorities, but Jesus' path does not lie in that direction either.[66] "The determination to disassociate Jesus from any revolutionary messianic movement pervades the passion story: Jesus is seized as a bandit (λῃστής, 14:48) and yet declines to make any effort at defense (14:65; 15:5); ironically, a real revolutionary is released (15:7), while Jesus is executed as a political leader (15:12, 18, 26) in the company of two insurrectionists (15:27)."[67]

The scriptures that are to be fulfilled are those about the eschatological cup of wrath, that life comes not from empirical victory over transience and death, but from within—from the acceptance of human being, of transience, of suffering for the sake of justice and truth (See *Isaiah* 53, *Psalm* 22). Jesus breaks the expectations of the scriptures, for he does not reverse the tables. There is no great day when the Lord comes in all his glory and gives Jesus' enemies what for. The eschaton comes in the everyday suffering and the everyday resurrection from that suffering. Mark has himself emphasized that those scriptures are fulfilled through Jesus' sufferings. It is not that Jesus comes to fulfill their glory expectations, but that their expectations are fulfilled in his deconstructive commitment to merely be human.

And so everyone abandons Jesus and runs away. Fighting will be of no avail. He submits to the arrest, but not meekly or masochistically. He does not want to experience the cup to come; that is clear from his Gethsemane prayer. Yet, he rejects violence, the only means available to counter the oppression of the authorities, with the understandable result that the disciples have no recourse but flight. They are indeed ready to resist, but not to abandon confidence in selfhood. The hour has come, but it does not bring the expected glorious battle. Indeed, in 13: 14 Jesus himself recommends eschatological flight. In fact, the fault of the disciples is not that they run away; not allowed to resist physically, what other course is open to them? Rather, their failure is that they fail to practice the path. They have all drunk of the cup of suffering, for they cannot avoid doing so. Yet they remain unawakened to the advent of the eschatological hour, and thus to the everyday presence of ultimate meaning in the "mere" conventionality of events.

The strange episode of the bare-bodied fellow is the most curious puzzle of this account. Various explanations are offered. Allusions to the Hebrew scriptures are not very helpful, although it may perhaps relate to the drinking of the cup of suffering. *Lamentations* 4: 21 says: "Rejoice, exult, daughter of Edom, you who reside in Uz! To you in turn the cup will pass; you will get drunk and strip yourself naked!" The daughter of Edom refers to the enemies of Israel, who will experience Yahweh's wrath. But, here the naked youth has been made to drink the cup of suffering, confused because of the events of Jesus' arrest, and reduced to drunken nakedness and shame.[68] *Ezekiel*

---

66. Collins, *The Beginning of the Gospel,* 109.
67. Kee, *Community of the New Age,* 32.
68. Tannehill, "The Disciples in Mark," 151: "The . . . flight of the naked young man probably dramatizes the shamefulness of the disciples' flight and satirizes the pretensions of Christians who claimed to be ready for martyrdom." Note 38 explains that the linen

23: 26–30 says: "They will strip off your garments . . . and leave you stark naked. And thus your shameful whorings will be exposed . . . because you have played the whore with the nations and defiled yourself with their foul idols." This passage is directed to the dwellers in Jerusalem who whore after other gods and practice idolatry—but that hardly seems applicable. The disciples, whose account has now been closed (14: 41), remain fixated on false ideas of power and status—less visible but more tenacious idols—but they all run away fully clothed. More to the point, *Amos* 2: 16 says that "he who is stout of heart among the mighty shall flee away naked in that day," in the day of the eschatological trials. "The word naked, on which the description ends, sums up effectively the pitiful helplessness of a man stripped of all the resources on which he counts to maintain himself when he faces the final catastrophe."[69] Jesus goes to his trial bereft of any support for selfhood, and so a lonely follower who initially does not run away must, when challenged, follow the disciples' example. There is no other recourse.

But what is this youth (νεανίσκος τις) doing there dressed only in a linen cloth around his naked body (σινδόνα ἐπὶ γυμνοῦ), having lost which, he has to flee in the all-together? Perhaps it is a scribal mistake.[70] Or perhaps it is a flash-forward to the young man in the empty tomb, for he also is covered with a white robe (16: 5, στολὴν λευκήν),[71] but he remains clothed. Where did this somebody (τις) come from and what is he doing here?

In 1958 Morton Smith discovered a few passages on the back of a letter from Clement of Alexandria, which purported to be from a *Secret Gospel of Mark*. It was to some an upsetting discovery, because the passages are not what one would expect. Rather, they give an only slightly masked erotic portrayal of a gnostic Jesus with a young man (ὁ νεανίσκος). One fragment says: "And they come into Bethany. And a certain woman whose brother had died was there. And, coming, she prostrated herself before Jesus and said to him, 'Son of David, have mercy on me.' But the disciples rebuked her. And Jesus, being angered, went off with her into the garden where the tomb was, and straightway a great cry was heard from the tomb. And going near Jesus rolled away the stone from the door of the tomb. And straightway, going in where the youth was, he stretched forth his hand and raised him, seizing his hand. But the youth, looking upon him, loved him and began to beseech him that he might be with him. And going out of the tomb they came into the house of the youth, for he was rich. And after six days Jesus

---

was used in the New Testament only in reference to burial, and thus suggests the young man was ready for burial, but chickened out when faced with actual arrest. For an alternate interpretation that sees the young man as a symbolic representation of Jesus himself, as well as neophytes in Mark's community, see Crossan, "Empty Tomb and Absent Lord," 147–48.

69. Fosbroke, *The Interpreter's Bible*, 6: 790.

70. Kermode, *The Genesis of Secrecy*, 33: "Anyway, why is the youth naked? Some ancient texts omit the phrase *epi gumnou*, which is not the usual way of saying 'about his body' and it is sometimes called a scribal corruption. . . ."

71. So Farrer, as reported by Kermode, *The Genesis of Secrecy*, 34.

told him what to do and in the evening the youth came to him, wearing a linen cloth over his naked body. And he remained with him that night, for Jesus taught him the mystery of the kingdom of God. And thence, arising, he returned to the other side of the Jordan."[72]

The question, of course, is what to make of this story. How does it relate to the present canonical text of Mark? Does it predate the present, canonical Mark? Or was it written after canonical Mark? Is it even authentic?[73] Crossan argues that our present text of Mark censored the above *Secret Mark.* I find his interpretation complex but cogent. He reconstructs the developments thus: "First, canonical Mark is a censored version of *Secret Mark,* so that 130 *Dead Man Raised* [1/2] (i.e., the complex of accounts on that theme found in John 1:1–57; *Secret Mark* lv20–2r11a, and Mark 14:51–52) was present in the first edition of Mark, the one that Clement calls *Secret Mark.* Second, it was probably used in the nude baptismal practice of his community and thereby received an erotic interpretation among some believers. The second-century Carpocratians known to Clement were not, in other words, the only or even the first early Christians with homosexual understandings of such baptisms. Proto-Carpocratians existed, as it were, within the immediate time and place of Mark's first composition. Third, and for that reason, the story was excised completely from the second edition, the one that we call canonical Mark. Fourth, I think that process happened very swiftly and that both editions may well have been done by Mark himself. Fifth, that censorship not only excised the story, it dismembered it, so that the miraculous raising devolved into Mark 16:1–8 within 275 *The Empty Tomb* [2/1] (complex of material) and the nocturnal initiation devolved into Mark 14:51–52 within 130 *Dead Man Raised* [1/2]. Such dismemberment indicates the censorship's strategy of making the story look like a pastiche rather than an excision from canonical Mark. Sixth, all three 'versions' continued in existence, so that, at least in Alexandria around the year 200 C.E., there was a *Secret Mark,* a canonical Mark, and an erotic Mark. Seventh, and finally, *Secret Mark* must have been important in the baptismal liturgy, or the simplest solution would have been to destroy it completely."[74]

---

72. M. Smith, *Secret Gospel,* 445–53. Cited in Crossan, *The Historical Jesus,* 329.

73. Quesnell, "The Mar Saba Clementine: A Question of Evidence," challenges its authenticity, thinks it a forgery. Neirynck, "La fuite," 33–66, thinks that the author of *Secret Mark* has brought together all occurrences about the young man (*neaniskos*) throughout the Synoptic gospels. Meier, *A Marginal Jew,* 123, against Crossan, judges not only *Secret Mark,* but all the apocryphal gospels to be patristic documents. In the passage cited above, it does seem that the story of the rich man who had kept the commandments and whom Jesus loved (10:17–22) has been extensively reworked. Perhaps *Secret Mark* has also reworked the brief references to the linen-clothed fellow in Mark 14 and the white-robed messenger at the empty tomb. Yet, that hardly explains how they came to be in canonical Mark in the first place. Above I follow Crossan.

74. Crossan, *The Historical Jesus,* 329–30. See *Four Other Gospels,* and *The Cross That Spoke,* 283. Koester, "History and Development of Mark's Gospel," first offered the thesis that canonical Mark was derived from Secret Mark.

Be that as it may, what significance does the naked runaway have in the present text of Mark? Even if he comes from the erotic milieu of *Secret Mark*, why does Mark bother to include him? "The discourse teases us with bits and pieces of a story about a *neaniskos* [young man] that has not been told to us and that therefore we can never fully understand. We may guess at what lies behind the veil, which is a reasonable response to a veil. Some interesting guesses have been made as to what lies behind the *neaniskos* veil, but the veil itself is never lifted or torn asunder in the narrative."[75] In effect, Mark has hidden the naked boy behind an overly-clothed story that prevents anyone from catching a glimpse of fleshy substance. But Mark has been doing that all along. Cameo characters pop into the story, only to be withdrawn immediately. We can remember the woman who anointed Jesus, but we do not know her name. Mark never told us the name of Jairus' little daughter. The healed usually just go on home once they have been healed. And here a naked youth, a follower of Jesus (συνηκολούθει αὐτῷ), runs away, shorn of all protective images of selfhood and social position. All Jesus' followers disappear from the scene. This young man probably went on home too, like most of the others.

The Sanhedrin Trial
14: 53–65

[53] They led Jesus off to the high priest; and all the chief priests and the elders and the scribes assembled there. [54] Peter had followed him at a distance, right into the high priest's palace, and was sitting with the attendants warming himself at the fire.

[55] The chief priests and the whole Sanhedrin were looking for evidence against Jesus in order to have him executed. But they could not find any. [56] Several, indeed, brought false evidence against him, but their evidence was conflicting. [57] Some stood up and submitted this false evidence against him, [58] "We heard him say, 'I am going to destroy this Temple made by human hands, and in three days build another, not made by human hands.' " [59] But even on this point the evidence was conflicting. [60] The high priest then arose before the whole assembly and put this question to Jesus, "Have you no answer to that? What is this evidence these men are bringing against you?" [61] But he was silent and made no answer at all. The high priest put a second question to him saying, "Are you the Christ, the Son of the Blessed One?" [62] "I am," said Jesus, "and you will see the Son of man seated at the right hand of the Power and coming with the clouds of heaven." [63] The high priest tore his robes and said, "What need of witnesses have we now? [64] You heard

---

75. Fowler, *Let the Reader Understand*, 216, who notes appreciatively the discussion in Kermode, *The Genesis of Secrecy*, 49–73, on "The Man in the Macintosh and the Boy in the Shirt."

*the blasphemy. What is your finding?" Their verdict was unanimous: he
deserved to die.*

*[65]And some began to spit on him, and to cover his face, and to strike him,
saying to him, "Prophesy!"[76] And the attendants struck him too.*

The first paragraph of this account of Jesus' confrontation is constructed
by Mark to set his theological stage.[77] Mark's concern is not to present an
eye-witness narrative about the legal proceedings to which Jesus was subjected, and indeed there are many discrepancies between the trial he outlines
and the procedures mandated in Jewish law. Debates about whether the trial
was legal in Jewish law are not then to the point. Mark was not there and
did not know the exact chain of events. If indeed the trial was held as
reported in Mark, then Mack's conclusion that it was a kangaroo court is
probably correct.[78]

The setting draws together in counterpoint the two parties who confront
and judge Jesus, the full assembly of religious authorities and his own disciples. Jesus is led to the high priest and Peter follows right into the high
priest's palace. The authorities play the role of unjust judges, arresting Jesus
and submitting him to trial and sentencing. Peter is associated with their
proceedings not only as an observer, but also as witness to and judge of

---

76. Following the more literal RSV.

77. Donahue, *Are You the Christ?* 102: "Marcan activity in the trial narrative can be
summarized briefly. He takes over traditions from the early Church's exegetical use of
the Old Testament and works them into a narrative of the formal trial of Jesus before the
Sanhedrin. This narrative then becomes the focus of theological concerns and the culmination of the interest in the fate of Jesus. The two main theological concerns are the
preoccupation with the temple which is paramount after chapter 11, and the Christological
question of who Jesus is, which is under the veil of secrecy throughout the gospel." See
Crossan, *The Cross That Spoke,* 45: "Donahue has argued most persuasively that Mark
himself created the process before the Jewish spiritual authorities for several important
reasons. First, Mark's juxtaposition of the witness of Jesus in 14:64 with the denial of
Peter in 14:66–72 is a graphic demonstration of the twin options confronting persecuted
Christians. And such persecuted people, as we know from 'with persecutions' in Mark
10:30, were very much in view in that Gospel. Second, the twin processes model the twin
situations foretold in 13:9: 'They will deliver you up to councils; and you will be beaten
in synagogues; and you will stand before governors and kings for my sake, to bear
testimony before them.' Third, but here I disagree with Donahue's details, it is 'false' to
claim that Jesus said he would destroy the temple, said in other words that parousia and
catastrophe were coincident. Mark had already gone to great trouble to separate Jesus'
prophecies of those two events in 13:14–20 ('such tribulation') and 13:24–27 ('after that
tribulation') with a warning against false parousia prophets in 13:21–23. He now attributes
such accusations to false and self-contradictory witnesses, as later he will attribute them
to mocking passersby at the Crucifixion in Mark 15:29. Fourth, the major titles of 'Christ'
and 'Son of God' in 14:63 are subsumed into that of 'Son of Man' in 14:64. In other
words, Mark has doubled the process into two distinct trials for theological reasons that
go to the very heart of his Gospel, but 'any attempt to find the historicity of the events
surrounding the death of Jesus must, in the future, renounce the Marcan trial as its principal
source' " (Donahue, *Are You the Christ?* 239).

78. See Mack, *A Myth of Innocence,* 293–94.

Jesus' career, for he also is questioned and forced to render his own judgment. The truth of the matter is found neither in the evil intent of the authorities nor in the good intentions of the disciples. It is obvious that Mark is painting the Sanhedrin as false judges, for they were looking for evidence to execute him.[79] But Peter comes off little better, despite being a follower of Jesus. Within his deluded perspective and with his hopes for a different, more glorious outcome, Peter is incapable of true witness and is already oriented toward denying Jesus. That has been the constant description of Peter and the disciples throughout the gospel. His courage is undoubted, for he does not simply flee but boldly follows Jesus right into the lion's den. He sits there, warming himself at the fire with the Temple attendants. Here two parallel trials are taking place, one inside and one outside.

In Mahāyāna thinking, the wisdom of awakening is beyond both evil and good, for both are seen as human constructs (*saṃskṛta*) in the service of self. What is needed is neither blind affirmation of establishment norms nor bold attacks against them, but conversion to the otherness of Abba, apart from all imagined realities. The authorities imagine Jesus to be a threat to true religion and thus want to eliminate him. Peter imagines Jesus to be an empirical messiah leading on to glory and thus already has disassociated himself from Jesus. Both the Sanhedrin and Peter are engaged in lying, whether they see Jesus as a dangerous rebel or as the expected messiah. One's viewpoint is not the issue, for Jesus has not come to give a viewpoint, but to issue a call for conversion. Psalm 27: 12 says that "false witnesses have arisen against me." In the event, both the Sanhedrin and Peter render that false witness.[80]

The Sanhedrin seeks evidence, i.e., two agreeing witness against Jesus (ἐζήτουν . . . μαρτυρίαν), but cannot find any two who agree (καὶ οὐχ ηὕρισκον). The false charge they come up with, that Jesus has said he will destroy the Temple, reflects chapter 13: 2, where Jesus says that the Temple will indeed be destroyed.[81] That statement is the beginning of the eschatologi-

---

79. Mack, *Myth,* 293: "The search for witnesses was used to scandalize the proceedings. Specifically, since Jewish law required that two witnesses agree, the failure to produce agreement meant that the trial was illegal. The ploy was doubly shrewd [on Mark's part], for witnesses who did not agree would be false witnesses, or accusers only. Because their accusations were false, Jesus should have been declared innocent."

80. Donahue, "Temple, Trial, and Royal Christology," 66, points out that "the parallels between the Wisdom of Solomon and the Passion Narrative are striking. In the Wisdom of Solomon the enemies lie in wait for the righteous man (2: 12) whose ways are strange (2: 15); he boasts that God is his father (2: 16); he is tested with insults and torture (2: 19) and condemned to a shameful death (2: 20). Nonetheless, the righteous sufferer will stand with great confidence in the presence of those who accuse him (5: 1–2); when they see him (cf. Mk 14: 62) they will be shaken with fear and amazed (cf. Mk 15: 5; 16: 6, 8); at his death he will be numbered among the sons of God (Wis 5: 5; cf. Mk 15: 39)." The contrast is between the wisdom of Jesus, who is accused, and the delusion of his accusers. See also, Donahue, *Are You the Christ?* 72–73, on the Markan development of false witnesses.

81. Crossan, *The Historical Jesus,* 357: "One should not, Mark insists, believe either false witnesses or mocking enemies [who repeat the charge in 15:29–30]. But all of that

cal discourse, about the time beyond time, about the ultimate truth that renders all conventions dependently co-arisen and thus transient. But here the charge reduces eschatological judgment about substituting one kind of temple for another. The temple made by hands (τὸν ναὸν τοῦτον τὸν χειροποίητον) is clearly the historical Temple institution, while the temple not made by hands is perhaps a cipher, without a clear referential analogue.[82] There are many riddles the Markan Jesus spreads about in this story, which should "encourage us to take the temple references of 14:58 and 15:29 as riddles worth serious consideration. Because the narrator gives no clear solution to the temple riddle, perhaps we can fairly say that the challenge represented by the riddle is more important to the narrator than a definitive solution."[83] Mark is telling kōans again: if you can sort it out on a gut level, you awaken to the meaning—not just of the riddle, but of your own original emptiness. Some interpret the temple not made with hands as the community of the faithful. The issue then becomes what it means to be a member of such a community. The only models left in the narrative, except Peter, have left the scene. How then could it be that Christians have now replaced the old institutions with their own institution? Rather, what is suggested is a community of those who are awakened to the ultimate meaning of Abba, not subject to human construction (ἄλλον ἀχειροποίητον), and who concretize the kingdom in their everyday lives.[84]

---

intensive damage control in Mark 13–15 simply underlines the fact that certain Christian circles, first, believed Jesus had said or done something concerning his destruction of the Temple and, second, interpreted that as the conjunction of siege and parousia in 70 C.E." Crossan thinks the root of that belief was found in Mark 11:15–19, where Jesus symbolically destroys the temple and its activities. Perhaps that is the case, but I do not think so. First, Jesus' temple action seems to me more of a rejection of the temple usurpation of ultimate meaning—to be emptied and negated, not destroyed (or cleansed). Second, a broader and more available source can easily be found in the group bias of any alienated (or not so alienated) community vis-á-vis other groups. The need for victory, so evident in Mark's portrayal of the disciples, must indeed have characterized Mark's contemporary Christians, and the victories could be over other peoples and their prized institutions. But note Juel, *Messiah and Temple,* 55–58, who argues that the charge that Jesus will destroy the temple is ironically true for Mark's readers, both at the mocking scene at the crucifixion and at the trial, for Mark clearly polemicizes against the temple throughout the narrative.

82. Donahue, *Are You the Christ?* 106.1, notes that the contrast between "made with hands" and "not made with hands" is not found in the Hebrew scriptures, where "made with hands" is used in reference to idols.

83. Fowler, *Let the Reader Understand,* 161.

84. Concurring with Malbon, *Narrative Space,* 112, who argues that the meaning of Jesus' temple metaphor, "presented but once in Mark—and then in a statement falsely attributed to Jesus," is not at all clear. No temple seems favored by Jesus' words, only the "house" of God for all the nations. See 135: "Both John Donahue and Donald Juel have argued that the temple 'not made with hands' (14: 58) signifies the Christian community. The present analysis concurs in significant ways with Donahue's analysis of the 'anti-Jerusalem and anti-Temple polemic which runs through the Gospel,' but diverges from his conclusion that Mark 'brings to a culmination' this polemic by attributing 14: 58 to Jesus as a true statement in reference to the new community. Indeed, the new community is opposed to the old community in Mark; and, indeed, the old community is signaled metaphorically by the 'temple.' But the evidence for the temple 'not made

The authorities see Jesus as claiming to be a supernatural destroyer of the traditions and a builder of a replacement temple. In 13: 26 Jesus did announce in startling images that they will see the son of man coming in the clouds with great power and glory to gather up his chosen from all the earth. And they take this literally, for they fail to differentiate the two truths. They do try to have witnesses testify to what he has in fact said, but they garble it—they can only understand things by clinging to their conventional frameworks, while Jesus has been speaking about a time beyond time, beyond all linear reckoning of time, when all imagined hopes are made desolate. The Sanhedrin takes his words within linear time and clings to their traditions. It is not that they are simply liars and evil persons, but that they cling to traditions as themselves absolute. They misconstrue the three days (8: 31; 9: 31; and 10: 34) of the resurrection predictions to refer to a conventional change of the Temple institution. Despite the fact that the passion predictions were made in private only to the disciples, the Markan false witnesses seem to have an insider's view on the matter, as if they were eavesdropping and could not hear quite clearly enough. In 9: 32, the disciples themselves do not understand what this is all about. Neither does the Sanhedrin. In Acts 6: 13–14 a parallel charge is made against the deacon Stephen: "And they put up false witnesses to say, 'This man is always making speeches against this Holy Place and the Law. We have heard him say that Jesus, this Nazarene, is going to destroy this place and alter the traditions that Moses handed down to us.' The members of the Sanhedrin all looked intently at Stephen, and his face appeared to them like the face of an angel." Yet the core message of Jesus and his followers is not the replacement of one set of traditions with another set, but with the awakening to the emptiness of all traditions, and thus to their dependently co-arisen validity. The charges are false and the prisoner innocent.[85]

---

with hands' as a metaphor for the new community comes not from Mark but from New Testament letters and Qumran documents. It seems likely that the Markan Gospel does suggest a theological response of the Christian community to the crisis of the destruction of the temple; but, on the basis of the entire system of architectural relations as well as the immediate context of 14: 58, it seems unlikely that Mark does so by 'creat[ing] a Christian exegesis of Temple expectations' and by imagining the Christian community as a new temple 'not made with hands.' [See Donahue, "Temple, Trial," 68–69.] But may it not be that the house, which replaces the synagogue and stands in opposition to the doomed temple in Mark, does suggest the early Christian community? With the destruction of the temple (13:2) and the rejection in the synagogue (13:9), the Christian community must come together in 'house churches.' " All those awakened and healed by Jesus are told to go home, for that is where they will find the community of the kingdom, i.e., the church.

85. Tannehill, "Tension in Synoptic Sayings," 150: "The dramatic tension of these events [of the two trials and the crucifixion] is heightened by a series of suggestions of ways in which Jesus might escape. Those inclined to seek such escape from death are enticed to false hopes: then hope is crushed as the ways of escape are closed one by one. Mark's readers must face the conflict between the way of Jesus and their own desire which will make them like the faithful disciples." The innocent Jesus should have been released, but the karmic events take little notice of legal necessities, then and now.

The chief priest demands an answer to the charges, but Jesus remains silent and does not respond at all (ἐσιώπα καὶ οὐκ ἀπεκρίνατο οὐδέν). Indeed, how can one respond to accusations that, not agreeing, are false under Jewish law?[86] But there is more to Jesus' silence, for there is no framework in which any answer can be given within the deluded context of those who cling to absolute conventions. His prediction of resurrection and glory is not an empirical foretelling of linear events. Rather, the resurrection stands as the breakdown of all conventional linear events and the breakthrough to awareness of the complete otherness of ultimate meaning. We are not dealing with a courtroom drama about guilt or innocence, but with the futility of all deluded attempts at self-justification. The Layman Vimalakīrti declared that emptiness has the sound of thunder. Here Jesus' silence stands opposed to the insistence on the absolute validity of fabricated traditions. To answer within that framework would be to acquiesce in that delusion. And so his silence is itself the answer.[87]

But religious personages are hardly ever silenced by silence, for their lives are built upon conventional speech. The question is pressed by the chief priest, "Are you the Christ, the Son of the Blessed One?"[88] In his framework that is the basic question: Do you embody the ultimate? Are you christ? The son of the Blessed One? This last phrase (ὁ υἱὸς τοῦ εὐλογητοῦ) ties in with 1: 11, where the voice from heaven declares that "You are my Son, the Beloved" (σὺ εἶ ὁ υἱός μου ὁ ἀγαπητός). The term "blessed one" is a circumlocution to avoid pronouncing the sacrosanct name of YHWH. Evidently, the chief priest equates being messiah with being the son of the blessed one, and perhaps saw the many candidate messiahs as usurpers of divine status. Thus in his context to claim to be the son of the blessed one is tantamount to blasphemy, for it assails the uniqueness of Yahweh. And that indeed is the bedrock tradition of Judaism, enshrined in the Shema Israel, "Hear Israel, the Lord your God is one."

Jesus' answer ties in with 12: 36 where the christ is the lord even of David, sitting at the right hand of the Lord God, as well as with 13: 26, where the

86. Mack, *Myth,* 294: "Mark used the motif of the false witnesses to create the illusion of a trial and develop a riddle of comparison between two contrasting kingdoms. Naturally Jesus will remain silent when asked to respond to such an accusation, a very clever introduction of the motif of silence before one's accusers."

87. See Nagao, "The Silence of the Buddha and Its Madhyamic Interpretation," on the Buddha's silence upon awakening and the notion of emptiness.

88. Donahue, *Are You the Christ?* 89, on the words "are you" (σὺ εἶ): "Mark uses the formula here as an initial Christological statement that he is about to give meaning and content to the two titles, Son of God and *Christos* which have been used earlier in his gospel (1: 11; 3: 11; 8: 29; 14: 61; 15: 2)." Again, 91: "In 14:62 the veil of secrecy surrounding Jesus which has dominated Mark's Gospel is lifted. . . . Mark is about to make the definitive Christological statement of his gospel." And 93: "In these verses [i.e., 13:6f about false christs, the phrase ἐγώ εἰμι] is a revelational formula, the content of which is not determined. We affirm that in 14:61 Mark uses ἐγώ εἰμι consciously as a revelational formula, the content of which will now be determined by the following verse."

Son of Man comes in the clouds with great power and glory.[89] Jesus' answer
"I am" (ἐγώ εἰμι) means that "that messiah is I," that the expected hope is
realized in his mere presence.[90] Yet, I do not think that Jesus is raising himself
to the exalted status of the expected messiah, but rather emptying that status
by identifying it with his concrete presence.[91] Throughout the gospel he has
been reticent about being messiah. Even at Peter's confession in 8: 29–30
Jesus does not accept the appellation, but enjoins his disciples not to talk
about him. Only now, when he is subjected to the power of the Sanhedrin
and about to suffer and die, does he admit the term, precisely because it is
now shorn of all imagined delusions. This is what the messiah means. Jesus
in Mark is a demythologized messiah. The interrogation has proceeded within
an imagined pattern of understanding about what the messiah means, and it
is within that pattern that he will be condemned. By claiming to be messiah,
Jesus in fact empties it of the conventional images: he stands there powerless

---

89. Donahue, *Are You the Christ?* 140, reports Perrin's explanation in "Mark XIV.62:
The End Product of a Christian Pesher Tradition?" and *Rediscovering the Teachings of
Jesus,* that "there is no pre-Christian Jewish apocalyptic expectation of the Son of Man
coming 'with the clouds,' and . . . the form of 14:62 found in Mark represents the end-
product of early Christian use of the Old Testament."

90. Numerous scholars see this confession of Jesus' messianic identity as the climax
of Mark's narrative. For example see Dibelius, *From Tradition to Gospel,* 182: "What
Mark means to describe in 14:61–63 is that a supernatural mystery flamed in the midst
of all the shame of Jesus and while the criminal was dying his heavenly future was
announced to the world." Donahue, *Are You the Christ?* 16, reports that in *Botschaft und
Geschichte,* 1:249, "Dibelius pictures a community which lives in expectation of the
imminent coming of the Lord, and which saw in his death and resurrection the eschatological event which brought history to a conclusion, and offered to men the promise of
salvation." In more awesome theological terms, Donahue, *Are You the Christ?* 181.1 cites
G. Minette de Tillesse, *Le Secret messianique,* "Le question solennelle du grand prête
et la non moins solennelle réponse de Jésus indiquent que là se trouve, *pour Marc,*
l'aboutissement et le term de tout son évangile. Tout cequi avait précédé tendait vers ce
moment suprême." Also see Donahue, *Are You the Christ?* 149: "A consensus among
virtually all commentators on the scene that the moment of the trial scene culminates in
Jesus' answer *ego eimi* and the saying of 14:62 gives content to the affirmation. Therefore,
the future Son of Man saying of 14:62 becomes a key to an understanding of the scene."

91. Donahue, *Are You the Christ?* 185: "He is the same Jesus about whom the gospel
is written, who suffered and died, but his work is incomplete. The parousia has not come;
it is still awaited. The community will be founded only at the return of Jesus. Therefore
Mark has given a radical eschatological dimension to his gospel." Rather, the eschatological
presence of the kingdom has been announced as present from the very inception of Mark's
narrative. Furthermore, the promise of Jesus' return does not, I think, fit well with the
notion of the parousia, the very term never being mentioned in Mark's text. Jesus'
uncompleted work is carried on in the return to the eschatological everyday of Galilee,
where by practice anyone may awaken to that presence. Eschatology functions in a linear
time flow only for the false prophets of chapter 13; for Mark it signifies the collapse of
all human structures of time and space in the wilderness depths of Jesus' spirituality.
Thus, in a linear time sense, it is not true that "the suffering of Jesus and the meaning
of his life will be clear when he returns" (Donahue, *Are You the Christ?* 181, cf. 178).
If that return is envisaged as already having taken place in Jesus' *going before* his disciples
to Galilee, how can one still await it in the future?

and inglorious. He is a rebutter of religious truth by embodying it in his actual presence. In saying: "and you will see the Son of man seated at the right hand of the Power and coming with the clouds of heaven," he applies to himself *Psalm* 110: 1, "Yahweh declared to my Lord, 'Take your seat at my right hand, till I have made your enemies your footstool,' " and *Daniel* 7: 13, "I was gazing into the visions of the night, when I saw, coming on the clouds of heaven, as it were a son of man. He came to the One most venerable and was led into his presence."[92] Psalm 110 is a royal song, celebrating the victorious enthronement of the king who is promised divine aid to overcome his enemies, for in the latter half of the Psalm the judgment of the Lord seals the victory of the king over his enemies.[93] If indeed the trial scene is a midrash on Psalm 110,[94] it is a most strange midrash, for Jesus is envisaged at the right hand of God in power at precisely the moment when he is most at the mercy of his enemies, whom he does not conquer. His eschatological victory takes place right in the middle of such trials, not in an imagined future. The passage is not to be read merely as irony, wherein the reader gets the point that the characters in the gospel misunderstand. Rather, this is the mother of all paradoxes: Jesus' kingdom is present at the very moment when he is most unlike a king, subjected to the political delusions of his day. The royal imagery does not promise a future comeuppance for the unfaithful, but empties all imagery in the bare figure of one who, saying that he will come seated on the clouds, stands defenseless in court.[95]

The chief priest asks if he is the son of the Blessed One, and Jesus,[96] alluding to *Daniel,* answers that he is the son of man, for his true being as the son of man is the conventional embodiment (*udbhāvanā-saṃvṛti*) of the

---

92. Donahue, *Are You the Christ?* 108: "The details which characterize the coming of the Son of Man—in glory (13:26, 8:38), on the clouds of heaven (14:62), with power (13:26), accompanied by angels (8:35) are peculiar to the Son of Man sayings as they are found in Mark and in the traditions dependent upon him." That is, they are the result of Mark's creative writing.

93. Mowinckel, *The Psalms in Israel's Worship,* 63–65.

94. Donahue, *Are You the Christ?* 173–74.

95. Sheehan, *The First Coming,* 187, notes that the early Christians "believed that when he was raised to heaven, Jesus had been *designated* or appointed for that role [of judge over the living and the dead], but that he would not begin exercising it until the end arrived." The postponement of the endtime is not, however, just a Christian delusion. Rather, the endtime is the dissolution of the reality of chronological time itself, in virtue of which the Markan christology does not move away from the presence of the kingdom to an imagined future, but toward the collapse of time into the very moment of the "now."

96. Humphrey, *He Is Risen,* 124, sees the reaction of the high priest not to Jesus' claim to be messiah, but to his claim to be the Son of the Blessed One. But note Mack, *Myth,* 294: "The charge is blasphemy. Blasphemy was a slander against God, thus it had to be spoken. The high priest underscores the point, 'Why do we still need witnesses? You have heard. . . .' Nevertheless, there is little to be gained in trying to figure out just what it was Jesus said that could have been labeled blasphemy. Popular messiahs did not get charged with blasphemy. Apocalyptic visionaries did not get killed for impiety. Sons of God were not considered profane. So something else is at work." Mack thinks it was Jesus' prior claim to have authority to forgive sins and his consequent breakdown of the religious and social barrier between sinners and the righteous.

already present kingdom. The point is emphasized by the contrast between Daniel and Mark. In *Daniel* the son of man is presented before the One most venerable, Yahweh, while Jesus is here presented before the deluded religious authorities. Jesus' assertion of his messiahship is not the revelation of a supernatural truth about the ordinary Jesus, but a concrete identification of the ground of all truth as worldly convention-only. He is the demythologized messiah, yet the power of such an ordinary presence thunders with the force of eschatological emptiness, at a time beyond time, as in the descriptions of *Daniel.* The final hour has arrived. In 8: 38 Jesus speaks about the coming of the son of man in the glory of the Father with the holy angels. In 13: 26–27, 30 he reiterates that message and announces that these things will have taken place before this generation has passed away. Here he directs his response to the high priest, telling him that he himself will see that coming. The final hour is not a future parousia. It would be stretching a sense of irony to think that Jesus' final revelation of his long-hidden messianic identity was made to the unbelieving high priest who wants him dead. The Markan discourse is here not ironical, but paradoxical and opaque.[97] The decisive moment of Jesus' response is found in the present moment.[98]

And this is what the authorities cannot abide, for it undermines the entire pattern of their understanding. If ultimate meaning is both completely other than conventional truth, and yet embodied in the present moment, then no tradition can be absolute. The chief priest accuses him of blasphemy and asks the Sanhedrin "What is your finding?" Literally, "How does it appear to you?" (τί ὑμῖν φαίνεται), for the whole gospel is about how truth does appear in the world. Jesus' embodiment of a deconstructed messiahship is blasphemy, for he negates the supernatural expectations of the entire tradition, Jewish and Christian. Thus he must appear to them either to be guilty of blasphemy or to be playing his cards right for his eventual victory. They must either condemn Jesus or see the emptiness of their traditions. This is why some began to spit at him,[99] and to cover his face (περικαλύπτειν

---

97. I thus disagree with Perrin, "The High Priest's Question and Jesus' Answer," 92: "If this saying is addressed to the readers of the Gospel, then it makes very real sense—as it does not, incidentally, if it is addressed to the High Priest." If one reads irony into Jesus' response, then indeed it makes sense only to the extrastory reader. But if it is paradox, it makes sense neither to the story's characters nor to the reader.

98. See Via, *The Ethics of Mark's Gospel,* 165–66.

99. Fowler, *Let the Reader Understand,* 199: "In the instant that Jesus is challenged to 'prophesy!' in the story, the reader realizes that Jesus' most significant prophecy in the Gospel, the prediction of his suffering and death, is in the process of being fulfilled in the story, even though no one in the story takes note of such fulfillment. The verbal ambiguity of 'prophesy!' at story level reverberates also at the level of discourse, at least as far back as the Passion prediction in Mark 10: 32–34, and perhaps even further. 'Prophesy!' entices the reader into a moment of far-ranging retrospection and prospection." Note that it is not just that the reader sees the fulfillment of Jesus' passion predictions, for those predictions remain as paradoxical as ever. One is immersed by an ironic insight into a deeper sense of the paradox of the entire story of the Markan Jesus.

αὐτοῦ τὸ πρόσωπον), for primal ignorance covers over (*saṃvṛ*) the presence of truth. And so they pronounce him deserving of the death penalty.

Peter's Witness
14: 66–72

⁶⁶While Peter was down below in the courtyard, one of the high priest's servant-girls came up. ⁶⁷She saw Peter warming himself there, looked closely at him and said, "You too were with Jesus, the man from Nazareth." ⁶⁸But he denied it. "I do not know, I do not understand what you are talking about," he said. And he went out into the forecourt, and a cock crowed. ⁶⁹The servant-girl saw him and again started telling the bystanders, "This man is one of them." ⁷⁰But again he denied it. A little later the bystanders themselves said to Peter, "You are certainly one of them! Why, you are a Galilean." ⁷¹But he started cursing and swearing, "I do not know the man you speak of." ⁷²And at once the cock crowed for the second time, and Peter recalled what Jesus had said to him, "Before the cock crows twice, you will have disowned me three times." And he burst into tears.

Mark's gospel is about how truth is revealed, how it is embodied. Not in religious authorities or in traditions. But not in Christian imaginings either. Peter, being indeed committed to Jesus and following him at great risk into the high priest's courtyard, does not have it within him to break with his version of worldly convention. He too hides from truth and fails to bear true witness to Jesus. He covers (ἐπιβαλὼν) his face and cries, for the verb translated in the Jerusalem Bible as "he burst into" tears is understood by other exegetes as "to cover one's head."[100] The point is dramatic and theological, not merely historical. Just after Jesus' face has been covered and the attendants begin to beat him, the servant girl stared (ἐμβλέψασα αὐτῷ) at Peter's face, and recognized him.[101] He hides his face from her by moving out of her

---

100. Bratcher and Nida, *A Translator's Handbook,* 472, reports that among other interpretations "*he covered his head and wept* is strongly defended by Field (*Notes,* 41–43) with his usual impressive array of supporting evidence; it is accepted by Rawlinson, and has been adopted by Zürich, *Und er verhüllte sich und weinte.*"

101. Meier, *A Marginal Jew,* 231.1, presents an interesting note on Aramaic pronunciation, on the name Yēšûaʻ, the more correct name for Jesus: "I say 'more correct' because the shorter form, Yēšû, comes from the loss . . . of the final Hebrew letter ʻayin. . . The rabbimic literature . . . associates it with the dialect of Galilee. . . . David Noel Freedman has suggested to me that . . . in the first century Jesus of Nazareth would have been called Yēšû by his Galilean neighbors, and only in more formal situations, or perhaps in Jerusalem, would the fuller form Yēšûaʻ have been used. The peculiarities of Galilean pronunciation probably lie behind the caustic remark to Peter in the story of his denial of Jesus in the Passion Narrative (Matt 26:73: 'Truly you also are one of them, for even your speech betrays you'). I say 'probably' because only Matthew focuses on the speech of Peter. Both Mark 14:70 and Luke 22:59 say simply: 'for you are [Luke: he is] a Galilean.' As usual, with his learned scribal tendencies Matthew draws what is probably a correct conclusion from his Marcan source. . . .''

immediate sight. Yet he cannot hide it from himself. The Gospel of Luke makes the point even more insistently by saying that, just after Peter has denied his Lord, "the Lord turned and looked straight at Peter, and Peter remembered the Lord's words" (22: 61). One's face is the manifestation of the inner person, yet here Peter must cover over and hide his inner person, just as the authorities have covered over the face of Christ with spittle, smug in their worldly and conventional ideas.

Just as the high priest pressed his questioning, so too the servant girl again urges her question.[102] She does know who Peter is, for she has recognized his face. The theme is picked up by the bystanders and Peter invokes a curse and swears that he does not know Jesus, speaking ironically but truly. He does not have a clue who Jesus is anymore. His own brave self-identity is on trial, for by following him into the courtyard, he is indeed sharing in Jesus' passion. Just as he swears his denial, Jesus, after his second questioning by the high priest, is accused of blasphemy for telling the plain truth. A curse for the Hebrews was the strongest possible way of expressing divine disapproval, and so Peter is calling God to witness to the truth of his lie. The second crowing of the cock signals the awakening of the dawn: perhaps Peter also begins to awaken, for his accustomed self-identity, which led in 14:31 to his boast to die with Jesus, has been demolished by a servant-girl.[103] He has discovered the emptiness of self (*ātmanśūnyatā*). That is why he weeps, for the loss of his previous life. He is perhaps now ready to follow Jesus back to Galilee.

---

102. Camery-Hoggatt, *Irony in Mark's Gospel,* 172: "In one sense, Peter's agitated behavior is a foil for the behavior of Jesus. Both are on trial. The object of the interrogation is roughly the same: who, after all, is Jesus, and what is the basis of his claim to exercise authority? Peter becomes more agitated as Jesus becomes more silent. There is a sense in which Peter's final disavowal (in v. 71) counterbalances Jesus' ultimate claim to authority as he answers—for the only time—the question of the high priest (in v. 62)."

103. Robbins, *Jesus the Teacher,* 184: "The system of thought and action taught to them by Jesus places them under a charge to save their lives by losing them for Jesus and the gospel. When the disciples fall away, they must all call this system of thought and action to remembrance. Peter begins this process when, finding himself in a situation where he denies any association with Jesus, he remembers Jesus' prediction of his denial, judges his own action as unacceptable and weeps (14: 71–72). From the perspective of the teacher/disciple cycle, Peter has reached a point of consciousness of his own activity whereby he brings the words of Jesus to remembrance, judges his activity according to the system of thought and action taught to him, and responds with the appropriate emotions." I see Peter's weeping as the breakdown of his very selfhood, not just his failure to live up to Jesus' system of thought and action.

15

Jesus' Death as Final Emptying

Trial Before Pilate
15: 1–5

¹First thing in the morning, the chief priests, together with the elders and scribes and the rest of the Sanhedrin, had their plan ready. They had Jesus bound and took him away and handed him over to Pilate.

²Pilate put to him this question, "Are you the king of the Jews?" He replied, "Are you saying it?"¹ ³And the chief priests brought many accusations against him. ⁴Pilate questioned him again, "Have you no reply at all? See how many accusations they are bringing against you!" ⁵But, to Pilate's amazement, Jesus made no further reply.

The early Church knew simply that Jesus had been arrested and executed. He was one of the many "desparecidos," countless throughout history. They did not know the details of just how it had all happened, for they were privy to no official proceedings. What was needed, desperately, was to see the inner meaning of those events, for their outward meaning was bleak indeed. No glory ensued, no angels came to aid the disciples, no group of believers rallied to their aid. Mark's narrative is concerned with these dilemmas, not with the newspaper facts.[2]

---

1. Following Fowler partially, *Let the Reader Understand,* 198: "Consider the brief conversation between Pilate and Jesus in 15:2. The English translation in the RSV reads: 'And Pilate asked him, "Are you the King of the Jews?" And he answered him, "You have said so." ' Ancient Greek texts had no question marks, and the phrasing of a question and a declarative statement in Greek is often identical. Pilate's 'question,' although clearly labeled a question by the narrator, is worded in such a way that it would work perfectly well as a statement of fact: *su ei ho basileus tōn Ioudaiōn.* Moreover, Jesus' 'answer' is worded in such a way that it would work equally well as a question: *su legeis?* To grasp the ambiguities of the Greek, an English speaker needs to read the following translation alongside the RSV's: 'And Pilate asked him, "You are the King of the Jews." And he answered him, "Are you saying so?" ' " I understand the passage as a parrying of questions.

2. For an attempt to reconstruct the historical facts beneath the many textual witnesses,

The light of the dawn (πρωΐ) has come, yet the darkened minds of the story level participants are still unawakened. The authorities have prepared the only plan (συμβούλιον ἑτοιμάσαντες) ever mentioned by Mark, to deliver Jesus to the Roman authority, Pilate, who has the proper authority to pronounce a sentence of execution. This is the operative plan in the passion narrative, not some divine plan according to which Jesus is sentenced to death by the Father in order to satisfy the needs of divine justice. Jesus is caught in the planning of others and dies because of their planning.[3] The authorities cling to devising stratagems, gripped in the blindness of primal ignorance. Pilate asks him if he is king of the Jews. Jesus' brief retort, "Are you saying so?," constitutes an enunciated silence, for again there is no effective response within that pattern of imagined reality. His silence is the silence of ultimate meaning before the hegemony of a false worldly and conventional view of affairs. It is not merely a refusal to deem Pilate worthy of a proper reply, for Jesus likewise remained silent before the Jewish authorities. His only response is to refuse to identify himself as the king of the Jews. "Are you saying so?" (σὺ λέγεις) means that Jesus does not enter into the question at all.[4] Later Christian exegesis saw his reply as ironic because, while Pilate and the Jewish authorities deride his claims to kingship, in fact Jesus is the king, not only of Israel, but of the entire cosmos.[5] Yet Jesus does not accept the title, for he does not function as a king at all, but as the servant of all, as he taught his disciples in 10:22. Indeed, Herod had tried to assume the identity of King of the Jews, and he is depicted as the murderer of the Baptist. Jesus' identity, however, remains ambiguous throughout, for all identities are fabricated from the rich complex of dependently co-arisen factors that cause us to be who we are. They are not genetically imposed or divinely determined. There is no permanent inner self. Jesus reveals who he is by mirroring the presence of Abba by his broken humanity, standing unprotected before the plans and machinations of deluded minds. And so he answers nothing, which makes Pilate marvel and be amazed (ὥστε θαυμάζειν), for Pilate cannot fathom anyone not moving within that same pattern of false consciousness.

---

see Crossan, *The Cross That Spoke.* It is speculative—how could any such reconstruction not be?

3. Illich, *In the Mirror of the Past,* mentions coming to the philosopher Jacques Maritain with the question of how to understand social planning in the traditional framework of Christian virtues. After some confusion and befuddlement, they reached the conclusion that it corresponded to arrogance.

4. Fowler, *Let the Reader Understand,* 198: "Any alert reader of Greek would have perceived that Pilate's question to Jesus is simultaneously the narrator's declaration to the reader and that Jesus' declaration to Pilate is the narrator's question addressed to the reader. The ambiguity of both Pilate's and Jesus' utterances allows the language to work at different levels and in different directions simultaneously."

5. Kelber, *Mark's Story of Jesus,* 82: "Pilate . . . is the first person to call him king (15:2). The crowd which demands the crucifixion is reported to have called him king (15: 12). The soldiers enact a cruel mock scene in which they salute him as king (15:

Realpolitik
15: 6–15

⁶At festival time Pilate used to release a prisoner for them, any one they asked for. ⁷Now a man called Barabbas was then in prison with the rebels who had committed murder during the uprising. ⁸When the crowd went up and began to ask Pilate the customary favor, ⁹Pilate answered them, "Do you want me to release for you the king of the Jews?" ¹⁰For he realized it was out of jealousy that the chief priests had handed Jesus over. ¹¹The chief priests, however, had incited the crowd to demand that he should release Barabbas for them instead. ¹²Then Pilate spoke again, "But in that case, what am I to do with the man you call the king of the Jews?" ¹³They shouted back, "Crucify him!" ¹⁴Pilate asked them, "What harm has he done?" But they shouted all the louder, "Crucify him!" ¹⁵So Pilate, anxious to placate the crowd, released Barabbas for them and, after having Jesus scourged, he handed him over to be crucified.

Who is bound and who is free? Jesus has been handed over and bound by the authorities, yet it is they who are bound by delusion and false planning. A custom intervenes to emphasize the point, for at festival time Pilate is to free a prisoner.[6] In 3: 17 Jesus says that in order to plunder a strong man's house one must first bind him. There the reference is to Satan, yet here it is the silent and free presence of truth that is bound, rendered mute, and held prisoner. Official religion, when it takes itself as absolute, binds up and covers over truth.

Yet the custom is to be observed, for Pilate knows that Jesus has been handed over to him because of the envy or jealousy (διὰ φθόνον) of the chief priests,[7] who then incite the crowd to ask for the freedom of the murderer

---

16–20). The temple authorities . . . ridicule him as king (15: 31–32). . . . [They] speak and enact the truth in ignorance and infamy."

6. Crossan, *The Historical Jesus,* 390, holds that Mark created this Barabbas incident, for such a custom to release anyone the crowd demanded goes against all known practices of Roman governors, and Pilate was considered a rather cruel governor. Rather, it symbolically presents the choice between Jesus and a bandit.

7. Humphrey, *He Is Risen,* 138, notes parallels to the *Book of Wisdom* 2: 21–22, 24, where it is said: "They were led astray, for their wickedness blinded them, and they did not know the secret purposes of God, nor hope for the wages of holiness, nor discern the prize for blameless souls; . . . but through the devil's *envy* entered the world." Humphrey comments: "*Is it only coincidence* that the fundamental motivation of the chief priests is perceived to be 'envy'? That word occurs nowhere else in Mark. It occurs only four times in the entire Old Testament, two of which are in the book of Wisdom. One text is that cited above in Wisdom 2:24; the other is Wisdom 6:23 and is equally suggestive: '. . . envy does not associate with wisdom.' What is coming to pass is the radical choice between the wisdom which is of God, found in Jesus, and the 'envy' which is 'of men' and binding them, driving them into unrighteousness." Barabbas is yet another example of such envy, countering the arrogance of the Roman occupiers by murder.

Barabbas.[8] The plan was to have Jesus executed because he threatened the religious hegemony. So the chief priests want Barabbas freed, despite the fact that he is an insurrectionist and as such threatens the political status quo. He was imprisoned because of an uprising in which murder had been done. Perhaps he belonged to the Sicarii, a band of political rebels.[9] That in itself probably made him popular with the Jews, who had suffered long under the yoke of Rome. When the excited crowd comes to "ask" or "entreat" (αἰτεῖσθαι) Pilate for Barabbas, they mimic the same verbal entreaty Herodias' daughter had used to her mother, "What shall I ask for?" just before she requests the head of the Baptist (6:24, τί αἰτήσωμαι).[10] When Pilate "placates" or "satisfies" the crowd, one hears undertones of sexual pandering: Jesus immediately becomes the object of sadistic torture by the entire Roman cohort.[11]

In choosing Barabbas, the crowd, encouraged by the chief priests, elect a path that in fact leads to the war with Rome and the destruction of the Temple.

---

8. Fowler, *Let the Reader Understand,* 110: "The other instance of a parenthetical comment introduced by *hostis* is in 15:7: 'And among the rebels in prison, *who had committed murder in the insurrection,* there was a man called Barabbas.' The parenthesis is intriguing in that it seems to allude to portions of Mark's story that have been submerged or suppressed. After encountering 15:7 we may well ask: What rebels? What insurrection? This verse lends support to readers such as Fernando Belo who see in Mark's discourse an 'erased' narrative about Zealotic insurgency against Rome. Jesus' disciples often advocate the Zealot point of view, Belo says, while Jesus distances himself from this perspective but perhaps not enough to avoid being crucified as a Zealot. (Belo, *A Materialist Reading,* 157, 224). Mark, the master of indirection, may tantalize us with traces of submerged or erased narratives."

9. Myers, *Binding the Strong Man,* 380: "Mark describes Barabbas in a manner that had concrete historical signification: as a Sicarius terrorist. Mark states matter of factly that he belonged to a cadre of imprisoned rebels 'who had committed murder in the insurrection.' . . . This is the only time Mark uses the explicit language of revolution, . . . and it may be that Mark is appealing to reader-recognition of a specific person or event, for there was constant insurrectionary activity in Jerusalem during the period. What Mark calls 'murder' (cf. *phonos,* 7.22) would have been characteristic of the modus operandi of the Sicarii, or 'dagger men,' who were infamous for their stealth in political assassination. Thus Mark's narrative concern here is to dramatize the choice. Jesus and Barabbas each represent fundamentally different kinds of revolutionary practice, violent and nonviolent, both of which have led to a common fate: prison and impending execution."

10. Myers, *Binding the Strong Man,* 381.

11. Hamerton-Kelly, *The Gospel and the Sacred,* 55: "The priests incite the mob to choose Barabbas. Mark rubs our noses in the fact that we prefer the murderer to the man of peace, the sacrificial order to the spirit of God. Pilate tries to withstand the demands of the mob, knowing that Jesus is innocent. He cannot, because his power, like that of the priests, arises out of the mob and must respect its source. And so he sacrifices Jesus to the mob. The text is quite explicit on this; it reads, ὁ δὲ Πιλᾶτος βουλόμενος τῷ ὄχλῳ τὸ ἱκανὸν ποιῆσαι ((15:15). The phrase ἱκανόν ποιῆσαι reflects the Latinism, *satisfacere alicui.* 'To satisfy the mob' means to propitiate it by throwing it a victim. The very language of the text, therefore, shows that it understands the mechanism at work between Pilate and the mob. . . . Pilate is coerced by the mob, like every politician before or since, and has to give it the victim it demands."

It was not Jesus who will destroy the Temple: he is here seen to be innocent of that charge once again. The contrast is drawn between Barabbas, an insurrectionist, and Jesus, who refuses to be identified as the king of the Jews. Jesus' death in the final outcome frees a political prisoner. It is perhaps significant that the name Barabbas means "son of Abba," a name associated with Jesus' title as son of God. He too leaves the scene, his part in the Markan drama ended.

Jesus is handed over to Pilate because the authorities fear he may disrupt the temple institution. They practice a realpolitik which sees the necessity of breaking eggs to make an omelet. Jesus must be sacrificed for the good of the Temple. Yet, clinging to that institution, they experience the complete destruction of the temple in 70 C.E., a fact that clearly was known to Mark and his community. The crowd chooses a revolutionary terrorist over Jesus, for Barabbas represents another version of the same realpolitik. The crowd does not care whether Jesus has done evil or not, and so do not answer Pilate's question, "What harm has he done?" (τί γὰρ ἐποίησεν κακόν). Crucify the ineffectual Jesus. The story character Pilate, on his side, wants to placate the crowd and quell their blood lust, lest a new uprising occur right there during the festival. Jesus is caught in the net of competing delusions, all masquerading as realpolitik. One of the many thousands of innocent persons who dare to speak truth within a context that has already assured its participants that truth is fully known.

Thus Jesus is handed over to suffering. This is not, however, the inevitable consequence of preaching the gospel.[12] Many Christians have followed Jesus' example to the point of martyrdom. Yet, many other Christians do preach that gospel without being arrested or executed. There is no inevitability about the course of human events, for there is no overarching plan that intervenes to direct or rearrange the dependently co-arisen course of events. Only human stratagems, either deluded or wise. In Mark Jesus' suffering comes from his constant emptying of all identity markers, both for himself and for society at large. Even his awareness of ultimate meaning in the silent presence of Abba is itself emptied, and he becomes bereft of all supports for selfhood. "Falsely confessed and falsely accused all his life, Jesus dies a victim of mistaken identity."[13] He is neither the king nor the messiah anyone expected. Yet, his sufferings do not thereby identify him as a different kind of messiah, who will snatch victory from apparent defeat. That version is still an imagined perspective, in light of which Christians may find yet another comforting viewpoint to bolster their own deluded belief in selfhood. Rather, Mark's suffering Jesus undermines all expectations, presenting himself as a question mark to all who read or listen, for the point is not that we really know who

---

12. Against Tolbert, *Sowing the Gospel,* 284: "Suffering, then, is the inevitable consequence of preaching the good news of God's imminent coup d'état in a world now oppressed by power-greedy human tyrants."

13. Kelber, *Mark's Story of Jesus,* 80.

Jesus is, but that we convert our minds from deluded knowing to an awakened awareness that recognizes who Jesus is. And practice the middle path of social reengagement.

Jesus' Royalty
15: 16–22

[16]The soldiers led him away to the inner part of the palace, that is, the Praetorium, and called the whole cohort together. [17]They dressed him up in purple, twisted some thorns into a crown and put it on him. [18]And they began saluting him, "Hail, king of the Jews!" [19]They struck his head with a reed and spat on him; and they went down on their knees to do him homage. [20]And when they had finished making fun of him, they took off the purple and dressed him in his own clothes.

They led him out to crucify him. [21]They enlisted a passer-by, Simon of Cyrene, father of Alexander and Rufus, who was coming in from the country, to carry his cross. [22]They brought Jesus to the place called Golgotha, which means the place of the skull.

After Jesus' trial in the Sanhedrin in verse 14: 65, some had spit on him and beat him, mockingly asking him to play the prophet, i.e., to speak God's truth. Here, in dramatic parallel, the Roman soldiers mock him as a political king, clothing him in royal purple and making him a sadistic crown.[14] All cling to the imagined pattern of false ideas. The Jews know what a prophet is, while the Romans are no less certain what a king is. Jesus leaves the high priest's court as a prisoner, not a prophet. He leaves the Roman praetorium not as a king, but as a condemned man being led to death. Jesus throughout the gospel is unconcerned with the titles others impute to him. He accepts the title of messiah only after redefining it to refer to his quite ordinary person, extraordinary only in the full dimension of his transparent mirroring of Abba. Here he remains silent; he is neither a supernatural prophet nor a heavenly king. The entire passion narrative depicts the sufferings of a human at the mercy of deluded men.

Mark is at work again with rhetorical subtlety, setting up his audience like bowling pins only to knock them down again, and again. "Irony is sophisticated art, a kind of verbal trickery. Sometimes it reflects remarkable subtlety or power. It is not surprising that users of irony themselves tend to be somewhat clever in their dealings with their audiences, setting them up for this or that reaction, then contravening those expectations."[15] Here Mark's

---

14. Tolbert, *Sowing the Gospel,* 279: Tolbert has clearly explained that "the crucifixion scene itself (15:16–39) is rhetorically shaped by blocks of parallel material arranged in a chiastic pattern with the events of the third to the ninth hour (15:25–34) at the center." See 279–88 for her interpretation of the contrasting elements.

15. Camery-Hoggatt, *Irony in Mark's Gospel,* 62.

skill focuses on the identity of Jesus, whom the soldiers hail as king of the Jews. The reader, for whom the issues are of mounting urgency, knows that Jesus is the bearer of the eschatological kingdom, and is led by the force of that awareness to affirm the reality of what the soldiers in their ignorance confess: Jesus is indeed king. Yet she also is aware that Mark is slippery about identifying titles for Jesus, simultaneously affirming them and negating their content. Jesus' ambiguous retort to Pilate: "Are you saying so?" appears to deny that he is any king at all. Yet the reader remembers that he is the son of man who will come in the clouds with great glory and power (13:26), whose words will not pass away (13:31). Jesus' rebuke to Peter in 8:32 distances him from the title of messiah, yet he explicitly accepts that title before the Sanhedrin, elaborating in imagery of great force, proclaiming not only that he is messiah, but that the Sanhedrin itself will see him, as son of man, seated at the right hand of power (14:62). When the rich man addresses Jesus as a good teacher in 10:17, Jesus objects that only God is good, yet from the very first verse of Mark we know that Jesus is God's son. The reader is positioned by these memories of the Markan story to affirm as true what the soldiers say by way of mocking denial, at the very narrative moment when Jesus is most unlike any king imaginable. He is not accompanied by supernatural forces. No angels come to assist him. Mark's affirmation of Jesus' identity is negated by Mark's descriptions of Jesus. No clear insider views of the truth of the matter avail: Jesus remains an unidentified enigma, even when we call him son of God and messiah.

The mocking adulation of Jesus by the soldiers as king at the beginning of his passion ordeal is reflected after his death in the centurion's confession that Jesus is indeed son of God. Yet the point is not to contrast two perspectives, one human and one divine.[16] That is to understand the cosmic and divine as a separate realm apart from the everyday life of humans, to establish a dichotomy between God and humans. The otherness of ultimate meaning is not such a realm. Rather, figured in eschatological symbols and parabolic images, it is the silence beneath and between all words, the otherness signified by every veiling.

Jesus' only assistance in his eschatological hour of trial comes not from the powerful God, but from a nondescript stranger, forced to assist him in the task of carrying his cross to Golgotha. Simon, otherwise unknown, appears precisely as a stranger, a poor fellow whose unlucky lot it was to be pressed into such a disagreeable service. " 'Simon' of *Cyrene* is forced to carry the cross in the absence of 'Simon' called and named Peter by Jesus in *Galilee*."[17] He is a fill-in character, an understudy waiting in the wings. Some scholars speculate that because Simon is identified as the father of Alexander and

---

16. Tolbert, *Sowing the Gospel*, 279: "The pervasive contrast is between events understood only in the limited, distorted view of this generation's human world and events directed toward and informed by the cosmic, divine realm."

17. Heil, *The Gospel of Mark as a Model for Action*, 330.

Rufus, they were known to Mark's community. If that is true, then the only persons to help Jesus during his ordeal were members not of the narrative drama, but of Mark's own community, the ordinary people who have read and understood the inner meaning of the narrative. Simon is yet another of those transparent cameo characters upon whom the reader can project herself.

With Simon of Cyrene and the reader in assistance, Jesus is led to the final place of torment, Golgotha. "Golgotha, naturally enough, is the final Markan geopolitical reference in the present time of the narrative. It is not, however, and significantly, the final geopolitical reference in Mark, being followed by seven geopolitical references that are flashbacks and one that is a flash-forward. In fact, in the final portion of the Markan Gospel (from 13:14 on) geopolitical flashbacks together with flash-forwards dominate present geopolitical references more than three to one. These past and future narrative facts or relations both integrate and extend the Markan story."[18] The story goes on, for in 14:28 and again in 16:7, we learn that Jesus will go before his disciples to Galilee, the place of their everyday lives.[19]

The Crucifixion
15: 23–32

[23]*They offered him wine mixed with myrrh, but he refused it.* [24]*Then they crucified him, and shared out his clothing, casting lots to decide what each should get.* [25]*It was the third hour when they crucified him.* [26]*The inscription*

---

18. Malbon, *Narrative Space,* 34–35.

19. Malbon, *Narrative Space,* 37: "The women at the tomb, and through them the disciples and especially Peter, are not *told* to go to Galilee—a fact usually overlooked, if not contradicted, by most commentators, but apparently observed by one commentator, R. H. Lightfoot, concerning the parallel statement at 14:28. Rather, the return of these Galileans to their homeland is assumed. Lightfoot also recognizes that the proper question to ask in determining the significance of 'Galilee' at 16:7 is 'In what light is Galilee regarded in the entirety of Mark's gospel?' In Galilee Jesus' followers had experienced the authority of teaching and the power of healing in Jesus. From Galilee they had ventured out to foreign regions, witnessing through Jesus' actions the breakdown of barriers—geopolitical, sociological, theological. In Galilee they had often been blind to Jesus—to his walking on the sea, to his multiplying the loaves, to his steadfastness in taking the way from Galilee to Jerusalem, from life to death. To this Galilee they must return. Jesus has been killed, but their lives go on. They have left everything to follow Jesus; they have only Galilee to which to return. The surprising and yet familiar thing, the promising thing, is that Jesus 'who was crucified' is going before them, 'going to Galilee,' going where they must go—home, to begin life anew. 'There,' the Markan young man tells them, 'you will see. . . .' " Yet, I think the significance of Galilee lies not only in recounting the events of Mark's narrative past about what happened there, in contrast with which Galilee is all they have left. Rather, Galilee becomes a spatial symbol inviting Jesus' disciples to reengage in their original lives by now 'seeing' the emptiness of all imagined ideas of seflhood and power. In that lies the effectiveness of their careers as disciples.

giving the charge against him read: "The King of the Jews." [27]And they crucified two bandits with him, one on his right and one on his left.[20]

[29]The passers-by jeered at him; they shook their heads and said, "Aha! So you would destroy the Temple and rebuild it in three days! [30]Then save yourself: come down from the cross!" [31]The chief priests and scribes mocked him among themselves in the same way with the words, "He saved others, he cannot save himself. [32]Let the Christ, the king of Israel, come down from the cross now, for us to see it and believe." Even those who were crucified with him taunted him.

Mark depicts Jesus' crucifixion in terms of Psalm 22, which describes the sufferings of the just.[21] Verse 18 says: "They divide my garments among them and for my raiment they cast lots." The scene is one of complete abandonment, naked and bereft of friends and supporters. Throughout the gospel, "Jesus' garments have functioned symbolically to indicate his power or state of being: touching the hem of his garments was sufficient to heal those with faith (5: 27–31; 6: 56); his garments became intensely white beyond the power of any human bleach as he was transfigured (9: 3); and just prior to dividing his garments, the soldiers had replaced them with purple robes to mock him as king (15: 16–20). His garments have been used, then, to symbolize who Jesus is and what state he is in (i.e., powerful healer, transfigured divine son, mocked human king). . . . Hence clothes in the Gospel of Mark generally bear emblematic connotations."[22] To strip Jesus of his garments is then to strip him of his previous identities. He hangs alone, the naked victim of sadistic torture, without any identity markers or any effective persona.[23] Again, Psalm 69: 21 says, "when I was thirsty they gave me vinegar to drink." Here they try to give Jesus wine mixed with myrrh, while in verse 36 they give him a sponge dipped in vinegar. Jesus dies on a sour note, forsaken, fulfilling nobody's cherished expectancies.

In chapter 10: 35–40, James and John had requested the positions on Jesus' right and left hand in his expected kingdom. Here, as it turns out, those for whom that place is reserved are two condemned bandits, who also revile Jesus. Yet, their positioning does not signify that the crucifixion itself is a glorious event, with Jesus enthroned paradoxically as king.[24] The cross remains a place of dereliction, not a logically absurd identification of victory

---

20. Some texts add a verse 28 similar to Luke 22: 37: "And the text of the scripture was fulfilled that says: He was taken for a criminal" (Is 53:12).

21. Mack, *A Myth of Innocence,* 257: ". . . the betrayal by friends at the meal, Jesus' silence at the trial, the mockery of the soldiers, and the distribution of Jesus' clothes were . . . motifs taken from the Psalms."

22. Tolbert, *Sowing the Gospel,* 280.

23. Tolbert, *Sowing the Gospel,* 280: "The dividing up of Jesus' human clothes at his death indicates figuratively his departure from the human world."

24. Tolbert, *Sowing the Gospel,* 32: "Later in the midst of the crucifixion, all the disciples having fled, the reader meets 'those for whom it has been prepared,' the robbers, not James and John, and the reader also realizes clearly that in the Gospel of Mark, despite what the disciples might wish, Jesus' coming 'in his glory' is Jesus crucified on a cross."

with defeat. There is no empirical victory at all, no grasping of triumph from the midst of defeat.[25]

Often in the gospel Jesus has been asked to give validating signs, and always he has refused, for there are no such signs that can be given. The kingdom is not validated by producing proofs and authenticating credentials. The truth of Jesus' message is not a supernatural something imported from another realm, but the very humanness of awareness of Abba as completely other and a commitment to the kingdom. The signs are the fruits of true practice, not wondrous events that might make people gasp in amazement. Once again at the end, both passers-by and authorities demand a supernatural sign, so that they might see and believe (ἵνα ἴδωμεν καὶ πιστεύσωμεν): they want to see Jesus effect an empirical reversal of his crucifixion.[26] They demand that, since he is messiah and king of Israel, he live up to that title and demonstrate his eschatological status.[27] That he somehow would raise himself above being human. Their mocking challenge echoes the mocking of the righteous in the *Book of Wisdom* 2:17–18: "Let us see if his words are true, and let us test what will happen at the end of his life; for if the righteous man is God's son, he will help him, and will deliver him from the hand of his adversaries." But no sign is given, for faith does not come within the imagined pattern of demanding signs.[28] His eschatological kingdom is a kingdom of nobodies, and he is their nobody monarch.

---

25. Hamerton-Kelly, *The Gospel and the Sacred,* 56: "Jesus rejects the Davidic interpretation of the Messiah conclusively by failing to come down from the cross in response to the challenge, 'Let the Messiah the King of Israel come down from the cross, so that we might see and believe' (15:32)."

26. Donahue, *Are You the Christ?* 197: "Both Taylor (*Mark,* 591) and Lohmeyer (*Markus,* 344) have remarked that the intention of the mockers in 15:29–30 (come down from the cross) is that Jesus perform an eschatological miracle which would save himself and enable them to believe."

27. Donahue, *Are You the Christ?* 201: "The title given by the high priest in 15:32 is primarily religious, not political, and in its religious sense addresses Jesus as the king of the eschatological Israel. In this case Mark is again putting a false eschatology on the lips of Jesus' opponents."

28. Tolbert, *Sowing the Gospel,* 99: "The irony of the Markan crucifixion scene is but one further demonstration of the unified point of view shared by narrator and reader." Also Fowler, *Let the Reader Understand,* 156: "The double irony of 15:32 is unmistakable. The high priests, with the scribes, 'mock' *(empaizō)* Jesus as 'the Christ, the King of Israel,' and thus they speak ironically, mouthing a title for Jesus that they believe to be false. Ironically, however, in Mark's Gospel this title describes exactly who Jesus is. The verbal ironies spoken insincerely at the story level are recognized by the narrator and narratee as—ironically—true statements. . . ." Yet, I do not think that any description tells the reader exactly who Jesus is, even though the reader has been informed from the very first verse of Mark that Jesus is christ and son of God. Any point of view misses the focus of the gospel on a conversion of consciousness to the presence of the kingdom, without which no verbal point of view suffices. Mark's irony not only provides the reader with inside information the story's characters sadly lack, but doubles back on the reader to render even that information opaque and unsatisfactory. Just as no sign shall be given, so no viewpoint is worth a tinker's damn, unless one awaken to the presence of the kingdom. In Mahāyāna all views are emptied of essential reference, only to be reclaimed as dependently co-arisen.

The mocking of the passers-by echoes the false charges made at Jesus' Sanhedrin trial, that he would destroy the temple made with hands and rebuild it in three days. This is usually taken in a connative sense: you who would destroy, who tries to destroy. Literally, however, the verb forms are present tense: you who are destroying the temple and building it again.[29] Yet another ironic identity marker for Jesus, for his persecutors seem to be giving him another title: "the one who destroys" (ὁ καταλύων) the temple and builds it (again) in three days."[30]

The wine offered in verse 22, intended to lessen his pain, is turned to vinegar in verse 36, marking for Mark the souring of all hopes for empirical deliverance. Jesus refuses the first offer, but apparently accepts the second. The clamor to crucify him in verse 14a is fulfilled in verse 37, where he cries out in a loud voice and dies. The division of his garments in verse 24b is mirrored in the unclothing of the holy of holies when the temple curtain is torn asunder.

Jesus' Death
15: 33–39

[33]*When the sixth hour came there was darkness over the whole land until the ninth hour.* [34]*And at the ninth hour Jesus cried out in a loud voice, "Eloi, Eloi, lama sabachthani?" which means, "My God, my God, why have you forsaken me?"* [35]*When some of those who stood by heard this, they said, "Listen, he is calling on Elijah."* [36]*Someone ran and soaked a sponge in vinegar and, putting it on a reed, gave it to him to drink saying, "Wait! And see if Elijah will come to take him down."* [37]*But Jesus gave a loud cry and breathed his last.* [38]*And the veil of the Temple was torn into two from top to bottom.* [39]*The centurion, who was standing in front of him, had seen how he had died, and he said, "In truth, this man was son of God."*

The darkness covering the land (σκότος ἐγένετο ἐφ᾽ ὅλην τὴν γῆν) signifies the eschatological abandonment of all support, the final rupture of conventional planning, whether the scheming of the authorities or the devices of the disciples.[31] The prophet Amos (8:9) describes the eschatological day as follows: "On that Day—declares the Lord Yahweh—I shall make the sun go down at noon and darken the earth in broad daylight." Jesus' dying is itself the eschatological hour, the time of final revelation. Yet, that revelation manifests only the darkening of imagined realities; to this point there is

---

29. Donahue, *Are You the Christ?* 197.

30. Bratcher and Nida, *Handbook,* 488. "The whole phrase is in the nature of a title, and to be taken as a vocative, in apposition to the subject of the verb 'save thou' in the next verse."

31. Note also that the presence of darkness implies that the moment of Jesus' death is not a time when the seeds of the gospel can grow.

nothing more. Heretofore, Jesus has been rejected by family, friends, and followers. Now, his rejection is extended even to God, for there is now nothing whatever to cling to, not even God. This cry of abandonment is Jesus' last word: one cannot count even on God to bring about empirical reversal to the dependently co-arisen course of human living. Commitment to truth does not ensure false victory, and no sign shall be given.

The bystanders, fulfilling the role of the departed disciples, hear Jesus' last words and mistake their import. Jesus has quoted the beginning of Psalm 22, which depicts the sufferings and final rescue from suffering of the virtuous person. It begins: "My God, my God, why have you deserted me?" and goes on to describe the anguish and pain of unjustly inflicted suffering. But it does not stop there, for it continues to recount just how Yahweh comes to the aid of his servant: "For he has not despised nor disregarded the poverty of the poor, has not turned away his face, but has listened to the cry for help" (verse 24). Some interpreters, remembering how this Psalm turns out, think that in Jesus' mouth it has the same meaning, that it does not represent a cry of dereliction, but would have been clearly understood by all bystanders to refer not only to the first verse of the psalm, but to its entirety, including the more fulsome outcome. Yet, that is unlikely, for in Mark the bystanders do not even understand the first verse properly.[32] They do not understand it as the first verse of Psalm 22, for they think he is referring to Elijah, not Eloi (my God).[33] Thus even at the very last moment of his life, they look for yet another empirical sign, the arrival of the rescuer Elijah, to show them whether or not Jesus is really the son of God. But Jesus, empty of all support and all religious comfort, cries out with a loud voice and dies, severing any

---

32. Tolbert, *Sowing the Gospel,* 283: "Some have argued that the whole psalm is being called to mind, and consequently the cry should be interpreted as triumph over desolation. Such a view, however, does little justice to the words as they stand. Had Mark wanted Jesus to express triumph or confidence from the cross, his final words could have been shaped quite differently, as in fact they are in the Gospels of Luke and John."

33. Fowler, *Let the Reader Understand,* 109: "The cry to God *(Elōi)* is misheard as a cry to Elijah *(Elias),* the prophet of old who folklore said was the rescuer of those in distress. Thus, this *ho estin* [i.e., 'which means'] translation is quite distinctive in the Gospel in that the reader is made to understand exactly what the strange Aramaic words signify, while the characters in the story demonstrate clearly that they thoroughly misunderstand the very same words. No one but the reader understands Jesus' dying words! In a profound sense, the only genuine witness to the crucifixion in Mark is the reader." Again, 122: "Only the reader, who has been given in a parenthetical comment the true meaning of the cry ('My God, My God, why have you forsaken me?'), truly hears and sees what happens. Those in the story do not really see or hear; they are really outsiders. We who are outside the story, separated from the scene by time and space, do see and hear and are made insiders by virtue of the insight that is given to us by the narrator." Yet Mark's story is not the recounting of a mythic tale from a past golden age, *in illo tempore,* and the point is not only to realize that one is in possession of privileged information. Rather, realizing what the import of Jesus' words are, the reader is thrown into shock: if Jesus is abandoned, what about her? Insider views are foisted on the reader by Mark to trigger confusion and the breakdown of all assumptions of selfhood.

hope that God is really listening to his cry. No sign shall be given to this adulterous generation. Mark's readers perhaps would have understood the entire Psalm. Yet the main point in Mark is that Jesus in fact dies on the cross and neither Elijah nor God comes to his rescue.[34] His cry of desolation ties in with the voice crying out in the wilderness (1: 3), for his dying is itself the sacrilege that makes desolate the temple (13: 14). It is a sacrilege (βδέλυγμα), for the attempt to eliminate Jesus' embodiment of ultimate awareness is detestable to Yahweh. It is a desolating sacrilege (βδέλυγμα τῆς ἐρημώσεως) for it empties all conventional significance, both the machinations of Jesus' persecutors and the expectations of his disciples, just as Jesus' wilderness (ἔρημος) experiences signal the dropping of all conventional realities in the face of the silence of ultimate meaning. Verses 26 and 32 picture Jesus ironically as King of the Jews. Now verses 33–34 darken the inner hope that he might really turn out to be a king. Instead he dies forsaken and desolate.

Witnessing that abandonment, the centurion confesses that "this man indeed was son of God." "The christological confession on the lips of the centurion (15:40) echoes the divine designation of Jesus (1:11; 9:7). This is the first use of the title on human lips (the title is used by demons in 1:24 and 5:7), and its narrative location is crucial. The human confession that Jesus is Son of God comes only at the end of the narrative, only in the shadow of the cross."[35] Previously, the title has been unacceptable because of its "linkage to miracle activity. The title is consistently suppressed within the narrative until it may be properly linked to the death of Jesus on the cross (15:39)."[36] Here, where no miracles happen, the centurion, not a disciple, sees the truth that Jesus, dying in abandonment of all self-support, is the son of God.

Nevertheless, the title itself remains ambiguous, meaning either that Jesus is indeed God's very son, or merely that he is a godly son, a good man.[37] In

---

34. Tolbert, *Sowing the Gospel,* 287: "What is separation from family and betrayal or denial by friends in comparison to that timeless moment of nothingness when God's Son is deserted by God?" Jesus' eschatological dying is then a time beyond linear time, signaling not the actual end of time, but the possibilities of every present moment. It is not a cosmic denouement, but an emptying of every expected denouement.

35. Broadhead, *Teaching With Authority,* 184.

36. Broadhead, *Teaching With Authority,* 90.

37. Fowler, *Let the Reader Understand,* 202–09, has an intriguing discussion on the ambiguity of the centurion's confession. First, presenting the reasoning of Colwell ("A Definite Rule") and Harner ("Qualitative Anarthrous Predicate Nouns"), he points out the grammatical ambiguity of the phrase itself, for Mark's anarthrous phrase υἱὸς θεοῦ (not ὁ υἱὸς θεοῦ) can signify either *the* son of God or simply *a* son of God, and concludes that Mark's "phrasing of the centurion's utterance studiously avoids clarity. Therefore, we must admit that we do not know with any degree of certainty what the centurion, at story level, is saying" (206). Second, Fowler questions the sincerity of the character of the centurion, who is probably the officer in charge of "a ruthless, callous execution squad" (207), who have mocked Jesus with honorific titles just before. Why should we trust his word? Third, on the discourse level, scholars see his confession as the denouement of the Gospel because of their own response to the entire narrative, spying in the centurion's

a Mahāyāna reading, it is because Jesus is not God's very son that he indeed is God's very son. That is, because in his simple humanity he perfectly mirrors Abba, Jesus is confessed as son of God and savior. It is only by negating the imagined pattern, with all its notions, however orthodox or however mistaken, that one can confess Jesus' conventional identity to be itself a revealer of the hidden God.

Yet a further Markan ambiguity asserts itself, for the centurion utters his confession when he has seen how (οὕτως) Jesus died. What is there in Mark's description about Jesus' death that suggests anything but abandonment? He cries out and breathes his last breath—that is all. Perhaps a clue is found in the phrase that the centurion "was standing in front of him" (ὁ παρεοτηκὼς ἐξ ἐναντίας αὐτοῦ), for the term αὐτοῦ is also ambiguous. It can mean, as usually translated, in front of Jesus, observing his dying. Or it can refer to its most immediate antecedent, the temple, and mean that the centurion was facing the temple itself.[38] Its very ambiguity suggests that he simultaneously witnessed both the splitting of the temple veil and Jesus' dying.

The splitting of the temple curtain signifies that Jesus' final emptiness in his death has collapsed the divide between the supernatural expectations of the Gospel actors, from high priests to disciples, and brought all down firmly to the dependently co-arisen world.[39] It is a collapsing of any double-decker world view. "The curtain separating the Holy Place from the Holy of Holies, then, signifies the barrier between the human world and the divine."[40] In dying Jesus brings down the curtain, manifesting the emptiness of imagined images and hopes and tracing the empty space in which the hidden God is made manifest.[41] Rending that curtain means uncovering the emptiness within, which to self-clinging is utter desolation, the despair brought about by insight into the meaninglessness of unawakened cultic performances. The verb "it was torn" (ἐσχίσθη) is used only one other time in Mark, in 1: 10, where the heavens are split apart (σχιζομένους) to reveal the presence of the Father.

---

words the true meaning that Jesus is son of God, however the story-level centurion may have meant them.

38. Fowler, *Let the Reader Understand,* 203.

39. Against Linnemann, *Studien zur Passionsgeschichte,* 157–58, who considers the splitting of the temple veil in 15:38 to be the high point of the account, for now the majesty of God appears to all people paradoxically at the death of Jesus.

40. Tolbert, *Sowing the Gospel,* 281. Also Malbon, *Narrative Space,* 109: "The Holy of Holies as a separate space is destroyed by the splitting of the curtain of the *naos.*" Also 139: "So when the temple curtain is split, the temple merchants and money-changers cast out, and the total destruction of the temple itself foretold, the distinction between the sacred and profane is undermined at its foundation."

41. Hamerton-Kelly, *The Gospel and the Sacred,* 57: "The death of the servant opens the way to God for all the world by exposing sacred violence and depriving the temple of its mystique. . . . the holy of holies has been exposed to public view, its mystery has been removed; the system has been demystified and so deprived of the efficacy that depended on its operating behind a veil." Yet, that exposure has its impact only on those whose hearts have softened from their attachment to imagined realities.

In this instance, however, there is no heavenly voice, only the dead Jesus.[42] The veil is rent and now we are immersed in the realm of worldly convention-only.[43] Jesus was accused of bringing down the Temple in 15: 29 (καταλύων τὸν ναὸν), and he himself was challenged to come down from the cross (καταβὰς ἀπὸ τοῦ σταυροῦ). The bystanders wait to see if Elijah will take him down (καθελεῖν). None of the above happens, but in dying Jesus brings down the temple veil from top to bottom (τὸ καταπέτασμα τοῦ ναοῦ ἐσχίσθη εἰς δύο ἀπ' ἄνωθεν ἕως κάτω).[44] In Mahāyāna terms, emptiness and dependent co-arising are identical, insight into which constitutes full awakening. The uncovering of the empty Temple is itself the fullness of

---

42. Tolbert, *Sowing the Gospel*, 281: "Moreover, the prologue to the Gospel (1: 1–13), which contains the account of the heaven's splitting, is itself, like the crucifixion scene, structured rhetorically by a chiastic pattern that generally contrasts the human and cosmic dimensions of Mark's story. In that initial chiasm the cosmic realm surrounded the human (AA' vs. BB'), while at the end of the story the chiasm moves from the human to the divine (ABC vs. C'B'A'), emphasizing through the events of the crucifixion the underlying cosmic import of Jesus' message, life, and death." I do indeed think that the crucifixion recapitulates the prologue, but that, rather than manifesting an underlying cosmic realm where all is deeply meaningful, it collapses all images of such a realm into the originally present, dependently co-arisen world as the ground for all Christian practice.

43. Weeden, "The Cross as Power in Weakness," discusses Schenke's interpretation of Mark's rewriting of an apocalyptic tradition of Jesus' death as "a drama unfolding according to the predetermined plan of God." Weeden writes, 130–31: "In the triumphant cry of Jesus [15: 34a], good, reversing its plunge toward apparent defeat, emerges victorious from the cosmic battle, and seals the final judgment and ultimate destruction of evil (rending of the temple veil; 15: 38). Schenke hypothesizes that the apocalyptic crucifixion tradition belonged to Christians who avouched a realized eschatology and who viewed Jesus' death as the final end time moment in which the old, evil age was destroyed and the new age of God irrupted in full realization." He critiques that view, 131: "By historicizing the tradition, i.e., setting the death of Jesus in the context of world history (15: 1–20, 43–45), and even viewing Jesus' death in historical retrospect (15: 44–45), Mk divests the elements in the tradition of their original apocalyptic function. The time notices no longer serve the reinforcement of apocalyptic determinism. They only mark the temporal span of the crucifixion event. Historicizing the death into the past has deeschatologized the tradition's realized-eschatological character of both the death of Jesus and the 'proleptic' Temple destruction. By historicizing the triumphant apocalyptic death cry and transforming it into the anguished prayer of a servant of God victimized by his enemies (Ps 22: 1), Mk robbed the cry of its triumphalist character. He has turned what was once a climactic moment of apocalyptic reversal into an expiring cry of dereliction." Thus, realized eschatology is more an emptied eschatology, which collapses any dichotomy between human and divine realms and promises no empirical golden age, but directs one's attention back to the beginning of the originally present, dependently co-arisen world itself. The eschatological rending of the Temple veil manifests ultimate meaning as itself empty of any conventional form, and therefore eschatology itself is emptied of linear and historical expectations.

44. Tolbert, *Sowing the Gospel*, 282. Collins, *The Beginning of the Gospel*, 116: "The term *eschisthē* should be translated 'was divided,' 'separated,' or 'opened.' The curtain before the Holy of Holies was opened, as the heavens were at the baptism of Jesus (*schizomenous tous ouranous*, 1:10). Both passages are taken from tradition. In both cases, the very *schizō* signifies the opening of that which normally hides the godhead. Both verses imply a theophany." Indeed, but a theophany of the everyday, for therein lies hidden the presence of the kingdom.

dependently co-arisen redemption. Thus, the centurion, immersed only in the events as they unfold and seeing nothing more than how Jesus dies, confesses that indeed he is a son of God, echoing Mark's initial confession in 1: 1 that Jesus is the son of God.[45] The centurion sees because he has no expectations. This then is how the Temple is destroyed by Jesus' death, for it no longer divides the ordinary world from the sacred. All such clear distinctions are darkened and emptied of any final significance.[46]

The Women and Jesus' Burial
15: 40–47

[40]*There were some women watching from a distance. Among them were Mary of Magdala, Mary who was the mother of James the younger and Joset, and Salome.* [41]*They used to follow him and look after him when he was in Galilee. And there were many other women there who had come up to Jerusalem with him.*

[42]*It was now evening, and since it was Preparation Day—that is, the vigil of the Sabbath,* [43]*there came Joseph of Arimathea, a prominent member of the Council, who himself lived in hope of seeing the kingdom of God, and he boldly went to Pilate and asked for the body of Jesus.* [44]*Pilate, astonished that he should have died so soon, summoned the centurion and inquired if he had been dead for some time.* [45]*Having been assured of this by the centurion, he granted the corpse to Joseph* [46]*who brought a shroud, took Jesus down from the cross, wrapped him in the shroud and laid him in a tomb which had been hewn out of the rock. He then rolled a stone against the entrance to the tomb.* [47]*Mary of Magdala and Mary the mother of Joset took note of where he was laid.*

These women represent the continuing response to Jesus of his followers, for the disciples have long since fled from the scene, not to return. But they have been with Jesus all along, even from the days back in Galilee.[47] These

---

45. Schweizer, "Mark's Theological Achievement," 56: "The first to recognize what has taken place is not the theologians and Jewish Church leaders but the gentile, the secular man who stands where it is impossible to keep one's hands clean and is up to his neck in the dirty and responsible questions of human politics, and even has to carry out executions."

46. Against Collins, *The Beginning of the Gospel,* 116: "This judgment [on the old temple] involves not so much the beginning of the destruction of the building as the loss of its function as the place of prayer and service of God. This loss is due to the death of Jesus, which means the end of the temple cult and of Judaism itself. Since God has left the temple, the place of the temple has been taken by the new community." Yet that new community itself can and has constructed temples of its own. The issue of the temple destruction is not about Christianity and Judaism, but about any attempt to freeze the divine presence in any circumscribed locale.

47. Fowler, *Let the Reader Understand,* 111.

are the women who will shortly visit the tomb to anoint Jesus and find the stone rolled back. But even being with Jesus from the beginning, ministering to him in Galilee, does not mean that they have yet understood, any more than the disciples.

Joseph of Arimathea is described as a prominent councilor (εὐσχήμων βουλευτής), i.e., a member of the Sanhedrin. It is unclear if he was party to the plot to execute Jesus at the trial, for the statement at 15:1 is that the whole Sanhedrin had their plan ready. He is described by Mark as looking for the kingdom of God, yet he made no outcry about the sentencing and execution of Jesus. Perhaps, as a devout Jew, he simply was aware of the Deuteronomic norm that prohibited the bodies of the executed from being exposed overnight, especially on Sabbath. (Deut. 21: 23). He does not anoint Jesus for burial, but simply covers him with a shroud and lays him in the tomb, capturing even the dead Jesus within the cultic norms of proper behavior.[48] By so doing, he sets up the need for the women to come later to perform the omitted liturgies for Jesus. He takes Jesus' corpse (σῶμα) from the cross, for there has been no reversal, as Psalm 22 might have suggested. It is not Elijah who takes Jesus from the cross, but a religious and devout Jew, a member of the Sanhedrin itself.[49]

Pilate is astonished or surprised (ἐθαύμασεν) that Jesus is already dead, which brings the centurion back into view and reminds the reader of how he died: a son of God whose death split the temple veil. But to Pilate, Jesus simply died as other men die. Nothing in particular to note. Pilate is unaware of the Temple curtain's being rent asunder. Indeed, the Temple authorities seem not to notice it either, for they make no move to sew it back together! For them, things go on as before and no final, eschatological event has occurred at all.

---

48. Brown, "The Burial of Jesus," 233–45, considers the burial by Joseph to be a dishonorable burial, the type afforded to a criminal, for Jesus is not anointed. Joseph performs the act because of his observance of Deuteronomy 21:22–23, which states that the body of a convicted criminal should not remain unburied.

49. See Crossan, *The Historical Jesus,* 392–94, for a discussion of the burial tradition. Crossan holds that Mark invented Joseph of Arimathea as "a perfect go-between figure" between Jesus' enemies and his friends. He concludes: "But all of those industrious redactions [in the burial tradition] set out to solve one simple problem. *Nobody knew what had happened to Jesus' body.* And the best his followers could initially hope for was that he had been buried out of Jewish piety toward Deuteronomy 21:22–23. If you turn from the burier to the tomb, exactly the same phenomenon occurs. In Mark 15:46 it was 'a tomb which had been hewn out of the rock.' In Matthew 27:60 it is Joseph's 'own new tomb.' In Luke 23:53 it is 'a rock-hewn tomb, where no one had ever been laid.' In John 19:41 it is 'a garden, and in the garden a new tomb where no one had ever been laid.' But no amount of damage control can conceal what its intensity only confirms. With regard to the body of Jesus, by Easter Sunday morning, those who cared did not know where it was, and those who knew did not care. Why should even the soldiers themselves remember the death and disposal of a nobody?"

16

Resurrection and Return

The Empty Tomb
16: 1–8

[1]When the Sabbath was over, Mary of Magdala, Mary the mother of James, and Salome, bought spices with which to go and anoint him. [2]And very early in the morning on the first day of the week they went to the tomb when the sun had arisen.

[3]They had been saying to one another, "Who will roll away the stone for us from the entrance to the tomb?" [4]But when they looked they saw that the stone—which was very big—had already been rolled back. [5]On entering the tomb they saw a young man in a white robe seated on the right-hand side, and they were struck with amazement. [6]But he said to them, "There is no need to be so amazed. You are looking for Jesus of Nazareth, who was crucified: he has risen, he is not here. See, here is the place where they laid him. [7]But you must go and tell his disciples and Peter, 'He is going ahead of you to Galilee; that is where you will see him, just as he told you.' " [8]And the women came out and ran away from the tomb because they were frightened out of their wits; and they said nothing to a soul, for they were afraid. . . .

They came at dawn, the time of awakening, Mary, the mother of Jesus, and a couple of friends.[1] To anoint Jesus' corpse, although it has already

1. Fowler, "Reader-Response Criticism," 76: " 'Mary the mother of James' in Mark 6:1 is well known. She is also described as 'Mary, the mother of Joses' in Mark 15:47 and as 'Mary, the mother of James the younger and of Joses' in Mark 15:40. Because the Gospel has already introduced us to a woman named Mary who has sons named James and Joses (Mark 6:3), it makes sense to conclude that these are all references to the same woman. This conclusion, however, yields some surprises. The Mary introduced in Mark 6:3, along with her sons James and Joses, is none other than Jesus' own mother. Why does Mark refuse to call her 'Mary, the mother of Jesus'?" To which, Fowler adds in 76.32: "Some clues: in Mark 3:21, Jesus' family come to take him home because they think he 'has gone out of his mind.' When his mother and brothers arrive to take him away, Jesus acknowledges that he is estranged from his family (Mark 3:33–35). This estrangement is alluded to again in 6:4. Altogether this suggests that Mark avoids calling

been anointed for burial in advance by the anonymous woman with the jar of precious spikenard. Yet, that was clearly a symbolic anointing, and now there is need for a real burial anointing. Joseph of Arimathea has neglected to do so; he has simply removed the body and buried it so it will not defile the Sabbath. The women then are on a funereal mission. But how indeed are they to roll back the stone? If it was so very large, they could not have done so without assistance.[2] How do they expect to gain access to the body? In composing his theological narrative,[3] Mark seals the tomb from any human power to open it and Jesus lies beyond any last farewells.

But the women find the stone already rolled back and discover within the tomb what they scarcely could have expected to find: another young man, dressed in white.[4] This figure is more easily identified than the fleeing youth in 14:51–52, for he is a well-recognized apocalyptic figure, the *angelus interpres,* a narrative role common in apocalyptic literature.[5] He is the bearer of apocalyptic messages, frightening to anybody's common sense worldviews. And he does both frighten the women and enjoin them to give the disciples

---

Mary 'the mother of Jesus' in 15:40, 47; 16:1 in order to imply to the reader that Jesus is still alienated from his mother and his brothers." Yet, in 15:41 Mary the mother of James the younger and Joset (Joses) is included among those who followed and ministered to Jesus when he was in Jerusalem. Ambiguity remains.

2. Fowler, "Reader-Response Criticism," 77: "Who will roll away the stone from the door of the tomb? (Mark 16:3) This question is an ironic reminder to the reader that Jesus had four brothers (Mark 6:3) who could have helped their mother with funeral observances for their dead brother. He also had twelve disciples who all said they would never forsake him (Mark 14:31). In Mark everyone seems to abandon Jesus, even God (15:34), but this question by the women in 16:3 points out especially the absence of men who might have accompanied the women in paying their last respects."

3. Collins, *The Beginning of the Gospel,* 145: "My working hypothesis in this essay is that Mark 16:1–8 is fiction. In composing the story of the empty tomb, the author of Mark interpreted the proclamation that Jesus had been raised." So Crossan, *The Historical Jesus,* 395–416.

4. His description reminds one of the account of the avenging angel who punished Heliodorus, as described in 2 *Maccabees* 3: 25–26: "Before their eyes appeared a horse richly caparisoned and carrying a fearsome rider. Rearing violently, it struck at Heliodorus with its forefeet. The rider was seen to be accoutered entirely in gold. Two other young men of outstanding strength and radiant beauty, magnificently apparelled, appeared to him at the same time, and taking their stand on either side of him, flogged him unremittingly, inflicting stroke after stroke." The high priest Onias is fearful that Heliodorus' thrashing might be blamed on the Jews and bring political trouble, and so offers a sacrifice for his recovery. Then in verses 33–34 we read: "And while the high priest was performing the rite of expiation, the same young men again appeared to Heliodorus, wearing the same apparel and, standing beside him said, 'Be very grateful to Onias the high priest, since it is for his sake that the Lord has granted you your life. As for you, who have been scourged by Heaven, you must proclaim to everyone the grandeur of God's power.' So saying they vanished."

5. Collins, *The Beginning of the Gospel,* 135–36. So Sheehan, *The First Coming,* 157: "The early Christians had seen him on stage, as it were, many times before in the intertestamental apocalyptic works such as *Tobit* or *Testament of Abraham,* and he always had the same role. He was the Apocalyptic Messenger, always disguised as a young man, always dressed in white robes, and he usually frightened those to whom he appeared."

the message about Jesus' resurrection. One expects something quite awesome and indeed, he does announce to the women that Jesus has risen and is not there in the tomb. Yet instead of a bright vision of the apocalyptic kingdom, he merely tells them that Jesus is going before them to Galilee, just as he told them. The future images of a world-shattering apocalyptic kingdom are emptied: just Galilee is left and that is the eschatological kingdom. Mark "meets the disconfirmation of Kingdom apocalypticism by restating old prophecy in the new configuration of time and space,"[6] and that new configuration is just Galilee as it has always been.

Still it is possible that this young man is related to the one in 14: 51–52, a young man dressed in linen who followed the just-arrested Jesus. He was caught but managed to wriggle out of his linen robe and flee naked. That event recalls the sealed prophecy of *Daniel* and the man dressed in linen who proffered that eschatological prophecy (*Daniel* 12: 7). In Mark 14, in contrast to *Daniel,* the young man dressed in the linen cloth tries to accompany Jesus in his eschatological hour but fails to deliver any prediction. He offers no sealed prophecy about Jesus' final revelation and presents no time reference, for the end time has already come in Jesus' eschatological dying and rising.[7] Bereft of any support, he flees nakedly disgraced at the hour of Jesus' arrest, thus attesting to the emptiness of all linear eschatology. The young man who appears to the women in the present account is again dressed in white, but far from announcing a linear eschatology, he presents the emptied eschatology of Jesus' resurrection. His shameful nakedness is now clothed in the radiance of Jesus' absence from the tomb. And that is the eschatological reality of the resurrection he announces: "He has risen. He is not here" (ἠγέρθη οὐκ ἔστιν ὧδε).[8]

Who then is Jesus? What is his identity now? The young man refers to him at first as Jesus of Nazareth, the most commonplace identity marker a

---

6. Kelber, *The Kingdom in Mark,* 142. Note that for Kelber, the kingdom is to be found in northern Galilee, not Jerusalem. See 131: "Mark redefines his own identity in opposition to a ruined tradition of the south and discovers the Galilean centrality in view of the broken center in Jerusalem." Again, 139: "Conversely, Mark rejects the traditional localization of the parousia in Jerusalem, holding the firm conviction that the traditional site of eschatological manifestation had become a broken center, void and empty. Thus when the evangelist gives his last directions in the so-called story of the Empty Tomb (16:1–8), he is disinclined to display the resurrected Christ in Jerusalem, for to him the city is the place of absence." But it is not that Kelber imagines a bright future in Galilee, since (142), "for Mark, not the permanent holiness of the temple, but the impermanency of the way is the catalyst of transcendence." In Mahāyāna terms, Galilee is the locus of the practice of the middle path, holding in creative tension insight into emptiness and reengagement in the dependently co-arisen world of everyday living.

7. Via, *The Ethics of Mark's Gospel,* 45–46: "In the last part of Mark's plot, history and myth are fused. The end of the story brings the end of world history, for resurrection belongs to the apocalyptic end of the world. Therefore the power of the end is predicated of an epoch in time." That epoch, however, can be any moment of awakening and rising with Jesus, in the ordinary life of Galilee.

8. Crossan, "Empty Tomb and Absent Lord," 148: "The *neaniskos*-messenger is . . . the neophyte in the Mkan community and therefore it is that community itself, including

person has: his home origin. "And at his entrance onto the narrative scene, Jesus is described as coming from Nazareth (1:9). At the tomb, where the women expect to see Jesus for the final time, Jesus is identified as 'of Nazareth.'.... At the very moment when it appears that Jesus has broken through the human boundaries of death, the title *Nazarēnos* reaffirms his humanity."[9] If that is who he is, no wonder he returns to Galilee! The young man further defines the risen Jesus as "he who was crucified." The emptying of all expectancies remains central to Jesus' titles; even after the resurrection, he is still to be identified as the crucified.[10]

The women are told not to be fearful nor amazed (μὴ ἐκθαμβεῖσθε). They are not to cling to conventional frameworks, for Jesus is not here within that framework.[11] He has arisen and can no longer be sought in ordinary terms, even ordinary supernatural terms. He is not where he was placed. Their fear and flight are not unfounded, for as humans they have no way to cope with such a message.[12] They are silent in the tomb, and

---

Mk. It is not the risen Lord and neither is it some accidental angel who delivers the message: it is the Mkan community of those reborn in the resurrected Christ." I would add that this Markan community is composed of those who return to the everyday Galilean practice of emptied eschatology.

9. Malbon, *Narrative Space,* 25–26.

10. Broadhead, *Teaching With Authority,* 185: "The grammar of these narrative defines the resurrection as an event, but it identifies Jesus in terms of the cross. . . . Through these narrative operations the passion of Jesus becomes the defining characteristic of his life, and thus, the central event of his story." Note 1 observes: "Jesus is the Crucified One. For Mark 16:1–8, the resurrection is a significant event in the life of Jesus, but the cross event becomes definitive of the identity of Jesus." Indeed, how can one define the identity of someone risen from the dead, when all identity markers are dependently co-arisen and conventional?

11. Tolbert, *Sowing the Gospel,* 207, sees the disciples' earlier failure to question Jesus about the resurrection from the dead at 9: 10 as "especially preposterous coming from these three disciples, for it was Peter, James, and John alone among all the disciples and the multitudes who were permitted to accompany Jesus to Jairus' house and see him *raise Jairus's daughter from death* (5: 37–42). . . . Furthermore, in the episode they had just witnessed, they had seen Elijah and Moses, two leaders who had died centuries earlier, *alive* and talking with Jesus. That these disciples should still be unsure after such outstanding proofs underlines yet again their failure: they have eyes that do not see and ears that do not hear." In a Mahāyāna interpretation, however, there are no such proofs, and the imagined pattern not only has no ability to understand, it cannot even formulate questions about that which is completely other. Mark cannot have the disciples enter into any conversation about what Jesus' prediction of resurrection might mean, for there is no such conversation. Neither can the women grasp what is ungraspable.

12. Sheehan, *The First Coming,* 143, argues that: "The listener is therefore meant to understand that *the women's confused flight and subsequent silence is in fact the appropriate response to the scene at the tomb.* It is rhetorically understandable that the women tell no one what they have heard and seen, for the point of the story is that the angel's words do not effect faith (they did not for the women in the legend, and they will not for the listeners) and that empty graves of themselves say nothing about a resurrection." For Sheehan, 169: "They found, quite simply, that Jesus was unfindable."

later silent about that silence.[13] They flee from the emptiness of the tomb back to society, not knowing what to say.[14]

The empty tomb itself proves nothing. An empty tomb merely means that there is no corpse in it. Mark is not trying to demonstrate the truth of the resurrection within the context of imagined thinking, for no such demonstration is possible. Rather, the point is that Jesus is not there within conventional frames of reference, and thus not within the realm of words and judgments that might be called upon to demonstrate his renewed existence.[15] In fact, he has no such renewed existence in Mark. Rather, he has risen from the dead. His absence signals his presence beyond imagined realities.[16] The dynamic tension between conventional living and resurrected life remains, for in overcoming death, Jesus does not merely pick up the temporarily interrupted continuity of his life. He has entered a dimension that is totally other, beyond thought and image. Thus, "at the end the resurrection is proclaimed to those who keep silent (16: 8)."[17]

And so the white-robed man tells the women to inform the disciples and Peter, who (again called by the name Jesus bestowed upon him) is thus singled out, that Jesus is going before them into Galilee, where they will see him.[18] This has baffled Christian thinkers, for it seems to imply that, although in Mark himself there are no resurrection appearances recorded in Jerusalem, yet there

---

13. Sheehan, *The First Coming,* 173: "The proper response to the empty tomb is silence, even silence about that silence. The women who came to the tomb had the correct reaction. They took the path that led away from the tomb and away from Jesus himself. They went back to their own lives and to the meaning that Jesus' message had taught them to find therein." Yet Jesus is not present in that tomb from which they fled. Perhaps Sheehan has in mind that they fled from any hero image of Jesus.

14. Malbon, *Narrative Space,* 117: "So the women, too, with 'trembling and astonishment' flee 'from the tomb' (16:8), flee from the space beyond society's boundaries, flee from the realm of the dead, flee to . . .?" Unlike the Gerasene demoniac, they take no delight in dwelling among the tombs. Again, 131: "But when, amazingly (16:5), the tomb is found empty, Jesus is known to be outside this inside, beyond all enclosure. This realization astonishes (16:8). Resurrection is the turning of expectations inside out."

15. Malbon, *Narrative Space,* 129: "They had gone outside the city to the tomb, beyond the boundaries of society to the realm of the dead, to follow Jesus. But Jesus was not in that space. Jesus, who had taught concerning the resurrection (12:18–27) that God 'is not God of the dead, but of the living' (12:27), was no longer in the tomb. Thus the women flee from the tomb, and therefore back into society and back among the living, with the promise for themselves and for the disicples, especially Peter, that 'there you will see him' (16:7)."

16. Via, *The Ethics of Mark's Gospel,* 55: "The announcement of the young man that Jesus has risen is concealed revelation. . . . The fear and silence of the women portray the concealed element in the Church's proclamation of the resurrection."

17. Via, *The Ethics of Mark's Gospel,* 176.

18. Tolbert, *Sowing the Gospel,* 294: "Their very act of buying spices and going to the tomb to anoint Jesus raises troubling questions. If they had followed Jesus in Galilee and heard his predictions, they, like the authorial audience, should expect that he will be raised in three days." In Mark, the women, as the disciples before them, function within an imagined pattern of misunderstanding, and cannot grasp what is totally other.

is this promise that Jesus will appear to them in Galilee.[19] Yet, I do not think that is correct. There are no resurrection appearances because Jesus is beyond empirical validation.[20] He will not "reappear" even in Galilee. The resurrected Jesus can be seen only upon the awakening of conversion that he came to preach about, not in some supernaturally perceptible coming back to show his new glorified body. That would hardly be in line with Mark's consistent rejection of empirical validation for Jesus and his teachings. Galilee then signifies not the site for magical appearances, but rather the everyday site of the practice of Jesus' middle path.[21] The end result is not a Jerusalem triumph, but a return home, there to take up the original task of announcing the kingdom of God and

---

19. Collins, *The Beginning of the Gospel,* 136: "Some scholars have argued that the renewed promise, 'there you will see him' (16:7), refers to the parousia, that is, to the return of Jesus on the clouds as Son of Man. This interpretation is unlikely because language of 'power' and 'glory' associated with the parousia elsewhere in Mark (9:1; 13:26; cf. 14:62) does not occur here. The parousia and Galilee are not associated anywhere else in the Gospel." In Mahāyāna terms, the parousia (a term never mentioned in Mark) occurs precisely in everyday Galilee, shorn of all power and all glory, simply as a return of the risen and awakened Jesus to the dependently co-arisen world.

20. Petersen, "When Is the End not the End?" 156, sees 16: 8 as "either an intentional reversal of expectations or an ironic substitute for the obvious continuation of events implied by the narrator." He rejects the former because that would imply that Jesus himself was mistaken, 161–63: "Because the twelve disciples, who alone among all men were expected to perceive things in terms of the things of God, fail to achieve the expected enlightenment, Jesus' intent, expectations, and predictions prove to have failed. Once Jesus is shown to have been deluded about the disciples, the sense we have had of him throughout the narrative is rendered a delusion and the tables of meaning are overturned. The disciples really completely abandoned Jesus (Mark 14), the establishment really succeeded in the execution of a deluded troublemaker (Mark 15), and the credibility of the young man's explanation of the empty tomb is shattered by his erroneous prediction about meeting in Galilee (Mark 16). And God made a really big mistake. . . . A reading of Mark's narrative predicated on a literal interpretation of its closure in 16: 8 is not literally impossible, but its results assault its own credibility." Thus, Petersen opts for the second alternative, that 16: 8 is intended ironically: "Our narrator does not mean what he says in Mark 16: 8. . . . The reader recognizes irony in 16: 8 because a literal reading of it makes nonsense of the narrator's previous generation of expectations and satisfactions, with the last satisfaction being enjoyed as recently as 16: 6, where the young man announces, 'he has risen.' . . . Mark 16: 6–7 thus directs the reader's imagination to provide the proper closure to the narrator's story by supplying the satisfaction of the expectation generated in the prediction of a meeting between Jesus and the eleven in Galilee." In the present Mahāyāna reading, it is precisely the imagined expectations of Jesus' followers that come under challenge, for the overall aim of Jesus' message is a conversion from that deluded pattern to wisdom and understanding. The pattern of Mark who "creates an expectation and then cancels it," need not lead "the reader to wonder why he raised the expectation in the first place."(154) The whole movement of the gospel is to sketch imagined expectations and then undermine them. To insist then that the reader supply the expected ending of a meeting between Jesus and the remaining disciples in Galilee is a failure to appreciate the import of Jesus' call for a changing of one's understanding, μετάνοια, and an insistence that one's imagined expectations be satisfied.

21. Camery-Hoggatt, *Irony in Mark's Gospel,* 12: "The closing irony of Mark is a reminder that the risen Christ is yet at work, and that he has summoned his followers back to their original discipleship."

calling for conversion. It is in that ordinariness that they will see Jesus, for he has indeed gone ahead of them into Galilee (προάγει ὑμᾶς εἰς τὴν Γαλιλαίαν).[22] Through his life and death, Jesus has resurrected the ordinary dependently co-arisen course of life, infusing it with his presence. That is perhaps why in 16: 6 the final title applied to Jesus by the young man is Jesus of Nazareth, the least theological title in Mark, thereby echoing 1: 9, where Jesus comes from Nazareth to be baptized by John.[23] Galilee means the everyday, and that is where the risen Jesus is to be found. Galilee is not a special new community, for there is nothing special about Jesus' resurrection.[24] "Not for [Matthew] nor

---

22. Malbon, *Narrative Space,* 113–15. Jesus sends all sorts of people home after benefiting them. The advice of 16:7 is not out of the ordinary for Jesus.

23. Dewey, "Peter's Curse and Cursed Peter," 99: "In fact, Nazarene is a characteristically Mkan title, appearing four times: 1: 24; 10: 47; 14: 67; 16: 6. Mk also discloses that Nazareth is the place of Jesus' origin (1: 9). Thus at the outset of the Gospel Jesus is linked with Galilee, but even more specifically with Nazareth. . . . The last reference to the Nazarene appears in the final verses of the Gospel (16: 6). Of all the titles applied to Jesus in Mk, here Jesus rises as the Nazarene. Mk has framed the entire Gospel and the ministry of Jesus with references to Jesus as the Nazarene (1: 9, 24; 16: 6) and with Jesus traveling from Galilee and back to it. That this framing is intentional, is indicated in the reaction of the women (16: 5–6: *exethambēthēsan, mē ekthambeisthe*) which parallels the crowd's reaction to the Nazarene (1: 27: *ethambēthēsan*)." There is also a doubling back in 16: 2, with its reference to "very early in the morning" (καὶ λίαν πρωῒ) to 1: 35, where in beginning his Galilean mission, Jesus arises "in the morning, long before dawn (Καὶ πρωῒ ἔννυχα λίαν ἀναστὰς). The dawning of Jesus' resurrection recovers the dawning of his initial journeying." See Crossan, "Empty Tomb and Absent Lord," 146–47.

24. The thesis of Kee, *The Community of the New Age.* Lohmeyer, *Galiläa und Jerusalem,* argues that the early Christian community had two origins, Galilee and Jerusalem. Developing this view, Kelber thinks that Mark constructed his gospel, after the destruction of Jerusalem, in order to explain why in fact the Jerusalem Church had been eliminated. Thus, *Mark's Story of Jesus,* 90: "Mark's combined critique of the twelve . . . is directed against people who are identifiable (from Luke and Paul) as representatives of the Jerusalem Church. The logic of Mark's critique is aimed at the very existence of the Jerusalem community. Jesus' closest followers . . . were then stalled in Jerusalem, never reaching the goal of Galilee." Thus, 87: "As a result of their [the women's] failure the disciples never do return to Galilee. The kingdom (i.e., the new eschatological community) will not be represented by the disciples. Not going to Galilee, they will do what they have always wanted to do, that is, stay in Jerusalem and wait there for the kingdom to come in power." Tolbert, *Sowing the Gospel,* 31, offers a telling critique of these views: "In other words, the reason why a certain part of the narrative exists is to be discovered within the narrative itself and not generally in some realm external to the narrative. For Mark such an assumption would again challenge the predominant tradition of Gospel research: form and redaction critics tend to move very quickly out from the text to the life of Jesus, the history of the early church, or theological issues in the Markan community. Indeed, the primary explanatory grid for any element in the Gospel is often an extratextual one." The absence of Jesus, the lack of appearances, and the return to Galilee constitute variations on the same theme: that ultimate meaning, Jesus raised from the dead, has no, and cannot have any, imagined signification. Thus, I agree that extratextual contextualizations are not the point, for they attempt precisely to imagine a context that renders the account intelligible in expected terms. Marxsen, *Mark the Evangelist,* 108, identifies references to Galilee as indicating a community awaiting Jesus' parousia: "The community in Galilee which awaits the Parousia and the community which journeys toward Galilee

for Mark was Galilee *terra Christiana;* it was no Messianic holy land in either Gospel. Failure as well as success marked the Galilean ministry from the start. That failure knew no geographic boundaries. There is no Galilean idyll for Jesus in Mark or Matthew. For them both, Galilee found much to object to in Jesus, as he found much to condemn in it."[25] Rather, going to Galilee is going back home, the only place where the disciples would go after having their false expectancies totally frustrated. Even if the women do not report the message, where else would they go? In fact, they have already been informed by Jesus himself in 14: 28 that, after his resurrection, he will go before them into Galilee.[26]

Nevertheless, the women do not fulfill the request of the young man. They are caught in fear and beside themselves with wonder (εἶχεν γὰρ αὐτὰς τρόμος καὶ 'ἔκστασις), for they have come into contact with that which is completely other. And so they run away at the eschatological climax, just as did the disciples at Jesus' eschatological trial. But they do not deny Jesus as Peter did. They are simply rendered mute by the event, as is Mark himself in ending his gospel on their note of dismay.

Mark ends on a non-ending, "for they were afraid . . ." (ἐφοβοῦντο γὰρ). He drops the reader into a state of confusion.[27] Are we to conclude that the disciples and Peter never in fact hear about Jesus' resurrection? Is Mark presenting such a bleak picture of them in order to vilify an opposing party in his own community? I doubt that, for all the readers of the gospel are told to go to Galilee. In telling the women, the white-robed man also tells all the readers of the gospel that they are also to go to Galilee, to the everyday living of resurrected life. Mark's abrupt ending embodies the silence of the risen Lord and issues a call for his followers to awaken to his presence in the everyday.[28] Such silence

---

for the Parousia make of the land a *terra christiana.* So it is with Mark." Mark himself never mentions the parousia, yet, if that be taken to refer to the everyday practice of the middle path in Galilee, and not to a supernaturally empirical advent of Jesus in the future, it is admissible.

25. Davies, *The Gospel and the Land,* 241, cited in Malbon, *Narrative Space,* 167.

26. Throughout the gospel, Jesus' course is portrayed in a series of journeys. Kelber, *Mark's Story of Jesus,* 9: "Mark's Gospel is viewed as a dramatically plotted journey of Jesus. Throughout the Gospel Jesus is depicted as being in movement from one place to another. He journeys through Galilee, undertakes six boat trips on and across the Lake of Galilee, travels from Galilee to Jerusalem, makes three trips to the temple, and toward the end signals the return to Galilee. Mark invites the reader to follow Jesus on this journey which leads through a series of unexpected experiences and crises." The journey of practicing the middle path leads through a series of deconfirmations of imagined fantasies back to the dependently co-arisen mind that has been present all along. Thus, Jesus' way leads from Galilee to the dramatic experiences in Jerusalem, back to the everyday practice of the Galilean origin.

27. Kermode, *The Genesis of Secrecy,* 67: "The text really does end, 'they were scared, you see,' and with *gar* as the last word, 'the least forceful word' Mark 'could possibly find'." Allusions in the last clause about the "least forceful word . . . possibly find" are to Joyce's ending of *Finnegan's Wake* on "this," as reported to Louis Gillet.

28. Tolbert, *Sowing the Gospel,* 289: "We are more aroused if raised expectations are dashed than if no expectations had been raised in the first place."

empties any closure or *telos* that might end the account within the Markan narrative.[29] Jesus is messiah, not as a king of great power and glory who brings everything to final grand victory, but as the embodiment of Yahweh's presence in his very transparent humanness.[30] The gospel ends abruptly because its endings have to be filled in by each and every reader. The story of Jesus has no final conclusion, for the resurrected life of Jesus is not a given data, once learned and perhaps imitated. Rather, it is the life story of each Christian, embodied in particular circumstances and taking specific courses, as needed and possible in different lives.[31] The Gospel is open-ended, for the action of the story depends on decisions which the Church, including the readers, must still make.[32] Stories end, but the gospel goes on (προάγει).

What is resurrected then is not the physical continuity of Jesus' molecular structure, but the reality of his presence. And that presence is not a supernatural addition to the everyday, but itself entails the recovery and resurrection of the everyday kingdom of dependent co-arising in all its emptiness and beauty. Jesus is the full affirmation of human life lived in the present and ordinary world, but forever going beyond to the direct awareness of Abba, Father. His resurrection is an awakening to the eschatological wisdom of God-awareness, empty of any identifying image or idea, and to the subsequently attained wisdom of reengaged world awareness, with all the images and ideas needed to live and witness to the gospel.

---

29. Culler, *Structuralist Poetics,* 244: "Closure . . . testifies to the presence of an ideology." Having no closure, Mark is thus not an ideology. Also Camery-Hoggatt, *Irony in Mark's Gospel,* 91: "Even though the meaning of the narrative may only become entirely clear in its *telos,* it is in the unfolding encounter with the parts that the reader's perceptions are informed and his reactions shaped." Yet I think that Mark's *telos* lies outside any literary encounter with his text, which twists the reader to empty any formed perceptions about her worldview. See Marxsen, *Mark the Evangelist,* 280–09: "In this very conclusive inconclusiveness lies the inner goal of the entire Gospel."

30. Crossan, "Empty Tomb and Absent Lord," sees Mark as arguing against interest in miracles and apparitions rather than in suffering and service, against lack of sympathy for the gentile mission as questioning the validity of the law, and against unfounded appeals to the Jerusalem church, represented by the disciples. Thus, 146: "Mark has a very serious problem in *ending* his Gospel. If we accept a skeletal sequence such as 1 Cor 15: 3–5a (death, burial, resurrection, and appearance/revelation to Peter) as a creedal summary on which a story *might* be constructed and the Gospel concluded, Mk would have been forced to end in a way that would negate the polemical thrust of the entire preceding Gospel. He would have had to conclude with an apparition and mandate for Peter/James and the twelve/Apostles. My thesis is that it was precisely to avoid and to oppose any such apparition to Peter or to the Apostles that he created most deliberately a totally new tradition (*traditio tradenda* not *traditio tradita*), that of the empty tomb."

31. Against Collins, *The Beginning of the Gospel,* 138: "Mark lacks such a satisfying denouement. One result is that the readers are asked to complete the story not only by imagining the fulfillment of the promise of appearances, as 14:28 and 16:7 should probably be interpreted, but also by imagining the fulfillment of the dramatic and vivid promises that the Son of Man would return (13:24–27; 14:62)." Rather, the point is not to imagine the story line into the future, but to turn from that story—driven perhaps by its discourse—to engage in whatever life circumstances one encounters.

32. Tannehill, "The Disciples in Mark," 152.

Bibliography of Works Cited

Achtemeier, P. J.
1970   "Toward the Isolation of Pre-Markan Miracle Catenae." *JBL* 89: 265–91.
1972   "The Origin and Function of the Pre-Markan Miracle Catenae." *JBL* 91: 198–221.
1975   "Miracles and the Historical Jesus: A Study of Mark 9:14–29." *Catholic Biblical Quarterly* 37: 471–91.
1978   " 'And He Followed Him': Miracles and Discipleship in Mark 10:46–52," *Semeia* 11: 115–45.
1978   "Mark as Interpreter of the Jesus Traditions." *Interpretation* 32.4.

Ahn, Byung-mu
1981   "Jesus and the Minjung in the Gospel of Mark." In *Minjung Theology: People as the Subjects of History.* Maryknoll, NY: Orbis Books.

Aitken, Robert, trans.
1990   *The Gateless Barrier: The Wu-men Kuan (Mumonkan).* San Francisco: North Point Press.

Altizer, Thomas J. J.
1989   "Emptiness and God." In *The Religious Philosophy of Nishitani Keiji: Encounter With Emptiness,* edited by Taitetsu Unno, 70–81. Berkeley: Asian Humanities Press.

Amore, Roy C.
1978   *Two Masters, One Message: The Lives and Teachings of Gautama and Jesus.* Nashville: Abingdon.

Anderson, Janice Capel
1992   "Feminist Criticism: The Dancing Daughter." In *Mark and Method: New Approaches in Biblical Studies,* edited by J. C. Anderson and S. D. Moore, 103–34. Minneapolis: Fortress Press.

Anderson, Janice Capel and Stephen D. Moore, eds.
1992   *Mark and Method: New Approaches in Biblical Studies.* Minneapolis: Fortress Press.

Aune, David E.
1980   "Magic in Early Christianity." *Aufstieg und Niedergang der römischen Welt* 2.23: 1507–57.

Barth, Karl
1936–   *Church Dogmatics.* Trans. G. T. Thomson. 4 vols. New York: Scribner.
1969

Bassler, Jouette M.
1986   "The Parable of the Loaves." *Journal of Religion* 66: 157–72.

Bauer, Walter
1957   *A Greek-English Lexicon of the New Testament and Other Early Christian Literature.* 4th edition. Translated and adapted by W. R. Arndt and F. W. Gingrich. Chicago: University of Chicago Press. [2nd rev. ed., 1979.]

Beardslee, W.
1970   *Literary Criticism of the New Testament.* Philadelphia: Fortress Press.

Beavis, Mary Ann
1987   "The Trial Before the Sanhedrin (Mark 14:53–65): Reader Response and Greco-Roman Readers." *Catholic Biblical Quarterly* 49: 581–96.
1989   *Mark's Audience: The Literary and Social Setting of Mark 8:11–12.* Sheffield: JSOT Press.

Belo, Fernando
1981   *A Materialist Reading of the Gospel of Mark.* Maryknoll, NY: Orbis Books.

Berg, Temma F.
1989   "Reading in/to Mark." *Semeia* 48: 187–206.

Berger, Klaus
1976   *Die Auferstehung des Propheten und die Erhöhung des Menschensohnes: Traditionsgeschichtliche Untersuchungen zur Deutung des Geschickes Jesu in frühchristlichen Texten.* Göttingen: Vandenhoeck & Ruprecht.

Berger, Peter L.
1969   *The Sacred Canopy: Elements of a Sociological Theory of Religion.* New York: Doubleday.

Best, Ernest
1965   *The Temptation and the Passion: The Markan Soteriology.* Cambridge: Cambridge University Press. 2nd ed.,1990.
1974   "Mark's Preservation of the Tradition." In *L'Évangile selon Marc. Tradition et Rédaction,* edited by M. Sabbe, 21–34. Leuven: University Press. Reprinted in *The Interpretation of Mark,* edited by William Telford, 119–134. Philadelphia: Fortress Press; London: SPCK Press, 1985.
1978   "The Miracles in Mark." *Review and Expositor* 75: 539–54.
1983   *Mark: The Gospel as Story.* Edinburgh: T. & T. Clark.
1986   *Disciples and Discipleship: Studies in the Gospel According to Mark.* Edinburgh: T. & T. Clark.

Bird, C. H.
1953   "Some *gar* Clauses in St. Mark's Gospel." *Journal of Theological Studies* 4: 171–87.

Black, C. Clifton
1988   *The Disciples According to Mark: Markan Redaction in Current Debate.* JSNT Sup 27. Sheffield: JSOT Press.
1991   "An Oration at Olivet: A Rhetorical Analysis of Mark 13." In *Persuasive Artistry: Studies in New Testament Rhetoric in Honor of George A. Kennedy,* edited by Duane F. Watson. Sheffield: JSOT Press.

Black, Matthew
1946   *An Aramaic Approach to the Gospels and Acts.* Oxford: Oxford University Press.

Boobyer, G. H.
1921   "The Redaction of Mark IV:1–34." *New Testament Studies* 6: 225–35.

Boomershine, Thomas E.
1974   "Mark, the Storyteller: A Rhetorical-Critical Investigation of Mark's Passion and Resurrection Narrative." Ph.D. dissertation, Union Theological Seminary.
1981   "Mark 16:8 and the Apostolic Commission." *Journal of Biblical Literature* 100: 225–39.

Boomershine, Thomas E., and Gilbert L. Bartholomew
1981   "The Narrative Technique of Mark 16:8." *Journal of Biblical Literature* 100.2: 213–23.

Boring, M. Eugene
1990   "Mark 1:1–15 and the Beginning of the Gospel." *Semeia* 52: 43–81.

Boucher, Madeleine
1977   *The Mysterious Parable: A Literary Study.* Washington, DC: Catholic Biblical Association of America.
Bowker, John W.
1974   "Mystery and Parable: Mark 4:1–20." *Journal of Theological Studies* 25.
Bratcher, Robert G., and Eugene A. Nida
1961   *A Translator's Handbook on the Gospel of Mark.* London, New York, Stuttgart: United Bible Societies.
Broadhead, Edwin K.
1992   *Teaching with Authority: Miracles and Christology in the Gospel of Mark.* Sheffield, England: Sheffield Academic Press.
Brooke Rose, Christine
1980   "Round and Round the Jakobson Diagram: A Survey." *Hebrew University Studies in Literature* 8: 153–82.
Brown, Raymond E.
1966–   *The Gospel According to John: I–XII and XIII–XXI.* 2 vols. 1970 with
1970   continuous pagination. Garden City: Doubleday.
1973   *The Virginal Conception and Bodily Resurrection of Jesus.* New York: Paulist Press.
1988   "The Burial of Jesus (Mark 15:42–47)." *Catholic Biblical Quarterly* 50: 233–48.
Brown, Raymond, Karl P. Donfried, Joseph A. Fitzmyer, and John Reumann
1978   *Mary in the New Testament.* Philadelphia: Fortress Press.
Bryan, Christopher
1993   *A Preface to Mark: Notes on the Gospel and Its Literary and Cultural Settings.* New York and Oxford: Oxford University Press.
Bultmann, Rudolf Karl
1958   *Jesus and the Word.* Trans. L. P. Smith and E. H. Lantero. New York: Scribner.
1963   *The History of the Synoptic Tradition.* Trans. John Marsh. New York: Harper & Row.
Camery-Hoggatt, Jerry
1992   *Irony in Mark's Gospel: Text and Subtext.* Cambridge, England: Cambridge University Press.
Campbell, Joseph
1949   *The Hero with a Thousand Faces.* New York: Pantheon.
1962   *The Masks of God. Vol. 2: Oriental Mythology.* New York: Viking Penguin.
Chatman, Seymour
1978   *Story and Discourse: Narrative Structure in Fiction and Film.* Ithaca: Cornell University Press.
Chronis, Harry L.
1982   "The Torn Veil: Cultus and Christology in Mark 15:37–39." *Journal of Biblical Literature* 101: 97–114.
Clark, K. W.
1962   "Galilee, Sea of." *Interpreter's Dictionary of the Bible* 2: 348.
Cobb, John B., and Christopher Ives
1990   *The Emptying God: A Buddhist-Jewish-Christian Conversation.* Maryknoll, NY: Orbis Books.
Cohen, Shaye J. D.
1987   *From the Maccabees to the Mishnah.* Philadelphia: Westminster Press.
Collins, Adela Yarbro
1992   *The Beginning of the Gospel: Probings of Mark in Context.* Minneapolis: Fortress Press.

Colwell, E. C.
1933   "A Definite Rule for the Use of the Article in the Greek New Testament."
        Journal of Biblical Literature 52: 12–21.

Conzelmann, von H.
1959   "Geschichte und Eschaton nach Mc 13." *Zeitschrift für die neutestamentliche
        Wissenschaft* 50: 210–21.

Cook, Francis H.
1977   *Hua-yen Buddhism: The Jewel Net of Indra.* University Park: Pennsylvania
        State University Press.

Corless, Roger J.
1989   *The Vision of Buddhism: The Space Under the Tree.* New York: Paragon
        House.

Cotter, Wendy J.
1989   "Children Sitting in the Agora: Q(Luke) 7:31–35." *Forum* 5.2: 63–82.

Countryman, L. W.
1985   "How Many Baskets Full? Mark 8:14–21: The Value of Miracles in Mark."
        Catholic Biblical Quarterly 47: 643–55.

Cranfield, C. E. B.
1959   *The Gospel According to Saint Mark: Introduction and Commentary.* Cam-
        bridge: Cambridge University Press.

Crenshaw, James L.
1976   *Studies in Ancient Israelite Wisdom.* New York: Ktav Press.
1981   *Old Testament Wisdom.* Atlanta: John Knox Press.

Crossan, John Dominic
1973   *In Parables: The Challenge of the Historical Jesus.* New York: Harper
        and Row.
1973   "The Servant Parables of Jesus." *SBL Seminar Papers.* Edited by George
        MacRae. Cambridge: SBL.
1975   *The Dark Interval: Toward a Theology of Story.* Allen, TX: Argus Communi-
        cations.
1976   "Empty Tomb and Absent Lord (Mark 16:1–18)." In *The Passion in Mark:
        Studies on Mark 14–16* , edited by Werner H. Kelber, 135–52. Philadelphia:
        Fortress Press.
1976   *Raid on the Articulate: Cosmic Eschatology in Jesus and Borges.* New York:
        Harper & Row.
1978   "Waking the Bible: Biblical Hermeneutics and Literary Imagination." *Inter-
        pretation* 32: 269–85.
1978   "A Form of Absence: The Markan Creation of Gospel." *Semeia* 12: 41–56.
1980   *Cliffs of Fall: Paradox and Polyvalence in the Parables of Jesus.* New York:
        Seabury Press.
1982   "Ruth Amid the Alien Corn: Perspectives and Methods in Contemporary
        Biblical Criticism." In *The Biblical Mosaic: Changing Perspectives,* edited
        by Robert M. Polzin and Eugene Rothman, 199–210. Philadelphia: Fortress,
        and Chico, CA: Scholars Press.
1985   *Four Other Gospels: Shadows on the Contours of Canon.* Minneapolis:
        Seabury/Winston.
1988   *The Cross That Spoke: The Origins of the Passion Narrative.* San Francisco:
        Harper and Row.
1991   *The Historical Jesus: The Life of a Mediterranean Jewish Peasant.* San
        Francisco: Harper.

Culler, Jonathan
1975   *Structuralist Poetics: Structuralism, Linguistics, and the Study of Literature.*
        Ithaca: Cornell University Press.

Cullmann, O.
   1959   *The Christology of the New Testament.* Trans. S. C. Guthrie and C. A. M. Hall. Philadelphia: Westminster Press.
Culpepper, R. Alan
   1978   "An Outline of the Gospel According to Mark." *Review and Expositor* 75: 619–22.
   1982   "Mark 10:50: Why Mention the Garment?" *Journal of Biblical Literature* 101: 131–32.
Davies, W. D.
   1974   *The Gospel and the Land: Early Christianity and Jewish Territorial Doctrine.* Berkeley: University of California Press.
Delling, G.
   1957   "Βάπτισμα βαπτισθῆναι," *Novum Testamentum* 2: 92–105.
Derrett, J. Duncan M.
   1970   "The Anointing at Bethany and the Story of Zacchaeus." In *Law in the New Testament,* 266–85. London: Darton, Longman & Todd.
   1973   "Figtrees in the New Testament." *Heythrop Journal* 14.3: 249–65.
   1979   "Contributions to a Study of the Gerasene Demoniac." *Journal for the Study of the New Testament* 3: 5ff.
Derrida, Jacques
   1976   *Of Grammatology.* Trans. G. C. Spivak. Baltimore: Johns Hopkins.
Dewey, Joanna
   1973   "The Literary Structure of the Controversy Stories in Mark 2:1–3:6." *Journal of Biblical Literature* 92.3: 394–401. Reprinted in *The Interpretation of Mark,* edited by William Telford. Philadelphia: Fortress Press and London: SPCK Press, 1985.
   1979   *Markan Public Debate: Literary Technique, Concentric Structure, and Theology in Mk 2:1–3:6.* SBLDS 48. Missoula, MT: Scholars Press.
   1982   "Point of View and the Disciples in Mark." *Society of Biblical Literature: 1982 Seminar Papers,* edited by Kent Harold Richards, 97–106.
   1989   "Oral Methods of Structuring Narrative in Mark." *Interpretation* 43: 32–44.
   1991   "Recent Studies on Mark." *Religious Studies Review* 17: 12–16.
   FC   "Mark as Interwoven Tapestry: Forecasts and Echoes for a Listening Audience." *Catholic Biblical Quarterly.*
Dewey, Kim E.
   1976   "Peter's Curse and Cursed Peter (Mark 14:53–54, 66–72)." In *The Passion in Mark: Studies on Mark 14–16,* edited Werner H. Kelber. Philadelphia: Fortress Press.
Dibelius, Martin
   1935   *From Tradition to Gospel.* Trans. B. L. Woolf. New York: Scribner's.
   1956   *Botschaft und Geschichte.* 2 vols. Tübingen: J. C. B. Mohr.
Dodd, C. H.
   1953   *The Interpretation of the Fourth Gospel.* Cambridge: Cambridge University Press.
   1961   *The Parables of the Kingdom.* Rev. ed. New York: Scribner's.
Donahue, John R.
   1973   *Are You the Christ?: The Trial Narrative in the Gospel of Mark.* SBLDS 10. Missoula, MT: Scholars Press.
   1976   "From Passion Traditions to Passion Narrative." In *The Passion in Mark: Studies on Mark 14–16,* edited by Werner H. Kelber, 1–20. Philadelphia: Fortress Press.

1976   "Temple, Trial, and Royal Christology (Mark 14:53–65)." In *The Passion in Mark: Studies on Mark 14–16*, edited by Werner H. Kelber, 61–79. Philadelphia: Fortress Press.

1978   "Jesus as the Parable of God in the Gospel of Mark." *Interpretation* 32: 369–86.

1982   "A Neglected Factor in the Theology of Mark." *Journal of Biblical Literature* 101.4: 563–94.

1988   *The Gospel in Parable: Metaphor, Narrative, and Theology in the Synoptic Gospels*. Philadelphia: Fortress Press.

Dowd, Sharyn Echols
1988   *Prayer, Power, and the Problem of Suffering: Mark 11:22–25 in the Context of Markan Theology*. Atlanta: Scholars Press.

Drury, John
1973   "The Sower, the Vineyard, and the Place of Allegory in Mark's Parables." *Journal of Theological Studies* 24: 367–79.

Dumoulin, Heinrich
1988   *Zen Buddhism: A History. India and China*. Trans. James W. Heisig and Paul Knitter. New York: Macmillan.

Eckel, Malcolm David
1992   *To See the Buddha: A Philosopher's Quest for the Meaning of Emptiness*. San Francisco: Harper.

Eliade, Mircea
1960   *Myths, Dreams, and Mysteries*. New York: Harper.
1961   *The Sacred and the Profane: The Nature of Religion*. Trans. W. R. Trask. New York: Harper Torchbooks.

Elliott, J. H.
1986   "Social Scientific Criticism of the New Testament: More on Methods and Models." *Semeia* 35: 1–33.

Farmer, William R.
1964   *The Synoptic Problem: A Critical Analysis*. Hillsboro, NC: Western North Carolina Press.
1974   *The Last Twelve Verses of Mark*. Cambridge: Cambridge University Press.

Farrer, Austin.
1952   *A Study in St. Mark*. New York: Oxford University Press.

Faure, Bernard
1991   *The Rhetoric of Immediacy: A Cultural Critique of Chan/Zen Buddhism*. Princeton: Princeton University Press.

Fensham, F. C.
1964   "Judas' Hand in the Bowl and Qumran." *Révue de Qumran* 5: 259–61.

Fisher, K., and V. C. von Wahlde
1981   "The Miracles of Mark 4:35–5:43: Their Meaning and Function in the Gospel Framework." *Biblical Theology Bulletin* 11: 13–16.

Fitzmyer, J. A.
1981–   *The Gospel According to Luke*. 2 vols. with continuous pagination. Anchor
1985   Bible 28–28A. Garden City, NY: Doubleday.

Fleddermann, Harry
1981   "The Discipleship Discourse (Mark 9:33–50)." *Catholic Biblical Quarterly* 43: 57–75.

Fowler, Robert M.
1981   *Loaves and Fishes: The Function of the Feeding Stories in the Gospel of Mark*. SBLDS 54. Chico, CA: Scholars Press.

1991   *Let the Reader Understand: Reader-Response Criticism and the Gospel of Mark.* Minneapolis: Fortress Press.

1992   "Reader-Response Criticism: Figuring Mark's Reader." In *Mark and Method: New Approaches in Biblical Studies,* edited by J. C. Anderson and S. D. Moore, 50–83. Minneapolis: Fortress Press.

Fuller, Reginald H.

1954   *Mission and Achievement of Jesus.* Chicago: Alenson.

1965   *The Foundations of New Testament Christology.* New York: Scribner's.

1971   *The Formation of the Resurrection Narratives.* London and New York: Macmillan.

Gasché, Rodolphe

1986   *The Tain of the Mirror: Derrida and the Philosophy of Reflection.* Cambridge, MA: Harvard University Press.

Gaston, Lloyd

1970   *No Stone Upon Another: Studies in the Significance of the Fall of Jerusalem in the Synoptic Gospels.* Leiden: Brill.

Girard, René

1984   "Scandal and the Dance: Salome in the Gospel of Mark." *New Literary History* 15: 311–24.

Greer, Rowan A., trans.

1979   *Origen: An Exhortation to Martyrdom, Prayer, and First Principles, Book IV: Prologue to the Commentary on the Song of Songs, Homily XXVII in Numbers.* Mahwah, NJ: Paulist Press.

Griffiths, Paul, Noriaki Hakamaya, John Keenan, and Paul Swanson

1989   *The Realm of Awakening: Chapter Ten of Asanga's Mahāyānasangraha.* New York: Oxford University Press.

Grosnick, William G.

1990   "Buddha Nature as Myth." In *Buddha Nature: A Festschrift in Honor of Minoru Kiyota,* edited by Paul J. Griffiths and John P. Keenan, 65–74. Reno: Buddhist Books International.

Guelich, Robert A.

1982   " 'The Beginning of the Gospel'—Mark 1:1–15." *Biblical Research* 27: 6–8.

Hakamaya, Noriaki

1984   "Kushō rikai no mondaiten" [Issues in Understanding Emptiness]. *Risō* 610: 50–64.

1989   *Hongaku shisō hihan* [Critique of Original Enlightenment Thought]. Tokyo: Daizō Shuppan.

1990   *Hihan bukkyō* [Critical Buddhism]. Tokyo: Daizō Shuppan.

1992   *Dōgen to bukkyō: Jūni kanbun Shōbōgenzō no Dōgen* [Dōgen and Buddhism: The Dōgen of the Twelve Fascicle Shōbōgenzō]. Tokyo: Daizō Shuppan.

Hakeda, Yoshito S., trans.

1967   *The Awakening of Faith.* New York: Columbia University Press.

Hamerton-Kelly, Robert G.

1994   *The Gospel and the Sacred: Poetics of Violence in Mark.* Minneapolis: Fortress Press.

Harner, Philip B.

1973   "Qualitative Anarthrous Predicate Nouns: Mark 15:39 and John 1:1." *Journal of Biblical Literature* 92: 75–87.

Harrington, Wilfrid

1979   *Mark.* Wilmington, DE: Michael Glazier.

Harrison, R. K., ed.

1985   *Major Cities of the Biblical World.* Nashville: Thomas Nelson.

Hartmann, Lars
1966   *Prophecy Interpreted: The Formation of Some Jewish Apocalyptic Texts and of the Eschatological Discourse Mark 13 Par.* Coniectanea Biblica, New Testament Series 1. Uppsala: Lund.
Hawkin, David J.
1972   "The Incomprehension of the Disciples in the Marcan Redaction." *Journal of Biblical Literature* 91: 491–500.
Hay, Lewis S.
1970   "The Son of Man in 2:10 and 2:28." *Journal of Biblical Literature* 89: 69–75.
Hedrick, Charles W.
1987   "Narrator and Story in the Gospel of Mark: *Hermeneia* and *Paradosis*." *Perspectives in Religious Studies* 14: 239–58.
Heil, John Paul
1992   *The Gospel of Mark as a Model for Action: A Reader-Response Commentary.* New York: Paulist Press.
Hengel, M.
1974   *Judaism and Hellenism.* Philadelphia: Fortress Press.
Hick, John, and Paul Knitter
1987   *The Myth of Christian Uniqueness.* Maryknoll, NY: Orbis Books.
Hiers, R. H.
1968   "Not the Season for Figs." *Journal of Biblical Literature* 87.4: 394–401.
Hirota, Dennis, trans.
1982   *Tannishō: A Primer.* Kyoto: Ryukoku University Translation Center.
Hollenbach, Paul W.
1981   "Jesus, Demoniacs, and Public Authorities: A Socio-Historical Study." *Journal of the American Academy of Religion* 99: 567–88.
1982   "The Conversion of Jesus: From Jesus the Baptizer to Jesus the Healer." *Aufstieg und Niedergang der römischen Welt* 2.25: 196–219.
Humphrey, Hugh M.
1992   *He Is Risen! A New Reading of Mark's Gospel.* New York: Paulist Press.
Huntington, C. W., Jr.
1989   *The Emptiness of Emptiness: An Introduction to Early Indian Mādhyamika.* Honolulu: University of Hawaii Press.
Hurtado, Larry W.
1983   *Mark.* New International Biblical Commentary. Peabody, MA: Hendrickson.
Hurvitz, Leon, trans.
1976   *Scripture of the Lotus Blossom of the Fine Dharma (The Lotus Sūtra).* New York: Columbia University Press.
Illich, Ivan
1970   "The Vanishing Clergyman," in *Celebration of Awareness: A Call for Institutional Revolution.* Garden City, NY: Doubleday.
1971   *Deschooling Society.* New York: Harper & Row.
1974   *Energy and Equity.* New York: Harper & Row.
1976   *Medical Nemesis: The Expropriation of Health.* New York: Random House.
1992   *In the Mirror of the Past.* New York & London: Marion Boyars.
Iser, Wolfgang
1981   "Talk Like Whales: A Reply to Stanley Fish." *Diacritics* 11: 82–87.
Jackson, Howard M.
1987   "The Death of Jesus in Mark and the Miracle from the Cross." *New Testament Studies* 33: 16–37.
Jeremias, Joachim
1972   *The Parables of Jesus.* 2nd ed. New York: Scribner's.

Johnson, Earl S.
1978   "Mark 10:46–52: Blind Bartimaeus." *Catholic Biblical Quarterly* 40: 191–204.
Johnson, Sherman E.
1960   *A Commentary on the Gospel According to St. Mark.* New York: Harper and Row.
1991   *The Griesbach Hypothesis and Redaction Criticism.* SBLMS. Atlanta: Scholars Press.
Juel, Donald H.
1977   *Messiah and Temple: The Trial of Jesus in the Gospel of Mark.* SBLDS 31. Missoula, MT: Scholars Press.
1988   *Messianic Exegesis: Christological Interpretation of the Old Testament in Early Christianity.* Philadelphia: Fortress.
1990   *Augsburg Commentary on the New Testament: Mark.* Minneapolis: Augsburg.
Kähler, Martin
1964   *The So-Called Historical Jesus and the Historic, Biblical Christ.* Philadelphia: Fortress Press.
Kealy, Seán P.
1982   *Mark's Gospel: A History of Its Interpretation from the Beginning until 1979.* New York: Paulist Press.
Kee, Howard C.
1968   "The Terminology of Mark's Exorcism Stories." *New Testament Studies* 14: 242 ff.
1977   *Community of the New Age: Studies in Mark's Gospel.* Philadelphia: Westminster Press.
Keenan, John P.
1989   *The Meaning of Christ: A Mahāyāna Theology.* Maryknoll, NY: Orbis Books.
1990   "The Doctrine of Buddha Nature in Chinese Buddhism—Hui-K'ai on Paramartha." In *Buddha Nature: A Festschrift in Honor of Minoru Kiyota,* edited by Paul J. Griffiths and John P. Keenan, 125–38. Reno: Buddhist Books International.
1991   *The Summary of the Great Vehicle by Bodhisattva Asanga, Translated from the Chinese of Paramārtha.* Tokyo and Berkeley: Bukkyo Dendo Kyokai.
1992   "The Emptiness of Christ: A Mahāyāna Christology." *The Anglican Theological Review* 75.1: 48–62.
Kelber, Werner
1974   *The Kingdom in Mark: A New Place and a New Time.* Philadelphia: Fortress Press.
1976   "The Hour of the Son of Man and the Temptation of the Disciples (Mark 14:32–42)." In *The Passion in Mark: Studies on Mark 14–16,* edited by Werner H. Kelber, 41–60. Philadelphia: Fortress Press.
1976   "From Passion Narrative to Gospel." In *The Passion in Mark: Studies on Mark 14–16,* edited by Werner H. Kelber, 153–80. Philadelphia: Fortress Press.
1979   *Mark's Story of Jesus.* Philadelphia: Fortress Press.
1983   *The Oral and Written Gospel: The Hermeneutics of Speaking and Writing in the Synoptic Tradition, Mark, Paul, and Q.* Philadelphia: Fortress Press.
Kermode, Frank
1979   *The Genesis of Secrecy: On the Interpretation of Narrative.* Cambridge and London: Harvard University Press.
1988   "Anteriority, Authority, and Secrecy: A General Comment." *Semeia* 43: 155–67.

Kertledge, Karl
1969 "The Epiphanies of Jesus in the Gospel (Mark)." In *Gestalt und Anspruch des Neuen Testaments*, edited by J. Schreiner, 153–72. Würzburg: Echter-Verlag. Reprinted in *The Interpretation of Mark,* edited by William Telford, 78–94. Philadelphia: Fortress Press and London: SPCK Press, 1985.
Kingsbury, Jack Dean
1979 "The Gospel of Mark in Current Research." *Religious Studies Review* 5: 101–07.
1983 *The Christology of Mark's Gospel.* Philadelphia: Fortress Press.
1989 *Conflict in Mark: Jesus, Authorities, Disciples.* Minneapolis: Fortress Press.
Kittel, G., and G. Friedrich
1964– *Theological Dictionary of the New Testament.* 10 vols. Trans. G. W.
1976 Bromiley. Grand Rapids, MI: Eerdmans.
Kloppenborg, John S.
1990 "Alms, Debt and Divorce: Jesus' Ethics in Their Mediterranean Context." *Toronto Journal of Theology* 6: 182–200.
Klosinski, Lee Edward
1988 *The Meals in Mark.* Ann Arbor, MI: University Microfilms International.
Knitter, Paul F.
1985 *No Other Name? A Critical Survey of Christian Attitudes Toward the World Religions.* Maryknoll, NY: Orbis Books.
Knitter, Paul F., and John B. Hick
1987 *The Myth of Christian Uniqueness.* Maryknoll, NY: Orbis Books.
Koester, Helmut
1983 "History and Development of Mark's Gospel (From Mark to Secret Mark and 'Canonical Mark')." In *Colloquy on New Testament Studies: A Time for Reappraisal and Fresh Approaches* , edited by Bruce Corley, 35–57. Macon, GA: Mercer University Press.
Kolenkow, Anitra Bingham
1973 "Beyond Miracles, Suffering and Eschatology." *1973 Seminar Papers*, edited by George MacRae, SBLASP 109, Society of Biblical Literature 2: 155–202.
Kraeling, C. H.
1951 *John the Baptist.* New York: Scribner.
Lafontaine, René, and Pierre Mourlon Beernaert
1969 "Essai sur la structure de Marc, 8,27–9,13." *Recherches de science religieuse* 57: 543–61.
Lamotte, Étienne
1988 *History of Indian Buddhism: From the Origins to the Śaka Era.* Trans. Sara Webb-Boin. Louvain-Paris: Petters Press. [Original French 1958].
Lampe, G. W. H.
1961 *A Patristic Greek Lexicon.* Oxford: Clarendon.
Lane, William L.
1974 *The Gospel According to Mark: The English Text with Introduction, Exposition and Notes.* Grand Rapids, MI: Eerdmans.
Legault, A.
1954 "An Application of the Form-Critical Method to the Anointings in Galilee and Bethany." *Catholic Biblical Quarterly* 16: 131–45.
Lightfoot, Robert H.
1950 *The Gospel Message of St. Mark.* Oxford: Clarendon Press.
Lincoln, Andrew T.
1989 "The Promise and the Failure: Mark 16:7,8." *Journal of Biblical Literature* 108: 283–300.

Lindars, Barnabas
1983   *Jesus the Son of Man: A Fresh Examination of the Son of Man Sayings in the Gospels in the Light of Recent Research.* London: SPCK Press.
Linnemann, Eta
1966   *Jesus of the Parables: Introduction and Exposition.* New York and Evanston: Harper and Row.
1970   *Studien zur Passionsgeschichte.* Göttingen: Vandenhoeck & Ruprecht.
Lohmeyer, Ernst
1935   *Galiläa und Jerusalem.* Göttingen: Vandenhoeck & Ruprecht.
1959   *Das Evangeliums des Markus.* Göttingen: Vandenhoeck & Ruprecht.
Lopez, Donald S., Jr., ed.
1988   *Buddhist Hermeneutics.* Honolulu: University of Hawaii Press.
Lopez, Donald S., Jr.
1988   *The Heart Sūtra Explained: Indian and Tibetan Commentaries.* Albany, NY: SUNY Press.
Mack, Burton L.
1988   *A Myth of Innocence: Mark and Christian Origins.* Philadelphia: Fortress Press.
Magness, J. Lee
1986   *Sense and Absence: Structure and Suspension in the Ending of Mark's Gospel.* Atlanta: Scholars Press.
Malbon, Elizabeth Struthers
1982   "Galilee and Jerusalem: History and Literature in Marcan Interpretation." *Catholic Biblical Quarterly* 44: 242–55.
1983   "Structuralism, Hermeneutics, and Contextual Meaning." *Journal of the American Academy of Religion* 51: 207–30.
1983   "Fallible Followers: Women and Men in the Gospel of Mark." *Semeia* 28: 29–48.
1984   "The Jesus of Mark and the Sea of Galilee." *Journal of Biblical Literature* 103: 363–77.
1985   "Tē Oikia Autou: Mark 2:15 in Context." *New Testament Studies* 31: 282–92.
1986   "Mark: Myth and Parable." *Biblical Theology Bulletin* 16: 8–17.
1986   *Narrative Space and Mythic Meaning in Mark.* San Francisco: Harper and Row. Reprint, Sheffield: JSOT Press, 1991.
1992   "Narrative Criticism: How Does the Story Mean?" In *Mark and Method: New Approaches in Biblical Studies*, edited by J. C. Anderson and S. D. Moore, 23–49. Minneapolis: Fortress Press.
Mann, C. S.
1986   *Mark: A New Translation with Introduction and Commentary.* New York: Doubleday, The Anchor Bible.
Mansfield, M. Robert
1987   *"Spirit and Gospel" in Mark.* Peabody, MA: Hendrickson.
Marcus, Joel
1986   *The Mystery of the Kingdom of God.* Atlanta: Scholars Press.
1992   "The Jewish War and the *Sitz im Leben* of Mark." *Journal of Biblical Literature* 111: 441–462.
Marxsen, Willi
1968   *Introduction to the New Testament.* Trans. G. Buswell. Philadelphia: Fortress Press.
1969   *Mark the Evangelist: Studies on the Redaction History of the Gospel.* Trans. J. Boyce, D. Juel, and W. Poehlmann. Nashville and New York: Abingdon Press.
Matsumoto, Shiro
1989   *Engi to kū* [Dependent Co-arising and Emptiness]. Tokyo: Daizō Shuppan.

Mauser, U.
1963   *Christ in the Wilderness: The Wilderness Theme in the Second Gospel and Its Basis in the Biblical Tradition.* Naperville, IL: Alec R. Allenson.
McCurley, F. R., Jr.
1974   " 'And After Six Days' (Mark 9:2): A Semitic Literary Device." *Journal of Biblical Literature* 93: 67–81.
McIndoe, J. H.
1969   "The Young Man at the Tomb." *Expository Times* 80: 125.
Meagher, J. C.
1979   *Clumsy Construction in Mark's Gospel: A Critique of Form and Redaktiongeschichte.* New York: Mellen.
Meier, John P.
1991   *A Marginal Jew: Rethinking the Historical Jesus.* Vol. 1: The Roots of the Problem and the Person. New York: Doubleday.
Meyer, Marvin W.
1990   "The Youth in the Secret Gospel of Mark." *Semeia* 49: 129–53.
Miller, Barbara Stoler, trans.
1986   *The Bhagavad-Gita: Krishna's Counsel in Time of War.* Toronto: Bantam Books
Minette de Tillesse, G.
1968   *Le Secret messianique dans l'Évangile de Marc.* Lection Divina vol. XLVII. Paris: Cerf.
Monier-Williams, Sir Monier
1960   *A Sanskrit-English Dictionary.* Oxford: Clarendon Press. [1899]
Moore, Stephen D.
1989   *Literary Criticism and the Gospels: The Theoretical Challenge.* New Haven: Yale University Press.
1989   "The 'Post-' Age Stamp: Does It Stick? Biblical Studies and the Postmodernism Debate." *Journal of the American Academy of Religion* 57: 543–59.
1991   *Mark and Luke in Poststructuralist Perspectives: Jesus Begins to Write.* New Haven: Yale University Press.
1992   "Deconstructive Criticism: The Gospel of the Mark." In *Mark and Method: New Approaches in Biblical Studies,* edited by J. C. Anderson and S. D. Moore, 84–102. Minneapolis: Fortress Press.
Motyer, S.
1987   "The Rending of the Veil: A Markan Pentecost." *New Testament Studies* 33: 155–57.
Mowinckel, Sigmund
1967   *The Psalms in Israel's Worship.* New York: Abingdon Press.
Munro, Winsome
1979   "The Anointing in Mark 14:3–9 and John 12:1–8." *Society of Biblical Literature 1979 Seminar Papers I,* edited by P. J. Achtemeier, 127–30. Missoula, MT: Scholars Press.
1982   "Women Disciples in Mark?" *Catholic Biblical Quarterly* 44: 225–41.
Myers, Ched
1988   *Binding the Strong Man: A Political Reading of Mark's Story of Jesus.* Maryknoll, NY: Orbis Books.
Nagao, Gadjin
1989   *The Foundational Standpoint of Mādhyamika Philosophy.* Trans. John P. Keenan. Albany: State University of New York Press.

1991   "Buddhist Subjectivity." In *Mādhyamika and Yogācāra: A Study of Mahāyāna Philosophies, Collected Papers of G. M. Nagao,* edited and trans. by Leslie Kawamura, 7–12. Albany: State University of New York Press.

1991   "The Silence of the Buddha and Its Mādhyamic Interpretation." In *Mādhyamika and Yogācāra,* 35–50.

Nāgārjuna
1977   *Stanzas on the Middle [Mūlamadhyamakakārikaḥ].* Sanskrit text edited by J. W. de Jong. Madras: Adyar Library and Research Center.

1978   *Overcoming Vain Discussions [Vigrahavyāvartanī]* (Sanskrit text and English trans.) In *The Dialectical Method of Nāgārjuna: Vigrahāvyavartanī.* Text critically ed. by E. H. Johnson and Arnold Kunst. Trans. by Kamaleswar Bhattacharya. Delhi: Motilal Barnarsidass.

Napier, A. David
1986   *Masks, Transformation, and Paradox.* Berkeley: University of California Press.

Neirynck, F.
1970   *Duality in Mark: Contributions to the Study of Markan Redaction.* BETL 31. Leuven: Leuven University Press.

1979   "La fuite du jeune homme en Mc 14,51–52." *Ephemerides theologicae Lovanienses* 55: 43–52.

Neusner, Jacob
1972   "Judaism in a Time of Crisis: Four Responses to the Destruction of the Second Temple." *Judaism* 21: 313–27.

Nineham, D. E.
1978   *The Gospel According to Saint Mark.* Philadelphia: Westminster Press. Reprint of *The Gospel of St. Mark.* Baltimore: Penguin, 1963.

Nishitani, Keiji
1982   "What Is Religion?" in *Religion and Nothingness.* Trans. Jan Van Bragt. Berkeley: University of California Press.

Ong, Walter J.
1987   "Text as Interpretation: Mark and After." *Semeia* 39: 7–26.

Osborne, B. A. E.
1973   "Peter: Stumblingblock and Satan." *Novum Testamentum* 15: 187–90.

Otto, R.
1938   *The Kingdom of God and the Son of Man.* London: Lutterworth Press.

Panikkar, Raimundo
1989   *The Silence of God: The Answer of the Buddha.* Maryknoll, NY: Orbis Books.

1993   *The Cosmotheandric Experience: Emerging Religious Consciousness.* Maryknoll, NY: Orbis Books.

Perrin, Norman
1966   "Mark XIV.62: The End Product of a Christian Pesher Tradition?" *New Testament Studies* 12: 150–55.

1967   *Rediscovering the Teachings of Jesus.* New York: Harper & Row.

1970   "The Use of (Para)didonai in Connection with the Passion of Jesus in the New Testament." In *Der Rif Jesu und die Antwort der Gemeinde: Festschrift für Joachim Jeremias.* edited by Eduard Lohse, 204–12. Göttingen: Vandenhoeck & Ruprecht.

1971   "The Christology of Mark: A Study in Methodology." *Journal of Religion* 51: 173–87.

1971   *Rediscovery of Apocalyptic.* Naperville: Alec R. Alleson.

1972   "The Evangelist as Author: Reflections on Method in the Study and Interpretation of the Synoptic Gospels and Acts." *Biblical Research* 17: 5–18.

1976   "The High Priest's Question and Jesus' Answer (Mark 14:61–62)." In *The Passion in Mark: Studies on Mark 14–16*, edited by Werner H. Kelber, 80–95. Philadelphia: Fortress Press.

1976   "The Interpretation of the Gospel of Mark." *Interpretation* 30: 115–24.

1976   *Jesus and the Language of the Kingdom: Symbol and Metaphor in New Testament Interpretation.* Philadelphia: Fortress Press.

1985   "The Christology of Mark: A Study in Methodology." In *The Interpretation of Mark,* edited by William Telford, 95–108. Philadelphia: Fortress Press; London: SPCK Press. Slightly revised from first appearance in *L'Évangile selon Marc. Tradition et rédaction,* 471–85. Leuven: University Press, 1974.

Pesch, Rudolph

1968   *Naherwartungen: Tradition und Redaktion in Markus 13.* Düssseldorf: Patmos-Verlag.

1976   *Das Markusevangelium.* Freiburg: Herder.

1976   "The Markan Version of the Healing of the Gerasene Demoniac." *Ecumenical Review* 23: 349–76.

Petersen, Norman R.

1978   "'Point of View' in Mark's Narrative." *Semeia* 12: 97–121.

1980   "When is the End not the End? Literary Reflections on the Ending of Mark's Narrative." *Interpretation* 34: 151–66.

Quesnell, Quentin

1969   *The Mind of Mark: Interpretation and Method Through the Exegesis of Mark 6:52.* Rome: Pontifical Biblical Institute.

1975   "The Mar Saba Clementine: A Question of Evidence." *Catholic Biblical Quarterly* 37: 48–67.

Räisänen, Heikki

1990   *The "Messianic Secret" in Mark.* Trans. Christopher Tuckett. Edinburgh: T. & T. Clark.

Reps, Paul, ed.

1961   *Zen Flesh, Zen Bones: A Collection of Zen and Pre-Zen Writings.* New York: Doubleday Anchor Books.

Rhoads, David

1992   "Social Criticism: Crossing Boundaries." In *Mark and Method: New Approaches in Biblical Studies*, edited by J. C. Anderson and S. D. Moore, 135–61. Minneapolis: Fortress Press.

1994   "Jesus and the Syrophoenician Woman: A Narrative Critical Study." *Journal of the American Academy of Religion* 62.2: 343–375.

Rhoads, David, and Donald Michie

1982   *Mark as Story: An Introduction to the Narrative of a Gospel.* Philadelphia: Fortress Press.

Robbins, Vernon

1973   "The Healing of Blind Bartimaeus (10:46–52) in the Marcan Theology." *Journal of Biblical Literature* 92: 224–43.

1976   "Last Meal: Preparation, Betrayal, and Absence (Mark 14:12–25)." In *The Passion in Mark: Studies on Mark 14–16*, edited by Werner H. Kelber, 21–40. Philadelphia: Fortress Press.

1984   *Jesus the Teacher: A Socio-Rhetorical Interpretation of Mark.* Philadelphia: Fortress.

1991   "Text and Context in Recent Studies of the Gospel of Mark." *Religious Studies Review* 17: 16 ff.

Robinson, James M.

1982   *The Problem of History in Mark and Other Marcan Studies.* Philadelphia: Fortress Press.

Robinson, William C., Jr.
1973   "The Quest for Wrede's Secret Messiah." *Interpretation* 27: 10–30.

Ryle, G.
1949   *The Concept of Mind.* New York: Barnes and Noble.

Sanders, E. P., and Margaret Davies
1989   *Studying the Synoptic Gospels.* London: SCM Press; Philadelphia: Trinity Press International.

Sandmel, Samuel
1971   "The Trial of Jesus: Reservations." *Judaism* 20: 74 ff.
1972   "Prolegomena to a Commentary on Mark." In *Two Living Traditions: Essays on Religion and the Bible,* 147–57. Detroit: Wayne State University Press.
1972   " 'Son of Man' in Mark." In *Two Living Traditions,* 166–77.

Saussure, Ferdinand de
1959   *Course in General Linguistics.* Trans. Wade Baskin. New York: Philosophical Library.

Schenke, Hans-Martin
1984   "The Mystery of the Gospel of Mark." *The Second Century* 4: 65–82.

Schierling, M.
1980   "Women as Leaders in the Marcan Communities." *Listening* 15: 250–56.

Schillebeeckx, Edward
1979   *Jesus: An Experiment in Christology.* Trans. H. Hoskins. New York: Seabury.
1980   *Christ: The Experience of Jesus as Lord.* Trans. J. Bowden. New York: Seabury.

Schmithals, Walter
1970   *Wunder und Glaube. Eine Auslegung von Markus 4:35–6,6a.* Neukirchen-Vluyn: Neukirchener.

Schmithausen, Lambert
1991   *Buddhism and Nature.* Tokyo: The International Institute for Buddhist Studies.

Schulz, Siegfried
1966   "Mark's Significance for the Theology of Early Christianity." *Studia Evangelica II* 1: 135–45. Reprint in *The Interpretation of Mark,* edited by William Telford, 158–166. Philadelphia: Fortress Press; London: SPCK Press.

Schweitzer, Albert
1966   The Quest of the Historical Jesus. Trans. W. Montgomery. 10th printing. New York: Macmillan. [First English edition, 1910.]

Schweizer, Eduard
1964   "Mark's Theological Achievement." *Evangelische Theologie* 24: 337–55. Reprint in *The Interpretation of Mark,* edited by William Telford, 42–63. Philadelphia: Fortress Press; London: SPCK Press.
1965   "Zur Frage des Messiasgeheimmisses bei Markus." *Zeitschrift für die Neutestamentliche Wissenschaft* 56: 1–8. English translation, "The Question of the Messianic Secret in Mark." In *The Messianic Secret,* edited by C. M. Tuckett, 65–74. Philadelphia: Fortress Press, 1983.
1970   *The Good News According to Mark.* Trans. Donald H. Madvig. Atlanta: John Knox Press.

Scott, Bernard Brandon
1989   *Hear Then the Parable: A Commentary on the Parables of Jesus.* Minneapolis: Fortress Press.

Scott, M. Philip
1985   "Chiastic Structure: A Key to the Interpretation of Mark's Gospel." *Biblical Theology Bulletin* 15: 17–26.

Selvidge, M.J.
    1984   "Mark 5:25–34 and Leviticus 15:19–28: A Reaction to Restrictive Purity
            Regulations." *Journal of Biblical Literature* 103: 619–23.
Senior, D.
    1984   "The Struggle to be Universal: Mission as Vantage Point for New Testament
            Investigation." *Catholic Biblical Quarterly* 46: 63–81.
Sheehan, Thomas
    1986   *The First Coming: How the Kingdom of God Became Christianity.* New
            York: Vintage Books, Random House.
Shibayama Zenkei
    1974   *Zen Comments on the Mumonkan.* Trans. Sumiko Kudo. New York:
            Harper & Row.
Smith, Jonathan Z.
    1978   *Map Is Not Territory: Studies in the History of Religions.* Leiden: Brill.
Smith, Morton
    1973   *The Secret Gospel: The Discovery and Interpretation of the Secret Gospel
            According to Mark.* New York: Harper and Row.
    1973   *Clement of Alexandria and the Secret Gospel of Mark.* Cambridge, MA:
            Harvard University Press.
    1980   "The Origin and History of the Transfiguration Story." *Union Seminary
            Quarterly Review* 36: 39–44.
Starobinski, J.
    1973   "The Gerasene Demoniac: Literary Analysis of Mk 5:1–20." *New Literary
            History* 4: 331–56.
Stein, R. H.
    1976   "Is the Transfiguration (Mark 9:2–8) a Misplaced Resurrection Account?"
            Journal of Biblical Literature 95: 79–96.
Steinhauser. M. G.
    1986   "The Form of the Bartimaeus Narrative (Mark 10:46–52)." *New Testament
            Studies* 32: 583–95.
Talmon, Shemaryahu
    1966   "The 'Desert Motif' in the Bible and in Qumran Literature." In *Biblical
            Motifs: Origins and Transformations*, edited by Alexander Altmann, 31–63.
            Cambridge: Harvard University Press.
Tanahashi, Kazuaki, ed.
    1985   *Moon in A Dewdrop: Writings of Zen Master Dogen.* San Francisco: North
            Point Press.
Tannehill, Robert C.
    1975   *The Sword of His Mouth.* Philadelphia: Fortress Press.
    1977   "The Disciples in Mark: The Function of a Narrative Role." *Journal of
            Religion* 57: 386–405. Reprinted in *The Interpretation of Mark*, edited by
            William Telford, 134–57. Philadelphia: Fortress Press; London: SPCK Press.
    1979   "The Gospel of Mark as Narrative Christology." *Semeia* 16: 57–95.
    1980   "Tension in Synoptic Sayings and Stories." *Interpretation* 34: 138 ff.
    1981   "Introduction: The Pronouncement Story and its Types." *Semeia* 20: 1–14.
    1981   "Varieties of Synoptic Pronouncement Stories." *Semeia* 20: 101–28.
    1982   "Reading it Whole: The Function of Mark 8:34–35 in Mark's Story." *Quar-
            terly Review* 2: 67–78.
Taylor, Vincent
    1952   *The Gospel According to St. Mark.* London: Macmillan.
Telford, W. R.
    1980   *The Barren Temple and the Withered Tree: A Redactional-Critical Analysis
            of the Cursing of the Fig-Tree Pericope in Mark's Gospel and its Relation
            to the Cleansing of the Temple Tradition.* Sheffield: JSOT Press.

1985   "Introduction: The Gospel of Mark," in *The Interpretation of Mark*. Philadelphia: Fortress Press: London: SPCK Press.

Theissen, Gerd
1973   "Wanderradikalismus: Literatursoziologische Aspekte der überlie ferung von Worten Jesu im Urchristentum." *Zeitschrift für Theologie und Kirche* 70: 245–71. English Translation in *Radical Religion* 2.2–3 (1975): 84–93.

Thomas, Edward J.
1975   *The Life of Buddha as Legend and History*. London: Routledge & Kegan Paul. [First edition 1927].

Thompson, Mary R.
1989   *The Role of Disbelief in Mark: A New Approach to the Second Gospel*. New York: Paulist Press.

Thurman, Robert A. F., trans.
1976   *The Holy Teachings of Vimalakirtī: A Mahāyāna Scripture*. University Park: Pennsylvania State University Press.

Tödt, Heinz E.
1965   *The Son of Man in the Synoptic Tradition*. Trans. Dorothea M. Barton. Philadelphia: Westminster Press.

Tolbert, Mary Ann
1989   *Sowing the Gospel: Mark's World in Literary-Historical Perspective*. Minneapolis: Fortress Press.

Ulansey, David
1991   "The Heavenly Veil Torn: Mark's Cosmic *Inclusio*." *Journal of Biblical Literature* 110: 123–25.

Unno, Taitetsu, ed.
1989   *The Religious Philosophy of Nishitani Keiji: Encounter With Emptiness*. Berkeley: Asian Humanities Press.

Unno, Taitetsu, trans.
1984   *Tannisho: A Shin Buddhist Classic*. Honolulu: Buddhist Study Center Press.

Vaage, Leif Eric
1987   *Q: The Ethos and Ethics of an Itinerant Intelligence*. Ann Arbor, MI: University Microfilms International.
1989   "Q1 and the Historical Jesus: Some Peculiar Sayings (7:33–34; 9:57–58, 59–60;14:26–27." *Forum* 5.2: 159–76.

Van Iersel, Bas
1983   "Locality, Structure, and Meaning in Mark." *Linguistica Biblica* 32: 45–54.

Vermes, Geza
1981   *Jesus the Jew*. Philadelphia: Fortress Press.

Via, Dan O., Jr.
1967   *The Parables: Their Literary and Existential Dimension*. Philadelphia: Fortress Press.
1975   *Kergyma and Comedy in the New Testament: A Structuralist Approach to the New Testament*. Philadelphia: Fortress Press.
1985   *The Ethics of Mark's Gospel—In the Middle of Time*. Philadelphia: Fortress Press.
1988   "Irony as Hope in Mark's Gospel." *Semeia* 43: 21–28.
1990   *Self-Deception and Wholeness in Paul and Matthew*. Minneapolis: Fortress Press.

Volz, P.
1903   *Jüdische Eschatologie von Akiba bis Daniel*. Tubingen.

von Rad, Gerhard
    1965   *Old Testament Theology.* 2 vols. Trans. D. M. G. Stalker. New York: Harper and Row.
Vorster, Willem S.
    1987   "Characterization of Peter in the Gospel of Mark." *Neotestamentica* 21: 57–76.
    1987   "Literary Reflections on Mark 13:5–37: A Narrated Speech of Jesus." *Neotestamentica* 21: 203–24.
Waetjen, Herman C.
    1989   *A Reordering of Power: A Socio-Political Reading of Mark's Gospel.* Minneapolis: Fortress Press.
Waldenfels, Hans
    1980   *Absolute Nothingness: Foundations for a Buddhist-Christian Dialogue.* Trans. J. W. Heisig. New York: Paulist Press.
Waldron, William
    1988   "A Comparison of Ālayavijnana with Freud's and Jung's Theories of the Unconscious." *Annual Memoirs of the Ōtani University Shin Buddhist Comprehensive Research Institute* 6: 109–150.
Watson, Burton, trans.
    1968   *The Complete Works of Chuang Tzu.* New York: Columbia University Press.
Weeden, Theodore J.
    1968   "The Heresy That Necessitated Mark's Gospel." *Zeitschrift für die neutestamentliche Wissenschaft* 59: 145–58. Reprinted in *The Interpretation of Mark*, edited by William Telford, 64–77. Philadelphia: Fortress Press; London: SPCK Press, 1985.
    1971   *Mark—Traditions in Conflict.* Philadelphia: Fortress Press.
    1973   "The Conflict Between Mark and His Opponents Over Kingdom Theology." *1973 Seminar Papers*, edited by George MacRae, SBLASP 109, Society of Biblical Literature, Vol. 2: 203–41.
    1976   "The Cross as Power in Weakness (Mark 15:20b–41)." In *The Passion in Mark: Studies on Mark 14–16*, edited by Werner H. Kelber, 115–34. Philadelphia: Fortress Press.
    1979   "Recovering the Parabolic Intent in the Parable of the Sower." *Journal of the American Academy of Religion* 47: 97–120.
Wiles, Maurice
    1992   *Christian Theology and Inter-religious Dialogue.* London: SCM Press; Philadelphia: Trinity Press International.
Williams, James G.
    1985   *Gospel Against Parable: Mark's Language of Mystery.* Sheffield: Almond, JSOT Press.
Wrede, William
    1972   *The Messianic Secret.* Trans. J. C. G. Greig. Naperville, IL: Alec R. Allenson. [1901.]
Wuellner, Wilhelm
    1967   *The Meaning of "Fishers of Men."* Philadelphia: Westminster Press.
Yates, J. E.
    1958   "The Form of Mark 1: 8b." *New Testament Studies* 4: 334–38.
Zerwick, Max
    1953   *Analysis Philologica Novi Testamenti Graeci.* Rome: Pontifical Biblical Institute.
Ziesler, J.A.
    1970   "The Transfiguration Story and the Markan Soteriology." *Expository Times* 81: 263–68.

Index

Scripture Index

OLD TESTAMENT

NEW TESTAMENT

Other Titles in the Faith Meets Faith Series